OCEAN

EAST SIBERIAN SEA

LAPTEV SEA

KOLYMA

ARCTIC CIRCLE

KAMCHATKA

LENA

Iakutsk

SEA OF OKHOTSK

SAKHALIN

Nikolaevsk

LAKE BAIKAL

IABLONOVYI MOUNTAINS

Blagoveshchensk

Nerchinsk   Aigun   Khabarovsk

Chita   AMUR   USSURI

Kiakhta

CHINESE EASTERN RAILWAY

Urga

GOLIA   MANCHURIA   Vladivostok

Harbin

GOBI DESERT   CHINA   SEA OF JAPAN   JAPAN

Mukden   Tokyo

Peking   Kyoto

circa 1900   YALU   KOREA   Otsu

Pt. Arthur   Seoul

2000

Kiaochow Weihawei

1000   TSUSHIMA Nagasaki

Toward the Rising Sun

DAVID SCHIMMELPENNINCK VAN DER OYE

Toward the Rising Sun

Russian Ideologies of Empire

and the Path to War

with Japan

Northern

Illinois

University

Press

Library of Congress Cataloging-in-Publication Data

Schimmelpenninck van der Oye, David.

Toward the rising sun : Russian ideologies of empire

and the path to war with Japan/David

Schimmelpenninck van der Oye.

    p. cm.

Includes bibliographical references and index.

ISBN0-87580-276-1 (alk. paper)

1. Russo-Japanese War, 1904–1905—Causes. 2.

Russo-Japanese War, 1904–1905—Diplomatic

history. 3. Russia—Foreign relations—Japan. 4.

Japan—Foreign relations—Russia. 5. Russia—Foreign

relations— 1894–1917. 6. Japan—Foreign

relations—1868–1912. I. Title.

DS517.13 .S37 2001

952.03'1—dc21   2001030466

Portions of this book originally appeared in slightly

different form in Catherine Evtuhov, Boris Gasparov,

Alexander Ospovat, and Mark von Hagen, eds.,

Kazan, Moscow, St. Petersburg: Multiple Faces of the

Russian Empire (Moscow: ITS-Garant, 1997) and in

Cahiers du Monde Russe (41, 1 [2000]: 57–78).

Reprinted by permission of the publishers.

Voor Vader, van wie ik heb leren schrijven.

Contents

Maps

Illustrations

Preface

$\mathcal{T}$his book could not have been written before 1991. While drawing on a wide variety of sources, it is firmly grounded in archival work. When I carried out my research in Russia from 1993 through 1998 for *Toward the Rising Sun,* virtually all relevant collections in Moscow and St. Petersburg were freely accessible.

It has become a cliché that scholarship about the Soviet Union is being revolutionized as historians can now actually work with primary sources. Yet Soviet archival reticence did not just affect research into the USSR's past. Until 1991 tsarist repositories were also often out of reach. Even those collections that were not entirely closed frequently kept large portions of their holdings off-limits. Meanwhile, Soviet archivists were forbidden to make their finding aids available to scholars, making research even harder. The result was that those who studied the history of Imperial Russia largely had to rely on published document collections, prerevolutionary accounts, and the work of trusted Soviet scholars. Archival secrecy was particularly strict for diplomatic sources.

How did the opening of the archives affect this book? In the first flush of excitement after the fall of the Soviet Union, many hoped that radically freer access to the sources would revolutionize Russian history by opening an armory of "smoking guns." On one level the reality has been more mundane. The first decade of relative scholarly liberty in Russia has not magically resolved the major controversies of that nation's past, anymore than a much longer tradition of open access to document collections in the West has entirely freed our own bygone years of their mysteries.

Yet the effect of archival freedom on our understanding of Imperial Russian history will ultimately prove to be no less profound. The ability to work unhindered with the letters, diaries, notes, memoranda, and other writings of important decision makers makes a proper study of their ideas feasible. Likewise, over time the presence of historians patiently toiling through the immense records of the tsarist ancien régime will fundamentally alter its historiography, as it becomes more firmly anchored in objective fact.

Despite newer hardships imposed by severe budgetary constraints, Russia's archives proved to be both hospitable and professional. I would like to thank the directors and staffs of the following for their hospitality: Archive of the Foreign Ministry of the Russian Empire (AVPRI), State Archive of the Russian Federation (GARF), Scientific Archive of the Russian Geographical Society, Pushkin House (IRLI), Russian State Archive of the Navy (RGAVMF), Russian State Historical Archive (RGIA), Russian State Military History Archive (RGVIA), and the St. Petersburg branch of the Archive of the Academy of Sciences, in addition to the manuscript divisions of the Russian State Library and the Russian National Library. A number of other institutions in Russia also provided invaluable assistance for my research, including the Institute of Russian History (both in St. Petersburg and Moscow), the Department of History of Moscow State University, the Smolensk Pedagogical Institute, and the Przhevalskii Museum.

In the United States, I was very lucky to have worked in two of its great Slavic collections, at Yale and at the New York Public Library. I am indebted to the highly knowledgeable assistance provided by their curators, Tatjana Lorkovic and Edward Kasinec, respectively, as well as their staffs.

The following institutions largely funded the five years it took to research and write this book:

The Bradley Foundation
The Fox Fellowship
The International Research and Exchanges Board
The Olin Institute for Strategic Studies
The Smith Richardson Foundation
The Social Science and Humanities Research Council of Canada
The United States Institute of Peace
Yale University

It goes without saying that the views expressed in the following pages are entirely my own.

Toward the Rising Sun was begun as my doctoral thesis at Yale University. One of the privileges of studying there was the chance to be the apprentice of some of its distinguished historians. The members of my dissertation committee—Paul Kennedy, Jonathan Spence, Mark Steinberg, and Mark von Hagen (at Columbia)—have all been more than generous with their time, advice, and encouragement. Above all, I must thank my *nauchnyi rukoviditel*, Paul Bushkovitch. He has taught me much.

The book was completed during a fellowship at Harvard University's Olin Institute for Strategic Studies. I benefited enormously from the challenges of trying to make my work relevant to the Institute's political scientists, not to mention the congenial atmosphere inspired by its director, Samuel Huntington, and his associate, Stephen Rosen.

Many other scholars also took a lively interest in my peculiar pursuits. I am especially grateful to the following individuals, who shared their wisdom and friendship: Oleg Airapetov, Vladimir Alexandrov, Boris Ananich, Alekander Andreev, Tom Barrett, Leonard Blussé, Aleksandr Bokhanov, Jay Carter, Choi Dokkiu, Nikolaos Chrissidis, Valentin Emets, Lee Farrow, Tatiana Fillipova, William Fuller, Liudmilla Gatagova, Rafail Ganelin, Andrea Graziosi, Mary Habeck, Peter Holquist, Anatoli Ignatev, Nanno in 't Veld, Maija Jansson, Fred Kagan, Aleksandr Kavtaradze, Vladimir Lapin, John LeDonne, Andrei Levandovskii, Dominic Lieven, David McDonald, Louise McReynolds, Bruce Menning, Sergei Mironenko, William Odom, Dmitrii Oleinikov, Robert Ponichtera, David Rich, Vasily Rudich, Heather Ruland, Irina Rybachenok, Lev Savitsky, Fernande Scheid, George Schoolfield, Denis Showalter, Jennifer Siegel, Jennifer Spock, Richard Stites, David Stone, Theodore Taranovskii, Robin Winks, David Wolff, and Richard Wortmann. They deserve much of any credit this book may receive, but none of the opprobrium.

I am also appreciative of Northern Illinois University Press, especially the director, Mary Lincoln, and my copyeditor, Kevin Butterfield. It was a pleasure to work with them.

Most important, I must acknowledge my wife, Marie. Her patience and good cheer throughout have been nothing short of angelic. She is all the more remarkable for having tolerated frequent, long absences during the first years of our marriage, when it often seemed that her husband preferred the company of spies, poets, diplomats, and the Tsar of All the Russias, to that of his bride. She knows that it isn't so.

Note

*D*ates are according to the Julian calendar, which was then being used in Russia. In the nineteenth century, this calendar was 12 days behind the Gregorian calendar commonly employed in the West, whereas in the twentieth century it followed by 13 days. For example, when Russians in St. Petersburg celebrated the New Year on January 1, 1895, it was already January 13, 1895, in Paris and London. A chronology of key events in both Julian and Gregorian dates is included at the back. For measurements, I employ the metric system, although in a few cases I refer to the prerevolutionary *verst*, a unit of distance roughly equivalent to the kilometer.

Transliterations from the Cyrillic alphabet adhere to a modified form of the U.S. Library of Congress system, except for names and words widely known in English by other spellings. Thus, Alexander III and Nicholas II, rather than Aleksandr III and Nikolai II. Where Russian surnames were adapted from German or other Western languages, I generally use the original to avoid such awkward transliterations as "fon Giubennet" in the case of the Transportation Minister Adolph von Hubennet. As for Chinese words, I follow the Pinyin system, again with the exception of very familiar names, such as Peking and Kiaochow.

Unless otherwise indicated, translations from European languages are my own.

Toward the Rising Sun

"Восток дело тонкое"

Introduction

Russia, you are like a steed!

Your two front hooves have leaped far off into the darkness, into the void, while your two rear hooves are firmly planted in the granite soil. . . .

Once it has soared up on its hind legs, measuring the air with its eyes, the bronze steed will not set down its hooves. There will be a leap across history. Great shall be the turmoil. The earth shall be cleft. The very mountains shall be thrown down by the cataclysmic earthquake. . . .

In those days all the peoples of the earth will rush forth from their dwelling places. Great will be the strife, strife the like of which has never been seen in the world. The yellow hordes of Asians will set forth from their age-old abodes, and will encrimson the fields of Europe in oceans of blood. There will be, oh yes there will—Tsushima! The will be—a new Kalka!

Kulikovo Field, I await you!

—**From *Petersburg* by Andrei Bely**

*A*ndrei Bely's *Petersburg* is arguably the most important novel to emerge from the Silver Age, prerevolutionary Russia's symbolist florescence. First written in 1911, the narrative is set in the tsarist capital six years earlier, in autumn 1905. "Those were foggy days, strange days." A year and a half before, Imperial Russia had gone to war in distant Manchuria with little-known Japan. Defeat in East Asia had led to unrest in the heartland. "Through all the long nights the sky shone bloody with the glow of conflagrations in the countryside."[1] The jacquerie even menaced the great city itself.

The story ostensibly revolves around the reactionary senator,

Apollon Apollonovich Ableukhov, and his son, Nikolai Apollonovich. A confused intellectual who reads Kant and still lives at home, Nikolai has been ordered by a shadowy revolutionary group to assassinate his father with a bomb fashioned from a sardine can. Other clichés of late-nineteenth-century Russian literature abound, including shabby conspirators, adulterous wives, and agents provocateurs. Yet these characters are entirely secondary. The novel's true protagonist is the eponymous metropolis, and the plot really focuses on St. Petersburg's struggle for existence against myriad destructive powers, a battle of cosmos versus chaos. One critic described the work as "a rendition of delirium unprecedented in literature."[2]

Tsar Peter the Great's creation, "the most abstract and intentional city on the globe," has many meanings. To Bely, the artificial capital represented, among other things, reason, order, symmetry, man's struggle to tame the elements, the Romanov autocracy, and the West. Likewise, a number of angry, apocalyptic forces were waiting to engulf St. Petersburg. Nature, the dark proletarian masses, revolution, and Dionysian excess all threatened to sweep it into the turbulent waters of the Neva River. But the most violent danger was Asia, the Orient whose Mongol warriors had destroyed Russia seven centuries earlier, and which stood poised once again to march westward. Tsarist defeat on the Pacific in 1905 was a harbinger of more troubled times: "Port Arthur has fallen. That region has been inundated by yellow-faced people. The legends about the horsemen of Genghis Khan have come to life. . . . Listen, listen closely: there is a sound of galloping . . . from the Ural steppes. It is horsemen."[3]

Andrei Bely was not the only Silver Age author to see danger in the East. As in western Europe's fin de siècle, the yellow peril captivated the "frenzied poets" of the age. Like their French contemporaries, they combined a pessimistic outlook with a fascination for the exotic and the sinister. But if Charles Baudelaire, Joris-Karel Huysmans, and Gérard de Nerval had no Asian blood in their veins, the Russian symbolists were fully conscious of their Oriental heritage. On the one hand, as the passage above suggests, the deep foreboding that suffused Western literature of the age manifested itself in such novels as *Petersburg* as an atavistic fear of a latter-day Tartar Armageddon. Yet their overly refined aesthetic sensibilities also encouraged Silver Age Russians to stress their ties with their kinsmen to the east, real or imagined.

This profoundly ambivalent view of Asia, both as an alien element of destruction and as part of Russia's own heritage, permeates Bely's novel too. (*Petersburg* was the second installment of an uncompleted trilogy, provisionally titled "East or West?") Yellow is a dominant color, "Mongol mugs" people the boulevards, and many of the characters have Oriental links. The obscurantist bureaucrat Apollon Apollonovich in fact descends from the Central Asian Kirghiz-Kaisak horde. Although Apollon's devotion to mathematical precision and "the plane geometry of the state" suggests an entirely European mentality, his son is returning to his Asian roots. Nikolai Apollonovich flirts with Tibetan Buddhism, and at night he sees Confucius and

Genghis Khan in his fevered dreams. Puttering about his study dressed in a Bukhara dressing gown, Turkestan skull cap, and Tartar slippers, "thus was a brilliant student transformed into an Oriental."[4]

Petersburg is the best literary work to emerge from Russia's catastrophic war with Japan of 1904–1905.[5] It is by no means a campaign novel. Unlike such well-known books as *Tsushima,* by the radical sailor Aleksei Novikov-Priboi, Bely entirely ignores the fighting in the Far East.[6] His impressionist narrative focuses instead on the effect of the military fiasco on the urban home front. What the author describes so well is the confused mind-set of the capital's inhabitants after tsardom's humiliating defeat on the Pacific and the inchoate revolutionary turmoil that threatened to rise up and destroy the autocracy. More important, *Petersburg* reminds us that Russians thought about the East in several very different ways—as an object of conquest, a Mongol specter, or an undeniable element of their own racial genealogy. For precisely this reason, Bely's novel is also an excellent starting point for considering the events that led up to the war with Japan.

*I*n 1895 Japan unexpectedly beat China in a brief war. Russian diplomacy, which had lain dormant for more than a decade, suddenly sprang back to life. Nicholas II had just begun his reign, and the Far East excited his imagination. The Middle Kingdom's troubles seemed to offer many opportunities to the ambitious young tsar. Like Bely's steed, his empire leapt into the void and began its eastward plunge.

Over the next nine years, Russia galloped deeper into Asia. Its path was highly erratic. First, in 1896 the tsar concluded a defensive alliance with China, promising to protect the Middle Kingdom from the other powers that preyed on its realms. The following year St. Petersburg abruptly veered, seizing some choice territorial morsels for itself on the Liaodong Peninsula, not far from Peking itself. Three years later, in 1900, Russia seemed to resume its original direction and professed to help a China racked by the Boxer rising against the Western nations out for its blood. Then Cossacks suddenly marched into the Qing dynasty's ancestral provinces of Manchuria. Although the tsar's government formally promised to evacuate, it seemed bent on annexing the region instead and even appeared to have designs on Korea. Finally, early in 1904 Russia stumbled into a war with Japan few foresaw and even fewer wanted.

Why such wandering? To many Russian observers, both before and after the revolution of 1917, the cause lay in the corruption of a decadent imperial court. According to this reasoning, the Far East inspired a variety of rival mercenary schemes promoted by shadowy intimates of the tsar and his ministers of state. One of the first proponents of the "scapegoat" school was the former war minister, General Aleksei Kuropatkin. Four years after the Russian defeat, he published an account of the conflict and its origins, *The Russian Army and the Japanese War.*[7] Trying to exculpate himself from the debacle, the general suggested that it had been caused by the provocative activities of a business enterprise, the Yalu forestry concession. Based on northern Korea's frontier, this Russian venture had been championed by an intimate of the tsar, Guards Captain Aleksandr Bezobrazov.

Several years later the Russian historian Boris Glinskii took a similar tack when he published *Prolog Russko-Iaponskoi voiny* (The Prologue of the Russo-Japanese War), a detailed diplomatic history of the prewar years.[8] The book's subtitle, "Materials from the Archive of Count Witte," reveals its strengths and weaknesses. The former finance minister, Sergei Witte, had granted Glinskii extensive access to his personal papers. As a result, Glinskii's account provides much useful primary material. At the same time, the historian's intimacy with Witte led him to agree with the latter's stress on "the Bezobrazov cabal."

Boris Romanov's *Russia in Manchuria* is the best-known study that follows this line of reasoning.[9] Published in Leningrad in 1928, it appeared in a time of relative academic liberalism, when many scholars still enjoyed fairly free access to prerevolutionary government archives. As a student of the "St. Petersburg School," which emphasized a thorough and critical examination of the sources, Romanov tried to make full use of the privilege (although the foreign ministry's records remained off-limits). Like Glinskii's *Prolog*, Romanov's *Russia in Manchuria* provides a detailed analysis of tsarist involvement on the Pacific, including exhaustive accounts of Sergei Witte's policies and the schemes of Guards Captain Bezobrazov.

Boris Romanov's demonology differs from Glinskii's. His villain is the former finance minister. Sergei Witte, who dominated Far Eastern affairs until his demise in 1903, comes across as devious and vain. According to Romanov, Witte bears much of the blame for involving the empire in a highly perilous undertaking. Thus the finance minister's policies in the region, including the Trans-Siberian Railway—a "driving belt to the machinery of world imperialism"—and his irresponsible East Asian diplomacy laid much of the groundwork for the conflict. Nevertheless, Romanov also points his finger at the "militarist clique" led by Captain Bezobrazov, which he concludes directly provoked Japan into the war.

United Government and Foreign Policy in Russia, a recent monograph by the Canadian scholar David McDonald, is the most objective version of the scapegoat interpretation.[10] The bulk of McDonald's narrative deals with ministerial politics after the empire's defeat on the Pacific. However, the first three chapters describe the bureaucratic infighting in the years leading up to the war, which McDonald argues lay at the heart of St. Petersburg's disastrous diplomacy.

Another approach to explaining the outbreak of the Russo-Japanese War has been to examine the diplomatic context. Rather than find fault with a certain individual or a particular regime, this method tries dispassionately to chronicle the past on the basis of as many sources as scholars can read, in the style of the nineteenth-century German historian Leopold von

Ranke. The work of Harvard's William Langer remains the model of this type of scholarship. His *Diplomacy of Imperialism,* while not solely concerned with Russian affairs in East Asia, covers some of the more important episodes up to 1902 in great detail.[11] An earlier essay, "The Origin of the Russo-Japanese War," takes the story up to January 1904.[12] William Langer's deep familiarity with the published sources provides a rich background of the relations among the great powers at the time. Unfortunately, he wrote his studies some time ago and therefore does not incorporate much of the post–World War II literature.

Andrew Malozemoff's *Russian Far Eastern Policy* is somewhat less detached, and it seems to have been intended as a rebuttal to Romanov's *Russia in Manchuria*.[13] Originally written in the early 1950s as a Berkeley dissertation, the monograph strives both to rehabilitate Sergei Witte and to downplay the impact of the Bezobrazov group. Disagreeing with Romanov, Malozemoff describes the finance minister as a competent and honorable statesman, and he considers Bezobrazov to be a figure of limited importance. According to Malozemoff, war with Japan came about largely because of diplomatic bungling. His prose is clearer and less tainted by vitriol than that of Romanov. Although Malozemoff was writing at a time when access to tsarist archives was strictly controlled, he did consult an impressive number of published sources.

Two recent books, S. C. M. Paine's *Imperial Rivals: China, Russia, and Their Disputed Frontier* and David Wolff's *To the Harbin Station: The Liberal Alternative in Russian Manchuria,* also belong in this category.[14] Paine carried out the bulk of her research in Russia in the early 1990s, when archival restrictions were just beginning to be eased. She was therefore one of the first Western scholars to benefit from even partial access to the relevant sources. Meanwhile, in addition to working in archives in the capitals, David Wolff traveled to local repositories in eastern Siberia. Their most important innovation, however, was to examine both Russian *and* Chinese sources in addition to the English-language literature.

The best study in the Rankean tradition is also the most obscure. In a footnote to "The Origins of the Russo-Japanese War," William Langer speculated about the existence of a manuscript by Major General Panteleimon Simanskii.[15] Simanskii was a member of the committee set up in 1906 by the imperial army to write an official history of the war. The group's aim was neither to glorify nor to defend Russian military performance in the Far East, but to write an unbiased postmortem to help guide necessary reforms.

Simanskii's orders were to study the events leading to the conflict. After the personal intercession of Tsar Nicholas II, the general was given entirely unrestricted access to all relevant government archives, including those of the army, navy, finance, and foreign ministry. When Foreign Minister Aleksandr Izvolskii read Simanskii's draft, however, he was horrified by the amount of classified information the officer disclosed from his department's closely guarded records. Izvolskii ordered Simanskii to cut most of this material, and a radically abridged version appeared as the first part of the army's multivolume history, *Russko-iaponskaia voina* (The Russo-Japanese War).[16] Nevertheless, Langer's hunch had been right. The original, unexpurgated version of Simanskii's manuscript was published after all, albeit in a strictly limited, secret edition, as *Sobytiia na Dalnem Vostoke* (The Events in the Far East). The General Staff's press printed only seven copies, which were presented to the tsar, a few ministers, General Gurko, and the author himself. Until very recently, surviving copies of the book were unavailable to scholars.[17]

The scapegoat and Rankean approaches both help explain Russia's role in the origins of its war with Japan. By looking at the political maneuvering of leading officials, members of the scapegoat school such as Glinskii, Romanov, and McDonald help explain the inconsistent course of Russian policy before the war. At the same time, the prodigious academic spadework of the Rankeans provides many insights into the background. Yet one important factor all of these works neglect is the intellectual motivation of the key decision makers. We cannot properly understand the inconsistent course of Russian diplomacy before 1904 without studying the different thoughts that inspired Nicholas II and his statesmen to turn to the East.

Since the 1960s, Western scholars have been paying considerable attention to the role of ideology in European diplomacy and imperialism. On both sides of the Atlantic, much has been written about the intellectual aspects of such phenomena as Spanish, British, and French colonial expansion as well as international relations more generally.[18] Meanwhile, throughout the Cold War, Soviet foreign policy was the subject of much debate among political scientists who emphasized Marxist-Leninist doctrine and their "realist" colleagues, who looked to the more pragmatic imperatives of national interest. But, as a factor in Russian diplomacy before 1917, ideology remains neglected. Even when academics have considered the intellectual underpinnings of tsarist imperialism, they have invariably reduced it to a single, dominant philosophy. The best example is the Russian variant of Pan-Slavism, the late-nineteenth-century notion of a mission to rule over ethnic cousins then under Ottoman and Hapsburg sway.

The credo of Russia's Asian territorial growth has been the subject of particularly creative speculation. Nineteenth-century American observers often recognized it as a worldview akin to their own "Manifest Destiny."[19] Lord George Curzon, one of Victorian Britain's leading Russophobes, saw every tsarist action east of the Ural Mountains as part of a sinister plan to conquer the entire continent, right up to the Indian Ocean. Meanwhile, Tsar Alexander II's foreign minister, Prince Aleksander Gorchakov, spoke of Russia's need to pacify the frontier, like "all civilized states that come into contact with half-savage, wandering tribes."[20] Many other explanations exist, but they also concentrate on one, single imperative.

In fact, tsarist diplomacy in Asia was very rarely driven by a solitary ideology. Like the behavior of most states, it was almost always shaped by several intellectual currents, some complementary and others contradictory. This was particularly true for the decade before the Russo-Japanese War. In an era of intense interest in East Asia, policy was shaped by competing philosophies, each of which represented a particular view of Russia's imperial destiny. At times one of these alone dominated, and on other occasions some of them jointly oriented St. Petersburg's actions. To understand why the tsar's government behaved as it did, it helps to identify these views and study how they interacted rather than to focus on a single ideology. A careful analysis of the ideas about Asia and empire that were current in St. Petersburg at the time, as well as how they affected and were affected by tsarist diplomacy, will shed much light on Russia's prewar policy.

Ideology is a notoriously slippery concept. Terry Eagleton, an Oxford literary scholar, identified no less than 16 meanings for this noun, while his university's dictionary contains four. In *Toward the Rising Sun* I employ the *Oxford English Dictionary*'s following definition of ideology: "A systematic scheme of ideas, usu[ally] relating to politics or society, or to the conduct of a class or group, and regarded as justifying actions. . . ."[21] Further muddying the waters are the different degrees to which ideology is believed to influence thought. For Marxists, it represents no less than the entire intellectual and cultural superstructure of the dominant class. Some twentieth-century ideologies, such as Marxism-Leninism under Joseph Stalin and Adolph Hitler's National Socialism, tried to put this theory into practice by imposing themselves on nearly all aspects of human thinking, albeit with varying degrees of success. One cliché has it that ideologies are "secularized religions." But, like religion, ideology is not always all-encompassing. In considering ideology, I tend to agree with the McMaster historian Alan Cassels, who adopts a less sweeping approach. In his book *Ideology and International Relations in the Modern World*, Cassels argues that, compared to the "totalitarian" belief systems of Stalin and Hitler, "partial, unsophisticated ideology . . . has brought just as much weight to bear [on international relations] and over a longer time span."[22]

Russian thinking about Asia also tells us something about the empire's sense of itself. When considering Russia's cultural geography, scholars usually study its relationship to the West. Comparatively little attention has been paid to Russia's ties to the East, although interest has been growing in recent years, most notably with the appearance of Mark Bassin's *Imperial Visions: Nationalist Imagination and Geographical Expansion in the Russian Far East.*[23]

The study of Western perceptions of the East has been strongly influenced by Edward Said. A professor of English and comparative literature at Columbia University in New York, Said first raised the question when he published *Orientalism* in 1978, arguing that the scholarly apparatus whereby the West studies the East is also a means for the former to control the latter.[24] Closely linked to these ideas about perception as oppression is his notion that Occidentals think about the Orient as the "Other," a mysterious, feminized, malevolent, and dangerous "cultural contestant." Said argues that Orientalists tend to see the world in Manichaean terms, with the West as intrinsically hostile to the East. Said's Orientalist thesis may be a useful starting point for reflecting on Russia's notions of the East. Some Russians, such as the bellicose explorer Nikolai Przhevalskii, easily fit into Said's schema of Europeans who are hostile to Asia and yearn to subjugate it. But for many of Przhevalskii's compatriots the matter was more complicated. Caryl Emerson, another literary scholar, points out: "Both culturally and politically Russia has genuine roots in . . . Asia, which made the Orient both self and other."[25]

Unlike the English or the French, whose views Said studies, some Russians have also been conscious of an Asian heritage. At times, the East has taken an important place in Russian intellectual life, especially in moments of ideological malaise and self-scrutiny. The early-twentieth-century poet Aleksandr Blok was not alone when he declared, "We are Asians too, from shores that breed squint eyes bespeaking greed!"[26] Ideas about an Oriental destiny, or even identity, were particularly prominent in the years before the war with Japan.

This book studies the interplay of ideology and foreign policy in Russia during the decade before the outbreak of war with Japan. The first section, "Ideologies of Empire," looks closely at four very different conceptions of imperial destiny that all influenced tsarist policy in Asia at the time. But it starts with a trip to Asia by the heir to the Russian throne, the future Tsar Nicholas II. Begun in 1890, the Oriental grand tour awoke the tsarevich to promises of glory and greatness on the Pacific. Although he rarely expressed any original ideas about his empire's role on the continent, there were others who readily gave voice to Nicholas's infatuation with Asia.

Many Russians, especially military men, saw the Far East as an object of conquest for the sake of conquest. The most eloquent exponent of this idea was the late-nineteenth-century Inner Asian explorer Nikolai Przhevalskii. Przhevalskii was by no means the originator of this ideology of "conquistador imperialism." His philosophy was often shared by Europeans in an age that saw the great (and not so great) powers scrambling for colonies in the weaker continents of Africa and Asia.

If Przhevalskii's ideas were not exclusively Russian, another dominant intellectual current was unique. "Asianism," the fin de siècle philosophy that stressed Russia's Asian heritage and destiny, had few parallels abroad. The poet, newspaper publisher, and intimate of Nicholas II, Prince Esper Ukhtomskii, was the leading advocate of this important but little-studied ideology. After the revolution of 1917, these notions would inspire a circle of émigré intellectuals, who developed a variation on Ukhtomskii's Asianist theme with their vision of Russia as "Eurasian."

The prince often found a political ally in Finance Minister Sergei Witte. Like Ukhtomskii, Witte opposed armed conquest in the East. But the minister's motives were very different. Arguing that Russia was fundamentally European rather than Asian, Witte proposed extending tsarist influence into the Far East through nonviolent, economic, and commercial means, or *pénétration pacifique* (peaceful penetration). Other ideologies also influenced Russia's turn to the East, and chapter 5 examines War Minister Aleksei Kuropatkin's fears of a yellow peril.

The book's second part, "The Path to War," explains how the empire became entangled in East Asia at the turn of the twentieth century. The story has often been told, but until very recently scholars virtually never enjoyed full access to the relevant tsarist archives. In describing the diplomacy, *Toward the Rising Sun* also examines how policy makers in St. Petersburg thought about those events. Government memoranda, "what one clerk wrote to another," provide important clues about "the official mind." However, the press, "thick journals," popular books, and even poetry also tell us much about these ideas. The narrative opens and closes with Admiral Togo's nighttime raid on Nicholas II's Pacific Fleet at Port Arthur on January 26, 1904, which began the war with Japan (all dates are according to the Julian calendar then in use in Russia). The concluding chapter, "Thinking about the Far East," examines more closely the interplay between ideas and the policies they inspired.

The first decade of Nicholas II's reign is an excellent test case for the study of Russian imperial ideologies. The nation's flirtation with the East was relatively brief. It began with the Sino-Japanese War of 1894–1895, when Japan's easy victories suggested opportunities for expansion into China, and ended with Russia's own defeat in Asia ten years later. At the same time, the various ideas that shaped policy all had eloquent proponents, who wrote at great length about their thoughts. Russia's fin de siècle was a period of fascination with the exoticism of the Orient, and thinking about Asia was also richly represented in the literature and art of the time. The recent opening of previously inaccessible archives now makes a proper analysis feasible.

The British diplomatic historian James Joll once famously urged his students to study "the unspoken assumptions" of Europe's statesmen.[27] But, for Russians, even the thoughts *publicly* expressed about their place in the world have been almost entirely ignored. *Toward the Rising Sun* examines some of their spoken assumptions.

Part One

Ideologies of Empire

CHAPTER ONE

The Grand Tour

Nicholas II

The great journey he undertook when he was still the heir to the throne gave Nicholas an unrealistic impression of Russia's omnipotence in the Far East. He travels for weeks on end in the boundless expanses of Siberia, so scenic, so immensely rich. Abroad, people hail him almost as a deity. . . . Here, in the Far East, the Tsarevich first understands his true destiny. Here, in the Orient, strong passions and bright colours first intrude into his quiet and drab existence.

—Georgii Ivanov

*O*n a gray, raw afternoon in late October 1890, a train pulled out of the small station at Gatchina Palace on the Warsaw Railroad, south of St. Petersburg. Its most important occupant was the 22-year-old heir to the Russian throne, Grand Duke Nicholas Alexandrovich. He had just completed his formal schooling, and his parents were rewarding him with the grand tour, still a traditional rite of passage for the wellborn at the end of the nineteenth century. Under the benevolent supervision of the aging Major General Prince Vladimir Bariatinskii, the tsarevich was accompanied by his younger brother, Grand Duke George Alexandrovich, three Guards officers, and a poet.

Typically a lavish and leisurely ramble on the Continent, the grand tour customarily included the great capitals, where the traveler would acquaint himself with international society and perhaps sow a few wild oats before assuming the responsibilities of adulthood. The trip's primary goal, however, was pedagogical. Obligatory sojourns would be made to important historical and cultural sites, like the cathedrals of medieval France and

Germany and the ruins of ancient Rome, in a pilgrimage to the wellsprings of Western civilization.[1] Yet, if Nicholas's journey bore all of the hallmarks of the ritual grand tour, with its formulaic itinerary of important cities, illustrious personages, and decaying monuments, the destination was decidedly unconventional, for instead of taking him to Europe, the tsarevich's voyage was meant to introduce him to Asia.[2]

The imperial train headed south, passing through Russian Poland, and crossed the Austro-Hungarian border at Szczakowa. Stopping briefly in Vienna to attend a state dinner hosted by Emperor Franz Joseph at Schönbrunn Castle, the travelers reached the Adriatic port of Trieste within three days. There they were greeted by Rear Admiral Vladimir Basargin of the Imperial Russian Navy, who escorted them aboard the frigate *Pamiat Azova*.[3] Along with the frigate *Vladimir Monomakh* and the gunboat *Zaparozhets*, the ship sailed to the Aegean, making land at Athens to pick up Nicholas's cousin, Crown Prince George of Greece, who joined the group.

Egypt was the grand tour's first destination. As the Russian squadron entered Port Said, naval salutes and the Russian and Greek national anthems filled the air. The Khedive Tewfik Pasha welcomed the royal visitors with the requisite round of parades, receptions, and other courtesies, and he generously lent his yacht for a cruise up the Nile. For more than two weeks the grand duke and his companions toured the country. In his diary, Nicholas duly described his excursions to the temple of Karnak, the tombs of the pharaohs, the bazaar at Aswan, and frequent after-dinner performances by the local belly dancers.[4]

At the end of November, the tsarevich reboarded the *Pamiat Azova* and continued southward. There was a brief stay in the British Red Sea port of Aden, and on December 11 the group arrived in Bombay, India. Although the "Great Game," an intense rivalry between England and Russia in Asia, was still at its height and London's colonial authorities looked on tsarist intentions in the region with great suspicion, they did their best to be hospitable. The young heir, on the other hand, betrayed little affection for the rival power. In a letter to his father from Bombay he complained that "our host the governor is simply an ass," and a few weeks later, in Delhi, he confessed "how intolerable it is to be once again surrounded by Englishmen and their scarlet uniforms."[5] Not surprisingly, the tsarevich was much more enthusiastic about the tiger hunts and treks into the interior. "To me, the most interesting [aspect of India] were our visits to the various maharajas. Their life has such an unusual and theatrical air; it reeks of antiquity," he wrote his sister.[6] On the whole, the heir enjoyed his six-week journey in the subcontinent, although he was saddened when, toward the end of January 1891, his younger brother was diagnosed with tuberculosis and had to return home.

The *Pamiat Azova*'s next port of call was in Ceylon, where Nicholas crossed paths with his cousin Sandro (Grand Duke Alexander Mikhailovich), who was taking an extensive cruise of his own, and joined him for an elephant shoot.[7] In mid-February the ship proceeded to Singapore. Two

The future Tsar Nicholas II

months of touring Britain's South Asian possessions had not left the tsare-vich with a favorable impression of the Royal Navy. "I was really surprised at the kind of rubbish [the English] send to the Orient," he reported to his fa-ther. "One would think that here they would keep a squadron more worthy of their maritime greatness. . . . This makes me all the happier, dear Papa, since we must be stronger than the British in the Pacific Ocean."[8]

While in the port, the Russian frigate made contact with a cruiser sent by the Siamese king to extend an official invitation to visit Bangkok. Squeezed by an aggressive English colonial presence in Burma to the west and the equally ambitious French in Cambodia on its eastern frontier, the Asian monarchy ex-isted precariously as one of the few independent nations in the region.[9] Its ruler, King Chulalongkorn, was eager to court a major power with no ambi-tions on his realm, in the hope that good relations with St. Petersburg might help deter the attentions of others.[10] Sailing by way of Batavia (now Jakarta) in the Dutch East Indies, where they spent a fortnight sightseeing and hunting crocodiles as guests of the governor general, C. H. Pijnacker Hordijk, the Russians reached the Siamese capital in early March. King Chulalongkorn pulled out all the stops, treating the tsarevich to marches-past of war elephants in his park at Chakra Kri Palace and a stay at the royal country residence of Bang-pa-in. The Siamese monarch broached the subject of closer ties, although it would take another seven years for the two nations to get around to exchanging legations.[11] Nevertheless, the stay proved to be one of the highlights of Nicholas's tour. "This nation is truly blessed," he wrote home, "for it is so far entirely unspoiled by the Europeans."[12]

From Bangkok, the *Pamiat Azova* went on to the French Indochinese city of Saigon and in late March steamed into Hong Kong harbor. "At last we have arrived in China, the land of mandarins, slippers, and pigtails," the tsarevich reported.[13] After the obligatory exchange of courtesies with British officials, Nicholas boarded a ship sent by Li Hangzhang, the viceroy of Canton, to take him to the mainland.[14] Although Li often spurned efforts by European dignitaries to visit him, he extended a warm welcome to the grand duke. Unlike the English, French, and Germans, whose merchants and missionaries were a noxious presence in the area, the Russians seemed more benign.[15] To be sure, Russia had joined in the free-for-all on the Middle Kingdom's territory in a previous decade, but ten years earlier their tsar had actually returned some lands to the Qing dynasty, an act virtually unprecedented in the troubled annals of nineteenth-century relations with the West.

Nicholas got on well with the old viceroy, who reminded him of an Orthodox cleric, and was not put off by the exotic fare at his banquet. His letters home, however, do not suggest that he particularly enjoyed Canton. The city was crowded, its streets unspeakably filthy, the surrounding waters infested with pirates.[16] Nicholas's initial impression of East Asia's people recalls a racist cliché: "What a strange impression this sea of yellow faces made on me; they all look alike!"[17] The tsarevich's Chinese stay also included a few days in the Yangzi River treaty port of Hankou, to greet its colony of Russian tea merchants.

The last leg of the Oriental tour was in Japan. The heir had long looked forward to this part of his journey, and at first he was not disappointed. As he wrote his sister: "Only a few days here and I'm absolutely in heaven."[18] Nagasaki was the first stop, but since it was the Russian Holy Week, the official welcome was put off for a few days until after Easter Sunday. The exigencies of Lent did not however prevent Nicholas from making frequent incognito forays onshore to shop for souvenirs. At the time Nagasaki served as the winter base for Russia's Pacific squadron and the grand duke was delighted to discover that a number of storekeepers addressed him in his native tongue.[19]

Although in the early 1870s relations had been strained over the ownership of Sakhalin Island and some Japanese politicians now fretted about tsarist designs on Korea, at the time of the heir's visit ties between the two

"The Welcome to Hankou"—One of many scenes in Prince Ukhtomskii's official account of the tsarevich's grand tour that suggests all Asia adored the Russian heir.

empires were relatively cordial. Both the government and the public generally saw the visit of a future monarch as an honor, and Nicholas was greeted politely.[20] On April 22, Easter Monday, Prince Arisugawa met the party on behalf of the mikado and escorted the Russians by rickshaw into Nagasaki past cheering crowds for a formal lunch with the governor. The following day, the tsarevich and his companions traveled to Kagoshima Island, where the Satsuma Prince Shimazu put on displays of sumo wrestling, kendo, and samurai drill.

From Kagoshima the *Pamiat Azova* sailed northward through the Strait of Shimonoseki and dropped anchor in Kobe. The passengers toured the port to lusty shouts of *"Kotaishi denka banzai!"* (Long live the Crown

Prince!) by students lining the streets and proceeded by train to the old capital of Kyoto.[21] Ever the enthusiastic tourist, Nicholas rejected the Western-style rooms his hosts had prepared for him there, asking to be put up in Japanese quarters instead. As in Siam, the grand duke enjoyed the city's thoroughly Asian ambiance: "I was pleased to notice a total absence of Europeans—only Japanese men and women and nothing else."[22] He especially appreciated the latter; he was quite taken by the geishas who danced for him in Kyoto's tea houses.[23] So far the tsarevich was having a good time: "On the whole we were so impressed by the Japanese, their hospitality, and all of their wares and knickknacks that we forgot all about the countries we had already seen."[24]

On Monday, April 29, Nicholas made a short trip to the nearby town of Otsu. As he rode through its streets in a rickshaw one of the constables guarding the street suddenly lunged and struck him on the head with his sword. The blade did not penetrate very deeply and, before he could make another try, the would-be assassin was wrestled to the ground by the rickshaw pullers. Rushed back to Kyoto on a special train, the grand duke was tended by surgeons from the Russian squadron, who sewed up the cuts with a few stitches. The wounds proved to be superficial, and he made a speedy recovery.[25]

On the whole, Nicholas took the incident in good stride. More than anything he seemed embarrassed at the public outpourings of contrition for the act and worried about his hosts' discomfort.[26] Back in St. Petersburg, however, the heir's parents were alarmed. Alexander immediately ordered his son back on board the *Pamiat Azova,* cutting the tour short.[27] Nevertheless, the diplomatic repercussions were slight. Dmitrii Shevich, the Russian minister to Japan, readily accepted official explanations that the attacker had been a lone "patriotic fanatic" and was impressed by the government's efforts to atone, and the tsar hastened to assure Tokyo that there would be no reprisals.[28] As for the tsarevich, he was quick to forgive. "Strange to say I like Japan just as much as before," he wrote his mother as he was leaving the country, "and the incident of April 29 left no hard feelings; I'm just not very fond of police uniforms anymore!"[29] Fourteen years later, in the second year of his reign, Nicholas would tell a German visitor: "Essentially I have much affection for the Japanese, despite the injury whose mark I bear." Pointing to the scar on his forehead, the tsar added: "This was the work of a fanatic."[30] He was well aware that political assassination attempts were not a custom exclusive to Japan.

In mid-May the grand duke was back on Russian soil, at the young Pacific port of Vladivostok. This was the first time the Far Eastern outpost had hosted a person of his stature, so the local citizens took advantage of the heir's presence to stage a number of civic celebrations, enlisting the tsarevich to unveil a statue and open construction of a new dry dock. The most important ceremony came on May 19, when Nicholas turned the turf to start work on the eastern end of the Trans-Siberian Railway. Only a few months earlier, Alexander III had announced the start of this enormous 8,000-kilometer project to span Asiatic Russia by rail. The scheme appeared well justified on strategic and economic grounds, but there were still some powerful opponents within the imperial administration. Involving the heir to the throne seemed to be a good way of underscoring the tsar's determination to see the plan through.[31] As Alexander wrote his son: "The important role you will play in beginning this national task that I have commanded will prove my sincere desire to bring Siberia closer to the rest of the Empire, thereby showing this region—so dear to my heart—my strong wish for its peaceful prosperity."[32]

A little more than a week after his arrival in Vladivostok, Nicholas was on his way back to Europe. He made the journey across Siberia in leisurely fashion, stopping in such towns as Blagoveshchensk, Irkutsk, and Omsk, where he reviewed local Cossack regiments and received delegations of Buriats, Kirghiz, and other nationalities professing loyalty to their future sovereign.[33] The grand duke was clearly in awe of the Asian realms he stood to inherit. In a letter to Sandro shortly after his return, he could barely contain his excitement about what he had seen during these final months:

> Everything I have witnessed has made such a deep impression that only by talking to you in person can I properly pass on my impressions about this rich and great land, which, sad to say, has until now been virtually unknown to us Russians! Not to speak of the future of eastern Siberia and, especially, the southern Ussuri region.[34]

Because of the war that would break out within the first decade of Nicholas II's reign, there has been much speculation about the effect of the Oriental grand tour on his thinking.[35] One émigré biographer argued that the tsar was "the first sovereign to traverse the entire breadth of Siberia. He was seized by the spirit of the pioneer and his juvenile imagination played with grandiose ideas."[36] Meanwhile, in his memoirs Sergei Witte concluded:

> When the young Tsarevich unexpectedly became Emperor because of the untimely death of his father, it seems justifiable to believe that as a result of the impressions produced on him by the journey he dreamed of expanding the great Russian Empire in the Far East by subordinating the Chinese Bogdykhan [emperor], as the Emir of Bukhara had been subordinated, and possibly adding such titles as Bogdykhan of China and Mikado of Japan to the titles he already held.[37]

Nicholas was notoriously reticent about such matters in his writings, and scholars have voiced much frustration in trying to make sense of his ideas from such sources.[38] In the main, the diary entries and letters Nicholas wrote during the journey are rather typical of a nineteenth-century European aristocrat. As a lad who had just finished his education,

Allegory of Nicholas's Asian grand Tour—As imagined by the artist N. Karazin in
Ukhtomskii's *Travels in the East of His Imperial Majesty.*

the grand duke was out to enjoy himself, and it was natural for his correspondence to dwell on big game hunts, escapades with his companions,
and the local women.[39] Nicholas's letters home also betray a fascination
with the exotic. His predilections for the pyramids of Giza, the elephants of
Siam, and the floating cities of Canton were characteristic of the well-bred
Victorian tourist. Much the same could also be said about the jingo patrio-

tism he expressed when scorning the British fleet in Singapore and Hong Kong. Nicholas's writings as tsar, after he inherited the throne in 1894, are no more enlightening. His letters, conversations, and the brief marginal notes he penciled on official paperwork continued to be laconic. The only way to understand how his subjects thought about their empire and its role in the Far East is to look at what more eloquent individuals had to say.

Nevertheless, as Nicholas's note to Sandro about Siberia suggests, the trip clearly aroused a strong interest for the East in his imagination. One of his first official duties as tsarevich came in 1893 with his appointment as chairman of the committee overseeing construction of the Trans-Siberian Railway, an assignment he carried out with great zeal.[40] When Nicholas inherited the throne a little more than a year later, advocates of a forward policy in Asia would begin to find a sympathetic hearing in their audiences with the new tsar. Prince Esper Ukhtomskii, the trip's official chronicler, hardly exaggerated when he wrote that "the journey of the Tsarevich through the civilised countries of the East is full of deep significance for Russia."[41]

CHAPTER TWO

Conquistador Imperialism

Nikolai Przhevalskii

Our military conquests in Asia bring glory not only to Russia; they are also victories for the good of mankind. Carbine bullets and rifled cannon bear those elements of civilization that would otherwise be very long in coming to the petrified realms of the Inner Asian Khans.

—**Nikolai Przhevalskii**

*I*n February 1952, the prominent Soviet director Sergei Iutkevitch released his first color film, an epic based on the travels of the nineteenth-century Russian explorer, Nikolai Mikhailovich Przhevalskii, into deepest Inner Asia. Appropriately titled *Przhevalskii,* this action-packed adventure followed the hero's exploits as he struggled against both the rigors of nature and the machinations of evil foes, such as reactionary geographers, Manchu officials, and the sinister British agent, Mr. Simon. Moviegoers also enjoyed footage of exotic wildlife, desert caravans, Mongolian yurts, vulture shoots, and the classical Chinese theater. Since the feature was produced at the height of Sino-Soviet concord, the explorer was naturally portrayed as a great friend of the Asian masses, championing the cause of oppressed Chinese and Korean peasants wherever he journeyed.[1] The Soviet Communist Party daily *Pravda* gave the movie a rave review, praising it above all for "showing that Przhevalskii's work expresses the progressive role of Russian culture in Asia."[2]

When Iutkevich first arrived in Beijing with his crew to carry out some shoots for the film, the director met with strong objections from Chinese authorities about the subject matter. These officials did not quite see Przhevalskii as a great humanitarian who trekked to Inner Asia to promote friendship between the peoples of Russia and China. In their eyes the geographer, who wore the uni-form of a tsarist army officer, was nothing more than a spy and an enemy of China. It was only after the intervention of the Soviet ambassador, who ap-pealed directly to Liu Shaoqi, secretary of the Chinese Communist Party's Central Committee, that work on the production was allowed to proceed.[3]

Moscow's diplomacy notwithstanding, the Chinese had an accurate view of the explorer's role and ideas. Although the Imperial Russian Geographi-cal Society sponsored his four journeys to Inner Asia during the 1870s and the 1880s, Przhevalskii was an officer attached to the Main Staff, the Russ-ian army's unit responsible for military intelligence. Przhevalskii's accounts of his trips, while largely read as contributions to geography, also served as reconnaissance reports for a possible campaign into China's borderlands during a time of heightened tension between the empires of the Romanov and Qing dynasties.[4]

The officials in Beijing who complained about Iutkevich's film project were also entirely on the mark when they characterized Przhevalskii as an enemy of their nation. Even the most cursory reading of the explorer's books reveals a profound contempt for China and its people. More to the point, on the question of Russian policy vis-à-vis the Celestial Empire, Przhevalskii was an outright hawk. When the War Ministry summoned him in 1886 to participate in a special committee to study Sino-Russian rela-tions, the officer advocated war to annex the Qing Dynasty's borderlands of Xinjiang, Mongolia, and Tibet.

During his lifetime, few of Przhevalskii's compatriots shared his bellicose views, but many Russians lionized him as a romantic hero. Like the Scottish missionary David Livingstone, his exploits were well covered by the popular press, and the books he wrote about his journeys were widely read. When Przhevalskii died in 1888, the novelist Anton Chekhov mourned him as a man Russia needs "as it needs the sun."[5] More important, the explorer did much to popularize notions of a special destiny in Asia. Within a decade of his death, as Russians turned their interest to the Far East, many began to share his sentiments. In the early years of Nicholas II's reign, Przhevalskii's ideology of imperial conquest, largely for the sake of conquest, would come to represent a highly aggressive strain in tsarist thinking about Asia. Advo-cates of an active forward policy in Manchuria and Korea often echoed the ideas and rhetoric of his "conquistador imperialism." Much as the tales of the Dark Continent's explorers helped inspire a "scramble for Africa" among Europeans in the 1880s, Przhevalskii's adventures drove not a few of his countrymen to seek similar glory in the Orient some twenty years later.

*E*very Russian schoolchild knows about Nikolai Przhevalskii. The future Inner Asian geographer was born into a household of minor landowners in the government of Smolensk in 1839.[6] As the surname suggests, Przheval-skii's ancestors had been polonized Cossacks, whose origins were somewhat to the west, in the lands that had come under Russian rule during the reign of Catherine the Great in 1772.[7] His grandfather, Kazimir Przewalski, readily switched his allegiance to the Romanov dynasty and was rebaptized into the Orthodox Church in the 1790s as Kuzma Fomich. The family proved to be loyal to their new sovereigns. Kuzma's son, Mikhail Kuzmich, served the tsar as a junior officer during the Polish rebellion of 1831 before retiring to his wife's modest estate of Otradnoe, not far from the provincial capital.

Nikolai Mikhailovich did not get to know his father well. Always sickly, the subaltern died when his son was only seven, leaving the boy entirely in the care of his capable and ambitious mother, Elena Alekseevna. She gave him an idyllic childhood that seems to have been largely spent outdoors. "I grew up in the countryside like a savage, with the most spartan upbringing," Przhevalskii once reminisced. "I was allowed out in all kinds of weather, and early on began to hunt."[8] At the age of ten, the lad was packed off to the *gimnaziia* (secondary school) in Smolensk for a proper education. Blessed with a photographic memory, Nikolai did well in school, and he graduated six years later, in 1855, near the top of his class. He was now sixteen and had only one ambition—to join "the heroic exploits of Sevastopol's defenders" in the Crimea, where Russia was then at war.[9]

Much to the teenager's disappointment, by the time he signed up the fighting was practically over. Instead, he began a succession of dreary small-town postings as a cadet in the infantry reserve. The tedium of provincial garrison life grated on Nikolai Mikhailovich. He loathed the traditional diversions of his fellow subalterns, "good-for-nothings, drunks, and gamblers," as he wrote his mother, and found peace only in such solitary pursuits as shooting game in the countryside or reading accounts of the African explorers.[10] The latter, combining high adventure and the struggle with nature at its most elemental, was particularly appealing to the young man's brooding, romantic temperament. As a junior officer in the Russian army, Przhevalskii understood that there was little chance of joining an expedition into the jungles of Africa. However, the tsar had just acquired his own uncharted wilderness, in the large territories along the Amur and Ussuri Rivers in the Far East ceded by China in 1858 and 1860.

In 1860, Nikolai Mikhailovich formally requested a transfer to the new Siberian regions. His commander had little patience for such temerity and answered by clapping the officer in the stockade for three days. Finally, a year later, Przhevalskii made good his escape by passing the entrance examination for the Nicholas Academy of the General Staff in St. Petersburg. Many of the courses taught there dealt with geography, topography, and the natural sciences and would prove useful to the future explorer.

At the academy, Przhevalskii committed a youthful political indiscretion by joining most of his classmates in signing a petition protesting the appointment of a reactionary editor at the army journal *Voennyi Sbornik* (Military Review).[11] Nevertheless, Przhevalskii proved to be an excellent student. His dissertation about the Amur region caught the eye of the Geographical

Nikolai Mikhailovich Przhevalskii

Society, and within a few years he convinced both his superiors in the military and the society's vice president, Petr Semenov-Tian-Shanskii, to let him make a proper topographical survey of the empire's new Pacific possession.

From June 1867 through spring 1869, Lieutenant Przhevalskii, assisted by two men and a pointer, mapped a region larger than Britain. The expedition more than proved the officer's talents as an explorer, and its successful completion earned him a promotion to staff captain and the Geographical Society's silver medal.[12] For Nikolai Mikhailovich, the journey had been nothing more than a dry run. His true interests lay in the immense uncharted terrain that separated Asiatic Russia from the more populated eastern half of the Chinese Empire.

*I*nner Asia, the region comprised by Xinjiang, Mongolia, and Tibet, was still largely terra incognita on European maps in 1870.[13] A few Westerners had made it to Tibet during the past two hundred years, but shortly after the travels of the French Lazarist priests Huc and Gabet in 1846, the Himalayan theocracy had placed a ban on all foreign contact.[14] Xinjiang and Mongolia were even more obscure, and the thirteenth-century Venetian

Marco Polo apparently was the only European to have seen much of the area. In the words of one scholar, at the time Inner Asia "was a region [about] which less was known than . . . darkest Africa."[15]

The "Western Regions," as Inner Asia was known to the Chinese, had only recently been incorporated into the Middle Kingdom. It had taken the three great Qing emperors, Kangxi, Yongzheng, and Qianlong, the better part of a century to subjugate the area, an objective finally achieved in 1759. Yet Peking's hold was tenuous at best, and by the mid-1800s it began to loosen. The disastrous Opium War with Britain in the early 1840s and the Taiping Rebellion that erupted during the following decade were clear indications that the Manchu had entered into the inevitable cycle of dynastic decay. Meanwhile, a major uprising of various Muslim peoples that by the 1860s engulfed much of Xinjiang and southern Mongolia further weakened imperial authority over the Western Regions. St. Petersburg was no idle bystander in the Middle Kingdom's travails. Russian setbacks in Europe during the Crimean War combined with the Manchu's growing infirmity to whet tsarist appetites for any territorial morsels that might be snatched in the East, and by 1860 it had managed to annex the Amur and Ussuri regions on the Pacific.

There was another reason China's western periphery was of interest to the tsar, for those years marked the height of the Great Game, the Anglo-Russian rivalry in Asia.[16] The Great Game coincided with an important development taking place in the nature of military intelligence.[17] This change resulted from an evolution in Russian military thinking that had begun with the Napoleonic Wars. Before this first "patriotic war," finding out about the enemy was largely accomplished by individual agents. Now a greater interest in the application of the scientific principles of warfare alerted strategists to the value of a proper study of topography and other geographical statistics as a vital component of preparing for battle. The most effective advocate for this new approach to intelligence was a professor at the Nicholas Academy of the General Staff, Dmitrii Miliutin. Eventually becoming a leading figure in Alexander II's Great Reforms, Miliutin was an innovative teacher with a strong interest in geography and strategic intelligence.[18]

In 1845 the Russian Geographical Society was chartered in St. Petersburg.[19] Much like Miliutin, its members advocated the systematic application of scientific principles to study the land and its inhabitants. As its long-serving vice president Petr Semenov-Tian-Shanskii stressed, the new organization practiced not just geography but *Erdkunde* (earth science), the discipline advocated by the early-nineteenth-century German academic, Karl Ritter. *Erdkunde* had much broader implications than geography, comprising topography, climatology, and other aspects of physical geography in combination with ethnography.[20] This more comprehensive approach was reflected in the varied professions of the founding members, which included astronomers, naval explorers, biologists, and ethnographers.

According to its founding principles, the Russian Geographical Society

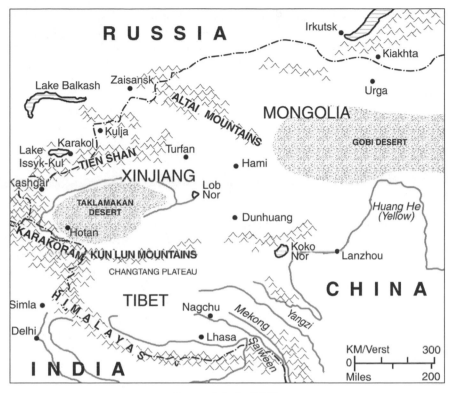

Inner Asia in 1880

was a scientific body established "for those who value and appreciate geography, ethnography, and statistics."[21] Yet, while the new organization was dedicated to the pursuit of knowledge, it also served the state. In its early years, its key bureaucratic sponsor was Nicholas I's moderately progressive minister of the interior, Lev Perovskii, who found the statistics the Geographical Society gathered about conditions within Russia very useful to help his officials prepare the reforms that would be undertaken during Alexander II's reign.[22]

In the late 1850s, the institution also began to take a strong interest in regions beyond the empire's borders. Much like the geographical societies that had been founded in the West somewhat earlier, its curiosity about foreign lands was more than purely academic. If there were strong political and economic grounds for the attention paid to Africa by the Société de Géographie de Paris, the Gesellschaft für Erdkunde zu Berlin, and the Royal Geographical Society in London during the latter half of the nineteenth century, much the same could be said about the interest the Russian Geographical Society began to take in Asia. Many of those who belonged to the Russian organization would heartily have agreed with the sentiments expressed in 1877 by the president of its Paris-based counterpart: "A country has no lasting value except by its force of expansion, and . . . the study of the geographical sciences is one of the most active elements of this expansion."[23] The novelist Joseph Conrad caustically referred to this nineteenth-century marriage of science and empire building as "militant geography."[24]

Under the patronage of a grand duke, the institution's first vice president was an admiral, and there were a number of other naval and army officers among its senior members. This heavy concentration of military men was no coincidence, since the society's interests and those of the army often overlapped.[25] Nowhere was this more evident than in Inner Asia. One scholar concluded that the Imperial Russian Geographical Society's "talented members played the Great Game of Central Asia."[26]

When a capable subaltern with proven topographical skills proposed to survey the Inner Asian frontier, the Geographical Society and the War Ministry had good reasons to support such a journey. It did not take long for both Semenov and War Minister Dmitrii Miliutin to give their assent. In 1870, a little more than a year after his return from the Ussuri, Przhevalskii set off anew, this time for Mongolia. Among his goals were mapping the Ordos Plateau to the north of the Great Wall and finding Koko Nor, the legendary "Blue Lake" at the meeting point of China, Mongolia, and Tibet. No doubt inspired by the "Nile Quest," the famous rivalry between Richard Burton and John Hanning Speke of the 1850s and 1860s, Przhevalskii hoped to identify the lake as the source of the Yellow River.

For nearly three years Nikolai Mikhailovich, now accompanied by two Cossacks, an assistant, and his trusty setter Faust, trekked on camel through "Eastern High Asia."[27] Starting at the Siberian frontier outpost of Kiakhta he crossed Mongolia's Gobi Desert to Peking, traversed the Ordos, and found Koko Nor at the boundary of northeastern Tibet. It was there, while camped on its shores, that Przhevalskii happened to cross paths with Kambi Nansu, Tibet's representative to Peking. The diplomat readily invited him to Lhasa, where, he assured the explorer, "the Dalai Lama would be very glad to receive Russians."[28] Unfortunately, by now the party had almost exhausted its silver and could not afford the 1,500-kilometer journey to the south. Przhevalskii reluctantly limited his travels to the plains of Tsaidam on Tibet's northern periphery and eventually returned to Irkutsk via the Mongolian capital of Urga.

Throughout the journey, Przhevalskii had to contend with bitterly inhospitable terrain, suspicious Chinese officials, and a frequently hostile native population. Although the local populace often posed the most formidable obstacle, he confidently shrugged off their attacks. "I know all about the unimaginably cowardly character of these peoples," he reported to the generals in St. Petersburg. "Anyway, we are all very well armed, and [rifle] fire . . . has a spellbinding effect on the half-savage natives."[29]

Covering more than 11,000 kilometers, the first Inner Asian expedition yielded a wealth of geographical discoveries about a region larger than western Europe. Meanwhile, zoologists and botanists at the Academy of Sciences in St. Petersburg acquired a collection of 200 animal skins, 1,000 bird specimens, 3,000 preserved insects, and 4,000 dried plants. Przhevalskii's journey also provided valuable intelligence about the Dungan revolt, a major rising among Muslims in western China, which was clearly appreciated by his superiors, who awarded him with a promotion to the rank of lieutenant colonel and the Order of St. Vladimir, Fourth Class.[30]

In summer 1876, Przhevalskii set off on a second Inner Asian expedition, this time approaching from the west. With a somewhat larger party and a rather more generous purse, he now planned to cross Xinjiang's notorious Taklamakan Desert, perhaps locate the Silk Road site of Lob Nor, the mysterious lake last described by Marco Polo, and cross the Kunlun range into Tibet.[31] Although Przhevalskii succeeded in finding Lob Nor, which turned out to be more of a marsh, disease and political complications kept him from proceeding much farther south. In all, his party had traveled less than 4,000 kilometers.[32]

The journey also had important intelligence aims. Much of the terrain to be covered was still in revolt, and St. Petersburg urgently needed details about the leader of the rising, Yakub Beg. Another General Staff officer, Aleksei Kuropatkin, had been ordered to meet with the rebel chief. However, Przhevalskii also made a point of seeing him, and he sent a detailed report to his superior, Count Fedor Heiden, after his encounter.[33] Titled "On the Current Situation in Eastern Turkestan," it painted a rather negative picture of Yakub Beg and his insurgent realm.[34] Describing him as "nothing more than a political impostor" who was thoroughly loathed by his subjects, Przhevalskii predicted his imminent fall.[35] The native population, he hastened to point out, had a much more favorable opinion of Russia: "The local inhabitants constantly cursed their government and expressed their desire to become Russian subjects. Rumors of how we brought order to [the Central Asian Khanate of] Kokand and Ili spread far. The savage Asiatic clearly understands that Russian power is the guarantee for prosperity."[36]

Przhevalskii's advice was to take full advantage of the situation and strike an agreement with the insurgent chief to annex territory: "The time is right for Russia to benefit from our relations with Chinese Turkestan. Yakub Beg will agree to every one of our demands."[37] Nothing came of the colonel's suggestion. Not long after Nikolai Mikhailovich's trip, Yakub Beg died, apparently of apoplexy, and his rebel kingdom rapidly fell to Chinese troops.

In 1878, Przhevalskii proposed an expedition devoted entirely to Tibet. His memorandum to the General Staff about the new journey listed a number of scientific goals, but the most important aim of the trip was strategic. Przhevalskii wrote: "Scientific research will camouflage the political goals of the expedition and ward off the interference of our adversaries."[38] He pointed out that Lhasa, the residence of Buddhism's most important spiritual leader, was Asia's Rome. In addition to being the temporal ruler of

Tibet itself, the Dalai Lama exercised enormous influence over the continent's 250 million Buddhists. If a Russian could reach the Potala Palace, he might well be able to sway the Oriental pontiff to do St. Petersburg's bidding. Time was of the essence, since the British were also trying hard to make their way to the Tibetan capital from India, and there were fears that the Himalayan theocracy might well join London's orbit.[39]

Being European, Przhevalskii recognized that it would be difficult to win the trust of the xenophobic Tibetans. He therefore proposed that, at the same time as he was setting off for Tibet, one or two lamas be dispatched to Lhasa by the Russian consul in Urga, Mongolia.[40] Traveling in the guise of a pilgrim to Tibet was hardly original. The British in Calcutta had been actively sending trained Indian scouts, disguised as "Pundits," or wise men, to gather information about the reclusive theocracy too.[41] The consul was ordered to recruit a suitable candidate, and a lama was hired to go to Lhasa in March of the following year.[42] What happened to this monk is not known, but he could not have met with Przhevalskii in the Tibetan capital. Much to Nikolai Mikhailovich's disappointment, his expedition was forced to turn back by the Dalai Lama's officials at Nagchu, less than 250 kilometers from the Potala.[43]

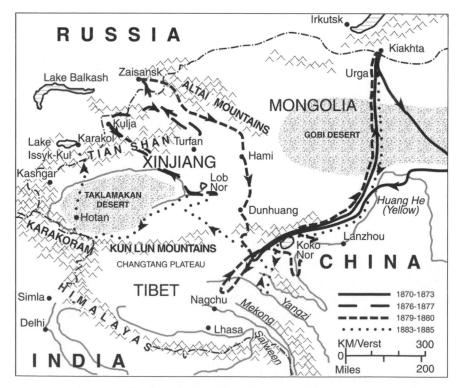

Przhevalskii's Inner Asian Expeditions

Nevertheless, the outcome of the expedition more than satisfied Przhevalskii's sponsors. Once again, he returned with a wealth of topographical, zoological, botanical, meteorological, and ethnographic data about enormous Inner Asian tracts hitherto almost entirely unstudied by European geography. It was on this trek that the explorer also made his best-remembered discovery, known to zoo visitors around the world, when he spotted an unknown species of wild horse on the Zunghar steppe of Mongolia's western frontier. The *takhi*, as local residents called it, is a muscular, pony-sized creature that very likely once roamed throughout Eurasia but by then had been nearly driven into extinction by the spread of civilization. Although he proved unable to shoot a specimen, Nikolai Mikhailovich got a skin from Kirghiz tribesmen, which he brought back to St. Petersburg, where zoologists named it *Equus przewalskii* in his honor.[44]

In 1883, within three year's of his return, Przhevalskii received permission for another expedition to Tibet. Despite generous funding and kitting by the army, his party had no better luck reaching Lhasa.[45] He came back to Russia with more new valuable scientific discoveries, however, including details about the source of the Yellow River.[46] Tsar Alexander III immediately promoted Przhevalskii to the rank of major general and invited him to give a report at a special audience at Anichkov Palace in January 1886.[47]

Two years later, in 1888, Przhevalskii set off on yet another trip "to have a look at the Dalai Lama."[48] Although he was not in the best of health, the journey was urgent because of news that a British embassy was on its way to Lhasa from its possessions to the south. Nikolai Mikhailovich wrote the war minister: "Aside from its scientific results, the trip will present a good opportunity to gather details about the activities of the English in Sikkim regarding Tibet."[49] He did not get very far. Still on Russian soil, near Lake Issyk Kul in the foothills of the Tian-Shan, Nikolai Mikhailovich Przhevalskii contracted typhoid fever and after a brief illness died. Karakol, the town where he died, was renamed Przhevalsk on Alexander III's orders in 1893. It is now again called Karakol.[50]

*I*n May 1886, as he was resting at his estate after the fourth Inner Asian expedition, Przhevalskii was summoned to the capital. A special committee at the War Ministry was discussing what should be done about China at a time of heightened tension between the two empires, and its members were interested in his opinion. Przhevalskii responded with a secret memorandum, "New Thoughts about War with China."[51] To reach a wider audience, he also gave an unclassified lecture at the Nicholas Academy on the same topic. The latter was subsequently published as "An Essay on the Current Situation in Central Asia" in a leading political journal in 1886 and as the final chapter of his next book two years later.[52] The Soviet reissue of the latter, published in 1948, omits this section.[53]

The two documents, the clearest statement of Przhevalskii's thinking about Russia's role in the Far East, are remarkable in their stridency. In the "Essay" Nikolai Mikhailovich exhaustively cataloged the many shortcomings of China and its army. The analogy with Ottoman Turkey, another waning Oriental empire, was strongly implied, and the author went on to predict that the Qing "may very likely one day form for Europe a new 'sick man.'"[54] As with Turkey, the only logical policy was to undertake a war of conquest, in this case into Inner Asia. Anyway, Przhevalskii pointed out, "China's hold over Mongolia, and even more, over Eastern Turkestan, is extremely shaky."[55]

Przhevalskii strongly criticized Russian diplomats for their undue passivity: "Beginning with our first embassy in 1635 . . . all our relations with the Middle Kingdom have been based on a 200-year-old policy of subservience and sycophancy."[56] Instead, he felt that "there are many scores to settle with our haughty neighbour, and we must show it that Russia's spirit and Russian courage know no match, whether at home or in the Far East." There was no alternative but to undertake hostilities. Turning an old folk saying on its head, he declared: "However evil war may be, a bad peace is far worse, as all Europe is finding out." To anticipate any objections to annexing the territory of another sovereign state, Przhevalskii cited the jurist Fedor Martens, who had written some years earlier about Central Asia that "international law does not apply to savages."[57]

Meanwhile, in his secret memorandum, Nikolai Mikhailovich sketched a detailed plan for attacking China from two directions. A modest contingent would enter Chinese Turkestan while a larger force struck from eastern Siberia into Mongolia. "In this way, slowly, like a threatening cloud, we will advance across the Gobi [to Peking]."[58] In both regions the local populations, which thoroughly despised their Qing overlords, would rise to a man to support the Russians.[59] Przhevalskii was certain of victory, as long as "the Maritime Powers" did not come to China's aid. Once the Bogdykhan sued for peace, the tsar could name his terms. In Przehvalskii's opinion, these would include the cession of eastern Turkestan, northern Tibet, and, if possible, large portions of Mongolia and a few revisions to the border on the Amur.[60] As for the ethics of Russian aggression, the answer was simple: "'The end justifies the means'— here's the motto of modern society and the modern state."[61]

Przhevalskii's essays well represented his thinking about China. While a geographer, he was first an officer, and this military affiliation strongly colored his views about the regions he explored. As he saw it, Chinese Inner Asia was not just an unknown region waiting to be opened to science but virgin territory to be conquered for the glory of Russia. Already in 1873 Przhevalskii had written a friend:

> Here you can penetrate anywhere . . . with money in your pocket, a carbine in one hand and a whip in the other. Europeans must use these to come here and bear away in the name of civilization all these dregs of the human race. A thousand of our soldiers would be enough to subdue all of Asia from Lake Baikal to the Himalayas. . . . Here we can still repeat the exploits of Cortez.[62]

In the nineteenth century, Russian Orientalists enjoyed a high reputation for their scholarship and their deep respect for the Asian civilizations they studied. Przhevalskii shared none of their sentiments.[63] As Vsevolod Roborovskii, his comrade on several expeditions, put it: "It was quite impossible for Nikolai Mikhailovich to have any fondness for the Chinese. He was angered by their mendacity and their hypocrisy. . . . He did his best to avoid meeting a Chinese and said that among them he saw nothing but unpleasantness."[64]

Przhevalskii recalled his first visit to Beijing, where he stopped on his way to Mongolia in 1871: "I may candidly confess . . . that the impression it left on my mind was far from agreeable; indeed a newcomer could hardly have been pleased with a city in which cesspools and crowds of naked beggars are the adjuncts of even the best streets."[65] In a letter to a friend at home, he complained that "crookery and fraud are developed to extremes. The Chinaman here is a Jew plus a Muscovite pickpocket both squared. But the lamentable thing is to see Europeans being polite to this rabble."[66] Even the food was distasteful: "I do not know how others may like the taste of Chinese cookery . . . but as for us . . . [it] was simply disgusting. . . . The Chinese show no repugnance for any kind of nastiness, and will even eat dog's flesh."[67]

Nor did Przhevalskii have much regard for the Middle Kingdom's culture. Semenov-Tian-Shanskii would recall that "Przhevalskii was reproached for his disdain for . . . Chinese civilization."[68] Przhevalskii himself was "convinced of the rotten state of China," going on to voice his contempt for those who had more positive views: "Nothing but ignorance on the part of Europeans could invest them with any of the attributes of power and majesty."[69] Bluntly put, "The Chinese people are a nation long past its prime."[70]

At times, Przhevalskii's ideas seem to have been taken straight from the writings of the nineteenth-century French racial theorist Joseph-Arthur comte de Gobineau, author of the *Essai sur l'inégalité des races*. For example, he strongly condemned the mixing of races. Writing about a people to the north of the Great Wall he noted: "Owing to their constant intercourse with the Chinese, the Chakhars of the present day have lost not only the character but also the type, of pure Mongols . . . and are degenerate mongrels."[71] He took another leaf from Gobineau when he exulted after winning a brief skirmish: "Such is the moral superiority of the European over the degraded inhabitants of Asia; such is the impression produced by resolution, energy, and unwavering courage of a superior race."[72]

The clearest indication of the Celestial Empire's decadence was the miserable condition of its army. Whenever Przhevalskii encountered Chinese troops, he saw only their more deplorable qualities. "The officers . . ." he once remarked, "are guiltless of any military training. Most are complete ignoramuses and, furthermore, as leaders actually corrupt the morals of their subordinates, rather than elevating them."[73] The other ranks were no better in his eyes. As he wrote Miliutin in 1879 from a Chinese garrison in Xinjiang: "Manchu soldiers remind us of loose-living women, which their indescribable

"Chinese at Tetun-gol"—Przhevalskii's contempt for the Chinese is clear in this drawing by a member of his 3rd Inner Asian expedition, V. I. Roborovskii.

habits make them resemble all the more."[74] On another occasion Przhevalskii observed that their "principal occupations consist of drinking tea, smoking opium and being fanned." Yet if Qing troops were idle and slothful, their principal failing was moral weakness: "Concepts like duty and honour are entirely alien to them. The Chinese soldier goes to battle only out of fear and in the hope of turning tail during battle."[75] A few years earlier he had remarked on the Chinese army's "moral and physical debility, and complete unfitness for the hardships and privations of warfare."[76]

Przhevalskii was firmly convinced that the Qing Dynasty could never hope to take on a Western power and win. Its forces were certainly no match for the Russian army. Already in 1873, after his first Inner Asian expedition, he wrote: "A bold, well-armed enemy might march into any part of the Middle Kingdom with perfect confidence of the result. He need not trouble himself about the number of his opponents; one wolf will put to flight a thousand sheep, and every European soldier is a wolf in comparison with Chinese soldiers."[77]

Although Przhevalskii rarely reflected on the morality of assaulting China, he was convinced that all of Inner Asia would welcome Russian rule. In 1886 he recalled: "In every one of our four expeditions we were constantly struck by the great sympathy and respect Russia enjoys among the natives."[78] During the Turkish war in 1877–1878, many Russians had believed that the conflict was entirely justified by the desires of Christians living in Ottoman Europe to come under Romanov rule. Now Przhevalskii argued that much the same applied to the inhabitants of Inner Asia: "The nomadic Mongols . . . the Muslim Chinese, and the inhabitants of Eastern Turkestan . . . all yearn to become subjects of the White Tsar, whose name, like that of the Dalai Lama, appears in the eyes of the Asiatic masses in a halo of mystic light."[79]

He wrote in his "Essay": "Through the mournful mists of a chaotic present and an equally clouded future shines the radiant light of a hope—Russia!"[80] The reason for his fatherland's popularity was simple: "The intolerable yoke of China on the one hand, and the renown of our humane rule over the natives of our Oriental possessions on the other, are the main reasons for the good reputation we enjoy even in the depths of the Inner Asian deserts."[81]

Przhevalskii's enthusiasm for conquest, his certainty in the superiority of the white man over the darker-skinned savage, his utter contempt for other civilizations, and the aggressive virility that permeate his prose were also characteristic of the way many Europeans wrote about Africa during the Victorian age. At the time the popular media in Paris, as throughout western Europe, frequently portrayed Africa as a "negative picture of barbarism, backwardness and despotism which was opposed to European civilisation and had to be dealt with by military force."[82] Having spent many years reading the accounts of the sub-Saharan explorers, Nikolai Mikhailovich instinctively imposed Western views about that region on Russia's own Dark Continent, Asia.

Like many of his European contemporaries, Przhevalskii was clearly influenced by social Darwinism.[83] Urging the war minister to attack China, he emphasized: "'The struggle for existence' seems to be coming to a head. The powerful weapons of science and technology only intensify the egotistical competition among the nations. . . . We must not tarry in our actions, never forgetting that might always and everywhere makes right." There were also glimmerings of *mission civilisatrice* and the *Kulturträger* in the explorer's opinions, and he made frequent references to the improvements Russian administration would bring to the existence of the Inner Asian nomad. "Our rule in China will bring a better life here," he promised.[84] If at times Przhevalskii sounded like the Central Asian conqueror, General Mikhail Skobelev, the confident, utterly unself-conscious expansionist attitudes that he expressed in his books and speeches were also spoken with the same voice as those of a Carl Peters, Cecil Rhodes, or Jules Ferry.

*P*rzhevalskii's superiors had the good sense to ignore his more extreme pronouncements. After politely hearing him out, the army's committee quietly relegated his memorandum to the oblivion of the archives.[85] War Minister Petr Vannovskii and his colleague at the Ministry of Foreign Affairs, Nikolai Giers, were simply too cautious to contemplate a war of aggression. Anyway, the emperor had made his will clear. On a telegram Przhevalskii had sent from Karakol in 1885, in which he argued that Chinese Turkestan was about to rise against Peking and suggested that this presented an excellent opportunity for an addition to the empire, Alexander III dryly noted: "I have my doubts about the benefits of such an annexation."[86]

On the other hand, the young tsarevich, Nicholas Aleksandrovich, was a great fan of Przhevalskii. Nicholas's mother, Empress Marie Fedorovna, on occasion summoned him to tutor her teenaged son about Inner Asia, and he was received at the imperial palace on a number of other occasions as well.[87] When Przhevalskii set off on his fourth expedition in 1883, the heir presented him with a precious aluminum telescope as a parting gift, and after the former returned to St. Petersburg Nicholas also provided a 25,000-ruble subsidy to publish the journey's account.[88]

At the request of his tutor, Aide-de-Camp General Grigorii Danilovich, Przhevalskii regularly sent letters to Nikolai Aleksandrovich about his exploits during the journey.[89] The explorer's lively pen described the many hair-raising exploits of his small party in the best style of the ripping yarn, and the young tsarevich thrilled to exciting tales, such as this account of an attack by 300 Tanguts, "the most notorious bandits of the Yellow River":

> Pouring down from the nearest mountain, they began their charge at a distance of a verst, shouting all the while. The hooves of their mounts sounded hollow on the damp earth. Their long spears glinted in the sunlight, and their robes and long, black hair flowed behind them in the rushing wind. Like a storm cloud the savage horde approached closer and closer. We could see the outlines of the horses and their riders growing sharper by the minute. Facing them, there were but fourteen of us, standing silently in front of our camp. We knew that the only outcome would be victory or death.
>
> When they were halfway to our position, I commanded "Fire!" and the first volley was loosed. Then my men began to shoot at will. . . . Our rifles took out forty of them and many of their horses, and we were lucky that our adversaries only managed to wound two of our horses.

In another letter, Przhevalskii assured the heir that Inner Asia's population wanted nothing more than to become subjects of the Romanovs:

> [Often] the inhabitants gave us a warm welcome. . . . They complained bitterly about their cruel overlords, and told us that they were ready to rise against their

Chinese oppressors. Elders at the oases and of the mountain tribes said that we merely had to give the signal, and they would lead their people in a general rising. "Our only wish is to have the Tsar as our sovereign," they explained. "We all know that he rules Russian Turkestan with fairness and justice, while here every Chinese official whips us mercilessly and robs us of our property, wives and children. . . . We are ready to rise. . . . All we need is someone to command us. Just give us one of your Cossacks to be our leader." We often heard such tales.[90]

The great explorer's exotic tales about the Orient sparked the lad's curiosity, and Przhevalskii's friendship with the heir to the Russian throne left its mark. As one scholar speculated, the tie "forged a link in a long chain of events and influences that involved Nicholas [II] deeply in Asia and interested him in ruling the non-Chinese people of Asia."[91]

Outside of the court, Przhevalskii's opinions horrified St. Petersburg's Orientalist establishment. In a review of the explorer's book about his third Inner Asian expedition, the distinguished Mongolian specialist Aleksei Pozdneev suggested that the volume belonged more to the belles lettres than to scholarship. Sarcastically describing its author as "among our best novelist-explorers," he savaged the account for being superficial, dogmatic, inaccurate, and thoroughly unscientific. Pozdneev concluded that "this kind of travel essay is even harmful . . . especially since it is based on the authority of the [famous] explorer himself."[92] Meanwhile the sinologist Sergei Georgievskii bitterly attacked Przhevalskii's "Essay" when it was published in Mikhail Katkov's conservative *Russkii Vestnik*.[93] Przhevalskii did not seem to lose much sleep over such criticism. He wrote a friend about Georgievskii's review: "Our views are entirely contradictory—his opinions are those of an ivory-tower humanitarian, while mine have been shaped by the harsh reality of life. His brain spews soap bubbles, which some would call ideals, whereas I believe that force is the only criterion for truth. . . . Time will tell who is right."[94]

Yet Przhevalskii's ideas were influential among the Russian educated public. His books and articles were avidly read, and his lectures were mobbed. As Miliutin wrote in his diary: "Przhevalskii more than anyone attracts audiences. The ladies are especially keen to learn from him."[95] The impression he made on the former governor of Moscow, Prince Vladimir Golitsyn, was typical: "It was fascinating to meet such a personality—how rarely we encounter such people!"[96] Przhevalskii's good friend, the geographer Mikhail Veniukov, was hardly exaggerating when he called him "the most celebrated traveler in Asia since Marco Polo."[97] When Nikolai Mikhailovich died, the public's response for money to build a monument in St. Petersburg was almost as enthusiastic as an earlier campaign to honor the great poet Aleksandr Pushkin.[98]

The author Anton Chekhov was particularly taken with the general. He wrote a friend: "People like Przhevalskii I loved without end."[99] The obituary he published in *Novoe Vremia* was nothing short of hagiography:

One Przhevalskii or one Stanley is worth ten institutes or a hundred good books. Their principles, their noble ambition, inspired by loyalty to the fatherland and to science, their stubborn determination, despite all hazards and despite the cost to personal happiness, to carry out a chosen goal . . . make them to the people heroes who embody a higher moral force. . . .

Reading his biography, no one wonders: "What for? Why? To what end?" They all say: "He is right."[100]

Above all, it was Przhevalskii's vigor that captured the imagination of his admirers. Miliutin recalled: "His words and his whole nature radiate pure energy."[101] In an age of stagnation and mediocrity, which was how many came to see the reign of Tsar Alexander III, Przhevalskii made a particularly strong impression on the Russian psyche.

Nikolai Przhevalskii is most often compared with David Livingstone. In terms of his thinking about Inner Asia, however, he was more like a General Skobelev. Przhevalskii's lectures and books overtly promoted Asiatic conquest. They assured their audience that such actions, desired by the local population, would be easy and were morally justified. The accounts of his expeditions, his intelligence reports to the War Ministry, and his letters all show him to be a would-be conquistador as well as a geographer. Przhevalskii personified Conrad's militant geography.

What inspired men like Przhevalskii? In his day, few wondered about such matters. When they did, their musings were rarely more profound than those of the German statesman Count Bernhard von Bülow, who once said that his government's actions overseas were motivated simply by "the principle that where I have planted my foot, there no one else shall be permitted to plant his."[102] The Canadian historian A. P. Thornton observed that "empires are not built by men troubled by second thoughts."[103]

Perhaps the best explanation was provided by the Austrian academic Joseph Schumpeter in his famous essay, "The Sociology of Imperialisms."[104] Written shortly after the First World War, it reflected on the violent passions that had inspired Europe's governments to consume their own continent in the bloody Armageddon of the recent conflict. Although he was an economist, Schumpeter believed that the Marxist analyses of the day were too narrowly focused. After all, finance capital and the relationship to the means of production could hardly account for a phenomenon that had long antedated the existence of merchant banks. Instead, Schumpeter looked to more primal urges.

The lust to acquire territory, Schumpeter believed, was "atavistic in character," driven by nothing more complicated than aggression for the sake of aggression. It was "non-rational and irrational, purely instinctual inclinations towards war and conquest," as he saw it. In short, there *was* no scientific explanation: "To look for deep-laid plans, broad perspectives, consistent trends is to miss the whole point." Schumpeter's description of a philosophy that "values conquest not so much on account of the immediate advantages . . . as because it *is* conquest, success, action," neatly characterizes the imperialism of Nikolai Przhevalskii.

Przhevalskii was not representative of Russian thinking in the 1880s. Yet his legacy left a deep imprint on the national psyche. The ministers of his day conducted a cautious policy vis-à-vis the Middle Kingdom and ignored Przhevalskii's more jingoistic pronouncements. The next generation, though, which had read his books at a more impressionable age, would prove itself to be more receptive to such sentiments. Przhevalskii's accounts helped inspire Russian involvement in China in the coming years. English literary scholars have studied the relationship of popular literature to British expansion overseas. "The adventure tales that formed the light reading of Englishmen . . . were, in fact, the energising myth of English imperialism," as one of them put it.[105] Przhevalskii's impact on Russia was similar.

Przhevalskii was one of the most eloquent proponents in Russia of the primal urges to conquest described by Joseph Schumpeter. His writings gave voice to the virile aggression that became fashionable once again as Russia entered the twentieth century. Przhevalskii's "conquistador imperialism," with its atavistic aggression and lust to subjugate, described one of the elements that drove Russian policy in the Far East at the start of Nicholas II's reign—and with disastrous consequences, as the events of 1904 and 1905 would show. These Schumpeterian sentiments were by no means exclusive to tsarist Russia. Rather, as the Harvard historian William Langer makes clear, they were an intellectual current that energized much of the developed world at the time:

> One cannot study this period without marvelling at the exuberance and optimism which went hand in hand with recklessness and confidence in the conduct of foreign affairs. It was taken for granted that the world was marked out by Providence for exploitation by the European white man and that the principle of every man for himself and the devil take the hindmost was natural law. . . . Even Lord Salisbury could see in the world nothing but a few virile nations and a large number of dying nations. The basic problem of international relations was who should cut up the victims.[106]

CHAPTER THREE

The Asianist Vision

Esper Ukhtomskii

You have your millions. We are hordes, and hordes, and hordes.

Just try it! Take us on!

Yes, we are Scythians! Yes, we're Asians too!

With slanting eyes bespeaking greed! . . .

Triumphant yet in sorrow,

Awash in dark blood,

[Russia] gazes, and gazes, and gazes upon you,

With hatred and with love!

—From "The Scythians" by Aleksandr Blok

*T*he Russian symbolist poet Aleksander Blok wrote "The Scythians" in January 1918. The Romanov dynasty had collapsed less than a year earlier, and Vladimir Lenin's Bolshevik Party now ruled the former empire. Shortly before he composed these lines, Soviet officials signed an armistice with Imperial Germany that took Russia out of the First World War. A little more than a month after Blok completed his famous poem, Lenin's infant regime concluded a peace at Brest-Litovsk with its Central European adversaries. The Treaty of Brest-Litovsk traded huge swaths of territory in the former Russian Empire's west for much-needed peace. The agreement also incurred the wrath of Russia's former allies, England and France.

"The Scythians" was both an appeal and a warning to Europe. Elsewhere in his poem, Blok beseeched the West to accept the Bolshevik revolution: "Come to us! Leave the war's horrors and join us in peace!" Were the Europeans to continue their hostility to Soviet Russia, they would only earn its undying enmity. "We have nothing to lose," Blok reminded the great Occidental powers. "Century upon century you will be cursed by your children's enfeebled progeny." No longer would Russia protect the civilized West against the barbarous East. Indeed, "We will turn our Asiatic face to you."[1]

Blok's notorious reference to the Scythians alluded to an aggressive Inner Asian nomadic people who had occupied Ukraine's steppes some 25 centuries earlier. Russians usually claim their heritage from the more peaceful and more Occidental Slavs. By reminding the world that "We are Scythians! We are Asians, too!" Aleksandr Blok's poem was an audacious response to the German notion of the Russians as barbarous Asiatics. Blok was mocking what had been a important theme of Wilhelmine propaganda during the war. Just as Great Britain called its adversary the Hun, to suggest that the Teuton was a savage Oriental ravaging the civilized West, the Germans similarly hurled Asian epithets at the enemy on *their* eastern front.

In proclaiming his Asiatic provenance, Aleksandr Blok was in a distinct minority among Russians. Certainly since their conversion to Christianity more than 10 centuries ago most would vehemently have denied being Oriental. In his frequent warfare with nomadic Asian tribes before, during, and after the Mongol invasion of the early thirteenth century, the medieval Russian saw himself as a true defender of the cross. Since the eighteenth century, when Peter the Great and his heirs strove to impose Western ways on their empire, educated Russians would have tended to agree with the Soviet leader Mikhail Gorbachev's assertion that "we are European."[2] Even the Slavophiles of the mid-nineteenth century, who stressed their nation's apartness from the West, never considered themselves to be Asian.[3]

Yet, in the 1890s, as Russian diplomacy and intellectual life marked a distinct eastward turn, some stopped regarding the epithet Asiatic as an insult. With Tsar Alexander III's decision to build a railway linking St. Petersburg to its distant Pacific territories, it seemed to them that the empire's future lay in Asia. In their eyes, Russia was Oriental rather than Occidental in character. Labeled *vostochniki,* or Asianists, those who subscribed to this peculiar offshoot of Slavophilism felt that Russia's roots also lay in the East. To the Asianists, it was the tsar's holy mission to "reunite" Russia with China, like some latter-day khan, with St. Petersburg as the new Xanadu. In addition to its influence on tsarist foreign policy, Asianism also reflected a profound unease with Russia's sense of itself and its place in the world. The pessimistic fin de siècle literature of St. Petersburg's Silver Age often brooded about the nation's Asian links.[4]

The Asianists strongly disagreed with Przhevalskii about Russia's continental identity. Advocates of conquistador imperialism such as Przhevalskii firmly identified with the other European powers when they called for conquest in Asia. They saw the Orient as weak, backward, and inferior. Armed conquest was entirely justified by virtue of the West's inherent superiority. By contrast, the Asianists highly respected the East's civilizations and did not necessarily consider them to be less important than those of the West. Moreover, Russia itself had strong Oriental roots. Asianists pressed for more involvement in the East, but they strongly opposed resorting to military means, which in any case was entirely unnecessary. According to their leading champion: "Russia in reality conquers nothing in the East, since all the alien races visibly absorbed by her are related to us by blood, in tradition, in thought. We are only tightening the bonds between us and that which in reality was always ours."[5]

These words were written by the newspaper publisher and poet Prince Esper Esperovich Ukhtomskii. As a well-connected dilettante with passion for Oriental art, Ukhtomskii had also secured an appointment as the tsarevich's tutor on his Asian grand tour, and the friendship that resulted from his shipboard intimacy with the heir enabled Esper Esperovich to exercise considerable influence on Nicholas in the early years of his reign. Like many journalists, Prince Ukhtomskii was a prolific author, devoting much of his pamphleteering to the Asianist cause. His most important work was a lavish three-volume account of the grand duke's trip, *Travels in the East of Nicholas II when Cesarewitch*. Written as a travelogue, the work essentially served as Ukhtomskii's Asianist manifesto.

Although few in number, the Asianists were influential. As one historian put it, their ideology evolved into "a policy which received ministerial and imperial sanction under Nicholas II."[6] The tsar's adventures in the East, culminating in the disastrous war with Japan of 1904, were in part a consequence of this fascination with the Orient.

*E*sper Esperovich Ukhtomskii was born in 1861 near the imperial summer retreat of Oranienbaum outside of St. Petersburg.[7] "Thirty generations from Riurik, on the Monomakh branch," the prince took great pride in his lineage, which boasted a moderately prominent boyar family in Muscovite times.[8] More recently, Ukhtomskii's ancestors had been involved in the navy. Esper Alekseevich, his father, had served as an officer in the Russian fleet at Sevastopol during the Crimean War and later helped establish a commercial steamship line, which linked St. Petersburg with India and China, and his mother descended from a long line of admirals of Scottish origin, the Greigs. Another Ukhtomskii, Pavel Petrovich, would serve as a vice admiral with the Pacific squadron during the Russo-Japanese War.

Like many of his estate, Ukhtomskii spent his childhood among tutors at home and often traveled to Europe with his parents. After more formal secondary schooling in a gymnasium, Esper Esperovich read philosophy and literature at the University of St. Petersburg. He graduated in 1884 with a silver medal for his master's thesis, "A Historical and Critical Survey of the Study of Free Will." During his student years Esper Esperovich also began to dabble in poetry. While still an undergraduate his work was published in the Pan-Slavist Ivan Aksakov's journal *Rus*. Throughout his career Ukhtomskii continued to write verse, which appeared on the pages of such periodicals as *Vestnik Evropy* (European Herald), *Russkaia Mysl* (Russian Thought), *Niva* (Corn Field), *Sever* (The North), and *Grazhdanin* (The Citizen).[9]

Perhaps inspired by his father's journeys to the Orient, Ukhtomskii developed a fascination for Russia's more exotic nationalities. After graduating, he was able to indulge these interests by landing a job with the Interior Ministry's Department of Foreign Creeds, which dealt with the empire's non-Orthodox faiths.[10] His early years were not particularly distinguished, but they did enable the prince to travel extensively to eastern Siberia, where he studied the Buriats, a nomadic people living around Lake Baikal. Numbering around 300,000, according the 1897 census, the Buriats were Siberia's largest non-Russian nationality.[11] Originally a Mongolian people, they had migrated north sometime before Russia extended its rule to the shores of the Pacific in the seventeenth century. When the Buriats first settled the Baikal steppes, their religious beliefs were shamanistic. During the eighteenth century, Lamaist missionaries converted many of them to Gelugpa Sect Buddhism, the "Yellow Hats" faithful to the Dalai Lama of Tibet.

Both for reasons of state—St. Petersburg's hold over its east was still somewhat tenuous—and a relatively tolerant attitude to other creeds at the time, tsarist officials did not actively discourage the new faith in the eighteenth century. In 1741, a date still commemorated as the anniversary of Buddhism in Russia, Empress Elizabeth officially recognized the Lamaist hierarchy and their right to practice.[12] Siberia's enlightened early-nineteenth-century governor, Mikhail Speranskii, confirmed the special status of the Buddhist nationality in his Statute of 1822, which legislated minimal interference in their spiritual affairs.[13] The dynasty's initially benign attitude to the Buriats and their confession helped earn their goodwill. Until the late nineteenth century, many even believed the Romanovs to be the "White Tsars" of Mongolian legend about which Przhevalskii had written.[14]

Prince Ukhtomskii also had a soft spot for the Kalmyks, another Lamaist people, who lived in European Russia.[15] Distant ethnic cousins of the Buriats, Kalmyk nomads had migrated from their ancestral homeland in Dzungaria around 1630 to the lower Volga steppe, just north of the Caspian seaport of Astrakhan. Over the next century their relationship with Russia's rulers was much stormier than those of their Siberian coreligionists. But by the 1800s the Kalmyks were relatively well integrated into the empire, having received a semiprivileged status like that of the Cossacks. As late as the Civil War (1918–1922), Kalmyks overwhelmingly sided with the anti-Bolshevik forces of General Anton Denikin.[16]

During the late 1880s Ukhtomskii made several trips to Russia's Asian domains as well as to China and Mongolia.[17] One was undertaken in 1886 to report on growing friction between Orthodox missionaries and the Buriats' Buddhist clergy. Tsar Alexander III's policy of aggressive Russification had started to affect the lives of Buriats, arousing great resentment. Violating treaties guaranteeing religious freedoms going back to 1689, Russian

Prince Esper Esperovich Ukhtomskii

Orthodox missionaries led by the zealous Archbishop Veniamin of Irkutsk
began forcibly converting the local inhabitants to Christianity. Meanwhile,
land-hungry peasants from European Russia traveled eastward in growing
numbers, competing with Buriat nomads for the steppe.[18]

Ukhtomskii's 1886 journey "to study the Lamaist question" lasted almost a year. Often traveling incognito, the prince visited 19 datsans
(monasteries), where he interviewed monks and studied Buriat archives. At
Lake Gusino Monastery there were lengthy talks with the Buddhist hier-
arch, the Bandido Khambo Lama, and Ukhtomskii ventured abroad to Urga
and Peking for meetings with senior Lamaist clergy there as well. Esper Esperovich also spoke with the region's two governors-general and Archbishop Veniamin, none of whom seemed overjoyed at having to deal with
the meddlesome Interior Ministry bureaucrat.

When he returned to the capital, Ukhtomskii wrote a memorandum for his superiors in the Department of Foreign Creeds that strongly con-demned the heavy-handed tactics of Irkutsk's Orthodox establishment.[19] Archbishop Veniamin and his priests, he concluded, were singularly unsuc-cessful in attracting converts, with new Christians nowhere making up more than 4 percent of the local population, according to Ukhtomskii's cal-culations. Those who had agreed to be baptized often did so only to collect the cash incentives offered by the Orthodox Church. In fact, despite Rus-sian proselytization, Esper Esperovich observed that Lamaism was undergo-ing a revival among the Buriats.

The note was typical of Ukhtomskii's tolerant views of Russia's non-Orthodox faiths. A brief he prepared for his department in 1889, "Mecca's Political and Religious Significance," was equally favorable about Islam. Written at a time when St. Petersburg was becoming increasingly worried about the loyalty of its Muslim subjects, the document sought to reassure its readers about their allegiance to the tsar: "Russian autocracy . . . is seen sympathetically. [Muslims] consider the conquest of Central Asia as some-thing miraculous, and they are prepared to reconcile themselves to it."[20] In later years, hypernationalists would revile Ukhtomskii for his sympathies to the empire's Poles and Jews.[21]

But Buddhism was Ukhtomskii's first love. While he remained Russian Orthodox, Esper Esperovich developed a deep respect early on for "the hu-mane creed of Gautama, second only to Christianity."[22] Buddhism, as he saw it, was a powerful doctrine, "which is bound by neither time nor space, and brings benefits wherever its faithful bring it."[23] There was much Rus-sia's Christians could learn from the Oriental faith's wisdom, tolerance, and respect for autocracy.[24] Above all, it was the religion's mystical streak that appealed to the poetically inclined prince: "There, in the Asia about which Europe knows nothing, the people have always been intimately influenced by otherworldly forces. They have been drawn to the ethereal planes of contemplation and prayer, to those luminous realms where hatreds and the fraternal quarrels among nations dissolve before divine power."[25]

Ukhtomskii was not the only Russian of his day to be entranced by Bud-dhism's esoteric side. He was the product of an age of profound disillusion-ment with the positivist faith in science and reason that had characterized much of the post-Romantic nineteenth century. As in Europe, at Russia's fin de siècle many sought solace on a more irrational and emotional plane.[26] Some returned to the church; others became intensely interested in spiri-tual arcana. The Russian philosopher Nikolai Berdiaev remembered the mood in St. Petersburg as "a time marked by a profound spiritual disquiet and religious searching, and by a wide-spread interest in mysticism and even occultism."[27] Silver Age poets and intellectuals were fascinated with the otherworldly, and seances, fortune tellers, and *radeniia* (sectarian ec-stasies) were all the rage among the public.[28] The most notorious example of this phenomenon was the popularity at the imperial court of such ques-tionable individuals as Philippe of Lyons, Peter Badmaev, and Grigory

"Buriat Lama on the Sino-Indian Border"—Ukhtomskii's fascination for Buddhism is conveyed by many such illustrations in his book about Nicholas's Asian grand tour.

Rasputin.[29] Theosophy, the strange blend of Hinduism, Buddhism, spiritualism, and other occult elements promoted by the enterprising Madame Blavatsky, was another manifestation of this trend.[30]

Yet Ukhtomskii's affection for Buddhism was not limited to its mystical charms. He also detected an important strategic purpose for the Buriats and their faith.[31] "Trans-Baikalia is the key to the heart of Asia, the vanguard of Russian civilization on the frontier of 'the Yellow Orient,'" Ukhtomskii pointed out.[32] Esper Esperovich saw the tsar's Buddhist subjects as an important tool for extending Russian influence into Inner Asia, albeit in a less bellicose way "as apostles of Russian commerce and our good reputation."[33] For this reason, Russian officials were wrong to try assimilating Buddhist *inorodtsy* (alien nationalities).[34]

Ukhtomskii's interests in the Orient extended well beyond its religions. He was also passionate about its culture, and during his journeys in the late 1880s he amassed a large collection of Tibetan and Chinese art.[35] Eventually numbering more than 2,000 pieces, Ukhtomskii's acquisitions were initially displayed at the Alexander III Museum in Moscow (now the State Historical Museum) and earned him a gold medal when they were shown in the Siberian pavilion of the Paris Universal Exposition of 1900. "Donated" to the Soviet government after 1917, they now form the core of the East Asian holdings at the Hermitage Museum in St. Petersburg.[36]

*P*rince Ukhtomskii's publications and his collection attracted the attention of St. Petersburg's Orientalist establishment. He was elected to membership of the Imperial Geographical Society, and the Foreign Ministry began to seek his advice on East Asian questions.[37] When plans were being made in 1890 to send the tsarevich on his grand tour of the East, Ukhtomskii's reputation as a connoisseur of Oriental art and his sterling social credentials made him an ideal companion for the journey.

Accompanying the heir was a good career move for Esper Esperovich. While the delicate prince was mercilessly teased by the *Pamiat Azova's* officers during the trip, Nicholas took a liking to him. The tsarevich wrote his sister Ksenia that "the little Ukhtomskii . . . is such a jolly fellow."[38] Upon his return to St. Petersburg in 1891, Esper Esperovich was rewarded with an honorary appointment as *Kammerjunker* (court chamberlain) and also served on the Siberian Railway Committee, which was chaired by Nicholas. At the same time, he got leave from the Interior Ministry to begin work on his account of the grand tour, *Travels in the East of Nicholas II.*

The book was written in close consultation with Nicholas, who personally read and approved each chapter.[39] It took six years to complete the work, which appeared in three volumes between 1893 and 1897. Lavishly illustrated and published by Brockhaus in Leipzig, the book saw four editions, despite the steep price of 35 rubles.[40] All efforts were made to ensure a broad distribution. Empress Alexandra Fedorovna bought several thousand copies for the Ministry of Education and other government departments.[41] A cheaper paperback version was printed to make it more accessible, and translations appeared in English, French, German, and even Chinese, which was presented to the Guangxu emperor and dowager empress by the Russian envoy Mikhail Giers in 1899.[42]

Ukhtomskii's close ties with Nicholas II enabled him to play an active part in East Asian politics during the early years of his reign. Auguste Gérard, the French minister to China, believed that "the tsar chose him to be the interpreter and principal artisan of Russia's East Asian policies."[43]

Although the diplomat overestimated Esper Esperovich's importance, he described him well: "[Ukhtomskii] was a curious man. Young, educated, with a lively and florid temperament, enthusiastic yet thoughtful, he had the temperament and the aspirations neither of a diplomat nor of a courtier. He was above all involved in the important questions of his country."[44]

The prince's most prominent role was as an apostle for closer ties with the Orient. In addition to writing his popular *Travels in the East of Nicholas II*, Esper Esperovich had frequently editorialized about Asian affairs in such publications as Prince Vladimir Meshcherskii's ultraconservative *Grazhdanin* in the early 1890s. Now Ukhtomskii had more ambitious hopes, and in 1895 he submitted to the tsar a plan to organize his own daily newspaper. He explained that the paper, "while adhering to a devoutly nationalist orientation and *vigorously warding off the cultural life of the West,* would also fulfill a political function by advocating the principles of our Eastern policy, as blessed by Yourself."[45]

Ironically, the vehicle for his scheme turned out to be the venerable *Sankt-Peterburgskie Vedomosti* (St. Petersburg Gazette), a daily that claimed descent from Russia's first newspaper, founded by the Westernizing Tsar Peter the Great in 1702. During the eighteenth century the paper was printed by the Academy of Sciences and edited by such intellectual luminaries as Mikhail Lomonosov. In the 1860s, under the liberal Baron V. F. Korsh, it was St. Petersburg's leading daily, the arch rival of Katkov's conservative *Moskovskie Vedomosti* (Moscow Gazette). Korsh's criticisms of prominent officials led to his ouster in 1874, however, and control over the publication was transferred to the Ministry of Education.[46] The ministry allowed the paper to languish, and by the 1890s its circulation was among the lowest of the capital's dailies.[47]

In October 1895 the minister of education, Count Ivan Delianov, wrote Ukhtomskii that, "with [Nicholas II's] approval," he was to be appointed editor of *Sankt-Peterburgskie Vedomosti,* with an annual subsidy of 35,000–45,000 rubles.[48] In the first issues after assuming control over the paper in January 1896, the prince explained his editorial policy. While *Sankt-Peterburgskie Vedomosti* would "calmly" debate the "radical-progressive press," it promised not to resort to knee-jerk conservatism. One of its special interests would be defending the rights of the empire's minorities.[49]

At the same time, the daily adopted a distinctly anti-European philosophy. Ukhtomskii warned his readers against "slavishly following the scientific path to the West," which he predicted would only lead to "catastrophes of a revolutionary character." The Russian Empire was fundamentally Asian rather than European: "Correct people, with a different patriotic spirit, say 'Russia and the Orient' as a concept are one, only temporarily not existing as an entity."[50] The newspaper's most important goal, Ukhtomskii stressed, was promoting Russia's eastward turn:

We must have broad horizons: Every great nation from time immemorial has been deeply convinced of their historical destiny to be greater and better than the others. . . . Russia, more powerful in Asia than the Europeans, casts its gaze to the East, which presents remarkable possibilities for the creative energies of the Russian people.[51]

Although it never recaptured the prominence it once held, during the first decade of Ukhtomskii's editorship *Sankt-Peterburgskie Vedomosti* developed a reputation as the most authoritative organ for Asian affairs.[52] It provided detailed coverage of the East, and its articles were often cited by other papers. Public awareness of Ukhtomskii's ties to the court and leading policy makers lent this paper the status of a semiofficial voice for St. Petersburg's Oriental entanglements. In one of his weekly columns in the conservative Berlin *Kreuzzeitung,* the German historian Theodor Schiemann called the prince "the editorial authority for all questions concerning 'Russia's Asian mission.'"[53]

The paper's relationship with the state was not entirely trouble free. Less than a year after becoming editor, Ukhtomskii was reprimanded by Count Delianov for being too soft on student unrest.[54] Not surprisingly, his calls for greater toleration of the empire's religious minorities also roused the ire of Russia's highest lay church official, the notoriously reactionary chief procurator of the Holy Synod, Konstantin Pobedonostsev.[55] Ukhtomskii's editorial policy drew fire from more right-wing colleagues as well. The editor of the Ukrainian daily *Iuzhnyi Krai* (Southern Land), V. M. Iuzefovich, condemned him as a "preacher of national discord" and arranged to have him removed from the board of a historical society.[56] Between 1898 and 1903 the paper was barred from Russian newsstands several times as punishment for what was deemed its overly progressive stance.[57]

Yet, until at least 1900, the tsar favored Ukhtomskii with his friendship. Esper Esperovich had easy access to Nicholas, and he freely gave him his advice about Asian policy.[58] According to *Novoe Vremia*'s editor Aleksei Suvorin, Ukhtomskii "tells the Sovereign everything," and War Minister Aleksei Kuropatkin described him as an "intimate of the emperor. . . . Influenced the tsar and this influence was harmful."[59] In the prince's own romantic imagination, he saw himself as a latter-day *oprichnik,* likening his role to that of Ivan the Terrible's political police.[60]

Foreign observers were divided over the extent to which Ukhtomskii held Nicholas's ear, but he was nevertheless regarded as an important figure during the years before the Russo-Japanese War. A French diplomat described him as "the interpreter and the principal artisan of the Russian program and policy in the Far East."[61] His British colleagues were somewhat more jaundiced in their assessment, calling him the "Miles Gloriosus" of Russian journalism, "a blind enthusiast, honest of purpose, but confused of ideas."[62]

One of the passions the prince and the emperor shared was Inner Asia.

Like Ukhtomskii, Nicholas II had a deeply mystical side. In Sergei Witte's words, "a soft haze of mysticism refracts everything [Nicholas] beholds and magnifies his own functions and person."[63] Although he always regarded himself as a devout defender of the Orthodox faith, the tsar also developed a strong interest in Buddhism and the nations where it was practiced.[64]

In the mid-1890s, Ukhtomskii became Nicholas's intermediary to the Buriat apothecary Peter Badmaev when the druggist traveled to the East to carry out his baroque schemes.[65] Esper Esperovich also tirelessly championed closer ties to Mongolia and Tibet. Ever sensitive to separatist sentiments among Mongolia's princes, Ukhtomskii did his best to promote their cause to the tsar.[66] In 1898, it was Ukhtomskii who introduced Agvan Dorzhiev, the Thirteenth Dalai Lama's emissary, to Nicholas II. A Buriat monk with close ties to the Tibetan ruler, Dorzhiev had been sent to St. Petersburg to seek Russian support against the British, who were suspected of having designs on the Himalayan theocracy. More cautious ministers dissuaded the tsar from becoming too actively involved, although he did authorize several covert intelligence-gathering missions as sepoys commanded by Colonel Francis Younghusband were shooting their way to Lhasa in 1903 and 1904.[67] General Kuropatkin, who strongly opposed such adventures, often worried about Ukhtomskii's influence on the tsar:

> The emperor is restless on foreign policy matters. I consider one of the sovereign's more dangerous character traits to be his love for mysterious lands and individuals such as the Buriat Badmaev and Prince Ukhtomskii. They inspire him with fantasies about the Russian tsar's greatness as ruler over all Asia. The emperor is drawn to Tibet and similar places. This is all very worrisome, and I shudder about the harm these delusions may cause to Russia.[68]

By 1900, Ukhtomskii's intimacy with the tsar was on the wane. He complained to a friend that the influence he once held was no longer, and thereafter he seems to have had much less contact with Nicholas.[69]

*E*sper Esperovich's interests also drew him close to Finance Minister Sergei Witte, the lead architect of the new forward policy in East Asia. According to the Soviet historian B. A. Romanov, the prince was "a great admirer of Witte," and Witte bragged to a colleague in 1897 that he and "the tsar's friend" were entirely in charge of Chinese affairs.[70] Although Witte was stretching the truth, the two men did collaborate on several important initiatives.

In 1896, when the Chinese statesman Li Hongzhang went to Russia to attend Nicholas II's coronation, Ukhtomskii accompanied the Chinese statesman for much of the trip and participated in the negotiations to secure a passage through Manchuria for the Trans-Siberian Railway.[71] The finance minister also arranged to have Ukhtomskii appointed as president of the Russo-Chinese Bank, although this position was largely honorary.[72] In the following year Witte entrusted him with an embassy to Peking for further talks with Li.[73] While the trip was officially undertaken to present gifts from the tsar to the Qing emperor and empress dowager, its real, unstated purpose was to reopen negotiations for a southward spur of the Chinese Eastern Railway (CER).[74]

News of Ukhtomskii's impending visit caused much excitement among the Chinese population of the capital. Rumors circulated that Manchuria was about to be annexed, that orders would be given to all male subjects to cut off their queues, and that their empire would become a Russian protectorate. The city's legations were puzzled and concerned. George Morrison, Peking correspondent for the *Times*, wrote back to London: "[Ukhtomskii] has no official rank and is not recognized by the diplomatic body. By the Chinese he is regarded as a 'brother of the Czar' if not the Czar himself. . . . There is great difficulty in learning what is the object of the mission."[75] The European diplomatic community's uncertainty was not allayed by officials of Russia's Foreign Ministry, who were annoyed at the intervention of the finance minister in what they regarded as their own, exclusive sphere.[76]

The emissary arrived in Peking on May 9, where he was feted by his friend Li Hongzhang. Ukhtomskii reciprocated with several elaborate receptions at the Russian mission, and he opened a branch of the Russo-Chinese Bank with much pomp and ceremony. There were also two audiences with the emperor, who graciously accepted lavish gifts of Fabergé crystal, Ovchinnikov silver, precious furs, and the Order of St. Andrew.[77] At first, the trip seemed to go quite well. The prince jubilantly cabled Witte: "Please inform the tsar. . . . Unprecedented welcome, strong expression of interest, even from the masses, Europeans positively embarrassed. . . . Our dealings with the Chinese were the best."[78]

Despite compliments of large diamonds to each of the ministers at the Zongli Yamen (China's foreign office), Ukhtomskii was unable to get their consent for a railway concession in southern Manchuria. Allowing a neighbor to take a shortcut through the region's northern barrens was one thing. Opening the much more populous and prosperous southern half of the dynasty's ancestral provinces to the foreign devils was quite another. Even Li, who had just received along with his new diamond the first one-million-ruble installment of his bribe for the CER concession, could not be swayed. He objected: "We have admitted you to the courtyard, now you wish to get to the rooms where we house our wives and small children."[79]

Ukhtomskii returned to St. Petersburg empty-handed, with nothing more than vague promises and the Qing's Order of the Double Dragon to show for his munificence.[80] Aside from presenting Nicholas II's gifts, the prince had failed to carry out any of his instructions, and his clumsy negotiating tactics and faux pas thoroughly alienated the Foreign Ministry.[81] One diplomat described the trip as "very regrettable and unfortunate," and the slippery finance minister quickly disowned any responsibility for the effort.[82]

Three years later, during the Boxer rising, Ukhtomskii was once again sent to China. The trip was undertaken in response to Li Hongzhang's request to Witte in June 1900 for Russian intervention to help head off the other powers.[83] Li, who was still waiting for the second installment of the bribe promised in 1896, urged the finance minister to send the prince "as soon as possible" to Shanghai.[84] At first, the plan was for Esper Esperovich to accompany the mandarin on a Russian warship from Shanghai to Peking, where Li would intercede with the empress dowager to put an end to the unrest.[85] Ukhtomskii undertook his mission "as a private individual," with funding from the tsar's private budget, and Witte ensured that both Russian diplomats and even his own agent in China, Dmitrii Pokotilov, were kept out of the picture.[86]

Ukhtomskii was entirely overtaken by events. By the time he arrived in Shanghai on September 16, 1900, the Boxers' siege of the legations had already been lifted for more than a month, and Peking was in Western hands.[87] After he made his way to Peking, the prince did offer to represent China in the talks with the occupying armies, but both Nicholas and Witte thought better of the idea, and Ukhtomskii returned to St. Petersburg.[88] After this quixotic mission, the finance minister no longer sought his assistance. Although Witte fondly recalled Ukhtomskii as "quite a decent man" in his memoirs, the two men were no longer close after 1900.[89]

Although Ukhtomskii's active role in affairs of state was over, he continued to editorialize about Asia for a few more years, cheering his countrymen on during the war with Japan.[90] The defeats at Tsushima and Port Arthur in 1904 snuffed out Russian dreams of Asian empire and also largely silenced Ukhtomskii's pen. He remained involved in St. Petersburg's Orientalist community, but during the postwar years Esper Esperovich primarily concerned himself with his paper, which he continued to edit until the fall of the Romanov dynasty in 1917.[91] Ukhtomskii survived the revolution, albeit in straightened circumstances. After 1917, he held various odd jobs in St. Petersburg's libraries and museums and met a peaceful end in 1921.[92]

*U*khtomskii was not the first Russian to reject his nation's European identity. One of the great debates among Russian intellectuals in the nineteenth century had been the Slavophile-Westernizer controversy. Westernizers, who hoped to draw their country closer to European culture, struggled against those who saw their country as fundamentally distinct from the sterile materialism and rationalism of the "Germano-Roman tribes." In foreign policy, a later variant of the Slavophile movement, Pan-Slavism, strove to liberate the western and southern Slavs from Hapsburg and Ottoman rule and to unite them into a greater Slavic condominium, "under the wing of the Russian eagle."[93]

In the second half of the nineteenth century, some scholars began to gaze farther east, to focus on Russia's Asian roots. Whereas the conventional historiography had always downplayed the role of the Tartars in Russian history, a few dissenters now thought otherwise. They believed that the Mongols, who had overrun Russia in the thirteenth century and controlled it for more than 200 years, had left a profound imprint on the national psyche, and this influence was not necessarily negative. Already in the early 1800s, the historian Nikolai Karamzin had written that "Russia owes its greatness to the Khans."[94] What Karamzin meant was that Muscovy's autocratic regimentation of society, which had enabled Russia to achieve its preeminence, had been directly adopted from the Mongol political tradition. The late-nineteenth-century history professor Vasily Kliuchevskii also taught that Russian absolutism was a legacy of the Golden Horde.[95]

To be sure, most nineteenth-century Russians were uncomfortable with the idea that any good had come from their ancestors' Tartar oppressors, and they downplayed Asiatic influences on the development of the Russian polity. When Nikita Muravev, one of the participants in the antidynastic Decembrist revolt of 1825, wrote that the tsarist autocracy was the offspring of Mongol despotism, he was not trying to make an objective statement of historical fact.[96] Nevertheless, for those who refused to side with either camp in the great Slavophile-Westernizer debate, there seemed to be a third alternative: Russia might find its true destiny by returning to its Eastern heritage.

In the troubled aftermath of the Congress of Berlin of 1878, when it became clear that Russian dreams of Pan-Slavic conquests in the Balkans would for now have to remain unrealized, it became even more appealing to imagine affinities with Asia. Meanwhile, the dawning of the Silver Age also marked a philosophical turn to the East. Such late-nineteenth-century thinkers as Nikolai Fedorov and Vladimir Solovev now looked to the Orient much as Slavophiles had stressed Russia's Slavic roots.

The eccentric librarian of the Moscow's Rumiantsev Museum (later the Lenin Library), Fedorov was an influential figure in late-nineteenth-century Russian intellectual life.[97] Like the Slavophiles, Fedorov believed that the peasant commune would be the empire's salvation from the evils of Western materialism. He took issue, though, with the Slavophiles' emphasis on the uniquely Russian character of the rural institution. In Fedorov's Manichaean conception, the world was divided into two implacably opposed civilizations: the agrarian cultures of Russia and Asia against a destructive coalition of Central Asian nomads and the Anglo-Saxon maritime powers. Russia stood in danger, Fedorov believed, of being destroyed by the latter. Its only hope for survival lay in joining forces with China, with which Russia had much more in common than the warlike, greedy English merchants. In a letter to a friend, Fedorov summoned his compatriots to join the "cult of the ancestors" in its struggle against the Anglo-American "cult of gold."[98]

The philosopher and poet Vladimir Solovev also foresaw a future menaced by apocalyptic struggles. To him, however, the threat was exclusively East Asian. Yet, while Solovev popularized the notion of the "yellow peril" among Russian thinkers of his day, the East also exerted a powerful fascination on him. His 1890 poem "Ex Oriente Lux" looked to Asia both as Russia's source of light and of power:

And the word is prophetic—it does not lie,
And the light from the East begins to glow,
And that which was impossible,
It promises and proclaims.

And, spreading out widely,
Flooding with banners and power,
That light, shining from the Orient,
Reconciles East with West.

O Russia! With lofty ambition
your thoughts are proudly filled;
Which East will you be:
The East of Xerxes or of Christ?[99]

Thus to Solovev the Orient was not only a tremendously destructive force but also his nation's destiny. In his universalist conception, Russia united the two continents into a greater whole: "The empire of the double-headed eagle is the world of East and West."[100] Vladimir Solovev strongly influenced the symbolist poets of the Silver Age. Like Fedorov, he also clearly left his mark on Prince Ukhtomskii, whom he had known in his student days.[101]

When Solovev called for a synthesis of East and West, he referred to Byzantium. This idea was developed more extensively by the self-proclaimed "Byzantinist," Konstantin Leontev. A precursor to Nietzsche, as Berdiaev described him, Leontev had spent some time as a consular official in the Near East in the 1860s before devoting himself to his philosophical and literary writings. He was eventually tonsured as a monk at Mount Athos in Greece.

In Leontev's proto-Spenglerian worldview, societies were inherently organic, inevitably maturing from feudalism to autocracy. Parliamentary democracy was the decadent stage of a culture. According to this logic, Ottoman Turkey and Qing China were more civilized than France or England. The only way Russia could stave off such degeneration was to infuse its political life with the essence of Byzantium, in other words, to stress autocratic rule and cast aside all notions of democracy, constitutions, and individual liberty. Ukhtomskii's sympathy for the Orient, albeit one farther east than Byzantium, was very similar to that of Solovev and Leontev in its strident rejection of Western materialism and democracy.

*E*sper Ukhtomskii's ideas about Russia's role in Asia are best expressed in *Travels in the East of Nicholas II.* It was an attractive book. With a newspaperman's flair for capturing the reader's attention, Ukhtomskii described the history, customs, religion, and art of the Orient's civilizations. Yet, among his exotic accounts of the pyramids of Egypt, the floating cities of Canton, and the geishas of Kyoto, the prince frequently editorialized about St. Petersburg's duties on the continent. "It is surely time for Russians to express some definite thoughts . . . on their great inheritance from Genghis Khan and Tamerlane," he wrote.[102]

Ukhtomskii's perspective was unusual, for unlike most travelogue writers of his generation he did not presume the superiority of Western civilization.[103] Implicit in his extensive digressions on Asia's history and his descriptions of its monuments was a belief that the Orient was Europe's cultural equal. Responding to contemporary criticism of Chinese backwardness, Ukhtomskii countered: "Have they really lived on in a state of incomprehensible stagnation, or have they lived a rich internal life of their own in no way inferior to Europe?"[104] On several occasions, he displayed his intense irritation at the efforts of colonial administrators and missionaries to impose their learning on societies with an equally distinguished past: "To educate the East up to a complete assimilation of Christian principles in our European life is beyond its powers. . . . The only thing is to regard this vast continent from a new and more humane point of view: Asia does not need the artificial inculcation of a baseless foreign culture."[105]

The clearest case of Western arrogance was British India. In Esper Esperovich's eyes, the English were an entirely alien presence: "at the present moment an immense gulf separates [the Indians] from the lordly masters of the land."[106] The colonial administration, he argued, had done little to better the lives of their Asian subjects:

> India lies crushed and dumb under the burden of exotic mushroom universities and expensive administrative reforms carried out with all the blind energy of self-sufficient ignorance. On the other hand, what irony lurks in such cheap catchwords as "native congresses," "a free native press," "the right of natives to be citizens of a great colonial empire."[107]

Condemning their rule as "unnatural" and "abnormal," Ukhtomskii strongly criticized the "rude egotism of the Anglo-Saxon and his impulse to rule over weaker races."[108] As he described a carriage ride along the streets of Calcutta, the prince sensed the restiveness of the native population: "Clearly history is preparing new and complex problems in the East for the colonising states of Western Europe, which are not really at home in Asia, but appear . . . as fortuitous and abnormal excrescences on her gigantic body."[109]

If the English were entirely foreign to the subcontinent, Ukhtomskii's compatriots were not. In his chapters on India, the prince stressed the similarities between the British colony and Russia. The Slavs and the Indians shared the same racial stock, both were ravaged by the Mongols, and neither had any affinity with the West: "For our own past, and the past of India . . . are similar and related. . . . They are equally confused and gloomy on the material side, and in an equal measure contain the spiritual promise of a renovated future."[110]

Ukhtomskii's descriptions of the tsarevitch's visits to Siam, the Dutch East Indies, and China abound with similar digressions about Russia's kinship with Asia: "The West is but dimly reflected in our intellectual life. The depths below the surface have their being in an atmosphere of deeply Oriental views and beliefs."[111] Much like the Slavophiles half a century earlier, the prince argued that the West's overreliance on reason was alien to the Russian soul. This was one of the characteristics that bound his countrymen to the Orient: "We feel our spiritual and political isolation from the Romano-Germanic countries overburdened by a too-exacting civilisation. For us . . . [as] for Asia, the basis of life is faith."[112]

Russia and the East were also united by a repugnance for crass materialism. At times, the diatribes against the colonialist West have a distinctly modern ring: "The strangers have dethroned and oppressed the East. Coming here to live and to make money, they do not find a home."[113] Much as the Soviet Union's propagandists would argue half a century later, Russia's aims on the continent were pure and disinterested, solely motivated by fraternal sentiments. St. Petersburg, Ukhtomskii reasoned, was Asia's natural ally, its soul mate, and its champion in the struggle against Western exploitation: "Russia has [no] solidarity of vital interests with those powers which feed on its blood and sweat."[114] In a remarkable passage elsewhere in his book, the author contrasts the benevolent Russian in Central Asia to the oppressive British in their colonies:

> While in our country, in the bazaars of Merv and Tashkent, a young soldier mingling with the throng of Asiatics behaves towards them in a friendly manner, and never dreams of hating them or despising them as savages, in India, the typical representatives of British power and prestige, the rank and file of the army, regard the natives as nearer animals than men.[115]

Scholars since the early-nineteenth-century historian Nikolai Karamzin had written that autocracy was the most important legacy of Russia's Asiatic past. Like Karamzin, Ukhtomskii was no democrat, and he strongly championed the monarchy throughout his career.[116] Part of Asia's appeal was the form of government that ruled over much of the continent. As the prince saw it, in addition to a deep spirituality and a strong aversion to materialism, Russians and Orientals both wanted firm rule: "The East believes no less than we do . . . [in] the most precious of our national traditions—autocracy. Without it, Asia would be incapable of sincere liking for Russia and of painless identification with her."[117]

Ukhtomskii's logic had a distinctly Slavophile flavor. Whereas the West represented the evils of republicanism, atheism, and revolution, the East preserved the ideals of the past. In drawing closer to Asia, Ukhtomskii implied, Russia would also renounce Peter the Great's reforms and return to its true roots:

> There, beyond the Altai Mountains and the Pamirs, lies really the same boundless, uninvestigated Russia as that of the ages before Peter the Great, with an untouched store of tradition and quenchless love for the marvelous, with its humble submission to the elemental . . . yet bearing the stamp of a stern majesty on every spiritual feature.[118]

Much like Przhevalskii, Ukhtomskii concluded that the peoples of Asia were instinctively drawn to the Romanov dynasty. Violated and exploited by the West, the Orient looked to the emperor in St. Petersburg for salvation: "The more actively Europe presses on Asia, the brighter becomes the name of the White Tsar in popular report and tradition."[119] This became a frequent theme of Ukhtomskii's editorials as well. In a collection of articles published shortly after the Boxer rising of 1900, for example, he argued that Mongolians and Tibetans both sought to come under Russian rule: "The troubles between us and the Chinese have convinced the Mongols to turn to Russia and the higher authority of the White Tsar. . . . The Tibetans, who maintain the closest ties with our Buriats, are slowly becoming convinced of the same idea."[120]

The construction of the Trans-Siberian Railway was a clear sign of where Russia's future lay, and Ukhtomskii appealed to his compatriots to fulfill their true destiny:

> From that remote period when our great golden-domed Moscow . . . received the blessing of the saints and was irradiated by the creative glow of the autocratic ideal, the East, advancing on us with fire and sword, has masterfully drawn toward it the eyes of the Russians . . . and now calls them onward to glory. . . . Properly speaking, in Asia we have not, nor can have, any bounds, except the boundless sea breaking on her shores.[121]

Ukhtomskii's statement that Russia has no boundaries in Asia can be taken two ways. On the one hand, it could be seen as a clarion call for ceaseless expansion. Indeed, elsewhere in the book, the prince writes that "beyond the Caspian, the Altai Mountains and Lake Baikal we cannot find a clearly-defined border . . . beyond which our rightful land ceases to be."[122] Yet at the same time the earlier citation can also be understood to mean that there is no separation between Russia and the Orient in the sense that both are fundamentally alien to the West. In an age when tsarist prerogatives were perennially under siege by calls for European-style reforms such as parliaments and constitutions, the Asianist ideology provided an attractive argument for maintaining the autocratic status quo.

*F*or a brief period at the turn of the century, the Orient exerted a peculiar fascination on the Russian imagination. Tiring of the endless debates as to whether their nation's true destiny lay with the West or in going back to its Slavic heritage, some pressed for a third course: Russia must return to its Asian roots. Two centuries of Mongol rule, this group believed, had brought Russia closer to the East than to Europe.

The poets of the Silver Age and the mystically inclined were attracted to what they believed was a more spiritually sound order. Meanwhile some conservatives believed that autocratic China was a more suitable soul mate for a Russia threatened by democratic pressures from the West. Others agreed with Prince Ukhtomskii's argument that Russia's Oriental nature gave it the moral right to seize territory in the Far East, since, in contrast to British colonialism, the tsar's intentions there were entirely benevolent.

To be sure, Esper Esperovich did not imply renouncing any annexations in the East. He predicted that the tsar would eventually add China to his dominions, but such a union would occur peacefully, according to the logic of a common heritage and similar interests. Even Nicholas II at times agreed with this view. For Finance Minister Witte, these ideas conveniently supported his own ambitions in Asia.

While Ukhtomskii's Asianist ideology was never the main driving force of tsarist involvement in the Far East, it reflected certain perceptions at court and among the educated public about Russia's place in the world. Furthermore, in the face of growing competition for influence in the Far East, Asianism was an attractive doctrine, because it saw Russia's role as legitimate and morally superior.

The ideology of the Asianists was too enticing for Russia's own good. Emboldened by such men as Ukhtomskii, the emperor set an increasingly adventuristic course in the East, culminating in the disastrous confrontation with Japan in Manchuria. Ultimately, as an element of Russian policy, Asianism foundered, along with the Baltic Fleet, in the Straits of Tsushima. Thus, Asianism did not survive the war with Japan. Its influence, however, long outlived the revolution of 1917. Throughout the twentieth century, Russians continued to believe—albeit using a different political vocabulary—that their country was one with Asia in its struggle against the decadent, materialist West.

CHAPTER FOUR

Pénétration Pacifique

Sergei Witte

We started the expansion of our influence over Manchuria not by taking the path of armed conquest but along the path of peace, by building the railway. And to consolidate our hold we must continue on this way to the end. This consolidation is only a matter of time, and we cannot . . . try to speed it along by force of arms.

—Sergei Witte

*I*n January 1904, shortly before war broke out with Japan, the Moscow Art Theater staged its first performance of Anton Chekhov's new play, *The Cherry Orchard*. The action, such as it is, revolves around the impending auction of an estate that bears the name of its fruit garden. Years ago, its cherries were sold throughout Russia and brought wealth, and the manor house's balls were attended by "generals, barons, and admirals." Now the property has fallen on hard times. Its owner, the frivolous Liuba Ranevskaia, cannot meet the payments due on some half-forgotten mortgage. Her soirees barely attract "the post office clerk and the stationmaster, and even they aren't all that keen to come."[1] The Cherry Orchard is an anachronism, fated to fall victim to the modern age, like the class that once derived its power and prosperity from such holdings. The new order even physically menaces the grounds: "Dark poplar trees loom on one side, and beyond them the cherry orchard begins. There is a row of telegraph poles in the distance and far, far away on the horizon are the dim outlines of a big town, visible only in very fine, clear weather."[2]

Chekhov's more recent productions, *Uncle Vania* and *The Three Sisters*, had been rather melancholic, but with *The Cherry Orchard* he hoped to offer something in a lighter vein. The author wrote his wife that "the whole play will be merry and giddy."[3] To a friend he described it as "a comedy, and in places even a farce."[4] Indeed, most of the characters are clearly lampoons, such as Madame Ranevskaia, the hopelessly impractical landowner whose purse is being drained by a worthless lover in Paris, and her equally feckless brother, Gaev, similarly impoverished after frittering away his assets on candy. There are also the high-minded, eternal undergraduate Trofimov, the eccentric German governess Charlotta, the ancient servant Firs, and other assorted caricatures.

One role was less ridiculous. Chekhov portrayed the merchant Ermolai Lopakhin as the only practical individual in the play. The son of the village shopkeeper, who has grown wealthy by dint of hard work and a good nose for business, Lopakhin is the quintessential self-made man, the direct antithesis of idle gentlefolk and fanciful intellectuals. He is well aware of his humble origins, and his ostensible social betters agree. Nevertheless, Lopakhin is fond of his snobbish friends and initially tries his best to help Ranevskaia out of her predicament. Yet, if his proposed remedies make sense, the intended benefactor cannot be bothered to follow his advice. When Lopakhin suggests that she could earn much-needed cash by renting some land to vacationing city folk, Ranevskaia is horrified: "Cottages, summer visitors. Forgive me, but all that's frightfully vulgar."[5]

To no one's surprise, the Cherry Orchard passes under the auctioneer's hammer. The buyer turns out to be the enterprising Lopakhin himself. He plans to realize his investment by razing the fruit trees and building cabins to let to the townsmen. In all of his other plays, Chekhov had used a gunshot to mark the dramatic climax. Now the plot is brought to a head by different means. After Ranevskaia has left her former patrimony, the curtain falls as "a distant sound is heard. It seems to come from the sky and is the sound of breaking string. It dies away sadly. Silence follows, broken only by the thud of an axe striking a tree far away in the orchard."[6]

If Chekhov hoped to amuse his audience, he was sorely mistaken. Although the play's theme—the decline of the Russian gentry—was hardly original, it struck a responsive chord. Konstantin Stanislavskii, the Moscow Art Theater's director, called *The Cherry Orchard* "a truly great tragedy."[7] Newspaper reviews tended to agree, and even the Bolshevik literary critic Anatoli Lunacharskii felt it was "unbearably sad."[8]

The play was disturbing because it so effectively voiced anxieties about the great changes in recent decades, as the end of serfdom and the transition to capitalism threatened to render the landed nobility superfluous. Rather than being a vaudeville, to many viewers the production was an elegy to a dying order, a nostalgic farewell to a way of life that was inexorably giving way to the modern age, where telegraph poles and smokestacks rather than cherry blossoms and ball gowns would rule the countryside.[9]

Theatergoers also disagreed with the playwright over Lopakhin. Chekhov, himself the son of a shopkeeper, could empathize with the entrepreneur. When he wrote the play, he meant to portray the merchant as "a decent fellow in every respect."[10] But others tended to see such figures in an entirely different light. The businessmen created by other nineteenth-century Russian writers, whether as Gogol's buffoonish townsman, Dostoevskii's vile bourgeois, or Nekrasov's grasping *kulak*, were usually greedy and boorish.[11] Even the part of Lopakhin himself, in the Moscow Art Theater's premiere of *The Cherry Orchard*, was portrayed by a second-rate actor with exaggerated coarseness, despite Chekhov's specific instructions that the character "must not be played as a loudmouth, he must not be the standard stage merchant."[12]

These negative attitudes toward businessmen and entrepreneurs in late Imperial Russia help explain the difficulties faced by Finance Minister Sergei Witte. In the eyes of his contemporaries, no other statesman came as close to being a real-life Lopakhin. Like Chekhov's merchant, the minister also seemed to have risen to prominence by his own abilities.[13] Sergei Witte began work as a railway clerk in Ukraine, and he enjoyed a successful business career until his abilities caught the eye of St. Petersburg. Witte, too, was a man of action, who got things done rather than mope about the past or philosophize about the future. And the finance minister similarly devoted his energies to transforming his environment into a more productive and efficient order.

Most important, Witte resembled Lopakhin in the way he was disdained by many of his contempories. Endowed with almost superhuman energy and abilities, Sergei Iulevich often swam against the current, as he struggled seemingly single-handed to drag an empire that was barely emerging from agrarianism into the capitalist era. As one biographer put it, in a government still dominated by a more traditionalist ethos, "he stood as an alien force."[14]

Witte also put his stamp on Russian foreign policy, particularly in its Far Eastern endeavors. For a while he succeeded. During his eleven years as finance minister, from the beginnings of the Trans-Siberian Railway in 1892 to his dismissal in August 1903, Sergei Witte was one of the leading architects of Russia's forward policy on the Pacific. Although his office was not formally linked to diplomacy, Witte participated in all important ministerial deliberations on Asian questions. Ambassadors frequently turned to him rather than the foreign minister in matters involving the East. More often than not, until he began to lose the confidence of the tsar in 1902, the finance minister's voice would decide the matter at hand. Meanwhile, by virtue of his enterprises, including the Trans-Siberian and the Chinese Eastern Railways, the Russo-Chinese Bank, and the port of Dalnii, Witte for a while directly controlled Russia's most ambitious foreign adventure of the age.

Witte's imperial vision was profoundly modern. Like many of his countrymen at the time, he advocated a vigorously expansionist course on the Pacific Ocean. But Witte's idea of *pénétration pacifique* ("peaceful penetration," or political influence through economic means rather than territorial conquest) was unique among Russians of the day. While Englishmen,

Germans, and others in the West understood the power of investments, railways, and banks in the scramble for Asia, most Russians still equated diplomatic muscle with more traditional means, such as armed might and annexation.

As the term suggests, Witte's ideology of *pénétration pacifique* shared Asianism's distaste for military aggression. Indeed, Witte and Ukhtomskii often cooperated in Russia's Far Eastern diplomacy. At the same time, the finance minister hardly considered the empire to be Oriental. Despite a youthful flirtation with the ideas of the Slavophiles, he strongly advocated a modern Russia that could compete with its Western rivals on their own terms.

Sergei Witte was the only important Russian champion of *pénétration pacifique* in East Asia at the turn of the twentieth century. Even the Marxist revolutionary Vladimir Lenin understood the unusual nature of Witte's ideas for his country. Writing in 1915 about the policies that had been largely directed by the finance minister, he observed: "In Russia, capitalist imperialism of the new type fully manifested itself with respect to Persia, Manchuria, and Mongolia, but Russia itself is generally dominated by [more archaic] feudal and military imperialism."[15]

*W*ith the possible exception of the tsar himself, no individual in Nicholas II's government aroused more controversy than Sergei Iulevich Witte. The Russian diplomat Baron Roman Rosen called him "the greatest man Russia has produced in a century."[16] To the American Senator Albert Beveridge, the finance minister was "Russia's master mind."[17] Others excoriated Witte, blaming him for the empire's financial difficulties in the latter years of his ministry, the war with Japan, the constitution of 1905, and a host of other ills. When Witte died in 1915, the right-wing paper *Russkoe Znamia* claimed to be quoting the tsar when it rejoiced that "Russia [now] has one less enemy."[18] The former foreign minister Aleksandr Izvolskii rightly observed that portraying Witte faithfully is "a most difficult task. . . . Few ministers have been more diversely judged, or with greater passion."[19]

Witte did not help matters by zealously trying to bequeath a positive image of himself. As finance minister, he clearly understood the value of a favorable press, and he actively courted journalists. Even then, he did not always enjoy a reputation for veracity. One St. Petersburg society matron echoed the sentiments of many when she said that the man "is not a liar. He is the father of all lies."[20] In retirement, Witte tirelessly devoted his energies trying to convince the world of his genius. The most ambitious effort in this regard was the series of memoirs he wrote in the last years of his life. Published after his death, Witte's reminiscences are highly polemical and need to be read with healthy doses of caution and skepticism. Even the British journalist Emile Dillon, a man otherwise highly sympathetic to him, warned that they were "disfigured by many concrete errors."[21]

There is less argument about the basic outline of Sergei Witte's life.[22]

Sergei Iulevich Witte

Sergei Iulevich was born in 1849 in Tiflis. Known today as Tbilisi, the capital of the Republic of Georgia, the city then was the headquarters for the long and difficult Russian campaign to "pacify" the mountain peoples of the Caucasus. Mid-nineteenth-century Tiflis had the air of a frontier outpost. Men and women of many nationalities mingled on its streets. Since the days of Aleksandr Pushkin and Mikhail Lermontov, the region held an exotic appeal in the minds of Russians back home.

Witte's father was a colonial official who had moved to the city to take up a post in the administration of Russia's new southern lands two years earlier. As his name—Christoph Heinrich Georg Julius Witte—suggests, he was of Germanic origin, raised in a Lutheran household in Courland and educated at the University of Dorpat as well as in Prussia. Sergei Iulevich was embarrassed by his Teutonic roots, and he preferred to stress his maternal ancestry.[23] Born Ekaterina Andreevna Fadeeva, Witte's mother had a more distinguished, Russian bloodline. Her mother was a Dolgorukaia, from one of the more venerable princely houses. Sergei's maternal grandfather, Andrei

Fadeev, had been the governor of Saratov Province before being posted to Tiflis.

The Fadeevs had the dominant influence on Sergei's upbringing. The boy was raised in his grandfather's household, based in a palatial mansion with more than eighty serfs in attendance. His more colorful relatives included his uncle, General Rostislav Fadeev, a veteran of various Caucasian and Turkish campaigns and subsequently a Slavophile author. Sergei's cousin Elena Petrovna was rather more notorious, having run away from an unhappy marriage and occasionally returning to Grandfather Fadeev's house to hold spiritualist seances. The lad remembered her as "quite stout and frowzy" and found her activities rather silly.[24] Like Sergei, she would also develop a fascination with Asia, albeit in a very different way, in the guise of the theosophist Madame Helen Blavatsky.

Witte began his schooling at home with a succession of foreign tutors and as a teenager audited classes at the Tiflis gymnasium. Although the latter were supplemented by private lessons from the school's teachers, this education was neither thorough nor effective. Sergei barely passed his school-leaving examination, and with some difficulty he managed to be accepted by the brand-new university in the Black Sea port of Odessa. Now he stuck to his books and graduated at the head of his class in 1870 with a degree in mathematics. At first, Sergei Iulevich hoped to stay on at the university as a professor, but his mother thought an academic career unbecoming of someone with his bloodline. Fortunately, Uncle Rostislav knew the minister of transportation, Count Aleksei Bobrinskii, and eventually a job materialized for his nephew on the Odessa Railway.

In those years Russia was in the midst of its first great railway boom. The disastrous war in the Crimea some twenty years earlier had made abundantly clear the need for a more effective transportation network within the empire. St. Petersburg was content to entrust the task of building railways to the private sector, encouraging it with generous financial support. As in America, the age gave birth to a new class of ambitious, freewheeling entrepreneurs, many of whom rose from humble origins to great wealth.[25] Despite fraud, waste, and corruption of epic proportions, the job got done: Between 1860 and 1880 Russian track grew more than seventeenfold, from 1,250 to 21,600 kilometers.[26]

Witte's own employer had begun as an enterprise of the crown. In 1877, however, the state privatized all of its railways, and the operation now landed in the hands of Jan Bloch. A wealthy banker and railway baron, Bloch had started out as a minor Jewish official in Poland. By now he owned a large rail network in Ukraine and Poland, which, along with his newly acquired line, he consolidated into the Southwestern Railway. Like all effective businessmen, Bloch had a good eye for talent. One of his protégés was another future finance minister, Ivan Vyshnegradskii.

Sergei Witte soon came to Bloch's attention as well. He had already more than proven himself during the Turkish War of 1877–1878, when the Odessa Railway was a key logistical link to the front. In his time as traffic manager for the line, Witte's remarkable competence had won him an accolade from the Russian army's commander, Grand Duke Nikolai Nikolaevich. Now Bloch began to appoint him to increasingly important positions. Within eight years Witte became chairman of the Southwestern Railway's board. The tycoon's confidence was well placed. His man put a money-losing concern comfortably into the black.

Witte also became actively involved in regulatory matters. Despite the fact that he had become a businessman, he enthusiastically welcomed state intervention. During the early 1880s, Sergei Iulevich took a leading role in an official commission to reconsider government involvement in his sector, and he strongly supported its conclusion that the crown take a firmer hand. In 1883, Witte further enhanced his reputation by publishing his *Printsip zheleznodorzhnykh tarifov po perevozkie gruzov* (Principle of Railway Freight Tariffs), which was the first serious treatment of the subject in Russia. The book is set against a confusing blend of Western economic thought and Slavophile ideas. Nevertheless, the underlying message is clear: Russia needed to develop a modern economy suited to its specific needs.[27]

Witte did not always approve of bureaucratic interference. In one famous incident in 1888, he clashed with the court over the details of the tsar's travels on the Southwestern Railway. Despite several warnings to travel more slowly, Sergei Iulevich's advice was sometimes ignored, and in October that year excessive speed caused the imperial train to jump the tracks near the eastern Ukrainian city of Kharkov. Alexander III and his family escaped injury in the wreck, and the accident did not damage Witte's standing. Instead, the tsar was favorably impressed by the man's obstinate refusal to yield to his officials' misguided demands.

When in the following year Alexander's finance minister, Ivan Vyshnegradskii, decided to set up a new railway office in his department, the obvious choice for its director was his former colleague. Despite a steep cut in pay, Witte eagerly made the move to the public sector. Rough-hewn in appearance, direct in his approach, and with the style and accent of the southern provinces, the new bureaucrat stood out glaringly from the polished officials of the imperial capital.[28] The French ambassador characterized him as "an eminent person, but his manners were blunt, his speech was crude, in his dealings with others he bristled; he was incapable of inspiring affection even when he tried. His massive physique only reinforced this impression; it was as if he had been shaped by axe, like some rudimentary sculpture."[29]

Alexander III, himself a man with little patience for overly refined courtier mannerisms, appreciated Witte's no-nonsense style and administrative talents. Within three years the tsar named him transportation minister and, in 1892, when failing health forced Vyshnegradskii into retirement, he asked Sergei Witte to take his place. At the relatively youthful age of 43, Witte held one of the most powerful posts in the realm.

Witte's new appointment was also perhaps the most challenging job in the imperial bureaucracy at the time. There were the serious problems that continue to plague finance ministers today, including budgets to balance, an enormous foreign debt, structural declines in key sectors, and intractable poverty among certain groups. But, over the longer term, the new minister knew that the Russian Empire faced a mortal dilemma. Recent conflicts, such as the American Civil War and Prussia's victories over Austria and France—not to mention Russia's own rout in the Crimea a little earlier—stressed the increasingly intimate link between industrial power and military might. Yet, as Russia approached the twentieth century, it was still predominantly agrarian. This was particularly evident in foreign trade, where grain sales alone contributed about half of the empire's export earnings, and other natural resources provided virtually all of the rest.[30] An old saw had it that "Russia's real finance minister was Lady Harvest."[31] Furthermore, with their heavy reliance on indirect taxes, the government's own shaky finances remained heavily dependent on the countryside too. Despite St. Petersburg's desire to remain a great power, its economy clearly was not up to the task.

Witte's two immediate predecessors, Nikolai Bunge and Ivan Vyshnegradskii, had both done their best to encourage the development of a manufacturing sector. While their efforts were beginning to bear some fruit, Russia's finances remained fragile and often seemed on the precipice of catastrophe. Bunge was removed from his post in 1886 when diplomatic crises led to a run on the currency. Six years later, the health and career of his successor, Vyshnegradskii, were destroyed by a disastrous combination of crop failures, famine, and a global industrial depression.

The new finance minister was therefore well aware that major structural changes were inescapable. He set his mind to the task with the same ferocious efficiency that had made him such a success in the private sector. Over the next decade, Witte implemented a sweeping range of reforms aimed at creating a modern, industrial economy worthy of the empire's status as a great power.[32]

Not surprisingly, one priority was the railway system. In European Russia, Witte began to buy up unprofitable railways and liberally subsidized others. There was a whole range of other measures to set up the infrastructure necessary for an industrial sector, including vastly improved technical schooling, a new bureau of weights and measures, and more sophisticated statistics. Witte also provided direct support to entrepreneurs through easier access to capital and steep protective tariffs. Meanwhile, of great psychological importance, the finance minister did his best to open lines of communication between Russian businessmen and his department. Under Witte, Finance became the bourgeois ministry par excellence.

Like Bunge and Vyshnegradskii, Witte understood that a strong, stable currency was a basic requirement of economic maturity. The finance minister's ambitious plans would require heavy borrowing abroad, and this was always risky, since the Russian ruble was not freely convertible on foreign money markets and its value could fluctuate wildly when it fell victim to speculators. After considerable effort to amass enough reserves of the precious metal, and despite strong opposition from his colleagues, in 1897 Witte was at last able to announce that the ruble would henceforth be freely convertible into gold. In his memoirs, Sergei Iulevich remembered establishing the gold standard as "my greatest achievement as minister of finance."[33]

One scholar aptly described Witte's domestic program as "railway construction plus capitalism plus the gold standard equals rapid industrialization."[34] The idea was that the state could create a manufacturing sector by simultaneously building railways to stimulate domestic coal, steel, and machinery production, encouraging initiative through government loans and protective tariffs, and building confidence in the ruble. Perhaps this approach did not mark a radical departure from the thinking of his precursors, Bunge and Vyshnegradskii. What was different was the robust determination with which he carried it out. A French historian remarked: "We cannot really call Witte the father of industrialization in Russia. But it is incontestable that he greatly helped it by systematically applying an array of measures that hitherto had only been ventured in timid and fragmentary fashion."[35]

If Witte looked to the gold standard as his greatest accomplishment, most Russians remember him for the Trans-Siberian Railway. The idea of joining the Pacific Ocean to Europe by track did not originate in Sergei Iulevich's imagination. Such proposals were already being discussed in St. Petersburg not long after Russia's Pacific provinces were wrested from China in 1860.[36] Yet the immense distances to be covered made the project seem far too costly for Russia's insecure finances. According to the most authoritative estimate, building the 8,000-kilometer track would require some 362 million rubles, an enormous sum when the imperial purse took in less than a billion rubles a year.[37] Predictably, the three finance ministers who preceded Witte all strongly opposed the scheme.

In the event, the railway was initially approved by Alexander III on strategic rather than economic grounds. During his reign, a sharp deterioration in relations with Peking had underscored St. Petersburg's weakness in the Far East. Russian generals recognized that, without an effective means for transporting an army to the Pacific, the region would be highly vulnerable should the Qing try to recover the provinces they had lost twenty years earlier.[38] In 1886, after receiving alarming reports from two governors-general in eastern Siberia about their desperate position, the emperor declared that "it is time, long since time."[39] Even with the sovereign's imprimatur, the railway still faced enormous bureaucratic resistance, especially from Vyshnegradskii. It was only when Witte took his place that the enterprise's completion was assured.

The new finance minister threw himself into the project with zeal. To finance its construction, Witte borrowed heavily on the Paris Bourse. Fortuitously, Alexander III had just concluded an alliance with the French Republic, making access to its money markets much easier. Meanwhile, Witte assured political support by setting up a Siberian Railway Committee of leading officials and cleverly arranging to have Tsarevich Nicholas as its head.[40] Despite immense hardships wrought by climatic extremes, forbidding terrain, a scarcity of skilled labor, bureaucratic incompetence, and the sheer scope of the enormous undertaking, a railway of sorts already linked Moscow to Vladivostok by 1901.[41]

Witte's Far Eastern projects eventually reached well beyond Siberia. In 1896, the finance minister negotiated a significant short-cut across Chinese territory in northern Manchuria for the Trans-Siberian. Two years later, after Russian warships seized two ports on the Liaodong Peninsula in southern Manchuria, he also arranged for a track to the new possessions. These new Manchurian railways were joined by a host of other enterprises in northern China, including a Russo-Chinese Bank, river and ocean fleets, and even new cities like Harbin, along with an army of border guards to protect them, all under the aegis of the Finance Ministry. For a while it seemed that, in the East, Witte's ambitions knew no bounds. Aleksandr Izvolskii hardly exaggerated when he wrote that Sergei Iulevich saw himself as a Russian equivalent of the builder of the British Empire, Cecil Rhodes, likewise creating "a veritable kingdom of which he was its own master."[42]

To his contemporaries, it appeared that Sergei Witte lacked a consistent ideology. Because of the volte-faces of his politics, a tendency to intrigue and self-aggrandizement, and an apparent absence of integrity, many concluded that the statesman acted entirely according to the dictates of his own ambition. One official who knew him wrote that "his political and economic conceptions . . . were not really inspired by an overall conception of the state or of the laws that govern human intercourse."[43] The economist Petr Struve believed that Witte "was by nature without principle or ideals."[44] Nevertheless, the finance minister's actions and writings show his policies were guided by a coherent logic.

The clearest statement of Witte's ideas is in a set of lectures he gave to the tsar's younger brother and heir, Grand Duke Mikhail Aleksandrovich, in 1901 and 1902. In 1900 the emperor had been ill with typhus, and it seemed appropriate to have the finance minister teach the tsarevich the basics about economics and government finance should worst come to worst. Subsequently published as *Konspekt lektsii o narodnom i gosudarstvennom khoziaistve* (Lessons on National and Government Economics), Witte's notes were a powerful manifesto for modernization along European lines.[45]

The finance minister's emphasis on Western notions of progress is not altogether surprising. He attended university in the 1860s, and, not unlike

American undergraduates a hundred years later, Russia's *shestidesiatniki* ("people of the sixties")—as the youth of that decade became known—were an intensely rebellious generation. With a passion for progress, materialism, and the primacy of scientific reason, they acquired the epithet "nihilist" for their fervent rejection of all traditional notions. The novelist Ivan Turgenev caricatured the type well in *Fathers and Sons* with his character Bazarov, the hyperutilitarian medical student who prefers dissecting frogs over poetry and romantic love. Although Witte disdained the rowdy politics of his more extremist university classmates, the age left its imprint on the mathematics student. Despite the occasional genuflection to Slavophile notions of Russian particularity, the finance minister firmly stood in the camp of the Westernizers.[46]

The overriding message of the *Lessons* is the primacy of economic forces. Like Karl Marx, Sergei Witte defined historical progress according to modes of production. He also agreed with Marx (while disagreeing about the end result) when he explained that all peoples advance along the same path, beginning at the most primitive level of hunter-gatherers, evolving to nomads, then to farmer-craftsmen, and ultimately reaching the apogee as a modern industrial-commercial order. That universal schema, Witte emphasized, applies to every nation, including Russia.

The final, industrial-commercial stage, is a desirable goal, for it alone affords a people true prosperity and control over their destiny. "Progress is nothing less than man's emancipation from the yoke of nature," as Witte put it.[47] In contrast, backward societies remained vulnerable. Without a proper manufacturing sector and a money economy, such societies could never fully realize their potential, no matter how populous or well endowed in natural resources. More important, as Witte frequently reminded his sovereign, there was a clear link between economic maturity and political power, since "finances are the nerve of war."[48] In a memorandum to Nicholas II in early 1900, he argued that "only economically independent states can exert their will in the world."[49]

Witte admired Britain and Germany as the most advanced nations. His own country, he taught the grand duke, still had some catching up to do. On an earlier occasion the finance minister put it more bluntly: "To this day Russia remains predominantly rural. Given the current international level of political and economic development, an agrarian nation that does not possess its own industry . . . cannot hope to remain sovereign."[50] The only solution was for Russia to become more like its rivals. With its parliamentary system and maritime geography, England might not be the best model. The German Empire, however, was another mighty continental power with a strong monarchy. Witte therefore taught that Russia must encourage modern industry along the lines so successfully adopted by its central European neighbour.

Witte's inspiration explicitly came from the early-nineteenth-century economist Friedrich List, "the prophet of Germany's present greatness."[51]

List had been an enthusiastic advocate of German economic unity as well as of railway construction. He is best known, however, for his *National System of Political Economy*.[52] Published in 1841, the book advocated high protectionist tariffs to speed up industrialization. Among its more important readers was the Prussian statesman Otto von Bismarck, whose economic policies were strongly influenced by its prescriptions. Witte was convinced that Russia could replicate German success by adopting List's advice.

The finance minister did not agree with List about everything. The German economist held somewhat liberal political views, and Witte was an unabashed monarchist.[53] On other occasions, the minister vehemently opposed institutions that might dilute the monarchy's power, such as the zemstvo system of local self-government.[54] Only a strong, centralized state could undertake the vital task of industrialization. He lectured Grand Duke Mikhail Aleksandrovich: "Every nation must . . . develop its economy, taking all possible steps to achieve this goal. . . . Individuals can never accomplish this on their own; this is a matter for the state . . . which acts as the intermediary between man and mankind."[55]

Witte also taught his august student about peace. One of the more worrisome developments of the modern age, he said, was the rise of large standing armies. Since the Napoleonic Wars at the start of the nineteenth century, and even more in recent decades, militarism was insinuating itself into European politics. The danger was great: "As governments are compelled incessantly to prepare for war, they have artificially created and strengthened a class of men devoted to it. Militarism increases the possibility and certainty of conflict."[56]

More to the point, militarization was a tremendous impediment to prosperity. "Among those factors that retard growth, the first place is occupied by militarism," Witte noted.[57] He reminded the grand duke that the expenses associated with armaments were a major drain on the economy, absorbing between one-fifth to one-third of governments' budgets. This was money entirely gone to waste: "When we consider that spending on the military deprives the state of cash it could devote instead to raising the cultural and productive level of its population, we see even more how heavily the burden of maintaining large armies weighs on the governments of Europe."[58] Its effect, he stressed, was pernicious: "The harm unrelentingly done by militarism to the economic well-being of European states is like a chronic illness, which slowly saps their productive vitality."[59] The danger to Russia was particularly great. Witte knew that the empire could not afford to squander its limited resources on the costly paraphernalia of war. "The art of our diplomacy," he never tired of reminding Nicholas, ". . . must be entirely devoted to preserving the status quo. With all our efforts we must play for time. Time is Russia's truest ally. Every year that your people live in peace accomplishes as much as a good battle."[60]

Witte's distaste for militarism strongly echoed that of his former employer, Jan Bloch. Like other tycoons of the era, such as Alfred Nobel and

Andrew Carnegie, during his later years Bloch had increasingly dedicated himself to promoting peace. In 1899, the Pole published a detailed six-volume warning about the dangers of armed conflict in the industrial age. *Budushchaia voina* (Future War) argued that recent technological developments, including smokeless powder, machine guns, and rapid-firing artillery, together with an increasing reliance on mass conscriptôn armies, entirely transformed the nature of combat.[61]

Bloch predicted that the twentieth century would witness wars that were total, mobilizing all aspects of society in confrontations of unprecedented violence, destruction, and duration. Moreover, the resulting stresses on the home front could lead to domestic unrest that might well topple some of the combatant regimes.[62] *Budushchaia voina* received considerable attention when it appeared, not least because some saw it as the inspiration for Nicholas II's conference in The Hague, also in 1899, to curb the arms race.[63] Bloch's impact on the finance minister is clear, especially with regard to the latter's thinking about the economic consequences of militarism.

Aside from being costly and dangerous, there was another reason Russia should avoid war, Witte taught the grand duke. The real contest among the powers was being fought in the economic arena. His lesson about the influence of trade on diplomacy has a familiar tone: "One of the priorities of commercial nations is to secure markets for their products. This effort . . . is particularly critical for those countries that, like England, possess an enormous industrial plant but must import raw materials from abroad."[64] Trying to sustain their industries, the rich countries were drawn in an "unceasing struggle to acquire commercial influence over nations that were at a lower level of development."[65] Meanwhile, this competition was increasingly being conducted by economic means, "since the authority of the metropolis over its colonies now more than ever is exercised not by force of arms but by trade."[66]

Those nations that could not keep up were bound to come under the control of their wealthier rivals. Russia had already suffered the political cost of its relative poverty when its richer neighbors had used loans to influence its diplomacy.[67] At times, Witte saw matters in an even more pessimistic light. He once told the tsar that "the economic relations of Russia with western Europe are fully comparable to the relations of colonial countries with their metropolises."[68]

Witte's conviction regarding the supremacy of economics also shaped his geopolitical views. Russian generals invariably thought in terms of military opportunities or vulnerabilities. The finance minister had a startlingly different conception of the empire's place in the world. As he saw it, a strong manufacturing sector was one characteristic of the modern great powers of the West. But another important feature was their role as entrepôts in global trade. Whether by developing a backward region overseas or simply transporting goods from one market to another, certain European states had grown tremendously rich. England was the most obvious example.

Russia lacked the maritime capability to establish a global colonial and shipping network like that of its great political rival. In Witte's opinion, however, the empire might well be able to turn its Eurasian geography to its advantage. He reminded Grand Duke Mikhail Aleksandrovich: "With its natural borders on Asian countries, Russia occupies an exceptionally favorable position both as a direct trade partner and as a transit point between the East and western Europe."[69]

This line of thinking lay behind Witte's rationale for the Trans-Siberian Railway. Whereas others had championed the project to help protect Russia's Pacific flank, the finance minister envisioned it as a means to bring prosperity to the empire. By linking European Russia with the Pacific Ocean, the Trans-Siberian would speed the development of Russia's own East Asian provinces and thereby "open abundant wellsprings of material prosperity for all people."[70]

Just as the recently completed Trans-Canada Railway had created new cities, brought prosperity to the prairies, and helped unify the young North American nation, this project would bestow similar benefits upon Russia's immense colony.[71] Once the tracks were laid, Siberia would inevitably become the most efficient transit route for Europe's commerce with the Orient. Russian merchants would then be able to wrest the fabled China trade from the hands of the British, who had dominated it for far too long.[72]

To Witte, the Trans-Siberian was built first and foremost to bring wealth to Russia: "Holding in its hands the means by which this rapprochement will take place, it has become the intermediary and must make sure that it profits from this position. Standing guard over the path it has opened between Europe and Asia, it can manipulate this rapprochement to its best advantage."[73]

Yet there were times when the finance minister mused about a higher purpose. Returning from a trip to the East along the railway in 1902, he wrote the tsar:

> The completion of the Siberian Railway opens a gate for Europe to this hitherto secluded world, putting it face-to-face with the innumerable tribes of the Mongol race. . . . Of course it is hard to predict exactly how the yellow and white races will come together, but Russia has a serious responsibility in bringing this about.

Meanwhile, he lectured the grand duke about the empire's obligations: "Russia's task abroad is both peaceful and, even more fundamentally, cultural in nature. Unlike the western European powers, who hope to exploit the Orient's peoples economically and often also politically, Russia's mission in the East must be to protect and enlighten them."[74] Sergei Iulevich also referred to a civilizing mission: "Russia long ago appeared among the Asian peoples on her border as the bearer of the Christian ideal, bringing the beginnings of Christian enlightenment to their midst."[75]

Like Nikolai Przhevalskii, Witte was convinced about the superiority of

Western civilization. He explained that Christian culture "was more powerful than the culture of the yellow nations, based on idolatry."[76] Although Russia was perhaps more benevolent than such western European rivals as England and Germany, this did not mean that its notions of progress should be fundamentally different. Just as he hoped to convert his own compatriots to Western ways, the finance minister was equally convinced about the desirability of modernizing the East along European lines. On this point, he strongly disagreed with the Asianist conception of Prince Ukhtomskii, which saw Russia and its eastern neighbors as thoroughly distinct from Europe. When Russians brought enlightenment to the Orient, Witte believed, they were extending Europe eastward. He wrote about the role his railways played in this important task: "At the pass in the Ural Mountains to the Siberian tract there still stands a sign. On one side is written 'Europe' and on the other 'Asia'. . . . For Russians, the boundary marker separating them, as a European race, from the peoples of Asia . . . will eventually stand at the end point of the Chinese Eastern Railway."[77]

This did not mean that Witte advocated territorial conquest. He reminded a Dutch journalist: "My motto is—up with trade and industry, down with the army!"[78] His distaste for militarism applied equally strongly to the Orient. Russia's role there, he emphasized, was to be a benevolent trading partner, not a conqueror. His was a vision of *pénétration pacifique*. Russia's expansion to the East was a natural process and would continue over time.[79] But, in the modern age, trade, banks, and railways, not troops, were the most effective means for extending Russian influence along the Pacific.

In fact, as Witte understood it, this economic goal of his Asian ambitions only reinforced its more humane aspects. England and the other Western powers established themselves in the Orient solely to profit themselves. Theirs was a zero-sum game. In contrast, Russia's relationship with its Asian neighbours was symbiotic; it turned to the East both to benefit its own people and those of Asia. This was particularly true of the Qing dynasty, with which Russia always had close ties. Witte stressed, "In our effort to fulfill [our] historic mission we have enjoyed the friendly assistance of the Chinese Empire."[80]

During the early years of Nicholas's reign, as St. Petersburg became more deeply involved in the Far East, Witte continued to stress the commercial aspects of the empire's interests. When in 1896 the possibility arose of an alliance with China, the finance minister pressed for a railway concession in northern Manchuria. "Building a railway track is one of the best ways to guarantee our economic influence in China," he told the tsar.[81] Four years later, after the war minister accused his colleague of trying to annex all of Manchuria, Witte protested:

> We *did not seize* Manchuria, and it would be best of all if we did not grab any territory, letting the battle for markets take place instead by trade. We proceeded

through all of Manchuria without making any [territorial] seizures. The Ministry of Finance has always insisted that, rather than take any land, we limit ourselves to establishing economic and political influence.[82]

A little more than a year before the outbreak of war with Japan, Sergei Iulevich once again underscored the peaceful nature of his enterprises: "As a result of the Chinese Eastern Railway [which was built under Witte's aegis] Russia will inevitably be drawn closer to Japan through our commercial and industrial interests. Building close ties among peoples this way is one of the best ways to avoid war."[83]

According to Witte, commerce and conquest were wholly antithetical. "Russia's movement to the East is fundamentally peaceful and cultural, and not one that involves annexation," he frequently reminded the tsar.[84] Both on the Pacific and elsewhere, the finance minister never ceased to oppose military adventures. The Soviet diplomatic historian Evgenii Tarle explained that "underscoring all of Witte's ideas about foreign policy is the deep conviction that Russia cannot and must not go to war."[85]

*F*or the first eight years of his tenure as finance minister, from 1892 through 1900, Sergei Witte's policies appeared to be a spectacular success. By many measures, the Russian economy boomed. Between 1890 and 1900 the production of iron and steel, crude oil, and coal all roughly tripled, the length of railway track increased by 50 percent, and the overall value of industrial output doubled. In all, growth rates averaged an impressive 8 percent per year, at the time the fastest pace in Europe. Meanwhile, investors both at home and abroad showed their faith in the empire's future prosperity by boosting purchases of Russian stocks from 60 million rubles in 1893 to more than 400 million by 1899.[86] As one economic historian put it, Russians were witnessing "the great upsurge of industrialisation."[87]

Alas, as with many booms, the decade ended in a bust. By 1900, the signs of a slump were unmistakable. The Russian countryside had seen mediocre crops in 1897 and 1898. Although yields improved somewhat in the next two years, falling grain prices continued to erode farm incomes. Compounding rural difficulties were the ongoing impoverishment of the landed nobility and the enormous taxes Witte levied on the empire's peasants to pay for his industrial plans. Meanwhile the West's economy, with which Russia was becoming increasingly integrated as a result of Witte's efforts, was once again mired in recession. The global downturn was accentuated by fewer orders for domestic heavy industry as work on the Trans-Siberian Railway neared completion.[88] This same unhappy coincidence of poor harvests at home and stagnation worldwide had torpedoed the ministry of his predecessor, Ivan Vyshnegradskii.

Prince Meshcherskii's *Grazhdanin,* a paper generally sympathetic to the finance minister, described 1901 as "a most difficult year for Russia's economy."[89] Share prices on the St. Petersburg Bourse plummeted, prompting intervention by the State Bank to prop up the market.[90] More ominously, throughout the empire many expressed their despair in increasingly violent ways. Student unrest had already been plaguing the universities since 1899. In spring 1902, angry peasants plundered dozens of manor houses in the Ukrainian provinces of Kharkov and Poltava.[91] The following year a general strike brought the Black Sea port of Odessa to a standstill. Assaults on the autocracy were also on the rise, with Socialist Revolutionary assassins alone claiming the lives of three of the tsar's ministers between 1901 and 1904.[92]

Around 1902, the increasingly apparent failure of Sergei Witte's economic policies was being paralleled by a dramatic erosion of his political standing. Vain, overbearing, and exceedingly arrogant, the finance minister had never been particularly popular in St. Petersburg. Other ministers often faced the choice of bowing to their domineering colleague or engaging in endless intrigues to undermine his authority. Over the years, officialdom's respect for Witte's talents diminished and resentments multiplied.

The capital's smart set sneered on the provincial's coarse ways. Fashionable society was shocked when he married a Jewish divorcée, Matilda Ivanovna, "a lady of acknowledged notoriety in the past," in the words of a British diplomat.[93] Although Alexander III's consort, Empress Marie Fedorovna, shared her husband's respect for his capable administrator, she refused to receive Matilda Ivanovna at court. The new tsarina, Alexandra Fedorovna, was even less forgiving and openly loathed the minister.[94]

There was a deeper reason for Witte's political ostracism. At the dawn of the twentieth century, Imperial Russia's elite was still predominantly aristocratic. Its economic base remained agrarian. Sergei Iulevich's plans to industrialize the empire therefore profoundly menaced their way of life. In the short run, the countryside bore the fiscal burden of the finance minister's costly initiatives, further impairing the nobility's precarious finances.[95] If Witte continued to have his way the future looked even bleaker, as a bourgeoisie inexorably edged out the aristocracy from its dominant position. Such concerns hardly reinforced the minister's appeal to the ruling class. A friend, State Councillor Aleksandr Polovtsov, wrote that "they are after Witte's head."[96]

As long as he enjoyed the confidence of the tsar, Witte could afford to ignore such feelings. But in the early 1900s he also began to alienate his master. Alexander III had valued his finance minister's iron will, and Nicholas II was thoroughly awed by his powerful official during the early years of his reign. But, as Nicholas grew into his role as autocrat, he became increasingly jealous of his own prerogatives. It was only a matter of time before the insecure monarch would summon the courage to defy the statesman. Witte described the dynamic of their relationship with uncanny accuracy when recounting the dismissal of another one of Alexander III's ministers:

He had lost the favour of the Emperor in part because, like so many of the ministers who had served under Emperor Alexander III and had known Emperor Nicholas II from the cradle, he could not immediately accept the fact that this young man had become the unlimited monarch of the greatest empire in the world and did not always speak to the young Emperor with the necessary respect.[97]

In August 1902 Sergei Witte celebrated the tenth anniversary of his appointment as finance minister. The press was full of flattering articles to mark the jubilee, and a few months later Nicholas II issued a rescript praising the official for a decade of loyal service.[98] Nevertheless, Witte was well aware that imperial favor was on the wane. The tsar had already made it clear that his domestic priorities lay not with industry but with the countryside during an address to noblemen in Kursk in September 1902. He added that "as for the landed gentry—the ancient stronghold of order and of the moral strength of Russia—it will be my constant concern to consolidate it."[99] Nicholas underscored this predilection by relying more and more on the advice of Viacheslav Plehve, the new minister of the interior and one of Witte's arch rivals.[100]

In early 1903, the finance minister discovered that his authority in East Asian matters was also fading. In February he complained to General Kuropatkin that Nicholas had not yet even deigned to return the report he had written about his trip to the Orient six months earlier.[101] Toward the end of July 1903, the tsar named a naval officer, Admiral Evgenii Alekseev, viceroy for the Far East. This move put Alekseev in charge of all of the empire's interests on the Pacific and was universally understood to be a slap in the face of Witte, who had hitherto dominated St. Petersburg's activities there.

Soon thereafter, on August 15, 1903, the finance minister delivered his weekly report to the emperor at Tsarskoe Selo. As the meeting drew to an end, Nicholas hesitated and grew visibly embarrassed. Suddenly he uttered: "Sergei Iulevich, I am asking you to take the post of chairman of the Council of Ministers and wish to appoint [Eduard] Pleske as minister of finance."[102] Technically, this was a promotion, but there was no question that Witte was being kicked upstairs.

Sergei Witte's career was not yet over. In August 1905, the emperor sent him to Portsmouth, New Hampshire, at the head of Russia's delegation to negotiate an end to the disastrous war with Japan. Witte's diplomatic abilities enabled St. Petersburg to extract itself from the military debacle with surprisingly light terms and won him the gratitude of Nicholas, who ennobled him with the title of count. Three months later, when the empire was paralyzed by a revolutionary general strike, Sergei Iulevich convinced the tsar that only serious political concessions could save the dynasty. Largely inspired by Witte, the manifesto Nicholas issued on October 17, 1905, effectively made Russia a constitutional monarchy by establishing an elected legislature and guaranteeing civil liberties. The former finance minister was then appointed to the considerably more substantial position of chairman of the Council of Ministers.

Witte's career as Nicholas's chief minister was brief and stormy. Within half a year, having once again lost the confidence of the tsar and alienated the public, he resigned. This time his retirement was permanent. Sergei Iulevich would live another nine years, engaging in futile polemics and vainly attempting to regain his former standing. He died on February 28, 1915.

*F*or a Russian official at the turn of the twentieth century, Sergei Witte had a strikingly modernist view of the world. According to his vision of *pénétration pacifique*, the fate of nations in the future would ultimately be decided by industrial might, not military prowess. Only those states that had the most advanced factories, the best commercial networks, and the fittest finances could expect to survive their grim contest for survival. Nowhere was this more true than in Asia, where St. Petersburg's imperial destiny lay. For these reasons, the tsar had to build a modern economy. The alternative was for Russia itself to succumb to the will of other powers. Witte summed up his ideas about reform, economic strength, and imperial power in a memorandum to Nicholas in early 1900:

> It is imperative for Russia . . . to base its political and cultural structure on sound economic foundations. . . . International competition does not wait. We must take vigorous and decisive steps now to ensure that within ten years our industry can produce goods to satisfy both the markets of Russia and of the Asian countries that we should influence. If this does not happen, rapidly growing foreign industries will penetrate our fatherland, as well as the Oriental nations in our sphere, thereby gradually also acquiring malign political influence. . . .
>
> I fear that the slow growth of our industry frustrates the great political tasks of Your Highness, that the ongoing industrial prostration of our nation saps its political power, that inadequate economic growth also leads to the country's political and cultural enfeeblement.[103]

The implications of *pénétration pacifique* for Russia's eastward drive were clear. Witte never doubted that the Romanov dynasty would eventually rule over China. "The extension of Russia's railway through Manchuria . . . was far from being the final step in our advance to the Pacific Ocean," he wrote. "By historical necessity we [are] obligated to go further."[104] But the empire had to do so peacefully and through economic means. Railroads, banks, and trading houses should conquer the Middle Kingdom, not troops. Territorial annexations by war, Witte believed, were antiquated and counterproductive. Besides, he often reminded the tsar, "for the sake of the general domestic situation in Russia it is exceedingly important to avoid anything that might lead to foreign complications."[105]

The idea that overseas expansion was driven by economic forces was hardly unique. A number of German Socialists, like Friedrich Engels and August Bebel, had already written about the links between capitalism and colonialism. In 1894, Engels had even predicted that "China is the only country left for capitalist production to conquer."[106] Six years later, the Fifth International Socialist Congress resolved "that the development of capitalism leads inevitably to colonial expansion."[107] In 1902, John Hobson, a British Liberal journalist, popularized the term "imperialism" in his treatise about the need for surplus investment to seek higher returns in underdeveloped areas abroad.[108]

Among tsarist statesmen, however, Witte was virtually alone in thinking about diplomacy in economic terms. To his colleagues in St. Petersburg, international power remained a matter of armies and navies. Although most of Nicholas's ministers were not particularly bellicose, few would have disagreed with the Clausewitzian notion that "war is a continuation of politics by other means." Even Russian businessmen failed to share the finance minister's interest in developing the Far East. Unlike western European countries at the time, where trade and industry often supported the acquisition of empire, there were few enthusiasts among entrepreneurs in Russia for Witte's foreign schemes.

Nevertheless, *pénétration pacifique* was one of the dominant ideologies driving tsarist expansion on the Pacific during the early years of Nicholas's reign. Unlike Przhevalskii and Ukhtomskii, Witte was influential not because he represented an idea that resonated with deeper intellectual currents in Nicholas II's realm. Instead, he was able to impose his vision by sheer force of will. From the beginnings of the alliance with Peking in 1896 through the early 1900s, Witte dominated St. Petersburg's policies in East Asia because of the authority he exercised over the emperor. After he fell from grace in 1903, virtually no official shared his beliefs. Ironically, it was one of the autocracy's most implacable foes who would once again revive the idea that economics drove foreign policy when in early 1917 Vladimir Lenin published *Imperialism: The Highest Stage of Capitalism.*

During the messy debates that followed Russia's defeat by Japan in 1905, Witte justifiably stressed that he had always been opposed to going to war. Indeed, throughout his years as finance minister, he did his best to avoid any fighting in the Orient. Witte well understood that a conflict would be disastrous for his fatherland. In a letter to the foreign minister, Count Lamsdorf, in 1901 he wrote:

> Military struggle with Japan in the near future would be a major calamity for us. I do not doubt the we would vanquish the foe, but our victory would come at the cost of many casualties as well as heavy economic losses. Besides, and most important . . . it would arouse the strong hostility of public opinion.[109]

At the same time, the finance minister was not entirely blameless for the eruption of hostilities in 1904. His ardor for the Trans-Siberian Railway, partnership with the Qing dynasty, and the Far East's *pénétration pacifique* all played a major role in arousing Nicholas's dreams for an empire on the Pacific Ocean. Witte admitted as much himself in a conversation with General Kuropatkin not long before the war broke out:

> Imagine that I invited some friends to the Aquarium [a nightclub in St. Petersburg], and they all proceeded to get drunk. Then, going on to a brothel, they ended up starting a fight there. Would I be responsible? I only took them to the Aquarium. They did the rest.[110]

CHAPTER FIVE

The Yellow Peril

Aleksei Kuropatkin

Panmongolism! Though the word be fierce

It is music to my ear

Like some portent

of God's awesome fate entire. . . .

From Malaysian waters to the Altai,

Chieftains from Eastern isles

Gather their hosts

At decadent China's walls. . . .

—From "Panmongolism" by Vladimir Solovev

*V*ladimir Solovev first began to worry about the Far East during a trip to Paris in 1888. The philosopher-poet had gone to France to promote his plans for the reunification of the Catholic and Orthodox churches. His proposals largely fell on deaf ears among the Latin clergy there while conservative officials back in St. Petersburg expressed their annoyance at the initiative. The increasingly evident failure of Vladimir Sergeevich's hopes for a reconciliation of Christendom's two great traditions weighed heavily on the sensitive bard.[1]

It was in this mood of gloomy contemplation that Solovev happened to attend a meeting of the Paris Geographical Society. Among the usual parade of academics, Egyptologists, explorers, and African dignitaries, one speaker caught his attention: Chen Jitong, China's military attaché in the French capital. A senior army officer, Chen was among the "self-strengtheners," those Qing officials who hoped to restore their empire's greatness by adopting the West's technological innovations. Chen's speech was a typical statement of the self-strengtheners' program:

> We will get from you everything we need, all the technology of your intellectual and material culture, but we will adopt not one element of your faith, not one of your ideas or even one of your tastes. . . . We applaud your progress, but we neither need nor want to be part of it: You are yourselves providing the means whereby we will vanquish you.[2]

Solovev was particularly alarmed at the audience's equanimity to the Chinese. "The Europeans greeted him with the same light-minded joy with which the Maccabean Jews hailed the Romans," he grimly remarked. The Russian philosopher considered Chen "the emissary of an alien, hostile world that menaces us more and more." He added that the attaché "unintentionally . . . recited the credo he shares with his 400 million compatriots." Vladimir Sergeevich hinted at "a dark cloud approaching from the Far East."[3]

Two years later, Solovev laid out his views more extensively in a lengthy essay, "China and Europe." As he saw it, Eurasia's extremities were polar opposites: "They represent two highly contradictory ideas: *order* [in the case of China] and *progress* [Europe]."[4] The term Solovev used to describe the former was *kitaishchina*. In the late-eighteenth-century Catherinian era the noun had referred to the fashion for all things Chinese, much like the French word *chinoiserie,* but in the nineteenth century *kitaishchina* acquired a much more derogatory connotation, evoking backwardness, reaction, cruelty, and tyranny.[5]

Like Nikolai Przhevalskii, Solovev held the Middle Kingdom's culture in low esteem. Based on ancestor worship and a slavish veneration of the past, its civilization was thoroughly ossified, Solovev explained. China, he wrote, "has given the world neither a single important idea nor any priceless creations. The Chinese nation may be big but it is not great."[6] Solovev concluded that, although the Oriental empire was dangerous, the West was not necessarily doomed: "If we, the European Christian world . . . remain true to ourselves, i.e., *true to ecumenical Christianity,* then China poses no threat to us."[7]

Solovev nevertheless continued to dread Asia. When severe drought led to a famine in 1891, he saw its cause in the East. "Inner Asia moves toward us with the spontaneous power of its deserts," he remarked.[8] In a review of Helen Blavatsky's *The Keys to Theosophy,* Solovev warned that the author and her followers were the instruments of "Buddhism's aggressive advance on the Western world."[9] Japan's surprising victory over China in 1895 inspired his poem "Panmongolism," with its ominous prophecy of Russia's invasion by a united Asian horde:

Panmongolism! Though the word be fierce
It is music to my ear
Like some portent
of God's awesome fate entire. . . .

From Malaysian waters to the Altai,
Chieftains from Eastern isles
Gather their hosts
At decadent China's walls.

Like locust swarm uncountable
And insatiable like it too,
By divine strength guarded,
Northward move the tribes.

O Russia! Forget your former glory:
The double-headed eagle is no more,
And yellow babes play
With the rags remaining from your flags.

Now knowing trembling fear and terror,
Who remembers commandments to love. . . .
And the Third Rome lies in ashes,
And a fourth will never be.

Vladimir Sergeevich's pessimistic musings were accompanied by other, equally foreboding thoughts. In 1897, he wrote a friend: "The approach of the end of the world is wafted to me as a kind of clear, though elusive breath—just as a wayfarer feels the sea air before the sea itself comes into sight."[10]

Solovev's best-known work about the Far East was his apocalyptic "Short Tale of the Antichrist." Published shortly before his death in 1900, the story was an appendix to his "Three Conversations," a meditation on the power of evil and the need to struggle against it. Supposedly written by the monk Pansophia, the "Tale" foresees the cataclysmic events at the end of history, including armed conflict, the coming of the Antichrist, his defeat by the united forces of Christianity and Judaism, and, ultimately, the thousand-year reign of Christ. The piece bears strong traces of the Bible, especially the book of Revelation, and once again pleads for the Eastern and Western churches to end their schism.

The most dramatic moment of the "Tale" is the start, which presages a period of wars and revolutions in the twentieth century, culminating in an assault from Asia. The protagonist was Japan:

> The imitative Japanese, with astonishing rapidity and success copied the material forms of European culture and adopted certain European ideas of a lower order. Having learned . . . about the existence in the West of Panhellenism, Pangermanism, Panslavism, Panislamism, they proclaimed the great idea of Panmongolism, which was the gathering into one, under their leadership, of all the peoples of Eastern Asia . . . [to] make a resolute struggle against . . . Europeans.[11]

It was not hard to enlist the Middle Kingdom:

> In the beginning of the twentieth century [the Japanese] began the realisation of a great plan—first, the occupation of Korea, then that of Peking, where, with the help of the progressive party in China they would depose the ancient Manchurian dynasty and put the Japanese in its place . . . the Chinese saw the delightful lyre of Panmongolism, which, moreover, in their eyes did away with the sad inevitability of European influence.[12]

Japanese officers now trained a vast army of Chinese, Manchurians, Mongolians, and Tibetans. The new confederation first drove the Europeans out from their colonies and concessions in Asia. The dynasty's next move was more sinister:

> [The new emperor] was Chinese on his mother's side, thus combining both the cunning and elasticity of the Chinese with the energy, mobility and enterprise of the Japanese. He mobilised an army of 4 million in Chinese Turkestan. The Zongli Yamen [China's foreign office] confidently informed the Russian Ambassador that this force was intended for the conquest of India. But the Emperor appears in our Central Asia, and having collected all its inhabitants, swiftly crosses the Urals and with his armies swamps all Eastern and Central Russia. . . . The fighting qualities of the Russian forces allow them only to perish with honour.[13]

Benefiting from old hatreds between the Germans and the French, the Asiatic hordes went on to conquer the rest of the continent. The new "Mongol yoke" held sway over the West for half a century before finally being driven out. Only Britain avoided occupation, by paying a tribute of a billion pounds.

When Solovev publicly read his "Tale" at the St. Petersburg Duma in February 1900, the Far East was still quiet. That summer, however, the papers were filled with reports of a violent outbreak of anti-European unrest in northern China at the hands of a bizarre xenophobic movement popularly dubbed "the Boxers." To the mystically inclined poet, this news confirmed his worst suspicions. In a letter to the journal *Voprosy Filosofii i Psikhologii* (Questions of Philosophy and Psychology) he wrote: "I certainly had foreknowledge and presentiments of these events and everything that will befall us thereafter . . . [already] ten years ago in my article 'China and

Europe.'"[14] Solovev viewed the Boxer rising as nothing less than the harbinger of the final cataclysm: "The historical drama has played out, and only the epilogue still remains. As with Ibsen, the story may extend over five acts, but we have already long known their contents."[15]

Solovev thought of the menace from the Far East as a biblical punishment, a sign of God's wrath against Christendom's quarrelsome believers. One scholar even compared the Asians to one of the Old Testament's seven plagues, noting that grasshoppers were an emblem of the medieval Mongols.[16] The philosopher Nikolai Berdiaev reflected: "Christian Russia and Christian Europe, as punishment for their sins, in the name of Christ . . . are menaced by Pan-Mongolism from the Far East, [those lands] up to now in slumber, the East we had forgotten."[17] Thus, Solovev's poem "Panmongolism" and his "Short Tale of the Antichrist" tried to warn Christians about the dangers they faced if they failed to reconcile their differences and reunite their churches.

While few heeded Vladimir Solovev's ecumenical summons, the idea of a danger from the East captured the imagination of many Russians. More than anyone else, Vladimir Sergeevich introduced the concept of a "yellow peril" to his compatriots. His apocalyptic musings found a receptive audience among the poets and philosophers of the Silver Age, especially in the troubled years after 1905.

Before the war with Japan such sentiments were rare among educated Russians. Nevertheless, some shared Solovev's deep forebodings about East Asia and its potential to cause great harm. The most influential among them in the tsar's government was War Minister Aleksei Kuropatkin. Notions of a yellow peril were not as important in East Asian policy at the turn of the century as the ideas considered in the previous three chapters, but they were an intellectual undercurrent whose influence was felt in St. Petersburg. Its leading proponent in official circles was General Kuropatkin.

*L*ike many of the Imperial Russian Army's officers, Aleksei Nikolaevich Kuropatkin was born into his caste.[18] Aleksei Nikolaevich entered the world on March 17, 1848, on his parent's estate in the village of Sheshurino, some 300 kilometers south of St. Petersburg, near Pskov. His father, Captain Nikolai Emelianovich Kuropatkin, taught geodesy, a form of mathematical geography, at various military schools in St. Petersburg. When Tsar Alexander II decreed the end of serfdom in 1861, Nikolai Emelianovich left active duty. Returning to the countryside, he devoted the rest of his life to local administration. The retired officer was particularly active in the newly created zemstva, institutions of rural self-government whose duties absorbed the energies of many liberally inclined landowners in the era of Alexander's Great Reforms.

Nikolai Emelianovich saw to it that his son received a proper military education. Aleksei Nikolaevich was enrolled in the capital's prestigious First

General Aleksei Nikolaevich Kuropatkin

Cadet Corps, going on to graduate from the Paul Junker Academy in 1866. In the 1860s, even the pupils of these aristocratic institutions were often imbued with the generation's radical thought. Years later, Kuropatkin recalled that, "until 1866, I was a *narodnik* [populist] of the old school."[19] The books that influenced him most strongly in those years were Ivan Turgenev's *Fathers and Sons* and Nikolai Chernyshevskii's *What Is to Be Done?* [20] Much like his father, as an adult Aleksei Nikolaevich held moderately liberal views and strongly supported the zemstvo.[21]

Upon completing school, Kuropatkin was commissioned as a subaltern in the First Turkestan Rifle Brigade, beginning a lengthy career in the empire's colonial wars. Russia had just started its campaign to conquer the khanates of Central Asia. After the demoralizing defeat in the Crimea some ten years earlier, the sands of Turkestan offered excellent opportunities for young officers eager to make their mark.

Second Lieutenant Kuropatkin was quick to distinguish himself. Over the next two years, he saw much action against the Khanate of Bokhara, including two assaults on the ancient city of Samarkand. By 1869 he had already become a company commander, and in 1871 he won admission to the Nicholas Academy of the General Staff. Kuropatkin proved to be equally adept in the classroom, graduating first in his class. This academic achievement earned him a tour abroad, with stops in Germany, France, and Algeria. Northern Africa was particularly interesting, since French armies there were fighting against Muslim desert nomads in a conflict resembling Kuropatkin's own combat in Turkestan.

Aleksei Nikolaevich returned to Russia with a *Légion d'honneur* for bravery in the Sahara as well as much to report about the French campaigns. Within a year he published an article in *Voennyi Sbornik* about camel transport in Algeria, followed by a series of "military statistical" essays about the region.[22] The officer's superiors quickly sent their man back into Turkestan, where he earned his first George's Cross—the tsarist equivalent of Britain's Victoria Cross—during a battle against Kokand, another khanate soon to be absorbed into the Russian Empire. In a move that was to prove extremely auspicious for his career, during the Kokand campaign Kuropatkin was made the chief of Major General Mikhail Skobelev's staff. Popularly known as the "White General," Skobelev was a flamboyant commander whose Central Asian exploits won him fame among the Russian public.

Kuropatkin also demonstrated his diplomatic talents when Konstantin von Kaufmann, Turkestan's governor-general, sent him on a delicate mission in 1876 to the Islamic rebel leader Yakub Beg to negotiate Russia's boundary with the latter's realm of Kashgaria in Xinjiang.[23] The undertaking was exceptionally hazardous, for much of the area was still in a state of unrest. Shortly after setting off, Kuropatkin was wounded when his party was attacked by Kirghiz horsemen in the Tian-Shan mountains, forcing him back to Russian territory for half a year to convalesce. His second attempt was more successful. Aleksei Nikolaevich spent the winter as Yakub Beg's guest, and he was able talk the insurgent chief into agreeing to most of St. Petersburg's territorial requests. Like Nikolai Przhevalskii, who had met the rebel a few months earlier, Kuropatkin also gathered extensive intelligence about the little-known region. The Imperial Geographical Society soon published Aleksei Nikolaevich's survey of Kashgaria and eventually awarded him a gold medal for his contribution to science.[24]

The following year Kuropatkin was tapped for service in the war that had just erupted in the Balkans with Ottoman Turkey. Once again appointed Skobelev's right-hand man, Kuropatkin played an active role in the White General's actions at Lovech and Plevna and in the difficult winter campaign.[25] After the hostilities, Aleksei Nikolaevich briefly served as head of the Main Staff's Asiatic Section, where Nikolai Przhevalskii was among his subordinates. But there were still laurels to be won in Turkestan. Kuropatkin returned just in time to participate in one of the last major battles of the Central Asian wars, General Skobelev's celebrated storming of Geok-Tepe in January 1881. It was Colonel Kuropatkin who led the final assault into the Turkoman fortress, garnering another George's Cross and a promotion to major general.

Over the next fifteen years the new general honed his administrative skills. His first assignment took him back to St. Petersburg to serve as deputy of the Main Staff's head, Adjutant General Nikolai Obruchev. Kuropatkin became intimately involved in Obruchev's work, including war planning, intelligence, training, logistics, and many other activities.[26] On one occasion, in 1886, Aleksei Nikolaevich even personally conducted a covert reconnaissance of the Bosphorus Straits near the Ottoman capital of Constantinople, a highly unusual undertaking for someone of his rank.[27] Four years later, the general was once again posted to Central Asia, to govern the tsar's new trans-Caspian possessions. He acquitted himself very well in this task too, considerably improving the area's economy and infrastructure. Even Sergei Witte, not one of his greatest admirers, commented that Kuropatkin "may have been the best governor the region ever had."[28]

The general also continued to publish prolifically. There were articles about artillery, hunting, and the Central Asian campaigns as well as a lengthy tome about the recent Turkish war.[29] Although the latter were military histories, their colorful prose was clearly meant for a broader public. Naturally, the White General featured prominently in such works, and, by glorifying Skobelev, Kuropatkin also enhanced his own reputation.[30] Aleksei Nikolaevich himself claimed: "Mikhail Dmitrevich [Skobelev] taught me a great deal, and I often copied him. More than anything, I learned to be decisive, true to my convictions, and confident in the abilities of the Russian soldier."[31] So closely was Kuropatkin linked to his erstwhile commander in the popular imagination that, when Kuropatkin was appointed head of the Russian army during the war with Japan in 1904, some peasant conscripts thought Skobelev was once again at their head, despite the fact that the White General had died more than twenty years earlier.[32]

In autumn 1897, not long into Nicholas II's reign, the aging War Minister Petr Vannovskii requested his sovereign's permission to retire.[33] Some had considered General Obruchev to be the natural candidate to replace Vannovskii, but Nicholas apparently wanted a younger man for the job. Kuropatkin's reputation as a "battle general" because of his association with the legendary Skobelev and his considerable popularity may also have been factors.[34] According to Witte, "Had there been an election for the post, [Kuropatkin] would have won."[35] On Christmas Eve 1897, Nicholas summoned General Kuropatkin to Tsarskoe Selo and told him that he was to succeed Vannovskii. "Serve righteously. Trust in God, and have faith in my confidence," the sovereign commanded his new minister.[36]

Kuropatkin's promotion came at a difficult moment for Russia's military. While the army had done much to recover the prestige it lost after the Crimean War more than 30 years earlier, the general was well aware of the empire's strategic vulnerability in the face of a steady arms buildup among its neighbors to the west. Matters were helped neither by the iron-willed parsimony of Finance Minister Sergei Witte nor by the seemingly endless fiscal gluttony of the imperial fleet.[37] One creative solution was to convince the other powers to end this expensive rivalry. When Austria-Hungary began to introduce new rapid-firing artillery early on in his ministry, Kuropatkin broached the idea of an arms pact to Nicholas, which eventually evolved into the Hague Peace Convention of 1899.[38] More realistically, Kuropatkin also endlessly campaigned for more resources to shore up defenses on the border with Germany and the Dual Monarchy.

In this context, the Far East was a costly distraction. As early as February 1898, in the midst of a crisis over Berlin's seizure of the port of Kiaochow in northern China, Kuropatkin urged his master to resist the temptation to involve himself in East Asia.[39] Oriental entanglements, he argued, could only benefit Germany, Russia's most dangerous strategic rival. In October 1902, at a time when the Pacific was becoming a heavy drain on Russian military resources, Kuropatkin wrote the head of the Main Staff, General V. V. Sakharov: "We have become so lost [in the Far East], and have squandered so much there, that we are fulfilling Germany's wildest hopes and dreams: Ensnare Russia in Chinese or Indian affairs, so as to enfeeble it in the West."[40] After a trip to Japan the following year, Kuropatkin again urged Nicholas not to waste his empire's precious military assets on the East. Although many of the tsar's advisors were pressing him to adopt an aggressive course there, the war minister still found Germany more menacing.[41]

There was another reason to resist the Pacific's siren song. In the past, Asians usually had yielded to Europe's small but technologically superior armies. As Japan had shown by annihilating vastly larger Qing forces in 1895, however, the East was quickly catching up. Already in 1887 Kuropatkin worried about the white man's narrowing military lead over other races:

> It is highly significant and ominous that recently, as Europeans fought in Asia and Africa, the foe has more and more proven to be their equals. British defeats in Afghanistan and the Sudan, and French setbacks in Tonkin, demonstrate that African and Asian peoples can battle Europeans with the hope of besting them.[42]

In early 1900, during a time of relative quiet in the East, the war minister warned Nicholas that his empire was particularly vulnerable to such developments because of its demographic deficit beyond the Urals:

> It is horrifying to contemplate what will become of Russia—the tears the Russian people will shed, the rivers of blood that will flow, the vast sums of money squandered, if we are taken on by 400 million Chinese or 300 million Indians. Russians only number 18 million on this populous continent.[43]

As minister, Aleksei Kuropatkin did not yet employ the phrase "yellow peril." He would first publicly write the words six years after he had been relieved from his post, in his *Zadachi Russkoi armii* (The Tasks of the Russian Army).[44] Before 1905, his language was more elliptical, consisting of such metaphors as "yellow floodwaters" and "yellow tidal wave." Nevertheless, the basic idea of the yellow peril—that Asia's masses threatened Europe— was already very much alive in his brain.

Kuropatkin's worries about the yellow peril seemed to be realized in 1904, when Japan went to war with Russia. Within days of the outbreak of hostilities, Nicholas put the war minister in charge of his armies in the East. Considered by many to be Skobelev's heir, Kuropatkin was a popular choice. Unfortunately, Aleksei Nikolaevich proved to be anything but a man of action. A pathological inability to make decisions combined with his severe doubts in the abilities of his troops and in his own talents to help ensure Russia's defeat in Manchuria. Not long after the disastrous battle of Mukden in March 1905, Kuropatkin was relieved of his command.

After the war, the former war minister engaged in an acrimonious polemic with Sergei Witte and others over the conflict. Spending most of his days at his estate, he also found the time to write several books. During the First World War, the general returned to active duty, eventually commanding Russian forces in the northern front against Germany. Once again, his performance in the field was less than distinguished, and in summer 1916 Nicholas posted him to Turkestan as governor-general. Kuropatkin's brief tenure there was taken up suppressing precisely the kind of rising by the non-Russian population he had often predicted. He held the post until the fall of the monarchy less than a year later.

For a former tsarist government minister and a senior general in the imperial army, Kuropatkin survived the onset of Soviet rule with relative ease. Despite entreaties from the French ambassador, Aleksei Nikolaevich even refused to emigrate, preferring to devote his days to a modest existence as a schoolteacher in his native Sheshurino. He died peacefully in January 1925.

*H*aving experienced nearly two centuries of Mongol rule, Russians should have had the strongest historical memory among Europeans of the danger that might strike them from the East. Chronicles, such as the fourteenth-century "Tale of the Destruction of Riazan by Batu [Khan]," and medieval *byliny* (epic folk songs) were filled with blood-curdling descriptions of the atrocities committed by Oriental horsemen during their invasion in the 1230s.[45] Yet by the nineteenth century popular attitudes about East Asia were relatively benign. The fabulist Ivan Krylov hardly inspired terror when he wrote:

> You haven't heard? Why yes, the China War
> To take away their tea and give it to the Tsar.[46]

When in the 1880s a group of schoolteachers polled Russian peasants about their knowledge of the world, they found that their respondents viewed the Middle Kingdom very favorably. To questions about which country was the strongest and which the wealthiest, in both cases China received more votes than any other, including Russia itself. Peasants often reasoned that China was rich and powerful because its emperor never squandered his resources on wars, in contrast to their own tsar. More striking was the fact that some identified with the Chinese as "a people which believes [*veruet*] as we do."[47]

Among the intelligentsia, attitudes were a little less positive. During the reign of Nicholas I (1825–1855) progressively minded authors began to equate China with lethargy, stagnation, and despotism. The poet Aleksandr Pushkin wrote about "the walls of unmoving China," and the radical literary critic Vissarion Belinskii remarked that, "from time immemorial, [the Asians] have been rotting in moral stagnation and repose in undisturbed slumber in the lap of Mother Nature."[48] Belinskii's friend Aleksandr Herzen also scorned the Middle Kingdom: "We cannot approve of the fact that China . . . will continue its alienated, reclusive, and inert existence for centuries to come."[49] To Westernizers like Belinskii and Herzen, who looked to Europe as their ideal, the eastern neighbor embodied everything they opposed. China was a warning for what Russia might well become itself. Foes of the autocracy even took to writing about the Qing in Aesopian critiques of the Romanov dynasty.[50]

On a few occasions, nineteenth-century authors portrayed East Asia in a more sinister light. Toward the end of Fedor Dostoevskii's novel *Crime and Punishment*, the homicidal protagonist Raskolnikov had a series of nightmares as he lay on his prison cot. During the last one, "he dreamt that the whole world was condemned to a terrible new strange plague that had come to Europe from the depths of Asia."[51] The character Nozdrev in Nikolai Gogol's novel *Dead Souls*, it has been suggested, was described with Asiatic garb and features to emphasize his violent behavior.[52]

Japan's startling debut as a Pacific power in the mid-1890s influenced anxieties about the yellow peril, as in Solovev's poem "Panmongolism." But the fear that Japan could lead an Oriental onslaught had already existed for some time. Among Russians, the notion probably originated with a book by Vasilii Golovnin, a naval officer who was captured by the Japanese along with his crew during a survey of the Kurile Islands in 1811. His account, written during his two years as prisoner, was one of the few detailed surveys that appeared in Europe during Japan's lengthy self-imposed isolation. On the whole, the captain presented a relatively objective view, even admitting that the Japanese were justified in seizing him. As he left Japan, he reflected: "We had endured much suffering [there], but . . . we had also experienced the generosity of a pacific people, whom some Europeans, perhaps less civilised, regard as barbarians."[53]

When it came to Japan's army, Golovnin concluded that "in the art of war they are still children."[54] This lack of military prowess was the result of the empire's isolation and aversion to innovation. In a passage that would strike readers after 1904 as eerily prophetic, he pointed out that the islands' inhabitants were not congenitally incapable of assimilating modern martial ways: "If the Japanese Government ever desired to have a navy, it would be very easy to form one upon the European system, and to bring it to the greatest perfection."[55] Captain Golovnin suggested that the other nations should count their blessings that Japan disdained contact with the West, for with good leadership ("like our own great Peter") Japan could dominate the Pacific. And, if Japan introduced European civilization, China would do the same, and the two nations might well give a different cast to European affairs.[56]

More than sixty years later, the exiled anarchist Mikhail Bakunin, who had also spent some time in Japan, made a similar prediction in a polemic against the Genoese revolutionary Giuseppe Mazzini. His tract, "Réponse d'un international à Massini" (An International's Reply to Mazzini), warned that England and Russia were pursuing a misguided policy in their "Great Game" for control over Asia. "Will they succeed?" he asked, going on to answer:

> They will not succeed for the simple reason that, being ambitious rivals, they fight in Asia to the death . . . conspiring, arming, and arousing Asian peoples against each other. Not meaning to, they nevertheless accustom these Orientals to our European ways of war and weaponry. Since Asiatics number in the hundreds of millions, the most likely outcome of these intrigues between England and Russia will be to awaken this hitherto immobile Asian world, which will . . . overrun Europe once again.[57]

Bakunin also respected the Japanese and similarly worried about their ability to inflict harm on Russia: "The Japanese do not resemble the Chinese in the least; they are not an old people. On the contrary, they are a virgin nation, barbarous, full of vigor, élan vital, and natural intelligence. They learn quickly. . . . Russians on the Amur River, beware! I give you but fifty years."[58]

Intelligence officers considered the potential for Asian powers to modernize their armies somewhat more scrupulously than the anarchist. From the 1880s onward, the pages of the Main Staff's *Sbornik* and related publications were rife with speculation about China's efforts to remake its armed forces along European lines. While few were as stridently contemptuous as the aggressive explorer Nikolai Przhevalskii, officers generally dismissed the possibility of a successful reform in the Qing military.[59] The Main Staff's most authoritative China hands respected the empire's imposing size but concluded that the Qing dynasty's innate conservatism seriously hampered any attempts at progress. In the words of one specialist, Lieutenant Colonel Butakov, "The Celestial Empire's army has hardly changed since the 1840s."[60] As for Japan, its armed forces received minimal attention until after it defeated China in 1895.[61]

Captain Golovnin and Mikhail Bakunin were therefore in a small minority when they worried about the Orient. Aside from some concerns during tensions with China in the 1880s, even most military men did not consider any Far Eastern powers to be potential aggressors. Until 1895, the over-whelming majority of Russians simply did not see East Asia as a threat.

*B*oth Russians and Europeans remembered Asia as a source of massive, destructive invasions. In antiquity the Orient had periodically menaced the West, starting with Persian attempts to conquer Greek states in the fifth century B.C. The Roman Empire's downfall was at the very least hastened by successive barbarian incursions from the East, most notoriously by Attila the Hun's assaults in the mid-fifth century. Eight hundred years later, in 1241, Batu Khan ravaged the central European kingdom of Hungary during the final stage of the march that had already annihilated Kievan Rus. The medieval world, which had at first hopefully imagined the Mongols to be subjects of the mythical Nestorian realm of Prester John, came to see them as the spawn of hell. It seemed to be no coincidence that "Tatar," a common synonym for "Mongol," was virtually identical to "Tartarus" (tartaroi), the infernal regions of classical mythology.[62] One chronicler wrote that the Mongols were "beasts rather than people, who quench their thirst with human blood and devour the flesh of dogs and men."[63]

As Denis Sinor points out, "The Mongol was the first Asiatic with whom the Occidental had any direct contact."[64] The next encounter with the Far East was more positive. Catholic missionaries who began to travel to China in the sixteenth century tended to idealize the exotic empire. Informed by the favorable accounts of Jesuits and others, seventeenth- and early-eighteenth-century philosophes like Voltaire saw the Middle Kingdom as the apotheosis of enlightened despotism.

Toward the end of the eighteenth century, more negative opinions resurfaced. Other French thinkers, such as Charles Baron de Montesquieu and Jean-Jacques Rousseau, began to equate the Qing dynasty with repression rather than reason. Montesquieu was also struck by the immense number of Chinese. In his *De l'esprit des lois* (Spirit of the Laws) he observed: "China's climate is highly favorable to the propagation of the human species. Women are endowed with a remarkable fertility that knows no equal on earth. The most cruel tyranny does nothing to inhibit this fecundity. . . . China's population is always growing."[65] By any measure, the Qing emperor ruled over many subjects. Whereas in 1800 France and Russia respectively counted 27 million and 35 million souls, there were estimated to be nearly 200 million Chinese. By 1900, China's population had more than doubled to about 400 million, compared to 41 million Frenchmen, 167 million Russians, and 76 million North Americans.[66]

At first, observations about this huge demographic disparity were just abstract statistical curiosities. But in 1798 a book by the English doomsayer Thomas Robert Malthus, *An Essay on the Principle of Population,* suggested that a high rate of reproduction was dangerous to the general welfare.[67] Such ideas about the hazards of overpopulation began to inspire increasing concern about the Orient's enormous masses toward the latter half of the nineteenth century, especially as large numbers of Chinese immigrants began to arrive on North America's Pacific coast and in Australia.[68]

Groups like the Committee for the Protection of the Anglo-Saxon Race began to agitate for strict controls on the admission of new Asians to the United States. Politicians of all stripes found vitriolic anti-Chinese rhetoric an excellent way to win votes, with even the future president Theodore Roosevelt railing against the "immoral, degraded, and worthless race."[69] Local newspapers, including William Randolph Hearst's *San Francisco Examiner,* boosted sales with lurid tales of "John Chinaman's" evil cunning and depraved ways.[70]

The Middle Kingdom's enormous population was a prominent leitmotiv of late-nineteenth-century Sinophobia. In the words of the British writer Rudyard Kipling, "There are three races who can work but there is only one that can swarm."[71] Legislators in Washington backed up arguments for restrictions on Asian immigration with dire warnings about a "Mongolian inundation." During a speech to Congress in 1892, a senator from Oregon thundered: "If those vast hordes of Chinese pagans, led on by the great Mongolian leader Tamerlane, over five centuries ago, could, not by military prowess, but by mere force of overpowering numbers, make a track of desolation through Russia and Turkey and Egypt and India . . . they may do it again."[72]

North American and Australian fears of an Asian demographic flood coincided with a growing sense of gloom among European intellectuals. In the final decades of a century that had seen the great powers amass huge empires overseas and provide unprecedented prosperity at home, many began to fear that Western civilization was fast drawing to an end as a result of its moral, social, physical, and religious decay. Literature saw the rise of the decadent movement, and books like Max Nordau's *Entartung* (Degeneration) and Brooks Adams's *Law of Civilisation and Decay* warned that the white man's world was passing into senescence and would soon be overrun by younger races.[73]

Charles Pearson, an Oxford-trained historian who had spent many years in Australia, fused the generation's ideas about the West's imminent decline with those about the dangers posed by the "yellow race" in his *National Life and Character.*[74] First printed in 1893, it was hailed by the future American president Theodore Roosevelt as "one of the most notable books of the end of the century."[75] Pearson agreed with Nordau and Adams that the European nations had passed their prime. Urbanization, weakening family bonds, and the "decay of character" were all sapping the West's vitality. Like an anemic, once-mighty noble lineage, white man was no longer capable of preserving his dominion. "In the long run the lower civilisation has a more vigorous life than the privileged," Pearson observed. "We shall wake to find ourselves . . . perhaps even thrust aside by peoples whom we looked down upon as servile, and thought of as bound to minister to our needs."[76]

According to Pearson, China stood to benefit most from the "Aryan race's" decline. For one thing, its population was remarkably resilient. Even during the Taiping Rebellion of the 1850s and early 1860s, which had claimed some 30 million lives, the Middle Kingdom had still managed to flood Southeast Asia, Australia, and North America with migrants. For now the primary threat was economic. Willing to work hard for wages at a fraction of those paid to whites, Chinese were bound to conquer the world's markets. But Pearson also detected a political danger over the horizon. Were its people to be properly unified and led, he speculated, "it is difficult to suppose that China would not become an aggressive military power, sending out her armies in millions to cross the Himalayas and traverse the Steppes."[77]

Charles Pearson's book aroused anxieties about China's masses among his readers, but no one did more to popularize notions of a yellow peril than Germany's Kaiser Wilhelm II.[78] In 1895, shortly after Japan had routed China in a brief war, the Prussian monarch instructed Professor Herman Knackfuß of the Cassel Art Academy to draw a picture. In the kaiser's own words, the illustration showed "the Powers of Europe represented by their respective Genii called together by the Arch-Angel Michael . . . to *unite* in resisting the inroads of Buddhism, heathenism and barbarism for the Defence of the Cross."[79] The caption appealed: "Nations of Europe! Defend your sacred patrimony!"[80]

Wilhelm ordered a wide distribution of the sketch. He had copies presented to his officials and foreign heads of state, prints were disseminated to the public, and the drawing even decorated steamers of Germany's East Asian Line.[81] The kaiser also laced his speeches and letters with florid bombast about the yellow peril, particularly during the Boxer rising of 1900 in China. That summer, as German troopships left Bremerhaven for East Asia, he told the officers: "You are going on a grave and portentous mission. . . . It may be the beginning of a great war between Occident and Orient."[82]

Colonel Count Helmuth von Moltke, the future chief of the German General Staff, was commanded to present the picture to the tsar in autumn 1895 as a memento of the two empires' intervention in East Asia along with France earlier that year. Eager to encourage his cousin's Pacific adventures, Wilhelm had already lectured him about "the great task of the future for Russia to cultivate the Asian Continent and to defend Europe from the inroads of the Great Yellow Race."[83] Over the next eight years, the kaiser continued to egg Nicholas on in the East with similar arguments. In a letter from Posen in summer 1902, the self-styled "Admiral of the Atlantic" warned the "Admiral of the Pacific" about Japanese military instructors in China: "20 to 30 Million of trained Chinese helped by half a dozen Jap. Divisions and led by fine, undaunted Christian hating Jap. Officers, is . . . the coming into reality of the 'Yellow Peril' which I depicted some years ago, and for which engraving I was laughed at by the greater mass of people."[84] Nicholas's laconic reactions to his cousin's rantings did not betray any similar worries about the yellow peril. The tsar had little patience for his overbearing Prussian relative.[85]

"Nations of Europe Defend Your Sacred Patrimony!"—Allegory of the Yellow Peril
drawn by Herman Knackfuß on Kaiser Wilhelm II's orders.

*A*leksei Kuropatkin strongly opposed the kaiser's clumsy efforts to engage Russia in Asia. As he saw it, the real danger was on the western border, in the form of Germany's own formidable army. The general often reminded Nicholas: "The more we squander our strength and our resources in the Far East, the weaker we will be on the Vistula and the Niemen [Rivers]."[86] Yet, at the same time, Kuropatkin was genuinely concerned about Asia's enormous population and its capacity to inflict harm on the Russian Empire. Throughout his tenure as war minister, he urged the tsar to avoid needlessly provoking the East's restive masses. Although Kuropatkin did not hesitate to use force in Asia when Russia's interests were threatened, he did so to defend the realm rather than to conquer new territory.

Like Nikolai Przhevalskii, Kuropatkin learned about the Orient's people through direct encounters. His appraisal of the Asian's martial prowess, however, was entirely different from that of the explorer. The accounts Kuropatkin published about his experiences in Kashgaria and Turkestan provide a more balanced portrait of their fighting men. Rather than being a rabble of lazy cowards, as Przhevalskii often characterized them, he saw them as effective warriors, regardless of any moral failings.

Writing about the Tekke Turkmen, a nomadic people he had fought in Central Asia, Kuropatkin described them as "very likable because of their bravery, hospitality, and love of their homeland." They were "blessed with superb physiques: Tall, athletically built, exceptionally strong and tough," but they were also "cruel, dishonest, mendacious, envious, and greedy."[87] Kuropatkin's assessment of Yakub Beg and his forces was much less contemptuous than Przhevalskii's. While he agreed that the rebel's rule would probably be "of short duration," Aleksei Nikolaevich nevertheless praised his "military accomplishments, his powers of organization, his personal bravery, his chaste life, his willpower, his iron energy."[88]

Kuropatkin worried that Asians would become better fighters over time as they acquired modern weapons. In the past, it had often been easy for Russia's Europeanized military to defeat the poorly equipped horsemen of the steppes. But Kuropatkin noticed that even in Central Asia tsarist generals could no longer take their paramountcy for granted: "In cities our foes proved to be better fighters and during our assaults there we suffered many casualties. The appearance of improved rifles in the hands of Oriental peoples made our job much harder."[89]

As for China, while Kuropatkin recognized that the Qing's army did not constitute an immediate threat to Russia, its size made it a force to be respected. He was also troubled by the Chinese soldier's indifference to his fate, his "ability calmly to face death."[90] The war minister was most bothered, though, by more peaceful invasions from the Middle Kingdom. The Amur region in eastern Siberia was already suffering from "a disturbing increase of the yellow population." Sounding a refrain familiar to late-nineteenth-century Californians, in 1903 Kuropatkin advised the tsar that Chinese migrants "monopolize trade; they constitute the majority of workers on the railways, construction sites, and the docks; they insinuate themselves everywhere as household servants; and, finally, yellow-faced tenants and laborers are replacing the Russians as farmers."[91] A year earlier the war minister had warned Nicholas of a sinister Qing plot to settle Manchuria and Mongolia, regions that previously had been largely off-limits to Han Chinese, with large numbers of migrants from China proper. This development was particularly ominous for eastern Siberia.[92] Kuropatkin sounded the alarm: "As northern Manchuria's inhabitants continue to grow, so does the danger that yellow floodwaters will inundate Priamuria's small Russian oases."[93]

Among the Asian powers, the war minister had the most respect for Japan. Already in March 1898, shortly after his appointment, Aleksei Nikolaevich expressed his concern about the possibility of a Japanese attack on the newly acquired naval station of Port Arthur.[94] Kuropatkin's closest look at the Pacific rival came in summer 1903, when Nicholas sent him to Japan on an extraordinary embassy.[95] The main purpose of the trip was to explain Russia's position on Manchuria and Korea during a time of great strain with Tokyo over these issues. The general also carried out a personal reconnaissance of the potential adversary. As the guest of the Japanese army, he visited military academies and arms plants, saw maneuvers, and inspected units in Tokyo, Nagasaki, Osaka, and elsewhere.

The island empire left a favorable impression. Kuropatkin wrote the tsar: "I was surprised at the high level of development in the places we saw along the way. There is no doubt that the population is almost as culturally advanced as Russians."[96] Japan's armed forces also got high marks. Although Kuropatkin detected some deficiencies in the cavalry and the officer corps, the infantry performed well both in the field and on the parade ground, troops were well fed, equipped, and trained, morale was high, and discipline effective. "On the whole, Japan's army struck me as an effective fighting force."[97]

If Kuropatkin shared none of Przhevalskii's contempt for the Asians as warriors, neither did he exhibit his friend's enthusiasm for conquest. The war minister's view of conflict was much more pessimistic. Modern states did not expand for the glory of acquiring new lands or for the riches they might bring. Instead, they did so to defend a tenuous border. Kuropatkin first explained this logic in his Algerian essays: "During 26 years of war the French, having at first only taken the city of Algiers, ended up gradually extending their control over all of Algeria. . . . Both the government and public opinion opposed acquiring new African territory, but [French rule] nevertheless expanded until it reached . . . the Sahara." The reason for this reluctant Gallic drive into Africa was to protect against hostile tribes on the frontier. Whenever French rule was established over a new territory, nomads across the border periodically launched raids into the recently pacified region, inevitably necessitating further annexations.[98]

Kuropatkin believed that Russia's eastward march was motivated by similar considerations. Like France in northern Africa, "Russian expansion into Central Asia . . . was not executed according to a specific plan and was opposed by the government."[99] He explained in an account of Russia's conquest of Turkestan that the border there was "perennially subject to attacks from nomadic tribes, who robbed the local population, stole its cattle, and reduced everyone to poverty."[100]

While there were also commercial motives, Kuropatkin stressed that the tsarist campaign was mainly undertaken to protect the southeastern frontier. It was "the unavoidable result of our proximity to the great steppe, inhabited by semisavage, ceaselessly warring Kirghiz and Turkmen."[101] Every advance exposed Russians to new foes, who then had to be subjugated too. There were no halfway measures, for "Asia recognizes only force."[102] "The move was a heavy burden on our own population," Kuropatkin added, "but was inevitable as long as our borders did not meet those of relatively strong and organized states (China, Persia, Afghanistan)." Only when all of the khanates were entirely subdued and incorporated into the empire during the 1880s did "Russia's difficult mission in Central Asia reach its natural end."[103]

Kuropatkin's thinking recalls the well-known circular of Alexander II's foreign minister, Prince Aleksander Gorchakov. Written in 1864, the document was distributed among Russian representatives abroad to justify a new campaign against the Kokanese city of Tashkent:

> The position of Russia in Central Asia is that of all civilized states that come into contact with half-savage, wandering tribes possessing no fixed social organization. It invariably happens in such cases that the interests of security on the frontier

> . . . compel the more civilized state to exercise a certain ascendancy over neighbors whose turbulence and nomad instincts make them difficult to live with. . . . Once this result is attained they become less troublesome, but in turn they are exposed to the aggression of more distant tribes. The state is obliged to defend them against these depredations and chastise those who commit them. . . .
>
> If we content ourselves with chastising the freebooters and then retire, the lesson is soon forgotten. Retreat is ascribed to weakness, for Asiatics respect only visible and palpable force. . . . The task has therefore to be performed over and over again.[104]

Many foreigners, especially Englishmen, cynically dismissed Gorchakov's letter as pure propaganda. More than a century later, shortly after Soviet troops had marched into Afghanistan, a magazine for American diplomats reprinted the circular in 1980 with the title "Déjà Vu: Russia in East Asia."[105] Some scholars debate whether even the foreign minister himself believed his words.[106] Whatever Gorchakov or his contemporaries in St. Petersburg thought about this rationale, Kuropatkin took it seriously.

Yet conquest did not necessarily liquidate the danger posed by alien peoples. According to Kuropatkin's gloomy reasoning, even after a foreign nation had been subdued and made subjects of the tsar, it might still remain a threat. In fact, within Russia's borders, a restive and violent foreign population could cause even more harm than on the outside. The only way to ensure domestic tranquility was to assimilate all non-Russian elements that inhabited the empire.

Kuropatkin proved to be a fervent advocate of Russification at a time of growing national consciousness among the empire's minorities. Finns remember the war minister as one of the leading players in tsarist efforts to eliminate the semiautonomous status of their military, starting in 1898.[107] Looking eastward, Kuropatkin often fretted about the intense religious fervor of the empire's Muslim subjects. In a report about his inspection of the Turkestan Military District in 1901, he wrote: "Turkestan's population . . . is basically peaceful. Nevertheless, by faith they are alien, and therefore require unflagging yet careful surveillance. We must always be prepared to deal with an outburst of religious fanaticism."[108]

As Kuropatkin saw it, Russians had only themselves to blame for their potential difficulties in Turkestan. The war minister felt that tolerating foreign creeds and customs was a recipe for disaster in a multinational empire. "We must remember that under the influence of Western ideas about religious tolerance," he wrote, "Russian officials in Siberia and in Central Asia during the eighteenth and nineteenth centuries became patrons for the proselytization of Islam."[109]

The war minister often sparred with his colleague Sergei Witte, who advocated a more benevolent attitude to the empire's other nationalities.[110] During a chat with Witte at the tsar's New Year's Day reception in 1902, Kuropatkin argued that it was the autocracy's mission to make its non-

Russian subjects "proud about the idea that they belong to the great Russian family."[111] A few years earlier, the war minister had advised Nicholas that he must "crush separatist dreams." Kuropatkin's ideal of Russia was the "melting pot" of the United States "whose people speak one language, have one school system and one law code."[112]

The implication of Kuropatkin's logic was obvious: If the Russian Empire was already having problems integrating its many alien nationalities, it made little sense to conquer new ones by further extending tsarist territory. "Woe betide us if we acquire new subjects, since we have not yet managed to strengthen our hold over the ones we already have," he once mused.[113] The clearest statement of Kuropatkin's strategic vision was his lengthy memorandum of March 1900 to the tsar on imperial defense. Written as a survey of the army's requirements in the twentieth century, the document provided a detailed description of the entire border, from the 870-kilometer frontier with Norway at the northwestern extremity through the 16 kilometers it shared with Korea in the east.[114] According to the author, Nicholas read the memorandum but confessed to having "trouble mastering the final chapter, with its many important ideas."[115]

The war minister began by describing the impressive growth of the tsar's patrimony since 1700: "Over the course of two centuries Russia has grown from being a state with 12 million inhabitants . . . into a great empire of 132 million souls . . . occupying one-sixth of the Earth's land."[116] The question was, "Are *we* now satisfied with our borders?"[117] Kuropatkin emphatically answered in the affirmative, arguing that Russia had long ago reached its natural boundaries. He urged his master to focus on protecting his current domains; holding onto what he already owned was hard enough. Any new conquests would only rouse the enmity of the other powers. Furthermore, the empire hardly needed to add to its restive national minorities.

In Asia, with the possible exception of the Bosphorus Straits near the Turkish capital of Constantinople, the tsar should certainly be content with his realm. Above all, Kuropatkin stressed, Nicholas had to resist any temptations in China. Despite the Middle Kingdom's infirmity, Russia simply could not afford to have a sullen and hostile empire along 9,000 kilometers of its eastern border. Although Kuropatkin would reverse his stance within less than a year as events related to the Boxer rising presented him with a fait accompli, the general strongly opposed any further expansion into Manchuria: "Not only would seizing one of its most important provinces irreparably harm our long-standing friendship with our neighbor, but it would bring Manchuria's huge population within our borders. . . . [Eastern Siberia's] small Russian population would drown in the onrushing tidal wave of the yellow race."[118]

Even when it came to India, supposedly long an object of Russian imperial desire, Kuropatkin felt that the tsar would be wise to abstain from any new conquests.[119] In fact, rather than competing with Albion for Asia, Russia should collaborate with its traditional rival there. In a remarkable passage, the war minister foresaw: "The twentieth century will witness the great struggle in Asia between Christians against non-Christians. For the good of humanity, we must ally ourselves with England against the Orient's heathen tribes."[120]

Kuropatkin's pessimism about Asia understandably intensified in the years after his Manchurian defeat. In 1910, as the former war minister brooded over the event at Sheshurino, he published *Zadachi Russkoi armii* (The Tasks of the Russian Army). Aimed at a broad audience, the massive, 1,600-page work followed a similar outline as Kuropatkin's March 1900 memorandum to Nicholas, including an overview of past wars and recommendations for the future. The message, however, was entirely different.

Adopting virulently nationalist and racist language, Kuropatkin now wrote about the many travails of the "Russian tribe" *(russkoe plemia)*. One of its gravest dangers, he suggested in a section titled "The Yellow Peril," lay to the east. "The battle is only just beginning," the author averred. "What happened in the fields of Manchuria in 1904–1905 was nothing more than a skirmish with the advance guard." Just as Solovev ten years earlier in his "Short Tale of the Antichrist" had called upon Christendom to set aside its quarrels and unite to face the new Mongol foe, Kuropatkin pleaded: "For the well-being of all of Europe, in the event of a new attack by the Japanese or the Chinese against Russia, Europe's forces must be deployed for us, not against us. . . . Only with a common recognition that keeping Asia peaceful is a matter of importance to all of Europe . . . can we keep the 'yellow peril' at bay."[121]

Kuropatkin's last major statement about Asia was his *Russko-Kitaiskii vopros* (The Russo-Chinese Question), a book that appeared two years later. The Qing dynasty had just collapsed, and the future of Russia's Oriental neighbor was uncertain. Repeating his dire warnings about the inevitable conflict "between the white and the yellow races," the retired general called upon Russians to take preventative measures against future assaults from the East.[122] They must seize a belt of Chinese territory in the sparsely populated steppes and deserts of Xinjiang, Mongolia, and Manchuria all along the Russian border and establish a cordon sanitaire. Thus could Russia, in the best tradition of Prince Gorchakov, guard itself against the yellow peril.

Aleksei Kuropatkin's imperial vision was profoundly pessimistic. He believed that the great powers of the modern age were increasingly threatened both by restive alien elements from within and by hostile, heathen races from without. Empires should therefore focus on defense rather than conquest. The general did not eschew annexations altogether but felt that they should be undertaken only to bolster the frontier against potential attacks from dangerous neighbors.

Kuropatkin was not the only Russian to articulate such a view—there are strong echoes of Prince Gorchakov's circular in his rhetoric—but he was one of the first to combine modern European beliefs about racial strife, *Kulturpessimismus,* and social Darwinism with more traditional ideas about the "turbulent frontier." He was also among the few tsarist government officials to refer to a yellow peril, even if he did not openly adopt the term itself until after his retirement.

Kuropatkin's notions of a yellow peril were largely imported from the West. It was no coincidence that Vladimir Solovev first began to think about the Orient's malevolence during a trip to France. Like many other elements of Russia's fin de siècle, these pessimistic ideas were strongly influenced by broader intellectual trends in the West, including a general feeling of unease as the century neared its end. Popular reactions against Chinese immigration to California, British Columbia, and Australia played a part as well. Even Sir Robert Hart, the long-serving British head of the Qing Imperial Maritime Customs and a man generally sympathetic to the Chinese, darkly predicted in 1900: "That the future will have a 'Yellow' question—perhaps a 'yellow peril'—to deal with, is as certain as that the sun will shine tomorrow."[123]

Russians themselves tended not to worry about the Orient's dangers at the turn of the twentieth century. Most speculation involving the menacing East took place in the rarefied circles of Silver Age poets inspired by Vladimir Solovev. Yet the idea of the yellow peril slowly percolated through Russian popular consciousness and manifested itself most prominently during the Sino-Soviet split of the 1960s.[124] A fascinating book of the time was an essay published abroad by the Soviet dissident Andrei Amalrik, *Will the Soviet Union Survive until 1984?*[125] Amalrik foresaw a disastrous war with China that would eventually lead to the Soviet Union's dissolution. In the event, the Asian power had very little to do with the USSR's demise in 1991. Nevertheless, at the dawn of the twenty-first century, in an age of deep insecurity and flagging imperial will, many Russians continue to eye their populous eastern neighbor with considerable unease.[126]

Part Two

The Path to War

Prologue / *Admiral Togo's Raid*

Japan broke off her diplomatic relations with Russia. In the roadstead at Port Arthur the explosions of Japanese mines resounded one dark night amidst the peacefully-sleeping warships. . . . The war began. What was this war about? Nobody knew. For half a year conversations, unintelligible to all, had been going on. . . . The clouds had been gathering heavier and heavier, and a storm was in the air. Our statesmen had been balancing the scales of war and peace with provoking hesitation.

—Vladimir Veresaev

*I*n St. Petersburg before the revolution, January was the height of the season for fashionable society.[1] Almost every evening some magnate hosted a lavish ball in his palace while *A l'Ours,* the *Restaurant de Paris, Akvarium,* and other establishments in the city bustled with activity. Meanwhile, the Imperial Ballet, the opera, and the theaters were all in full swing. As if to compensate for the anemic pallor that illuminates the Baltic metropolis during winter's few, fleeting hours of daylight, those with the means to do so spent their nights in a blaze of artificial light and glitter.

The evening of Monday, January 26, 1904, was much like any other that month in the northern capital. The highlight was a benefit for the Marinskii Theater's choir, which staged a performance of Aleksandr Dargomizhskii's opera, *Rusalka.* Tsar

Nicholas II was in attendance, along with his consort, Tsarina Alexandra, and his mother, the Empress Dowager Marie Fedorovna. The celebrated bass Fedor Chaliapin had consented to travel from Moscow to play the role of the miller, as did the lyric tenor Leonid Sobinov, who sang as the prince. While their voices won rave reviews, the choir disappointed the critics.[2]

To be sure, many in the audience had their minds on the brewing diplomatic crisis. Two days earlier, Japan had severed ties with Russia and recalled its representatives to express displeasure at the course of negotiations over the two empires' roles in Korea and Manchuria. As the bourse opened for business on Monday morning there had been a mild panic, and Nicholas had once again conferred with his ministers about the Far Eastern question, albeit without resolving to do much of anything.[3] Nevertheless, the common assumption in St. Petersburg was that the troubles in Asia would eventually blow over, an opinion held by the emperor as well. At most, the mighty Pacific Squadron would once again be called upon to teach the upstart islanders to respect Russia's will, much as it had done nine years earlier at Zhifu.[4] During the opera's second intermission, the public turned to the imperial loge, repeatedly breaking out into spontaneous choruses of the national anthem, "God Save the Tsar," along with patriotic hurrahs. After the final curtain, the tsar escorted his mother back to her apartments at Anichkov Palace, where he stayed for tea and a chat before returning to the Winter Palace around midnight.[5]

Some 8,000 verst to the east, in Russia's recently acquired Yellow Sea naval station of Port Arthur, the evening began equally unremarkably. The quarrel with Japan did not particularly worry the town's inhabitants. Although the Asiatic rival was no more than two days' sailing away, and the Russian naval attaché had been frantically cabling from Tokyo with reports about preparations for war throughout the island empire, there seemed to be no need to be concerned.[6] The new Russian viceroy for the Far East, Admiral Evgenii Alekseev, whose headquarters were at Port Arthur, did not even trouble to communicate the news about the rupture of diplomatic relations to his officers.[7]

No special preparations were made for the possibility of hostilities: The shore battery remained at rest, its guns heavily greased and covered with tarpaulins to protect them from the winter, and the powerful lighthouse at the tip of Tiger's Tail Peninsula continued to beckon ships to the port's entrance. Because much of the harbor was innavigable at low tide, the 16 ships of the impressive flotilla assembled at the station were neatly ranged by row in the open waters offshore. To avoid encumbering their movement, the vessels did not deploy their antitorpedo netting. At the same time, more worried about collisions with their neighbors than enemy attacks, some captains switched on their lights after dark.[8]

As dusk fell over the Pacific garrison, its Chinese residents began to celebrate the start of their new year. Among the European population, some had plans to attend Baratorskii's circus, which was in town, while others

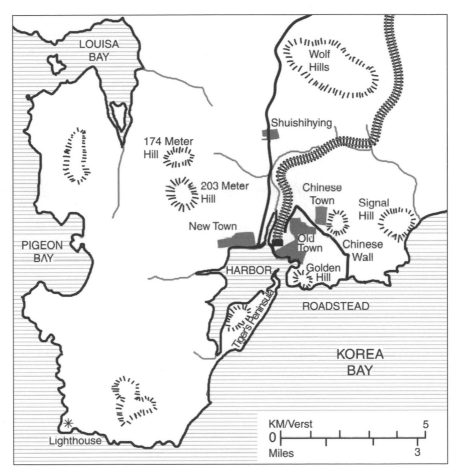

LOUISA
BAY

Wolf
Hills

Shuishihying

174 Meter
Hill

203 Meter
Hill

Chinese
Town

Signal
Hill

New Town

Old
Town

Chinese
Wall

PIGEON
BAY

HARBOR

Golden
Hill

Tiger's Peninsula

ROADSTEAD

KOREA
BAY

KM/Verst   5
0 |⎯⎯⎯⎯⎯⎯⎯⎯⎯⎯⎯⎯⎯
Miles   3

Lighthouse

Port Arthur in January 1904

contemplated less wholesome amusements in the port's taverns and broth-els. Vice Admiral Oskar Stark, who headed the naval detachment offshore, found the time to host a small name-day dinner for his wife.[9] In his orders for the night he had warned his officers to be on the lookout for trouble. However, the conscientious admiral's wishes were generally ignored, in the belief that he merely had another tiresome training exercise in mind. As usual, two destroyers were tasked to perform picket duty by patrolling the surrounding seas within a 30-kilometer radius.[10]

The night was cloudless, calm, and chilly. The waxing moon had just en-tered its first quarter and would not rise until after daybreak. The only light over the black waters was cast by the lighthouse and the Russian vessels. Shortly before midnight, as Admiral Stark was conferring with his staff in his quarters aboard the *Petropavlovsk*, he heard an explosion outside. The sound came from the direction of the *Retvizan,* another battleship less than a kilometer away. Since the latter's sailors had spent the day priming their torpedoes, Stark's first inclination was to dismiss the disturbance as an accidental detonation. It was only when two more blasts followed in rapid succession that the admiral realized his fleet was under attack.[11]

The assault came from torpedo boats of the Japanese navy. Two days earlier, when Tokyo had broken ties with Russia, two fleets under the command of Vice Admiral Togo Heichahiro steamed out of the base of Sasebo on the southern island of Kyushu. One of them made its way to the Korean port of Chemulpo (known today as Inchon), right outside of Seoul, where it incapacitated the Russian ships at anchor there and secured control of the maritime approach to the Korean capital.[12] A larger force headed for the Liaodong Peninsula, where the signal station at Port Arthur and the searchlights of the Russian fleet greatly assisted navigation. Striking in two waves, the Japanese flotilla launched 19 torpedoes, three of which found their mark, damaging the battleships *Retvizan* and *Tsesarevich* as well as the cruiser *Pallada.*[13]

Nicholas learned of the attack when he got back home from the opera. As the tsar entered the Winter Palace, a *feldjäger* (military courier) handed him a decoded cable:

> About midnight on January 26th Japanese destroyers made a sudden attack on the squadron anchored in the outer roadstead of Port Arthur. . . . The importance of the damage is being ascertained. I [will] report further details to your majesty in due course. Equerry General Alekseev.[14]

Before retiring that evening, the emperor summarized the telegram in his diary, adding, "And this without a declaration of war!"[15]

Many historians have likened Japan's surprise attack on Port Arthur to its raid on the American base of Pearl Harbor 37 years later.[16] In terms of the disbelief and denial with which Nicholas greeted the start of the war, an even better comparison might be made with Stalin's reaction to Hitler's invasion of the Soviet Union, also in 1941. However, there was an important difference between the tsarist contest with Japan and the American and Soviet responses to their uninvited entry into the Second World War. Unlike the latter conflict, in 1904, aside from an initial frisson of patriotic fervor, there was little support among Russia's public for the Manchurian campaign. Maurice Bompard, France's ambassador to St. Petersburg at the time, recalled:

> Never has war been so unpopular as it was from the start in Russia. . . . People understood neither its origins nor its aims. . . . Of course the army carried out its duty, but only out of discipline and without any enthusiasm whatsoever. . . . As for the population, which had to give the army over a million of its sons, it entered into a deep depression as a result of this inexplicable conflict, made all the worse by the inability of their emperor to explain the need for their sacrifices.[17]

The physical damage inflicted by the nighttime raid on Russia's naval station was modest. None of the craft was sunk, and loss of life was minimal.[18] But the psychological injury was immense, and the tsarist military never fully recovered from the shock to its morale. Throughout the conflict, Japan retained the initiative. The actions at Port Arthur and Chemulpo won Admiral Togo's fleet mastery of the northeastern Pacific, enabling the Japanese army to land troops on the Asian mainland. Russian attempts to resist were beset by ineffective command, dispirited soldiering, and logistical difficulties. Within little more than a year, both Korea and the Liaodong Peninsula were in Japanese hands, Russia's Baltic Fleet had been sunk at the Straits of Tsushima, and tsarist forces in Manchuria were humiliated. Meanwhile, the bad news from the front led to serious unrest at home, threatening the very existence of the Romanov dynasty. By 1905, Russian dreams of an Asian destiny had metamorphosed into a nightmare of military defeat and revolution.[19]

Back in the late 1890s, in the first years of Nicholas II's reign, Russia's position in the East had seemed unassailable. In sharp contrast to the western frontier, where it was very much on the defensive, on the Pacific St. Petersburg appeared to be the power of the future. China had just joined it in a defensive alliance, which held the promise of a mighty combination of the two greatest autocracies of the Eurasian landmass. Some, like Prince Ukhtomskii, even fantasized about a renaissance of Genghis Khan's empire, with the Romanov tsar as the Mongol's logical heir. Britain and Japan, the only two nations that were in a position to check tsarist ambitions in Asia, were momentarily cowed. Ambitious plans were made by Finance Minister Sergei Witte to develop the tsar's Pacific possessions into a showcase of enterprise and prosperity. Both at home and abroad, many spoke of Russia's Far East as a second California. While Witte thought only in terms of a *pénétration pacifique,* of dominion through the less violent weapons of modern capitalism, in the minds of others danced visions of quick glory and easy annexations in Asia. Przhevalskii's call to conquistador imperialism reawoke with a vengeance. Only a few, like General Kuropatkin, looked eastward with anxiety rather than excitement. In the first half of this book, we examined the ideologies of empire inspired by Russia's turn to the east. How St. Petersburg first rose to and then fell from grace on the Pacific during the nine short years between 1895 and 1904 is the subject of the following chapters.

CHAPTER SIX

The Turn to the East

*T*he grand tour the future Tsar Nicholas II took to Asia is most notable for what it tells us about the changing focus of Russian imperial interests in the late 1800s. During the first half of the nineteenth century, St. Petersburg's attention had very much been fixed on Europe. Tsarist diplomacy was particularly occupied by efforts to profit in the Balkans and the Near East from the Ottoman Empire's infirmity. When Nicholas's grandfather, Alexander II, succeeded to the throne in 1855, however, his realm was reeling from a major military setback in the Crimea after a conflict involving Ottoman Turkey backed by other powers.

Russia lost the war largely as a result of the nation's backwardness in relation to its principal adversaries, England and France. The new tsar understood that, if his realm were to avoid the ignominious fate of such senescent powers as Ottoman Turkey, major changes were needed, and he turned his attention to internal development. Alexander told one of his diplomats upon inheriting the crown: "After her recent trials, Russia must concentrate on her own affairs and seek to heal by domestic measures the wounds inflicted by war."[1] The Great Reforms of his reign, which would see the peasantry emancipated and the introduction of local self-government and trial by jury as well as important military improvements, left little time for foreign complications.[2] The new foreign minister, Prince Alexander Gorchakov, did his best to keep the empire at peace, adhering to a policy that would come to be known as *recueillement* (gathering one's strength).[3] Gorchakov's *recueillement* did not imply a complete suppression of expansive urges but rather redirected them to parts of the world where they posed little danger of provoking a risky war. Effectively thwarted in the Near East, St. Petersburg turned its attention deeper into Asia.[4]

*R*ussians were no strangers to the continent. During the Kievan era more than six centuries earlier, they had waged a ceaseless struggle against a succession of Turkic and Mongol tribes sweeping westward from the Inner Asian steppes. The chronicles of that age are often nothing more than a litany of nomadic incursions; "The Tale of Prince Igor," recounting a disastrous twelfth-century campaign against the Asiatic Polovitsians, is the best-known example of this somber literature.[5] Russia's darkest years began in the thirteenth century, when Mongol horsemen routed the Kievan princes and subjugated the Russian people for nearly two hundred years.

The *reconquista* began in 1480, when the Muscovite Grand Prince Ivan III successfully renounced Mongol rule. By the 1550s, his descendant Ivan the Terrible vanquished the Tatar strongholds of Kazan and Astrakhan on the Volga River, eliminating the threat from Asia. From the sixteenth century on, Russia inexorably advanced eastward. This expansion took on a dual character, with one axis driving directly east across the Siberian taiga and the other southeast into the Central Asian steppe.

In the north, a band of Cossack adventurers led by Ermak Timofeevich, in search of precious furs, breached the Urals in 1581.[6] Encountering little resistance from the indigenous nomads, his successors rapidly took possession of the Siberian subcontinent, much as pelt would lure New France's coureurs de bois across the breadth of Canada.[7] Within less than 70 years, Russians had reached the Pacific.[8] From then on, further territorial gains in the Far East came only at the expense of the Chinese Empire to the south. When the Middle Kingdom was strong, Russian ambitions were held in check. Thus, after the Treaty of Nerchinsk with the Emperor Kangxi's emissaries in 1689, the East Asian border saw little change for the next century and a half.[9]

At the time, Russia's relationship with the Qing dynasty was unique. Before the mid-nineteenth century, Russia was the only European power that China recognized as an equal by signing treaties and conducting diplomatic missions with it. While Russian envoys were made to kowtow to the Son of Heaven, Kangxi and his descendants acknowledged that the neighboring empire was not a tributary state.[10] An agreement concluded at Kiakhta in 1727 granted the unprecedented right to maintain an ecclesiastical mission in Peking, which also functioned as a language school, listening post, and unofficial embassy.[11]

Until the late nineteenth century, the Qing saw their continental neighbor in an entirely different light than the Portuguese, Dutch, and English foreign devils who clamored to land on their shores. Before the establishment of a foreign office, the Zongli Yamen, in 1861, relations with the latter were conducted by the Ministry of Rituals, since they were regarded as tributaries to the Son of Heaven. The Russians, on the other hand, were handled through the Lifan Yuan (the Bureau of Border Affairs), an institution established by the Ming in the early seventeenth century to deal with the Mongols and other nomads beyond the Great Wall.[12] To be sure, China's attitude was shaped by pragmatic considerations. Unlike the overseas maritime states, Russia directly bordered on the Middle Kingdom.

Moreover, during the dynasty's early years, its neighbor's neutrality was important to complete the conquest of the northwestern frontier, which lay between them.[13]

Chinese perceptions were not entirely negative. Ho Qitao's *Comprehensive Account of the Northern Regions,* a thorough compendium of all available materials about Russia, which was presented to the emperor in 1860, provided a fairly good indication of official views.[14] Its author reproached others for suggesting that the northern state was entirely uncivilized. In Ho's opinion, the fact that its ruler regularly sent subjects to Peking to learn helped redeem it:

> Admiring our Dynasty's civilizing virtue, [the Russians] annually send their most excellent students to our capital to study the Manchu and Chinese writings and recite the histories and classics. . . . Now our Dynasty's civilizing influence has spread afar, slowly turning men toward benevolence and righteousness. . . . For two hundred years [Russia] has been slowly transformed by this influence, and thus their literature has flourished increasingly.[15]

In the main, the two empires coexisted in relative harmony until the 1850s.[16]

The Opium Wars of the 1840s and the Taiping Rebellion that erupted ten years later altered some basic assumptions about the Qing's ability to maintain their empire's cohesion. Like the Ottomans, China's emperors now seemed less able to resist territorial encroachment. The first Russian to take advantage of this was the new governor-general of eastern Siberia, Count Nikolai Muravev. Seeking in part to frustrate the Russian-American Company's activities across the Bering Strait, Muravev began aggressively to colonize the Amur River region on the Pacific Coast in the early 1850s. Although largely undertaken on the count's own initiative, St. Petersburg did not disapprove. When a subaltern claimed a position on the mouth of the Amur for his country in 1849, against specific orders from his commanders to the contrary, Tsar Nicholas I accepted the move, declaring, "Where the Russian flag has once flown, it must never be lowered."[17]

By signing the Treaty of Nerchinsk nearly two hundred years earlier, Peter the Great's government had recognized Chinese sovereignty over these sparsely populated maritime provinces. The Manchus had now begun their inevitable slide into dynastic decay, however, and were in no position to oppose Muravev. Thus, in 1858, as an English force occupied Canton and the Taiping seized Nanjing, the beleaguered Qing had no alternative but to accept Muravev's demands for control over the region. According to the treaties signed in Aigun that year and in Peking in 1860, Russia acquired the west bank of the Amur, from the northwestern tip of Manchuria to the Pacific, as well as the area east of the Ussuri River.[18] To underscore his ambitions, Muravev christened a new port on the Pacific Vladivostok ("Ruler of the East").

*A*fter 1860, Prince Gorchakov's Asian diplomacy became more cautious. In Turkestan, aggressive generals like Skobelev vigorously pressed forward where tsarist territory abutted onto small, independent fiefdoms, such as the khanates of Khiva, Kokand, and Bokhara. Yet, when more established powers were involved, St. Petersburg avoided the risk of another war. Nowhere was this clearer than in the lengthy wrangling with Peking over the Ili question during the latter years of Alexander II's reign.[19]

One of Central Asia's most fertile oases, the valley irrigated by the Upper Ili River on China's northwestern frontier was of great strategic and commercial importance.[20] During a major Muslim rising in Chinese Turkestan in the 1860s, rebels had driven the Qing administration from the region and threatened to incite their coreligionists across the border in Russian Turkestan as well. Although without orders from his superiors to do so, in 1871 General von Kaufmann directed his forces to seize the valley. Tsarist troops easily defeated the insurgents, and their commander, General Gerasim Kolpakovskii, declared Ili to be occupied "in perpetuity."[21] The Russian minister in Peking, Gerasim Vlangali, laconically told the Zongli Yamen that Kolpakovskii had "recovered" the region from the Muslim rebels, conveniently omitting any reference to the general's claim to annexation. Instead, based on previous Chinese requests for assistance in putting down the rising, the action was presented more as a friendly gesture, and Alexander II publicly declared that Ili would be restored to Peking as soon as the latter had pacified Xinjiang.

There was considerable doubt that Russia would ever honor its word and lower its flag in the valley. Yet by 1878 Qing armies under the efficient General Zuo Zongtang finally crushed the rebellion. Despite great reluctance and three years of protracted negotiations, tsarist diplomats agreed to evacuate most of Ili on terms acceptable to China, in the Treaty of St. Petersburg on February 12, 1881.[22]

The decision to retreat from Chinese Turkestan was taken because of a profound malaise in St. Petersburg as the result of another reverse involving the Ottoman Empire. When Alexander II did reluctantly allow his realm to be dragged into a new Turkish war in 1877, later events only confirmed the wisdom of his pacifist instincts. Unlike the Crimean conflict twenty years earlier, Constantinople now fought largely unaided, and by early 1878 tsarist troops had reached its gates. However, alarmed at the terms extracted from the Porte in the Peace of San Stefano, Britain and Austria-Hungary forced Russia back to the bargaining table. Too weak to take on the other powers, Alexander was forced to scale down his demands and agreed to a substantial revision of the treaty at the Congress of Berlin in May 1878.[23]

This diplomatic reverse was taken as a major setback in the capital, angering the public and further disrupting Russia's increasingly shaky civil order.[24] The rising wave of terrorism, culminating in the assassination of Alexander II on March 13, 1881, eerily seemed to recall the prediction made to Tsarevich Alexander Alexandrovich by his tutor Konstantin Pobedonostsev: "The people of Russia will regard [the Congress of Berlin] as a stain on the honor of the nation. I can only foresee harmful and ominous consequences as a result of the treaty."[25]

Alexander III, who would rule from 1881 through 1894, seemed to be the opposite of his father. Stolid and unimaginative, but endowed with a certain native shrewdness, the profoundly conservative autocrat appeared to embody many of the qualities of the archetypal muzhik. The new tsar strongly disagreed with his predecessor about domestic policy and would reverse, or at least blunt, a number of his father's reforms. At the same time, he very much concurred with Alexander II on the need to avoid war. In his summary of Alexander III's reign, one foreign ministry official described the goal of his diplomacy as putting Russia "back on its feet among the nations of this world, so that it might regain order, recover from the trauma it had sustained, and redirect its energies to restoring its greatness. . . . Above all, Emperor Alexander III's foreign policy was directed at peace."[26] In this the emperor was successful. Ably assisted by his foreign minister, Nikolai Karlovich Giers, Alexander III set something of a record by avoiding armed conflict during the thirteen years of his rule.

As the son of a Lutheran postmaster, Giers was in a different league from the aristocratic dilettantes who traditionally dominated the Foreign Ministry, located at the Choristers' Bridge.[27] Yet he had extensive experience abroad and was "probably the most seasoned and able statesman of his time in Europe, after Bismarck," in one scholar's estimation.[28] Like his master, Giers was primarily interested in stability, and he pursued a policy of moderation and restraint, adhering to the motto: "Above all, avoid unnecessary and untimely complications."[29] Germany's future chancellor, Count Bernhard von Bülow, noted that "Giers clearly understands that a foreign defeat will drag Russia into a revolutionary tempest of such magnitude that the Paris Commune will look like child's play in comparison."[30] The foreign minister's only significant quarrel with the tsar was over the decision to ally with France in the early 1890s, but he loyally carried out Alexander's wishes.

In Asia, Alexander III put a stop to Russia's advance. Aside from some clashes with Afghanistan in the Pamirs, his armies largely stood at ease. Instead, the new tsar turned his attention to developing his possessions. His most ambitious undertaking there was the start of the Trans-Siberian Railway in 1891. Inspired in part by the Trans-Canada Railroad, which had created new cities, brought prosperity to the Prairies, and helped unify the young North American nation, this project was expected to bestow similar benefits on Russia's immense colony.[31] More important, the project was also meant to consolidate military control over the Pacific territories.

Beyond its borders in the Far East, Alexander III's Russia remained very much on the defensive. When in the mid-1880s an opportunity presented

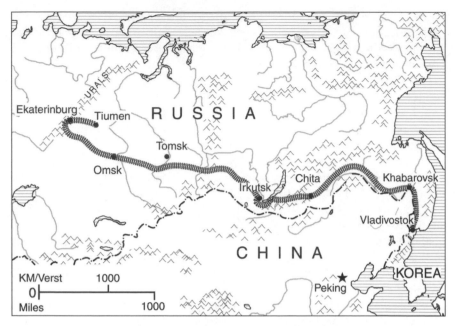

The Siberian Railway as Planned in 1892

itself to seize an ice-free port in Korea, St. Petersburg refused to become enticed, reasoning that such a move would overextend its forces on the Pacific.[32] Meanwhile, Giers was far too concerned with aggression from China to contemplate opportunities for further territorial expansion there.[33] Both the minister and the tsar, as noted earlier, rejected Przhevalskii's urgings for conquest. Despite the growing intimacy with France, Giers even rejected a request from Paris in 1891 to sign a protocol to protect Christian missionaries in China, on the grounds that Russia must be prudent vis-à-vis the Middle Kingdom.[34] For a while, Russian prestige in Peking seemed to be slipping. One tsarist diplomat recalled: "Over several years [before 1891, Russia's] standing had greatly declined [in China], and other, weaker powers were pulling ahead of us."[35]

Giers did try to improve matters by naming a highly competent representative to the Qing in 1891.[36] Count Arthur Pavlovich Cassini, the new minister, had extensive experience at the German courts and was well regarded by his colleagues.[37] Count Vladimir Nikolaevich Lamsdorf, one of his superiors, expressed delight at the appointment, describing him as "very clever and a keen observer."[38] The grandson of an Italian diplomat who had entered Russian service in the reign of Alexander I, Cassini was a cosmopolitan of the old school. He spoke French flawlessly, Russian with an accent, and, despite a good command of English, made a point of using an interpreter when dealing with Anglophone colleagues.[39] Unhindered by a private life one visitor to Peking described as "une chronique scandaleuse," the count proved quite adept at navigating the intrigues of his new posting, considerably restoring Russia's luster there.[40]

During the reign of Alexander III, the emphasis was on avoiding war abroad to put matters right at home. Yet, while the "Tsar Peacemaker" suppressed the expansionist urges of his more aggressive subjects, he did not altogether snuff out their dreams of empire.[41] His rule witnessed a major transformation of these ambitions. Under Alexander II, Central and East Asia had served as safety valves for ambitious generals frustrated by the impossibility of conquest in the Ottoman Empire after the Crimean War. To paraphrase one scholar, these campaigns were an expression of "compensatory imperialism."[43]

While Skobelevs and Muravevs won glory on the Central Asian steppes and the shores of the Pacific, their countrymen's most fervent desires were still about "Tsargrad," as they called Constantinople. The humiliating setback suffered at the Congress of Berlin, however, did much to diminish the attraction of the Porte's realms. As a result, during the reign of Alexander III, those who yearned for imperial conquest now began to look at the Far East not for compensation but as their true destiny. Writing at the turn of the twentieth century, an editor of the liberal daily *Rossiia* recalled:

> Until [the Turkish War of 1877–1878] most people thought that history summoned Russia to fulfill its duty in the Eastern question and once and for all restore the cross to the Hagia Sofia. After the Congress of Berlin, thoughtful men began to say that, although we cannot for now nail our shield to the gates of Tsargrad, destiny still calls Russia to the East, but now to another East. The masses are moving beyond the Urals, and the government must follow them, or even take the lead. There, beyond the Urals, unfolds an immense expanse that beckons Russia's might. Our future is not in Europe, which prevented us from projecting our rule in any direction.[44]

CHAPTER SEVEN

Intervention

*A*lexander III firmly resisted the temptation to pursue imperial glory in Asia, but his heir proved much more susceptible to its charms. Immediately upon succeeding to the throne in October 1894, the new tsar was confronted by a crisis on his eastern frontier as Japanese troops battled with China over the reclusive kingdom of Korea. When hostilities had broken out a few months earlier, St. Petersburg initially adopted an attitude of cautious neutrality. It would not take much for Nicholas II to set Russia on a more aggressive course.

Korea had long been a bone of contention between China and Japan. In the eyes of the late-nineteenth-century Qing, the peninsula was its vassal. This attitude dated to around 1400, when, in the early days of Korea's reigning Yi Dynasty, the emperor of China had deigned to accept the king's oath of fealty. As with their other tributaries, the Chinese stationed a representative in the capital of Seoul who meddled in local affairs when able. Peking's main obligation as suzerain was military protection, a duty most recently invoked in the 1590s, when Ming armies helped to repel an invasion by Japan's ambitious ruler, Hideyoshi Toyotomi. This was by no means the first time the two nations had sparred over Korea. However, in the two-and-a-half centuries after Hideyoshi's defeat, as shogunate Japan retreated into self-imposed isolation, the islands were content to limit their dealings with their overseas neighbor to informal commercial and diplomatic ties. During this time, Korea largely cut itself off from the world as well, earning the sobriquet of "the Hermit Kingdom."[1]

After the Meiji Restoration of 1868, an increasingly outward-looking and self-confident Japan renewed its interest in Korea. At first, King Kojong's government firmly rejected these advances, but it could not ward them off for long. Taking a leaf from U.S. Commodore Matthew Perry, Japanese gunboats in 1876 forced the Hermit Kingdom to open itself to foreign trade, and within a generation the island empire thoroughly dominated its economy.[2] At the same time, Japanese attempts to influence Korean politics led to a vigorous countereffort by China to assert its hold over the kingdom. In the wake of a failed coup in 1884, which had received unofficial backing from Tokyo, the Qing statesman Li Hongzhang, together with the assistance of his energetic proconsul Yuan Shikai, tightened Peking's grip.[3] For the next decade Li rightly boasted: "I am king of Korea, whenever I think the interests of China require me to assert the prerogative."[4]

Chinese interference in Korean affairs did not necessarily lead to better government. In the early 1890s, drought, oppressive taxes, and corruption set off a revolt by the reformist Tonghak sect in the south.[5] When in spring 1894 the insurgents seized a provincial capital, King Kojong turned to Peking for military assistance. Li was quick to respond and, duly informing Tokyo according to the terms of an agreement with Japan, ordered 1,500 men to the peninsula.[6] The same convention stipulated that both signatories could send troops to Korea in case of unrest, a provision Japan promptly invoked by dispatching a force of its own to the troubled kingdom. By July 20, 1894, the two empires were at war.[7]

Officials at the Choristers' Bridge had known for some time that trouble was brewing in Korea. In early February, the Russian minister in Tokyo, Mikhail Aleksandrovich Hitrovo, heard rumors about preparations for an insurrection on the peninsula.[8] A month later, Cassini reported that "for a while all of Korea has been in the grip of a . . . steadily growing disquiet that may easily erupt into public disorder," which he worried might invite Chinese and Japanese involvement.[9] Meanwhile, in Seoul, the chargé d'affaires, Karl Ivanovich Weber, at first accepted the assurances of the Korean foreign office that there were no grounds for concern and told his superiors not to worry.[10] By May 20, however, Weber also became alarmed: "The unrest in southern Korea is taking a more serious turn," he wired. "China's interference is possible. It would be advisable to send a warship to observe matters."[11]

Aside from passing Weber's request on to the navy, not much action was taken in St. Petersburg on the worsening situation in Korea.[12] As Chinese and Japanese troops were landing in the kingdom, Li Hongzhang tried to solicit Russian mediation in the crisis.[13] Giers initially welcomed the opportunity to increase his government's influence in the region and, perhaps more important, "prevent the possibility of English meddling."[14] Yet, when Japanese Foreign Minister Mutsu Munemitsu firmly rejected Hitrovo's invitation to the bargaining table, Giers did not press the matter.[15] While Nikolai Karlovich was concerned about the possibility of war, he did not want his country to be seen as China's handmaiden.[16] As he warned his envoy in Peking, overly active involvement "could, against our will, easily make us the open enemy of Japan, under the banner of China and the cunning viceroy of Pechili."[17] For the time being, Russia would limit itself to joining the diplomatic efforts of Britain and the other major European powers to resolve the conflict.[18]

The cautious stance taken by Alexander III's government when war broke out in July 1894 between China and Japan was confirmed in a special conference on August 9.[19] Chaired by the foreign minister, the council included Petr Vannovskii, Nikolai Chikhachev, and Sergei Witte (his colleagues from the ministries of war, navy, and finance, respectively) and two senior diplomats, Deputy Minister Nikolai Shishkin and the head of the Asiatic Department, Count Dmitrii Kapnist.

At the start of the meeting, Nikolai Giers summarized the events to date. Without identifying an aggressor, he explained that the war had resulted from a long-standing rivalry between China and Japan over the peninsula. Giers stressed his efforts to halt the conflict and expressed some frustration that Tokyo had rejected Hitrovo's offer to mediate. Nikolai Karlovich concluded that Russia must maintain strict neutrality. Nevertheless, he added, a Japanese seizure of southern Korea would be dangerous to Russia. It was therefore essential to maintain the kingdom's status quo. The foreign minister accordingly proposed that Russia coordinate its diplomacy with the other interested powers, including Great Britain.

His colleagues largely agreed, although Finance Minister Sergei Witte worried about London "and its selfish plans" while War Minister Vannovskii suggested moving more forces to the Korean border.[20] As for the possibility of snatching any territorial morsels for Russia, when the subject of a Korean port came up, the navy's chief, Admiral Nikolai Chikhachev, opposed the idea. There were superb anchorages on the peninsula, but Chikhachev argued that the burden of defending a new base would far outweigh any advantages. After some discussion the conference resolved to support Giers's tack, and over the next few months St. Petersburg continued to remain largely aloof from the war.[21]

Because of its proximity to the region, Russia was the European power with the most at stake in the conflict, and some later criticized its inactivity. One diplomat with much experience in Asia complained that "there was a total absence of any clear conception of what the aims of our Far Eastern policy should be."[22] To be sure, the political situation in 1894 only exacerbated the restraint of Alexander III's foreign ministry.[23] For several months, the emperor had been gravely ill, and he would die in October of that year. The septuagenarian Giers was also ailing, which left Russian diplomacy to his somewhat ineffectual deputy, Nikolai Pavlovich Shishkin.[24]

The outbreak of hostilities did not generate a great sense of crisis in St. Petersburg. Fashionable society joked that "la chicorée m'intéresse plus que la Corée" (I'm more concerned about chicory than Korea).[25] Tokyo had gone out of its way to assure Western powers that it was not interested in annexing the kingdom.[26] Anyhow, like most European observers, Russian officials generally expected China to win, leaving East Asia much as it had been before the war. Even Hitrovo predicted a Japanese defeat. "Perhaps they will have momentary successes, but in the end the Chinese will prevail," he wrote in June 1894.[27] Assessments of the Middle Kingdom's military potential had changed little from the days of the Ili crisis. While intelligence analysts recognized that the armies of the Qing were poorly led and inadequately armed, they still respected the immense size of the empire.[28] Some Russians even remained a little fearful of their populous neighbor to the East, as an article in the September issue of the liberal monthly *Vestnik Evropy* (The European Herald) suggested: "With its countless masses, China ominously menaces Europe . . . the sooner we are rid of this nightmare, the better the European nations will be able to rest at night."[29]

Events in Korea soon proved such views to be very much mistaken. Even before war was formally declared in July, Japanese forces had marched into the capital and seized the royal palace. In early September, the two adversaries confronted each other in a major battle in Pyongyang, which saw the Chinese driven back across the Yalu River onto their own soil.[30] As Marshal Yamagata's First Army pushed the Qing forces deep into Manchuria, the Second Army under Marshal Oyama landed on the Liaodong Peninsula and rapidly overran the strategically important base of Port Arthur. By January 1895 Japanese troops also captured the naval stronghold of Weihawei at the northern tip of Shandong Province, which together with Port Arthur controlled the maritime approaches to the Chinese capital. This action seemed almost superfluous, since control over the seas had already been assured in early September, when Admiral Ding Ruchang's well-regarded squadron had been routed by a much lighter Japanese fleet in the Yellow Sea. Before the fall of Weihawei, the Zongli Yamen had already decided to send a peace mission to Japan.[31]

China's abysmal performance in the field and at sea earned it the disdain of Russian observers. In November, having just seen the battle of Pyongyang, the military attaché, Colonel K. I. Wogack, wrote that the Chinese were "beneath all contempt," adding that "the troops, not excluding the generals and officers, are such a disorderly rabble, that they do not even deserve to be called soldiers." When attacked by the Japanese, they "evidently thought of nothing else but beating the quickest path back to their border."[32] Several months later, after the battle of Weihawei, Cassini reported that Qing forces were "entirely lacking in training and practically unarmed."[33] By early February, the count began to despair of the Qing's continued survival. "In the near future we may well see the collapse of the dynasty, the disintegration of the empire, and the slaughter of foreigners," he cabled St. Petersburg.[34]

As for China's adversary, many were beginning to regard it with new esteem. Colonel Wogack had spent most of the war observing the action from Japanese lines, and his reports to the General Staff were full of enthusiastic praise for the martial efficiency of his hosts. He was particularly impressed by the quality of the officers and the discipline of the men. "Japan and its armed forces merit the most careful attention from our camp," Wogack concluded, "for they are a power with whom we must now reckon very, very carefully."[35] The editor of *Novoe Vremia*, a daily said to have close ties with the Choristers' Bridge, agreed. "What can we anticipate from Japan's victory over China?" Alexei Suvorin asked his readers.

"In my opinion, the consequences are enormous: There has appeared a new nation, a new people, and besides, in the consciousness of the European, a new race—the yellow!"[36]

The rapid turn of events in Korea and Manchuria called for a fresh look at the problem, and the new tsar ordered another conference on January 20, 1895. The first council, in August of the previous year, had been dominated by the foreign minister. This second group had a stronger military presence. Its chairman now was Nicholas's uncle, Grand Duke Aleksei Aleksandrovich, who also served as titular head of the navy, and participants included the ministers of war and the navy, as well as their chiefs of staff, in addition to the finance minister. The foreign ministry was represented by Shishkin, the acting foreign minister since the death of Giers earlier that month, and Count Kapnist.[37]

The primary aim of the January 20 meeting was to decide whether to change Russian policy in light of Japan's unforeseen success in the conflict. Much of the deliberation consisted of discussing various contingencies, since it was still unclear what Japan's territorial claims would be. The participants continued to worry about the role of Britain, although they agreed that it was preferable to continue cooperating with London as long as the British continued to "act correctly."[38] As for Japan, Shishkin was confident that it would not break its promise to respect Korea's territorial integrity. Witte added that, should Tokyo act otherwise, appropriate steps could then be taken.

Meanwhile, the navy was much more eager about acquiring a Korean port than it had been in August. Grand Duke Aleksei Aleksandrovich raised the matter several times and hinted that Nicholas had been considering the matter. Chikhachev had changed his mind and now also favored the idea, even suggesting seizing some territory in Manchuria.[39] His colleagues, however, opposed such a move. Shishkin, for one, urged the council to "demonstrate that we have no aggressive designs on the Pacific's shores," stressing the need to remain on friendly terms with Japan.[40] General Obruchev, the head of the army's General Staff, also objected to a Korean base, pointing out that a station so far removed from Russian territory would be extremely difficult to defend.[41]

Despite the navy's desires, the council voted to stay the course and continue joint diplomacy. Nevertheless, to have a more convincing voice in the region it was also decided to beef up the Pacific squadron "so that it might exceed that of Japan."[42] The two resolutions were duly implemented. Chikhachev promptly ordered ships from the more modern Mediterranean squadron to Pacific waters, substantially increasing Russia's naval presence there, while the Foreign Ministry sought to enlist British and French support in pressuring the Japanese to conclude a peace.[43]

As China and Japan were moving to parley, both sides began an intense diplomatic effort in February to win the sympathies of the major powers. In Tokyo, Foreign Minister Mutsu became alarmed at the prospect of Anglo-Russian cooperation, which would prove a formidable combination in the region. He therefore hastened to repeat his assurances to Hitrovo that Japan had no designs on Korea but was primarily interested in Formosa (Taiwan), an island he knew was of little importance to Russia.[44] In St. Petersburg, Nicholas II received an envoy from the Chinese emperor at Anichkov Palace, who pleaded for his intercession. The dignitaries showed little subtlety when they began their audience by first politely inquiring after the tsar's health following the attack in Otsu four years earlier.[45] For his part, in the Chinese capital Li Hongzhang once again solicited Cassini's support, arguing that Russia should prefer "a quiet and peace-loving neighbor" to the dangerous Japanese upstarts.[46]

Neither the Japanese nor the Chinese approach met with a definitive response from St. Petersburg. Cassini consistently brushed off Li's pleas, telling him that Russia would intervene in the conflict only insofar as its own interests were affected.[47] Although the young tsar sympathized with the Chinese, he was as yet undecided about what course, if any, he should take.[48] For now, the conflict still seemed too distant to require any immediate action.

The other European powers were equally reluctant to involve themselves in the negotiations. As a result, when the talks finally got underway in earnest in the Japanese city of Shimonoseki in March, the Chinese delegation, led by Li Hongzhang, faced its counterpart alone. Japan's price for peace was finally communicated on March 18, and Li made sure that the European legations were quickly apprised. In addition to the usual indemnity and commercial concessions, Tokyo insisted on a formal renunciation of all Chinese claims to Korea. The most alarming provisions, however, were the territorial cessions it demanded: Formosa and the Pescadores Islands in the south as well as the entire Liaodong Peninsula, with its important naval base of Port Arthur.[49] To Cassini the latter was particularly ominous for Russia. He told the foreign minister that the possession of Port Arthur "will put in their hands such strong political and economic power that Japan will inevitably acquire a voice and authority second to none over the Chinese government, and in my opinion severely limit the influence of other powers that have political and trade interests in China."[50] In St. Petersburg the war no longer seemed so far off.

The prospect of a Japanese foothold on the Asian continent quickly developed into the first diplomatic crisis of Nicholas II's reign. Alexander III died on October 20, 1894, and the heir initially seemed utterly bewildered by his new responsibilities as Tsar of All the Russias. His father, who had never held the tsarevich in particularly high esteem, had done little to prepare him for the task of ruling the empire. When Giers delivered his first report to his new master, Nicholas moaned: "I know absolutely nothing. The late emperor did not foresee his end and did not initiate me into anything."[51] But the tsar soon recovered from the shock, and he rapidly turned his attention to ruling his realm.

Nicholas's first instincts as Russia's new ruler were to follow in his father's footsteps. He retained the finance minister, Sergei Witte, whose influence would only grow during the first years of his reign. Although Nicholas was not particularly fond of the imperious statesman, Witte's forceful personality easily prevailed. As many were soon to discover, the young sovereign was pathologically averse to confrontation, and he initially found it easier to yield to Sergei Iulevich's commanding ways.[52] For a while, Witte would even come to have a strong voice in foreign policy, which under Alexander III had always been firmly in the hands of the emperor and his foreign minister.[53]

When Giers died in January, the choice for his replacement also marked no radical departure. At first, the ambassador to London was approached, but at 73 years Egor Staal's only ambition was a comfortable retirement, and he politely declined the offer.[54] The next man on the list was another career diplomat with a long and distinguished service, Prince Aleksei Borisovich Lobanov-Rostovskii, who was currently posted to the court of Vienna. A dandy and a consummate snob, Lobanov had not been highly regarded by his predecessor, who was reputed to have said: "What do you expect, he's only been consul-general all of his life."[55] Although the prince had also served in Constantinople, he was primarily interested in European affairs, and officials at the Asiatic Department complained that the new foreign minister knew little about the East. Baron Rosen recalled: "[Lobanov] was quite ignorant of Far Eastern affairs, which was very natural, seeing that he belonged to a generation whose ideas of China and Japan were mostly connected with pictures of pig-tailed mandarins on boxes of tea, or red lacquer cups and saucers brought home by bold travellers."[56] Nevertheless, Lobanov earned the respect of his contemporaries and, during his brief tenure, proved to be a competent foreign minister.

One important way in which Nicholas differed from Alexander III was his willingness to pursue an aggressive diplomacy. Unlike his father, he had come to the throne when the empire seemed strong and again commanded the respect of the other powers. At home, the economic boom engineered by Finance Ministers Vyshnegradskii and Witte had put the government's finances in good shape. Meanwhile, the alliance concluded the previous year with France meant that Russia was no longer isolated. Throughout the difficult years after the Congress of Berlin, military planners had been obsessed about the danger of an assault from the west by the newly powerful German empire. Partnership with Paris entirely altered this gloomy strategic landscape and seemed to give St. Petersburg more latitude.[57]

There was also something in Nicholas's personality that made him more prone to taking risks abroad. One scholar rightly described him as "somewhat naive and over-optimistic. . . . As regards diplomacy, he did not always distinguish between hopes and practical possibilities."[58] Throughout his rule, officials would often complain that the tsar was easily seduced by foreign adventures of the most baroque kind. As one foreign minister put it, "It was precisely the fantastic and adventurous aspect of [a] project that captivated Nicholas II, who was highly receptive to chimerical ideas."[59]

The first major foreign policy decision confronting the new Russian emperor involved the peace talks at Shimonoseki. The approaches China and Japan had both made to his government suggested that he had one of two options: Either Russia could side with Tokyo and join the territorial free-for-all on the Middle Kingdom, or it could support Peking in its efforts to resist the Japanese demands, thereby attempting to preserve the status quo in the region. As the new foreign minister put it, "The choice between China and Japan as Russia's future ally depends entirely upon which policy we want to pursue after the Sino-Japanese War: Passive or more or less aggressive."[60]

Advocates of a vigorous forward policy argued that the Qing dynasty was breathing its last. Russians should therefore befriend Japan and seize a part of the disintegrating empire while the pickings were still good. An editorial in one of the capital's more liberal dailies, *Novosti* (The News), put the case well:

> The Chinese question is clearly analogous to the Eastern question. If it seemed possible to redistribute a significant part of Turkey, the same is all the more true for China. . . . Now is the most opportune moment to cast aside all hesitation and finish off China, redividing it among the interested European powers . . . China delenda est![61]

Commentators rushed to present their wish lists. In January *Grazhdanin* suggested extending the entire Siberian border southward, absorbing large portions of northern Xinjiang, Mongolia, Manchuria, and Korea, while letting Japan annex the southern halves of Manchuria and Korea.[62]

Those with more modest appetites focused on an ice-free outlet into the Pacific. Since its establishment in 1860, Vladivostok had seemed unsatisfactory as the main naval base in the Far East, because the surrounding seas were frozen for four months in the year. Among other things, this meant that Russia's Pacific squadron wintered in Japanese ports, an option that depended too much on the goodwill of a potential rival.[63] Also, the start of work on the Trans-Siberian Railway made the need for a warm-water port all the more urgent, as its Pacific terminus.[64]

In early 1895, a spate of editorials appeared in the capital's papers clamoring for a resolution of this vexing matter. "Now is the time to obtain at relatively little cost an ice-free port on the Pacific," one writer in *Novoe Vremia* intoned, "and we must not let this opportunity pass, just as we let slip our chance a few years ago to do the same in Korea."[65] This argument predictably found many supporters in the navy, including Grand Duke Aleksei Aleksandrovich and Chikhachev. Another enthusiastic fan of the idea was the tsar himself, who noted: "Russia absolutely requires year-round a free and open *port*. This port must be on the *continent* (southwest

Korea) and has to be linked to our current territory by *a strip of land.*"[66]

In a memorandum to Nicholas II shortly after Japan's harsh terms were divulged at Shimonoseki, Lobanov suggested that one response might be to make an arrangement with Tokyo for "an ice-free port on the Pacific, and a harbor in Manchuria to serve the Siberian Railway."[67] He added that another advantage of such an alliance was that the rising naval power would be an excellent partner against Russia's principal adversary: "Our relations with Japan always became a matter of concern whenever hostilities with England loomed on the horizon."[68]

This line of thinking was remarkably similar to that of a popular book that had appeared shortly after the outbreak of the war, *Nashi zadachi na Tikhom Okeane* (Our Aims on the Pacific).[69] Its author, Aleksandr Maksimov, a retired naval officer with experience in the Far East, argued that Russia's real foe in Asia was the Middle Kingdom. Although they were not performing brilliantly in the field at the moment, in time the Qing would successfully reform their armies and, supported by Britain, might well turn on Russia: "On the horizon of our relations with China there will always be a menacing cloud, which may easily burst out into a savage war . . . and drive us from the Far East."[70] The only option was to upgrade Russia's own military there and join forces with Japan. Maksimov repeated: "Japan is our only true ally on the shores of the Pacific; our friendship is as precious to us as it is to her. We must, if at all possible, be in solidarity with this power, since we share many common political goals."[71]

Lobanov was much more cautious when it came to the Far East; his proposal had merely been one of several options the foreign minister had dutifully presented to the emperor. However, within his ministry there were enthusiastic advocates of a pro-Japanese orientation, such as Hitrovo and Count Kapnist.[72] As late as 1896, Hitrovo was still calling for a compact with the island empire, and there are indications that Tokyo might well have welcomed such a move.[73] Rosen probably exaggerates when he suggests that the Japanese public hoped for Russia's friendship in the early days of the war.[74] Nevertheless, on the day after Japan's conditions for peace were announced, a Japanese diplomat in Berlin hinted that his government would not oppose a Russian move to secure a portion of northern Manchuria and a Korean port, as long as Japan's demand for the Liaodong Peninsula was assured.[75]

Yet, for every person who cheered the victories of Japan's armies in Manchuria, there were others who worried about the threat to Russia's Pacific provinces. Furthermore, many regarded Manchuria as part of their nation's own legitimate sphere of interest in China, and they saw any Japanese presence there as an unwarranted intrusion.[76] *Sankt-Peterburgskie Vedomosti* repeatedly warned that Tokyo's territorial demands at Shimonoseki were an ominous development. "Now that the war is over, the real problems in the Far East are only starting," one of its reporters fretted.[77] *Novoe Vremia* took a similar stance:

National pride, the desire to lead the great struggle of the yellow races against the white . . . this is what compels the Japanese to strive to make Port Arthur their Gibraltar on the sea lanes to our Siberian shores. . . . Even a few square feet of the Liaodong Peninsula in the hands of Japan will always be a thorn in our side . . . which we will sooner or later have to take out.[78]

Even *Grazhdanin*'s Prince Vladimir Petrovich Meshcherskii now reviled Japan as a "nation of pirates and bandits" and began to shift in favor of the Chinese.[79] By mid-February, he was openly calling for an alliance with Peking: "It would be good for us to join forces in the Orient with China, and especially with China, with its imposing and mighty uniformity. Together China and Russia will prove an invincible combination against our eternal Asiatic foe—England!"[80]

In the foreign ministry, Count Cassini predictably supported a pro-Chinese orientation.[81] The most powerful advocate of an entente with Peking, however, was Finance Minister Sergei Witte, who saw a closer relationship with the Qing as an essential element of his ambitious economic plans. Witte's active involvement in the Trans-Siberian Railway since its inception had excited his imagination with visions of the Far East's vast potential. Whereas others had championed the project to help protect Russia's Pacific flank, the finance minister saw it more as a means to bring prosperity to the empire. By linking European Russia with the Pacific, the railway would considerably hasten the development of Russia's own East Asian provinces and thereby "open abundant wellsprings of material prosperity for all people."[82] At the same time, once the tracks were laid, Siberia would inevitably become the most efficient transit route for Europe's commerce with the Orient. Russian merchants would then be able to wrest the fabled China trade from the hands of the British, who had dominated it for far too long.[83]

Witte also foresaw that "building the Great Siberian Railway will force Russia to take a more active part in the life of the Asiatic East."[84] Initially his conception of what this role should entail was somewhat vague, although his vision of the East implied a special relationship with Peking. As the new railroad drew Russia eastward, Witte reasoned, China would evolve into both an object of commercial expansion and an economic partner against England.[85]

Unlike the more enthusiastic hawks of the day, Witte adamantly opposed any territorial acquisitions in East Asia. To realize his ambitious aims, it was critical to retain the Qing dynasty's goodwill. In his words, the goal was strictly one of the Orient's *"pénétration pacifique."* At the same time, attempts by any other powers to gain a foothold on Chinese soil threatened Russian access to the Middle Kingdom and had to be firmly resisted.[86] Witte stressed: "We have to stand firm for the principle of China's integrity, just as firmly as the United States stand for the Monroe Doctrine. And, what is more, we ourselves must respect China's integrity."[87]

The choice between China and Japan was finally made at a third special conference, on March 30, 1895.[88] Once again, the group included the ministers of war, the navy, finance, and foreign affairs and was chaired by Aleksei Aleksandrovich. As the grand duke told the assembled officials at the start of the meeting, the tsar was inclined to side with Japan. Since the island empire was a strong naval power, it would invariably become Britain's rival. The best option, Aleksei suggested, was to negotiate a compact with Tokyo. By means of a "secret agreement," St. Petersburg could let Japan have its way in China in exchange for a support of "our interests" in the region. Russia could thereby acquire both an ice-free port and a strong ally against England.[89]

War Minister Vannovskii was the first to object, and even Lobanov cautioned that Japan was untrustworthy, but the most determined opposition came from Witte. Arguing that Japan had really gone to war with China to preempt Russia in the Far East before the Siberian Railway could be completed, he stressed that an understanding was out of the question. The finance minister warned: "Japan's hostility is directed mainly against us. Its plans to occupy southern Manchuria, if carried out, will be a menace to us in the future and will probably be followed by the annexation of Korea as well . . . [eventually the Japanese] will attract the martial Mongols and Manchus to their side and start a new war."[90] Russia's interests would be far better served by opposing any Japanese annexations on the mainland and calling on the navy to support this stance by force if necessary. "We will thereby become the savior of China," he concluded, "which would appreciate our services and eventually agree to a peaceful correction of our border."[91]

In the end, despite Nicholas's sentiments, the finance minister's arguments carried the day. Although some fretted that Russian forces in East Asia were not up to fighting a war there, and Lobanov doubted that Japan would step down peacefully, the ministers agreed to back Witte. As a result, the council resolved to "advise Japan, at first in a friendly way, not to occupy southern Manchuria, since this would interfere with our interests as well as being a permanent menace to the peace of the Far East."[92]

The emperor, who had not attended the meeting, still preferred a deal with Tokyo.[93] When Lobanov submitted his minutes of the conference to Nicholas four days later, the tsar evidently remained reluctant to abandon his desire for an ice-free port.[94] In order to reconsider the matter, Nicholas summoned his leading ministers for an informal meeting at Anichkov Palace on April 4. "After a long discussion" he finally gave in to Witte, albeit not without some trepidation. "God preserve us from getting into a war!" the emperor noted in his diary that day.[95]

*I*n addition to his desire for a naval station, Nicholas may also have been concerned about his army's ability to stand up to Japan in the distant Far East. His foreign minister worried that Tokyo could decide to resist a Russian ultimatum, and if matters came to a head it would be hard to drive the Japanese from the Asian mainland.[96] Compared to Japan's 84 battalions in Manchuria, the tsar could at most spare 22 from his forces in eastern Siberia. As Hitrovo warned, "We are still far from ready to undertake something as serious as a campaign against Japan.[97] The obvious solution was to convince the other powers to join Russia in putting pressure on Japan. Even before the council met on March 30, Lobanov had approached Britain, France, and Germany to determine whether they would support a démarche urging Tokyo to withdraw its demand for the Liaodong Peninsula.[98]

Great Britain seemed to be a logical partner. Besides Russia, it was clearly the European nation most intimately involved with East Asia. Although no longer as dominant as it had been during the Opium Wars some fifty years earlier, the Royal Navy was still a powerful presence. With more than four-fifths of Chinese foreign trade in British hands, London was keenly interested in the course of the war.[99] Indeed, the Foreign Office had led the Western effort to negotiate a cease-fire in the summer and autumn of 1894. During the early days of the conflict, English public opinion had tended to side with China.[100] Yet, as a Japanese victory began to seem certain, there was a noticeable change of heart in London. By February 1895, the leading papers were increasingly cheering on the aggressors as they marched through Manchuria. There was much admiration for the plucky successes of a fellow island-based maritime empire.[101] At the same time, as Prime Minister Rosebery put it, a strong Japan would be very useful as a "bulwark against Russia," still England's arch rival on the continent.[102]

When Foreign Secretary Lord Kimberley approached the Russian ambassador in late 1894 to request his government's backing in a peace effort, the latter had seemed somewhat coy.[103] Several months later, it was Staal's turn to be the frustrated suitor. Toward the end of March 1895, as the diplomat invited London to join in putting pressure on Japan, he was surprised to be met with an "unexpected volte-face." Lord Kimberley told him with some embarrassment that the cabinet had decided not to oppose Tokyo's demands at Shimonoseki. His colleagues felt that the draft treaty's commercial clauses would benefit English commerce, and the territorial cessions on the mainland were too far from Britain's own interests in the Yangzi River valley and Hong Kong to be a threat. Repeated appeals for support during the following weeks would prove equally unsuccessful as London adopted an attitude of benevolent neutrality. Lobanov reluctantly came to accept that Britain would not cooperate with his efforts.[104]

If England proved to be a disappointment to the foreign minister, he was pleasantly surprised by the stance taken in Berlin. When hostilities first broke out, Germany's Kaiser Wilhelm II took great pride in the successes of the Japanese army, which had been trained by Prussian advisors, and he directed his government to remain aloof from the conflict.[105] Yet he soon grew apprehensive about British and Russian involvement in the crisis. Their diplomacy, he reasoned, was motivated by something other than altruism. Above all Wilhelm worried that any postwar settlement would yield territorial benefits for those who had taken an active role. "Under no circumstances can we be left out or let ourselves be taken unawares," he insisted. "We must likewise have a foothold in China."[106]

Like his cousin, Nicholas II, the kaiser was also eager to acquire a naval station in Pacific waters.[107] At the time, German colonial interests in Asia were minimal, and St. Petersburg did not even regard Berlin as a major player in the region.[108] Germany did however have substantial trade ties with the East. More important, the kaiser was no longer content to play second fiddle to the more established Pacific powers. With his young empire's status as one of Europe's leading continental forces fully confirmed by the 1890s, Wilhelm began to dream of a more global role for Germany. The war seemed an excellent opportunity to insinuate himself into East Asian affairs.[109] Therefore, by March, the German ambassador had already let it be known to Lobanov that his government would gladly join in any Russian mediation.[110]

Germany's favorable response made it difficult for France to reject Lobanov's invitation. With its colonies in Indochina, the republic was equally unhappy about Japan's territorial demands at Shimonoseki, especially those involving Formosa and the Pescadores Islands just to the north of its own possessions.[111] The difficulty was that the Chamber of Deputies was not particularly eager to become involved in another Pacific war. Another concern was the attitude of London. France was as much a rival of the British Empire as Russia, but the playing fields of its contest lay in Africa. On other continents, it was reluctant to provoke England. As a result, the French Foreign Ministry at the Quay d'Orsay tried as far as possible to maintain a hands-off attitude in the Sino-Japanese conflict.[112]

When in early April the Russian foreign minister first discussed the Japanese demands with the French ambassador, Marquis de Montebello, the latter initially proposed taking a passive stance, as he worried that England might well oppose any pressure on Tokyo.[113] The news that Germany had enthusiastically supported Lobanov's proposal came as an unpleasant surprise.[114] Despite all of its reservations, the French government could ill afford to jeopardize the recently concluded alliance with St. Petersburg by publicly parting ways over the issue, especially when its Prussian nemesis was already on board.[115] With some reluctance, Paris signaled its readiness to participate in the Russian action as well.[116]

*I*n Shimonoseki the talks were coming to a head. Although the former German minister told Li Hongzhang that he could now count on the support of several European powers while Cassini urged him not to cede the Liaodong Peninsula, the Chinese statesman nevertheless gave in to Japan's demands and signed the peace on April 5.[117] As he was returning home to present the treaty to his emperor for ratification, the Triplice (triple intervention) of Russia, Germany, and France began to exert pressure on Tokyo.

On April 11, within a week of Li's capitulation, in a carefully scripted diplomatic maneuver, representatives of the three nations successively paid calls on Vice Foreign Minister Count Hayashi Tadasu, each handing him an identically worded note: "We find that the possession of the Liaodong Peninsula by Japan would be a constant menace to the Chinese capital and would render the independence of Korea illusory, thereby becoming a permanent obstacle to the peace of the Far East."[118] The Triplice was in a good position to make its voice heard. Together, their Far Eastern squadrons numbered 38 ships weighing some 95,000 tons, compared to a much lighter 57,000-ton Imperial Japanese fleet of 31 ships.[119]

For a few days, the Japanese government hesitated. Public passions ran high, since many felt that the peace terms were already insufficient reward for the military's victories on the mainland.[120] At first, the government offered to return most of the Liaodong Peninsula, with the exception of Port Arthur. But this solution was hardly acceptable to St. Petersburg, which mobilized its Triplice partners to express their dissatisfaction. Meanwhile, April 26, the Japanese deadline for ratification of the treaty, was fast approaching.

As delegates of the two warring sides were convening in the Chinese port of Zhifu to carry out this formality, Russian forces stepped up the pressure. In eastern Siberia, General Sergei Dukhovskoi mobilized the Priamur Military District and made preparations to march his forces into Manchuria.[121] Offshore, the tsarist navy was also getting ready to engage the Japanese. On April 10, Admiral P. P. Tyrtov, the Russian naval commander in the Pacific, had already received orders that "in case of hostilities the main objective must be to take active measures against the Japanese fleet and ports as well as to interdict Japanese communication with the shores of [the Asian mainland]."[122]

Ironically, at the time the bulk of Tyrtov's squadron was wintering in the harbors of Nagasaki, Yokohama, and Kobe. "It is inconvenient to menace a country while enjoying its hospitality," the admiral declared, and he ordered his ships out of Japanese waters. Two weeks later, nearly twenty Russian warships, torpedo boats, and other vessels were anchored at Zhifu.[123] An eyewitness described the scene:

> The Russian government concentrated there the most formidable squadron which had ever been assembled in Chinese waters . . . with the hope of still inducing China not to take the final step to put the treaty into operation. To make this demonstration more impressive, as each vessel came to anchor it immediately proceeded to don the war-paint of dark gray and strip for action, using the shore just in front of the hotel in which the Japanese Treaty Commission was quartered for the storage of boats, sails, and other superfluous paraphernalia.[124]

The Japanese government took the hint. On April 25 Tokyo declared that it would retrocede Liaodong in exchange for a more generous indemnity.[125]

CHAPTER EIGHT

Asian Alliance

T sarist intervention in the Sino-Japanese War earned the gratitude of Peking. Although France and Germany also participated in the Triplice, Chinese officials were well aware that Russia had headed the effort that led to the return of their lost territory. In summer 1895, Count Cassini gloated: "Since the days we first established diplomatic relations with the Celestial Empire, our position and prestige in China had never attained the prominence they acquired after . . . our decision to lend a rescuing hand to our great and feeble neighbour. At this hour, Russian supremacy in China is challenged by no one."[1]

The other Western powers fully acknowledged Russia's ascendancy. Auguste Gérard, Cassini's French colleague and good friend, happily recalled that in 1895 "Russia above all others had the initiative, the will, and the authority" in China.[2] Others found less joy in this development. English commentators such as Henry Norman and the *Times*'s Valentine Chirol expressed great alarm at Russia's intimacy with the Qing.[3] Even the long-serving British director of China's Imperial Maritime Customs, Sir Robert Hart, while not normally Russophobic, worried that "the Liaotung intervention put Russia into a terribly commanding position. . . . You may guess my anxiety!"[4]

English concerns were understandable. During much of the nineteenth century, the nation had been the most influential Western power in the Middle Kingdom. The reticence of Russia's rival during the recent war, however, greatly eroded its former preeminence, and British diplomats now found themselves shunted to the sidelines of Peking politics.[5] The state of affairs deteriorated to the point that, when the British minister, Sir Nicholas O'Conor, lost his temper during a meeting in June with the Zongli Yamen, the latter demanded and secured his recall.[6] Cassini was only mildly exaggerating when he reported that "there is hardly a trace left of the fascination and authority England exercised for so many years in . . . China."[7]

The new alignment seemed to be confirmed when Russia succeeded in arranging a major loan to the Chinese government in July 1895. Among the terms for peace with Japan at Shimonoseki was an indemnity of 250 million Kuping taels, or roughly £38 million. Since the central government's annual revenues at the time averaged 90 million taels, there was no other choice but to turn to international capital markets.[8] China's foreign debt at the time was relatively modest, and English, German, and French bankers hastened to offer their services.[9] The Hongkong and Shanghai Bank, long the leading financier in the region, was the first to approach Peking, but its agents' overconfidence as well as Chinese annoyance at London did not make the British institution a particularly attractive lender.[10] English bankers soon realized that they were out of the running, effectively clearing the field for German and French houses.[11]

Russia had not initially been involved in the scramble for the transaction.[12] In fact, news about the negotiations first reached the Choristers' Bridge via Berlin rather than from Peking.[13] This omission was hardly surprising, since Russia had little capital to provide and was a major borrower on Europe's money markets itself.[14] When St. Petersburg was asked whether it would consider joining France in a Chinese loan, the answer was noncommittal at first.[15] Nevertheless, Russian diplomats were not blind to the potential advantages of such a move, and Witte soon began to favor it too.[16] Here was a splendid opportunity to extend tsarist influence in the Middle Kingdom as well as to beat Britain, long the most prominent financial player there, at its own game. Lobanov explained the "political key" of his aims: "It is vital for our future plans to make China somehow dependent on us and to prevent England from extending its influence there."[17]

In mid-May, the finance minister instructed his Paris agent to seek the assistance of French bankers, and Lobanov told Montebello that Russia would be happy to participate in a deal, provided neither London nor Berlin were invited.[18] Despite frantic efforts in Peking by Sir Robert Hart and the German minister to convince the Chinese not to borrow from Russia, within little more than a month Cassini was able to report that the Zongli Yamen had agreed to the Russo-French offer.[19] On June 24, 1895, Chinese representatives signed a contract in Prince Lobanov's office for a loan of 100 million gold rubles at 4 percent with a maturity of 36 years. Equivalent to 100 million taels, the funds would cover two-fifths of the indemnity owed to Japan. The bulk of the issue was bought up by a syndicate of eight French banks, and the Russian government undertook to guarantee the loan.[20] The terms were quite favorable to China, which had been borrowing at rates of 7 percent in recent years.[21] On the other hand, July was a quiet month on the Paris Bourse and Russian backing made the issue an attractive investment.[22] As a result, the offering was oversubscribed by nearly 15 times when it appeared on the market.[23]

*A*lthough France put up the money, Russia organized the loan. The transaction was generally seen as a major coup for tsarist Far Eastern diplomacy, much to the annoyance of Britain and Germany.[24] *Sankt-Peterburgskie Vedomosti* hailed it as "a great success for Russia" and emphasized its "moral-political significance."[25] In his column, *Grazhdanin*'s Prince Meshcherskii argued that the deal "may be considered the start of a new era in our foreign relations." As he saw it, "Russia has now become China's closest partner. We are bound not only by friendship but also by common interests. Intimacy with Russia will enable China to resist the perfidious predacity of the other European powers."[26]

Count Lamsdorf took a more cynical view. Asked by Lobanov to write a favorable article about the loan in the Foreign Ministry's *Journal de St.-Pétersbourg,* he bit his tongue when his chief cited Count Nikolai Ignatev as an example in the Russian tradition of disinterested help to the Middle Kingdom. Lobanov was referring to the crafty diplomacy of Ignatev as minister to China at the time of the Second Opium War. In autumn 1860, as British and French troops had burned the Chinese emperor's Summer Palace and stood at the walls of Peking, Ignatev cleverly played off the adversaries, convincing both sides he was operating on their behalf. Acting as go-between, through a brilliant combination of charm, Macchiavellian guile, and deceit, the envoy both egged on the Anglo-French force and then took full credit for their decision to sign a peace treaty and evacuate their troops. Within a fortnight of the European retreat, Ignatev's "disinterested" mediation was rewarded by the Treaty of Peking, whereby the Chinese emperor fully confirmed Russia's claims to the territories seized by Muravev on the Pacific a few years earlier.[27]

Prince Lobanov gave a rather generous interpretation of the episode in some notes to guide Lamsdorf in writing the piece for the ministry's paper:

> Russia has always shown itself to be a disinterested friend of China. This is proved by our actions during the Anglo-French attack on China [of 1860]: Russia's representative [Ignatev] intervened in a semiofficial and friendly way with the warring nations to help bring them to peace, without any securing any special advantages for his own country.

The count indignantly protested in his diary: "But this is hardly true; all of Ignatev's efforts were motivated by the concrete advantages Russia would gain for his services. Here we can say: 'Qui s'excuse, s'accuse.'"[28]

Along with many others, Lamsdorf saw a parallel between the diplomat's maneuvers in 1860 and Russian assistance to China 35 years later. The decision to intervene at Shimonoseki and the loan to Peking were neither premeditated nor part of some meticulous tsarist plan to dominate the Far East. Yet both moves were made in the expectation of gaining advantages in China. As Lord Curzon put it, "Russia does not render this assistance from a superfluity of unselfishness, or for no end. She has her price, and she will receive her reward."[29]

In a dispatch to Prince Lobanov, Cassini confirmed that Peking was well aware that those who had assisted it would soon call the favor. "It seems that the Chinese government clearly understood that sooner or later each of the powers that supported China will remind it of their services and expect some form of compensation," the count wrote.[30] The only question was what form the reward would take. Some officials, such as the governors-general of the Steppe and Priamuria, advocated boundary changes.[31] But, since the Russian government had made so much of its role as the Middle Kingdom's protector at Shimonoseki, it was hardly convenient to emulate Ignatev and arrange for more annexations at Peking's expense.

Moreover, in the eyes of men like Witte, seizing more Far Eastern territory was entirely superfluous. Britain, Germany, and France had in recent years acquired great influence over foreign lands by commercial means rather than direct conquest. Through banks, railways, trade, and other financial activities, these European powers extended their sway overseas in a variety of areas, from Persia and Ottoman Turkey to Argentina. The object was to acquire "spheres of influence," or, as modern historians have it, "informal empires," which exercised economic and political sway indirectly, without the complicated business of stationing troops and setting up colonial administrations.

China was a good example.[32] Although the British Crown owned only a few specks of rock in the mouth of the Pearl River at Hong Kong, its commercial and financial activities enabled it to acquire an influence over Chinese affairs vastly out of proportion to its minuscule territorial presence.[33] To Sergei Witte it seemed logical to follow a similar tack and compete with Britain by establishing Russian enterprises in China.

The first step the finance minister took in this direction was to set up the Russo-Chinese Bank. England had long had its Hongkong and Shanghai Bank, and German and even Japanese capital was also well established in China, but Russia had yet to gain a financial foothold there.[34] In 1894 a delegation of Russian tea merchants from Hankou, complaining about the steep commissions charged by British banks for foreign currency transactions, had petitioned Witte for such a move.[35] At the same time, a new bank could help exports of kerosene and other Russian business activities in the Middle Kingdom.[36] However, Witte did not have only commerce in mind. In a memorandum to the tsar, he suggested that "the Russo-Chinese Bank, aside from promoting Russian trade with China, should also support the strengthening of our economic and political influence in the Middle Kingdom."[37] The minister added in another note that "one of the bank's tasks must be to . . . counter the enormous economic weight of the English there."[38]

Witte broached the idea for such an institution on June 24, 1895, when meeting with French bankers to conclude the Chinese loan. Immediately after the Parisian financiers had agreed to the terms of the transaction, he proposed that they form a partnership with some of their St. Petersburg–based counterparts and his ministry to help penetrate the Chinese market.[39] Much like the loan itself, this institution would largely use

"Honey, *My* Honey!"—Britons reacted to news of Russia's loan to China in 1895 with envy and cynicism, as this cartoon from the satirical weekly *Punch* suggests.

republican francs to further tsarist interests in the Far East. Nevertheless, in Paris a venture backed by the Russian government was regarded as an excellent confederate in its own commercial competition against the British and the Germans.[40] By September a consortium of French houses signaled their readiness to help, and four months later, in January 1896, the Russo-Chinese Bank officially came into being with a share capital of six million gold rubles. Although five-eighths of this money came from French investors, it was clear that the new corporation was firmly in Russian hands: A majority of the board was Russian, as was the working language.[41]

The bank opened its first office in Shanghai, and branches were soon added in Hankou, Tianjin, Vladivostok, and Peking.[42] In addition to taking deposits and making loans, the company's statutes also empowered it to provide insurance, transport goods, buy and sell real estate, issue currency, and even collect taxes.[43] One diplomat accurately likened its ambitions to Cecil Rhodes's South Africa Company.[44] Yet, although it was officially chartered as a private corporation, in practice the Russo-Chinese Bank worked as an arm of the Finance Ministry, and its head, Prince Esper Ukhtomskii, was of course an intimate of both the tsar and Witte. During the early years of its existence the bank would acquire considerable influence with the Qing government. The Peking branch's location directly across the street from the legation neatly symbolized the institution's function as a twin of tsarist diplomacy.[45] Its able director, Dmitrii Pokotilov, arrogated considerable authority, and during his tenure it often seemed that it was he rather than Russia's officially accredited representative who spoke for St. Petersburg.[46]

The Russo-Chinese Bank was one means to insinuate Russia into the Middle Kingdom. Another favorite weapon in the arsenal of informal empire was the steam locomotive. For nearly thirty years Britons and other Europeans had been trying to negotiate concessions to construct railways in China. Well aware of the potential of trains to bear Western civilization's poisonous seeds into the empire's interior, China's conservative mandarins had firmly resisted such attempts.[47] In 1894, half a century after the start of the railway age, a little more than 300 kilometers of track had been laid in China.[48] On the eve of the war with Japan there were signs that this attitude was slowly changing. Self-strengthening reformers such as Li Hongzhang began to consider railroads as a necessary innovation to bring their realm into the modern era, but even the most progressive officials preferred to build these without excessive involvement from abroad.[49]

China's weakness after the war encouraged foreign concession hunters to redouble their efforts. The ink on the Peace of Shimonoseki had barely dried when Peking was flooded by British, German, Belgian, French, and American engineers and speculators peddling their proposals for new railroads.[50] The first to meet with success was Auguste Gérard, who claimed a new line on the Indo-Chinese border in the south as partial reward for France's participation in the Triplice's intervention.[51]

For Sergei Witte, the new state of affairs provided an excellent opportunity to press the Qing for permission to make a shortcut for the Trans-Siberian Railway through northern Manchuria. There had already been several proposals for such a move long before the outbreak of the Sino-Japanese war. In the late 1880s, as the debate about the merits of the Siberian Railway was moving into its final stage, Rear Admiral Nikolai Kopytov suggested that the project would be much better served by building its eastern section from the old trading town of Kiakhta to Vladivostok straight across the Manchurian province of Heilongjiang, rather than following the northward bulge of the border along the Amur River as the Ministry of Transport was planning. He argued that this would cut that portion of the route by nearly a third, from some 2,000 to 1,400 kilometers, considerably reducing costs, in addition to bringing benefits to China. Furthermore, the transportation needs of towns of eastern Siberia were already adequately being served by river shipping. Other officials, fearing the diplomatic complications that might arise from this intrusion into the Qing empire, opposed the move, and Adolph von Hubbenet, transportation minister at the time, decided to stick to his ministry's original plan and keep the railway on Russian soil.[52]

Sergei Witte, who briefly succeeded Hubbenet in 1892 before his appointment as finance minister, initially agreed with his predecessor. However, he was not categorically against a subsidiary line across the Chinese border. He expressed his optimism that "the construction of such a branch would hardly meet serious obstacles in the near future," adding that it would promote Russian trade with the Middle Kingdom, "both boosting the profitability of the Siberian Railway's main line and strengthening our role in China's international commerce."[53] Two years later, engineers surveying the Shilka and Amur River valleys began to report on the difficulties of laying tracks in the region. Much of the terrain was either very hilly or subject to flooding, and the inhospitable climate made food scarce and disease plentiful.[54] Meanwhile, an unofficial reconnaissance by Lieutenant Colonel Strelbitskii indicated that the terrain in Heilongjiang was much better suited to railway construction.

The colonel's report convinced Witte, who now entirely came around to Admiral Kopytov's plan. In February 1895, during the extraordinary embassy to Nicholas II from Peking, the finance minister suggested asking the diplomats for a concession to take the railroad over Chinese territory, although he did not pursue the idea at the time.[55] A year later, in a memorandum to the tsar, Witte set out his thinking about the diversion into China in greater detail.[56] In addition to simplifying work on the Siberian Railway, it would make Vladivostok northern Manchuria's most important port and would tie the region closer to Russia economically. "The railroad," he noted, "has not only economic but also political and strategic importance."[57] The army would be able to transport troops to the region more efficiently, and Russia's presence in Heilongjiang would greatly increase tsarist power in the Far East. As Witte stressed, however, "the proposed Chinese Eastern Railroad . . . should under no circumstances be used as a tool for annexations."[58]

Most contemporary observers saw the project primarily as an instrument of influence. The French student of Russian affairs Anatole Leroy-Beaulieu, for example, remarked that, "if the government of the tsar has decided to build a Manchurian line, it is not just to simplify construction but above all for the great political advantages that will result."[59] Yet even some English-men could not deny the logic of such a move. Sir Frank Lascelles, Britain's ambassador to Berlin, said in March 1895 that he would not oppose a Russian annexation of part of Manchuria to shorten the Siberian railroad, and Lord Beaconsfield, in a celebrated speech later that year, generously declared, "In Asia there is room for us all."[60]

By May 1895, within three months of Witte's initial proposal, Prince Mikhail Khilkov, the new transportation minister, obtained Nicholas's approval for a more thorough survey of Manchuria. In August, a "private" expedition of some ministry engineers "on leave" set off to plan the route.[61] Neither Witte nor Lobanov were told about the mission, and in September Cassini wired St. Petersburg puzzled and alarmed at complaints from the Zongli Yamen about local reports of Russian officers and engineers traveling in Heilongjiang Province.[62]

Cassini's cable in November announcing the success of his French colleague in negotiating a railway concession in Yunnan galvanized the tsar's resolve, and he immediately ordered Lobanov to meet with Witte to discuss how Russia could obtain a concession in Manchuria.[63] Agreeing with his master that "it is important to take advantage now of our political standing in China," Lobanov duly instructed Count Cassini in early December to begin talks in Peking for a Russian concession.[64] Despite his initial optimism, the count found the Qing foreign office to be considerably less pliant than he had expected. It took him until April 1896 even to be able to make a formal proposal to the head of the Zongli Yamen.[65] On April 18, the Yamen informed Cassini that the emperor had decided that a Russian railway would violate his sovereignty over Manchuria. However, the Son of Heaven allowed that, if St. Petersburg were willing to provide the engineers and the money, he would be happy to command his government to build one to join the Siberian Railway.[66]

Cassini's setback did not mean that a concession was entirely out of the question. Another excellent opportunity to get China's consent came with the embassy Peking would send to Moscow in May 1896 to attend Nicholas II's coronation. Etiquette demanded that foreign governments honor such an august occasion by dispatching suitably prominent dignitaries to be present at the ceremonies. Japan, for example, planned to delegate Marshal Yamagata and a prince of the imperial blood. The Qing were well aware that the festivities would likely be accompanied by an attempt to wrest a railway concession from their ambassador. At first they sought to evade the question by appointing Wang Jichun, an official whose relatively modest status as the retired treasurer of Hubei Province would not give him the authority to discuss such weighty matters. Still, Cassini brought considerable pressure to bear on Peking. Recalling the services his government had provided at Shimonoseki, the minister finally prevailed, and an imperial rescript was issued appointing Li Hongzhang as the Middle Kingdom's representative to the coronation.[67]

*D*espite the reluctance to open Manchuria to the steam dragons of the Russian foreign devils, closer ties with their tsar seemed reasonable in Peking. As many Chinese contemporaries noted, the Qing's predicament recalled that of previous dynasties menaced by powerful enemies, such as the Sung 800 years earlier.[68] Facing a variety of hostile nomadic states to the north, Sung emperors had resorted to the tactic of *yi yi zhi yi,* or "playing off the barbarians." This intricate diplomacy consisted of bribing one adversary to help resist an even more menacing one. Assistance inevitably came at a steep price, often in treasure or territory, and never brought lasting peace. As the distinguished statesman Zeng Guofan had warned in 1860: "From time immemorial barbarian assistance to China, when followed by barbarian success, has always involved unexpected demands."[69] In the case of the Sung, it could not save the dynasty from Kublai Khan's horsemen in the thirteenth century. *Yi yi zhi yi* was a measure of last resort, and its adoption always involved a certain degree of fatalism.[70]

The tactic was clearly on the minds of many Qing officials in the wake of the disastrous war. During the negotiations at Shimonoseki, one provincial governor, Zhang Zhidong, sent a memorial to the emperor suggesting that he appeal to Britain and Russia for help against Tokyo, in exchange for some choice morsels of Chinese soil.[71] After the Triplice's intervention, many began to call for a pact with St. Petersburg. Another governor, for example, bluntly acknowledged that the empire was in a weak position: "We estimate that our power is inferior to theirs, so we must quickly make an international alliance as a means for seeking international assistance [against further attacks by Japan]." He added that the tsar would be the least likely to make onerous demands in return, since "Russia's territory is already very large."[72] Zhang Zhidong now agreed that Russia was the least objectionable barbarian. Britain, he pointed out, was friendly with Japan, and anyway its merchants had always been rapacious. Meanwhile, France "uses religion to entice people," Germany had no colonial interests in the region, and the United States was too reluctant to become involved.[73]

The most distinguished champion of alliance with Russia was Li Hongzhang. Aged 72, Li was the dynasty's leading elder statesman. Having first come to prominence as a highly effective general in the campaigns against the Taiping and Nian rebellions of the 1860s, he had been appointed in the following decade to the important posts of viceroy of the capital region of Zhili and commissioner of northern ports. A loyal servant of the Qing, Li was a strong advocate of modernization through "self-strengthening," or "learning the superior techniques of the barbarians to control the barbarians."[74] During his 20-year tenure as viceroy, Li enthusiastically developed arsenals, coal mines, telegraphs, railways, and a host of other enterprises. He set up a military academy and sent promising young men abroad for study. Like Tsar Peter the Great, he understood that his empire required a progressive army and navy, supported by an adequate industrial base, if it were to hold its own against its more advanced adversaries.[75]

Although technically a provincial official, Li Hongzhang also came to dominate China's relations with the outside world. His responsibilities as commissioner of northern ports brought him into frequent contact with the major maritime states, and over the years Li took the lead in resolving major disputes with Japan, France, and others, effectively relegating the Zongli Yamen to the background.[76] Because of its aggressive thrusts into Korea and the North Pacific, Japan caused him the most vexation. "Japan is as near as in the courtyard," he worried. "Undoubtedly she will become China's permanent and great anxiety."[77] At the same time, the official was much less troubled about Russia's capacity for harming the Middle Kingdom, and he became convinced that St. Petersburg would be a logical partner.[78] Nevertheless, there was little naïveté about his sentiments, as one biographer suggested:

> How far Li himself believed in the possibility of disinterested Russian "friendship" must remain a matter for surmise . . . [but] it seems reasonable to believe that he was under no delusions in the matter; that he made friends with the mammon of Muscovy simply because friends of some sort were imperatively required in 1895, and because he hoped to find some means to evade full payment on the day of reckoning.[79]

Peking had already begun considering the idea of an alliance with Russia during the latter part of the recent war. In late April 1895, before the Treaty of Shimonoseki had been ratified, its minister in St. Petersburg, Xu Jingcheng, was instructed to offer a secret pact between the two empires in exchange for support against Japan.[80] A year later, although now at peace, Tokyo was still regarded as the main threat. At the same time, the Qing understood that they could not indefinitely put off Russian demands for a Manchurian railway. It therefore seemed logical in Peking to agree to the construction in exchange for tsarist protection.[81]

*I*n March 1896, Li Hongzhang boarded a French steamer in Shanghai accompanied by an impressive entourage, his English physician, and an empty coffin, just in case.[82] The statesman's journey was not limited to Moscow; after the Romanov coronation there would also be other stops on the Continent as well as in England and North America to pay courtesy calls and discuss a variety of issues.[83] Considerable intrigue preceded his departure as rival diplomats jockeyed to change the itinerary. With some difficulty Cassini managed to convince Li to keep to the original plan and make Russia his first stop.[84] To circumvent any last-minute surprises, as well as to begin lobbying him, Witte commissioned Prince Ukhtomskii to meet "the old man" at Port Said and complete the voyage aboard a ship of the tsarist Volunteer Fleet.[85]

After landing at Odessa, where an honor guard provided a regal welcome, the Chinese party proceeded to St. Petersburg in a private train Witte put at their disposal. Three weeks remained before the coronation in Moscow, and the finance minister lost no time beginning his discussions with Li.[86] It took the men a little patience to adjust to each other's negotiating styles. Witte recalled:

> When Li Hung-chang paid his first call, he was ushered into my reception room. . . We greeted each other effusively, bowed low to each other. Then I took him into another reception room and ordered tea. I sat and he sat, but the members of his suite and my associates remained standing. Then I asked him if he wished to smoke. He thereupon began to make sounds like those of a stallion neighing. Immediately two Chinese came in from the other room, one carrying a hookah, the other tobacco. There followed the smoking ceremonial: with great reverence they lit the hookah, held the pipe to his mouth while he sat very still, making no motion except to inhale, have the pipe taken from his mouth, exhale, then permit the pipe to be put back into his mouth. He was obviously trying to make a strong impression on me with ceremonials of this kind, but I naturally reacted very coolly and gave the impression that I paid no attention to such things. It goes without saying that we did not touch on business at all during our first meeting, but just chattered away.[87]

At the following rendezvous the finance minister and his visitor dispensed with the pleasantries and got to the matter at hand. Suggesting that a shortcut through Manchuria would enable the tsarist government to send troops to the Far East and thereby come to China's aid more efficiently in the future, Witte repeated Cassini's request for a railway concession. At first Li's answer was no different from the Zongli Yamen's rebuff earlier that year: Allowing Russians to lay tracks on Chinese soil would only encourage the other Europeans to demand similar rights. Peking would build its own railway.[88]

Witte now tried a different tack, quickly arranging for his guest to have a private audience with the tsar. Possibly at the suggestion of Ukhtomskii, when Nicholas received Li Hongzhang on April 25 he openly linked the request for the railway to Russian military protection in case of another war with Japan. Meanwhile, to downplay the role of the tsarist government, it was suggested that the Russo-Chinese Bank be put in charge of the project.[89] This was more to Li's liking, and he did not reject the idea out of hand. A few days later, at a dinner hosted by Prince Lobanov, Witte presented a draft for a mutual defense treaty the Russian government was prepared to offer in exchange for the concession. "The treaty is not very objectionable," the viceroy cabled Peking; "if we reject it, it will certainly spell the end of our amicable relations with Russia and this would be prejudicial to the general situation."[90]

Witte encouraged Li's goodwill with the promise of a three-million-ruble bribe. Yet it is unclear that being "materially interested" played a decisive role in Peking's decision to sign the treaty. As an American scholar points out: "The Chinese documents . . . prove that it was the Empress Dowager, not Li, who made the final decision to sign the treaty. Therefore, even if Li did receive a bribe, its effect on the negotiations was inconsequential."[91]

After some wrangling over the terms, the Zongli Yamen essentially accepted the Russian proposal, and the Empress Dowager Cixi, China's de facto ruler, authorized Li Hongzhang to conclude the alliance. On May 22, 1896, a week after Nicholas's coronation, Witte, Lobanov, and Li signed a treaty in Moscow pledging the assistance of their governments' armed forces against "every aggression directed by Japan."[92] The agreement was meant to last for 15 years and would be invoked immediately in case of a Japanese attack on "Russian territory in East Asia, or against the territory of China or of Korea." In time of war, China would also put its ports at the disposal of the tsarist navy.

"To facilitate the access of Russian land troops," Peking consented "to the construction of a railway line across the Chinese provinces [of Heilongjiang and Jilin] in the direction of Vladivostok." This would be done via the Russo-Chinese Bank according to a contract to be negotiated, and the treaty stressed that the concession "shall not serve as a pretext for any encroachment of Chinese territory." Much like the alliance it had concluded with France three years earlier, Russia's pact with Peking was meant to be secret. Nevertheless, apocryphal versions of a "Cassini Convention" appeared in the foreign press within a few months, and the existence of some form of agreement between the two empires soon came to be taken for granted.[93]

As for the railway, all that remained now was to work out the details. One problem was the track width. Russian trains ride on a broader gauge than the 1.44-meter European standard that China had also adopted.[94] Peking naturally preferred to use the latter, but it eventually yielded and accepted the Russian width for the concession in Heilongjiang. A more contentious matter was Witte's desire to add a branch from his proposed railway south to a port on the Yellow Sea. Although Li was not opposed to this addition in principle, he categorically refused to agree to accept the Russian gauge on this new line, and the idea was shelved.[95] Finally, on August 27, Xu Jingcheng, Prince Ukhtomskii, and Adolph Rothstein, another associate of Witte, put their signatures on a contract for the construction of the Chinese Eastern Railway (CER), as the new enterprise was christened.[96]

Witte bragged to the tsar that his success in securing Peking's consent to build the CER marked "one of the most splendid pages in the history of Russia in the Far East."[97] For once the vainglorious finance minister was not being immodest. More than 1,500 kilometers long, the concession was by far the largest the Qing would ever accept. By comparison, the French line in Yunnan measured some 460 kilometers and the tiny British-owned Canton-Kowloon Railway only 35 kilometers.[98]

The contract also gave the CER extremely generous privileges. All government land needed for the tracks would be given free of charge, and private property could be bought or rented at prevailing prices. The operation was exempt from all taxes, and goods transported on the line from one Russian point back into Russia would not be subject to Chinese duties. Meanwhile duties paid on goods imported and exported by rail would be 33 percent lower than those transported by sea. Although Peking technically retained jurisdiction over security and the administration of justice on the CER's lands, Article 5 implied a way around this: "Criminal cases, lawsuits, etc., upon the territory of the railway must be settled by the local authorities in accordance with the stipulations of the treaties." This provision was soon further diluted when the CER's statutes, which Nicholas initialed in early December, allowed the railway to organize its own police force on the concession.[99] The concession was granted for 80 years, with an option for the Chinese government to buy the railway in 36 years, albeit for a very steep price.[100]

Technically, the CER was a publicly held company, whose shares could be bought by Russians and Chinese alike. The initial offering on the St. Petersburg Bourse was not handled in a way to encourage broad ownership. The only announcement was a small notice in the December 17 issue of the official daily, *Pravitelstvennyi vestnik* (Government Herald). It stated that subscriptions for the stock would be accepted starting at 9 A.M. that same morning. The cold northern dawn in the week before Christmas was not a time calculated to attract a large number of investors, and the entire issue was immediately scooped up by the Russian government and the Russo-Chinese Bank.[101]

There was the appearance of Chinese participation in the venture. Xu Jingcheng was appointed president, and the CER's flag combined the tsarist white-blue-red with the yellow imperial Chinese standard.[102] But the composition of the board of directors showed who was really in charge. Aside from the Chinese diplomat, its other members were all Witte's men, including his deputy, P. M. Romanov, the ubiquitous Prince Ukhtomskii, Rothstein, Pokotilov, and two railway engineers who had worked with Witte during his days at the Transportation Ministry.[103] In fact, the enterprise was firmly in the hands of Sergei Witte, who jealously guarded against any encroachments by other governments or even rival ministers.[104]

It would take several years of surveying and preliminary construction before the CER's presence was felt, but in time Witte's project would develop into a semi-independent fiefdom on Chinese soil, with its own cities, government, and police. Also operating mines, ships, telegraphs, and lumber mills, it came to dominate much of Manchuria, especially the more sparsely populated north.[105] "In a word, Witte built up and directed a veritable kingdom in the Far East," one tsarist official recalled.[106]

Five years later, when Russian troops held the region after suppressing an indigenous rebellion, a diplomat ventured that, "in principle, the decision

The Chinese Eastern Railway Concession in 1896

to occupy Manchuria was taken in 1896 (when the contract for building the railway was signed)."[107] There is no doubt that the military action might very well not have happened without the start of work on Witte's railway; once it was in place, it became very difficult for St. Petersburg to ignore any threats to such a massive investment of Russian manpower and money. Yet it is equally clear that the finance minister did not have the annexation of Chinese territory in mind when he undertook his project. General Simanskii more accurately characterizes Witte's intentions: "[The CER] began the peaceful conquest of Manchuria. . . .Instead of Siberian infantry rifles here the engineer's compass and the pickaxe did their work, commanded not by an army general but by a finance minister."[108]

*S*ometime after the revolution of 1917, a former official at the Russian legation in Peking recalled the events of April 1895. "We have sown the wind," he gloomily concluded, "and sure enough, we are reaping the whirlwind now."[109] The implication was that tsarist interference at Shimonoseki was the start of a chain of events that led to the disastrous war of 1904 with Japan, the First World War, and, ultimately, the overthrow of the Romanov dynasty. While the retired diplomat was being melodramatic, he was right in stressing the significance of the Russian-led démarche.

The most important event in Russia's relations with the West during the last decade of the nineteenth century was the conclusion of an alliance with France. For a few years after Shimonoseki, it seemed as if an equally momentous combination might be forming in the East. Largely through the efforts of Sergei Witte and Li Hongzhang, the Romanov and Qing dynasties formed a partnership that promised protection for the latter and economic and strategic benefits to the former. The Asiatic alliance made sense as long as Russians held their territorial appetites in check, and for a while St. Petersburg's standing in China was unparalleled.

To be sure, most Chinese officials saw the compact as a temporary expedient to preserve the Middle Kingdom from dismemberment by even more wicked barbarians.[110] Yet it was an epochal development. The conclusion of a formal defensive pact was unprecedented in Chinese history, much as at Nerchinsk two centuries earlier the Emperor Kangxi had deigned to accept the first treaty that dealt with another power on an equal footing.

The year 1895 also marked the start of a decade of intense interest, sometimes bordering on obsession, in the affairs of the Far East in the highest circles of St. Petersburg's court and officialdom. Prince Lobanov's diplomatic success excited the imagination, aroused visions of imperial greatness, and reanimated long-slumbering expansionist passions. Some voices cautioned restraint while others urged attention to the empire's many domestic ills. However, until Russian blood began to be shed in the snows of Manchuria nine years later, China's infirmity, in the words of another former diplomat, "opened wide new vistas for our foreign politics."[111] Prince Radolin, the German ambassador, captured the mood at the time:

> Recently highly placed officers have spoken to me with pride and self-importance about the great mission of Russia in Asia and the dawn of a new era that will make Russia a civilized nation of the first rank. . . . In short, everything I hear blends into one single voice, which says that in time Russia is destined for world domination, starting with the East and Southeast, which are as yet unspoiled by the cancer of European civilization. . . . I never thought it possible that such fevered fanaticism as I see now could ever take hold of Russia. These are not just a few single exalted individuals who think and speak this way—this is the general view that one encounters everywhere.[112]

CHAPTER NINE

Kaiser Wilhelm and Port Arthur

*L*ike nature, diplomacy abhors a vacuum. This was especially true of China after its defeat by Japan in 1895. The Qing's
inability to ward off the armies of the much smaller island
neighbor thoroughly confirmed their helplessness, and the decadent empire soon began to attract the attentions of the European powers. In the previous decade, bursting with expansionist
energies, the great nations of the West had raced to divide the
African continent among themselves.[1] Now the scramble for
China had begun.

During the first few years after the Peace of Shimonoseki, the
powers generally refrained from annexing any land. After all,
upholding the Middle Kingdom's territorial integrity had been
the reason for the Russo-Franco-German Triplice's intervention.
Instead, they jockeyed for economic advantages through railway
and telegraph concessions, mining rights, and trading privileges.
Britain, France, Germany, Russia, the United States, Japan, and
even Denmark and Belgium all joined in the fray. Count Münster, a German diplomat, expressed sentiments common to
many of his European contemporaries: "In China a whole new
world for colonial and industrial activity has been opened.
There, and not in Africa, lies the future for German commercial
and entrepreneurial spirit."[2] An editorial in the *Chicago Inter-
Ocean* said much the same: "The time is propitious . . . to an
opening of the vast area of China to the commerce and civilization of the Aryan race."[3]

For a while events seemed to confirm Lord Beaconsfield's
promise that there was "room for us all" in China. Auguste
Gérard, the French minister, acted quickly to claim France's reward for its participation in the Triplice. By June 1895, the
diplomat had already negotiated a demarcation favorable to
Paris on the Indo-Chinese border as well as permission to build
railways from the French colony into southern China.[4] The following year, Gérard also secured a license to operate the arsenal
at Fuzhou and important economic rights in Yunan and
Sichuan Provinces.

"Someone's pulling a fast one."—This cartoon by *Novoe Vremia*'s Soré in 1901
shares the common Russian view that the West exploited China.

Britain likewise improved its commercial position in the Middle Kingdom. In early 1896 the foreign secretary appointed a new minister to
Peking, Sir Claude MacDonald. A former Highland officer with extensive
service in the African wars, but little schooled in high diplomacy, he was regarded as an eccentric choice by many. However, Sir Claude's direct manner
and youthful energy enabled him to recover some of the ground lost in the
wake of London's reluctance to back China at Shimonoseki.[5] Within the
first two years of his posting, MacDonald convinced the Zongli Yamen also
to grant Britain a number of railway concessions and to confirm its economic preeminence in the prosperous Yangzi River valley.[6]

With its ambitious Chinese Eastern Railway project, Russia led the pack in
the race for commercial favors from the Qing, and its privileged standing in
Peking aroused much jealousy from its rivals. Sir Robert Hart sighed: "'The
Star of Empire' glittering in the *East* is distinctly Russian!"[7] The years 1896
and 1897 clearly marked the apogee of China's regard for St. Petersburg.[8] The
Zongli Yamen readily granted permission to a battalion of Cossacks to traverse Manchuria, and for tsarist ships to winter in Qingdao harbor, at Kiaochow (Jiaozhou) Bay on the Shandong Peninsula southeast of Peking.[9] In
1896, Qing officials even turned to Count Cassini for military assistance to
suppress a rebellion in Manchuria's remote northern mountains.[10] Neverthe-

less, there was a limit to the lengths Peking would go to indulge its new ally. Tsarist diplomats made little headway in their efforts to replace Englishmen in Chinese government service with Russians, and repeated offers to provide military instructors in Manchuria tended to fall on deaf ears.[11]

The European gentleman's agreement to refrain from any land grabs in China did not last long. Germany was the first to transgress. A parvenu to overseas imperialism with freshly aroused ambitions for *Weltpolitik*, Berlin had become increasingly dissatisfied with its modest standing in the Middle Kingdom. Although the Germans had a substantial economic presence there, they owned no territorial concessions and, aside from the privilege of providing military instructors to the Qing, enjoyed few other advantages. The boisterous and bombastic Kaiser Wilhelm II felt particularly aggrieved in the years following the Peace of Shimonoseki. His diplomats had supported the Russian intervention with considerably more enthusiasm than the French but, unlike the latter, had so far failed to derive any material benefits from their participation.[12] Above all, the kaiser longed for a naval station in Pacific waters. Britain already had an excellent network of such depots around the world, and the French were also fairly well-off in this regard. Despite a modest colonial empire of its own, Berlin possessed few satisfactory overseas bases. This lacuna was particularly galling in China, where German vessels had to rely on the hospitality of the British colony of Hong Kong for fuel and provisions.[13]

Already during the early days of the Sino-Japanese War, Wilhelm had begun to consider how he could benefit from the conflict to rectify the matter. "We must not permit ourselves to fall short," he wired his chancellor, Prince Chlodwig zu Hohenlohe-Schillingsfürst, in 1894. "We also need a strong base in China, where our trade is worth some 400 million [marks]."[14] The kaiser's ready participation in the Triplice the following year was obviously motivated by the hope he would receive a coaling station in return.[15] After peace was restored, Germany's minister to Peking, Baron Gustav-Adolph von Schenck zu Schweinsberg, tried to negotiate a lease for a suitable base with the Zongli Yamen. Schenk's ineffectual style did not get him very far, and in summer 1896 he was replaced with the more energetic Baron Edmund von Heyking. The new envoy was well aware of his principal duty. "The idea of a naval station is after all the only reason for being in this dreadful posting. If acquiring it for Germany proves to be impossible, I'll be at my wit's end about how we can bear life here any longer," his wife confided to her diary.[16]

In spring 1896, an ambitious Prussian admiral, Alfred von Tirpitz, was ordered to reconnoiter China's shores for a suitable military and commercial base. His choice fell on the port of Qingdao on the Shandong Peninsula's Kiaochow Bay. "The unset pearl of Qingdao" met all of his requirements: The harbor was well protected from the open sea, Shandong's hinterland was populous and held good possibilities for economic development, and there were rich coal deposits in the area. Most important, with its northerly location, Qingdao was far from British interests around the Yangzi River.[17]

The only complication was that it appeared that St. Petersburg might have a prior claim to Kiaochow Bay. In December 1895, with Peking's reluctant consent, a gunship flying the St. Andrew's standard of the Russian navy had briefly anchored in its waters.[18] Eight months later, after Baron Heyking "confided" to Count Cassini about his government's desire to secure Qingdao as a coaling station, Cassini suggested that his German counterpart look farther south, since St. Petersburg had already been granted use of the port.[19] On the other hand, when Li Hongzhang passed through Berlin earlier, in summer 1896, on his way back from Nicholas's coronation, he had emphatically denied that Russia had any rights to Kiaochow.[20] And, in the following year, during a dinner in Vladivostok with Rear Admiral Evgenii Alekseev, the commander of the Russian Pacific Fleet, Admiral Tirpitz was assured by his host that the tsarist navy did not have the slightest interest in the Chinese bay.[21]

As a result there was some confusion at the Wilhelmstrasse (the location of Germany's foreign ministry) about Russian rights to Kiaochow when the German kaiser set out on a state visit to the newly crowned tsar in July 1897. Although the two sovereigns were related and had known each other since childhood, Nicholas viewed the arrival of the arrogant Prussian monarch with much trepidation.[22] Eight years older than the tsar, and given to hectoring his younger cousin about how he should rule his empire, Wilhelm had never endeared himself to Nicholas.[23] The latter was particularly put out by the kaiser's childish insistence to be named an admiral of the Russian fleet. As Nicholas complained to his mother: "Alas, I now have to appoint Wilhelm to the rank of one of our admirals. . . . *C'est à vomir* [It makes you vomit]."[24]

At one point during the kaiser's stay, the two emperors had a private conversation as they rode unaccompanied in a carriage to the Great Palace at Peterhof. According to a German account of the talk, Wilhelm asked his companion if the Russian government had any claims to Kiaochow.[25] Nicholas answered that, although St. Petersburg did not consider the Chinese bay to be a Russian possession, it reserved the privilege of direct access until a more suitable Pacific naval station could be found for his fleet. Acknowledging Russia's right to Kiaochow, Nicholas's guest then inquired whether he would object if German ships used the facilities at Qingdao "in case of need" and "after having secured the consent of Russian naval authorities." The tsar vaguely mumbled that he might be prepared to approve of such a move. Nicholas's uncomfortable utterances were more than enough for the German kaiser. Wilhelm immediately ordered his chancellor, Prince Hohenlohe, to draft a précis of the conversation. To make sure that there would be no misunderstanding, Hohenlohe also read the text to the new Russian foreign minister, Count Nikolai Muravev, and handed him a copy.[26] Later dubbed the "Peterhof Declaration," this document was soon put to the test.

A little more than a month after the kaiser's visit to Russia, Berlin gave notice of its intention to anchor at Kiaochow. On September 4, Prince Radolin handed Foreign Minister Muravev a communication from Berlin stating that "conformant to the talks at Peterhof" German navy ships "may" winter in the bay but would first inform the Russian commander at the port.[27] The letter put the Choristers' Bridge in an awkward position. It was eager to claim northern China as its exclusive sphere of influence. Yet, since there were no Russian ships at Kiaochow, no tsarist admiral would be present to welcome the kaiser's vessels.[28] Moreover, the Zongli Yamen made it quite clear that St. Petersburg had no say in the disposition of a Chinese harbor.[29] Any Russian benediction of a German naval visit to Kiaochow would obviously compromise the tsar's honor as an ally of the Qing; a monarch who professed to protect the Middle Kingdom's territorial integrity could hardly claim the right to allow foreign warships anchorage in his partner's ports. Muravev's deputy, Count Lamsdorf, therefore replied evasively to Prince Radolin's note, pointing out that Russia had no jurisdiction over the territory.[30]

The embarrassed statements by the tsar and his officials about Kiaochow convinced Berlin that Russia would pose no major obstacle to planting the German flag on the bay's shores. As for China itself, all that was needed was an adequate pretext to satisfy international opinion.[31] On October 18, a Chinese mob in the Yangzi River port of Wuchang threw some rocks at sailors of the German gunship SMS *Cormoran*. Vice Admiral Otto von Diederichs, Tirpitz's successor as head of the Pacific squadron, immediately wired his commander to ask whether this altercation might justify seizing the bay. He was told to hold off for the time being.[32]

Two days later, on the night of October 20, a more suitable occasion presented itself when some Chinese peasants murdered two German Catholic missionaries as they slept in a small village in Shandong Province some 400 kilometers west of Kiaochow.[33] This was the excuse for which Wilhelm had been itching. When news of the incident reached him five days later, the emperor immediately ordered his Pacific squadron to occupy Kiaochow and back up demands for reparations and other punitive measures by force. "I have resolutely decided to abandon for once and for all our hypercautious diplomacy, which is scorned throughout East Asia as a sign of weakness," he impatiently cabled the Wilhelmstrasse. "Now is the time to show the Chinese firmly and, where necessary, with merciless brutality that the German kaiser will not be taken for a fool."[34]

"Willy" also sent his Russian cousin "Nicky" a personal telegram to apprise him of his intentions:

> Chinese attacked German missions Shantung, inflicting loss of life and property. I trust you approve according to our conversation Peterhof my sending German squadron to Kiautschou, as it is the only port available to operate from as a base against marauders. I am under obligations to the Catholic party in Germany to show that their missions . . . are really safe under my protectorate.[35]

Once again, the reply from St. Petersburg disclaimed any responsibility for the bay. "Cannot approve nor disapprove Your sending German squadron to Kiautchou as I have lately learned that this harbour only had been temporarily ours in 1895–1896," Nicholas wired back, adding that he worried about the impact seizing the bay might have on relations with Asia: "I am afraid that strong punishing measure may create disturbances and uneasy feelings in the Far East and perhaps make the precipice between Christians and Chinese still deeper than it was now."[36]

Despite this caveat, the kaiser took his cousin's response to be an indication of Russian assent.[37] On November 2, within a fortnight of the murders, Admiral Diederichs of the German Imperial Navy sailed into Kiaochow Bay, secured the garrison and port of Qingdao with a modest force of some 700 men, and proclaimed himself the area's governor.[38]

*F*eelings in St. Petersburg about the German annexation proved to be considerably more ambiguous than Wilhelm presumed. China was after all Russia's ally. To be sure, the secret treaty signed in the previous year by Li and Lobanov only pledged support against a *Japanese* attack.[39] However, some felt a moral obligation to protect the Qing against other aggressors as well. Prince Ukhtomskii, for one, railed against Germany in the pages of his daily: "And so at a historic juncture in our rather friendly relations with the realm of the Bogdykhan, the Germans—solely in the spirit of naked aggression . . . like the marauding Vikings of yore turn to the helpless Orient. . . . China is guilty only of the fact that German appetites for its territory have been whetted."[40] In another editorial, the prince insisted that "Asia must not become another Africa, which exists purely for the white man to exploit."[41]

Others were nervous that any German encroachments into northern China would introduce a nettlesome new European rival to a region Russia hoped to dominate. Diplomats such as Count Cassini, who had just ended his posting in Peking, pointed out that "Kiaochow is right next to our sphere of influence. . . . Germany's acquisition of Kiaochow is diametrically opposed to our interests as well as to our role . . . in China."[42] Russia's military attaché in Berlin, Lieutenant Colonel V. V. Muravev-Amurskii, also fretted about the new colony. "Along with greater prestige in the Far East, Germany has gained an important economic asset and a base for further strengthening of its political and commercial influence in China," he wrote in a dispatch. Elsewhere in his report, the colonel cautioned that Germans would soon begin to demand the same privileges Russia enjoyed in China, "forgetting our long-standing historic rights."[43] On the whole, educated opinion in St. Petersburg was very much against the taking of Kiaochow.[44]

The most resolute opponent to the German seizure was Finance Minister Sergei Witte. His vision of the steady advance of Russian economic and political influence over its eastern neighbor was predicated upon a weak and pliant but sovereign China. Like Count Cassini and Colonel Muravev-Amurskii, he was not overjoyed at the prospect of an energetic new competitor in the region. Witte also worried that Germany's move would set off a race for other land grabs among the great powers. In a private conversation with the German ambassador, the finance minister warned that an occupation of Kiaochow would necessarily lead to a similar move by Russia, resulting in a host of complications in the East.[45]

Yet there were also powerful champions of just such a scenario. In an age when navalism was highly fashionable, and Captain Mahan's *The Influence of Sea Power upon History* was required reading for strategists—armchair and otherwise—worldwide, many Russians still clamored for an ice-free port on the Pacific. Vladivostok continued to be regarded as desperately inadequate for the imperial navy, especially now that the admiralty, like Germany's, was about to boost the size of its fleet. For Russia to be a major player in the Far East, its Pacific Squadron needed a port that was both in warmer waters and closer to the action.

In fact, during the previous year Russia had become embroiled in a messy contest with Japan over Korea that was partially motivated, on St. Petersburg's side, by the attraction of the peninsula's excellent ports. The squabble included the murder of Korea's Queen Min by pro-Japanese assassins, the dramatic flight of her husband, King Kojong, to the Russian legation, and underhanded efforts by both powers to extend their influence over the Hermit Kingdom's army and economy.[46] The Japanese proved to be vexedly tenacious, and by 1897 it had become clear to Russian diplomats that their rival was not about to give up without another fight.[47]

When Britain also started opposing Russian efforts to draw Korea into its sphere, foreign ministry officials began to consider whether it was wise to take on both Tokyo and the Royal Navy. Perhaps it might be preferable to concentrate instead on northern China, where Russia seemed to be better placed to influence events. Such sentiments were seconded by Witte, who felt that Russia was overextending itself in Korea as well as needlessly antagonizing Japan.[48] While the admirals still yearned for a Korean port, others now sniffed an excellent opportunity in the Kiaochow imbroglio for Russia's navy to snatch a base from China instead.[49] Nicholas's new foreign minister, Mikhail Muravev, soon became the most ardent advocate of this view.

Count Mikhail Nikolaevich Muravev succeeded the deceased Prince Lobanov-Rostovskii in early 1897. The incoming minister was neither a diplomat of particular ability nor a man of principle. Many suspected that he owed his promotion solely to his prior appointment as ambassador to Copenhagen, which had enabled him to ingratiate himself to the Danish-born Empress Dowager Marie Fedorovna.[50] In a profession where mendacity and cynicism are common occupational hazards, the count shocked even his colleagues. Charles Hardinge, first secretary at the British embassy during much of Muravev's tenure, saw him as "a pleasant man . . . but hopelessly untruthful."[51] Alfred von Kiderlein-Wächter, an official at the Wilhelmstrasse, was rather more direct: "As a character, he is a swine. . . . He has no political convictions of any kind. . . . He will *only* conduct a policy which he believes will make him the most popular in St. Petersburg."[52] As these observations suggest, the count was a skillful courtier, whose principal talent was reading the mood of his sovereign and acting accordingly.

Muravev's actions during the Kiaochow crisis were fully in keeping with the ungenerous assessments of his contemporaries. When he first heard about Germany's plans to take the bay, the foreign minister balked. He immediately notified the German government that he "deplored" this step. Furthermore, should Berlin send ships into Kiaochow Bay, the Russian navy would do likewise, *"pour afirmer priorité de mouillage"* (to affirm the right of first anchorage).[53]

Muravev's insistence that Russia had rights to the bay infuriated the kaiser. "Unbelievably insolent," he angrily jotted in the margin of this communication.[54] Wilhelm emphatically reiterated that his admiral would occupy Kiaochow. More ominous, he had his chancellor inform the Russian ambassador that "he [Wilhelm II] dreaded the complications that would arise from the simultaneous presence into the bay of both squadrons, complications for which he disavows in advance all responsibility."[55] Within days of receiving the note, the foreign minister began to see the matter in a different light. During his next weekly report to the emperor, on November 4, Muravev wondered whether "we should maybe let them have Kiaochow." "It might be more advantageous to seize another port at the earliest opportunity," he added.[56]

A week later, the count put his thoughts in writing. In a memorandum to the tsar, Muravev argued that the increasing instability of the Far East required a strong naval presence in the region, which in turn called for a properly equipped, ice-free port. As for the location of such a facility, he ruled out Korea, on the grounds that it was too far from the Trans-Siberian Railway. Meanwhile, since Kiaochow had been deemed unsuitable by the Russian admiralty, Germany might as well have it. Muravev's choice fell on Dalien and Port Arthur, the stations on the southern tip of the Liaodong Peninsula occupied by Japan during the recent war. In addition to offering harbors well suited to modern battleships, the Yellow Sea ports could easily be connected to the Chinese Eastern Railway already under construction. The foreign minister stressed that now was the time to act, while the situation was favorable. Finally, he dismissed any possible complaints from the Chinese government: Russian diplomats could argue that such a base was necessary to help defend the Qing against aggression in the future. At any rate, it was best to deal firmly with Peking, for "history teaches that the Oriental respects strength and might above all else."[57]

Count Muravev rightly anticipated the wishes of his master. Nicholas enthusiastically penciled on the memorandum: "Absolutely correct."[58] Returning the document to Muravev, he attached a note instructing him to summon the ministers of finance, war, and the navy three days later to discuss the matter at a special council. "I have always been of the opinion that our future open port *must be* either on the Liaodong Peninsula or in the northeast corner of the Korean Gulf," the emperor added.[59]

On November 14, Sergei Witte, Nikolai Muravev, War Minister Vannovskii, and acting Navy Minister Pavel Petrovich Tyrtov took the train to the imperial residence of Tsarskoe Selo for the meeting, which was chaired by Nicholas II. Although he knew very well where the tsar's sympathies lay, Witte led the offensive against Count Muravev's proposal. The finance minister strongly opposed the seizure of the Liaodong ports on the grounds that it would violate the defensive alliance with China, at least in spirit if not directly. Above all, Witte emphasized, the success of Russia's future in East Asia hinged on maintaining Peking's confidence:

> The acquisition of an outlet on the Pacific must not be carried out by force, but by friendly agreement. If the Europeans commit indignities, it does not follow that we should do so as well, for the European powers are newcomers to China, while we are long-standing neighbors, and our ties to this empire are wholly unique. If we stay on the course of our traditionally friendly intercourse with China, and refrain from violence and contempt, we will invariably achieve better results than the Europeans.[60]

Seconding the finance minister, Admiral Tyrtov questioned the utility of Liaodong to the navy and argued that Russia should hold out for a Korean port. In the end, Muravev found himself outvoted three-to-one. The ministers resolved not to occupy Port Arthur and Dalien out of respect for the alliance with China. Nicholas reluctantly accepted the advice of his council. For the time being, his desire for a warm-water port would remain unfulfilled.[61]

The finance minister had his way, and the special relationship with the Qing seemed secure. Witte was therefore flabbergasted when his sovereign told him shortly after the session: "Sergei Iulevich, I have decided to take Port Arthur and Dalien. . . . I have already sent warships with a complement of troops there."[62] It emerged that Muravev had received alarming reports from his consul at Zhifu that some ships of the British Royal Navy were steaming toward the Liaodong Peninsula.[63] If Russia did not take the ports first, the foreign minister insinuated to the tsar, Albion would surely deprive his Pacific fleet of a superb base. It might be a long time until such a good opportunity to acquire an ice-free station in the Far East would arise again. Muravev added that his move would also get Germany off Nicholas's back. Besides, the count pointed out, had not Li Hongzhang offered a port to help the Russian navy protect China?[64]

The foreign minister was being disingenuous. Some British ships had indeed left Zhifu in November, but they were headed to Chemulpo, where London was gathering a fleet to discourage Russian machinations in Korea, not Liaodong.[65] Muravev may not have known the destination of the British navy's ships, but when it came to China he was under no illusions that the Middle Kingdom was about to make a present of any harbors to the tsar. From the start, Li Hongzhang had sought St. Petersburg's help in expelling the Germans from Kiaochow, suggesting that the Pacific squadron temporarily use Chinese naval bases in the region. At the same time, the Zongli Yamen remained adamant that Russia evacuate such facilities as soon as the crisis was resolved.[66]

At any rate, it had not taken long for the count to convince Nicholas. By late November, the German embassy reported a softening of Russian opposition to the action at Kiaochow.[67] Nicholas and Wilhelm even began to speak about a "Hand-in-Hand Politik" in the Far East.[68] Meanwhile, on December 1, a little more than a fortnight after the council, Rear Admiral Reunov, a naval officer stationed at Nagasaki, received orders to proceed to Port Arthur in the strictest secrecy.[69] Commanding three ships—the cruisers *Admiral Nakhimov* and *Admiral Kornilov* and the gunboat *Otvazhnyi*—Reunov reached the harbor on December 4, where the local Chinese authorities cordially placed their facilities at the admiral's disposal.[70] Wilhelm gleefully cabled his cousin: "Please accept my congratulations at the arrival of your squadron at Port Arthur. Russia and Germany at the entrance of the Yellow Sea may be taken as represented by St. George and St. Michael shielding the Holy Cross in the Far East and guarding the gates to the Continent of Asia."[71] There was no sign of the Royal Navy.[72]

Admiral Reunov had been rightly told that his entry was fully in accordance with Peking's wishes. A week earlier, on November 23, the Zongli Yamen had happily consented to Russia's request that all ports in the region be made accessible to the tsar's navy. The Chinese ministers added that they hoped their ally would quickly succeed in clearing Kiaochow of the noxious Teutons.[73] But the welcome soon began to sour. Repeated requests from Li Hongzhang over the next few months for assurances that Russia would eventually leave the Liaodong Peninsula were either shrugged off or ignored altogether.[74] When the German minister, Baron von Heyking, began to press for a long-term lease for Kiaochow, Alexander Pavlov, the acting Russian representative, demanded the same for Liaodong.[75] Bribes were once again liberally distributed to Li and his associates, more ships were dispatched to Port Arthur, and St. Petersburg threatened to cancel the defense pact with China.[76] It soon became evident to the Qing that their guests were here to stay. Bowing to the inevitable, on March 11, 1898, Peking reluctantly agreed to yield the southern tip of the Liaodong Peninsula.[77]

The lease for Port Arthur and Dalien was signed in a somber ceremony at the Zongli Yamen on March 15, 1898.[78] According to its terms, China would yield Port Arthur and Dalien, as well as the surrounding area, for 25 years. The new Russian colony, which would eventually come to be known as Kwantung, was to be separated from the Chinese mainland by an even larger "neutral zone." Furthermore, the agreement gave the Chinese Eastern Railway a concession to build a branch to Port Arthur, in effect linking St. Petersburg by rail to Russia's new "window on the East."[79] The tsar had at last won his ice-free port on the Pacific. But he also lost an ally.

Germany's heavy-handed acquisition of Kiaochow and Russia's copy-cat lease of the Liaodong ports sparked a free-for-all among the other powers to secure similar privileges.[80] On May 15, two months after Port Arthur and Dalien were formally yielded, the French government demanded a naval station in the south at Kwangchow Bay, for 99 years. A few weeks later, Britain extorted leases for territory around its colony of Hong Kong as well as the base of Weihawei near Kiaochow. Even European nations not traditionally major players in the Middle Kingdom joined in the fray. The Dutch minister, F. M. Knobel, proposed a concession at Swatow "to raise the prestige of the Netherlands," and his American colleague, Edwin Conger, also thought that "at least one good port" might be a good idea for the United States. Both were wisely turned down by their superiors back home.[81] Italy's comic opera attempt in February 1899 to obtain Sanmen Bay was the only land grab the Qing successfully resisted.

Chinese and foreigners alike began to doubt the continued existence of the Middle Kingdom. In the West maps began to appear showing the Asian empire entirely divided into various European "spheres of influence," as did books with titles such as *The Break-Up of China*.[82] Perhaps even more alarming

The Leases in Northern China in 1898

to Peking was the rumor of an agreement between England and Russia, arch rivals in Asia for most of the century, to respect each other's respective "zones."[83] It seemed that the age-old policy of playing off the barbarians had seen its day, and the foreign devils were about jointly to devour the Chinese Empire. One leading Confucian scholar wrote:

> [The emperor] saw his country about to sink in the earth, about to be buried in ruins, about to burst like an egg, about to be divided up, about to mortify, about to be torn up into shreds, about to become like India, or Annam, or Burma—a dependent of another Power. His ancestors' heritage was to fall to such a depth! The myriad people of the Celestial Empire henceforth were to sink to oblivion . . . our imperial palaces to become cultivated cornfields.[84]

With a reference to their most dreaded form of execution, Chinese took to calling these indignities "slicing the melon."

The recent turn of events had two important consequences. First, it effectively killed the Sino-Russian alliance. Russia's prestige at the Qing court after its aid to China during the war with Japan three years earlier had been unprecedented. For the first time in its modern history, China signed a formal defensive pact with another power. When St. Petersburg failed to support its Asiatic neighbor against the kaiser's predacity, helping itself to some territorial morsels instead, the Qing's confidence vanished. In Peking's eyes, the tsar now was no better than any other greedy Occidental. As Gabriel Hanotaux, the French foreign minister, said with respect to Port Arthur, "Russia has lost China."[85]

But the most significant outcome of Europe's incursions was the blow to the Middle Kingdom's pride. An editorial in the English-language *North-China Herald* caught the mood when Admiral Diederichs first sailed into Kiaochow Bay:

> Humiliating to China as was her easy conquest by the previously despised Japanese, her present situation is infinitely more humiliating. A foreign Power with three ships and six hundred men finds no difficulty in effecting a descent on the shores of a country of three hundred millions, whose nominal army is counted by the hundreds of thousands, and establishes itself within three hundred and fifty miles from the capital.[86]

Some observers understood that such humiliation could easily turn to rage. In spring 1898 a German journalist asked Prince Ukhtomskii for his opinion about the recent events in the Far East. Ukhtomskii answered:

> I am against the occupation of Port Arthur. I condemned the German occupation of Kiaochow. [Instead] we must do everything to strengthen the Peking regime. If disorder erupts in China, the Manchu dynasty will be overthrown, and a fanatic national reaction will succeed it . . . when the dynasty collapses, foreigners will be butchered.[87]

The coming years would prove the prince to be prescient.

CHAPTER TEN

Righteous and Harmonious Fists

*T*he last Year of the Dog during the Guangxu emperor's reign, known to Europeans as 1898, began inauspiciously in Peking. Late afternoon on the Chinese New Year's Day, its residents interrupted their merrymaking to see the sun vanish and the heavens darken. For a moment the imperial capital was black as night. When the sun reappeared in the western sky, at first it looked like the new moon. Robert Hart sensed a mood of "general gloom and depression" among the population and reported that, to the emperor, the solar eclipse "foreboded calamity."[1] Other foreigners also felt that somehow all was not well. A few months later, the Russian legation's physician, Dr. Vladimir Korsakov, recalled that, "despite an outward calm, life in Peking . . . seemed to be pregnant with impending upheaval."[2]

Events at the Qing court during the coming months appeared to confirm the ill omen. Formally all power in the Middle Kingdom rested with the Son of Heaven, the Guangxu emperor. Yet China's real ruler was the 24-year-old monarch's aunt and former guardian, the Dowager Empress Cixi. In spring 1898, alarmed at the prospect that the Western powers might soon eviscerate his realm, much as they had India, Burma, and Indochina, Guangxu began seriously to consider radical reforms. There was probably also a desire to shake free from his overbearing aunt. By June, the emperor started issuing edict after edict in an effort to shock China into the modern age.

For some hundred days Guangxu had his way, but on September 2 Cixi reasserted herself. Within days, she had her nephew isolated in his palace under guard, executed a number of his leading advisors, and proclaimed that, owing to his "weakness" and "inexperience," Guangxu was imploring his aunt to resume her regency.[3] Although there was some unrest in the streets of Peking, no one doubted who was once again in charge in the Forbidden City.[4]

Most Europeans were dismayed by the dowager's coup. Their sympathies lay with the young sovereign who had hoped to refashion his empire along Western lines, much like a latter-day

Peter the Great or Meiji emperor.[5] On the other hand, the acting Russian minister was delighted with the failure of the "Bogdykhan's childish attempt to emancipate himself from the Dowager Empress."[6] In Pavlov's view, had Guangxu succeeded, the Middle Kingdom would have come under the sway of progressive officials much more sympathetic to England and Japan than to Russia.[7] Pavlov also probably agreed with one of the tsarist army's leading China-watchers, General Staff Colonel Dmitrii Putiata, who had written not long ago: "Left to its own devices, China will never be a dangerous neighbor to Russia. Under the charge of foreign agents, furnished with their weapons, instructors, and strategic plans, in league with the West—for this kind of China we would have to be on our guard."[8]

One clear indication of the reformers' hostility to St. Petersburg had been the ouster in August from the Zongli Yamen of Li Hongzhang, "the only Chinese official . . . able to sway his government in our favor," Pavlov lamented.[9] Now, with the Guangxu emperor out of the way, the diplomat expected his country to regain the high standing it had until recently held in Peking.[10]

Nevertheless, Cixi's restoration did not return Russia to favor with the Qing. When the new minister, Mikhail Giers, finally arrived in the Chinese capital in early 1899, he found the Zongli Yamen to be growing increasingly hard-line.[11] This development was reflected in the mood of the dowager's new counselors, such as her favorite, the Manchu general Zhunlu, who were highly isolationist in their outlook. To the Russians it seemed that the only foreigners still welcome in Peking were the Japanese; in the current climate of xenophobia at the court, there was much respect for the Asiatic neighbor's accomplishments. Giers was particularly alarmed to learn of a covert mission by Chinese officials bearing a letter from Cixi to the emperor of Japan, as well as about rumors of Japanese instructors in China's armed forces.[12] By December 1899, the new minister began to suspect the existence of a secret alliance between Peking and Tokyo.[13] As for Li Hongzhang, the dowager packed off the aging mandarin away from the capital on a mission "to measure the Yellow River's current" in autumn 1898, and the following year sent him even farther afield, to become viceroy of Canton.[14]

The Year of the Dog proved to be unhappy outside Peking too. There was unrest throughout much of China: harvests failed in Zhejiang, and open rebellion broke out around Canton as well as in Hubei and Sichuan.[15] To the peasants in the countryside south of the capital, it must have seemed that the gods were particularly angry. Heavy summer rains caused the Yellow River's waters to rise, until the dikes burst in July, flooding much of Shandong's northern plain and driving more than a million farmers from their homes. Meanwhile, the province's south continued to be in the grip of a severe drought.[16] As if these natural disasters were not enough,

Shandong's inhabitants were also subjected to a host of man-made calamities. The recent war with Japan had exerted severe fiscal pressures on the economy, leading to higher taxes, inflation, and large-scale troop cuts.[17] Thus a large population of dissatisfied former soldiers was added to the restive legions of farmers driven from their homes by floodwaters and crop failures. It was an explosive mixture.

It was not uncommon in China for hardship, whether brought about by nature or misrule, to translate into antidynastic insurrection. Shandong was particularly prone to unrest. The province had seen several major uprisings during the past century alone, including a rebellion by the millenarian White Lotus sect in the early 1800s, followed by the Eight Trigrams shortly thereafter and the Nian insurgency some fifty years later. Invariably such revolts were carried out by impoverished peasants, in league with bandits and others at the margins of existence, under the slogan "Revive the Ming, Destroy the Qing."[18]

In 1898 a new threat to the established order emerged in Shandong in connection with a group dubbed *Yihequan*. Variously translated as "Righteous and Harmonious Fists" or "Boxers United in Righteousness," the name derived from a system of exercises involving highly ritualized arm and leg movements, controlled breathing, and meditation, not unlike the *Taiqiquan* inoffensively practiced by millions in twenty-first-century China.[19] Along with their esoteric calisthenics, the Boxers, as they came to be called in the West, also engaged in shamanistic mass spirit possession, invulnerability rituals, and an ascetic way of life. Yet, while these Boxers combined many elements of traditional popular rebellion, they also introduced one very important innovation, for unlike previous, antidynastic uprisings the new movement had a different battle cry: "Support the Qing, Destroy the Foreign."

The patriotic folk of Shandong, which had given China its two great sages, Confucius and Mencius, had much reason to be angry with the big-nosed barbarians. Germany and England just seized leaseholds at Kiaochow and Weihawei, cutting like deep sores into the peninsula's shoreline. The rest of the province was invaded by overseas goods like machine-made cotton cloth, wreaking havoc on the cottage industries that supplemented meager peasant incomes, and many bargemen on the Grand Canal were put out of work by new steamship lines along the coast. The most intrusive European import, however, was the militantly exclusionary faith of its missionaries.

Traditionally, China accommodated various denominations, from Confucianism, Daoism, and Buddhism to a host of more informal peasant creeds.[20] Chinese often adopted elements from all of these beliefs in their own daily lives, a practice tolerated by the authorities, as long as the dynasty itself was not questioned.[21] What made Christianity so objectionable was its insistence that adherents reject all other forms of spirituality. "Superstitions," such as ancestor worship, kowtowing to idols, and festivals honoring local deities, were all condemned by the alien priests as incompatible with their doctrine. The refusal of Chinese converts to participate in such traditional rites made their neighbors resentful and suspicious. Further fueling animosities were the privileges Western clergy bestowed upon those who agreed to be baptized in their creed, such as food or help in resolving legal disputes before the magistrate. Thus villagers grew both contemptuous and envious of these "rice Christians" while officials began to see the missionaries as meddlesome or even subversive. As a contemporary Russian sinologist observed: "Little by little Chinese became convinced that no respectable man could possibly be a Christian."[22]

Although there were missionaries in much of China, they seemed to be particularly intrusive in Shandong. Jesuits had been active there in the early seventeenth century, and after the Middle Kingdom was officially opened to Christian proselytization in the 1840s the province became home to a variety of French Catholics, Scottish Presbyterians, English Baptists, and American Congregationalists as well as Bishop Johann Baptist von Anzer's militantly aggressive German Catholic Society of the Divine Word, the S.V.D. (it was the murder of two S.V.D. priests that had led to the seizure of Kiaochow). In this atmosphere of territorial violations, economic dislocation, hostility to Christianity, and gentry xenophobia, Shandong's masses readily concluded that the foreign devils were behind the natural calamities that befell their province in the late 1890s. The "Righteous and Harmonious Fists" had little difficulty attracting recruits to their ranks with proclamations such as the one found by a Russian diplomat in Port Arthur:

> Three times on the night of the fourth day of the fourth moon Prince Qing had the following dream: God came to him and said that, by the Almighty Creator's wishes, Chinese must not go over either to Catholicism or to other Christian beliefs . . . otherwise they will be severely punished. The spread of Catholicism and other forms of Christianity are very harmful and untrue, and they must be stopped and eliminated throughout China.
>
> Therefore we have imposed this divine sanction: The snows and the rains have ceased. God has sent eight million heavenly warriors to earth, to protect the Chinese people and help them expel all foreigners. Every misfortune will be imposed on those who do not obey this notice, as well as on their ancestors.[23]

*T*he Boxers first became troublesome in spring 1898, when their members began assaulting Chinese Christians in western Shandong. At first they attracted little notice on Peking's Legation Street. Diplomats had long ago become inured to reports of violence against their coreligionists in the countryside. Aside from the Catholic French, most representatives tended to shrug off such outrages as one of China's many quotidian hazards.[24] Besides, the disturbances in Shandong tended to involve native converts rather than Europeans.

For Mikhail Giers at the Russian mission such matters were doubly irrelevant, since the Orthodox Church had never really joined the Western competition for Chinese souls.[25] At any rate, the new minister had more pressing concerns: the endless negotiations involving his government's activities in Manchuria, resistance to encroachments by the other powers into Russia's northern Chinese sphere, and his intense efforts to restore St. Petersburg's standing at the Qing court.[26]

The legations did take note when the Boxers murdered their first foreigner, a British missionary, in December 1899. Several governments pressed the Zongli Yamen to quash the organization.[27] Giers refused to join these complaints, reasoning that they were merely excuses to exact more concessions from the Chinese government.[28] When some of the powers carried out a naval demonstration off the fortress of Dagu in February to underscore their concerns, Russian warships did not participate. As Giers commented: "It is not in our interest to take part in the protests of the other powers. Russia's goal in the Orient differs fundamentally from the politics of the European governments."[29]

By spring 1900, the rising had spread well beyond Shandong province. In April Boxers were already disrupting life on the outskirts of Peking. Like its southeastern neighbor, Zhili also proved to be fertile ground for the rebellious group, with its large Christian population, the foreign enclaves in Peking and the port of Tianjin, and the railways and telegraphs that cut across the province.[30]

Another reason the Boxers were able to move northward with such ease

"It's boiling over!"—A typical example of Russian schadenfreude at the foreigners' predicament in Peking during the Boxer rising of 1900, as drawn for *Novoe Vremia* (labels added).

was the reluctance among many mandarins to resist them. Although officially proscribed as a "heterodox sect," the insurgents found much sympathy at Cixi's court, which largely shared their rabid hatred of the foreigners. Imperial decrees banning the troublemakers alternated with indications of the government's favor. At times even the dowager empress appeared to look upon the Boxers with a benevolent eye.[31] Western complaints only seemed to intensify Cixi's fondness for the rebels, and in May her officials actually considered recruiting them into the militia.[32]

In early May news of increasing Boxer activity in the capital itself began to alarm the small Western community in the Legation Quarter.[33] When diplomats met on May 7 to discuss the situation, Giers now supported summoning a modest contingent of troops from the nearby port of Tianjin to supplement the missions' guards. He did so reluctantly, however, and anguished about the consequences. "In my opinion," he wrote Muravev, "the prospect of such an extreme step is one of the most serious, if not the most serious, dangers of the current situation."[34] Meanwhile, the Russian envoy continued his own diplomacy, trying to convince moderates at the Zongli Yamen that only decisive action against the rebels would forestall intervention by the powers.[35] On May 14, Giers told the Chinese ministers:

> I stand outside of the whole conflict. But because our relations are the very best, and since our two empires both operate under an autocratic government, I can only hope that China will restore order by itself. For were the other powers to intervene, China would suffer far greater calamities than the one being caused by the Boxer uprising.[36]

Although Europeans fretted about their own physical safety, Russians were still relatively sanguine. A Finance Ministry official wrote a friend back home: "The disorders in this country do not affect us. Don't believe the newspapers, which repeat the false British and German reports."[37] Nevertheless, the situation in Peking worsened steadily. On May 21, Boxers murdered two more British missionaries, and the following day severed the only railway to the city. Throughout the capital, walls were plastered with posters calling upon the citizenry to expel all foreigners and Christians. And it became evident that the insurgency's supporters had the upper hand in Cixi's court.

Giers became concerned as well. When Boxers torched an Orthodox church in the countryside and menaced the venerable Ecclesiastical Mission northeast of the Forbidden City, he understood that his countrymen were not exempt from their xenophobic fury. Resigned, he informed Muravev on May 27: "The role of the diplomats in Peking is over, and matters must now be turned over to the admirals. Only the speedy arrival of a strong force can save the foreigners here."[38] Two days later, Dmitrii Pokotilov, who managed the local branch of the Russo-Chinese Bank, wired that the Russian legation was under siege.[39] It was the last cable from

Peking that would reach St. Petersburg for a while. Within hours the only remaining telegraph link to the outside world was cut.[40]

The events in China aroused little outrage in the Russian press. "What a cruel irony this confrontation is for the Europeans now, after they condemned the Middle Kingdom's millennial somnolence for so many years," Prince Meshcherskii sniggered.[41] Newspapers had no compassion for the foreigners who suffered the wrath of the Boxers. *Novoe Vremia*'s Soré often poked fun at their predicament in his cartoons, and one of the paper's writers argued: "If we examine China, and consider what the Jesuits, preachers, and merchants have wrought there, it is not hard to understand why the Chinese joined together and took up arms. . . . Europe is paying the price in China for its sins."[42]

The rapacity of the "capitalist powers" was a common theme among conservatives and liberals alike. One leading editorial writer, Vlas Dorosevich, pressed this point in a highly polemical piece in the progressive daily *Rossiia*. Describing a trip to China, he quoted an acquaintance, who told him: "Did you know that colonial troops like to go on a 'Chinaman hunt'? . . . In the colonies, they hunt people much more often than tigers." Dorosevich condemned "a whole army of missionaries," whose preaching did more harm than good and disrupted people's lives. There was also strong criticism for the opium dealers, merchants, and factory owners, "who come from London and Paris to China, where they live like princes by exploiting the Chinese." Dorosevich indignantly concluded:

> [The Boxer] rising is an outcry of horrible, unbearable pain, whose origins are in Europe, which has plunged its filthy, greedy claws into China. And these filthy claws of exploitation we call the benevolent hand of Civilization. Don't fool yourselves! Europe is lying when it calls this supposed need to shed blood as a "war for Civilization." No. This is a war for exploitation. And no "Boxers," no "Society of Harmonious Fists," . . . no corrupt mandarins can rightfully be accused for this war. We must really blame the dirty paws of the European gentlemen, evil, cruel, treating people like dogs.[43]

To the editorialists, the Chinese grievances seemed entirely justified. Like the Boers battling the British in the Transvaal, the Boxers were characterized as patriots who were fighting for their freedom against exploitative colonial powers.[44] The journalist Aleksandr Amfitreatov invoked a metaphor closer to home: "What is happening [in China] is really a people's war. [As Russians] we cannot deny the great significance of people's wars: In 1812 we won a people's war against Europe and crossed its territory to the very capital of the world . . . Paris."[45] As tsarist troops joined the other powers to save the legations, another commentator reminded his readers who Russia's true foes were: "So, you see, the Chinese are not our enemies; [our real enemies are] those countries that try to cause enmity between us and our neighbors."[46]

These sentiments were shared by many of the tsar's senior officials. Even Nicholas himself never condemned the Chinese. While he worried about the fate of his envoy in Peking, the emperor blamed Catholic missionaries, rather than the Boxers, for being at "the root of all this evil." Along with Western commerce, it was they who had "awakened China's hatred toward the Europeans," by exploiting them "in the Holy name of Christ."[47]

Sergei Witte predictably opposed harsh measures against the Boxers. In his opinion, Russia's occupation of the Liaodong Peninsula had contributed to China's xenophobic revolt. The only way for St. Petersburg to salvage its interests, the finance minister reasoned, was to refrain from further aggression on the Pacific. The best tack was to support the Qing and to restrain the Europeans. Besides, the monarchy simply could not afford the risk of another Eastern adventure. Reminding the tsar of the unrest that had disrupted the empire after the Crimean and Turkish imbroglios some decades earlier, Witte advised him that "for the sake of the domestic situation . . . it is exceedingly important to avoid any actions that might lead to complications abroad."[48]

In sharp contrast to his position three years earlier, when he had championed taking Port Arthur, the foreign minister now also favored a soft line in the Far East. As the crisis came to a head, Muravev devoted his energies to preserving his government's special relationship with Peking. His pronouncements repeatedly stressed the centuries of peaceful relations between the two autocracies. Like Witte, Count Muravev resisted military intervention as long as possible. When in early June the count could no longer reasonably abstain from sending troops to the region, he instructed Admiral Evgenii Alekseev, the Russian commander in the Far East: "You must bear in mind that our units are on Chinese territory without any hostile intentions toward our traditional friend on the eastern border. It is entirely in our interests, as soon as the disorders have been put down, to reestablish the friendliest relations possible."[49]

Yet Muravev did not escape criticism for having bungled in China. Witte had never forgiven him for tricking the tsar into seizing Port Arthur and Dalien. While he supported the count's current position, the finance minister saw a perfect opportunity to lambaste his colleague for the consequences of the earlier action.[50] The most devastating rebuke, however, came from his chief. Muravev had long prided himself on his ability to retain the emperor's confidence and affection, and Nicholas generally backed the broad lines of his policies in China. As the Boxers were laying siege to the legations in Peking, however, Nicholas faulted the count for having minimized the seriousness of the unrest there. He was particularly displeased that Muravev had not ordered the mission's staff to evacuate the capital earlier in the year, while there was still time. When the foreign minister died suddenly on the night of June 8, 1900, after a heated argument with Witte over the Chinese question, it was believed that somehow his demise was linked to the events on the Pacific.[51]

Muravev's successor, Count Vladimir Nikolaevich Lamsdorf, made no major changes in his approach to the Far Eastern crisis. If Muravev had been the archetypal courtier, Lamsdorf was the consummate functionary. Unlike many of his predecessors to the post, Vladimir Nikolaevich had not been stationed abroad. In fact, Lamsdorf never even seemed to leave the ministry's building on Palace Square, where he kept both his office and his apartment. "A strange-looking man," "very pale," and "exquisitely perfumed," the count was gossiped to have a predilection for the handsome young nobles who had recently been recruited into the chancellery.[52] It was more likely that he simply had no private life. Like Akaky Akakevich, Gogol's caricature of the faceless bureaucrat in his short story "The Overcoat," the new foreign minister lived solely for his career in the imperial civil service.[53] Vladimir Nikolaevich's credo, as recited in his diary, was simple: "I ask for *nothing*. I wish only to act in a manner in which I can be most useful to the interests of my service. . . . It is not my place to judge whether I can be useful, nor where or in what capacity; just decide everything and I will follow my assignment with gratitude and the best goodwill."[54]

A French diplomat once described Lamsdorf as a foreign minister "à la russe." By this he meant that the count had no say in determining policy and was responsible "solely for Russian diplomacy, and adapting it to the former."[55] In the case of China, Lamsdorf accepted that the decisions were made by Witte, and for the first three years of his appointment he would almost entirely subordinate his will to that of the finance minister.[56]

There were advocates of a tougher stance in the Orient. Colonel Wogack, the Russian military attaché in China, had been sending alarming reports about the rising since early 1899.[57] At Port Arthur, Admiral Alekseev thoroughly disdained the appeasement of the diplomats and was eager to teach the Chinese a lesson.[58] The war minister also advocated firmness. In contrast to the officials at the Choristers' Bridge, General Kuropatkin argued that the special relationship with the Qing was no more. After the dowager's coup in 1898, Peking had become hostile to all foreigners, including Russia. "Our former peaceful and friendly relations with our Asiatic neighbor changed several years ago," Kuropatkin explained to the tsar. "The [Boxer] movement . . . has a patriotic and anti-Christian character and is directed against us just as much as against the other powers." Russia, he concluded, was now involved in a conflict with all of China: "From a political perspective, it has been useful for us to continue asserting that we are fighting a rebellious army [in China] . . . but in fact we are waging war with the government of China."[59] Not all Russian generals shared these views. Vannovskii, the former war minister, strongly disagreed with his successor's opinions, and he accused Kuropatkin of cynically fabricating the war so that he might "upgrade his George's Cross."[60]

As the crisis deepened in summer 1900, the tsar tended to support those ministers who counseled moderation in China. The British embassy observed: "The policy followed has . . . been directly inspired by the peaceful disposition of the Emperor, and initiated by His Majesty with the warm support of M. Witte and Count Lamsdorff, who have thus formed a potent party of peace, and whose policy the powerful military party has strongly but so far ineffectually opposed."[61] Nicholas would eventually sanction military participation in the intervention against the Boxers and took pride in the performance of his troops during the Chinese campaign.[62] Yet the emperor repeatedly pointed out that his government had a special mission in the Middle Kingdom. "Russia and the other powers have entirely different goals in the Far East," he wrote his mother. "What's good for us is bad for the rest and doesn't suit them; this has long been apparent."[63]

*N*icholas was forced to intervene in the Boxer crisis against his will. When on May 25 the British minister, Sir Claude MacDonald, took the unprecedented step of asking Giers to supply 4,000 troops from the Port Arthur garrison, his superiors in St. Petersburg felt obligated to comply.[64] A few days later, Russian sailors joined a British-led multinational force as it set out from Tianjin in a vain effort to reach the beleaguered legations in the Chinese capital.[65] In early June, Russian ships joined five other navies in seizing Dagu's fortifications at the mouth of the Peiho River, and during much of that month Siberian infantry played a leading role in the battle for Tianjin.[66]

Every action was accompanied by solemn pronouncements that Russia bore no malice toward the Qing. The speech given by Vice Admiral Iakov Hildebrandt to sailors of the *Petropavlovsk* as they were about to set off for Dagu in late May was typical:

> Lads! Not far from us . . . an uprising of Chinese rebels has broken out, which threatens the capital of the Bogdykhan. . . . His majesty the emperor . . . sends his troops to Peking . . . to protect his representative to the emperor of China, Russian subjects, as well as all foreigners, and to help the Chinese government, whose army cannot subdue the rebels on its own. So you are not being ordered to China for war, but in the interests of peace.[67]

After the failure of the first attempt to reach the missions, Nicholas dithered for weeks about whether his forces should join a second international expedition to Peking. He agreed to do so only when news reached him in mid-June that Boxers had murdered the new German minister, Baron Clemens von Ketteler.[68] Even then the tsar and his foreign minister agonized over who should command this force. Kuropatkin's suggestion that Admiral Alekseev have that honor was deemed inappropriate, given Russia's aspirations to a special relationship with China. Yet, when Tokyo volunteered one of its generals, Lamsdorf was horrified. Ultimately, a German officer, Field Marshal Count Alfred von Waldersee, turned out to be the least objectionable man for the job.[69]

Meanwhile, St. Petersburg continued its own diplomacy. After the telegraph was cut, negotiating with the government in Peking became impossible. Li Hongzhang, however, reemerged from semibanishment in Canton and was drafted to offer his services as intermediary to the Qing. In a cable to Witte on June 13, Li proposed to intercede with the dowager empress to suppress the Boxers, if the Russian tsar helped restrain the Europeans.[70] Nicholas declared this idea "very desirable," and Witte promptly instructed Prince Ukhtomskii to join the "old man" in China and ordered the Russian navy to place a cruiser at Li's disposal for the journey to Peking.[71] In the event, the initiative came to nothing, since the other powers were skeptical of the notoriously pro-Russian official. By the time Li arrived in the Chinese capital in mid-September, Western troops had already been there for more than a month.[72]

In the early afternoon of August 1, a multinational force finally rescued the legations. Comprising mainly Japanese, Russian, British, and American units, the 20,000-man expedition had taken 10 days to battle its way from Tianjin. Ironically, the first troops to reach to the besieged compound were not Europeans but sepoys of the 1st Sikh and 7th Rajput Infantry Regiments. The siege had lasted nearly two months and took 76 foreign lives, including 5 Russians. Damage to the Russian compound was relatively light, although the Russo-Chinese Bank's building and the Ecclesiastical Mission were destroyed. With the capture of Peking, Cixi fled westward with her court to Xi'an, the capital of Shaanxi Province. It did not take long thereafter for the Boxer rising in Zhili to come to an end.[73]

The attention of the foreign powers now turned to exacting suitable compensation from the Qing for the troubles. For more than a year complicated negotiations were carried out between the so-called Allies, Li Hongzhang, and the exiled Qing court, resulting in the "Boxer Protocol" of August 1901. Its terms were draconian, dictating the execution of leading antiforeign officials, severe restrictions on Chinese defenses, monuments to commemorate the European victims, and the replacement of the Zongli Yamen with a Western-style foreign ministry. The most burdensome provision was a massive 450-million-tael indemnity—more than twice that imposed by the Japanese five years earlier and more than four times the annual revenues of the central government.[74]

In the months following the capture of Peking, Giers continued to exasperate his colleagues by his reluctance to punish the Chinese.[75] On August 12, St. Petersburg issued a statement explaining that its only goals had been to protect Russian subjects and to help the Chinese government to restore order.[76] Meanwhile, tsarist officials expressed strong disapproval of Field Marshal Waldersee's sorties into the countryside during the fall, and they were the first to withdraw their troops from the capital. As for the talks themselves, Nicholas remarked that "the Europeans have drunk enough

Chinese blood already." The tsar's instructions to his envoy were clear: "I want Giers to lessen his participation in the collective efforts by the Europeans to impose such severe conditions on the Chinese. It's time for us to separate ourselves from the Western powers in the Far East."[77] Within weeks of the siege's end, the minister fulfilled the emperor's wishes quite literally, by temporarily moving his legation to Tianjin on the grounds that its presence in Peking was dilatory as long as Cixi's court remained in Xi'an. Robert Hart muttered, "The Russians are playing their own game."[78]

St. Petersburg's dovish stance infuriated the West. Britain's prime minister, Lord Salisbury, at one point felt that "Russia, not China, seems to me to be the greatest danger."[79] Kaiser Wilhelm II dismissed Lamsdorf's statements as "rubbish any self-respecting secretary from one of our legations wouldn't dream of writing."[80] Even a French diplomat charged that, "if it did not directly provoke [the Boxers, Russia] has perhaps encouraged them. It well knows how to benefit from the situation."[81]

*T*hroughout the Far Eastern troubles of 1900, Russia kept its distance from the other powers. When unrest was first reported at the start of the year, its diplomats dismissed the news as alarmist and refused to consider expressing its displeasure to the Qing. As the disorders grew into a full-scale rising and the legation came under siege that summer, the tsar hesitated, temporized, and only participated in the multinational march on Peking with the greatest reluctance. During the fall and into the following year, Russia's envoy pleaded with his colleagues to soften their demands for retribution from the Qing.

Early in August 1900, shortly after foreign troops had stormed Peking, Count Lamsdorf directed his department's legal expert, Fedor Martens, to compose a memorandum with his thoughts about the Boxer rebellion. Martens was one of the leading authorities on international law and had published a standard textbook about the subject. From time to time he also wrote about pressing diplomatic issues of the day. These pieces, such as "England and Russia in Central Asia," "Russia and China," and "The African Conference in Berlin," were often published abroad, and many considered them to be authoritative statements of the Russian Foreign Ministry.[82]

Martens duly submitted a note, "Europe and China," which formed the basis of Lamsdorf's circular of August 12. While it said nothing particularly new, the document provided the clearest insight into official tsarist thinking about the recent events. As its author explained, the siege of the legations was only a minor aspect of the problem. The real issue was the endless, "brazen exploitation of the Chinese by the Europeans." For decades now "the European-American peoples" had been destroying the Middle Kingdom with its opium and missionary activity. Small wonder then that mandarins and Chinese patriots had played leading roles in the "people's war." "Russia's relationship with China has been entirely different," Martens stressed. "To [the Europeans] China is a colony, which must be exploited in all respects. To Russia, China is a great neighboring state, which has every right to an independent existence."[83]

Tsarist thinking about the Boxer rising, as illustrated in the memorandum by Fedor Martens, was condemned abroad as pure propaganda. Yet to dismiss it as such would be too simplistic. Russians were entirely right when they pointed out that they exported neither opium nor missionaries to China. Furthermore, conservative officials could easily sympathize with the plight of another autocracy being polluted by Western ideas and goods.

With the possible exception of Li Hongzhang, there was no sympathy in Peking any more for an alliance with the Romanov tsar. In St. Petersburg, however, the idea of a special relationship remained very much alive. Russian policy throughout the Boxer crisis was a determined effort to revert to the line adopted five years earlier during the talks at Shimonoseki, when China's northern neighbor had offered to be the Qing's guardian. At the same time, there were other, powerful motives for keeping on friendly terms with China.

CHAPTER ELEVEN

Manchurian Quicksand

*B*eyond the Great Wall, on the northeastern edge of the Chinese pale, lies Manchuria. It is huge, covering an area roughly equal to France and Great Britain combined. Nineteenth-century Europeans knew the region as the ancestral homeland of the Manchus. Distant ethnic cousins of the Mongols, in the seventeenth century they had swept southward to dethrone the Ming emperor and proclaim their own, establishing the Qing dynasty.

Chinese called Manchuria "outside the Eastern Pass," or "the northeastern provinces," referring to the aggregation of Fengtien (now Liaoning), Jirin, and Heilongjiang. Unlike Europeans, they traditionally saw it not as a distinct geographic entity but as a frontier, a periphery inhabited by increasingly barbaric tribes, more or less subject to the Son of Heaven. This view more accurately reflected the varied population, which at the turn of the century included Han Chinese in the Liaodong Peninsula in the south, Mongols, Manchus, and Koreans in the stretch bounded by Inner Mongolia and Korea, and, in the forests and mountains to the north, a number of different peoples, including the Daurs, Solons, Golds, and Giliaks.

Even at the height of the Qing dynasty, the northeastern provinces were a classic imperial borderland. The authority of the state diminished the farther one traveled northward, and with a population variously estimated at 6 million to 10 million around 1900 the region was much less densely peopled than the Chinese heartland.[1] Yet the lands also held many treasures. The mountains were rich in gold and fur-bearing animals. Valuable ginseng root abounded in Manchuria's forests, and pearl-bearing oysters inhabited its waters. The central plains were covered in fertile black soil, which received plenty of rain.[2]

Manchuria held a special place in the affections of the Qing, for whom it was their lineage's womb, "the place where the dragon rose."[3] In 1895, when Japanese troops occupied parts of the region after routing the Chinese, Shandong's patriotic governor Li Bengheng memorialized the throne:

The three eastern provinces are the places from which our dynasty issued. The frontier pass to this base and the capital are bound together. Moreover, the Imperial tombs are there; the comforts of the spirits of successive ancestors depends on them. Suddenly they are given over to a tribe of dogs and sheep. The Imperial spirits will certainly blush and not be at peace.[4]

Manchuria in 1903

By the nineteenth century Qing emperors largely neglected their north-eastern provinces. As with all of the Middle Kingdom's conquerors, the Manchus' priorities now lay with China proper.[5] Britain's seizure of tiny Hong Kong in 1841 had been much more traumatic to them than St. Petersburg's annexation of the vast Amur and Ussuri region on Manchuria's northern marches twenty years later. Peking's policy of the day was to treat the three provinces largely in defensive terms. The American sinologist Owen Lattimore explained that Manchuria was "a buffer region where the encroachment of another power would cause apprehension, but where the responsibility of occupation and government was by all means to be avoided, short of the most imperative necessity."[6]

The Qing's ambivalence toward their dynastic fatherland was shown by their demographic policy. Shortly after seizing Peking in 1644, the new dynasty began to build "Willow Palisades" to block Han Chinese migration to Manchuria. Actually a series of deep trenches lined by willow trees guarded by occasional garrisons, the line was meant to keep the Manchus' homeland ethnically pure by containing the historically Chinese population of the Liaodong Peninsula.

Like American efforts in the late twentieth century to fence off its southern border from illegal Mexican immigration, the effort failed. Over the next two hundred years, Chinese who sought a better life on the northern frontier crossed the divide with relative impunity. After 1860, however, worries that Russians would not stop at the Amur and Ussuri rivers led the Qing to abandon their exclusionary policy and consider opening Manchuria to Han settlers. By the 1890s much of the region was legally accessible to colonists from the rest of China.[7]

Concerns about St. Petersburg's intentions were not misplaced. Around 1900, Russians were already well established in Manchuria. During the four years after the finance minister won a concession to build a railway in the north, "Witte's kingdom" had flourished. Work on the Chinese Eastern Railway proceeded at a frantic pace, with more than 1,300 kilometers of the projected 2,500-kilometer line already on the ground by summer 1900.[8] The CER's headquarters, which were initially set up in an old distillery at the intersection of the Sungari River and the future track in spring 1898, soon became the center of a boomtown. Despite its Manchurian name of Harbin, the new city was largely Russian in appearance and character.[9]

Meanwhile, a maritime branch of the railway and the Odessa-based Volunteer Fleet, also controlled by the Finance Ministry, dominated shipping in Manchuria. Other CER subsidiaries began to exploit the region's lumber and coal.[10] At the southern tip of the Liaodong Peninsula, near the new tsarist naval station of Port Arthur, Witte had equally ambitious plans to turn the harbor of Dalien, now officially renamed Dalnii ("Far away"), into a major commercial entrepôt.[11] To protect it all, the finance minister commanded an ever-expanding security force. Largely staffed by former Siberian troops, on the eve of the Boxer rising its numbers had already grown to

5,000 men. Wags dubbed the unit "Matilda's Guards," after Witte's wife, Matilda Ivanovna.[12]

The huge scope of the finance minister's Manchurian projects and the colossal sums involved—in the first three years of its existence, the CER had already spent more than 100 million rubles—suggested that his countrymen planned to stay.[13] The American Senator Albert Beveridge, who traveled to the area in 1901 and soon thereafter wrote an account of his trip, remarked:

> It is all quite "temporary" of course. . . . But the Slav root strikes quickly into new soil, and having struck, history tells us that, usually, it stays. . . . Great railways through the heart of Manchuria . . . brick and stone buildings, homes of officials, cottages of peasants, the blond wives . . . and, above all, Russian churches, raising their semi-Oriental spires to heaven in the centre of every Russian town, point to the permanency of Russian occupation.[14]

Furthermore, it was obvious that Witte's enterprise was more than purely commercial. General Aleksei Kuropatkin reminded the tsar: "Despite the name 'Chinese-Eastern,' depite the external appearance of a commercial enterprise, despite the participation of some Chinese on its board, and, finally, despite the fact that its guards masquerade in uniforms adorned with dragons, everyone in Manchuria and China clearly understands that this is a Russian government railway."[15]

While more sophisticated citizens of St. Petersburg and Moscow considered Manchuria to be the boondocks, to other Russians it held the promise of an East Asian Klondike. Railway engineers, government clerks, army veterans, workers, peasants, gold hunters, adventurers, and "café singers" all made their way to the east in search of better pay and the excitement of life on the frontier.[16] Many of those who stayed home took pride in what some began to call a "colony."[17]

Sergei Witte's lavish spending on his Far Eastern adventure also benefited the indigenous population. Although far below those paid to European laborers, the wages earned by native laborers working on the CER were generous by local standards.[18] From their employers' perspective the workers had the added advantage of being far less troublesome than the obstreperous Russian proletarian, with the latter's irksome notions of strikes and worker's rights.[19] Chinese from as far as Zhifu and Shandong trekked north to make a living on the railway, which in 1900 employed close to 100,000 local men.[20] Witte courted native goodwill. He ordered his railway to treat its Chinese employees well and to respect shrines and tombs in the area.[21] Foreign travelers were often struck by the cameraderie between Russians and Asians working on the CER.[22]

Relations with Chinese officials proved more difficult. Although the CER's dealings with the local administration were relatively good, especially when it took care to "interest" them "materially," Peking was rather less enthusiastic about the venture.[23] Negotiations in the capital between the Russian minister and the Zongli Yamen for various details involving the railway and other Russian ventures in Manchuria inevitably became mired in evasions, delays, and obstructions. There were also periodic fears that the Qing planned to flood the provinces with Han Chinese to frustrate any Russian annexation.[24] When in November 1899 Mikhail Giers, the Russian envoy, told the Yamen of his intentions to send a consular official to Heilongjiang and Jirin, one of its ministers acidly inquired whether that individual's title would be "governor."[25]

*T*he Qing's growing hostility to Russia's presence in Manchuria came to a head during the Boxer rising of 1900. As unrest erupted in Peking that spring, at first it seemed that the three northeastern provinces would be spared. Despite occasional brushes with the notorious "Red Beards," bandits who had long been the scourge of Manchuria's countryside, the CER's guards were still largely kept busy with the more mundane police work of any frontier.

The local population remained generally well disposed toward the Russians and seemed content to make a living from the new interlopers.[26] The Reverend Dugald Christie, a Presbyterian missionary who had been living in the Manchu capital of Mukden (now Shenyang) since 1882, remembered that at the time "in Manchuria all was quiet, and very little anti-foreign feeling existed. The Russian railway and the presence of the Russians were sullenly accepted as facts which could be neither denied nor altered."[27] As late as June 1, when Boxers were already besieging Peking's legations less than 600 kilometers to the east, the Scottish minister was enjoying a peaceful church picnic on a river bank near Mukden.[28]

The three provinces' governors-general also initially opposed the Boxers. Even after the allied naval assault on Dagu on June 8, when the Empress Dowager Cixi issued a decree ordering them to arms against the foreigners, they prevaricated.[29] Meanwhile, Sergei Witte was doing his best to keep the conflict from spreading to Manchuria. In mid-June he authorized generous credits for the CER's chief engineer to distribute at his discretion among the local administration.[30] Aside from augmenting his guards, the finance minister preferred diplomacy for the time being. For much of the month, he engaged in a war of memoranda to the tsar with General Kuropatkin, who was much more anxious about the threat to Russian lives and property in the region.[31] Witte repeatedly advised Nicholas that intervention would only "harm the good relations" that still existed between his subjects and Chinese in Manchuria.[32]

Toward the end of June, the situation began to deteriorate. In the southern province of Fengtien, where many men from Shandong were working on the CER, Boxer emissaries began to find a sympathetic hearing. Unlike the area around Peking, however, the deciding factor here was the Qing central government itself, which was now insisting that its governors drive out the Russians by force. Fengtien's weak-willed governor-general, Zengqi, eventually gave the insurgents his halfhearted support, but his radical lieutenant, Jinchang, proved to be much more zealous. On June 22 Jinchang arrested his superior and took command of a joint force of regular soldiers and Boxers. Over the next few days reports of attacks all along the CER's southern line began to pour into the headquarters at Harbin. Within a week, Aleksandr Iugovich, the chief engineer, ordered his staff to evacuate the railway, and by June 27 Harbin itself was under siege and its telegraph out of service.[33]

Witte now knew he had no alternative. On June 26 he reluctantly gave General Kuropatkin his consent to send troops into Manchuria against the Boxers. That day, a contingent of Cossacks, infantry, and artillery under the command of Major General V. V. Sakharov set off by steamer and barge up the Sungari River from Khabarovsk to relieve Harbin. It would take another three weeks to organize a larger force for the overland invasion of Manchuria.

July was a month of uncertainty, confusion, and panic among the Russians in Siberia. While their compatriots in Manchuria survived the disturbances relatively unscathed, pogroms within Russia killed hundreds of Chinese.[34] The worst excesses took place at the town of Blagoveshchensk on the Amur River. On July 4 the local commander, made jittery by artillery bombardment from the Manchurian bank, ordered the Chinese population to cross the Amur, which at that point was about 200 meters wide and more than 2 meters deep. More than 3,000 men, women, and children entered the fast-flowing waters. Qing soldiers on the opposite bank, who mistook them for a tsarist assault, and the Russians themselves both opened fire on the struggling mass. There are no reliable statistics about how many made it to the other side.[35]

In mid-July, more than 100,000 troops from the Siberian and Amur Military Districts crossed into Manchuria in five separate columns. The Russians sliced through the three provinces like knives through soft butter. General Sakharov's flotilla lifted the siege of Harbin on July 22. Three weeks later, on August 15, Cossacks under the command of Major General P. K. Rennenkampf stormed Qigihar, the fortified capital of Heilongjiang, and on September 18 Lieutenant General D. I. Subbotich marched unopposed through the gates of Mukden. The operation had taken less than three months and cost about 200 Russian lives.

Lacking proper leadership, weapons, and support from the local populace and provincial governors, the Chinese were easily crushed. At times it seemed that the commanders of the five Russian units spent more energy bickering among themselves than defeating the Boxers.[36] When it was all over, grateful generals liberally distributed George's Crosses among the participants, priests celebrated Te Deums, and Nicholas expressed his relief that the fighting was behind him.[37] In fact, Manchuria had only begun to give the tsar headaches.

*I*f invading Manchuria had been easy for Russia, evacuating it would prove more difficult. The situation was strikingly reminiscent of Russia's march into the Ili Valley in 1871. Then as now, the tsar had ordered his troops onto Chinese soil to quell disorders that threatened to spill across the border. Once in place, generals worried about the chaos that might again erupt after their departure. Russian diplomats of the day were eager to stay in the Qing's good graces, but others had a visceral objection to yielding territory won in battle.[38] As they would in 1900, many officers then recalled Nicholas I's promise that, "where once the Russian flag has flown, never shall it be lowered." It had taken ten years to return the Ili Valley to China.

From the first, Nicholas II's ministers assured the world that their country's troops had every intention of leaving the three provinces in the near future. Already on August 12, 1900, Count Lamsdorf asked his ambassadors to distribute a circular to foreign governments explaining the occupation as a temporary measure, which would end as soon as life was back to normal. "Russia has no designs of territorial acquisitions in China," he pledged.[39] Two days later, the finance minister instructed Iugovich to make a similar proclamation to the local population in Manchuria.[40]

Yet Russian officials were also eager to win something in return for handing the region back to China. Although the tsarist army sustained remarkably light casualties, the operation had been expensive, and the railroad claimed extensive damage at the hands of the Boxers. More important, officials wanted to be sure popular unrest would never again pose a threat to Russian lives and property.

Opinions in St. Petersburg about the Manchurian question followed three lines of thought. Men like Count Lamsdorf and Sergei Witte were embarrassed about the invasion and hoped to restore the status quo as soon as possible. Opposing them, a number of army and navy officers adopted a highly aggressive stance. War Minister Kuropatkin, though, took a more moderate position than such subordinates.

The finance minister's attitude was clear. As Witte would repeat in his letters and at ministerial conferences over the next three years, Russia had to regain Peking's trust. "It is in our interests above all to restore a government that is capable of reestablishing order [in China]," he advised the tsar in a memorandum on August 11, 1900. "Instead of exacting harsh demands, we must give it [our] moral and material support. This is how we will make the dynasty dependent upon us."[41]

Reviving an argument he had advanced three years earlier when trying to convince his sovereign not to seize Port Arthur, Witte warned that annexing Manchuria would only encourage the other powers to slice away at the melon:

> The signal will be sounded for Germany to expand its possessions in Shandong, Britain will take the Yangzi River valley and other places, France will seize more

in the south, and other nations will want their own share. The most dangerous
of these will be Japan, which may well occupy Korea. All of this will set off the
breakup of China.[42]

This was a recipe for disaster, Witte felt. Just as Russia's premature grab of
the Liaodong Peninsula had angered the Middle Kingdom's government
and people, helping to incite the Boxer rebellion, so too would new incursions guarantee hostility for years to come: "Instead of our familiar neighbor . . . in Asia we will find ourselves bordering on a mighty and aggressive
power. Then our troubles will really begin."[43] Besides, the finance minister
reminded his sovereign, there were more pressing matters at home. Given
current economic problems in Russia itself, it would be better to keep the
Far Eastern border at peace.

Witte by no means felt that Russia should abandon its Chinese enterprises. On the contrary, he emphasized that St. Petersburg must maintain
its dominion over the three provinces, but through indirect means: "By dis-
arming Manchuria, intersecting it by Russian railways, [and] guarding [the
CER] with Russian troops."[44] History had shown, Witte lectured the tsar,
that by patiently waiting for the natural course of events the Russian empire was destined to continue growing in Asia. Premature territorial grabs
were invariably counterproductive.

Count Lamsdorf, never a particularly forceful figure, entirely deferred to
Witte on Far Eastern matters.[45] Yet, whereas Witte had stressed the financial
burden and the damage to relations with China of a continued occupation
of Manchuria, the foreign minister was more worried about angering
Tokyo, which was becoming increasingly militant about Russian intentions.
In a letter to Kuropatkin in March 1902, the count wrote that "it would be
advisable for us to evacuate Manchuria sooner, if possible, so as not to . . .
provoke war with Japan at a time of heightened national pride, self-confidence, and self-sacrifice."[46]

Meanwhile, among military men a hard line was emerging. Senior officers in the Far East were particularly scrappy. Many had begun their careers
during the reign of Alexander II in Turkestan, where it had been somewhat
of a tradition for local commanders to seize territory for the tsar on their
own initiative. Already within days of the invasion of Manchuria, upon
crossing the Amur River at Blagoveshchensk, Lieutenant General K. N.
Gribskii declared the river's Chinese side to be Russian territory as well. His
commander enthusiastically approved the action and wired the war minister: "Fifty years ago Captain Nevelskoi raised the Russian flag at the mouth
of the Amur on its right bank. . . . Now, after hard fighting, we have taken
possession of the left bank." Kuropatkin did not concur.[47]

When one officer, Ivan Balashev, wrote a memorandum to the tsar in
1902 urging him not to evacuate Manchuria, his rationale was straight out
of Przhevalskii. Russia's occupation was fully justified, he argued, both on
the grounds of "the timeless logic of things" and the perfidy and weakness

of China: "No one ever doubted that Manchuria must ultimately belong to Russia."[48] Anyway, Balashev maintained, the local population rightly understood its destiny. "The Manchurians," he wrote, ". . . like their Mongolian neighbors and all other Asiatic tribes, are firmly convinced that fate has ordained them, sooner or later, to come under the rule of 'THE WHITE TSAR' . . . [who] will satisfy their vague yearnings for truth and justice on Earth."[49]

The most prominent hawk was Admiral Evgenii Alekseev. Based at Port Arthur, the naval officer had authority not only over the Pacific Fleet but over the garrison on the Liaodong Peninsula. He also commanded Russian forces in the Far East during the Boxer rebellion. Short, stout, with a generous black beard and a domineering personality, Alekseev was a controversial figure.[50] His mercurial temperament, ambition, and rumors that he was the illegitimate son of Alexander II earned him the dislike of many contemporaries, especially Sergei Witte, who regarded him as a dangerous rival in Russia's Far East. "A man with the mentality of a sly Armenian rug dealer . . . that egregious careerist Admiral Alekseev," the finance minister sniffed.[51] Lamsdorf also distrusted him, fretting to a friend about "our new Pacific commander, who has an unfortunate propensity for adventures."[52] The count was particularly offended at Alekseev's habit of bypassing the Russian minister in Peking and meddling in Far Eastern diplomacy.[53]

Over the next three years, Alekseev would emerge as the most forceful advocate for retaining Manchuria. He often argued that quitting the region would only make Russia more vulnerable to another rebellion as well as to an increasingly aggressive Japan.[54] Yet, if the admiral seemed to worry about defending his position on the Pacific, the international repercussions of a prolonged occupation did not bother him in the least. As he wrote the war minister: "Despite their protests against our intention to retain Manchuria, they have long ago reconciled themselves to the matter."[55]

General Kuropatkin himself took an intermediate position on the Manchurian question. When the unrest first broke out, he strongly supported intervention, and he would come to oppose withdrawing the army prematurely. There were times when Kuropatkin was inclined to keep troops stationed in northern Manchuria, where the Chinese population was much smaller than in the southern province of Fengtien. Even then, however, he wavered between a full annexation of the north and making it a semi-independent vassal, like the Central Asian Khanate of Bokhara.[56]

The war minister's attitude was completely different from the brash confidence of such men as Admiral Alekseev. Kuropatkin had a much more pessimistic worldview and saw China not as an antiquated and degenerate Oriental empire ripe for Russian conquest, as did many of his officers. Instead, he viewed it as a potentially dangerous foe, whose millions, if roused, could swamp Russia's Far East in a "yellow tidal wave."[57]

In a note to the tsar at the start of the Russian invasion, Kuropatkin agreed with Witte that by taking Port Arthur St. Petersburg had contributed to the cause of the Boxer rising: "With this step we finally broke our venerable traditions, and in the eyes of the Chinese we became neighbors who deal with China at our pleasure and in the name of right substitute might."[58] Like Witte, he pressed for a strong presence along the CER: "We must act to ensure that a disarmed Manchuria, intersected by Russian railways and guarded by Russian troops, safely covered by the Amur Military District, would give this important Russian region the chance to develop quietly and peacefully." He allowed that "Manchuria can nevertheless entirely remain part of the Chinese state."[59] Unlike his colleague at the finance ministry, however, Kuropatkin was under no illusions about Peking's sentiments: "From a political perspective, it has been useful for us to continue asserting that we are fighting a rebellious army, but in fact we are waging war with the government of China, only without a formal declaration of war."[60]

There was also a very practical reason for not annexing Manchuria. During a conversation in summer 1900 with the French ambassador, Marquis de Montebello, Kuropatkin assured him that Russia would never retain the provinces, since it would open Siberia to a flood of Chinese migrants: "If this salutary frontier did not exist, and were Manchuria to become Russian territory, how would we prevent our new subjects from invading regions where we want to retain the purity of our race? What problems would we cause these millions with whom we have absolutely no racial affinity?"[61] As a determined advocate of Russifiying Finland and other European borderlands, the general hardly wanted to worry about assimilating peoples who were even more alien to his own countrymen. "Woe to us if we take on new subjects, having not yet integrated the minorities over which we already rule," he had warned the tsar earlier that year.[62]

*E*ven before the invasion of Manchuria was complete, St. Petersburg began negotiations with the Chinese government for handing back the region. A more pressing concern, however, was the administration of Manchuria during the occupation. On October 31, 1900, Witte, Lamsdorf, and Kuropatkin met to discuss the matter at the Black Sea resort of Yalta, where the three had joined the court for its traditional autumn holiday. Together they drafted the "Principles for Russian Control over Manchuria." Largely written by Kuropatkin, the document confirmed that the provinces were part of the Chinese empire. As long as Russian troops were stationed in the region, civilian authority would be restored to the local administration, but its power to police was strictly circumscribed.[63]

Meanwhile, on orders of Kuropatkin, Admiral Alekseev also began talks in October with Fengtien's governor, Zengqi, to establish a modus vivendi for the Russian occupation of his province. The agreement, which was signed on November 13, contained terms similar to the "Principles" drafted at Yalta and explicitly temporary in nature.[64] Yet Alekseev's impatience and bullying during the talks thoroughly alienated the Qing. Although Zengqi reluctantly put his seal to the pact, the court immediately disowned its governor and threatened to sack him.[65]

A reasonably accurate copy of the text, which was meant to be secret, was soon leaked to Dr. George Morrison of the *Times*, who wired it to London. His paper gleefully announced the "Manchurian Agreement" to the world in late December, conveniently neglecting to state that it was provisional. Because of the clause that provided for a Russian resident in Mukden with unspecified "general powers of control," the daily readily concluded that there were plans to turn Manchuria into a tsarist protectorate.[66]

British hackles had already been raised over a number of jurisdictional squabbles with the Russians in Zhili Province. The mysterious talks between Li Hongzhang and Prince Ukhtomskii and the fact that the Chinese minister in St. Petersburg had been the only foreign diplomat to be invited to Yalta that fall only further aroused London's suspicions. Finally, Englishmen as well as other foreigners were perturbed by Russia's declaration in mid-August that it would soon withdraw its troops from Peking. Lord Selborne, Britain's first lord of the admiralty, complained: "The Russian army people have indulged into a Saturnalia of lies . . . and dishonourable tricks." He added: "No one can prevent her from absorbing Manchuria."[67]

The power most disturbed by Russia's Asian ambitions was Japan. Along with Russia it had the strongest alien presence in the continent's northeast. By 1900, Tokyo's economic and political influence over Korea was unparalleled.[68] Although Witte had basically abandoned it to concentrate on Manchuria in 1898, other Russians still coveted the peninsula. Naval officers, including Admiral Alekseev, remained keen to win a station and almost succeeded in getting a lease to the southern port of Masampo in spring 1900. Japanese public opinion bristled at such incursions into what they felt to be their rightful sphere. After all, many reasoned, Russians should be content with Manchuria.

Russian diplomats in Tokyo were well aware of their hosts' sensitivities and hoped to conclude an agreement recognizing their government's dominance over Manchuria in return for giving Japan a free hand in Korea.[69] This had been a Japanese demand since the days after Shimonoseki. Indeed, *Man-Kan kokan* (Manchuria for Korea) had become one of the island empire's leading foreign policy imperatives by the late 1890s.[70] Referring to the French provinces ceded to Germany in 1871, a Japanese diplomat told a journalist: "Korea, you understand, is Japan's Alsace-Lorraine."[71]

In 1896, when he traveled to Russia for Nicholas II's coronation, Marshal Yamagata had tried to negotiate a *Man-Kan kokan* arrangement with Russia. Although he managed to sign a pact with Foreign Minister Lobanov, its terms disappointed his government.[72] Two years later, on April 13, 1898, Baron Rosen, the Russian envoy, and Japan's foreign minister, Nishi Tokujiro, signed a similar protocol in Tokyo. The deal gave Japan slightly better terms, including recognition of economic dominance over Korea, but pledged both signatories to upholding the kingdom's political sovereignty.

Rosen himself dismissed it as "a rather lame and pointless convention," and the Japanese were hardly more enthusiastic.[73]

During the next four years, as Russia largely withdrew from Korean affairs, there were repeated efforts to win its formal recognition of Japan's primacy there. However, Russian diplomats were unable to receive authorization from their government for such a deal. Alexander Izvolskii, then the minister to Tokyo, explained his dilemma: "We could give [Japan] carte blanche in commercial, economic, and financial matters in Korea, but we could never countenance its occupation by Japanese troops or any attempt to infringe the peninsula's political independence."[74] The problem was that both the tsar and his admirals "attach an overly sentimental importance to Korea." Izvolskii and his chief, Count Lamsdorf, had no such qualms. The former remarked that "allowing Japan to occupy Korea will only weaken it militarily and make it more vulnerable to Russia."[75] Meanwhile, Lamsdorf feared Japanese hostility. If Russia did not appease the dangerous new rival, he warned in letters to Witte, Kuropatkin, and Navy Minister Tyrtov, there was "a clear danger of armed conflict with Japan."[76]

As long as Marquis Ito Hirobumi led the Japanese government, cooler heads prevailed in Tokyo. Although he was hardly pro-Russian, the prime minister had great respect for his nation's rival. Since the time of the negotiations at Shimonoseki in 1895, he had tended to be cautious vis-à-vis Russia. One of the most eminent Meiji statesmen, Ito was highly regarded both by other politicians and by the emperor.[77] In May 1901, however, his administration lost the confidence of the diet, and a new prime minister, Count Katsura Taro, took office. On average a decade younger in age than their predecessors, the members of Katsura's cabinet were much more aggressive toward Russia.[78]

Many Japanese began to press at this time for an even more militant policy in China. In September 1900, Prince Konoe Atsumara, a member of the powerful Fujiwara clan and the president of the House of Peers, helped found the *Tai-Ro Kokumin Domekai* (Anti-Russian National League). Other influential Russophobic groups that emerged at the time included the hard-line *Kokuryukai,* or Amur River Society, which advocated expelling Russia from northern Manchuria. Its goals were straightforward: "In view of the situation in East Asia and the mission of imperial Japan . . . and to promote the . . . prosperity of East Asia, it is the urgent duty of Japan to fight Russia and expel it from the East, and then to lay the foundation for a grand continental enterprise linking Manchuria, Mongolia, and Siberia as one region."[79]

Marquis Ito, now out of government, tried to salvage his country's peace with Russia by undertaking a private mission to St. Petersburg in November 1901. Although he had received the new government's approval for the trip, it was entirely at his own initiative. The elder statesman received a warm welcome, and Nicholas awarded him the Order of St. Alexander Nevsky. In meetings with both Witte and Lamsdorf, Ito pleaded for a Korean-Manchurian deal. Although the finance minister was sympathetic to such an arrangement, the foreign minister turned him down.[80] Lamsdorf was clearly heeding the wishes of his sovereign. Earlier that month, Nicholas had told his cousin, Prince Henry of Prussia: "I don't want Korea for myself, but neither can I countenance that the Japanese set foot there. Were they to try this, it would be a casus belli for Russia. A Japanese presence in Korea would be like a new Bosphorus for us in East Asia. Russia can never accept this."[81]

If Marquis Ito had hoped to accomplish a rapprochement with Russia, Count Katsura's administration took a radically different tack. As Ito conferred with the tsar and his officials, the Japanese minister in London, Count Hayashi Tadasu, was secretly negotiating a defensive pact with the British government.[82] When the Anglo-Japanese alliance was announced to the world in January 1902, Russian diplomats were caught entirely off guard.[83] Lamsdorf publicly shrugged off its importance and advised his

"A Man of his word"—Few expected Russia to leave Manchuria voluntarily after its occupation in 1900, as this cartoon in *Punch* shows.

diplomats to "keep their sangfroid."[84] Nevertheless, the new combination was an alarming one for Russia. Now its two most formidable opponents in the Far East had joined forces, changing the Pacific's strategic landscape.

Russia's inability to compromise with Japan was not its only diplomatic setback in the Far East. The negotiations with China over the evacuation of Manchuria were equally troubled. Matters were not simplified by the court's lengthy exile in Xi'an and ongoing talks between the Qing and the occupying powers in Zhili Province. When by fall 1900 it became clear that Prince Ukhtomskii's dealings with Li Hongzhang were getting nowhere, Witte decided to move the talks to St. Petersburg. The finance minister wanted to keep his diplomacy entirely separate from that of the other powers. Anyway, the Chinese minister, Yangyu, seemed to be an agreeable fellow.[85]

Witte's measure of the man proved to be wrong. On January 4, 1901, he presented Yangyu a provisional list of 13 conditions for the tsarist army's withdrawal from Manchuria. The terms seemed draconian and essentially amounted to continued Russian control over the three provinces' army, police, and economy.[86] Although they were meant to be only a starting point, Witte's sweeping demands shocked the Chinese diplomat: "It is apparent that Russia will seize this occasion to realise her designs in China. . . . The situation will be unbearable if we are deprived of all our rights in Manchuria. . . . If one country does this, others will follow. How could China be preserved?"[87]

Yangyu advised his government to postpone the talks, and they were duly suspended that month. When Lamsdorf proposed a somewhat milder version in early February, it was also rejected. At the end of the month, the count gave Yangyu his final offer. The envoy had 15 days to make up his mind. At the same time Witte's agent Pokotilov stepped up the pressure on Li, threatening to break off ties, which would essentially leave Russia in control of Manchuria. Despite such threats, the Chinese government refused to budge.[88]

China's resolve had been stiffened by the active intervention of the other powers.[89] Just as Russia had urged the Qing not to yield its Manchurian ports to Japan in 1895, now it was the turn of Japan and Britain to support Chinese territorial integrity in the face of Russian encroachments. In February 1901, Japan's foreign minister approached the British minister, Sir Ernest Satow, and suggested "an effective opposition [to Russia's demands] by a combination of the other powers."[90] Meanwhile the powerful Yangzi viceroys, Zhang Zhidong and Liu Kuni, also strenuously opposed any arrangements that would dilute Chinese sovereignty over Manchuria. Zhang reasoned: "If Russia becomes angry, we would lose only the three Eastern provinces; but if all the other powers become angry, the eighteen provinces would at once be lost."[91] When Li Hongzhang died on October 25, 1901, St. Petersburg was deprived of its only important friend in the Chinese government.[92]

The Anglo-Japanese alliance galvanized St. Petersburg. Witte, Lamsdorf, and Kuropatkin worried increasingly about their government's diplomatic isolation in the Far East, and the new minister in Peking, Pavel Lessar, was instructed to speed up the negotiations.[93] Finally, on March 26, 1902, an agreement was signed in the Chinese capital. Russia pledged to evacuate Manchuria in three phases. Within six months, on September 9, 1902, the army would pull out of the southwestern part of Fengtien province. On March 26, 1903, troops would evacuate the rest of Fengtien and Jirin. The remaining province of Heilongjiang was to be cleared on September 29, 1903. The rest of the terms were considerably less harsh than the proposal Witte had initially presented to Yangyu in Peking fourteen months earlier: Russia's special position in Manchuria was confirmed without giving the tsar strong powers to intervene in the provinces' internal affairs after Chinese rule was restored.[94] Lessar concluded:

> At first glance it's not much. But Russia had no alternative. Staying in Manchuria would have aroused China's anger for a long time to come. . . . All the foreign representatives, except the French, gave advice hostile to us, the Chinese listened to them and became more and more convinced that we were their only foes. Finally, inspired by the Anglo-Japanese accord, they began to dream about driving us out of Manchuria with the help of the other foreigners without even signing any agreement whatsoever.

All was not lost. "There is an out," Lessar added. "Russia can halt its evacuation 'in case of any disturbances.'"[95]

CHAPTER TWELVE

The Last Lap

*R*ussia's promise to evacuate Manchuria came at a time when East Asia's allure was beginning to fade. By 1902, even once-enthusiastic advocates of Russia's Oriental destiny like Ukhtomskii were more muted in their pronouncements. With the exception of the prince's *Sankt-Peterburgskie Vedomosti*, the media's foreign coverage now stressed issues closer to home, such as the Balkans and the Near East. As for Manchuria, the enormous expenses of the CER were coming under increasing criticism. Many Russians felt that domestic problems were simply more pressing than costly adventures on the Pacific. In an editorial in February 1903, Suvorin urged: "What really matters is central Russia. This is where the government must spend its money. . . . Let us allow these far-reaching plans in the Far East to rest for now. We have to concentrate on our home and on the present, not on some distant land and the future, not two birds in the bush, but one in the hand."[1]

As newspapers grew bolder in their attacks on the finance minister's East Asian enterprises, enemies at the court and the bureaucracy were doing their best to undercut his authority.[2] Matters were not helped by a prolonged recession in Russia.[3] More ominously, Witte was gradually losing his hold over the tsar. In the earlier years of his reign, Nicholas's respect for his father and lack of self-assurance had usually enabled Witte to get his way. Now, as the emperor grew more confident of his abilities, he began to resent his domineering finance minister.[4]

For the tsar, the Asian dream was still very much alive, and his interest was being reawakened from an unexpected quarter. It all began in 1896 with a forestry concession in Korea. At the time, St. Petersburg dominated the kingdom's affairs, and Russian entrepreneurs were being strongly encouraged to establish themselves there. One such foothold was obtained by a Vladivostok-based merchant, Iulius Briner, who won the right to exploit an enormous tract of woods on the banks of the Yalu and Tumen Rivers along Korea's northern border. The business never got off the ground, and a year later he divested himself of his concession.[5]

In 1899, the project ended up in the hands of a group of aristocratic investors and Guards officers with close ties to the court. The leading men in this group were Vladimir Vonliarliarskii, a retired colonel of the exclusive Chevalier Guardes turned business promoter, and Aleksandr Bezobrazov, a former captain in the same regiment. Vonliarliarskii was on particularly good terms with Viacheslav Plehve, the future interior minister, as well as Grand Duke Aleksandr Mikhailovich. He used these connections to try to interest such august personages as Sergei Witte and the emperor in his "East Asian Development Company," which by now had become a curious hybrid of commerce and strategic vanguard, self-consciously modeled on the British East India Company.[6]

Witte saw the affair as a threat to his own Far Eastern ventures, and he lent it no support. The project did, however, capture the imagination of Nicholas II. Over the next few years, he occasionally dabbled in the venture, authorizing funds for a survey of the region covered by the concession and personally acquiring shares. His brother-in-law was even more enthusiastic. Aleksandr Mikhailovich, who acted as Vonliarliarskii's intermediary to Nicholas, wrote a memorandum in 1899 advocating using the company to secure a hold over northern Korea. As he warned the emperor: "Sooner or later we will have to contend with the Japanese. It would be better to lay our cards on the table now, to prevent any misunderstandings in the future."[7]

Witte was nevertheless able to stymie this potential rival, and for the next two years the East Asian Development Company languished. Then, suddenly in January 1903, the tsar instructed his finance minister secretly to open a two-million-ruble credit "for purposes known to His Majesty" in the name of Guards Captain Bezobrazov, who had by then become the company's leading promoter. Nicholas added that Bezobrazov was unlikely to spend the entire sum, but the large amount was necessary "to give weight and importance to his mission." What precisely his task entailed remained unstated.[8]

During the previous months, Bezobrazov had managed thoroughly to ingratiate himself to the tsar. The two often spent hours in conversation together. Nicholas was very much attracted to his optimism and enthusiasm about Russia's place in the East, which were so much more appealing than the gloomy pessimism of his ministers.[9]

Bezobrazov used the money to undertake a lavish tour of Manchuria. Finance Ministry employees followed him closely. On January 24, a report came in from an official in Mukden: "Life here continues to revolve around Bezobrazov [and his group]. . . . There are lunches, dinners, counter-lunches, counter-dinners, and toasts to the union of China and Russia."[10] In another letter the functionary wrote: "[Bezobrazov] arrived . . . surrounded by a halo of two million rubles accompanied by a glittering suite. . . . After many dinners and the like and generous financial gifts and donations to Chinese and Russians alike . . . he finally left for Port Arthur and Peking for further talks. What results he achieved here, I cannot yet say."[11] Four days later, Bezobrazov was in Dalnii: "Being of a very vain character, he no doubt has very good connections, since everyone waits on him hand and foot. He does not refrain from criticizing the Finance Ministry," another Finance Ministry employee advised.[12]

Bezobrazov's largesse was impressive. He donated money to hospitals and Port Arthur's newspaper, bought a coal mine, made plans for a power station and a telephone service in Mukden, made agricultural settlements, established a ship line, and offered well-paying jobs all around.[13] The former officer also began work on the Yalu lumber concession, but he paid considerably more attention to organizing a security force than to cutting trees.[14] By July virtually the entire two million rubles had been spent.[15]

Dmitrii Pokotilov, Witte's most senior agent in China, traveled from Peking in February to try to make sense of these activities. It was not easy. He cabled St. Petersburg about their first talk: "I am in a fog right now and am at a loss for words about him. In any case, I find it hard to take seriously anyone who finds it necessary to speak for hours on end about all manner of subjects without himself posing any questions."[16]

A few days later he met again with Bezobrazov, and after twelve hours of conversation over the space of two days was able to comprehend his plans. Essentially the aim of the Yalu concession was to form a defensive screen stretching from Vladivostok to Port Arthur, to guard Manchuria against any Japanese attacks. The main unit would be stationed at the mouth of the Yalu River "disguised as forestry guards."[17] In a somewhat briefer chat with Iugovich a few weeks later, Bezobrazov said much the same, adding that Russia must under no circumstances clear Manchuria. As for the treaty with China signed the year before, he argued that force of arms would take care of that minor detail.[18]

Bezobrazov also met with Admiral Alekseev, who initially formed a negative opinion of the bombastic subaltern. He wrote Lamsdorf that he feared the Yalu enterprise was inopportune and could complicate negotiations with the Chinese.[19] When reports of Alekseev's concerns reached Nicholas, he decided to recall his protégé to St. Petersburg for an explanation.[20]

Bezobrazov nevertheless retained the tsar's good graces for a few more months. In May, Nicholas even promoted him to the high bureaucratic rank of state secretary. There would be another trip to the Far East in June, and the Guards captain continued to flood his sovereign with memoranda outlining his thoughts about the need for a powerful military presence in Manchuria and Korea.[21] But by summer 1903 his role was becoming increasingly marginalized. Although Bezobrazov got his way at a ministerial conference on the Yalu question in May, his voice was barely heard at a series of discussions in Port Arthur the following month.[22] Even Nicholas began to tire of his rantings. In August, during a conversation with Kuropatkin, the tsar remarked that he had once liked Bezobrazov's critiques but now found them grating.[23] By fall, the officer's initial two-million-ruble appropriation exhausted, the Finance Ministry turned down a plea for more money.[24] Bezobrazov decided to go on a lengthy trip abroad.[25]

Bezobrazov's role in Russian politics has received considerable attention. To his foes, like Witte and Kuropatkin, he was a convenient scapegoat for the outbreak of the war with Japan. But the importance of the Guards captain and his activities should not be exaggerated. Baron Rosen, the minister to Tokyo at the time, pointed out that the Japanese government did not even seem to pay much attention to his notorious forestry venture: "The question of the Yalu timber concession was never raised nor even alluded to in the course of negotiations preceding the outbreak of war. . . . Therefore the accusation of having been directly instrumental in bringing about the rupture with Japan . . . necessarily falls to the ground."[26]

At the same time, Bezobrazov was symptomatic of the emperor's increasing tendency to bypass his ministers for advice on important questions of state. Although he listened to their weekly reports and dutifully read their memoranda, at times Nicholas seemed to find the ideas of such men as Bezobrazov rather more congenial. In March 1903, Kuropatkin despaired that "two policies have arisen in the Far East: The 'imperial' and the 'Bezobrazovian.'"[27]

*A*lthough Bezobrazov's role was ephemeral, there were others who shared his uncompromising stance during the increasingly bitter debate about the evacuation of Manchuria in 1903. The whole year became an endless succession of conferences about the matter, each one of which seemed to be less conclusive than the preceding one. Even the Japanese foreign minister, Baron Komura, spoke of a "serious diversity of opinion in the counsels of Russia."[28]

On September 26, 1902, the first phase of the evacuation agreement was carried out, and Russian troops withdrew from the southern half of Fengtien, including the provincial capital of Mukden. Not long thereafter, Sergei Witte, Count Lamsdorf, General Kuropatkin, and the new interior minister, Viacheslav Plehve, gathered in Yalta on Nicholas's orders to discuss measures to assure continued control over the CER. The question arose after Priamuria's governor-general, N. I. Grodekov, reported that Peking might be encouraging massive migration to Manchuria.[29] While they unanimously decided that, "undoubtedly, in the future Manchuria will either have to be joined to Russia or become entirely dependent on it," the ministers could not agree on any measures to ensure that this would happen. Most likely, this statement was only meant to reassure the tsar, since the foreign ministry continued to confirm St. Petersburg's intention to pull its troops out of Manchuria. Even Grodekov's idea of settling the land along the railroad with Russian peasants, which Kuropatkin had formally proposed at the meeting, was deemed impractical, since that territory technically belonged to the Chinese government.[30]

Three months later, on January 25, 1903, Lamsdorf, Witte, and

Kuropatkin continued the debate in another conference in St. Petersburg.[31] Joined by Admiral Tyrtov and various diplomats, the officials were now charged with drafting new instructions for the envoy in Peking. The second phase of the Russian withdrawal was two months away, and mounting concerns over the unsettled state of affairs in the region had led to a reevaluation of the question at the Choristers' Bridge. Although diplomats agreed that Russia was obligated to restore the provinces to China, they proposed negotiating with Peking for additional guarantees to ensure dominance even after the evacuation.[32]

The ministers also briefly discussed Japan. Lamsdorf announced that Tokyo had offered in July 1902 once again to trade control over Korea for Manchuria but that he had turned it down. Most of the participants agreed that it would be desirable to reach an agreement with their Pacific rival. Lamsdorf decided that it was preferable to wait for another approach, lest Russia appear too eager.

As for the March 1902 agreement, General Kuropatkin repeated his concerns about "the rush of the Yellow Race" into eastern Siberia. The only way to protect Asiatic Russia, he argued, would be to retain control over northern Manchuria. He therefore proposed to implement only half of the upcoming second evacuation. Witte and Lamsdorf both disagreed, pointing out that China and the other powers would strongly oppose a prolonged Russian presence. Kuropatkin did not get his way, although the instructions agreed upon for the new talks in Peking were sufficiently strict to make agreement difficult. The terms included a promise that no Manchurian territory would be handed over to a third party, a prohibition on consulates and commerce by any other foreigners, and pledges to ensure that the provinces would remain within Russia's sphere.[33]

The Russian chargé d'affaires, G. A. Plançon, took his time presenting the new demands to the Chinese, who responded with an equivalent absence of alacrity, and in early May Plançon broke off the talks. If Peking was in no hurry to settle the matter, he pouted, then neither was his government. Meanwhile, the second phase of the withdrawal would be delayed indefinitely.[34] When P. M. Lessar, the new minister in Peking, returned from a trip to St. Petersburg later that month, he reopened the negotiations.[35] Still, his Chinese counterpart, Prince Qing, proved unready to yield. At the end of June, as Russia stepped up the pressure by ordering more troops to eastern Siberia, it was Prince Qing's turn to walk out. He assured Lessar that his government was willing to discuss the new Russian proposals, but only after Manchuria had been cleared of all foreign troops.

Both sides were growing more intractable by the day. China continued to solicit the help of the other powers in standing up to its northern neighbor, and in Russia some began to press for even stricter terms for the withdrawal.[36] Bezobrazov, recently returned from the Far East, was now at the height of his standing while his chief rival, Sergei Witte, was rapidly falling from imperial favor. More important, Admiral Alekseev was beginning to emerge as the man Nicholas most trusted for his Far Eastern policy.

The emperor called the hard line set in spring 1903 "the new course."[37] Its purpose, as he explained in a telegram on May 2 to his commander on the Pacific, was to ensure that there would be "no penetration of foreign influence into Manchuria . . . in any form whatsoever."[38] Russian determination, he wrote Alekseev, would be underscored by stepping up their military and commercial presence in East Asia. Nicholas promised: "We will upgrade our armed forces in the Far East as soon as possible, and without regard to budgetary prudence, to the level demanded by our political and economic tasks, thereby proving to the world our steadfast determination to defend our right to exclusive influence over Manchuria."[39] As if to emphasize his ambivalence and uncertainty, the tsar added that his "new course" would be implemented "in connection with our final decision to comply with the agreement of March 26, 1902."[40]

Five days later, on May 7, 1903, Nicholas convened another meeting to discuss these issues.[41] There was a new political constellation, with Bezobrazov and Colonel Wogack, who was now in the retired Guards captain's pay, joining the usual ministers, Witte, Lamsdorf, and Plehve.[42] Chaired by the emperor, this session confirmed the points he had set out in his telegram to Alekseev. More disturbing for Witte and Lamsdorf, Nicholas also seemed to sanction Bezobrazov's Yalu forestry concession as one of the primary means toward this end. Nevertheless, the tsar did promise not to make any final decisions until after he had received Kuropatkin's and Alekseev's views.

Lamsdorf was shocked. He complained that "a new era in our foreign policy" had begun and submitted his resignation to the tsar (which was declined).[43] To many it seemed that the former Guards captain and his questionable enterprise now ruled over Russia's Far East. In fact, Bezobrazov's standing had peaked, as events during the following month would show. At the same time, it was clear that Witte was being supplanted by Admiral Alekseev as the leading voice on East Asian affairs. Over the next months two alliances emerged, with Lamsdorf, Witte, and Kuropatkin advocating caution and Alekseev and Plehve supporting a less conciliatory approach toward China and Japan.

Bezobrazov suffered a major setback in June at Port Arthur, where he had arrived to participate in yet another discussion on Far Eastern matters. General Kuropatkin, just back from a visit to Japan, had been ordered to chair a 10-day conference attended by Admiral Alekseev, Colonel Wogack, and various diplomatic officials in addition to the Guards captain. Its purpose, as Kuropatkin explained on June 18, the opening day, was "to study Russia's position in Manchuria, in light of the emperor's will, and reconcile the treaty of 26 March 1902 with the need to preserve Russia's dignity and to assure it a presence in the region corresponding to the expenses it has made there."[44]

The two most important matters on the agenda were the evacuation agreement with China and the Yalu enterprise. On neither matter did Bezo-

Cossack thrashing a Japanese officer—This Russian *lubok* conveys the military's optimism before 1904 that any confrontation with its East Asian rival would be "a splendid little war."

brazov have a significant impact. The forestry concession was only discussed on the sixth day, when the other participants rapidly decided to relegate it to a "purely commercial" venture, thereby significantly reducing its status.[45] Meanwhile, the officials reaffirmed the need to demand more exacting conditions from Peking in exchange for leaving Manchuria. These conditions included prohibiting China from stationing any troops or (non-Russian) foreign military advisors in Manchuria while allowing Russia to keep soldiers along the CER and in various posts along the Amur River's right bank. To Lessar's objection that China was unlikely to accept these severe new terms, Kuropatkin replied that his forces would simply stay put until an agreement was reached.[46]

Once again, the sessions' results were mixed. Although Bezobrazov's ambitious plans were rebuffed, on the other matters the participants largely agreed to disagree. Lamsdorf wrote the tsar that it was "clearly evident that the aforementioned conference did not attain the desired unanimity, and every one of the participants stuck to their own opinions."[47]

The talks did lead Nicholas to make one important decision. Tiring of the endless squabbling between his ministers, on July 30, 1903, Nicholas issued a decree appointing Admiral Alekseev as his viceroy of the Far East. As Nicholas explained to his new deputy, the post essentially made him the tsar's personal representative on the Pacific, with full authority for all policy in the region. All other officials, including diplomats, financial agents, and military officers, were answerable to him, not their own ministers in St. Petersburg. The emperor was emphatic about Alekseev's new authority: "My viceroy of the Far East is the true commander of all army and naval forces in the region . . . and serves to guard our natural interests on the shores of the Pacific Ocean. The viceroy I have appointed is also the political chief, executing my will on diplomatic, administrative, and economic matters."[48] Two weeks later, on August 15, Nicholas removed Alekseev's chief rival by dismissing Sergei Witte from his post as finance minister.[49] Witte understood the reason for his removal: he "was too sharp" with the tsar, he wrote, and "loyal subjects should learn to control themselves in his presence."[50]

Alekseev's new appointment also came as a major blow to Kuropatkin and Lamsdorf. The war minister considered resigning, complaining to the tsar that he had evidently lost his master's confidence.[51] As for the foreign minister, he went into a depression after the announcement. Ivan Korostovets, a diplomat who had served in Port Arthur, wrote Alekseev that the count's pride had been shattered by the news. His colleagues at the Choristers' Bridge bitterly joked that London had requested accreditation for an ambassador to Port Arthur.[52] When Nicholas asked Lamsdorf for his thoughts about Asia in mid-September, he replied: "It is difficult for me to give any opinion, Sire, as of late I have been in darkness as to our policy in the Far East and have lost the drift of things."[53]

Nicholas's decision to promote Alekseev also had severe repercussions abroad.[54] Sir Charles Scott, the British ambassador, wrote that the move indicated that "the Emperor has decided to attach greater weight to the views of the military authorities in the Far East than to . . . diplomatic and financial considerations." Now the situation, he felt, was "most serious and pregnant with the seed of fresh complications and dangers to the peace of the Far East."[55] Japan saw the appointment as highly provocative. As Baron Rosen reported, naming a viceroy for the Far East was taken as an aggressive act.[56] The Japanese were particularly offended, since the decree came only two weeks after their government had swallowed its pride and proposed new negotiations.[57]

Throughout 1903 foreign statesmen were confused, alarmed, and often angered by the frequent reversals in tsarist policy, further isolating Russia diplomatically. England and Japan, newly emboldened by their alliance, were the most troublesome powers, and they did their best to disrupt Russian negotiations with China. Meanwhile Germany was cynically playing off its European rivals by alternately assuring St. Petersburg of its support and promising strict neutrality to London and Tokyo.[58]

The United States, whose secretary of state, John Hay, had taken the moral high ground by declaring China's doors open to all foreign commerce in 1899, expressed its indignation at Russia's continued attempts to close Manchuria to American business. Count Cassini, who was now the ambassador in Washington, observed, "Hay is in an aggressive mood." The American public, which had been aroused by news of recent anti-Semitic pogroms in the southwestern town of Kishinev, was also hostile. Cassini advised that "the United States will certainly not join in a war against us, but her morale and probably also financial support will go to Japan."[59]

Even France opposed complications on the Pacific. Paris's partnership with St. Petersburg was meant to contain Germany, not Japan. Still smarting over Russia's lukewarm support of its African interest during the Fashoda Crisis five years earlier, the Quay d'Orsay let it be known that it would do little more to assist its ally in the Far East.[60] Chinese diplomats were well aware of the other powers' sentiments, and their intractability over the Manchurian question was largely a result of the support given by foreign diplomats opposed to a Russian presence in the northeastern provinces.

China's military weakness severely hampered its bargaining position. Writing a survey about the situation in July 1903, a British intelligence officer described the Russian buildup and the acquiescence of Manchuria's inhabitants. "They [the Russians] are perfectly earnest in their intention to gradually obtain the mastery over the country until it shall have, by force of circumstances, become a Russian province," he observed. But supremacy was not necessarily assured: "Russian ascendance as the chief political and future governing power, in the three Eastern provinces, is assured—for at least as long as no power shall drive her out at the point of a bayonet."[61]

In autumn 1903, Japan's government finally lost its patience. When Russia failed to observe the third phase of its evacuation of Manchuria on September 26, having audaciously reoccupied Mukden less than three weeks earlier, it became clear that there was no alternative. On January 24, 1904, Tokyo ordered its troops to fix bayonets and commanded Admiral Togo to set sail for Port Arthur.

Conclusion

Thinking about the Far East

*I*n his book about rivalry among the great powers during the early twentieth century, *Imperialism in Manchuria,* the Soviet historian Vladimir Avarin argued that China's northeastern provinces were the battleground of two types of expansionism. Business interests and nations such as the United States were engaged in "modern capitalist imperialism" while others were exponents of "military-feudal imperialism."[1] According to Avarin, tsarist Russia was primarily driven by the latter.

Avarin's dichotomy is too crude to explain the ideological motives of Russia's involvement in the Far East. The German scholar Jürgen Osterhammel captured the intellectual complexities of St. Petersburg's Pacific entanglements more accurately:

> We find all forms of . . . imperialism in China, from the prototypical informal empire and missionary work, to advanced finance imperialism, to unique types of commercial and industrial colonies (Taiwan, Manchuria), and, finally, to the more modern manifestations of violent conquest. China has been the proving ground for the greatest variety of imperialisms in history.[2]

Osterhammel was referring to all of the powers that were active in the Middle Kingdom over the past two hundred years, including Britain and France in the nineteenth century and the United States and Japan during the twentieth. Yet his observation is particularly apt for Russia around 1900.

In 1894, when Tsar Nicholas II inherited the throne, St. Petersburg's Asian politics awoke from a long slumber. Finance Minister Sergei Witte already had ambitious plans for developing with his Siberian railway the huge territories Russia acquired on the Pacific in Alexander II's reign. Japan's easy victory over China during their brief war aroused greedier appetites. The Qing dynasty's decadence was now evident to all, and many Russians began to fantasize about their empire's brilliant destiny in the Far East.

As we have seen, these dreams took on many different guises. Witte envisaged China as an arena for *pénétration pacifique*. His was the doctrine of establishing economic and political influence over foreign lands without directly governing them as colonies. To his colleague at the war ministry, Aleksei Kuropatkin, Russia's eastern neighbor provoked nightmares about a yellow peril. According to the general's pessimistic worldview, China's 400 millions were a potential "yellow tidal wave" that could easily engulf the few million whites living in Russian Siberia. Kuropatkin's imperialist vision for East Asia was entirely defensive.

The two most influential ideas in the shaping of Russia's policies in the Far East were also the most divergent. Even though he belonged to an earlier generation, Nikolai Przhevalskii represented an important intellectual current of Russian imperialism in East Asia. Better known as the great Inner Asian explorer, Przhevalskii unabashedly championed annexing vast tracts of China's borderlands. In his eyes, China was a place for quick glory and new conquests, much like Turkestan had been in General Skobelev's day.

The East also inspired another way of thinking. Tiring of the endless debates about whether their nation's true destiny lay with Europe or with its Slavic heritage, men like the newspaper publisher Prince Esper Ukhtomskii pressed for a third course: Russia must return to its Asian roots. The prince believed that two centuries of Mongol rule had brought Russians much closer to the East than the West. He saw Russia's soul as essentially Oriental in its spirituality, aversion to crass materialism, and yearning for autocratic rule. This Eastern heritage, Ukhtomskii stressed, gave St. Petersburg the moral right to a more active role in Asia. Though Britain, Germany, and the other capitalist powers merely sought lucre there, Russia's intentions on the continent were entirely benevolent.

As Russia turned to the East in the 1890s, were there others within the government who shared any of these four conceptions of imperial destiny? Did such notions evoke any response among the educated public? Finally, what role, if any, did these ideas—the beliefs of Przhevalskii, Ukhtomskii, Witte, and Kuropatkin—play in tsarist policy on the Pacific?

*T*he generation that was raised on Nikolai Przhevalskii's tales remembered the explorer when Japan and China went to war in 1894. The ease with which the small island empire shattered the Middle Kingdom's forces fully confirmed Nikolai Mikhailovich's earlier appraisal of the Chinese military. Dispatches from the army's attaché in East Asia, Colonel Wogack, echoed Przhevalskii's assessment of the Qing's utter inability to fight. Meanwhile, journalists repeatedly cited the explorer's claim that a handful of Cossacks could march to Peking without any trouble.[3] At the turn of the twentieth century, such views were also common in the army. The future war minister, Aleksandr Rödiger, recalled: "Since the days of Przhevalskii, we were convinced that we could penetrate all China with just one battalion."[4]

In 1900, Russian troops occupied Manchuria to protect the Chinese Eastern Railway from the Boxers. The operation met with hopelessly ineffectual resistance, again proving the martial incapacity of the Asian neighbor and reinforcing the tsarist military's contempt for Asian combatants. One good example is the account of a junior officer who took part in the action, Captain Konstantin Kushakov's *Iuzhno-manchzhurskie besporiadki v 1900 godu* (The Southern Manchurian Disorders of 1900).[5] Like Przhevalskii, Kushakov saw the Chinese troops as undisciplined and cowardly and their commanders as thoroughly incompetent. Whenever Russian troops attacked them, the soldiers threw away their weapons to flee the battlefield all the more quickly.[6]

Other themes of Przhevalskii's writings found their way into Kushakov's narrative as well. Thus the local population thoroughly despised Qing officials. It was their cruelty, not the Europeans, that had largely led to the Boxer revolt. Kushakov's instincts in dealing with them strongly resembled those of Przhevalskii: "We must thrash the mandarins' fat brains."[7] Like Przhevalskii, the author stressed that Manchurians preferred the Russians to their own government for the order they brought to their region, and they were much more content to live under the White Tsar.[8]

Many of the officers who served in the Far East, such as Admiral Alekseev and his lieutenants in Manchuria, fully shared Przhevalskii's robust imperialism. Alekseev's mouthpiece, the Port Arthur newspaper *Novyi Krai* (The New Land), strongly endorsed Russia's imperial drive in the Orient. Editorials championing a more aggressive course for St. Petersburg frequently appeared on its pages. "Russia's Eastern Century," a piece in the 1901 New Year's issue, was typical:

> Constrained by a 9,000-verst Russian ring, China is hemmed in by the tsar's realms on its western, northern, and northeastern borders. [The Boxer rebellion] showed that between China and the [European] whites there exists an insurmountable gulf of racial enmity and hatred. To us, on the other hand, heathen China offers untold opportunities for Christian missions and Russian enlightenment. And so, from Teheran to Peking in the north, from Tibet to the Great Wall, there can be no power except that of Russia.[9]

The strident jingoism of Guards Captain Bezobrazov and his confederates similarly echoed Przhevalskii's bellicose sentiments. If Bezobrazov proposed slightly less overt forms of conquest in the East, such as his notorious scheme for occupying the Yalu River basin with a heavily armed logging enterprise, his enthusiasm for stripping weaker Asian neighbors of their borderlands was no less fervent than that of Przhevalskii. In Avarin's words, the guardsman was a typical example of "military-feudal imperialism."[10]

Bezobrazov fully shared the explorer's belief that "might makes right." Brushing aside Peking's concerns about the legality of his operations on their soil, the retired officer sniffed: "Only the bayonet can guarantee the success of our . . . activities in Manchuria."[11] Nor was Bezobrazov particularly bothered by diplomatic niceties. "As for treaties and agreements," he once remarked, "we should never let them stand in the way as we fulfill our historic destiny in the Far East."[12]

When one official close to Bezobrazov, Ivan Balashev, wrote a memorandum to the tsar in 1902 urging him not to evacuate Manchuria, his rationale was pure Przhevalskii. Russia's occupation was fully justified, he argued, both on the grounds of "the timeless logic of things" and the perfidy and weakness of China: "No one ever doubted that Manchuria must ultimately belong to Russia." Anyway, Balashev maintained, the local population rightly understood its destiny: "The Manchurians . . . like their Mongolian neighbors and all other Asiatic tribes, are firmly convinced that fate has ordained them, sooner or later, to come under the rule of "THE WHITE TSAR" . . . [who] will satisfy their vague yearnings for truth and justice on Earth."[13]

In the years before 1904, even intelligence assessments of the Japanese often shared Przhevalskii's disdain for Asian martial prowess. More perspicacious diplomats and other officials were well aware of Tokyo's military capabilities. Men like Baron Rosen and Aleksandr Izvolskii repeatedly urged Nicholas not to antagonize his offshore rival. Yet others, especially army and navy officers in the Far East, failed to distinguish between the decrepit Qing and the modern troops of Meiji Japan.

The perceptions of the army's attaché to Tokyo, Lieutenant Colonel V. P. Vannovskii, were typical of this attitude. In 1903 he reported that "[while] no longer the rabble of an Asiatic horde . . . [the Japanese military] is nevertheless no modern European army. . . . It will take them another ten, perhaps a hundred years."[14] As Russian officers began to contemplate the possibility of fighting Japan, many believed that it would be enough to "pelt them with our caps" (shapkami zakidaem); the mere sight of a Cossack's scruffy shapka would send Japanese troops fleeing in terror.[15]

The most curious advocate of Przhevalskii's ideas was the Buriat apothecary Peter Badmaev. Born Zhamsaran Badmaev, he ran a fashionable clinic on the outskirts of St. Petersburg that used Tibetan herbal medicine to treat "serious cases of stubborn nervous diseases, mental maladies, and disturbances of the female physiology."[16] Badmaev's impeccable connections—Tsar Alexander III had stood as his godfather when he converted from Buddhism to Orthodoxy—and a good nose for business had earned him a thriving practice. Much as a similar enterprise might flourish today in a trendy, upscale North American community, the practice and its exotic remedies were avidly patronized by the imperial capital's Brahmins. Among its illustrious clientele were Finance Minister Sergei Witte and, later, the legislature's president, Mikhail Rodzianko. The society doctor used his access to Nicholas II and the upper echelons of officialdom to play an unusual role in Russia's Far Eastern policy at the turn of the century.

In 1893, Badmaev approached Alexander III with an eccentric plan to conquer China.[17] His scheme was to add a spur to the Trans-Siberian Railway, then being built, to connect the Buriat homeland on the shore of Lake Baikal to the western Chinese city of Lanzhou, some 1,800 kilometers across the Gobi Desert. The southern terminus would become a dispersal point for thousands of Buriat fifth columnists, who would agitate their Lamaist coreligionists in Tibet, Mongolia, and Xinjiang. Eventually raising a force of a half-million horsemen, the tsarist agents would march on the Forbidden City and overthrow the Qing dynasty. Having seized power, "selected members of the Mongolian, Tibetan, and Chinese nobility and leading Buddhist priests would set off for St. Petersburg *to supplicate the White Tsar to accept their submission*."[18] Much like Bezobrazov's Yalu timber concession some ten years later, Russian subversion would be conducted under the cover of a legitimate commercial enterprise.

At first, Witte strongly endorsed the proposal. Appealing to Russia's "special role in world history" and "her cultural-enlightening mission," the finance minister urged the tsar to consent to Badmaev's project.[19] Alexander was rather more skeptical, commenting that "this is all so new, strange, and fantastic that it is difficult to consider its feasibility."[20] Nevertheless, Witte did convince the sovereign to provide Badmaev with a two-million-ruble subsidy to set up the enterprise. "P. A. Badmaev and Co." was duly incorporated later in 1893, with offices in St. Petersburg and the Buriat city of Chita.

The enterprise was neither a commercial nor a political success. When its owner requested a second two-million-ruble infusion a few years later, even Witte turned him down.[21] By 1900 Badmaev himself abandoned the scheme.[22] Aside from vague references to clandestine groups of Buriat agents, there is little evidence to believe that it achieved much beyond a few investments in Chita and Peking. The Bolshevik editor of his papers was close to the truth when he suggested that the "fairy-tale plan" was an elaborate swindle, whose object was not to join Inner Asia to Russia but to "unite . . . a few million rubles to Badmaev's pocket."[23]

Despite the meager results of his eccentric project, Badmaev managed to retain the court's good graces and took care to befriend Nicholas II. Having known him since childhood, the new emperor readily turned to the Buriat for advice on Far Eastern policy. Badmaev was never shy about expressing his opinions. He continued to urge Nicholas to detach Mongolia and Tibet from China, reminding the tsar of his destiny: "Peter the Great opened a window on Europe, and Petersburg has become the symbol of Russian might. . . . [Now you] have opened a window on the Chinese East."[24]

Even though Witte had decided by 1896 that the Buriat was a quack and a charlatan and had ordered him to cease his activities in the Far East, Nicholas continued to grant him audiences.[25] General Kuropatkin also saw him as a fraud and repeatedly expressed his exasperation at "Badmaev's wild ravings."[26] Yet Badmaev rose in the tsar's esteem in direct proportion to the ministers' complaints. Although Badmaev's direct influence on Russian policy was slight, his intimacy with the court heightened the tsar's receptivity to Przhevalskian ideas of Asian conquest, as Kuropatkin's famous diary entry of early 1903 makes clear: "Our sovereign has grandiose plans in his head: to absorb Manchuria into Russia, to begin the annexation of Korea. He also dreams of taking Tibet under his orb. He wants to rule Persia, to seize both the Bosporus and the Dardanelles."[27]

*W*hen war broke out between China and Japan in 1894 and Russians began to discuss the merits of backing one or the other combatant, Prince Ukhtomskii's views also entered the debate. St. Petersburg's decision the following year to side with China was taken largely at the urging of Sergei Witte, whose plans for economic development in the Far East were predicated on good relations with Peking. Nevertheless, Ukhtomskii's ideas of a Russo-Chinese condominium dovetailed with the finance minister's plans. In the excitement about Russia's future on the Pacific that followed the successful intervention at Shimonoseki, the prince's pronouncements often drew the attention of other journalists. Commentators in Britain, Germany, and France looked to his editorials as an authoritative voice on tsarist policy in the Far East.

Two years later St. Petersburg implicitly canceled its alliance with Peking by seizing Port Arthur and Dalnii. The initial opposition to the possibility of such a move in fall 1897 among the Russian public suggests the extent to which Ukhtomskii's vision of intimacy between Asia's two great empires was shared by educated opinion. Although leasing the Liaodong Peninsula in March 1898 disillusioned the Qing, Russian sympathies for the Middle Kingdom remained strong. The clearest indication was the response to the Boxer rising of 1900.

Even the writer Lev Tolstoy joined the chorus. In "Thou Shalt Not Kill," an article published in August 1900, he thundered against the German kaiser, who had been one of the most vehement exponents of foreign intervention: "Let [Wilhelm II] say that in China the army must not take any captives, but it must kill all men. He is not put in an insane asylum. Instead [his troops] shout 'Hurrah!' and sail for China to execute his command."[28]

A month later, after Western troops had seized Peking, Tolstoy expressed his thoughts in an unpublished "Letter to the Chinese": "Armed people, calling themselves Christians, are now committing the greatest crimes among you. Do not believe them. These people are not Christians but a gang of the most terrible, shameless criminals . . . [who] now wish to lay hands on you, rob you, subject you, and, above all, corrupt you."[29] At the same time, Tolstoy was no apologist for Russian policy, and Nicholas II also drew his opprobrium for "causing the Chinese slaughter."[30]

Internal government communications were also sharply critical of the West. The Foreign Ministry's classified annual report for 1900 entirely blamed the foreigners: "The causes of this evil lie in the influence of west

European culture on Chinese life."[31] Even some of the more thoughtful minds in the military could not fault Russia's Asian neighbor. One General Staff colonel argued: "The fundamental origins of the recent events in China, the so-called 'Boxer Rising' . . . can be traced to the growth of capitalist production, which ultimately drove domestic goods from the markets and forced people to buy foreign imports."[32]

A brochure written for public consumption by General Evgenii Bogdanovich's prolific pen told a story very similar to Ukhtomskii's.[33] Issued by the Red Cross, it was meant to explain the events to the common man. Bogdanovich knew Ukhtomskii well.[34] He also had close ties to the court, and his pamphlet, like the many others he published, can basically be read as the official line.[35] According to the general, Nicholas thanked him warmly for issuing the booklet.[36]

Titled *Rossiia na Dalnem Vostoke* (Russia in the Far East), it shows the Boxer rising to be an outburst of popular anger against the depredations of the West. The violence, while regrettable, was understandable: "[The Boxers] represent the deep and long-standing hatred of the Chinese toward the Europeans who . . . by means of threats and war violently opened China to their trade and imports. . . . Making themselves at home, they unceremoniously lord it over them, with thorough contempt for the ancient traditions and beliefs of the Chinese." The author found the Catholic and Protestant missionaries particularly offensive. Not only did their arrogant meddling in the affairs of the Chinese emperor's subjects disrupt civic order, but they were not even motivated by a sincere love of God. It was no coincidence that preachers, trade, and opium all forced their way into the countryside simultaneously.[37]

China, General Bogdanovich stressed, is a great civilization, distinguished by its antiquity and respect for tradition. It was also Russia's peaceful neighbor, with whom it shared an almost 10,000-kilometer-long border. And its relations with Russia were entirely different from those with the Europeans:

> The Chinese never confuse Russians with the other foreigners. . . . We won their respect long ago, thanks to the confederates of the Mongols, who in their day told the Chinese good things about the Russians. More recently, their descendants spread reports of the White Tsar's glorious name throughout the Middle Kingdom. They say that, like a powerful *bogatyr* [medieval warrior] on the battlefield, he bears peace, justice, and order all over the world.

Furthermore, unlike the invidious Western preachers, Russian Orthodox priests did not force their faith on the Chinese.[38] When Russia's tsar did command his armies to intervene in China, he did so only to help their emperor restore order and to protect him against the retribution of the Europeans.[39]

St. Petersburg's more conservative press also followed this line of reasoning. Dailies like *Novoe Vremia* and *Grazhdanin* could hardly restrain their schadenfreude at the sufferings the insurgents wrought on the Europeans in Peking. Like Ukhtomskii's paper, they also expressed their sympathy for China as well as their distaste for the missionaries and traders the West had inflicted on its masses. *Sankt-Peterburskie Vedomosti* was not exaggerating when it declared that, at first, Russian journalists were united in their distaste for Russian intervention.[40] Many of these themes reflected the Asianist view.

One of Ukhtomskii's most loyal editorial allies was Prince Vladimir Petrovich Meshcherskii. While his *Grazhdanin* was not one of the capital's biggest newspapers, it enjoyed a select readership that included the emperor.[41] Vladimir Petrovich also had a notorious reputation for intrigue, and it would be hard to say whether his editorials shaped policy or skillfully adjusted to it. Nevertheless, his column, "The Diary," reflected official thinking with uncanny accuracy. It was therefore significant that Meshcherskii often expressed his agreement with Ukhtomskii.

When Esper Esperovich was put in charge of *Sankt-Peterburskie Vedomosti*, the liberal *Vestnik Evropy* expressed great surprise at the warm welcome the reactionary Meshcherskii extended to his new colleague, a man noted for his tolerance of minorities.[42] Yet, despite this seeming incongruity, Ukhtomskii's Asianism had many virtues to someone with the highly conservative views of Vladimir Petrovich. Prince Meshcherskii's reaction to the Boxer rising is a good example of this logic.

Like Ukhtomskii, Meshcherskii had great respect for China's culture: "If we set aside . . . W. C.'s and other modern inventions, as well as military technology, and look at civilization in the spiritual sense, then we can hardly consider China to be beneath Europe, whose Christian foundation is disfigured, exhausted, and maimed by lies and depravity."[43] China, in its unwavering conservatism, was even superior to the West:

> European civilization has advanced so far from its original state, while China progresses so slowly, that after its long journey, the West has regressed to barbarism in the moral sense, while China remains cultured. . . . Russia alone grasped this great truth, and on the basis of this understanding is founded its friendship with China and its strength in the East.[44]

Thus, as a monarchy loyal to autocratic principles, Russia had much in common with its Oriental neighbor.

Prince Meshcherskii was aghast at the West's arrogance in trying to impose its decadent culture on the East. "What right has Europe to force China to yield to its civilization?" he asked.[45] It was no surprise that the Chinese had risen in anger against these interlopers. Ultimately, by trying to convert them to Western ways, Europeans were hoist by their own petard:

> Not once did Europe stop to consider the question: Against whom is it arming China, training it in the arts of war and destroying its instinctive love of peace! Now . . . China answers it herself. Stricken with terror, Europe nervously babbles

... that it was silly to send their missionaries to the Chinese, and even more stu-
pid to furnish them with weapons and military instructors.[46]

The Boxer rising was a cautionary tale for the prince's countrymen. It was
the natural and inevitable outcome of Europe's pernicious influence, he
suggested:"Who is better: The impoverished Chinese, who can look upon
the rest of the world with a confident sense of his moral superiority, or the
prosperous, semicivilized Russian intelligent, always seeing everything
through ambitious or atheistic eyes?"[47]

Meshcherskii felt that the crisis should teach Russians not to reject the
old order for the newfangled ways of the West. Looking back on history, he
agreed with Ukhtomskii that his country's place was in Asia, not Europe:

> Siberia's conquest during Ivan IV's reign changed nothing in the structure of the
> Muscovite order, and Russia continued its natural progress. . . . For three cen-
> turies this task [of joining with its Asian province] was carried out. Then there
> was an event of an entirely different character: Peter the Great's rush to build a
> new capital on the Finnish Gulf, which altered the course of Russian history and
> arrested the development of the old heartland for a long time.[48]

*I*n the early days of Sergei Witte's tenure as finance minister, many
shared his zeal for the economic prospects of the Far East. During the
1880s, well before he was appointed to the post, interest groups such as the
Society for the Promotion of Russian Industry and Commerce were already
enthusiastic about developing commercial links to Asia.[49] Businessmen
cheered Witte's ambitions in the East in the early 1890s. As the decade pro-
gressed, the economic boom generated by capital spending on the Siberian
Railway only intensified their ardor. In the Marxist jargon of A. Popov, an
early Soviet expert of East Asian diplomatic history, "The state's decision to
play an active role in the Far East found support not only among the land-
owning classes but among the higher echelons of the bourgeoisie as well."[50]

The recession that set in around 1900 did much to dampen Russian optimism about any prosperity the Pacific might yield.[51] Russian industrialists,
who had been among the project's most fervent backers, began to have second thoughts about the Trans-Siberian Railway's economic viability. In a
study for the Orientalist Society, the head of the group's trade and industry
section declared that the track was suitable only for passenger traffic, mail,
and precious cargo.[52] Another commentator concluded, "The railway has
no relevance to international transportation. . . . Shipping goods by sea
through the Suez [Canal] will always be cheaper."[53]

At the same time, the private sector no longer shared the finance minister's hopes for the fabled China trade. By now the Society for the Promotion of Russian Industry and Commerce believed that prospects for sales to
the Middle Kingdom were minimal at best.[54] Businessmen knew that, de-

spite Witte's efforts to rouse the commercial interest of their eastern neighbor, exports never really took off. At the turn of the twentieth century, the value of Russian goods sold there barely exceeded seven million rubles a year, ranking Russia seventh among China's trading partners, just ahead of Belgium.[55] Russian factories were incapable of making goods Chinese wanted, and merchants had no interest in developing this market. A correspondent for a newspaper reported from Shanghai:

> [I didn't find] a single Russian sign, or one Russian shop, with the exception of an insignificant little establishment, hidden away in some alley, bearing the name "Keeper's General Store, Boon Road No. 3." There I found some Russian tobacco and salted pickles (40 kopeks per pound). . . . I give you this address with pride, so that, when visiting Shanghai, you can acquaint yourself with the pioneer and flag-bearer of Russian trade and industry in the commercial capital of the Far East, pay it well-deserved respect, and also buy some salted pickles.[56]

In the last years before the war with Japan, the Russian press largely shared this gloomy assessment. Rather than look to the East as a source of riches, editorials now saw the region as a tremendous drain on the tsarist purse. Influential commentators like *Novoe Vremia*'s Suvorin began to invoke economic arguments in calling for disengagement from Asia. Even *Sankt-Peterburgskie Vedomosti*, traditionally the finance minister's staunch ally, was losing faith: "To think that we will win the Chinese market is wrong. . . . Our only exports there are more troops and more money."[57]

Cyclical factors played a part in the public's rejection of Witte's plans for Asia's *pénétration pacifique*. But there was a more fundamental reason for the poor reception of the finance minister's ideas. More than any European nation around 1900, Russian educated society was still dominated by an aristocratic, preindustrial ethos that disdained merchants and entrepreneurs as nouveaux riches. To paraphrase the Princeton historian Arno Mayer, nowhere did the old regime persist more tenaciously than in the empire of the Romanovs.

A good example of the finance minister's difficulties was a malicious anecdote about a meeting he staged in Nizhnii-Novgorod between Nicholas II and representatives of the merchant class in summer 1896. As part of the festivities surrounding the tsar's coronation that year, Witte had organized a lavish Exposition of Trade and Industry in the historic market town. In the minister's words, the fair was to showcase "the success of our industry" and "the great political wisdom" of his program.[58] No expense was spared to impress visitors. To encourage attendance, students and workers were offered free train trips from anywhere in Russia.[59]

Witte hoped to inspire respect for the *kupechestvo*, the old merchant estate, and to remind the public of their nation's commercial heritage. A regional paper gushed: "The merchant class stands in closed communion with the genuine spirit of Russia and constitutes its strongest component."

The implication was that, with its European ways, the nobility had ceded its leading role. "Because of changing conditions," the editorial went on, "many estates no longer possess the vitality that was theirs in former times."[60]

The highlight was a visit by the newly crowned imperial couple in July. Nicholas and Alexandra were welcomed by the curious spectacle of an honor guard composed of merchants' sons in medieval Muscovite velvet and fur garb. Making small talk, the tsar asked the lads about their names. "Knoop!" proudly answered the first. "Von Einem!" replied the second, followed by "Schulz!" "König!" and a variety of other Germanic surnames. Nicholas was not impressed.[61]

The story is apocryphal, but it illustrates Russian feelings about the finance minister's ideas. Sergei Witte's vision of Russia as a modern commercial power stood as much chance of taking root in his compatriots' imaginations as an orchid shoot planted in Siberia's taiga.

*I*f many Russians grew enthusiastic about the Far East when Nicholas became their tsar, reports of complications on the Pacific in 1894 aroused fears in the minds of others. A writer for *Vestnik Evropy* fretted about the immense population of the troubled Asian neighbor: "With its innumerable masses China gravely threatens Europe. . . . The sooner the European nations are delivered from this nightmare, the better."[62] "Sigma," who frequently commented about East Asia in *Novoe Vremia,* invoked Vladimir Solovev's famous poem: "I beseech Russian society, Russian writers, and Russian journalists to pay heed to what is now happening in the East and to prepare for battle with the approaching Pan-Mongolist [threat]. It menaces not just our Pacific provinces or even Siberia but our very historical existence."[63]

China's speedy rout soon put such fears to rest. But over the coming years the Middle Kingdom awakened anxieties of another kind. As on North America's West Coast, during the latter years of the nineteenth century the influx into eastern Siberia of *manzy,* as Chinese migrants were popularly known there, was not universally welcomed by the local Russian population.[64] Newspapers in Vladivostok began pressing authorities to "support the Russian worker's struggle against the harmful effects of Chinese immigration and their competition for manual labor."[65]

General Kuropatkin was not alone in sounding the alarm against "the yellow tidal wave." The February 1897 issue of *Russkaia Mysl* complained that "Siberia is becoming entirely non-Russian," going on to implore: "We must keep every Siberian *desiatina* in Russian hands."[66] Another periodical, *Sibirskii Vestnik* (The Siberian Herald) remarked a year earlier: "The Chinese are playing a similar role on our eastern frontier as the Jews in our western borderlands, with all of the same consequences."[67] On occasion Russian papers even reprinted Western anti-immigration diatribes.[68] Yet, when compared to the vitriol of William Randolph Hearst's *San Francisco Examiner,* the Russian press tended to be much less alarmist about the *manzy* in Vladivostok and Khabarovsk than North American dailies were about the changing ethnic mix of California or British Columbia.

The Boxer rising naturally heightened worries about the restive Oriental empire, especially among authors and artists. The radical literary critic Nikolai Mikhailovskii, for one, was convinced that Vladimir Solovev's direst predictions were coming true. "We are beginning to realize that the dismal literature about the Mongol flood and its danger to Europe is hardly far-fetched," he warned in an article.[69]

Another cultural figure who was concerned about the Boxers was the well-known war painter Vasilii Vereshchagin.[70] In summer 1900 he published a long series of articles about a recent Far Eastern journey that betrayed fears bearing a remarkable resemblance to Kuropatkin's. Perhaps the Orient had a similar effect on Vereschagin's imagination because of a shared past. The two men had made their careers in the Central Asian wars of the 1870s and 1880s and were friends in later years.[71] At the same time, in the public's imagination their names were both firmly linked to Turkestan. If Kuropatkin was the chronicler of its conquest, Vereshchagin was the campaign's most famous artist.

Although some of Vereshchagin's earlier paintings might have seemed to glorify the combat in Central Asia, now his distaste for Oriental conquest was unambiguous.[72] In one of the articles he recalled that he had opposed the annexation of China's Ili Valley in 1883.[73] The artist also strongly objected to any land grabs in Manchuria or Xinjiang during the Qing's current difficulties. "What good would [such acquisitions] do us?" Vereshchagin asked. "They would only bring a host of heavy complications. Even immense and mighty Russia lacks the strength to pacify and civilize several tens of millions of people from an alien race." He concluded: "The smaller our population of men with queues, the better."[74]

Like the war minister, Vasilii Vereshchagin was obsessed by demographics. He often worried about the tremendous disparity between the white race and Asia's "600 million yellow faces and pairs of slanting eyes."[75] Vereshchagin believed it would be impossible to defeat such a populous adversary:

> It is difficult to imagine how we could inflict harm on [the Chinese]. Killing 20,000, 50,000, or even 100,000 of them is literally a drop in the ocean. With their philosophical indifference to death, they will just keep coming at our cannon and our rifles. They will march in the hundreds of thousands, in the millions![76]

The painter agreed with Kuropatkin that the Occident would witness another great Oriental attack in the new century: "It seems to me . . . that the danger of a new assault from the east is very great, and virtually inevitable in the future. The only question is when it will happen."[77] He repeated that Russians must be careful to avoid needlessly provoking their Asian neighbor by annexing its territory. Vereshchagin also echoed the war minister's appeal to the white nations for unity in the face of this grave danger: "It is in Europe's interest . . . to prevent the coming to life of 'the yellow specter' until the time Russia is strong enough to absorb the dragon's first blows."[78] By not joining its forces, Christendom stood to suffer the very fate that befell the quarrelsome Kievan principalities nearly seven hundred years earlier: "If Europeans respond to the threat of a multimillion yellow-faced army with as little unanimity of resolve as the Russian appanage princes when they were attacked by the Asiatic hordes in another age, the former will surely experience the same sad consequences."[79]

Unfortunately, on a personal level, the artist's worries about the yellow peril proved to be well founded. Vereshchagin met his end along with Vice Admiral Stepan Makarov on the Pacific Fleet's flagship, *Petropavlovsk,* which was sunk by a mine off Port Arthur in March 1904 during the Russo-Japanese War.

Kuropatkin's views were nevertheless in a distinct minority among Russians at the time. Editorials in the press generally betrayed little concern that the Boxer rising might pose a threat outside of China. As we have seen, many more commentators shared Ukhtomskii's sympathy for the Chinese than the war minister's worries about a yellow peril. Even when Russian interests were directly menaced by the disturbances in Manchuria, those who did react tended to do so with anger rather than fear. The response of Port Arthur's hawkish *Novyi Krai* was typical when it announced that "Russians must forget about their long friendship with China's Bogdykhan" and "gather its armed forces" to teach "the yellow race" a lesson.[80]

Some Russians did worry about Japan as the new yellow peril. In 1895 the newspaper editor Suvorin warned, "The white-faced diplomacy of Europe is having to contend with the tide of the Japanese yellow race. And it seems to me that this is the harbinger of difficult times."[81] One curious article in *Novoe Vremia* suggested that Genghis Khan's birthplace, long a source of speculation, actually lay in the island empire, thereby implying that Meiji Japan was the natural heir of the Mongol Horde.[82]

To some, Solovev's prediction that Japan might join forces with China and lead a Pan-Mongolist march through the Eurasian continent seemed the most frightening possibility. In a book about the new Russian tsar published in France in 1895, Nicolas Notovitch likened the recent advent of Japan on the world stage to Gog and Magog, the biblical enemies of the kingdom of God. He also drew another parallel with the past: "And the ferocious Scythians, the pitiless Turanians seem ready once again to launch their sanguinary sweep across the world." Were Tokyo to take command of the Middle Kingdom's masses, the consequences would be cataclysm: "Imagine the unstoppable power of such a force, drawn from two nations that together can field some two hundred million troops, as it advances . . . over the [Inner Asian] desert into the plains of Turkestan. These were the very routes traversed by Genghis Khan."[83]

In "Poslednie ogonki" (The Last Glimmerings), a fairy tale published in 1897, Dmitri Mamin-Sibiriak told of Europe's conquest from a large island off the coast of East Asia: "This last attack, inflicted on Europe by the yellow-faced barbarians, was the inevitable consequence of all of the West's policies. Indeed, for several hundred years Europeans had taught the yellow race the arts of destruction. . . . This was the real flood of barbarism surging over the continent with the most modern weapons."[84] The fate of Mamin's Europeans was not quite as grim as that suffered in Solovev's "Short Tale of the Antichrist." Here the Asians sold the continent to some American billionaires who turned it into a giant park for their hunting vacations.

Another author who feared Japan was the Port Arthur–based journalist I. S. Levitov. The author of alarmist tracts, including "The Yellow Race," "The Yellow Bosphorus," and "Yellow Russia," Levitov avidly spread notions of a yellow peril.[85] In his "Yellow Bosphorus," for example, he warned that Tokyo hoped to seize the Korean peninsula. In addition to hemming in the Russian Pacific Fleet, a firm footing on the Asian continent would place Japan in an excellent position to influence the Qing. "Europe must finally understand the consequences should a China, armed by Japan, begin to use its newfound military might to insist on equality with the European powers," Levitov pointed out.[86] It would be far better, he felt, to strike a deal with England to keep Japan in check.[87]

Russian diplomats were not above using the yellow peril to defend tsarist ambitions on the Pacific. In May 1901, Foreign Minister Count Lamsdorf instructed his ambassadors in Europe to tell their hosts that a Japanese attack on Russia would jeopardize the West as well. "The governments must not lose sight of the fact," he wrote, "that such a war would unleash a powerful patriotic outburst, which would undoubtedly be transformed into an uprising of the entire yellow race against the hated Europeans."[88] There is no evidence to suggest that Lamsdorf himself believed such rhetoric.

Notovitch and Levitov were exceptions among their countrymen. Japan, like China, did not worry many, as shown by the tsarist military's spectacular failure to heed the threat of war before January 1904. On the whole, it seems that the yellow peril exerted a much stronger fascination in cultural circles, such as the Silver Age poets, than among the general public. Even then, those who invoked the yellow peril sometimes did so in an ironic sense. After all, even Solovev had been ambiguous in his famous poem of 1895. If the first line read: "Panmongolism! Though the word be fierce," the second suggested a less hostile attitude: "Yet it caresses my ear."

*T*he ideas expressed by Przhevalskii, Ukhtomskii, Witte, and Kuropatkin all shaped the Russian consciousness during its fin de siècle infatuation with the Far East. One obvious case was the tsar himself, whose inconsistent East Asian politics betrayed the contradictory elements of various ideologies. Nicholas's contempt for the Asians' martial talents, his faith in the superiority of Russian arms, and his lust for empire in the East were all characteristic of Przhevalskii's conquistador imperialism. Yet the tsar's response to the Boxer rising shows that he also shared Ukhtomskii's enthusiasm for Russia's Oriental destiny and the Middle Kingdom. And, very early in his reign, before Nicholas had lost faith in his finance minister, he was intrigued about the economic possibilities the Trans-Siberian Railway might open for his empire.

As with the tsar, the ideas we have studied also played a part in the actions of his government. Witte's ambitions for *pénétration pacifique* were joined with Ukhtomskii's Asianism in predisposing St. Petersburg toward its secret alliance with Peking in 1896. Asianism was also very much in evidence four years later, when Russian opinion and policy remained sympathetic to the Chinese during the Boxer crisis. Meanwhile, the tsarist government took an entirely different tack in response to Germany's seizure of Kiaochow in 1897. Rather than stand by its Asian partner, Nicholas allowed his administration to be seduced by Przhevalskian conquistador imperialism, greedily taking its own slice of Qing territory. The yellow peril had a weaker impact on the Russian imagination at the time than some of the other ideologies. Yet its specter nevertheless haunted War Minister Kuropatkin and made him reluctant to play more than a purely defensive role in East Asia.

We do not know enough about the way foreign policy was shaped in St. Petersburg to describe the interplay between ideas and diplomacy more precisely. But a look at Russia's turn to the East during the short decade from 1895 to 1904 suggests two conclusions. First, it is clear that foreign policy is influenced by ideas. This is not to say the way a state sees the world entirely determines how it behaves among other nations. The role of ideology in diplomacy is more complicated than mere cause and effect. The historian Gordon Craig once remarked: "To establish the relationship between ideas and foreign policy is always a difficult task."[89]

St. Petersburg's interest in the Pacific was awakened by events over which it had no control, namely, China's spectacular defeat in its brief war with Japan in 1894–1895. The decision to seize Port Arthur three years later would clearly never have been taken without Germany's sudden grab of Kiaochow. By the same token, the long and painful debate over evacuating Manchuria only occurred after the Boxer rising drew tsarist troops into China's northeastern provinces in the first place. Yet in each case St. Petersburg's response to these episodes was determined not just by circumstance alone. It was also shaped by the way leading officials thought about such events.

This study also underscores the futility of trying to distill diplomatic behavior to a single ideological essence. The actions of states are rarely if ever entirely driven by one idea. In his intellectual history of American foreign policy, *Promised Land, Crusader State,* the University of Pennsylvania scholar Walter McDougall identified no less than eight important strains of thought during the two centuries of the republic's existence.[90] By the same token, Russian perceptions of its place in the world have never been monopolized by a solitary ideology, be it an "urge to the sea," "Third-Rome Messianism," "pacifying the frontier," or some other notion.

While this has been a study of events that occurred in another age, under a very different political order, some of the ideas we encountered remain alive at the turn of the twenty-first century. To local officials in the Russian Federation's Pacific regions, who anxiously compare their nation's waning power to populous China's waxing self-confidence, the yellow peril has risen from the grave. Meanwhile, in Moscow some politicians call for closer ties with Peking and other Asian states on the grounds that Russia has more in common with them politically, economically, and culturally than "Atlanticists" like the United States. At the same time, many intellectuals are increasingly fascinated by Eurasianism, the twentieth-century offshoot of Asianism. Others, in response to the territorial indignities inflicted on their empire since 1991, have reacted by glorifying the Skobelevs and other conquerors of a more confident past. As Russia grapples for a new sense of itself after the collapse of Communism's ideological certainties, we can only expect older notions to reassert themselves.

Appendix

Chronology

	("Russian") Julian *calendar*	(Western) Gregorian *calendar*
Alexander III resolves to build Trans-Siberian Railroad	Dec. 16, 1886	Dec. 28, 1886
Tsarevich Nicholas begins grand tour of Asia	Oct. 23, 1890	Nov. 4, 1890
Japanese policeman attacks Nicholas at Otsu	Apr. 29, 1891	May, 11, 1891
Japan declares war on China	July 20, 1894	Aug. 1, 1894
Alexander III dies, Nicholas II becomes tsar	Oct. 20, 1894	Nov. 1, 1894
China and Japan sign Treaty of Shimonoseki	Apr. 5, 1895	Apr. 17, 1895
Russia, Germany, and France warn Japan	Apr. 11, 1895	Apr. 23, 1895
Russia lends 100 million rubles to China	June 25, 1895	July 6, 1895
Russia and China conclude secret alliance	May 22, 1896	June 3, 1896
German navy seizes Kiaochow Bay	Nov. 2, 1897	Nov. 14, 1897
Russian squadron anchors off Port Arthur	Dec. 4, 1897	Dec. 16. 1897
Russians found Harbin	May 28, 1898	June 9, 1898
Empress dowager quashes Hundred Days' reforms	Sep. 9, 1898	Sep. 21, 1898
Boxers murder German diplomat	June 6, 1900	June 19, 1900
Chinese bombard Blagoveshchensk	July 2, 1900	July 15, 1900
Russians begin invading Manchuria	July 13, 1900	July 26, 1900
Allies reach Peking legations	Aug. 1, 1900	Aug. 14, 1900
Ito arrives in Russia for private peace mission	Nov. 12, 1901	Nov. 25, 1901
Britain and Japan conclude alliance	Jan. 17, 1902	Jan. 30, 1902
Russia pledges Manchurian evacuation	Mar. 26, 1902	Apr. 8, 1902
Bezobrazov arrives in Port Arthur	Jan. 30, 1903	Feb. 12, 1903
Russians ignore evacuation's second phase	Mar. 26, 1903	Apr. 8, 1903
Yalu timber partnership chartered	May 31, 1903	June 13, 1903
Nicholas appoints Alekseev viceroy of Far East	July 30, 1903	Aug. 12, 1903
Nicholas fires Witte	Aug. 15, 1903	Aug. 28, 1903
Russians reoccupy Mukden	Oct. 15, 1903	Oct. 28, 1903
Japanese attack Port Arthur	Jan. 26, 1904	Feb. 8, 1904

Notes

Abbreviations

I use the following abbreviations for archives, document collections, and some periodicals. Citations for Russian archives generally follow this format: f. o. d. l.—with f. representing *fond* (fund), o. = *opis* (register), d. = *delo* (file), and l. = *list* (page). When citing the same archival source more than once, I abbreviate it to author, type of document, date, and page number.

AVPRI	Arkhiv vneshnei politiki Rossiiskoi Imperii (Archive of Foreign Policy of the Russian Empire, Moscow)
BA	Bakhmeteff Archive, Columbia University, New York
BDFA	Kenneth Bourne and D. Cameron Watt, eds., *British Documents on Foreign Affairs: Reports and Papers from the Foreign Office Confidential Print*, pt. 1, ser. A, E ([Frederick, Md.]: University Publications of America, 1983–1989)
BDOW	Great Britain. Foreign Office, *British Documents on the Origins of the War, 1898–1914*, ed. G. P. Gooch and Harold Temperley, vols. 1–2 (London: His Majesty's Stationery Office, 1926–1938)
BE	*Entsiklopedicheskii slovar*, 82 vols. (St. Petersburg: Brokgauz i Efron, 1890–1905)
DDF	France. Ministère des affaires étrangères, *Documents diplomatiques français (1871–1914), 1ère série (1871–1900)*, vols. 11–16 (Paris: Imprimerie nationale, 1929–1959)
GARF	Gosudarstvennyi arkhiv Rossiiskoi Federatsii (State Archive of the Russian Federation, Moscow)
GP	Germany. Auswärtiges Amt, *Die grosse Politik der Europäischen Kabinette, 1871–1914: Sammlung der diplomatichen Akten der Auswärtigen Amptes*, ed. Johannes Lepsius et al., vols. 9, 12–14, 16, 18 (Berlin: Deutsche Verlagsgesellschaft für Politik und Geschichte, 1922–1927)
IRLI	Institut russkoi literatury (Pushkinskii dom) (Institute of Russian Literature [Pushkin House] of the Russian Academy of Sciences, St. Petersburg)

Izvestiia   *Izvestiia Imperatorskago Russkogo Geograficheskago Obshchestva* (in the Soviet period, *Izvestiia Vsesoiuznogo Geograficheskago Obshchestva*)

KA   *Krasnyi Arkhiv,* 106 vols. (Moscow: Tsentralnyi arkhiv RSFSR, 1922–1941)

NCH   *The North-China Herald*

NV   *Novoe Vremia*

RAN   Sanktpeterburgskii filial Arkhiva Rossiiskoi Akademii Nauk (St. Petersburg Branch of the Archive of the Russian Academy of Sciences)

RGAVMF   Rossiiskii gosudarstvennyi arkhiv Voenno-Morskogo Flota (Russian State Archive of the Navy, St. Petersburg)

RGB   Otdel rukopisei, Rossiiskaia gosudarstvennaia biblioteka (Manuscript division of the Russian State Library, Moscow)

RGIA   Rossiiskii gosudarstvennyi istoricheskii arkhiv (Russian State Historical Archive, St. Petersburg)

RGO   Nauchnyi arkhiv Rossiiskogo Geograficheskogo obshchestva (Scientific Archive of the Russian Geographical Society, St. Petersburg)

RGP   *Rijks Geschiedkundige Publicatiën, grote serie,* vols. 100, 138 (The Hague: Martinus Nijhoff, 1905–)

RGVIA   Rossiiskii gosudarstvennyi voenno-istoricheskii arkhiv (Russian State Military-Historical Archive, Moscow)

RNB   Otdel rukopisei, Rossiiskaia natsionalnaia biblioteka (Manuscript division of the Russian National Library, St. Petersburg)

Sbornik   Russia. Generalnyi shtab, *Sbornik geograficheskikh, topograficheskikh i statisticheskikh materialov po Azii* (St. Petersburg: Voen. tip., 1883–1914), 87 vols.

SPBVed   *Sankt-Peterburgskie Vedomosti*

VE   *Vestnik Evropy*

Introduction

1. Andrei Bely, *Petersburg,* trans. Robert A. Maguire and John E. Malmstad (Bloomington: Indiana University Press, 1978), 51, 64–65.

2. Konstantin Mochulsky, *Andrei Bely: His Life and Works,* trans. Nora Szalavitz (Ann Arbor, Mich.: Ardis, 1977), 147.

3. Bely, *Petersburg,* 238–39.

4. Ibid., 27.

5. For a survey of Russian literary responses to the conflict, see David Wells, "The Russo-Japanese War in Russian Literature," in David Wells and Sandra Wilson, eds., *The Russo-Japanese War in Cultural Perspective* (New York: St. Martin's Press, 1999), 108–33.

6. Properly speaking, the region should be called East Asia. Since this work is written largely from the perspective of St. Petersburg, however, I use the terms Far East and East Asia interchangeably.

7. Aleksei Nikolaevich Kuropatkin, *The Russian Army and the Japanese War*, trans. A. B. Lindsay, 2 vols. (New York: E. P. Dutton, 1909).

8. Boris Borisovich Glinskii, ed., *Prolog Russko-Iaponskoi voiny: Materialy iz arkhiva Grafa S. Iu. Vitte* (Petrograd: Brokgauz-Efron, 1916). An abridged French translation also exists: Pierre Marc, *Quelques années de la politique internationale: Antécédants de la guerre russo-japonaise* (Leipzig: K. F. Koehler, 1914).

9. Boris Aleksandrovich Romanov, *Russia in Manchuria, 1892–1906*, trans. Susan Wilbur Jones (Ann Arbor, Mich.: Edwards, 1952).

10. David Maclaren McDonald, *United Government and Foreign Policy in Russia, 1900–1914* (Cambridge, Mass.: Harvard University Press, 1992).

11. William L. Langer, *The Diplomacy of Imperialism*, 2 vols. (New York: Alfred A. Knopf, 1956).

12. William L. Langer, "The Origins of the Russo-Japanese War," in Carl E. and Elizabeth Schorske, eds., *Explorations in Crisis: Papers on International History* (Cambridge, Mass.: Harvard University Press, 1969), 3–45.

13. Andrew Malozemoff, *Russian Far Eastern Policy, 1881–1904: With Special Emphasis on the Causes of the Russo-Japanese War* (Berkeley: University of California Press, 1958).

14. S. C. M. Paine, *Imperial Rivals: China, Russia, and Their Disputed Frontier* (Armonk, N.Y.: M. E. Sharpe, 1996); David Wolff, *To the Harbin Station: The Liberal Alternative in Russian Manchuria, 1898–1914* (Stanford, Calif.: Stanford University Press, 1999).

15. Langer, "Origins," 7n.15.

16. V. A. Avdeev, "'Sekrety' Russko-iaponskoi voiny," *Voenno-Istoricheskii Zhurnal*, no. 9 (1993): 87–88.

17. Panteleimon Nikolaevich Simanskii, *Sobytiia na Dalnem Vostoke*, 3 vols. (St. Petersburg: Voennaia tipografiia, 1910). The entire text was recently republished in a single volume: V. A. Zolotarev, ed., *Rossiia i Iaponiia na zare XX stoletiia* (Moscow: Abrizo, 1994); Avdeev, "'Sekrety,'" 89n.39. I am aware of two copies of the original, which can now be freely read. The tsar's personal edition, bound in dark-green Morocco leather, with gilded pages and the bookplate of his Winter Palace Library, is now held at the Russian State Library in Moscow (formerly the Lenin Library). Until a few years ago it had been locked up in the library's *spetskhran* (restricted collection). RGVIA possesses another, somewhat less luxurious version in f. VUA, o. 6, d. 1.

18. The best treatment of the former is Anthony Pagden, *Lords of All the World: Ideologies of Empire in Spain, Britain, and France, c. 1500–c. 1800* (New Haven, Conn.: Yale University Press, 1995). Two studies of ideology in international relations in the modern era are Heinz Gollwitzer, *Geschichte des weltpolitischen Denkens* (Göttingen: Vandenhoeck & Ruprecht, 1972); and Alan Cassels, *Ideology and International Relations in the Modern World* (London: Routledge, 1996). Another useful work is Eric Carlton, *War and Ideology* (Savage, Md.: Barnes and Noble Books, 1990).

19. See, for example, Andrew H. White to John Foster, dispatch, Feb. 16, 1893, in Harold Perry Ford, "Russian Far Eastern Diplomacy: Count Witte and the Penetration of China, 1895–1904" (Ph.D. diss., University of Chicago, 1950), 47–48.

20. A. M. Gorchakov, memorandum, Nov. 21, 1864, *BDFA*, pt. I, ser. A, 1:287.

21. Terry Eagleton, *Ideology: An Introduction* (London: Verson, 1991); *Oxford English Dictionary,* 2d ed., s.v. "ideology." This definition is very close to that in the *Dictionary of the Social Sciences:* "A pattern of beliefs and concepts . . . which purport to explain complex social phenomena with a view to directing and simplifying socio-political choices" (J. Gould, "Ideology," in J. Gould and W. Kolb, eds., *Dictionary of the Social Sciences* [London: Tavistock, 1964], 315, cited in Carlton, *War and Ideology,* 20).

22. Cassels, *Ideology,* 242.

23. Mark Bassin, *Imperial Visions: Nationalist Imagination and Geographical Expansion in the Russian Far East, 1840–1865* (Cambridge: Cambridge University Press, 1999). Other recent books include Milan Hauner, *What Is Asia to Us? Russia's Asian Heartland Yesterday and Today* (Boston: Unwyn Hyman, 1990); Daniel Brower and Edward J. Lazzerini, eds., *Russia's Orient: Imperial Borderlands and Peoples, 1700–1917* (Bloomington: Indiana University Press, 1997); Susan Layton, *Russian Literature and Empire: Conquest of the Caucasus from Pushkin to Tolstoy* (Cambridge: Cambridge University Press, 1994); Kalpana Sahni, *Crucifying the Orient: Russian Orientalism and the Colonization of Caucasus and Central Asia* (Bangkok: White Orchid Press, 1997).

24. Edward Said, *Orientalism* (New York: Vintage, 1979).

25. Caryl Emerson, *Boris Godunov: Transpositions of a Russian Theme* (Bloomington: Indiana University Press, 1986), 245.

26. Aleksandr Blok, "Skify," in *Polnoe sobranie stikhotvorenii v dvukh tomakh,* vol. 1 (Leningrad: Sovetskii Pisatel, 1946), 585.

27. James Joll, "1914: The Unspoken Assumptions," in Hans-Joachim Wolfgang Koch, ed., *The Origins of the First World War: Great Power Rivalry and German War Aims* (New York: Taplinger, 1972), 309–16.

1: The Grand Tour

1. Georgii Ivanov, *Kniga o poslednem tsarstvovanii* (Orange, Conn.: Antiquary, 1990), 85–87; Geoffrey Trease, *The Grand Tour* (New York: Holt, Rinehart and Winston, 1967), 1–4; R. S. Lambert, ed., *Grand Tour: A Journey in the Tracks of the Age of Aristocracy* (New York: E. P. Dutton, 1937).

2. The standard account is Prince Esper E. Ookhtomsky [Ukhtomskii], *Travels in the East of His Imperial Majesty Czar Nicholas II of Russia, when Cesarewich, 1890–1891,* 2 vols. (Westminster: Constable, 1900). Quotes are from this English translation. The Russian original is Ukhtomskii, *Puteshestvie.* Nicholas's own diaries are rather laconic (GARF, f. 601, o. 1, dd. 225–26). For an official summary of the first leg of the journey, see Vasilii Silovich Krivchenko, *Puteshestvie Ego Imperatorskago Vysochestva Naslednika Tsesarevicha na Vostok ot Gatchiny do Bombeia* (St. Petersburg: Tip. Min. Vnutrennykh Del, 1891). Although Nicholas Alexandrovich was the first tsarevich to travel to Asia overseas, his grandfather, Alexander II, ventured into Siberia as far as Tobolsk in spring 1837 during a lengthy tour of Russia as heir; see Otto Hoetzsch, *Rußland in Asien: Geschichte einer Expansion* (Stuttgart: Deutsche Verlags-Anstallt, 1966), 31.

3. For a detailed itinerary, consult the *Pamiat Azova*'s logs, RGAVMF, f. 417, o. 1, d. 558.

4. Nicholas II, *Dnevnik Imperatora Nikolaia II* (Berlin: Slovo, 1923), 39–40.

5. Nicholas to Alexander III, letter, Dec. 24, 1890, GARF, f. 677, o. 1, d. 919, l. 132; Nicholas, *Dnevnik,* 40.

6. Nicholas to Alexander, letter, Jan. 20, 1891, GARF, f. 677, o. 1, d. 919, l. 142;

Nicholas to Ksenia, letter, Jan. 22, 1891, GARF, f. 662, o. 1, d. 186, l. 53.

7. The trip is described in Gustav I. Radde, *23,000 mil na iakhte "Tamara": Puteshchestvie ikh Imperatorskikh Vysochestv Velikikh Kniazei Aleksandra i Sergeia Mikhailovichei v 1890–1891 gg.,* 2 vols. (St. Petersburg: tipografiia Eduarda Roppe, 1892).

8. Nicholas to Alexander, letter, Mar. 7, 1891, GARF, f. 677, o. 1, d. 919, l. 156.

9. The background is sketched out in Chandran Jeshurun, *The Contests for Siam, 1889–1902* (Kuala Lumpur: Penerbit University Kebangsaan Malaysia, 1977).

10. Marina Georgievna Kozlova, *Rossiia i strany Iugo-Vostochnoi Azii* (Moscow: Nauka, 1986), 198–99; Andrei Lobanov-Rostovsky, *Russia and Asia* (Ann Arbor, Mich.: George Wahr, 1951), 209–10; A. S. Guzin, "Tailandskii vopros na rubezhe XIX i XX vv. i pozitsiia Rossii," in *Vzaimotnosheniia narodov Rossii, Sibirii i stran Vostoka: Istoriia i sovremennost* (Irkutsk: Irkutskii gos. ped. institut, 1995), 140–43.

11. Nicholas to Alexander, letter, Mar. 20, 1891, GARF, f. 677, o. 1, d. 919, l. 165; Andrew D. Kalmykow, *Memoirs of a Russian Diplomat: Outposts of the Empire, 1893–1917* (New Haven, Conn.: Yale University Press, 1971), 101. On Nicholas's relations with King Chulalongkorn, see Roy D. R. Betteley, *Fabergé* (Bangkok: Chitralada Palace, 1986), 49–55.

12. Nicholas to Alexander, letter, Mar. 20, 1891, GARF, f. 677, o. 1, d. 919, ll. 165–66. Nicholas expresses similar sentiments in his diary; see diary, Mar. 13, 1891, GARF, f. 601, o. 1, d. 225, l. 108.

13. Nicholas to Marie Fedorovna, letter, Mar. 31, 1891, GARF, f. 642, o. 1, d. 2321, l. 148.

14. Li Hangzhang was the brother of the more well-known statesman Li Hongzhang.

15. Jürgen Osterhammel, *China und die Weltgesellschaft* (Munich: C. H. Beck, 1989), 104.

16. Nicholas to Marie Fedorovna, letter, Mar. 31, 1891, GARF, f. 642, o. 1, d. 2321, ll. 150–52; Nicholas to Ksenia, letter, Apr. 2, 1891, GARF, f. 662, o. 1, d. 186, l. 63.

17. Nicholas, diary, Mar. 24, 1891, GARF, f. 601, o. 1, d. 225, l. 125.

18. Nicholas to Ksenia, letter, Apr. 26, 1891, GARF, f. 662, o. 1, d. 186, l. 64.

19. Ibid., l. 67.

20. George Lensen, *The Russian Push toward Japan: Russo-Japanese Relations, 1697–1875* (Princeton, N.J.: Princeton University Press, 1959), 437–46; Hosoya Chihiro, "Japan's Policies toward Russia," in James Morley, ed., *Japan's Foreign Policy, 1868–1941: A Research Guide* (New York: Columbia University Press, 1974), 351; Leonid Nikolaevich Kutakov, *Rossiia i Iaponiia* (Moscow: Nauka, 1988), 207–10. At the time, Japanese public opinion was much more wary of China. Tokyo had witnessed an anti-Russian demonstration by Japanese students in November 1890, but this was more an expression of dislike for the West than Russophobia. See Vladimir Nikolaevich Lamsdorf, *Dnevnik 1891–1892* (Moscow: Academia, 1934), 7; and George Lensen, "The Attempt on the Life of Nicholas II in Japan," *Russian Review* 20, no. 3 (July 1961): 234–35. On Japanese suspicions of Russian designs in East Asia at the time of Nicholas's visit, see Robert Britton Vaillant, "Japan and the Trans-Siberian Railroad, 1885–1905" (Ph.D. diss., University of Hawaii, 1974), 47–67; Simanskii, *Sobytiia,* 1:22.

21. Lensen, "Attempt," 238.

22. Nicholas to Marie Fedorovna, letter, May 8, 1891, GARF, f. 642, o. 1, d. 2321, l. 184.

23. Ibid. Apparently the tsarevich's admiration of the local women was not limited to passively enjoying the geishas' company. Japanese police reports record that at night he ventured to establishments "where sailors usually go" (Marc Ferro, *Nicholas II: The Last of the Tsars* [London: Penguin, 1991], 20).

24. Nicholas to Marie Fedorovna, letter, May 8, 1891, GARF, f. 642, o. 1, d. 2321, l. 185.

25. Nicholas to Marie Fedorovna, letter, May 2, 1891, GARF, f. 642, o. 1, d. 2321, ll. 175–76; Nicholas to Alexander, letter, May 2, 1891, GARF, f. 677, o. 1, d. 919, l. 175; Lensen, "Attempt," 240.

26. Nicholas to Alexander, letter, May 7, 1891, GARF, f. 677, o. 1, d. 919, l. 186. Nicholas wrote his mother that he was "very touched that Japanese lined the streets along the train on their knees with such sad expressions . . . [he] received 1,000 telegrams expressing sympathy from various Japanese" (Nicholas to Marie Fedorovna, letter, May 2, 1891, GARF, f. 642, o. 1, d. 2321, l. 176; D. E. Shevich to N. K. Giers, letter, May 2, 1891, AVPRI, f. 138, o. 467, d. 114/121b, l. 14).

27. Lamsdorf, *Dnevnik 1891–1892,* 121.

28. D. E. Shevich to N. K. Giers, letter, May 2, 1891, AVPRI, f. 138, o. 467, d. 114/121b, ll. 13–16; Lamsdorf, *Dnevnik 1891–1892,* 119. Lamsdorf also took pity on "the poor Japanese [who] are doing everything to be forgiven" (120). Peter Yong-Shik Shin argues that the Japanese government was actually deeply involved in the attack in "The Otsu Incident: Japan's Hidden History of the Attempted Assassination of Future Emperor Nicholas II of Russia in the Town of Otsu, Japan, May 11, 1891, and Its Implication for Historical Analysis" (Ph.D. diss., University of Pennsylvania, 1989). Simanskii hints at this as well (*Sobytiia,* 1:22). On suggestions that the attempted assassination was the work of revolutionaries, see Kniaz U . . . [S. D. Urusov], *Imperator Nikolai II: Zhizn i deianiia Ventsenosnago Tsaria* (Nice: Imprimerie russe, 1910), 24–28.

29. Nicholas to Marie Fedorovna, letter, May 8, 1891, GARF, f. 642, o. 1, d. 2321, l. 183.

30. Hohenlohe-Schillingsfürst to Wilhelm II, letter, Sep. 12, 1895, *GP,* 9:360.

31. Steven G. Marks, *Road to Power: The Trans-Siberian Railroad and the Colonization of Asian Russia, 1850–1917* (Ithaca, N.Y.: Cornell University Press, 1991), 94–114 ; Vaillant, "Japan," 1–20; Harmon Tupper, *To the Great Ocean: Siberia and the Trans-Siberian Railway* (Boston: Little, Brown, 1965), 82.

32. A. I. Dmitriev-Mamonov, ed., *Ot Volgi do Velikogo okeana: Putevoditel po Velikoi Sibirskoi zheleznoi doroge s opisaniem Shilko-Amurskago vodago puti i Manchzhurii* (St. Petersburg: T-vo khudozh. pechati, 1900), 52; Glinskii, *Prolog,* 8; Tupper, *To the Great Ocean,* 82–83; Michael Myers Shoemaker, *The Great Siberian Railway: From St. Petersburg to Pekin* (New York: G. P. Putnam's Sons, 1903), 1–2.

33. The itinerary of the journey's Siberian leg is described in great detail in a guide commissioned for the tsarevich's journey: Russia, Tsentralnyi statitisticheskii komitet M. V. D., *Ot Vladivostoka do Uralska: Putevoditel k puteshchestviiu Ego Imperatorskago Vysochestva gosudaria nasliednika tsesarevicha* (St. Petersburg: Tip. T-va A. Transhel, 1891).

34. Nicholas to Aleksandr Mikhailovich, letter, Aug. 13, 1891, GARF, f. 645, o. 1, d. 102, l. 90.

35. V. N. Lamsdorf, *Dnevnik 1894–1896* (Moscow: Mezhdunarodnye otnosheniia, 1991), 145; Vladimir Iosifovich Gurko, *Features and Figures of the Past: Government and Opinion in the Reign of Nicholas II* (Stanford, Calif.: Stanford University Press, 1939), 256; Malozemoff, *Russian Far Eastern Policy,* 50; Nicolas Notovich, *L'Empereur Nicolas II et la politique russe* (Paris: Paul Ollendorf, 1895); Marks, *Road to Power,* 136.

36. Constantin de Grunwald, *Le Tsar Nicolas II* (Paris: Berger-Levrault, 1965), 123.

37. Sergei Iulevich Witte, *The Memoirs of Count Witte,* trans. and ed. Sidney Harcave (Armonk, N.Y.: M. E. Sharpe, 1990), 127. On the other hand, Nicholas's letters clearly contradict Witte's assertion that the attack in Otsu "left the Tsarevich with an attitude of hostility toward and contempt for Japan and the Japanese" (126).

Bogdykhan is an archaic Russian designation for the Chinese emperor.

38. Andrew M. Verner, *The Crisis of Russian Autocracy: Nicholas II and the 1905 Revolution* (Princeton, N.J.: Princeton University Press, 1990), 9–10, 61n.30. Even the editor of Nicholas's diaries makes this complaint. See Nicholas, *Dnevnik*, 40. Along with Verner, another good analysis of Nicholas's thinking is in Mark D. Steinberg and Vladimir M. Krustalëv, eds., *The Fall of the Romanovs: Political Dreams and Personal Struggles in a Time of Revolution* (New Haven, Conn.: Yale University Press, 1995), esp. 1–37.

39. Just before his departure, Nicholas pleaded with the British ambassador not to burden him with too many official obligations when he traveled in India, in order to leave as much time as possible for sightseeing (British ambassador to N. K. Giers, letter, Dec. 18, 1890, AVPRI, f. 138, o. 467, d. 114/121b, l. 7). Once he was abroad, the heir was frequently admonished by his mother to be more conscientious about his responsibilities. See Edward J. Bing, ed., *The Letters of Tsar Nicholas and Empress Marie* (London: Ivor Nicholson & Watson, 1937), 47, 57–58.

40. Marks, *Road to Power*, 139.

41. Ukhtomskii, *Travels*, 2:35.

2: Conquistador Imperialism

1. N. M. Przhevalskii to F. L. Heiden, report, June 6, 1877, RGO, f. 13, o. 1, d. 26, ll. 2–3; *Przhevalskii*, directed by Sergei Iutkevitch (Mosfilm, 1952). For details about the film, see N. Vaganova, ed., *Przhevalskii, Zametki o filme* (Moscow: Goskinoizdat, 1952).

2. Nikolai Mikhailov, "'Przhevalskii' Novyi khudozhestvennyi film," in *Pravda*, Feb. 28, 1952, 3.

3. Sergei Iutkevich, *Sobranie Sochinenii*, vol. 2 (Moscow: Iskusstvo, 1991), 319; Iu. M. Galenovich, *"Belye piatna" i "bolevye tochki" v istorii Sovetsko-Kitaiskikh otnoshenii* (Moscow: Institut Dalnago Vostoka, 1992), 38. Iutkevich makes no mention of these problems in the essay he wrote at the time of the movie's release, "The Project and Its Execution," in Vaganova, *Przhevalskii*, 25–40. One wag claimed that Chinese objections were dropped after strong pressure from Stalin, out of supposed filial piety. See Iurii Borev, "Staliniada," *Daugava* (1990): 49. Because of Przhevalskii's strong physical resemblance to the Georgian, and since he apparently visited the latter's birthplace in the Caucasus nine months before Stalin was born, Soviet mythology has it that Nikolai Mikhailovich was Stalin's real father. See Edvard Radzinskii, *Stalin: The First In-Depth Biography Based on Explosive New Documents from Russia's Secret Archives* (New York: Doubleday, 1996), 21–22. A spirited rebuttal of the legend is given by the director of the Przhevalskii museum, Evgeniia Gavrilenkova, "Spletnia: Przhevalskii i Stalin. Pochemu sviazyvaiut eti imena?" *Raboche-kretstianskii korrespondent*, no. 2 (1990): 26–29.

The explorer's private life has been the subject of considerable speculation in other respects as well. One woman in Smolensk claimed to be his illegitimate daughter. See Marfa Kirillovna Batseva, "Vospominaiia o Przhevalskom," manuscript, 1963–1964, RNB, f. 656, k. 1, n. 1; Boris Mikhailovich Ovchinnikov, "Zapis o znakomstve s docheriu Przhevalskogo," manuscript, Aug. 24, 1964, RNB, f. 656, k. 2, n. 3; B. M. Ovchinnikov, "Taina serdtsa Przhevalskogo," manuscript, 1963, 1966; RNB, f. 656, k. 2, n. 2. However, the facts that Przhevalskii was vehemently opposed to marriage and that only young men accompanied him on his travels have also led some to argue that Nikolai Mikhailovich's tastes were a little divergent from the norm. See Simon Karlinsky, "Gay Life before the Soviets," *Advocate*, Apr. 1, 1982, 31–34.

4. Edwin George Bilof, "The Imperial Russian General Staff and China in the Far East, 1880–1888" (Ph.D. diss., Syracuse University, 1974), 56.

5. [Anton Pavlovich Chekhov], *NV,* Oct. 26, 1888, 1, republished in A. P. Chekhov, *Polnoe sobranie sochineii i pisem,* vol. 15 (Moscow: Nauka, 1979), 236–37. Also cited in Donald Rayfield, *The Dream of Lhasa: The Life of Nikolay Przhevalsky (1839–88), Explorer of Central Asia* ([Athens]: Ohio University Press, 1976), 203–4.

6. The definitive biography remains Nikolai Fedorovich Dubrovin, *Nikolai Mikhailovich Przhevalskii, Biograficheskii ocherk* (St. Petersburg: Voennaia Tipografiia, 1890). A reasonable, albeit rather hagiographic, Russian work is A. V. Zelenin, *Puteshestviia N. M. Przhevalskago* (St. Petersburg: Soikin, 1900). Two of his collaborators also wrote about him. See Petr Kuzmich Kozlov, *Nikolai Mikhailovich Przhevalskii: Pervyi izsledovatel prirody Tsentralnoi Azii* (St. Petersburg: N. Ia. Stokovaia, 1913); Vsevolod Ivanovich Roborovskii, "Nikolai Mikhailovich Przhevalskii v. 1878–1888 gg.," *Russkaia Starina* 23, no. 1 (January 1892): 217–38; 23, no. 3 (March 1892): 653–74. For details about his earlier life, see the brief autobiography, N. M. Przhevalskii, "Avtobiografiia N. M. Przhevalskago," *Russkaia Starina* 19, no. 11 (November 1888): 528–43, republished as "Avtobiograficheskii rasskaz," *Izvestiia* 72, nos. 4–5 (1940): 477–87; as well as the largely autobiographical "Vospominaniia okhotnika," *Izvestiia* 72, nos. 4–5 (1940): 488–500. The entry "Przhevalskii," in A. A. Polovtsov, ed., *Russkii biograficheskii slovar,* vol. 14 (St. Petersburg: Skorokhodov, 1903), 763–83, provides a good summary. The only English-language biography is Rayfield, *Dream.* For details about his military career, see RGVIA, f. 400, o. 21, d. 1692. Diaries, correspondence, and much other valuable material can be consulted in his papers, RGO, f. 13.

7. Sven Hedin is inaccurate when he writes that the explorer descended from "an old Russian noble lineage" (*General Prschewalski in Innerasien* [Leipzig: F. A. Brockhaus, 1928], 9).

8. Przhevalskii, "Avtobiografiia," 529.

9. Przhevalskii, "Vospominaniia," 494.

10. Rayfield, *Dream,* 8.

11. One of its editors until 1862 had been the radical novelist Nikolai Chernyshevskii. The monthly's new head became the more politically safe Maj. Gen. Prince Sayn-Wittgenstein-Berleburg. See ibid., 12.

12. For a full account of the expedition, see N. M. Przhevalskii, *Puteshestvie v Ussuriiskom Krae, 1867–1869 gg.* (St. Petersburg: N. Nekliudov, 1870).

13. In the nineteenth century the area was also called Central Asia. However, this term now applies more to the Turkic republics of the former Soviet Union. Good surveys of the region include Denis Sinor, ed., *The Cambridge History of Early Inner Asia* (Cambridge: Cambridge University Press, 1990); and Owen Lattimore, *Pivot of Asia: Sinkiang and the Inner Asian Frontiers of China and Russia* (Boston: Little, Brown, 1950).

14. John MacGregor, *Tibet: A Chronicle of Exploration* (London: Routledge & Kegan Paul, 1970), 248. The story is also engagingly told in Peter Hopkirk, *Trespassers on the Roof of the World: The Race for Lhasa* (London: John Murray, 1982).

15. Rayfield, *Dream,* 50.

16. Although written from a British perspective, the most readable account is Peter Hopkirk, *The Great Game: On Secret Service in High Asia* (London: John Murray, 1990). A more recent book by an American couple adds some details about the Russian involvement: Karl E. Meyer and Shareen Blair Brysac, *Tournament of Shadows: The Race for Empire and the Great Game in Central Asia* (New York: Counterpoint, 1999). See also David Gillard, *The Struggle for Asia, 1828–1914: A Study in British and Russian Imperialism* (London: Methuen, 1977). Two earlier works tell the Russian side of the story: Andrei Evgenevich Snesarev, *Indiia kak glavnyi faktor v Sredne-Aziatskom voprose* (St. Petersburg:

A. E. Suvorin, 1906); and V. T. Lebedev, *V Indiiu: Voenno-statisticheskii i strategicheskii ocherk* (St. Petersburg: Tipografiia A. A. Pokhorovshchikova, 1898).

17. M. I. Veniukov, "Ob organizatsii voenno-statisticheskikh rabot po izucheniiu gosudarstv Srednei i Vostochnoi Azii," manuscript, n.d., RNB, f. 363, k. 3, n. 40; Bilof, "Imperial Russian General Staff," xii; K. K. Zvonarev, *Agenturnaia razvedka*, vol. 1 (Moscow: IV upravlenie shtaba Rab.-Kr. Armii, 1929), 1–26; Mikhail Alekseev, *Voennaia razvedka Rossii ot Riurika do Nikolaia II*, vol. 1 (Moscow: Russkaia Razvedka, 1998), 29–44, 51–73. The development of intelligence in the nineteenth century is described more generally in Roger Faligot, *Histoire mondiale du renseignement*, vol. 1 (Paris: R. Laffont, 1994).

18. Dmitrii Aleksandrovich Miliutin, "Kriticheskoe izsledovanie znacheniia voennoi geografii i voennoi statistiki," *Voennyi Zhurnal*, no. 1 (1846): 124–25; S. G. Kliashtornyi and A. I. Kolesnikov, *Vostochnyi Turkestan glazami russkikh puteshestvennikov* (Alma Ata: Nauka, 1988), 62; Bruce Menning, *Bayonets before Bullets: The Russian Imperial Army, 1861–1914* (Bloomington: Indiana University Press, 1992), 10; David Alan Rich, *The Tsar's Colonels: Professionalism, Strategy, and Subversion in Late Imperial Russia* (Cambridge, Mass.: Harvard University Press, 1998), 52–54; Mikhail Rafailovich Ryzhenkov, "Vklad i izuchenie Vostoka diplomaticheskogo i voennogo vedomstv," in A. A. Vigasin et al., eds., *Istoriia otechestvennogo vostokovedeniia s serediny XIX veka do 1917 goda* (Moscow: Vostochnaia Literatura, 1997), 135.

19. The Geographical Society's official history, written for its fiftieth anniversary, provides a detailed institutional account: Petr Petrovich Semenov-Tian-Shanskii, *Istoriia poluvekoi deiatelnosti Imperatorskago Russkogo Geograficheskago Obshchestva, 1845–1895*, 3 vols. (St. Petersburg: V. Bezobrazov, 1895). More recently, the Geographical Society commissioned briefer studies to mark its centennial and sesquicentennial. See, respectively, Lev Semenovich Berg, *Vsesoiuznoe geograficheskoe obshchestvo za sto let* (Moscow: Akademiia Nauk SSSR, 1946); and Anatolii Grigorevich Isachenko, ed., *Russkoe Geograficheskoe Obshchestvo: 150 let* (Moscow: Progress, 1995). There is also much valuable detail in Nathaniel Knight, "Constructing the Science of Nationality: Ethnography in Mid-Nineteenth-Century Russia" (Ph.D. diss., Columbia University, 1995).

20. Semenov, *Istoriia*, 1:xvii-xxi. I am indebted to Firoozeh Kashani-Sabet for explaining the term *Erdkunde* to me.

21. Berg, *Vsesoiuznoe*, 31.

22. Knight, "Constructing," 228–29.

23. Agnes Murphy, *The Ideology of French Imperialism, 1871–1881* (New York: Howard Fertig, 1968), 19. Murphy's work is an excellent study of the links between French geography and colonialism. See also Anne Godlewska and Neil Smith, eds., *Geography and Empire* (Oxford: Blackwell, 1994), esp. 1–8, 56–127; Heinz Gollwitzer, *Europe in the Age of Imperialism, 1880–1914* (New York: W. W. Norton, 1969), 102–3, 161–63.

24. Joseph Conrad, "Geography and Some Explorers," in *Last Essays* (Garden City: Doubleday, Page, 1926), 9, cited in Godlewska and Smith, *Geography and Empire*, 1.

25. Rich, *Tsar's Colonels*, 59–62.

26. Hauner, *What Is Asia*, 41.

27. N. M. Przhevalskii, *Mongolia, The Tangut Country, and the Solitudes of Northern Tibet*, trans. E. Delmar Morgan, 2 vols. (London: S. Low, Marston, Searle, & Rivington, 1876).

28. Ibid., 2:154.

29. N. M. Przhevalskii to Main Staff, report, Apr. 28, 1871, RGVIA, f. 447, o. 1, d. 8, l. 9.

30. F. L. Heiden to M. Kh. Reutern, memorandum, Jan. 20, 1874, RGVIA, f. 400, o. 1, d. 368, ll. 1–10.

31. The published account of the expedition is N. M. Przhevalskii, *From Kulja, across the Tian Shan to Lob-Nor,* trans. E. Delmar Morgan (London: S. Low, Marston, Searle, & Rivington, 1876). Przhevalskii's diary was also published: N. M. Przhevalskii, "Dnevnik vtorogo puteshestviia N. M. Przhevalskogo v Tsentralnuiu Aziiu," *Izvestiia* 72, nos. 4–5 (1940): 501–606.

32. Przhevalskii's claims were energetically disputed by the German explorer Baron Ferdinand von Richthofen, who asserted that, based on Chinese maps, the lake lay farther north than the Russian reported. Przhevalskii stuck to his guns and eventually *both* were proven correct when subsequent geographers determined that the lake had moved several times (Rayfield, *Dream,* 110). Richthofen's critique and Przhevalskii's rebuttal are included in the English translation of Przhevalskii's second Inner Asian expedition (Przhevalskii, *From Kulja,* 135–65). My understanding of this question was also helped by an undergraduate essay: Andrea Tokheim, "Przhevalskii: Journey to Lob Nor," (Unpublished paper, Yale University, 1993).

33. N. M. Przhevalskii to Main Staff, memorandum, June 6, 1877, RGO, f. 13, o. 1, d. 26, l. 1–6. Another copy can be found in RGVIA, f. 400, o. 1, d. 438, ll. 132–8. The report was also published as an appendix in Dubrovin, *Przhevalskii,* 570–77.

34. Nineteenth-century Russians knew Xinjiang as "Eastern Turkestan" to distinguish it from "their" Turkestan. The largely Muslim northwestern borderlands were conquered by the Qianlong emperor in the 1750s, who named the region Xinjiang (the "New Territories").

35. Przhevalskii, memorandum, June 6, 1877, l. 2.

36. Ibid., l. 2.

37. Ibid., l. 2.

38. Przhevalskii, memorandum, Aug. 25, 1878, RGVIA, f. 400, o. 1, d. 553, ll. 3–4.

39. Kuropatkin, now head of the Asiatic Section of the army's Main Staff and Przhevalskii's direct superior at the time, confirmed the army's interest in a report to the emperor: "The object of this research will be Tibet. Along with scientific aims, it is suggested that, as much as may be possible, the expedition also gather intelligence about the political situation in Tibet. . . . Such an effort . . . may open the way to our influence over all of Inner Asia, right through to the Himalayas", (Kuropatkin to Alexander II, report, November 1878, RGVIA, f. 400, o. 1, d. 553, l. 24).

40. Przhevalskii, report, Nov. 16, 1878, RGVIA, f. 400, o. 1, d. 553, l. 10. Urga is known today as Ulan Bator.

41. A good description is given in Derek Waller, *The Pundits: British Exploration of Tibet and Central Asia* (Lexington: University Press of Kentucky, 1990). For a first-hand account, see Sarat Chandra Das, *Journey to Lhasa and Central Tibet* (London: John Murray, 1902).

42. N. K. Giers to Ia. P. Shishmarev, secret telegram, Dec. 9, 1878, RGVIA, f. 400, o. 1, d.553, l. 15; Ia. P. Shishmarev to N. K. Giers, secret telegram, Mar. 23, 1879, RGVIA, f. 400, o. 1, d. 553, l. 37a.

43. The explorer describes these travels in Przhevalskii, *Iz Zaisana cherez Khami v Tibet* (St. Petersburg: V. S. Balashev, 1883).

44. For details about the horse, see ibid., 40–42; L. S. Poliakov, "Loshad Przhevalskogo, zoologicheskii ocherk," *Izvestiia* 17, no. 1 (January 1881): 1–20; Lee Boyd and Katherine A. Houpt, eds., *Przewalski's Horse: The History and Biology of an Endangered Species* (Albany: State University of New York Press, 1994); Erica Mohr, *Das Urwildpferd* (Wittenberg: A. Ziemsen Verlag, 1959); Suzanne Possehl, "Rare Przewalski's Horse Returns to the Harsh Mongolian Steppe," *New York Times,* Oct. 4, 1994, B9; Ewoud Sanders, "Przewalskipaard," *NRC Handelsblad,* Sep. 2, 1996, 18.

45. P. S. Vannovskii, report, Apr. 2, 1883, RGVIA, f. 401, o. 4/928, d. 36, ll. 19–21.

46. The journey is described in Przhevalskii, *Ot Kiakhty na istoki Zheltoi Reki* (St. Petersburg: V. S. Balashev, 1888).

47. P. S. Vannovskii to Alexander III, memorandum, Jan. 22, 1886, RGVIA, f. 401, o. 4/926, d. 36, l. 130; N. N. Obruchev to Przhevalskii, letter, Jan. 21, 1886, RGVIA, f. 401, o. 4/928, d. 36, l. 134.

48. Rayfield, *Dream,* 191.

49. Przhevalskii to P. S. Vannovskii, report, Mar. 10, 1888, RGVIA, f. 401, o. 4/928, d. 40, l. 4. See also P. S. Vannovskii, report, Mar. 14, 1888, RGVIA, f. 401, o. 4/928, d. 40, l. 11.

50. The city's name is a good weather vane for Russian nationalist sensibilities. V. I. Lenin changed it back to Karakol in 1921, but Stalin again decreed the use of Przhevalsk, to mark the centenary of Nikolai Mikhailovich's birth. Finally, in 1991 the Republic of Kyrgyzstan, which now governs the city, restored the name Karakol. The diary the explorer kept at the start of this journey was published: Przhevalskii, "Dnevnik poslednego puteshestviia N. M. Przhevalskogo v 1888 g.," *Izvestiia* 72, nos. 4–5 (1940): 630–40.

51. Przhevalskii to Main Staff, "Novaia soobrazhenii o voine s Kitaem," memorandum, June 25, 1886, RGO, f.13, o. 1, d. 43; also in RGIA, f. 971, o. 1, d. 181. A somewhat similar plan was sketched out earlier in his classified article, "O vozmozhnoi voine s Kitaem," *Sbornik,* 1:293–321.

52. M. I. Dragomirov to F. A. Feldman, letter, Nov. 6, 1886, RGVIA, f. 401, o. 4/928, d. 36, l. 194; Przhevalskii, *Ot Kiakhti,* 493–536. The essay also appeared in Katkov's thick journal: N. M. Przhevalskii, "Sovremennoe polozhenie Tsentralnoi Azii," *Russkii Vestnik* 186 (1886): 473–524; an English translation, "General Prjevalsky on Central Asia," was published in *Asiatic Quarterly Review* 4 (October 1887): 393–452.

53. Nikolai Mikhailovich Przhevalskii, *Ot Kiakhti na istoki zheltoi reki,* ed. Eduard Markovich Murzaev (Moscow: OGIZ, 1948). The editor of this edition pointed this discrepancy out to me during a conversation in July 1993.

54. Przhevalskii, *Ot Kiakhti,* 502.

55. Ibid., 509.

56. Ibid., 530.

57. Ibid., 536. Przhevalskii conveniently ignores the fact that Martens was much more sympathetic to China, which the jurist certainly acknowledged as an ancient civilization worthy of respect. See Fedor Fedorovich Martens, *Le conflit entre la Russie et la Chine* (Brussels: Librairie C. Muquardt, 1880).

58. Przhevalskii, "Novaia," l. 83.

59. Ibid., ll. 52–99.

60. Ibid., ll. 91–96.

61. Ibid., l. 98.

62. Dubrovin, *Przhevalskii,* 161.

63. Ibid., 145.

64. Roborovskii, "Przhevalskii," 655–56.

65. Przhevalskii, *Mongolia,* 1:91.

66. Rayfield, *Dream,* 69.

67. Przhevalskii, *Mongolia,* 1:43.

68. Semenov, *Istoriia,* 1:545.

69. Przhevalskii, *Mongolia,* 2:128.

70. Przhevalskii, *Ot Kiakhti,* 501.

71. Przhevalskii, *Mongolia,* 1:32–33.

72. Ibid., 2:100.

73. Przhevalskii, *Ot Kiakhti*, 516.

74. Rayfield, *Dream*, 124.

75. Przhevalskii, *Iz Zaisana*, 52.

76. Przhevalskii, *Mongolia*, 2:131.

77. Ibid., 2:133.

78. Przhevalskii, *Ot Kiakhti*, 509.

79. Ibid.

80. Ibid., 511.

81. Ibid., 510.

82. William H. Scheider, *An Empire for the Masses: The French Popular Image of Africa, 1870–1900* (Westport, Conn.: Greenwood Press, 1982), 154.

83. Social Darwinism did not get an easy reception in tsarist Russia. The American historian of Russian science Alexander Vucinich points out that virtually all sociologists of the day opposed the notions of social Darwinism then fashionable in the West, as well as such thinkers as Nikolai Danilevskii and the anarchist Prince Petr Kropotkin. One contemporary scholar said that the philosophy was "a doctrine that considers collective homicide the cause of human progress." Cited in Alexander Vucinich, *Darwin in Russian Thought* (Berkeley: University of California Press, 1988), 385.

84. Przhevalskii, notes, n.d., RGO, f. 13, o. 1, d. 55, l. 1.

85. Przhevalskii claims that the committee chaired by Gen. Nikolai Obruchev approved the document. See Przhevalskii to V. I. Roborovskii, letter, June 6, 1886, RGO, f. 13, o. 1, d. 39, l. 16.

86. P. S. Vannovskii to N. K. Giers, letter, Nov. 5, 1885, RGVIA, f. 401, o. 4/928. d. 36, l. 124.

87. N. N. Obruchev to G. G. Danilovich, memorandum, Feb. 7, 1886, RGVIA, f. 401, o. 4/928, d. 36, l. 157; D. A. Miliutin, note, Jan. 17, 1881, RGVIA, f. 400, o. 1, d. 553, l. 314; Head of Main Staff to Przhevalskii, letter, July 27, 1883, RGO, f. 13, o. 2, d. 141, l. 15; Dubrovin, *Przhevalskii*, 354, 361, 419, 433.

88. Przhevalskii to P. S. Vannovskii, letter, June 3, 1888, RGO, f. 13, o. 1, d. 93, l. 29; RAN, f. 4, o. 2-1887, d. 58; Dubrovin, *Przhevalskii*, 379.

89. G. G. Danilovich to Przhevalskii, letter, Aug. 17, 1883, RGO, f. 13, o. 2, d. 61, l. 7.

90. Przhevalskii to G. G. Danilovich, letters, 1884–1885, GARF, f. 601, o. 1, d. 1329. This file contains five letters about the expedition addressed to Gen. Danilovich, "for report to the Imperial Heir." Some of these letters were also published in *Izvestiia* 21, no. 3 (May 1885): 235–240; 21, no. 12 (November 1885): 558–76.

91. Rayfield, *Dream*, 151.

92. A. M. Pozdneev, "Tretie puteshestvie v Tsentralnoi Azii," *Zhurnal Ministerstvo Narodnago Prosveshcheniia* 232 (March 1884): 316–51.

93. S. M. Georgievskii, "Dva izsledovatelia Kitaiskoi Imperii," *VE* 24, no. 8 (August 1887): 777–806.

94. Dubrovin, *Przhevalskii*, 428. See also Przhevalskii's spirited rebuttal to Georgievskii: "Otvet na kritiku o Kitae," *NV*, Oct. 14, 1887, 2.

95. Dmitrii Alekseevich Miliutin, *Dnevnik*, vol. 1 (Moscow: Bilioteka im. Lenina, 1947), 144.

96. V. M. Golitsyn, diary, Feb. 21, 1881, RGB, f. 75, 10:484.

97. M. I. Veniukov to 3ème Congrès de Géographie, letter, 1881, RGO, f. 13, o. 2, d. 41, l. 16.

98. Daniel Brower, "Imperial Russia and the Orient: The Renown of Nikolai

Przhevalsky," *Russian Review* 53, no. 3 (July 1994): 367; "Smes," *Istoricheskii Vestnik* 46 (November 1891): 546; K. G. Sokol, *Monumenty Imperii* (Moscow: Geos, 1999), 202–4.

99. Nikolai Mikhailovich Karataev, *Nikolai Mikhailovich Przhevalskii: Pervyi issledovatel prirody Tsentralnoi Azii* (Moscow: Akademiia Nauk SSSR, 1948), 267n.1.

100. [Anton Pavlovich Chekhov], *NV*, Oct. 26, 1888, 1. Chekhov respected Przhevalskii as the archetypal man of action and the antithesis of the Ivanovs and Uncle Vanyas, the "superfluous men" he gently mocked in his stories and plays. As several literary critics have suggested, one of the protagonists of Chekhov's novella *The Duel* was largely inspired by Nikolai Mikhailovich. See A. G. Hornfeld, "Przhevalskii i Chekhov," manuscript, 1938, RNB, f. 356, k. 10, n. 8; Donald Rayfield, *Chekhov: The Evolution of His Art* (London: Paul Elek, 1975), 7, 114, 124; Rayfield, *Dream*, 203–4; E. Gavrilenkova, "Chekhov i Przhevalskii," *Rabochii Put*, Aug. 23, 1980, 3. Rayfield believes that one of the characters in Vladimir Nabokov's *The Gift*, a novella written forty years later, also "bears the imprint of Przhevalsky" (*Dream*, 204).

101. Miliutin, *Dnevnik*, 1:144.

102. Mary Townsend, *The Rise and Fall of Germany's Colonial Empire* (New York: Macmillan, 1930), 56.

103. A. P. Thornton, *Doctrines of Imperialism* (New York: John Wiley & Sons, 1965), 47.

104. Joseph Alois Schumpeter, "The Sociology of Imperialisms," in Heinz Norden, trans., *Imperialism and Social Classes* (Fairfield, N.J.: Augustus M. Kelley, 1989), 3–130.

105. Martin Green, *Dreams of Adventure, Deeds of Empire* (London: Routledge & Kegan Paul, 1979), 3. See also Susanne Howe, *Novels of Empire* (New York: Columbia University Press, 1949).

106. Langer, *Diplomacy*, 2:797.

3: The Asianist Vision

1. Aleksandr Blok, "Skify," *Stikhotvoreniia i poemy* (Moscow: Khudozhestvennaia Literatura, 1968), 231. Commentaries about the Asian motif in Blok's "The Scythians" include Ivanov-Razumnik, "Ispytanie v groze i bure. ('Dvenadtsat' i 'Skify' A. Bloka)," in *Aleksandr Blok Andrei Bely* (Letchworth: Bradda Books, 1971), 129–173; Rolf-Dieter Kluge, *Westeuropa und Rußland im Weltbild Aleksandr Bloks* (Munich: Verlag Otto Sagner, 1967); Avril Pyman, "The Scythians," *Stand* 8:3 (1966–1967): 23–33; George Nivat, "Du 'Panmogolisme' au mouvement Eurasien," in *Vers la fin du mythe russe: Essais sur la culture russe de Gogol à nos jours* (Lausanne: L'Age d'homme, 1988), 126–42.

2. Liah Greenfield, *Nationalism: Five Roads to Modernity* (Cambridge, Mass.: Harvard University Press, 1992), 191.

3. Emanuel Sarkisyanz, *Russland und der Messianismus des Orients* (Tübingen: J. C. B. Mohr, 1955), 203–4; Sarkisyanz, "Russian Attitudes toward Asia," *Russian Review* 13, no. 4 (October 1954): 245; Nicholas V. Riasanovsky, "Asia through Russian Eyes," in Wayne S. Vucinich, ed., *Russia and Asia: Essays on the Influence of Russia on the Asian Peoples* (Stanford, Calif.: Hoover Institution Press, 1972), 9–10.

4. Nivat, "Du 'Panmogolisme,'" 126.

5. Ukhtomskii, *Travels*, 2:55.

6. Malozemoff, *Russian Far Eastern Policy*, 46.

7. The only published biography is the essay by a Hermitage curator, G. A. Leonov, "K istorii lamaiskogo sobraniia gosudarstvennogo ermitazha," in R. E. Pubaev, ed., *Buddizm i literaturno-khudozhestvennoe tvorchestvo narodov Tsentralnoi Azii* (Novosibirsk: Nauka, 1985), 101–15. Ukhtomskii compiled a short autobiography in 1899: "Av-

tobiografiia," 1899, IRLI, f. 326, o. 1, d. 72. There are also some details about his life in his personnel records at the Ministry of Internal Affairs: Department of Spiritual Affairs, "Ukhtomskii," RGIA, f. 821, o. 12, d. 546, and in a brief entry in *BE*, 35:102.

8. Ukhtomskii, "Avtobiografiia," l. 2. The family took its name from its ancestral property on the Ukhtoma River, which flows into Lake Beloe, some 500 kilometers east of St. Petersburg. See Departament geroldii, *Obshchii Gerbovnik dvorianskikh rodov Vserossiiskaia Imperiia*, 11 vols. (St. Petersburg, 1798–1862), 4:3; R. J. Ermerin, *La noblesse titrée de l'empire russe* (Sarau: Emile Zeidler, n.d.), 221–22; Patrick de Gmeline, *Dictionaire de la nobless Russe* (Paris: Contrepoint, 1978), 449–50; P. K. Grebelskii, ed., *Dvorianskie rody Rossiiskoi imperii*, vol. 1 (St. Peterburg: Vesti, 1993), 302–5.

9. Ukhtomskii, "Avtobiografiia," ll. 2–3

10. Details about Ukhtomskii's bureaucratic career are in Department of Spiritual Affairs, "Ukhtomskii," ll. 1–127.

11. Emanuel Sarkisyanz, *Geschichte der orientalischen Völker Rußlands bis 1917* (Munich: R. Oldenbourg, 1961), 369–87; Russia, Pereselencheskoe Upravlenie, *Aziatskaia Rossiia*, 3 vols. (St. Petersburg: A. F. Marks, 1914), 1:132–43, 225–31; M. N. Bogdanov, *Ocherki istorii buriat-mongolskogo naroda* (Verkhneudinsk: Buriat-mongolskoe izd-vo, 1926); Galina Rinchinovna Galdanova et al., *Lamaizm v Buriatii XVIII-nachala XX veka* (Novosibirsk: Nauka, 1983); John Snelling, *Buddhism in Russia: The Story of Agvan Dorzhiev, Lhasa's Emissary to the Tsar* (Shaftesbury: Element, 1993), 1–10.

12. Galdanova et al., *Lamaizm*, 17–18, 26. For a general study of Russian prerevolutionary nationalities policy, see Andreas Kappeler, *Russland als Vielvölkerreich: Entstehung, Geschichte, Zerfall* (Munich: C. H. Beck, 1993); on Buddhism, see 127. For a more polemical description of tsarist treatment of its Siberian minorities, see Nikolai Mikhailovich Iadrintsev, *Sibir kak koloniia* (St. Petersburg: I. M. Sibiriakov, 1892), 146–89.

13. Speranskii's policies are described in Helen Sharon Hundley, "Speransky and the Buriats: Administrative Reform in Nineteenth-Century Russia" (Ph.D. diss., University of Illinois at Urbana-Champaign, 1984). See also Marc Raeff, *Michael Speransky: Statesman of Imperial Russia* (The Hague: Martinus Nijhoff, 1969), 252–79; Kappeler, *Russland*, 140–41.

14. Sarkisyanz, *Russland*, 378–80; Snelling, *Buddhism in Russia*, 10.

15. E. E. Ukhtomskii to Nicholas, letter, Jan. 5, 1900, RGIA, f. 1072, o. 1, d. 21, l. 6[b]. See Ukhtomskii's account of a trip taken from Kalmykia to Bukhara in 1889 in his *Ot Kalmytskoi stepi do Bukhary [Putevye ocherki]* (St. Petersburg: Kniaz V. P. Meshcherskii, 1891).

16. The story is told in Michael Khodarkovsky, *Where Two Worlds Met: The Russian State and the Kalmyk Nomads, 1600–1771* (Ithaca, N.Y.: Cornell University Press, 1992). See also Dittmar Schorkowitz, *Die soziale und politische Organisation bei den Kalmücken (Oiraten) und Prozesse der Akkulturation von 17. Jahrhundert bis zur Mitte des 19. Jahrhunderts* (Frankfurt a/M: P. Lang, 1992); Kappeler, *Russland*, 46–47; Sarkisyanz, *Geschichte*, 252–64; Hans-Heinrich Nolte, *Religiöse Toleranz in Rußland 1600–1725* (Göttingen: Musterschmidt, 1969), 36–52. Thomas De Quincy's narrative verse about the events of 1771, *Flight of a Tatar Tribe* (Boston: Heath, 1897), is somewhat too fanciful.

17. Department of Spiritual Affairs, "Ukhtomskii," l. 58.

18. I. Shpitsberg, ed., "Tserkov i russifikatsiia buriato-mongol pri tsarizma," *KA*, 53:100–26; Robert Rupen, *Mongols of the Twentieth Century*, 2 vols. (Bloomington: Indiana University Press, 1964), 1:7–9; Kappeler, *Russland*, 217, 246.

19. Ukhtomskii to Department of Spiritual Affairs, memorandum, Apr. 7, 1888, RGIA, f. 821, o. 133, d. 420, ll. 1–15. A version of this report was subsequently published: E. E. Ukhtomskii, *O sostoianii missionerskago voprosa v Zabaikale, v sviazi s prichinami, obuslovlivaiushchimi malouspeshnost khristianskoi propovedi sredi buriat* (St. Peters-

burg: Sinodalnaia tipografiia, 1892).

20. Ukhtkomskii to Department of Spiritual Affairs, "Mekka v politicheskom i religioznom otnoshenii," memorandum, 1889, RGIA, f. 821, o. 8, d. 1174, l. 111.

21. A good example of such attacks was an editorial in the rightist daily *Znamia*, which charged that Ukhtomskii "flirts with the Poles and the Chinese and the Jews." See Vika, "Kniaz Meshcherskii 'Opyt nekrologii,'" *Znamia*, Apr. 16, 1903, 2; V. P. Meshcherskii, "Dnevnik," *Grazhdanin*, Sep. 21, 1897, 16; Meshcherskii, "Dnevnik," *Grazhdanin*, June 25, 1902, 17.

22. Ukhtomskii, *Travels*, 2:12.

23. E. E. Ukhtomskii, "Préface," in Albert Grünwedel, *Mythologie du Bouddhisme en Tibet er Mongolie basée sur la collection lamaïque du Prince Ukhtomsky* (Leipzig: F. A. Brockhaus, 1900), xvi.

24. Ibid., xvii, xxxii.

25. Ibid., xviii.

26. Bernice Glatzer Rosenthal, *Dmitrii Sergeevich Merezhkovsky and the Silver Age: The Development of a Revolutionary Mentality* (The Hague: Martinus Nijhoff, 1975), 5–8.

27. Nikolai Berdiaev, *Dream and Reality: An Essay in Autobiography*, trans. Katharine Lampert (London: Geoffrey Bles, 1950), 141.

28. James Webb, *The Occult Establishment* (LaSalle, Ill.: Open Court, 1976), 145–211; Bernice Glatzer Rosenthal, ed., *The Occult in Russian and Soviet Culture* (Ithaca, N.Y.: Cornell University Press, 1997), 1–32, 135–52; Maria Carlson, *"No Religion Higher than Truth": A History of the Theosophical Movement in Russia, 1875–1922* (Princeton, N.J.: Princeton University Press, 1993), 3–14.

29. Robert D. Warth, "Before Rasputin: Piety and the Occult at the Court of Nicholas II," *Historian* 47, no. 3 (May 1985): 323–37.

30. In 1891, Ukhtomskii visited the Theosophical Society's headquarters in Madras, India, during the tsarevich's Asian cruise and later met with Helen Blavatsky's associate, Col. Henry Steel Olcott, in Colombia, Ceylon. He was enthusiastic about "the new and original brotherhood," praising its founder as "a Russian lady who knew and has seen much" (Ukhtomskii, *Travels*, 2:76–77; K. Paul Johnson, *Initiates of Theosophical Masters* [Albany: State University of New York Press, 1995], 124–37). The author James Webb speculates that Ukhtomskii may also have had links with the émigré mystic George Gurdjieff, who apparently based the character "Prince Lubovedsky" in his *Meetings with Remarkable Men* on Esper Esperovich. See James Webb, *The Harmonious Circle: The Lives and Work of G. I. Gurdjieff, P. D. Ouspensky, and Their Followers* (Boston: Shambala, 1987), 73.

31. René Pinon, *La lutte pour le Pacifique: Origines et résultats de la guerre russojaponaise* (Paris: Perrin, 1906), 55–56.

32. Ukhtomskii, "Préface," in Grünwedel, *Mythologie du Bouddhisme*, ix.

33. Ibid., xii.

34. Ukhtomskii, *Ot kalmytskoi*, 16, 25.

35. The collection is described in Grünwedel, *Mythologie du bouddhisme;* and in Marilyn M. Rhie and Robert A. M. Thurman, *Wisdom and Compassion: The Sacred Art of Tibet* (New York: Abrams, 1991), 85.

36. Museum of Anthropology and Ethnography, memorandum, May 7, 1920, RGIA, f. 1072, o. 1, d. 4, ll. 2–3; S. F. Oldenburg to his mother, letter, Mar. 10, 1902, RAN, f. 208, o. 2, d. 45, l. 63; *Vostokovedenie v Petrograde, 1918–1922* (Petrograd, 1923), 61; Leonov, "K istorii," 101, 109–10.

37. Leonov, "K istorii," 104.

38. Nicholas Aleksandrovich to Grand Duchess Ksenia, letter, Nov. 4, 1890,

GARF, f. 662, o. 1, d. 186, l. 41.

39. The subtitle of the book's English edition states: "Written by Order of His Imperial Majesty" (Ukhtomskii, *Travels*, 1:title page). Ukhtomskii's salary, while he was on leave, was paid directly by the Imperial Chancellery. See Department of Spiritual Affairs, RGIA, f. 821, o. 12, d. 546, l. 64. On Nicholas's involvement with the book, see Ukhtomskii to Nicholas, letter, Apr. 18, 1895, GARF, f. 601, o. 1, d. 1370, l. 13–14; Witte, *Memoirs*, 126.

40. Leonov, "K istorii," 104.

41. V. N. Lamsdorf to Ukhtomskii, letter, July 20, 1899, IRLI, f. 314, o. 1, d. 68, l. 3–4.

42. M. N. Giers to N. M. Muravev, dispatch, Sep. 30, 1899, AVPRI, f. 143, o. 471, d.116, ll. 151–152.

43. Auguste Gérard, *Ma mission en Chine, 1894–1897* (Paris: Plon, 1918), 214.

44. Ibid., 220.

45. Ukhtomskii to Nicholas, letter, Aug. 15, 1895, GARF, f. 601, o. 1, d. 1370, l. 21. Emphasis in original.

46. Effie Ambler, *Russian Journalism and Politics, 1861–1881: The Career of Aleksei Suvorin* (Detroit: Wayne State University Press, 1972), 76–78. For details about the paper's earlier years, see Gary Marker, *Publishing, Printing, and the Origins of Intellectual Life in Russia, 1700–1800* (Princeton, N.J.: Princeton University Press, 1985), 48–49.

47. In 1903 the paper's circulation was 7,000, compared to 130,000 for the business daily *Birzhevye vedomosti* and 71,500 for Suvorin's *Novoe Vremia*. See Louise McReynolds, *The News under Russia's Old Regime* (Princeton, N.J.: Princeton University Press, 1991), 97–99.

48. Ukhtomskii to Nicholas, letter, Oct. 22, 1895, GARF, f. 601, o. 1., d. 1370, l. 31.

49. [E. E. Ukhtomskii], "Ot redaktsii," *SPBVed*, Jan. 3, 1896, 1.

50. [E. E. Ukhtomskii], "Ot redaktsii," *SPBVed*, Jan. 6, 1896, 1.

51. Ibid.

52. On the newspaper's role, see Irina Sergeevna Rybachenok, "Dalnevostochnaia politika Rossii 90–kh godov XIX v. na stranitsakh russkikh gazet konservativnogo napravleniia," in A. L. Narochnitskii, ed., *Vneshniaia politika Rossii i obshchestvennoe mnenie* (Moscow: Institut Istorii SSSR, 1988), 125–46.

53. Theodor Schiemann, *Deutschland und die große Politik*, 14 vols. (Berlin, Georg Reimer, 1902–1915), 1:251.

54. I. D. Delianov to Ukhtomskii, letter, Dec. 21, 1896, RNB, f. 244, o. 1, d. 4, l. 9.

55. Schiemann, *Deutschland*, 1:366.

56. V. M. Iuzefovich, notice, Nov. 7, 1897, RGIA, f.1088, o. 2, d. 26, l. 2; Iuzefovich to Ukhtomskii, letter, Oct. 29, 1897, RGIA, f.1088, o. 2, d. 26, ll. 4–5.

57. Aleksei Sergeevich Suvorin, *Dnevnik* (Moscow: L. D. Frenkel, 1923), 127; *BE*, 35:102; Leonov, "K istorii," 107.

58. See Ukhtomskii's extensive correspondence with Nicholas during 1895 in GARF, f. 601, o. 1, d. 1370. Nicholas's diary entries for 1896 indicate that he received Ukhtomskii on a number of occasions; see, for example, Nicholas, *Dnevnik*, 188.

59. Suvorin, *Dnevnik*, 113; Kuropatkin, diary, Apr. 7, 1898, RGVIA, f. 165, o. 1, d. 1871, l. 19.

60. Suvorin, *Dnevnik*, 224.

61. Ford, "Russian Far Eastern Diplomacy," 165–66.

62. W. H. W. Waters to W. E. Goschen, letter, Oct. 13, 1896, *BDFA*, pt. I, ser. A, 2:310.

63. Emil Joseph Dillon, *The Eclipse of Russia* (New York: George H. Doran, 1918), 327. Nicholas described his own intense religious feelings in a letter to his mother:

Nicholas to Marie Fedorovna, letter, Apr. 5, 1900, GARF, f. 642, o. 1, d. 2326, l. 56.

64. Kuropatkin recalled that Buddhism was a subject of lunchtime conversation with the imperial family; see his diary, July 14, 1898, RGVIA, f. 165, o. 1, d. 1871, ll. 23–24.

65. This is the subject of many of Ukhtomskii's letters to Nicholas from 1894 through 1896; see RGIA, f. 601, o. 1, d. 1370.

66. Ukhtomskii to Nicholas, letter, May 2, 1900, RGIA, f. 601, o. 1, d. 21, l. 7; Ukhtomskii to Nicholas, letter, June 9, 1900, RGIA, f. 601, o. 1, d. 21, l. 8; Ukhtomskii to V. N. Lamsdorf, letter, July 16, 1900, GARF, f. 568, o. 1, d. 823, l. 1; Ivan Iakovlevich Korostovets, *Von Cinggis Khan zur Sowjetrepublik: Eine kurze Geschichte der Mongolei unter besonderer Berücksichtigung der neuesten Zeit* (Berlin: Walter de Gruyter, 1926), 123. See also E. E. Ukhtomskii, *Pered groznym budushchim. K russko-iaponskomu stolknoveniu* (St. Petersburg: Vostok, 1904), 13–14.

67. Despite his diminished stature at the Russian court, Ukhtomskii was actively involved in the Tibetan question up to at least 1907. See Kaznakov to P. K. Kozlov, letter, 1899, RGO, f. 18, o. 3, d. 265, ll. 20–21; Ukhtomskii to Nicholas, letter, Jan. 11, 1904, RGVIA, f. 165, o. 1, d. 1036, l. 2. The Russian Foreign Ministry's records of the Dorzhiev embassy are in AVPRI, f. 143, o. 491, ff. 1488–89. See also minutes, council of June 6, 1906, on Tibetan affairs, f. 143, o. 491, d. 1468, ll. 8–11. I have described this episode in greater length in "Tsarist Military Intelligence and the Younghusband Expedition of 1904," in Jennifer Siegel, ed., *Intelligence and International Politics from the Civil War to the Cold War* (Wesport, Conn.: Greenwood, forthcoming in 2002).

68. Kuropatkin, diary, Sep. 22, 1899, RGVIA, f. 165, o. 1, d 1889, l. 36.

69. Leonov, "K istorii," 107; Aleksandra Viktorevna Bogdanovich, *Tri poslednykh samoderzhtsa* (Moscow: Novosti, 1990), 287.

70. Romanov, *Russia in Manchuria*, 80; Kuropatkin, diary, Dec. 20, 1897, RGVIA, f. 165, o. 1, d. 1871, l. 5.

71. Russia. Ministerstvo Finansov, *Istoricheskaia spravka o vozhneishikh dlia Rossii sobytiiakh na Dalnem Vostoke v trekhletie 1898–1900 gg.* (St. Petersburg: V. F. Kirshbaum, 1902), 80–82; Witte, *Memoirs*, 230; Romanov, *Russia in Manchuria*, 78–81, 85–86.

72. The real chief was A. Iu. Rotshtein (Romanov, *Russia in Manchuria*, 81).

73. S. Iu. Witte to Nicholas, memorandum, Feb. 28, 1897, RGIA, f. 560, o. 38, d. 177, l. 31; Ministry of Foreign Affairs, Annual Report, 1897, AVPRI, f. 137, o. 475, d. 124, l. 194. A good description of the trip is given by the *Novoe Vremia* correspondent Sigma [S. N. Syromiatnikov], "V gostiakh u Bogdykhana," manuscript, May 1897, GARF, f. 543, o. 1, d. 171. Portions of this were also published in *Novoe Vremia* in July and August 1897. See also Ukhtomskii to Nicholas, letter, May 21, 1897, GARF, f. 543, o. 1, d. 171, ll. 5–8; Vladimir Vikentevich Korsakov, *Pekinskiia sobytiia: Lichnyia vospominaniia uchastnika ob osade v Pekine* (St. Petersburg: A. S. Suvorin, 1901), 199–213; Iurii Iakovlevich Solovev, *Vospominaniia diplomata 1893–1922* (Moscow: Sotsialno-ekonomicheskaia literatura, 1959), 94–97; A. Gérard to G. Hanotaux, dispatch, June 5, 1897, *DDF*, 13:421–23; Gérard, *Ma mission*, 214–25.

74. Ukhtomskii's instructions are in Romanov, *Russia in Manchuria*, 124.

75. R. Hart to J. D. Campbell, letter, May 23, 1897, in Sir Robert Hart, *The I. G. in Peking: Letters of Robert Hart Chinese Maritime Customs, 1868–1907*, 2 vols. (Cambridge, Mass.: Harvard University Press, 1975), 2:1119–20; Lo Hi-min, ed., *The Correspondence of G. E. Morrison*, vol. 1 (Cambridge: Cambridge University Press, 1876), 52. See also F. M. Knobel to J. Röell, dispatch, July 1, 1897, *RGP*, 138:516.

76. Solovev, *Vospominaniia*, 94–95.

77. Ukhtomskii to Nicholas, letter, May 21, 1897, GARF, f. 543, o. 1, d. 171, ll. 5–8;

"Utrennaia pochta," *NV*, Aug. 26, 1897, 1. The *Times* (London) foreign editor Valentine Chirol maliciously noted that he had seen the Ovchinnikov piece in the silversmith's Nevskii Prospect shop window in St. Petersburg several years earlier. The sculpture had initially been an allegory celebrating the liberation of Bulgaria. After the item was commissioned, however, the kingdom had become estranged from Russia, and it was never presented. Before Ukhtomskii's trip, Ovchinnikov's craftsmen recycled the sculpture for its new diplomatic purpose "with some of the minor figures deftly converted from Bulgars into Manchus and a suitable inscription in which China was substituted for Bulgaria." See Sir Valentine Chirol, *Fifty Years in a Changing World* (New York: Harcourt, Brace, 1928), 205; Vladimir Vikentevich Korsakov, *V starom Pekine* (St. Petersburg: Trud, 1904), 203.

78. Ukhtomskii to Witte, telegram, May 14, 1897, RGIA, f. 560, o. 28, d. 177, l. 48.

79. Romanov, *Russia in Manchuria,* 125.

80. Ukhtomskii to P. A. Romanov, telegram, [probably May or June 1897], RGIA, f. 632, o. 1, d. 1, l. 62; Ukhtomskii to Witte, telegram, June 20, 1897, RGIA, f. 632, o. 1, d. 1, l. 77; A. I. Pavlov to M. N. Muravev, dispatch, Aug. 10, 1897, AVPRI, f. 143, o. 491, d. 114, pt. 2, ll. 98–108.

81. Romanov, *Russia in Manchuria,* 124–25.

82. P. A. Romanov to D. D. Pokotilov, telegram, Aug. 1, 1897, RGIA, f. 560, o. 28, d. 13, l. 89; A. P. Cassini to Lamsdorf, letter, June 12, 1897, GARF, f. 568, o. 1, d. 527, l. 43; Ukhtomskii to M. N. Muravev, letter, May 20, 1897, GARF, f. 543, o. 1, d. 171, ll. 10–11. See also Solovev, *Vospominaniia,* 94–98.

83. Li Hongzhang to Witte, telegram, June 13, 1900, RGIA, f. 560, o. 28, d. 190, l. 1; Witte to Li Hongzhang, telegram, June 14, 1900, RGIA, f. 560, o. 28, d. 190, l. 2.

84. Li Hongzhang to Witte, telegram, June 1900, RGIA, f. 560, o. 28, d. 190, l. 9.

85. Witte to Nicholas, memorandum, July 13, 1900, RGIA, f. 560, o. 28, d. 190, ll. 37–42; Witte to Li Hongzhang, telegram, July 20, 1900, RGIA, f. 560, o. 28, d. 190, l. 35.

86. M. Shipov, note, July 18, 1900, RGIA, f. 560, o. 28, d. 190, l. 26; P. A. Romanov to Pokotilov, telegram, Sep. 12, 1900, RGIA, f. 560, o. 28, l. 190, l. 85; Ukhtomskii to Witte, telegram, Sep. 24, 1900, RGIA, f. 560, o. 28, d. 190, l. 99; Lamsdorf to M. N. Giers, telegram, Sep. 26, 1900, RGIA, f. 560, o. 28, d. 190, l. 103. The money for the mission came from Nicholas's special 12-million-ruble appropriation "for purposes known to His Majesty."

87. Ukhtomskii to Witte, telegram, Sep. 16, 1900, RGIA, f. 560, o. 28, d. 190, l. 86.

88. Ukhtomskii to Witte, telegram, Oct. 21, 1900, RGIA, f. 560, o. 28, d. 190, l. 111; Witte to Ukhtomskii, telegram, Oct. 21, 1900, RGIA, f. 560, o. 28. d.190, l. 112.

89. Witte, *Memoirs,* 126; Romanov, *Russia in Manchuria,* 81.

90. A collection of articles with his thoughts about the Russo-Japanese War was published in Ukhtomskii, *Pered.*

91. Ukhtomskii took an active role in supporting a controversial project to build a Buddhist temple in St. Petersburg on the eve of the First World War. See Aleksandr Ivanovich Andreev, *The Buddhist Shrine of Petrograd* (Ulan Ude: EcoArt Agency, 1992), 89.

92. E. E. Ukhtomskii to A. A. Ukhtomskii, letter, 1920, RAN, f. 749, o. 2, d. 354, l. 20; E. E. Ukhtomskii to S. F. Platonov, letter, Nov. 10, 1919, RNB, f. 585, d. 4484, ll. 1–2. His descendants had a more difficult time in the 1930s. His daughter-in-law, Natalia Dmitrieva, née Princess Tsertelevaia, was banished from Moscow by the OGPU in 1932 (M. V. Ukhtomskaia to OGPU, petition, May 17, 1932, RNB, f. 384, k. 12, n. 18, l. 1).

93. Andrzej Walicki, *The Slavophile Controversy: History of a Conservative Utopia in Nineteenth-Century Russian Thought,* trans. Hilda Andrews-Rusiecka (Oxford: Oxford University Press, 1975), 502.

94. George Vernadsky, *The Mongols and Russia* (New Haven, Conn.: Yale University Press, 1953), 333.

95. Karl A. Wittfogel, "Russia and the East: A Comparison and Contrast," *Slavic Review* 22, no. 4 (1963): 627.

96. Sarkisyanz, *Russland,* 204.

97. George M. Young, Jr., *Nikolai F. Fedorov: An Introduction* (Belmont, Mass.: Nordland, 1979), 8, 37–52, 60–71; Stephen Lukashevich, *N. F. Fedorov (1828–1903): A Study in Russian Eupsychian and Utopian Thought* (Newark: University of Delaware Press, 1977), 20–23. See also Michael Hagemeister, *Nikolaj Fedorov: Studien zu Leben, Werk un Wirkung* (Munich: Otto Sagner, 1989). I am grateful to Dr. Hagemeister for clarifying some points about Fedorov's ideas.

98. N. A. Setnitskii, *Russkie mystliteli o Kitae (V. S. Solovev i N. F. Fedorov)* (Harbin: n.p., 1926), 5–14; Young, *Fedorov,* 126–44; Sarkisyanz, *Russland,* 210; Hauner, *What Is Asia,* 53–54. Nikolai Fedorov's hostility to the venality of the West's commercial ethos is best expressed in his highly sarcastic article, "Vystavka 1889 goda, ili nagliadnoe izobrazhenie kultury, tsivilizatsiia i ekspluatatsiia," in *Sobranie sochinenii v chetyrekh tomakh,* 2 vols. (Moscow: Progress, 1995), 1:442–63.

99. Vladimir Sergeevich Solovev, *Chteniia o Bogochelovechestve; Stati; Stikhotovreniia i poema; Iz trekh razgovorov* (St. Petersburg: Khudozhestvennaia literatura, 1994), 385.

100. V. S. Solovev, "Mir Vostoka i Zapada," in *Sochineniia v dvukh tomakh,* 2 vols. (Moscow: Pravda, 1989), 2:602.

101. N. K. Nikiforov, "Peterburgskoe studenchestvo i Vlad. S. Solovev," in B. Averin et al., eds., *Kniga o Vladimire Soloveve* (Moscow: Sovetskii pisatel, 1991), 182.

102. Ukhtomskii, *Travels,* 2:35.

103. Dominic Lieven, *Nicholas II: Emperor of All the Russias* (London: John Murray, 1993), 38.

104. Ukhtomskii, *Travels,* 2:301.

105. Ibid., 2:145.

106. Ibid., 2:38.

107. Ibid., 2:4.

108. Ibid., 2:286.

109. Ibid., 2:35.

110. Ibid., 2:2.

111. Ibid., 2:287.

112. Ibid., 2:32.

113. Ibid., 2:143.

114. Ibid., 2:244. Ukhtomskii was not the first to portray Russia as Asia's protector. As early as 1880, the diplomat and legal scholar Fedor Martens, in *Le conflit entre la Russie et la Chine,* argued that it was St. Petersburg's place to defend the Middle Kingdom against Western colonialism.

115. Ukhtomskii, *Travels,* 2:55. Perhaps the prince was not completely off base. Eugene Schuyler, who journeyed to Turkestan in the 1870s, reported that the Russians "have not so much that contemptuous feeling towards the natives which is so marked in the dealing of the Anglo-Saxon race with people of lower culture and civilisation" (*Turkistan: Notes of a Journey in Russian Turkistan, Kokand, Bukhara, and Kuldja,* 2 vols. [New York: Scribner, Armstrong, 1876], 2:233).

116. Suvorin, *Dnevnik,* 224. See also Bogdanovich, *Tri poslednykh,* 269.

117. Ukhtomskii, *Travels,* 2:446.

118. Ibid., 2:2.

119. Ibid., 2:143.

120. E. E. Ukhtomskii, *K sobytiiam v Kitae. Ob otnosheniiakh Zapada i Rossii k Vostoku* (St. Petersburg: Vostok, 1900), 49.

121. Ukhtomskii, *Travels,* 2:379, 444.

122. Ibid., 2:287.

4: Pénétration Pacifique

1. Witte to Nicholas, memorandum, 1902, RGIA, f. 1622, o. 1, d. 711, l. 41; also in Glinskii, *Prolog,* 242; Anton Chekhov, *The Cherry Orchard,* in Ronald Hingley, trans. and ed., *The Oxford Chekhov,* vol. 3 (Oxford: Oxford University Press, 1965), 181.

2. Ibid., 162.

3. Ernest J. Simmons, *Chekhov: A Biography* (New York: Atlantic Monthly Press, 1962), 604.

4. David Magarshack, *Chekhov the Dramatist* (London: John Lehmann, 1952), 264.

5. Ibid., 166.

6. Ibid., 198.

7. V. S. Pritchett, *Chekhov: A Spirit Set Free* (New York: Random House, 1988), 220.

8. Harvey Pitcher, *The Chekhov Play: A New Interpretation* (Berkeley: University of California Press, 1985), 162.

9. Simmons, *Chekhov,* 615; Aimée Alexandre, *A la recherche de Tchékhov* (Paris: Editions Buchet/Castel, 1971), 257. After 1917, many came to see the play as a metaphor for the ancien régime. The Englishman Maurice Baring, for one, wrote, "It summed up the whole of pre-Revolutionary Russia . . . all of them dancing on the top of a volcano which is heaving and already rumbling with the noise of the coming convulsion" (*The Puppet Show of Memory* [London: W. Heinemann, 1922], 268). See also Princess Nina Andronikova Toumanova, *Anton Chekhov: The Voice of Twilight Russia* (New York: Columbia University Press, 1937), 205.

10. Magarshack, *Chekhov,* 275.

11. Eugen Häusler, *Der Kaufmann in der russischen Literatur* (Königsberg: Gräfe und Unzer Verlag, 1935), 29–127.

12. Chekhov preferred Stanislavskii, who was also of peasant and merchant origins, for the role. However, the latter was aghast at the thought of being portrayed in this humble station, and he chose to play Gaev instead. See Laurence Senelick, *The Chekhov Theatre: A Century of Plays and Performance* (Cambridge: Cambridge University Press, 1977), 68–69.

13. His maternal grandmother, though, came from an old princely family.

14. Theodore H. von Laue, *Sergei Witte and the Industrialization of Russia* (New York: Atheneum, 1974), 194.

15. V. I. Lenin, "Sotsializm i voina," in *Sochineniia,* vol. 21 (Moscow: Ogiz, 1948), 277.

16. Baron Roman Romanovich Rosen, *Forty Years of Diplomacy,* vol. 1 (London: Allen & Unwyn, 1922), 62.

17. Albert J. Beveridge, *The Russian Advance* (New York: Harper, 1903), 53.

18. Boris Vassilevich Ananich and Rafail Sholomovich Ganelin, *Sergei Iulevich Vitte i ego vremia* (St. Petersburg: Dmitrii Bulanin, 1999), 7; A. P. Korelin and S. A. Stepanov, *S. Iu. Vitte: Finansist, politik, diplomat* (Moscow: Terra, 1998), 6.

19. A. P. Izvolskii, *Mémoires de Alexandre Iswolsky: Ancien ambassadeur de Russie à Paris* (Paris: Payot, 1923), 149.

20. Evgenii Viktorovich Tarle, *Graf S. Iu. Vitte: Opyt kharakteristiki vneshnei politiki* (Leningrad: Knizhnye novinki, 1927), 3.

21. E. J. Dillon, "Two Russian Statesmen," *Quarterly Review* 236, no. 469 (October 1921): 404. A similar assessment is made by other reviewers, such as Maurice Bompard, "Les mémoires du comte Witte," *La revue de Paris* 28, no. 5 (September–October 1921): 19–33; and Johannes Delquist, "Graf Wittes Memoiren," *Preußische Jahrbücher* 191, no. 2 (February 1923): 129–46; Korelin and Stepanov, *Vitte*, 294–310. For a more detailed study of this vexing source, see B. V. Ananich and R. Sh. Ganelin, *S. Iu. Vitte: Memuarist* (St. Petersburg: Sankt-Peterburgskii filial Instituta rossiiskoi istorii RAN, 1994).

22. The definitive biography is Ananich and Ganelin, *Vitte* (1999). A more popular account of the statesman's life is Korelin and Stepanov, *Vitte*. The only English-language biography remains Laue, *Sergei Witte and the Industrialization of Russia,* although it mainly focuses on his economic policies. Another biography is currently being written by the Vanderbilt University historian Frank Wcislo. For studies of specific aspects of Witte's career, see Dietrich Geyer, *Russian Imperialism: The Interaction of Domestic and Foreign Policy, 1860–1914* (New Haven, Conn.: Yale University Press, 1987), esp. 125–245; Tarle, *Vitte;* Anatolii Venediktovich Ignatev, *S. Iu. Vitte: Diplomat* (Moscow: Mezhdunarodnye otnosheniia, 1989); I. Ia. Korostovets, *Pre-War Diplomacy: The Russo-Japanese Problem* (London: British Periodicals, 1920); Howard D. Mehlinger and John M. Thompson, *Count Witte and the Tsarist Government in the 1905 Revolution* (Bloomington: Indiana University Press, 1972). Witte's personal papers are preserved in RGIA, f. 1622, and at Columbia University's Bakhmeteff Archive. The latter contains Witte's memoirs, which have not been published in their entirety.

23. According to Sergei Iulevich, his "ancestors were Dutch who had settled in the Baltic provinces when they still belonged to Sweden" (Witte, *Memoirs,* 3). At one point, Witte even petitioned the minister of the court, Count I. I. Vorontsov-Dashkov, for permission to change his surname to Witte-Fadeev, but was turned down (Ananich and Ganelin, *Vitte,* 32).

24. Witte, *Memoirs,* 9; Marion Meade, *Madame Blavatsky: The Woman behind the Myth* (New York: G. P. Putnam's Sons, 1980), 82–84.

25. J. N. Westwood, *A History of Russian Railways* (London: George Allen and Unwin, 1964), 64–78.

26. *Istoricheskii ocherk razvitiia zheleznykh dorog v Rossii,* vol. 2 (St. Petersburg: Tipografiia Ministerstva Putei Soobshcheniia, 1899), 593.

27. S. Iu. Vitte, *Printsip zheleznodorzhnykh tarifov po perevozkie gruzov* (St. Petersburg: Brokgauz-Efron, 1910).

28. Korelin and Stepanov, *Vitte,* 22.

29. Maurice Bompard, *Mon ambassade en Russie (1903–1908)* (Paris: Plon, 1937), xxix. Izvolskii invokes a very similar metaphor when he describes Witte's physique (*Mémoires,* 150).

30. Leo Pasvolsky and Harold G. Moulton, *Russian Debts and Russian Reconstruction: A Study of the Relation of Russia's Foreign Debts to Her Economic Recovery* (New York: McGraw-Hill, 1924), 73.

31. Stanislav Maksimilianovich Propper, *Was Nicht in die Zeitung Kam: Erinnerungen des Chefredakteurs der "Birschewyja wedomosti"* (Frankfurt a/M: Frankfurter Societäts Druckerei, 1929), 138.

32. Ananich and Ganelin, *Vitte,* 67–122; Laue, *Sergei Witte,* 71–119; Korelin and Stepanov, *Vitte,* 25–70; Werner E. Mosse, *Perestroika under the Tsars* (London: I. B. Tauris, 1992), 95–135; Roger Portal, *La Russie industrielle de 1881 à 1927* (Paris: Centre de

documentation universitaire, n.d.), 34–50.

33. Witte, *Memoirs,* 249. For a recent analysis of the question, see Paul Gregory, *Before Command: An Economic History of Russia from the Emancipation to the First Five-Year Plan* (Princeton, N.J.: Princeton University Press, 1994), 55–80.

34. Laue, *Sergei Witte,* 114.

35. Portal, *Russie,* 50.

36. Marks, *Road to Power,* 58.

37. Ibid., 105; Peter Gattrel, *The Tsarist Economy, 1850–1917* (London: B. T. Batsford, 1986), 219.

38. A senior British military intelligence official in 1886 concluded that "there should be no special difficulty in striking a serious blow at Russia in the Pacific" (Maj. Gen. Henry Brackenbury, preface to "Report on Russian Pacific Provinces," May 1, 1886, *BDFA,* pt. I, ser. A, 2:123). Russian generals concurred with this gloomy assessment. In a report on the defense of the border with China written in 1883, Maj. Gen. L. N. Sobolev warned that "nothing can guarantee that in five or ten years, when the Chinese army will be rearmed and trained, it will consider it possible to demand from us the return of the Ussuri region and the Amur basin" (Bilof, "Imperial Russian General Staff," x). On the strategic rationale for the Siberian Railway, see Witte to Nicholas, memorandum, June 30, 1896, RGIA, f. 560, o. 22, d. 201, l. 56; Obshchaia Kantseliaria Ministra Finansov, "Istoricheskaia spravka o sooruzhenii velikago sibirskago zheleznodorozhnago puti," memorandum, 1903, RGIA, f. 1622, o. 1, d. 936, ll. 7–9; Marks, *Road to Power,* 35–45; Langer, *Diplomacy,* 1:171.

39. Marks, *Road to Power,* 94.

40. Korelin and Stepanov, *Vitte,* 104.

41. Regularly scheduled service did not begin until summer 1903.

42. Izvolskii, *Mémoires,* 162.

43. Ibid., 152.

44. Petr Struve, "Graf S. Iu. Vitte: Opyt Kharakteristiki," *Russkaia Mysl* 36, no. 3 (March 1915): 9.

45. S. Iu. Witte, *Konspekt lektsii o narodnom i gosudarstvennom khoziaistve, chitannykh Ego Imperatorskomu Vysochestvu Velikomu Kniaziu Mikhailu Aleksandrovichu v 1900–1902 gg.* (St. Petersburg: Brockhaus i Efron, 1912).

46. Witte, however, had been more sympathetic to the ideas of the Slavophiles in younger years. See Ananich and Ganelin, *Vitte,* 30–33, 53; Korelin and Stepanov, *Vitte,* 11.

47. Witte, *Konspekt,* 66.

48. Witte to Nicholas, memorandum, Aug. 11, 1900, RGIA, f. 560, o. 28, d. 218, l. 70.

49. S. Iu. Witte, "Dokladnaia zapiska Vitte Nikolaiu II," *Istorik Marksist,* nos. 2–3 (February–March 1935): 133.

50. Witte, "Dokladnaia zapiska," 133.

51. S. Iu. Witte, *Po povodu natsionalizma: Natsionalnaia ekonomiia i Fridrikh List* (St. Petersburg: Brokgauz i Efron, 1912), 11. The essay is also appended to Korelin and Stepanov, *Vitte,* 311–74.

52. Friedrich List, *The National System of Political Economy,* trans. Sampson S. Lloyd (Fairfield, N.J.: A. M. Kelley, 1991).

53. Gregory Guroff, "The State and Industrialization in Russian Economic Thought, 1909–1914" (Ph.D. diss., Princeton University, 1970), 34–35.

54. See his impassioned critique of this institution in Sergei Iulevich Witte, *Samoderzhavie i zemstvo* (Stuttgart: J. H. W. Dietz, 1903); Ananich and Ganelin, *Vitte,* 100–10.

55. Witte, *Konspekt,* 199.

56. Ibid., 81.

57. Ibid., 80.

58. Ibid., 82. Witte voices very similar sentiments in a letter to V. P. Meshcherskii (Ananich and Ganelin, *Vitte*, 89).

59. Witte, *Konspekt*, 82–83.

60. Witte to Nicholas, memorandum, Nov. 12, 1896, RGIA, f. 1622, o. 1, d. 4, l. 1.

61. Ivan Stanislavovich Bliokh (Jan Bloch), *Budushchaia voina v tekhnicheskom, ekonomicheskom i politicheskom otnosheniiakh*, 6 vols. (St. Petersburg: Tip. I. A. Efrona, 1899). A one-volume English-language version claims to be a translation of the concluding volume but is a somewhat clumsy abridgement of the entire work: Jean de Bloch, *The Future of War in Its Technical, Economic, and Political Relations* (Boston: Ginn, 1903). For a good summary see Adolph G. Rosengarten, "John Bloch: A Neglected Prophet," *Military Review* 37, no. 1 (April 1957): 27–39.

62. After the First World War erupted, many writers commented about the eerie accuracy of Bloch's prophetic warnings. The British author Capt. B. H. Liddel Hart remarked: "[Bloch] was near 80 percent on the main factors—whereas the contemporary manuals were far more often wrong than right" (B. H. Liddel Hart, "John Bloch: A Neglected Prophet," *Military Review* 37, no. 3 [June 1957]: 31).

63. For a list of contemporary reactions, see Peter van den Dungen, *A Bibliography of the Pacifist Writings of Jean de Bloch* (London: Housmans, 1977). Witte modestly took full credit for the idea himself (*Memoirs*, 284–85).

64. Witte, *Konspekt*, 202.

65. Ibid., 202.

66. Witte, "Dokladnaia zapiska," 133.

67. Laue, *Sergei Witte*, 13–14.

68. Witte to Nicholas, memorandum, Mar. 22, 1900, in Theodore H. von Laue, ed., "Sergei Witte on the Industrialization of Russia," *Journal of Modern History* 26, no. 1 (March 1954): 66.

69. Witte, *Konspekt*, 217.

70. Glinskii, *Prolog*, 10.

71. Geyer, *Russian Imperialism*, 188–89.

72. Witte to Nicholas, memorandum, October 1902, RGIA, f. 1622, o.1, d. 711, l. 1; Glinskii, *Prolog*, 10–14; Romanov, *Russia in Manchuria*, 39–45; Laue, *Sergei Witte*, 81–82; Marks, *Road to Power*, 142–45; Ford, "Russian Far Eastern Diplomacy," 19–24.

73. Witte to Nicholas, memorandum, October 1902, l. 1.

74. Witte, *Konspekt*, 203.

75. V. P. Semennikov, ed., *Za kulisami tsarizma: Arkhiv tibetskago vracha Badmaeva* (Leningrad: Gosudarstvennoe izdatelstvo, 1925), 78.

76. Witte, *Memoirs*, 237.

77. Witte to Nicholas, memorandum, October 1902, l. 41.

78. A. Popov, "Dalnevostochnaia politika tsarizma v 1894–1901 gg.," *Istorik Marksist* 11, no. 11 (November 1935): 56.

79. This idea was eloquently expressed by Witte in a survey of Russia's eastward expansion, which describes it as a gradual, inevitable process that began with the merchants of twelfth-century Novgorod (Witte to Nicholas, memorandum, Aug. 11, 1900, ll. 67–69).

80. Laue, *Sergei Witte*, 155.

81. Witte to Nicholas, memorandum, Mar. 31, 1896, *KA*, 52:95.

82. Witte, marginal note on Kuropatkin to Nicholas, memorandum, Mar. 14, 1900, RGIA, f. 1622, o. 1, d. 269, l. 164. Emphasis in original.

83. Witte to Nicholas, memorandum, October 1902, l. 30.

84. Witte to Nicholas, memorandum, Aug. 11, 1900, l. 70.

85. Tarle, *Vitte*, 10.

86. Portal, *Russie,* 51; Mosse, *Perestroika,* 107; Alexander Gerschenkron, "Russia: Patterns of Economic Development, 1861–1958," in Gerschenkron, ed., *Economic Backwardness in Historical Perspective* (Cambridge, Mass.: Harvard University Press, 1962), 129. For a more recent economic history of the period, see Gregory, *Before Command.*

87. Gerschenkron, "Russia," 130.

88. Portal, *Russie,* 105–12; Laue, *Sergei Witte,* 211–14; Mosse, *Perestroika,* 119; Gershchenkron, "Russia," 132.

89. V. P. Meshcherskii, "Dnevnik," *Grazhdanin,* Jan. 8, 1902, 41.

90. Gattrel, *Tsarist Economy,* 169.

91. Sergei Sergeevich Oldenburg, *Last Tsar: Nicholas II, His Reign, and His Russia,* 4 vols. (Gulf Breeze, Fl.: Academic International Press, 1975), 2:15–16.

92. Lieven, *Nicholas II,* 90.

93. Charles Hardinge, *Old Diplomacy: The Reminiscences of Lord Hardinge of Penhurst* (London: John Murray, 1947), 75.

94. Lamsdorf, *Dnevnik 1894–1896,* 131, 143; Ford, "Russian Far Eastern Diplomacy," 26.

95. Laue, *Sergei Witte,* 277–78; Guroff, "State and Industrialization," 35–38.

96. A. A. Polovtsov, diary, July 22, 1901, *KA,* 3:99.

97. Witte, *Memoirs,* 263.

98. See, for example, "Ministr finansov stats-sekretar Vitte (1892–1902)," *NV,* Aug. 30, 1902, 1–2; V. P. Meshcherskii, "Dnevnik," *Grazhdanin,* Sep. 5, 1902, 22ff.; Witte, *Memoirs,* 310.

99. Gurko, *Features and Figures,* 228.

100. Edward H. Judge, *Plehve: Repression and Reform in Imperial Russia, 1902–1904* (Syracuse, N.Y.: Syracuse University Press, 1983), 151–53.

101. Kuropatkin, diary, Feb. 16, 1903, *KA,* 2:31.

102. Witte, *Memoirs,* 315.

103. Witte, *Dokladnaia zapiska,* 133.

104. Witte to Nicholas, memorandum, Aug. 11, 1900, l. 69.

105. Ibid., l. 71.

106. Wolfgang Mommsen, *Theories of Imperialism,* trans. P. S. Falla (Chicago: University of Chicago Press, 1982), 32–33.

107. D. K. Fieldhouse, "Imperialism: An Historiographical Revision," *Economic History Review,* 2d ser., 14, no. 2 (1961): 187–209.

108. John A. Hobson, *Imperialism: A Study* (London: George Allen & Unwin, 1902).

109. Witte to Lamsdorf, letter, Nov. 22, 1901, BA, Witte Papers, f. 24, n. 6.

110. Kuropatkin, diary, Dec. 3, 1903, *KA,* 2:91.

5: The Yellow Peril

1. Solovev, "Panmongolism," in *Chteniia,* 392–93; D. Strémooukhoff, *Vladimir Soloviev et son oeuvre messianique* (Lausanne: L'Age d'Homme, 1975), 188–217; S. M. Solovev, *Zhizn i tvorcheskaia evoliutsiia Vladimira Soloveva* (Brussels: Zhizn s Bogom, 1977), 277–89.

2. V. S. Solovev, "Kitai i Evropa," in *Sobranie sochinenii Vladimira Sergeevicha Soloveva,* vol. 6 (St. Petersburg: Prosveshchenie, n.d.), 94. Earlier during his posting to Paris the officer published a less belligerent book, about "China as it is": Tcheng-Ki-tong, *Les chinois peints par eux-mêmes* (Paris: Calman Lévy, 1884).

3. Solovev, "Kitai i Evropa," 6:94.

4. Ibid., 6:147; Evgenii Trubetskoi, *Mirosozertanie Vl. S. Soloveva,* 2 vols. (Moscow:

A. I. Mamontov, 1913), 2:300–2.

5. M. P. Alekseev, "Pushkin i Kitai," *A. S. Pushkin i Sibir* (Moscow: Vostsiboblgiz, 1937), 115; Barbara Widenor Maggs, *Russia and 'le rêve chinois': China in Eighteenth-century Russian Literature* (Oxford: Voltaire Foundation, 1984), 109–11; Bassin, *Imperial Visions*, 50. In Russian, the suffix "-shchin(a)" often implies the sway of something noxious. Thus the Russian word for a violent peasant uprising, *pugachevshchina*, after the eighteenth-century rebel Emelian Pugachev, and *ezhovshchina*, the term used to describe the height of the Stalinist terror led by Nikolai Ivanovich Ezhov, from 1936 to 1938 the head of the NKVD (the Soviet Commissariat of Internal Affairs, responsible for the secret police), etc. See N. Iu. Shvedov et al., eds., *Russkaia grammatika*, vol. 1 (Moscow: Nauka, 1980), 180. The grammarian Tatiana Iurevna Pozdniakova of the Russian Academy of Sciences' Institute of Russian Language kindly clarified this point.

6. Solovev, "Kitai i Evropa," 6:139.

7. Ibid., 6:150.

8. V. S. Solovev, "Vrag s Vostoka," *Sochineniia v dvukh tomakh*, 2:480

9. V. S. Solovev, "Zametka o E. P. Blavatskoi," *Sobranie Sochineniia*, 6:395.

10. S. L. Frank, ed., *A Solovev Anthology*, (London: SCM Press, 1950), 26–27.

11. V. S. Solovev, *War and Christianity: From the Russian Point of View* (New York: G. P. Putnam's Sons, 1915), 145.

12. Ibid., 145.

13. Ibid., 147–48 (translation modified for clarity).

14. V. S. Solovev, "Po povodu poslednikh sobytii, *Sobranie Sochineniia*, 8:584.

15. Ibid., 586.

16. Strémooukhoff, *Soloviev*, 289.

17. Nikolai Berdiaev, "Problema Vostoka i Zapada v religioznom soznaniia Vl. Soloveva," in *Sbornik pervyi o Vladimire Soloveve* (Moscow: Tipografiia Imperatorskogo Moskovskogo Universiteta, 1911), 125.

18. Kuropatkin's personal papers are in RGVIA, f. 165. This extensive collection includes many diaries covering much of the officer's career. Small portions, from 1902 to 1904, were published in *Krasnyi Arkhiv* 2 (1922): 5–117. Kuropatkin's papers also include his memoirs, *70 let moei zhizni* (70 Years of My Life), which are scheduled to be published in the near future. Some useful biographical details can be gleaned from essays in RGVIA, f. 165, o. 1, d. 35; *Voennaia Entsiklopediia* (St. Petersburg: I. D. Sytina, 1914); *Stoletie voennago ministerstva* (St. Petersburg: M. O. Volf, 1907); "A. N. Kuropatkin," *Razvedchik* 11, no. 378 (Jan. 13, 1898): 25–27. See also Aleksandr Valerevich Sharov, "Zabytii General Kuropatkin," *Kommunist Vooruzhennykh sil*, no. 12 (June 1991): 61–67; V. A. Avdeev, "Ternovyi venets Generala A. N. Kuropatkina," *Voenno-Istoricheskii Zhurnal*, no. 4 (1995): 68–75; "A. N. Kuropatkin," *NV*, Jan. 2, 1898, 2; Sven Hedin, "General Kuropatkin," *Times* (London), Nov. 1, 1904; R. M. Portugalskii et al., *Pervaia mirovaia v zhizneopisaniiakh russkikh voenachalnikov* (Moscow: Elakos, 1994), 247–66. I am grateful to Geoffrey Parker for his suggestion that I include Gen. Kuropatkin in my study.

19. Avdeev, "Ternovyi venets," 69.

20. Ibid., 69.

21. Kuropatkin to Witte, letter, Dec. 30, 1901, RGVIA, f. 165, o. 1, d. 1861, l. 62. A Soviet author would make much of Kuropatkin's anticapitalist sentiments, but these were probably more an indication of aristocratic distaste for the vulgar bourgeois. See Petr Andreevich Zaionchkovskii, *Samoderzhavie i russkaia armiia na rubezhe XIX-XX stolety* (Moscow: Mysl, 1973), 70.

22. A. N. Kuropatkin, "Ocherki Alzhiri (verbliuzhii oboz)," *Voennyi Sbornik*, no. 2

(February 1875): 273–297; "Alzhiriia: Voenno-statisticheskii obzor," *Voennyi Sbornik,* nos. 3–7 (March–July 1876); "Pishcha frantsuskikh voisk v Alzhirii," *Voennyi Sbornik,* no. 4 (1877).

23. Kuropatkin to K. P. von Kaufman, report, 1877, RGVIA, f. 165, o. 1, d. 222.

24. A. N. Kuropatkin, *Kashgaria: Istoriko-geograficheskii ocherk strany, eia voennyia sily, promyshlennost i torgovlia* (St. Petersburg: V. S. Balashev, 1879).

25. A. N. Kuropatkin, *Lovcha, Plevna i Sheinovo: Iz istorii Russko-Turetskoi voiny* (St. Petersburg: V. A. Poletika, 1881).

26. Rich, *Tsar's Colonels,* 173–91. According to George Curzon, Kuropatkin also drew up plans to invade British India at the time, an activity the general vigorously denied in later years (*Russia in Central Asia in 1889 and the Central Asian Question* [London: Longmans, Green, 1889], 331).

27. The diary entries for this eccentric expedition were published in a Russian military journal: A. N. Kuropatkin, "Razvedivatelnaia missiia v Turtsiu," *Voenno-Istoricheskii Zhurnal,* no. 4 (1994): 68–77.

28. Witte, *Memoirs,* 109.

29. A. N. Kuropatkin, "Artillereiskie voprosy," *Voennyi Sbornik,* no. 5 (1885); A. N. Kuropatkin, "Ocherk voennykh deistvii v Srednei Azii s 1839 do 1836," in G. A. Leer, ed., *Obzor voin Rossii ot Petra Velikogo do nashikh dnei,* vol. 2, pt. 3 (St. Petersburg: Izd-vo. Glav. upr. voenn-ucheb. zavedenii, 1889); A. N. Kuropatkin, "Ocherk dvizheniia russkikh voisk v Sredniuiu Aziiu," in *Voennyia besedy ispolnennyia v shtabe voisk gvardii i peterburgkago voennago okruga v 1885–1887 gg.,* vol. 1 (St. Petersburg: Voisk Gvardiia, 1887), 105–18; A. N. Kuropatkin, *Deistviia otriadov generala Skobeleva v Russko-Turetskoiu voiny 1877–78 godov: Lovcha i Plevna* (St. Petersburg: Voennaia Tipografiia Glavnogo Shtaba, 1885).

30. Freiherr von Tettau, *Kuropatkin und seine Unterführer* (Berlin: Ernst Siegfried Mittler, 1913), 22. A good example of Kuropatkin's growing renown at the time is in the chapter about him in *L'Armée russe et ses chefs en 1888* (Paris: Librarie Moderne, 1888), 252–93.

31. Portugalskii, *Pervaia mirovaia,* 249.

32. Leonid Heretz, "Russian Apocalypse, 1891–1917: Popular Perception of Events from the Year of Famine and Cholera to the Fall of the Tsar" (Ph.D. diss., Harvard University, 1993), 212.

33. The septuagenarian general cited fatigue, but the real reason lay with the growing involvement of the tsar's uncles in military affairs. Whereas Alexander III had kept them on a short leash during his reign, his insecure young heir lacked the will to curb the meddlesome grand dukes. See Zaionchkovskii, *Samoderzhavie,* 65.

34. Kuropatkin, diary, Dec. 24, 1897, RGVIA, f. 165, o. 1, d. 1871, ll. 9–10; V. P. Meshcherskii, "Dnevnik," *Grazhdanin,* Jan. 4, 1898, 26–27. For a contemporary assessment of Kuropatkin in the years immediately preceding his appointment as war minister, see Notovitch, *Nicolas II,* 196–97.

35. Witte, *Memoirs,* 265.

36. Kuropatkin, diary, Dec. 24, 1897, RGVIA, f. 165, o. 1, d. 1871, ll. 8–9.

37. William C. Fuller, *Strategy and Power in Russia, 1600–1914* (New York: Free Press, 1992), 329.

38. Irina Sergeevna Rybachenok, "Rossiia i gaagskaia konferentsia po razoruzheniiu 1899 g.," *Novaia i Noveishaia Istoriia,* no. 4 (1996): 173.

39. Kuropatkin, diary, Feb. 21, 1898, RGVIA, f. 165, o. 1, d. 1871, l. 17.

40. Kuropatkin to A. N. Sakharov, letter, Oct. 21, 1895, RGVIA, f. 165, o. 1, d. 1871, l. 95.

41. Kuropatkin to Nicholas, memorandum, July 27, 1903, BA, Witte Papers, d.

27, n. 2. Kuropatkin's report about the journey is in Kuropatkin to Nicholas, memorandum, Dec. 8, 1903, RGVIA, f. 165, o. 1, d. 957.

42. Kuropatkin, "Ocherk dvizheniia," 118.

43. Kuropatkin to Nicholas, notes of report, Feb. 8, 1900, RGVIA, f. 165, o. 1, d. 594, l. 22.

44. A. N. Kuropatkin, *Zadachi Russkoi armii,* vol. 3 (St. Petersburg: V. A. Berezovskii, 1910), 252.

45. Several scholars have suggested that, after the Mongol invasion, the interaction between Russians and their rulers was not as hostile as such literature would suggest. A good historical study is Charles Halperin, *Russia and the Golden Horde: The Mongol Impact on Medieval Russian History* (Bloomington: Indiana University Press, 1985). Better known but somewhat idiosyncratic is Vernadsky, *Mongols and Russia.* For an examination of the chronicles and *byliny* as historical sources, see Peter Voorheis, "The Perceptions of Asiatic Nomads in Medieval Russia: Folklore, History, and Historiography" (Ph.D. diss., Indiana University, 1982).

46. Ivan Andreevich Krylov, "The Three Townies," in Bernard Pares, trans., *Krylov's Fables* (Westport, Conn.: Hyperion, 1977), 253.

47. Heretz, "Russian Apocalypse," 205–8.

48. Alekseev, "Pushkin i Kitai," 139; Bassin, *Imperial Visions,* 51.

49. Aleksandr Ivanovich Herzen, "Kontsy i nachala (Pismo shestoe)," *Kolokol,* no. 149 (Nov. 1, 1862): 1.

50. Bassin, *Imperial Visions,* 52.

51. Fedor Mikhailovich Dostoevskii, *Crime and Punishment,* trans. Constance Garnett (New York: Macmillan, 1928), 489.

52. Barbara Heldt, "'Japanese' in Russian Literature: Transforming Identities," in J. Thomas Rimer, ed., *A Hidden Fire: Russian and Japanese Cultural Encounters* (Stanford, Calif.: Stanford University Press, 1995), 170.

53. Vasilii Mikhailovich Golovnin, *Japan and the Japanese: Comprising the Narrative of a Captivity in Japan,* 2 vols. (London: Colburn, 1853), 2:74.

54. Ibid., 2:101.

55. Ibid., 2:191.

56. Lensen, *Russian Push,* 252–53.

57. Mikhail Bakunin, "Réponse d'un international à Massini," in *Michel Bakounine et l'Italie 1871–1872* (Leiden: E. J. Brill, 1961), 69.

58. Ibid., 70.

59. One dissenting opinion was voiced by Maj. Gen. L. N. Sobolev. In a report in 1883 about the Russo-Chinese border, he fretted that "nothing can guarantee that in five or ten years, when the Chinese army will be rearmed and trained, it will not consider it possible to demand from us the return of the Ussuri region and the Amur basin" (Bilof, "Imperial Russian General Staff," x).

60. Butakov, "Vooruzheniia sili Kitaia i Iaponii," *Sbornik* 3 (1883): 24. Dmitrii Vassilevich Putiata makes a very similar assessment in *Kitai: Ocherki geograficheskago sostoianiia administrativnago i voennago ustroistva Kitaia* (St. Petersburg: Voennaia tipografiia, 1895), 170–72. See also his *Vooruzhenyia sily Kitaia* (St. Petersburg: Voennaia tipografiia, 1889).

61. One of the few occasions the Main Staff's 87-volume *Sbornik* studied Japan was in vol. 3, which devoted 16 pages to the nation (Butakov, "Vooruzheniia sili," 1–16).

62. Denis Sinor, "Le mongol vue par l'Occident," in *Studies in Medieval Inner Asia,* vol. 9 (Ashgate: Variorum, 1997), 62. See also Axel Kloprogge, "Das Mongolenbild im

Abendland," in Stephan Conerman and Jan Kusber, eds., *Die Mongolen in Asien und Europa* (Frankfurt a/Main: Peter Lang, 1997), 81–101.

63. Sinor, "Le mongol," 61.

64. Ibid., 68.

65. Charles Baron de Montesquieu, *De l'Esprit des lois,* vol. 1 (Paris: Gallimard, 1995), 282–84; Jonathan D. Spence, *The Chan's Great Continent: China in Western Minds* (New York: Norton, 1998), 81–100; Colin Mackerras, *Western Images of China* (Oxford: Oxford University Press, 1989), 28–41. See also Virgile Pinot, *La Chine et la formation de l'esprit philosophique en France (1640–1740)* (Geneva: Slatkin Reprints, 1971); Guy Basil, *The French Image of China before and after Voltaire* (Geneva: Institut Voltaire, 1963); Song Shun-Ching, *Voltaire et la Chine* (Aix-en-Provence: University de Provence, 1989).

66. Louis Garros, "Le péril jaune," *Historama* (May 1966): 12.

67. Thomas Robert Malthus, *An Essay on Population,* 2 vols. (London: J. M. Dent, 1960–1961).

68. Heinz Gollwitzer, *Die Gelbe Gefahr* (Göttingen: Vandenhoeck & Ruprecht, 1962), 14–15; Richard Austin Thompson, *The Yellow Peril, 1890–1924* (New York: Arno Press, 1978), 31–32.

69. Robert McClellan, *The Heathen Chinee: A Study of American Attitudes toward China, 1890–1905* (Columbus: Ohio State University Press, 1971), 70.

70. Thompson, *Yellow Peril,* 7–11; Gollwitzer, *Gelbe Gefahr,* 26–27; Jonathan Spence, *The Search for Modern China* (New York: Norton, 1990), 213–15; Spence, *Chan's Great Continent,* 185. For a more detailed study, see Elmer Clarence Sandmeyer, *The Anti-Chinese Movement in California* (Urbana: University of Illinois Press, 1991).

71. McClellan, *Heathen Chinee,* 207.

72. Ibid., 232. Similar comparisons are still being made a century later. Recently, a columnist for the *Washington Times,* the Korean evangelist Sun Myung Moon's conservative daily, wrote about immigration to the United States: "Not since Genghis Khan rode out of the Asian steppes has the West . . . encountered such an alien invasion." Quoted in Matthew Connelly and Paul Kennedy, "Must it Be the Rest against the West?" *Atlantic Monthly* 274, no. 6 (December 1994): 69.

73. Koenraad W. Swart, *The Sense of Decadence in Nineteenth-Century France* (The Hague: Martinus Nijhoff, 1964), 122–92; Jean Pierrot, *The Decadent Imagination, 1880–1900,* trans. Derek Coltman (Chicago: University of Chicago Press, 1981), 45–49; George Ross Ridge, *The Hero in French Decadent Literature* (Athens: University of Georgia Press, 1961), 13–20; George Schoolfield, *A Baedeker of Decadence* (New Haven, Conn.: Yale University Press, forthcoming); Max Nordau, *Degeneration* (New York: Howard Fertig, 1968). Nordau was the synonym of Max Simon Südfeld, a friend of the Jewish nationalist Theodor Herzl and an ardent Zionist. Ironically, Nordau's objections to artistic modernism were enthusiastically appropriated by Germany's Nazis in their campaign against *entarte Kunst* ("degenerate" art). See also Brooks Adams, *The Law of Civilisation and Decay: An Essay on History* (London: Swan Sonnenschein, 1895), 294–95.

74. Charles H. Pearson, *National Life and Character: A Forecast* (London: Macmillan, 1893).

75. Theodore Roosevelt, "National Life and Character," *Sewanee Review* 2, no. 3 (May 1894): 13.

76. Pearson, *National Life,* 68, 85.

77. Ibid., 132.

78. Gollwitzer, *Gelbe Gefahr,* 42–43; Thompson, *Yellow Peril,* 1–4. In 1907 Wilhelm proudly boasted to an American dentist that "it was I, who originated the phrase

'yellow peril'" (Gollwitzer, *Gelbe Gefahr*, 420).

79. Wilhelm II to Nicholas, letter, Sep. 26, 1895, in Wilhelm II, *Letters from the Kaiser to the Czar* (New York: Frederick A. Stokes, 1920), 17. Italics added.

80. Arthur Diósy, *The New Far East* (London: Cassell, 1904), 335.

81. Gollwitzer, *Gelbe Gefahr*, 207.

82. Wilhelm II, *The Kaiser's Speeches,* trans. and ed. Wolf von Schierbrand (New York: Harper & Brothers, 1903), 260.

83. Wilhelm reassured Nicholas: "I shall certainly do everything in my power to keep Europe quiet and also guard the rear of Russia so that nobody shall hamper your action toward the Far East!" (Wilhelm II to Nicholas, letter, Apr. 16, 1895, *Letters from the Kaiser,* 10).

84. Wilhelm II to Nicholas, letter, Sep. 2, 1902, *Letters from the Kaiser,* 86.

85. Some of Nicholas's replies to Wilhelm's telegrams were published in Mikhail Nikolaevich Pokrovskii, ed., *Perepiska Vilgelma II s Nikolaem II* (Moscow: Gosudarstvennoe izdatelstvo, 1923). Chapter 10 addresses this topic in greater detail.

86. Kuropatkin to Nicholas, memorandum, Oct. 15, 1903, GARF, f. 543, o. 1, d. 182, l. 3.

87. A. N. Kuropatkin, *Zavoevanie Turkmenii* (St. Petersburg: V. Berezovskii, 1899), 94–95.

88. Kuropatkin, *Kashgaria,* 59.

89. Kuropatkin, *Zavoevanie Turkmenii,* 117.

90. A. N. Kuropatkin, *Russko-kitaiskii vopros* (St. Petersburg: A. S. Suvorin), 183.

91. Kuropatkin to Nicholas, memorandum, Oct. 15, 1903, GARF, f. 543, o. 1, d. 182, l. 5.

92. Kuropatkin, diary, Oct. 20, 1902, RGVIA, f. 165, o. 1, d. 1871, ll. 91–92.

93. Kuropatkin, memorandum, Oct. 15, 1903, l. 5.

94. Kuropatkin, diary, Mar. 21, 1898, RGVIA, f. 165, o. 1, d. 1871, l. 19.

95. The official report is in Kuropatkin to Nicholas, report, Dec. 8, 1903, RGVIA, f. 165, o. 1, d. 957. For Kuropatkin's instructions, see ibid., l. 2. The diaries for the trip were not included in *Krasnyi Arkhiv's* second volume but recently appeared in a new Russian document collection: A. N. Kuropatkin, "Iaponskie dnevniki A. N. Kuropatkina," *Rossiiskii Arkhiv* 6 (1995): 393–444.

96. Kuropatkin to Nicholas, report, Dec. 8, 1903, RGVIA, f. 165, o. 1, d. 957, l. 4.

97. Ibid., l. 9.

98. Kuropatkin, "Alzhiriia," 226–27.

99. Kuropatkin, *Russko-kitaiskii vopros,* 52.

100. A. N. Kuropatkin, "Ocherk dvizhenii," 105.

101. Ibid., 109.

102. A. N. Kuropatkin, *Zavoevaniia turkmenii* (St. Petersburg: V. Berezovskii, 1899), 11.

103. Kuropatkin, "Ocherk dvizhenii," 115.

104. Gorchakov, memorandum, Nov. 21, 1864, *BDFA*, pt. I, ser. A, 1:287.

105. A. M. Gorchakov, "Déjà Vu: Russia in East Asia," *Foreign Service Journal* (June 1980): 27–28, 44.

106. Hopkirk, *Great Game*, 304–5.

107. Tuomo Polvinen, *Imperial Borderland: Bobrikov and the Attempted Russification of Finland, 1898–1904* (London: Hurst, 1995), 54–70.

108. A. N. Kuropatkin, *Otchet o sluzhebnoi poezdke Voennago Ministra v Turkestanskii voennyi okrug v 1901 godu* (St. Petersburg: Voennaia Tipografiia, 1902), 93.

109. Kuropatkin, *Russko-kitaiskii vopros,* 71.

110. Witte, *Memoirs*, 261.

111. Kuropatkin, diary, Jan. 1, 1902, RGVIA, f. 165, o. 1, d. 1871, l. 63.

112. Kuropatkin, diary, Sep. 22, 1899, RGVIA, f. 165, o. 1, d. 1889, l. 40.

113. Kuropatkin, notes of report, Feb. 8, 1900, RGVIA, f. 165, o. 1, d. 594, l. 22.

114. Kuropatkin to Nicholas, memorandum, Mar. 14, 1900. Copies of this memorandum are in GARF, f. 601, o. 1, d. 445; and RGVIA, f. 165, o. 1, d. 602. The latter was unavailable in winter 1996. The versions at RGIA (in Witte's personal papers) and at GARF (in Nicholas II's papers) include marginal comments by Witte. For a brief summary, see Fuller, *Strategy and Power*, 377–79.

115. Kuropatkin, diary, Oct. 10, 1900, RGVIA, f. 165, o. 1, d. 1868, l. 45.

116. Kuropatkin to Nicholas, memorandum, Mar. 14, 1900, l. 24.

117. Ibid., l. 25. Emphasis in original.

118. Ibid., l. 54.

119. Ibid., l. 52.

120. Ibid., l. 52.

121. Kuropatkin, *Zadachi Russkoi armii*, 3:255.

122. Kuropatkin, *Russko-kitaiskii vopros*, 27.

123. Robert Hart, "The Peking Legations," *Cosmopolitan*, 30, no. 2 (December 1900): 136.

124. Heinz Brahm, "Sowjetische Intellektuelle über die 'chinesische Gefahr,'" *Berichte des Bundesintitutes für ostwissenschaftliche und internationale Studien*, no. 60 (1977).

125. Andrei Amalrik, *Will the Soviet Union Survive until 1984?* (New York: Harper & Row, 1981).

126. A remarkable artifact of such alarmist views is Boris Diachenko, ed., *Zheltaia opasnost* (Vladivostok: Voron, 1996). For a good summary of post-Soviet demographic developments in eastern Siberia, see Elizabeth Wishnick, "Russia in Asia and Asians in Russia," *SAIS Review* 20, no. 1 (winter–spring 2000): 87–101.

Part Two: Prologue

1. Vikentii Vikentevich Veresaev, *In the War: Memoirs of V. Veresaev* (New York: Mitchell Kennerley, 1917), 1.

2. Nicholas, *Dnevniki Imperatora Nikolaia II* (Moscow: Orbita, 1991), 193; *NV,* Jan. 28, 1904, 13; A. K., "Teatr i muzyka," *SPBVed,* Jan. 28, 1904, 11.

3. "Birzhevaia khronika," *SPBVed,* Jan. 27, 1904, 5; A. N. Kuropatkin, "Dnevnik Kuropatkina," *KA,* 2:107–9.

4. Kuropatkin, "Dnevnik," 95, 109; Lieven, *Nicholas II,* 100.

5. Aleksandr Aleksandrovich Savinskii, *Recollections of a Russian Diplomat* (London: Hutchinson, 1927), 79–80; Irina Sergeevna Rybachenok, "Nikolai Romanov i Ko. Put k katastrofe," in Anatolii Venediktovich Ignatev et al., eds., *Rossiiskaia diplomatiia v protretakh* (Moscow: Mezhdunarodnye otnosheniia, 1992), 299–300.

6. Aleksandr Ivanovich Rusin, "Iz predistorii russko-iaponskoi voiny: Doneseniia morskogo agenta v Iaponii A. I. Rusina (1902–1904 gg.)," *Russkoe proshloe* 6 (1996): 55–86. Captain Rusin's penulitmate telegram to St. Petersburg, sent on January 24, the day Japan broke off relations, read: "General mobilisation. Rusin" (ibid., 86); A. I., "Beglyi ocherk morskikh operatsii russko-iaponskoi voiny," *Morskoi Sbornik* 370, no. 6 (June 1912): 54–55; Gurko, *Features and Figures*, 285; D. V. Nikitin, "Kak nachalas voina s Iaponiei," in *Port-Artur: Vospominaniia uchastnikov* (New York: Chekhov, 1955), 44.

7. Aleksandr Ivanovich Sorokin, *Russko-Iaponsaia voina 1904–1905 gg.* (Moscow:

Ministerstva Oborony Soiuza SSR, 1956), 69.

8. Ivan Ivanovich Rostunov, ed., *Russko-iaponskaia voina 1904–1905 gg.* (Moscow: Nauka, 1977), 119; A. I., "Beglyi ocherk," 59–64. In a remarkably prescient letter sent to the navy minister earlier that very day, on January 26, the commander of the Baltic Fleet, Vice Adm. Stepan Makarov, wrote: "Were Japan not to possess protected harbors either, and like us had to keep all of its ships at anchor in open water, then our tactic, on the very first night after breaking diplomatic ties, would have to be to carry out the most energetic strike on their fleet. The Japanese will not let pass by such a wonderful opportunity to do us harm. I even think that one of the motives for declaring war is the hope to damage our fleet in a nighttime assault. If we had a large roadstead inside of Port Arthur, out of which the squadron might sail at any moment, the Japanese would have thought twice about declaring war" (64).

9. P. Larenko, *Stradnye dni Port-Artura: Khronika voennykh sobytii i zhizni v osazhennoi kreposti s 26–go ianvaria 1904 g. do 9–e ianvaria 1905 g.*, vol. 1 (St. Petersburg: Tip. Shedera, 1906), 47; Richard Connaughton, *The War of the Rising Sun and the Tumbling Bear* (London: Routledge, 1991), 29–31. Accounts claiming that all of the base's senior officers were attending a ball that evening to honor Madame Stark's name day are apocryphal. See Nikitin, "Kak nachalas," 43; Grigorii Antonovich Planson, "V shtabe adm. E. A. Alekseeva," *KA*, 41–42:163; J. N. Westwood, *Japan against Russia, 1904–1905: A New Look at the Russo-Japanese War* (Albany: State University of New York Press, 1986), 40.

10. Julian S. Corbett, *Maritime Operations in the Russo-Japanese War, 1904–1905* (Annapolis, Md.: Naval Institute Press, 1994), 92–93; A. I., "Beglyi ocherk," 63.

11. A. I., "Beglyi ocherk," 72.

12. The maneuver had taken place earlier on January 26. Cable links with Port Arthur were cut, however, because the Korean telegraph monopoly was in Japanese hands. As a result, Alekseev remained entirely ignorant of the attack (Westwood, *Japan against Russia*, 42).

13. A. I., "Beglyi ocherk," 67–71.

14. Bing, *Letters of Tsar Nicholas and Empress Marie*, 176.

15. Nicholas, *Dnevnik*, 193.

16. The raid on Port Arthur was not the first time Japan attacked an advesary before formally declaring war. Belgium's perceptive minister to Tokyo at the time, Baron Albert d'Anethan, wrote to Brussels on January 24, the day his host broke diplomatic relations with St. Petersburg: "As of now, the Government considers itself to be in a state of war with Russia. Hostilities are thus imminent and we shall probably have the declaration after the first act or engagement of war. At the time of the war with China [in 1894], the Emperor did not proclaim the declaration of war until after the attack on the Chinese transport *Kowshing*" (George Alexander Lensen, ed., *The d'Anethan Dispatches from Japan, 1894–1910: The Observations of Baron Albert d'Anethan, Belgian Minister Plenipotentiary and Dean of the Diplomatic Corps* [Tokyo: Sophia University Press, 1967], 180).

17. Bompard, *Mon ambassade*, 52–53

18. Sir Cyprian Bridge, "The Russo-Japanese Naval Campaign of 1904," in T. A. Brassey, ed., *The Naval Annual 1905* (Portsmouth: J. Griffin, 1905), 117–18.

19. The best accounts of the war are A. A. Svechin, *Russo-Iaponskaia voina* (Oranienbaum: Izdatel'stvo Ofitserskoi Strelkovoi Shkoli, 1910); and Nikolai Arsenevich Levitskii, *Russo-Iaponskaia voina 1904–1905 gg.* (Moscow: Gosudarstvennoe voennoe izdatel'stvo, 1936). Good English-language histories include Westwood, *Japan against Russia;* and Connaughton, *Rising Sun.* For a more detailed narrative of the land war, see the Russian Army's nine-volume official study, edited by Lt. Gen. V. I. Gurko: Russia,

Voenno-istoricheskaia komissiia po opisaniiu Russko-Iaponskoi voiny, *Russko-iaponskaia voina 1904–1905 gg.* (St. Petersburg: A. S. Suvorin, 1910). Summaries of the land war are given in Menning, *Bayonets,* 152–99; and my "The Russo-Japanese War," Frederick Kagan and Robin Higham, eds., *The Military History of Tsarist Russia* (New York: St. Martin's Press, forthcoming). The naval conflict is covered in Corbett, *Maritime Operations.*

6: The Turn to the East

1. Werner E. Mosse, *The European Great Powers and the German Question, 1848–1871* (Cambridge: Cambridge University Press, 1958), 73.

2. Fuller, *Strategy and Power,* 268–70; Geyer, *Russian Imperialism,* 17–32.

3. Based on his celebrated phrase "La Russie ne boude pas, mais se receuille" ("Russia is not sulking. It is merely gathering its strength.") See Barbara Jelavich, *A Century of Russian Foreign Policy* (Philadelphia: J. B. Lippincott, 1964), 134; Fuller, *Strategy and Power,* 270.

4. Two surveys of Russia's push into the continent during Alexander II's reign are Hoetzsch, *Russland in Asien;* and Kappeler, *Russland,* 141–76. For an institutional history, see Galen B. Ritchie, "The Asiatic Department during the Reign of Alexander II, 1855–1881" (Ph.D. diss., Columbia University, 1970).

5. Vladimir Nabokov, trans., *The Song of Igor's Campaign* (New York: McGraw-Hill, 1960).

6. Ruslan Grigorevich Skrynnikov, *Sibirskaia ekspeditsiia Ermaka* (Novosibirsk: Nauka, 1982); John F. Baddeley, ed., *Russia, Mongolia, China: Being Some Record of the Relations between Them from the Beginning of the XVIIth Century to the Death of Tsar Aleksei Mikhailovich,* 2 vols. (London: Macmillan, 1919), 1:lxix-lxxiii. On the importance of furs to the medieval Russian economy, see Janet Martin, *Treasure of the Land of Darkness: The Fur Trade and Its Significance for Medieval Russia* (Cambridge: Cambridge University Press, 1986), 151–66; and more generally Raymond H. Fischer, *The Russian Fur Trade, 1550–1700* (Berkeley: University of California Press, 1943).

7. Pierre Leroy-Beaulieu, *La rénovation de l'Asie: Sibérie—Chine—Japon* (Paris: Armand Colin, 1900), 3.

8. George V. Lantzeff and Richard A. Pierce, *Eastward to Empire: Exploration and Conquest on the Russian Open Frontier to 1750* (Montreal: McGill-Queen's University Press, 1973), 82–182.

9. As late as 1853, Russia's Foreign Minister Count Nesselrode acknowledged the validity of the Treaty of Nerchinsk to the Chinese government (Paine, *Imperial Rivals,* 39). For the text of the Treaty of Nerchinsk, see P. E. Skachkov and V. S. Miasnikov, eds., *Russko-kitaiskie otnosheniia 1689–1916: Ofitsialnye dokumenty* (Moscow: Izd-vo. vostochnoi literatury, 1958), 9–11; Sergei Leonidovich Tikhvinskii et al., eds., *Russko-kitaiskie otnosheniia v XVII veke. Materialy i dokumenty,* vol. 2 (Moscow: Nauka, 1972), 645–46; P. J. B. Du Halde, *Description géographique, historique, chronologique, politique et physique de l'Empire de la Chine et de la Tartarie Chinoise,* vol. 4 (Paris: P. G. Lemercier, 1735), 201–2.

10. Immanuel C. Y. Hsü, *The Rise of Modern China* (Oxford: Oxford University Press, 1983), 117.

11. I. Ia. Korostovets, "Russkaia dukhovnaia missiia v Pekine," *Russkii Arkhiv* 31, no. 9 (1893): 57–86; Ieromonakh Nikolai (Adoratskii), "Istoriia Pekinskoi Dukhovnoi Missii v pervoi period ee deiatelnosti (1685–1745)," in Sergei Leonidovich Tikhvinskii et al., eds., *Istoriia Rossiiskoi Dukhovnoi Missii v Kitae: Sbornik Statei* (Moscow: Sviato-Vladimisrskoe

Bratstvo, 1997), 14–164; Eric Widmer, *The Russian Ecclesiastical Mission during the Eighteenth Century* (Cambridge, Mass.: Harvard University Press, 1961); Albert Parry, "Russian (Greek Orthodox) Missionaries in China, 1689–1917: Their Cultural, Political, and Economic Rôle" (Ph.D. diss., University of Chicago, 1938). The treaty itself is reproduced in Tikhvinskii et al., *Russko-kitaiskie*, vol. 2; Skachkov, *Russko-kitaiskie otnosheniia*, 17–22.

12. Spence, *Search for Modern China*, 67. The Zongli Yamen, "The Bureau for the Management of Relations with Foreign Countries," was China's foreign office from 1861 to 1901. See S. M. Meng, *The Tsungli Yamen: Its Organization and Functions* (Cambridge, Mass.: Harvard University Press, 1962); Immanuel C. Y. Hsü, "The Development of the Chinese Foreign Office in the Ch'ing Period," in Zara Steiner, ed., *The Times Survey of Foreign Ministries of the World* (London: Times Books, 1982), 119–33.

13. Immanuel C. Y. Hsü, "Russia's Special Position in China during the Early Ch'ing Period," *Slavic Review* 23, no. 4 (1964): 688.

14. There were some inaccuracies. For example, Peter the Great was identified as the *daughter* of Tsar Alexis Mikhailovich. See Don C. Price, *Russia and the Roots of the Chinese Revolution, 1896–1911* (Cambridge, Mass.: Harvard University Press, 1974), 29–32.

15. Ibid., 30.

16. For studies of Sino-Russian relations before the 1850s, see Gaston Cahen, *Histoire des relations de la Russie avec la Chine sous Pierre le Grand (1689–1730)* (Paris: E. Alcan, 1912); M. Veniukov, *Starye i novye dogovory Rossii s Kitaem* (St. Petersburg: V. Bezobrazov, 1863); Vasilii Pavlovich Vasilev, "Russko-kitaiskie traktaty," in *Otkrytie Kitaia* (St. Petersburg: Izd. zhurnala Viestnik vsemirnoi istorii, 1900), 63–105; Nikolai Vasilevich Kiuner, *Snosheniia Rossii s Dalnim Vostokom na protiazhenii tsarstvovaniia doma Romanovykh* (Vladivostok: Vostochnyi Institut, 1914); Vladimir Stepanovich Miasnikov, *The Ch'ing Empire and the Russian State in the Seventeenth Century* (Moscow: Progress Publishers, 1985); Clifford M. Foust, *Muscovite and Mandarin: Russia's Trade with China and Its Setting, 1727–1805* (Chapel Hill: University of North Carolina Press, 1969); Mark Mancall, *Russia and China: Their Diplomatic Relations to 1728* (Cambridge, Mass.: Harvard University Press, 1971).

17. G. I. Nevelskoi, *Podvigi russkikh morskikh ofitserov na krainem Vostoke Rossii 1849–1855* (St. Petersburg: A. S. Suvorin, 1897), 112; Russia, *Aziatskaia*, 1:517. Captain Nevelskoi's words also form the inscription on his statue in Vladivostok, which Tsarevich Nicholas Alexandrovich unveiled in 1891 (Sokol, *Monumenty imperii*, 201).

18. The treaties themselves are in Ervin Davidovich Grimm, ed., *Sbornik dogovorov i drugikh dokumentov po istorii mezhdunarodnikh otnoshenii na Dalnem Vostoke (1842–1925)* (Moscow: Institut Vostokovedeniia, 1927), 54–55, 71–76; Skachkov, *Russko-Kitaiskie otnosheniia*, 29–30, 34–41; William Frederic Mayers, *Treaties between the Empire of China and Foreign Powers* (Shanghai: North-China Herald, 1906), 100, 105–12. For a good account, see R. K. I. Quested, *The Expansion of Russia in East Asia, 1857–1860* (Kuala Lumpur: University of Malaysia Press, 1968). A fascinating intellectual history of Russian interest with the Pacific at the time is Bassin, *Imperial Visions*.

19. Although its author did not have access to the tsarist foreign ministry's files, the most thorough study of this episode remains Immanuel C. Y. Hsü, *The Ili Crisis* (Oxford: Oxford University Press, 1965). A recent account based on Russian archival sources is Alexei D. Voskressenski, *The Sino-Russian St. Petersburg Treaty of 1881: Diplomatic History* (Commack, N.Y.: Nova Science Publishers, 1986). See also D. M. Pozdneev, "Istoriia Sankt-Peterburgskogo dogovora 1881 goda," manuscript, 1911, RNB, f. 590, o. 1, d. 35; Charles and Barbara Jelavich, eds., *Russia in the East, 1876–1880* (Leiden: E. J. Brill, 1959); Paine, *Imperial Rivals*, 110–73; B. P. Gurevich, "History of the 'Ili Crisis,'" in

Sergei Leonidovich Tikhvinsky, ed., *Chapters from the History of Russo-Chinese Relations, 17th-19th Centuries* (Moscow: Progress Publishers, 1985), 301–26.

20. Hsü, *Ili Crisis*, 16–18; Paine, *Imperial Rivals*, 112–13.

21. Hsü, *Ili Crisis*, 31.

22. Grimm, *Sbornik dogovorov*, 84–88; Skachkov, *Russko-kitaiskie otnosheniia*, 54–60; Mayers, *Treaties*, 271–77.

23. William L. Langer, *European Alliances and Alignments, 1871–1890* (New York: Alfred A. Knopf, 1931), 121–66.

24. Irene Grünig, *Die russische öffentliche Meinung und ihre Stellung zu den Großmächten 1878–1894* (Berlin: Ost-Europa Verlag, 1929), 52–63; Boris Nolde, *L'alliance franco-russe: Les origines du système diplomatique d'avant-guerre* (Paris: Librairie Droz, 1936), 199–206; Langer, *European Alliances*, 171–72; George F. Kennan, *The Decline of Bismarck's European Order: Franco-Russian Relations, 1875–1890* (Princeton, N.J.: Princeton University Press, 1979), 27–39; Geyer, *Russian Imperialism*, 82–85. For a discussion from an official perspective, see V. N. Lamsdorf, "Istoricheskii obzor politicheskoi obstanovki v Evrope posle Berlinskogo kongresa," memorandum, 1878, GARF, f. 568, o. 1, d. 52. The general mood in St. Petersburg at the time is well covered in Petr Andreevich Zaionchkovskii, *The Russian Autocracy in Crisis, 1878–1882* (Gulf Breeze, Fl.: Academic International Press, 1979), 33–91.

25. Nolde, *L'alliance*, 209.

26. V. N. Lamsdorf, "Obzor vneshnei politiki Rossii za vremia tsarstvovaniia Aleksandra III," manuscript, n.d., GARF, f. 568, o. 1, d. 53, l. 1.

27. The tsarist Ministry of Foreign Affairs was located near the Choristers' Bridge in St. Petersburg. Just as Frenchmen referred to the Quai D'Orsay and Germans to the Wilhelmstrasse, Russians often spoke about the Choristers' Bridge when talking about their foreign ministry. See Dominic Lieven, *Russia and the Origins of the First World War* (New York: St. Martin's Press, 1983), 61; Helene Iswolsky, *No Time to Grieve: An Autobiographical Journey* (Philadelphia: Winchell, 1985), 31.

28. George F. Kennan, *The Fateful Alliance* (New York: Pantheon Books, 1984), 10.

29. I. S. Rybachenok, "Brak po raschetu. N. K. Girs i zakliuchenie russko-frantsuzkogo soiuza," in Ignatev et al., *Rossiiskaia diplomatiia*, 258. Other good portraits of the foreign minister are given in Ada von Erdmann, "Nikolaj Karlovic Giers, russischer Außenminister 1882–1895: Eine politische Biographie," *Zeitschrift für Osteuropäische Geschichte* 9 (1935): 481–540; Barbara Jelavich, "Giers and the Politics of Russian Moderation," in Robert B. McKean, ed., *New Perspectives in Modern Russian History* (Houndmills: Macmillan, 1992), 25–42.

30. Bülow to Bismarck, letter, Oct. 27, 1887, *GP*, 5:308.

31. Geyer, *Russian Imperialism*, 188–89.

32. "Zhurnal osobogo soveshchaniia," Apr. 26, 1888, *KA*, 52:54–61; Russia, Istoricheskaia Komissiia pri Generalnom Shtabe, *Russko-Iaponskaia voina 1904–1905 gg. Vvedenie chast 1-ia. Russkie morskie sily na Dalnem Vostoke s 1894 do 1901 gg.* (Petrograd: Morskoi generalnyi shtab, 1918), 21–22; Lensen, *Balance*, 1:31–86; J. E. Hoare, "Komundo-Port Hamilton," *Asian Affairs* 17, pt. 3 (October 1986): 298–308; Langer, *Diplomacy*, 1:168–69; Malozemoff, *Russian Far Eastern Policy*, 27–33.

33. In a letter to Finance Minister Ivan Alekseevich Vyshnegradskii in 1890, Giers worried that "it is impossible not to predict that our foes will try to attack us precisely from that side" (Simanskii, *Sobytiia*, 1:5).

34. Malozemoff, *Russian Far Eastern Policy*, 51; Pierre Guillen, *L'Expansion 1881–1898* (Paris: Imprimerie nationale, 1984), 370.

35. Cassini to Lamsdorf, letter, Mar. 1, 1893, GARF, f. 568, o. 1, d. 526, l. 10.

36. Henri Cordier, *Histoire des relations de la Chine avec les puissances occidentales, 1860–1902,* vol. 3 (Paris: Félix Alcan, 1902), 66–67.

37. He was equally well regarded by his adversaries. The long-serving British head of the Chinese Imperial Maritime Customs, Sir Robert Hart, also grudgingly respected his abilities (R. Hart to J. D. Campbell, letter, Dec. 8, 1895, *I. G. in Peking,* 2:1044).

38. Lamsdorf, *Dnevnik 1891–1892,* 18.

39. "Kassini," *BE,* 15:682; Solovev, *Vospominaniia,* 70.

40. Ukhtomskii to Nicholas, letter, Sep. 28, 1895, GARF, f. 601, o. 1, d. 1370, l. 27. Cassini's extracurricular activities had more than earned the displeasure of his superiors. The count did not endear himself to the empress by eloping "briefly and inconclusively" with one of her ladies-in-waiting, nor did he help his career by divorcing Gorchakov's niece (Marguerite Cassini, *Never a Dull Moment: The Memoirs of Countess Marguerite Cassini* [New York: Harper & Brothers, 1956], 10). See Cordier, *Histoire des relations,* 3:348; Auguste Gérard, *Memoires d'Auguste Gérard* (Paris: Librairie Plon, 1928), 266. Cassini's next posting would be as Russia's first ambassador to the United States.

41. Alexander III's success in avoiding war earned him the epithet of *Tsar Mirotvorets* (Tsar-Peacemaker), much as Alexander II was referred to as the "Tsar-Liberator" for abolishing serfdom.

42. Geyer, *Russian Imperialism,* 205.

43. "Vostochnoe napravlenie," *Rossiia* (St. Petersburg), June 18, 1900, 2. The Edwardian Russia watcher, Sir Bernard Pares, put it a little differently: "Rebuffed in Europe after a victorious war by an ignominious treaty enforced by non-combatant powers, Russia under Alexander III sulked. . . . This sulking attitude, in the official creed of [Konstantin] Pobedonostsev, became a theory of Russia's apartness from the rest of the world [and] of her mission in Asia" (Bernard A. Pares, *A History of Russia* [New York: Alfred A. Knopf, 1926], 409).

7: Intervention

1. William Woodville Rockhill, *China's Intercourse with Korea from the XVth Century to 1895* (London: Luzac, 1905); M. Frederic Nelson, *Korea and the Old Orders in Eastern Asia* (Baton Rouge: Louisiana State University Press, 1945), 28–57, 68–85; Hae-jong Chun, "Sino-Korean Tributary Relations in the Ch'ing Period," in John K. Fairbank, ed., *The Chinese World Order: Traditional China's Foreign Relations* (Cambridge, Mass.: Harvard University Press, 1968), 90–111; Andrew C. Nahm, *Korea: Tradition and Transformation: A History of the Korean People* (Elizabeth, N.J.: Hollym International, 1988), 94–143.

2. In 1893, 91 percent of Korean exports (primarily rice and soybeans) went to Japan, which produced 50 percent of Korea's imports. See Ki-baik Lee, *A New History of Korea* (Cambridge, Mass.: Harvard University Press, 1984), 282.

3. Yuan Shikai would later head the powerful Beiyang (North China) army. After playing a major role in the overthrow of the Qing dynasty in 1912, he proclaimed himself the new emperor in 1915, but died not long thereafter, in 1916.

4. Lensen, *Balance,* 1:23.

5. C. I. Eugene Kim and Han-kyo Kim, *Korea and the Politics of Imperialism, 1876–1910* (Berkeley: University of California Press, 1967), 74–77; Chong-sik Lee, *The Politics of Korean Nationalism* (Berkeley: University of California Press, 1963), 19–33. Although the Tonghaks were fiercely nationalist, some have seen Japan's hand in the rising. See Hosea Ballou Morse, *The International Relations of the Chinese Empire,* vol. 3

(Taipei: Ch'eng Wen Publishing Company, 1978), 20; Malozemoff, *Russian Far Eastern Policy*, 52; John K. Fairbank, ed., *The Cambridge History of China*, vol. 11, pt. 2 (Cambridge: Cambridge University Press), 105.

6. The Treaty of Tientsin was signed in April 1885 by Ito Hirobumi and Li Hongzhang to resolve the dispute that arose over the failed coup attempt in 1884. The agreement stipulated that both China and Japan were to withdraw their troops from Korea and that the kingdom could only engage military instructors from third powers. In case of unrest, however, the signatories retained to right to send forces to the region, provided they notified the other party. Text in Cordier, *Histoire des relations*, 3:221–22; Max von Brandt, *Drei Jahre ostasiatischer Politik 1894–1897* (Stuttgart: Strecker & Moser, 1898), 221–23.

7. For a good summary of the events leading up to the war, see Alfred Vagts, "Der chinesisch-japanische Krieg 1894/95," *Europäische Gespräche* 9, no. 5 (May 1931): 234–52; no. 6 (June 1931): 285–301.

8. M. A. Hitrovo to K. I. Weber, letter, Feb. 9, 1894, *KA*, 50–51:4–5.

9. Cassini to N. K. Giers, dispatch, Mar. 10, 1894, *KA*, 50–51:5–6.

10. V. P. Nikhamin, "Russko-iaponskie otnosheniia i Koreia, 1894–1895 gg." (Candidate's diss., Vysshaia diplomaticheskaia shkola, 1948), 20.

11. K. I. Weber to Ministry of Foreign Affairs, telegram, May 20, 1894, *KA*, 50–51:7.

12. Alexander III to N. K. Giers, marginal note, May 1894, *KA*, 50–51:7; Kapnist to Kerberg, telegram, May 27, 1894, *KA*, 50–51:8.

13. Cassini to N. K. Giers, June 10, 1894, *KA*, 50–51:16.

14. N. K. Giers to Alexander III, memorandum, June 10, 1894, *KA*, 50–51:15–16.

15. M. A. Hitrovo to N. K. Giers, telegram, June 24, 1894, *KA*, 50–51:28; Giers to Cassini, telegram, June 28, 1894, *KA*, 50–51:32.

16. Giers may also have been irritated by Li Hongzhang's diplomatic double-dealing. Both Hitrovo and Count Dmitrii Kapnist, the head of the Asiatic Department, accused Li of deception, and Giers was likely well aware that the Chinese official was playing a similar game with Britain. See M. A. Hitrovo to N. K. Giers, telegram, June 13, 1894, *KA*, 50–51:18; D. A. Kapnist, memorandum, June 18, 1894, *KA*, 50–51:21.

17. I.e., Li Hongzhang. See N. K. Giers to Cassini, letter, July 27, 1894, *KA*, 50–51:59.

18. "Otchet MID," 1894, AVPRI, f. 137, o. 475, d. 118, ll. 205–6.

19. In autocratic Russia, the emperor could convene a special conference *(osoboe soveshchanie)* of ministers and other senior bureaucrats to discuss an important question. While the tsar retained the final say, and at times rejected the advice he was given by his ministers, the minutes of such a meeting were a good indication of official thinking. See V. A. Emets, "Mekhanizm priniatiia vneshnepoliticheskikh reshenii v Rossii do i v period pervoi mirovoi voiny," in Iu. A. Pisarev and V. L. Malkov, eds, *Pervaia mirovaia voina: Diskussionye problemy istorii* (Moscow: Nauka, 1994), 60–64. For the minutes of the August 9 conference, see "Zhurnal Osobogo soveshchaniia (21) 9 avgusta 1894 g.," *KA*, 52:62–67.

20. Ibid., 65.

21. Ibid., 66–67; "Otchet MID," 1894, ll. 207–8; Lamsdorf, *Dnevnik 1894–1896*, 156–57.

22. Rosen, *Forty Years*, 1:134. One senior British official expressed surprise that, two months after the outbreak of the war, the Russian ambassador in London still had "no instructions about China" (Keith Neilson, *Britain and the Last Tsar: British Policy and Russia, 1894–1917* [Oxford: Oxford University Press, 1995], 149).

23. Rybachenok suggests that the weakness of Russia's military presence in the Far East may also have contributed to St. Petersburg's caution. The Pacific Squadron

had only half the tonnage of British ships in the region, the army was quite weak, and, with at least 5 more years to complete the Trans-Siberian Railway, logistics were a problem as well. See Irina Sergeevna Rybachenok, *Soiuz s Frantsiei vo vneshnei politiki Rossii v kontse XIX v.* (Moscow: Institut istorii SSSR, 1993), 36.

24. Count Lamsdorf, for one, was not impressed by the deputy minister: "What a shame such a splendid fellow has such a weak head!" (Lamsdorf, *Dnevnik 1894–1896,* 129).

25. *Moskovskie vedomosti,* Apr. 15, 1895, 3.

26. Langer, *Diplomacy,* 1:134.

27. M. A. Hitrovo to N. K. Giers, telegram, June 19, 1894, *KA,* 50–51:23. Even after the first Japanese advances in Korea, the British minister to Peking, Sir Nicholas O'Connor, still expected that "the Chinese anvil was bound to wear out the Japanese hammer in the end" (Chirol, *Fifty Years,* 181). See also Beveridge, *Russian Advance,* 94; Langer, *Diplomacy,* 1:174.

28. The best published source for late-nineteenth-century Russian assessments of Chinese and other Asian armed forces is the *Sbornik geograficheskikh, topograficheskikh i statisticheskikh materialov po Azii,* a classified digest of intelligence reports and translations of Western articles, regularly issued by the army's General Staff between 1883 and 1914. An authoritative description of the Chinese armed forces was considered to be G. Sh. Podpolkovnik Putiata, "Vooruzheniia sili Kitaia 1888–1889," *Sbornik* 39 (1888): 1–87; An expanded version of this is Putiata, *Kitai.*

29. "Innostrannyi obzor," *Vestnik Evropy,* September 1894, 379–81.

30. A good account is provided by the dispatches of the Russian military attaché, Col. K. I. Wogack, which were reprinted in *Sbornik* 60–61. See also Vladimir [pseudonym for Zenone Volpicelli], *The China-Japan War* (New York: Charles Scribner's Sons, 1896). For a brief survey by a British military intelligence officer, see N. W. H. du Boulay, *An Epitome of the Chino Japanese War, 1894–95* (London: Her Majesty's Stationery Office, 1896).

31. Cassini to N. P. Shishkin, dispatch, Jan. 19, 1895, AVPRI, f. 143, o. 491, d. 113, ll. 16–19.

32. K. I. Wogack to Cassini, letter, Oct. 30, 1894, AVPRI, f. 143, o. 491, d. 113, ll. 88–96. Published in *Sbornik* 60 (1895):169–181. Wogack's sympathies distressed both Li Hongzhang and Russian diplomats in Peking, as Cassini complained to Lamsdorf (Cassini to Lamsdorf, letter, Feb. 19, 1897, GARF, f. 568, o. 1, d. 527, l. 27).

33. Cassini to Shishkin, Jan. 19, 1895, l. 19.

34. Lamsdorf, *Dnevnik 1894–1896,* 140.

35. K. I. Wogack to Cassini, Oct. 30, 1894, ll. 88–96. Lensen suggests that the colonel was overly sympathetic to the Japanese during the war (*Balance,* 1:203–4).

36. A. S. Suvorin, "Malenkie pisma," *NV,* Mar. 4, 1895, 1.

37. "Zhurnal Osobogo soveshchaniia (1 fevralia) 20 ianvaria 1895 g.," *KA,* 52:67–74.

38. Ibid., 68.

39. Ibid., 69.

40. Ibid., 68.

41. The general was not categorically opposed to territorial seizures. When the Sino-Japanese War broke out, he wrote a report suggesting annexing portions of northern Manchuria and northern Korea in order to make the Far Eastern border more defensible (Paine, *Imperial Rivals,* 183).

42. "Zhurnal . . . 20 ianvaria 1895 g.," 73.

43. Komissiia, *Russkie morskie sily,* 45–47. Russia's naval dispositions at this time are also given in "S teatra iaponskoi voiny" *NV,* Apr. 9, 1895, 2. For good measure, the

army strengthened its forces in the Far East and mobilized the Priamur Military District. See *Vsepodaneishnyi otchet Voennago Ministra za 1895 g.* (St. Petersburg: Voennaia tipografiia, 1896), App. 1, p. 52; "Otchet MID," 1895, AVPRI, f. 137, o. 475, d. 120, l. 151; Langer, *Diplomacy,* 1:176.

44. Lamsdorf, *Dnevnik 1894–1896,* 138.

45. Ibid., 143–44.

46. Cassini to N. P. Shishkin, dispatch, Feb. 11, 1895, AVPRI, f. 143, o. 491, d. 113, l. 46.

47. Ibid., ll. 44–48; Cassini to N. P. Shishkin, telegram, Feb. 11, 1895, AVPRI, f. 143, o. 491, d. 85, l. 10; Cassini to Shishkin, dispatch, Feb. 21, 1895, AVPRI, f. 143, o. 491, d. 113, ll. 50–55.

48. Lamsdorf, *Dnevnik 1894–1896,* 157.

49. Cassini to A. B. Lobanov, dispatch, Mar. 28, 1895, AVPRI, f. 143, o. 491, d. 113, ll. 101–7. The terms are also in Vladimir, *China-Japan War,* 405–11. Rybachenok suggests that the Japanese minister had already informed the Russian Foreign Ministry about his government's demands in early February (*Soiuz s Frantsiei,* 41).

50. Cassini to Lobanov, dispatch, Mar. 28, 1895, AVPRI, f. 143, o. 491, d. 113, ll. 105–106.

51. Nicholas was even not informed about the terms of the secret military alliance with France, which Giers communicated to his new master only upon his succession to the throne (Lamsdorf, *Dnevnik 1894–1896,* 85).

52. The emperor was well aware of this deficiency. He wrote his uncle, Grand Duke Vladimir Aleksandrovich: "In order not to quarrel . . . I continually give way and in the long run I remain an idiot, without will or character" (*KA,* 17:220). He also complained to one of his ministers: "Why do you constantly argue? I always agree with everyone on everything and then do as I like" (Ford, "Russian Far Eastern Diplomacy," 8).

53. McDonald, *United Government,* 11–17; Boris Aleksandrovich Romanov, "Vitte kak diplomat (1895–1903 gg.)," *Vestnik leningradskogo universiteta,* nos. 4–5 (1946): 150–72.

54. Lamsdorf, *Dnevnik 1894–1896,* 148–49.

55. Konstantin Apollonovich Skalkovskii, *Vneshnaia politika Rossii i polozhenie inostrannykh derzhav* (St. Petersburg: A. S. Suvorin, 1897), xxiii. For other views by his contemporaries, see Witte, *Memoirs,* 220–21, 227–29; A. S. Suvorin, *NV,* Mar. 4, 1895, 1; Neilson, *Britain,* 64; Hatzfeld to Holstein, telegram, May 18, 1895, *GP,* 9:353–54. Aside from his responsibilites as diplomat, the prince was passionately interested in genealogy, and shortly after his appointment as foreign minister he published a two-volume reference work on the great families of Russia: Aleksei Borisovich Lobanov-Rostovskii, *Russkaia Rodoslovnaia Kniga,* 2 vols. (St. Petersburg: A. S. Suvorin, 1895). Count Lamsdorf, who was not insensitive to such matters, was furious to discover that the book ignored his own lineage (*Dnevnik 1894–1896,* 173).

56. Rosen, *Forty Years,* 1:134. Witte said much the same thing: "He was very well educated . . . but knew nothing about the East, in which he ever had any interest. He knew as much about Manchuria, Mukden, Kirin as a second-year *gymnaziia* student" (*Memoirs,* 227–28).

57. Fuller, *Strategy and Power,* 366–67.

58. Lieven, *Russia,* 66. The same point is made in Raymond A. Esthus, "Nicholas II and the Russo-Japanese War," *Russian Review* 40, no. 4 (October 1981): 397.

59. Izvolskii, *Mémoires,* 290.

60. Lobanov to Nicholas, memorandum, Mar. 25, 1895, AVPRI, f. 143, o. 491, d. 143/146, l. 4; also in *KA,* 52:75.

61. Popov, "Dalnevostochnaia," 42–43; Oldenburg, *Last Tsar*, 1:121; Ford, "Russian Far Eastern Diplomacy," 100.

62. "Mozhet li Rossiia dovolit Iaponii pered Koreeiu ?" *Grazhdanin*, Jan. 4, 1895, 2.

63. The naval commentator A. E. Belomor pointed out that the only friendly port on the Pacific was distant Saigon ("Morskie voprosy" *NV*, Mar. 3, 1895, 2).

64. Simanskii, *Sobytiia*, 1:11–12.

65. "Eshche o nezamerzaiushchem porte," *NV*, Mar. 27, 1895, 1.

66. Nicholas to Lobanov, marginal note, ca. Mar. 25, 1895, AVPRI, f. 143, o. 491, d. 143/146, l. 4. Emphasis in original.

67. Lobanov to Nicholas, Mar. 25, 1895, AVPRI, f. 143, o. 491, d. 143/146, l. 4. Nicholas enthusiastically noted in the margin, "Exactly."

68. Ibid., l. 5.

69. Aleksandr Iakovlevich Maksimov, *Nashi zadachi na Tikhom Okeane*, 4th ed. (St. Petersburg: K. L. Pentkovskii, 1901).

70. Ibid., 44.

71. Ibid., 58.

72. Hitrovo suggested allowing Japan to have the Liaodong peninsula in exchange for Russian control over Korea (Simanskii, *Sobytiia*, 1:41). In a letter to Giers in October 1894, Hitrovo argued: "I am deeply convinced that Japan will not only prove to be our natural and true ally, but that it is in a position, so to speak, to be our *avant garde* in that part of the world" (ibid., 1:66). On Kapnist, see Lamsdorf, *Dnevnik 1894–1896*, 168.

73. M. A. Hitrovo to Lobanov, letter, Apr. 30, 1896, AVPRI, f. 138, o. 467, d. 153/159, ll. 2–9. Nicholas noted with some annoyance in the margin: "And the alliance with China ?!!!"

74. Rosen, *Forty Years*, 1:135–36.

75. Viscount Aoki, the Japanese minister to Berlin, told the Wilhelmstrasse that Tokyo would also be amenable to annexations by Germany of a province in southwestern China and a Korean island by Britain. See Von Mühlberg, memorandum, Apr. 2, 1895, *GP*, 9:260; Langer, *Diplomacy*, 1:181.

76. One editorial complained that "it doesn't seem to bother [the Japanese] that Manchuria has been in Russia's commercial sphere for a long time, and in no case may be yielded to Japan" (Editorial, *NV*, Mar. 1, 1895, 1). Shishkin even felt that the Gulf of Chili lay "more or less in the sphere if influence of Russia" (*KA*, 52:68–69).

77. "Evropa i Iaponiia," *SPBVed*, April 10, 1895, 1.

78. *NV*, Apr. 8, 1895, 1.

79. V. P. Meshcherskii, "Dnevnik" *Grazhdanin*, Feb. 21, 1895, 3.

80. V. P. Meshcherskii, "Dnevnik" *Grazhdanin*, Feb. 11, 1895, 3.

81. Cassini to N. K. Giers, dispatch, Jan. 8, 1894, AVPRI, f. 143, o. 491, d. 113, ll. 13–14; *KA*, 50:30; Lamsdorf, *Dnevnik 1894–1896*, 156–57.

82. Glinskii, *Prolog*, 10.

83. Witte, memorandum, 1902, RGIA, f. 1622, o. 1, d. 711, l. 1; Glinskii, *Prolog*, 10–14; Romanov, *Russia in Manchuria*, 39–45; Laue, *Sergei Witte*, 81–82; Marks, *Road to Power*, 142–45; Ford, "Russian Far Eastern Diplomacy," 19–24.

84. Semennikov, *Za kulisami tsarizma*, 81.

85. Romanov, *Russia in Manchuria*, 45.

86. Geyer, *Russian Imperialism*, 187–95.

87. Dillon, *Eclipse*, 246.

88. "Zhurnal Osobogo soveshchaniia," Mar. 30, 1895, AVPRI, f. 143, o. 491, d. 145/148, ll. 2–11; also in *KA*, 52:78–83.

89. Ibid., l. 3.

90. Ibid., l. 6.

91. Ibid., l. 7.

92. Ibid., l. 11.

93. When Lobanov sent him a note two days after the meeting about a conversation he had had with the French Ambassador, Nicholas penciled in the margin: "I agree with [the] . . . proposal that we, in agreement with France, not oppose the Sino-Japanese peace treaty, but that we obtain as compensation an open port" (KA, 52:77).

94. DDF, 11:692.

95. Nicholas, Dnevnik, 115; Witte, Memoirs, 228; Romanov, Russia in Manchuria, 56–59; DDF, 11:708.

96. KA, 52:74.

97. Simanskii, Sobytiia, 1:45.

98. "Otchet MID," 1895, AVPRI, f. 137, o. 475, d. 120, l. 154; Langer, Diplomacy, 1:182.

99. Leonard Kenneth Young, British Policy in China 1895–1902 (Oxford: Clarendon, 1970), 1–15.

100. The Foreign Office was more even-handed in its approach. As an English diplomatic historian puts it: "There is no evidence in the archives that Britain gave her favour either to China or Japan. . . . The actions which Britain took before and during the war were not so much pro-Chinese or anti-Japanese as pro-British" (Ian H. Nish, The Anglo-Japanese Alliance: The Diplomacy of Two Island Empires, 1894–1907 [London: Athlone Press, 1966], 25).

101. Ibid., 23–26; Young, British Policy, 18–19; Otto Franke, Die Großmächte in Ostasien von 1894 bis 1914 (Brunswick: Verlag Georg Westermann, 1923), 66–68; Brandt, Drei Jahre, 115–18; Langer, Diplomacy, 1:174. One good example of this new attitude is in George N. Curzon, Problems of the Far East: Japan—China—Korea (London: Longmans, Green, 1895), 392–93.

102. Neilson, Britain, 148.

103. Ibid., 148–50; Rybachenok, Soiuz s Frantsiei, 39.

104. Alexandre Meyendorff, ed., Correspondance diplomatique de M. de Staal (1884–1900), 2 vols. (Paris: Marcel Rivière, 1929), 2:266–68; Neilson, Britain, 154–60; Young, British Policy, 16–19.

105. Gérard, Ma mission, 46; GP, 9:245n.

106. Hohenlohe to Marschall, telegram, Nov. 17, 1894, GP, 9:245–46.

107. Arthur Julius Irmer, "Die Erwerbung von Kiautschou, 1894–1898" (Inaugural diss., Rheinischen Friedrich-Wilhelm Universität zu Bonn, 1930), 8–9; A. Harding Ganz, "The German Navy in the Far East and the Pacific: The Seizure of Kiaochow and After," in J. A. Moses and P. D. Kennedy, eds., Germany in the Pacific and Far East, 1870–1914 (St. Lucia: University of Queensland Press, 1977), 120. A more popular account of the kaiser's global ambitions is given in Robert K. Massie, Dreadnought: Britain, Germany, and the Coming of the Great War (New York: Random House, 1991).

108. When Cassini commented on the reaction of European diplomats in Peking to the talks at Shimonoseki, he did not even trouble to mention the German minister (Cassini to Lobanov, dispatch, Apr. 6, 1895, AVPRI, f. 143, o. 491, d. 113, ll. 114–17).

109. The war was also a good way to obtain a naval station. When Hohenlohe suggested that German participation in a démarche could be rewarded by a port, the kaiser noted, "Correct" (Hohenlohe to Wilhelm II, memorandum, Mar. 19, 1895, GP, 9:254). See also GP, 9:266; DDF, 14:6.

110. "Zhurnal Osobogo soveshchaniia," Mar. 30, 1895, l. 2; Marschall to H.

Tschirsky, telegram, Mar. 23, 1895, *GP,* 9:258–59.

111. *DDF,* 11:623–24.

112. Guillen, *L'Expansion,* 339–44, 370–73; Rybachenok, *Soiuz s Frantsiei,* 46–47.

113. Lobanov to Nicholas, memorandum, Apr. 2, 1895, AVPRI, f. 143, o. 491, d. 143/146, l. 8; also in *KA,* 52:71; Montebello implies that it was Lobanov who made this objection (*DDF,* 11:691–92).

114. *DDF,* 11:646–47, 673.

115. Looking back a month later, the French ambassador to Berlin, Jules Herbette, expressed his irritation that France "was forced to support Russia in the Japanese question in order to keep it from throwing itself in the arms of Germany" (*DDF,* 12:26). Lamsdorf caustically suggested that France and Germany both acted solely to preempt their rival: "In essence the two powers participated in this risky adventure with misgivings, each of them satisfied only by the knowledge that they had kept us from greater intimacy with the other" (*Dnevnik 1894–1896,* 177).

116. Guillen, *L'Expansion,* 373; Gérard, *Ma mission,* 42–43; Langer, *Diplomacy,* 1:185.

117. Cassini to Lobanov, dispatch, Apr. 3, 1895, AVPRI, f. 143, o. 491, d. 113, ll. 108–10; Cassini to Lobanov, dispatch, Apr. 6, 1895, AVPRI, f. 143, o. 491, d. 113, ll. 111–13; Gérard, *Ma mission,* 38. Rybachenok suggests that Cassini's hints of Russian support gave Li the confidence to sign the treaty, in the knowledge that European diplomatic pressure would eventually lead to a revision of its terms (*Soiuz s Frantsiei,* 41). For a copy of the treaty, see *BDFA,* pt. I, ser. E, 5:372–77; Cordier, *Histoire des relations,* 3:281–86.

118. Foreign Minister Mutsu was ill at the time. See Cassini to Lobanov, telegram, Apr. 7, 1895, AVPRI, f. 143, o. 491, d. 85, l. 31; Cassini to Lobanov, dispatch, Apr. 22, 1895, AVPRI, f. 143, o. 491, d. 113, ll. 134–37; *DDF,* 11:694–695; Gutschmidt to Hohenlohe, memorandum, Apr. 24, 1895, *GP,* 9:275–78; A. M. Pooley, ed., *The Secret Memoirs of Count Tadasu Hayashi* (New York: G. P. Putnam's Sons, 1915), 82–85.

119. According to Grand Duke Aleksei Aleksandrovich, Britain, which steadfastly maintained an attitude of strict neutrality, disposed of 15 ships with a total weight of 66,000 tons in regional waters (Simanskii, *Sobytiia,* 1:43). A British diplomat in Tokyo estimated the combined strength of the Russian, French, and German fleets in the Far East at 40 ships, adding, "In resisting Russia, Japan would probably be defeated" (*BDFA,* pt. I, ser. E, 5:308).

120. Lensen, *The d'Anethan Dispatches,* 48; Mutsu Munemitsu, *Kenkenroku: A Diplomatic Record of the Sino-Japanese War, 1894–1895* (Princeton, N.J.: Princeton University Press, 1982), 248–54.

121. Cassini to Lobanov, telegram, Apr. 23, 1895, AVPRI, f. 143, o. 491, d. 85, l. 37; Cassini to Lobanov, dispatch, Apr. 27, 1895, AVPRI, f. 143, o. 491, d. 113, ll. 141–42.

122. P. P. Tyrtov, memorandum, Apr. 24, 1896, GARF, f. 601, o. 1, d. 434, l. 15.

123. Ibid., ll. 15–21; Russia, Istoricheskaia Komissiia pri Morskom Generalnom Shtabe, *Russko-Iaponskaia voina 1904–1905 gg. Deistviia flota,* ed. A. F. Heiden et al., pt. 1-a (Petrograd: Morskoi generalnyi shtab, 1918), 56–57. French support was notably lacking in enthusiasm, much to Tyrtov's irritation. In his report about the operation, the admiral noted that his French counterpart, Rear Adm. de Beaumont, initially declined to join his squadron, on the grounds that he lacked instructions. "I became convinced . . . that the French would hardly be our ally in the imminent hostilities" (Tyrtov, memorandum, Apr. 24, 1896, l. 19). Beaumont did finally get orders to put his ships at Tyrtov's disposal. See *DDF,* 11:726–27, 738, 743, 745–46; Russia, *Russko-Iaponskaia voina,* pt. 1-a, 51; Rybachenok, *Soiuz s Frantsiei,* 46–49; Simanskii, *Sobytiia,* 1:44.

124. John W. Foster, *Diplomatic Memoirs,* 2 vols. (Boston: Houghton Mifflin, 1909), 2:151; also cited in Langer, *Diplomacy,* 1:187. The British consul at Zhifu gives a

similar account. See *BDFA,* pt. I, ser. E, 5:408–9.

125. Cassini to Lobanov, dispatch, Apr. 27, 1895, AVPRI, f. 143, o. 491, d. 113, ll. 138–40; Tyrtov, memorandum, Apr. 24, 1896, l. 21.

8: *Asian Alliance*

1. Cassini to Lobanov, letter, Aug. 7, 1895, AVPRI, f. 143, o. 491 , d. 113, ll. 112–13.
2. Gérard, *Memoires,* 266.
3. Chirol, *The Far Eastern Question* (London: Macmillan, 1896), 63–64; Henry Norman, *The Peoples and Politics of the Far East* (New York: C. Scribner's, 1895).
4. Hart, *I. G. in Peking,* 2:1060.
5. Young, *British Policy,* 2–7, 19; Mary H. Wilgus, *Sir Claude MacDonald, the Open Door, and British Informal Empire in China, 1895–1900* (New York: Garland, 1987), 12–32; Chirol, *Far Eastern Question,* 2–3.
6. Cordier, *Histoire des relations,* 3:309–10.
7. He added that Englishmen were even turning to him for help in interceding with the Chinese government. The tsar penciled in the margin of this dispatch cataloging Britain's woes in Peking: "delightful!" (Cassini to Lobanov, dispatch, July 6, 1896, AVPRI, f. 143, o. 491, d. 114/1, ll. 109–12). The travails of England's minister were a favorite theme in the count's reports to St. Petersburg in 1895 and 1896. See Cassini to Lobanov, dispatch, Aug. 8, 1895, AVPRI, f. 143, o. 491, d. 113, ll. 203–5; Cassini to Lobanov, dispatch, Oct. 7, 1895, AVPRI, f. 143, o. 491, d. 113, ll. 210–13; Cassini to Lobanov, dispatch, June 25, 1896, AVPRI, f. 143, o. 491, d. 114/1, l. 108.
8. C. M. Hou, *Foreign Investment and Economic Development in China, 1840–1937* (Cambridge, Mass.: Harvard University Press, 1965), 27. Imperial Chinese public finance is treated in greater detail in Wen Ching Yin, *Le système fiscal de la Chine* (Paris: Imprimerie du Montparnasse et de Persan Beaumont, 1929); and Joseph Edkins, *The Revenue and Taxation of the Chinese Empire* (Shanghai: Presbyterian Mission Press, 1903).
9. Between 1861 and 1893 China had borrowed 85 million taels abroad, according to Hou. (*Foreign Investment,* 29). During the war with Japan, two more international loans totaling 30 million taels were made. Cassini estimated China's foreign debt in May 1895 at 45 million taels, a sum equivalent to half of the central government's annual revenues (Cassini to Lobanov, dispatch, May 28, 1895, AVPRI, f. 143, o. 495, d. 113, ll. 168–69).
10. The Hongkong and Shanghai Bank had already made two loans during the war. See Arthur Gardiner Coons, *The Foreign Public Debt of China* (Philadelphia: University of Pennsylvania Press, 1930), 5; Twitchett and Fairbank, *Cambridge History of China,* vol. 11, pt. 2:67.
11. Cassini to Lobanov, dispatch, Apr. 29, 1895, AVPRI, f. 143, o. 495, d. 113, ll. 143–47; Lamsdorf, *Dnevnik 1894–1896,* 209; Young, *British Policy,* 27; Neilson, *Britain,* 179. A British scholar implies that Russian intrigue torpedoed the Hongkong and Shanghai Bank's offer, but Cassini makes no mention of such machinations in his dispatches. See D. McLean, "The Foreign Office and the First Chinese Indemnity Loan, 1895," *Historical Journal* 16, no. 2 (June 1973): 308, 313–316.
12. In early May, Cassini was still asking if his government would consider entering the competition (Cassini to Ministry of Foreign Affairs, telegram, May 4, 1895, AVPRI, f. 143, o. 495, d. 85, l. 41).
13. Romanov, *Russia in Manchuria,* 65; Rybachenok, *Soiuz s Frantsiei,* 51. Montebello claims that China approached Russia for the loan, but there does not seem to be any evidence in the tsarist foreign and finance ministry archives that Chinese officials

made any advances in St. Petersburg (*DDF,* 12:81).

14. Lensen, *Balance,* 2:480; Langer, *Diplomacy,* 1:188.

15. *DDF,* 12:19–20; Romanov, *Russia in Manchuria,* 66.

16. In late April, Cassini was already urging the foreign minister to participate in the loan. See Cassini to Lobanov, dispatch, Apr. 29, 1895, AVPRI, f. 143, o. 495, d. 113, l. 147; Witte, *Memoirs,* 229.

17. Meyendorff, *Correspondance de M. de Staal,* 2:274; also cited in Lamsdorf, *Dnevnik 1894–1896,* 176. Montebello said much the same: "There is no doubt that if Russia assists China today it is not without anticipating some benefits in the future" (*DDF,* 12:83).

18. Witte's agent Rothstein first turned to Alphonse de Rothschild in Paris. Rothschild was Russia's lead banker, and the head of the British Rothschilds was Lord Rosebery's father-in-law. Alphonse's cousin in London came under pressure from the British government not to assist the Russians in the deal, and Alphonse turned him down. Messrs. Hottinguer, the Banque de Paris et des Pays-Bas, and the Crédit Lyonnais had no such scruples and readily offered their services. See *DDF,* 12:24n., 34, 62, 82; Cordier, *Histoire des relations,* 3:305; Neilson, *Britain,* 179; Rybachenok, *Soiuz s Frantsiei,* 52, McLean, "Foreign Office," 309.

19. Cassini to Lobanov, dispatch, June 27, 1894, AVPRI, f. 143, o. 495, d. 113, ll. 177–82. Cassini complained in one telegram that "the Anglo-German intrigues surpass the bounds of reason" (Cassini to Ministry of Foreign Affairs, telegram, June 9, 1895, AVPRI, f. 143, o. 495, d. 85, l. 64). Meanwhile, Hart sighed, "China's excessive gratitude seems bent on putting on Russia's golden fetters, and all I can do is to stiffen China against accepting killing conditions" (*I. G. in Peking,* 2:1021).

20. Cordier, *Histoire des relations,* 3:305–6; Romanov, *Russia in Manchuria,* 67. For the terms of the loan, see Grimm, *Sbornik dogovorov,* 56–60, also 104–5; Skachkov, *Russko-kitaiskie otnosheniia,* 67–69; Cordier, *Histoire des relations,* 3:307 8; John V. A. MacMurray, *Treaties and Agreements with and concerning China, 1894–1919,* vol. 1 (New York: Oxford University Press, 1921), 35–42.

21. Cassini to Lobanov, dispatch, Apr. 28, 1895, AVPRI, f. 143, o. 495, d. 113, ll. 168–169. A historical table of the rates paid by the central government of China is provided by Hou, *Foreign Investment,* 31.

22. René Girault, *Emprunts russes et investissements français en Russie 1887–1914* (Paris: Librairie Armand Colin, 1973), 306.

23. Cordier, *Histoire des relations,* 3:306.

24. It was his fury at China's decision to borrow from Russia that caused the British minister Nicholas O'Conor to lose his temper at the Yamen and insult the emperor (Lensen, *Balance,* 2:486). Lamsdorf repeatedly fretted in his diary about the damage done to relations with the two nations. As he wrote in early July: "The ill-starred Chinese loan, which we guaranteed, hurt our ties with Germany and England" (*Dnevnik 1894–1896,* 231; see also 193–200, 202–3). Germany, which had enthusiastically supported the Triplice, was particularly vexed and now began advising Tokyo to tarry in evacuating the Liaodong peninsula (Marschall to Gutschmid, telegram, June 7, 1895, *GP,* 9:301). Neilson downplays London's annoyance at the Russian loan (*Britain,* 181).

25. "Politicheskoe obozrenie," *SPBVed,* June 23, 1895, 1; "Po povodu kitaiskago zaima," *SPBVed,* June 27, 1895, 1.

26. V. P. Meshcherskii, "Dnevnik," *Grazhdanin,* June 26, 1895, 3.

27. The best study of these negotiations is Baron Aleksei Buksgevden (Buxhoevden), *Russkii Kitai: Ocherki diplomaticheskoi snoshenii Rossii s Kitaem* (Port Arthur: Novyi Krai, 1902).

28. "He who excuses himself, implicates himself" (Lamsdorf, *Dnevnik*

1894–1896, 208–9).

29. Curzon, *Problems,* 279.

30. Cassini to Lobanov, dispatch, July 6, 1896, AVPRI, f. 143, o. 495, d. 143, l. 114.

31. Simanskii, *Sobytiia,* 1:70.

32. Soviet scholars have studied the race for informal empires in the Far East in considerable depth. Some characteristic works include Vladimir Iakovlevich Avarin, *Imperializm v Manzhurii,* 2 vols. (Moscow-Leningrad: Ogiz, 1934); Mikhail Nikolaevich Pokrovskii, "Vneshniaia politika Rossii v kontse XIX veka," in *Diplomatiia i voiny tsarskoi Rossii v XIX stoletii* (Moscow: Krasnaia Nov, 1923), 302–78; V. P. Potemkin, ed., *Istoriia diplomatii,* vol. 2 (Moscow: Ogiz, 1945), 107–59. The subject is also covered quite well in Osterhammel, *China,* 125–201.

33. On Britain, see, for example, Wilgus, *MacDonald;* and E. W. Edwards, *British Diplomacy and Finance in China, 1895–1914* (Oxford: Oxford University Press, 1987).

34. Siberian Railway Committee, minutes, Nov. 29, 1895, RGIA, f. 560, o. 28, d. 52, l. 54; Glinskii, *Prolog,* 26; Hou, *Foreign Investment,* 43.

35. Finance Ministry, "Istoricheskaia spravka," 68; Glinskii, *Prolog,* 26–27.

36. Witte to Nicholas, memorandum, Aug. 14, 1895, RGIA, f. 560, o. 38, d. 175, l. 68.

37. Witte to Nicholas, memorandum, Sep. 30, 1895, RGIA, f. 560, o. 38, d. 175, l. 81.

38. Witte to Nicholas, memorandum, Aug. 14, 1895, RGIA, f. 560, o. 38, d. 175, ll. 68–69.

39. Romanov, *Russia in Manchuria,* 67–68.

40. Girault, *Emprunts,* 306–7; Olga Crisp, "The Russo-Chinese Bank: An Episode in Franco-Russian Relations," *Slavonic and East European Review* 52, no. 127 (April 1974): 198–99.

41. This caused some distress to its French directors, some of whom did not speak the language (Crisp, "Russo-Chinese Bank," 203). A list of the board is given in Romanov, *Russia in Manchuria,* 397n.27. See also Witte to Nicholas, Sep. 30, 1895, l. 78; *DDF,* 12:236–37.

42. By 1901, the bank had 31 branches, of which 16 were in China. For a partial list, see Rosemary Quested, *The Russo-Chinese Bank: A Multinational Financial Base of Tsarism in China* (Birmingham: University of Birmingham, 1977), 33.

43. Glinskii, *Prolog,* 28–29.

44. Solovev, *Vospominaniia,* 71.

45. Korsakov, *V starom Pekine,* 211.

46. Solovev recalled that from the date of Pokotilov's arrival in 1896 Russian policy in the Chinese capital was carried out by both the Foreign and Finance Ministries (*Vospominaniia,* 71).

47. Ronald E. Robinson, "Railways and Informal Empire," in Clarence B. Davis and Kenneth E. Wilburn, Jr., eds., *Railway Imperialism* (New York: Greenwood Press, 1991), 191; Cheng Lin, *The Chinese Railways: A Historical Survey* (Shanghai: China United Press, 1935), 12–13.

48. By comparison, in 1894 there were more than 280,000 kilometers of track in the United States. See Ralph William Huenemann, *The Dragon and the Iron Horse: The Economics of Railroads in China, 1876–1937* (Cambridge, Mass.: Harvard University Press, 1984), 46–47.

49. Ibid., 37–47; Percy H. Kent, *Railway Enterprise in China* (London: Edward Arnold, 1908), 1–35; Clarence B. Davis, "Railway Imperialism in China 1895–1939," in Davis and Wilburn, eds., *Railway Imperialism,* 155–173

50. Malozemoff, *Russian Far Eastern Policy,* 77.

51. Gérard, *Ma mission,* 55–67; Langer, *Diplomacy,* 1:394.

52. E. Kh. Nilus, ed., *Istoricheskii obzor Kitaiskoi vostochnoi zheleznoi dorogi, 1896–1923 gg.,* vol. 1 (Harbin: Tipografiia K.V.Zh.D., 1923), 5; Glinskii, *Prolog,* 29–30; Marks, *Road to Power,* 42–44; Romanov, *Russia in Manchuria,* 62.

53. Glinskii, *Prolog,* 30; Nilus, *Istoricheskii obzor,* 1:14.

54. Glinskii, *Prolog,* 30–31; Tupper, *To the Great Ocean,* 235.

55. Simanskii, *Sobytiia,* 1:71–72; Malozemoff, *Russian Far Eastern Policy,* 72. Prince Meshcherskii was another enthusiastic supporter of this idea, and in March 1895 he was already proposing that Russia make its diplomatic support of Peking at Shimonoseki contingent upon the railway concession. See V. P. Meshcherskii, "Dnevnik," *Grazhdanin,* Mar. 15, 1895, 3.

56. Witte to Nicholas, memorandum, Mar. 31, 1896, *KA,* 52:91–102.

57. Ibid., 91.

58. Witte, *Memoirs,* 237.

59. Leroy-Beaulieu, *La rénovation,* 141.

60. Ford, "Russian Far Eastern Diplomacy," 133–34. Lord Salisbury said much the same at his Guildhall speech of 1895, adding that "good Anglo-Russian relations are more important than keeping Russia out of Asia" (Neilson, *Britain,* 182).

61. Nilus, *Istoricheskii obzor,* 1:41; Lamsdorf, *Dnevnik 1894–1896,* 282; R. K. I. Quested, *"Matey" Imperialists? The Tsarist Russians in Manchuria, 1895–1917* (Hong Kong: University of Hong Kong, 1982), 21–22.

62. Cassini to Ministry of Foreign Affairs, telegram, Sep. 27, 1895, AVPRI, f. 143, o. 491, d. 85, l. 87; Malozemoff, *Russian Far Eastern Policy,* 72–73.

63. Lamsdorf, *Dnevnik 1894–1896,* 315.

64. Ibid., 327–28; Cassini to Lobanov, dispatch, Mar. 19, 1896, AVPRI, f. 143, o. 491, d. 114/1, l. 37.

65. Cassini to Lobanov, dispatch, Apr. 9, 1896, AVPRI, f. 143, o. 491, d. 114/1, ll. 43–46.

66. Cassini to Ministry of Foreign Affairs, telegram, Apr. 19, 1896, AVPRI, f. 133, o. 470, d. 143, ll. 16–17; Casssini to Lobanov, dispatch, Apr. 20, 1896, AVPRI, f. 143, o. 491, d. 114/1, ll. 63–69.

67. Cassini to Lobanov, dispatch, Feb. 20, 1896, AVPRI, f. 143, o. 491, d. 114/1, ll. 27–32; Marcella Bounds, "The Sino-Russian Secret Treaty of 1896," *Papers on China* 23 (July 1970): 113–114; Cordier, *Histoire des relations,* 3:340–41; Solovev, *Vospominaniia,* 67.

68. One example is a memorial cited in Bounds, "Secret Treaty," 110.

69. Mary Clabaugh Wright, *The Last Stand of Chinese Conservatism: The T'ung-Chih Restoration, 1862–1874* (Stanford, Calif.: Stanford University Press, 1957), 218.

70. Ibid., 121; Mark Mancall, *China at the Center: 300 Years of Foreign Policy* (New York: Free Press, 1984), 32. Twenty years earlier the Hong Kong–based journalist Wang Tao had likened the Europeans to the foes of the Chou dynasty in its Warring States period (403–221 B.C.). See Paul A. Cohen, "Wang T'ao's Perspective on a Changing World," in Albert Feuerwerker et al., eds., *Approaches to Modern Chinese History* (Berkeley: University of California Press, 1967), 140–44. Another commentator, Liang Chichao, found an equally ominous precedent in European history when he drew a parallel with the partition of Poland in the late eighteenth century (Price, *Russia,* 75).

71. Bounds, "Secret Treaty," 111.

72. Ssu-yü Teng and John K. Fairbank, eds., *China's Response to the West: A Documentary Survey, 1839–1923* (Cambridge, Mass.: Harvard University Press, 1954), 127–28.

73. Bounds, "Secret Treaty," 111–12.

74. Hsü, *Rise of Modern China*, 277.

75. Li deeply admired Peter the Great. See Arthur W. Hummel, ed., *Eminent Chinese of the Ch'ing Period*, vol. 1 (Washington, D.C.: U.S. Government Printing Office, 1943), 464–71; Stanley Spector, *Li Hung-chang and the Huai Army* (Seattle: University of Washington Press, 1964). On self-strengthening, see Wright, *Last Stand*.

76. Edwin Pak-wah Leung, "Li Hung-chang and the Liu-ch'iu (Ryukyu) Controversy, 1871–1881," in Samuel C. Chu and Kwang-Ching Liu, eds., *Li Hung-chang and China's Early Modernization* (Armonk, N.Y.: M. E. Sharpe, 1984), 170–71; Meng, *Tsungli Yamen*, 58–59.

77. Teng and Fairbank, *China's Response*, 119.

78. As early as 1874, when China faced aggression both from Russia in Xinjiang and Japan on the northern coast, Li downplayed the threat from the former and tried to convince the emperor that the real enemy was Tokyo. See Immanuel C. Y. Hsü, "The Great Policy Debate in China, 1874: Maritime Defense vs. Frontier Defense," *Harvard Journal of Asiatic Studies* 25 (1965): 212–28.

79. J. O. P. Bland, *Li Hung-chang* (New York: Henry Holt and Company, 1917), 210–11.

80. Bounds, "Secret Treaty," 112–13.

81. "Istoricheskaia spravka," 72; Langer, *Diplomacy*, 1:402, Romanov, *Russia in Manchuria*, 79. The instructions to Li Hongzhang for the embassy to Moscow make no mention of such a trade, but Bounds does suggest that the viceroy discussed the idea of an alliance with a number of officials before his departure ("Secret Treaty," 114).

82. Bland, *Li Hung-chang*, 182.

83. Cordier, *Histoire des relations*, 3:342; Morse, *International Relations*, 3:102–3; Gérard, *Ma mission*, 125, 149–52.

84. Pokotilov to Witte, dispatch, Mar. 4, 1896, RGIA, f. 560, o. 28, d. 640, l. 38; Solovev, *Vospominaniia*, 67; Glinskii, *Prolog*, 35.

85. "Istoricheskaia spravka," 74, 80–82; Ignatev, *Vitte*, 46; Romanov, *Russia in Manchuria*, 81; Witte, *Memoirs*, 230.

86. "Istoricheskaia spravka," 75–76. Witte claimed that "Prince Lobanov-Rostovskii took no part in the negotiations at the time . . . [being] neither informed about nor interested in Far Eastern politics" (*Memoirs*, 231). This appears to be one of the many instances that the finance minister exaggerated his role, since Lamsdorf's diary, generally a more reliable source, mentions that his chief met with Li (*Dnevnik 1894–1896*, 380). Nevertheless, it is clear that Witte was in charge of the talks and that he did his best not to involve his colleague at the Choristers' Bridge more than was absolutely necessary.

87. Witte, *Memoirs*, 231.

88. Romanov, *Russia in Manchuria*, 82; Ignatev, *Vitte*, 47.

89. Nicholas, *Dnevniki*, 139–40; Witte, *Memoirs*, 232; Lensen, *Balance*, 2:499. Nicholas received Ukhtomskii a number of times to discuss the negotiations with Li. See Ukhtomskii to Nicholas, letter, Mar. 21, 1896, RGIA, f. 1072, o. 2, d. 21, l. 2; Ukhtomskii to Nicholas, letter, May 12, 1896, GARF, f. 543, o. 1, d. 171, ll. 1–3; Nicholas, *Dnevniki*, 139.

90. Bounds, "Secret Treaty," 118.

91. Ibid., 119; Langer, *Diplomacy*, 1:403–4. On the bribe itself, see Cassini to Lamsdorf, letter, Feb. 19, 1897, GARF, f. 568, o. 1, d. 527, l. 26; Romanov, *Russia in Manchuria*, 84–85, 402–3n.74.

92. The text of the Sino-Russian treaty and related correspondence are in AVPRI, f. 138, o. 467, d. 151/157. For published versions, see Romanov, *Russia in Manchuria*, 400–2n.68; Grimm, *Sbornik dogovorov*, 105–6; Skachkov, *Russko-kitaiskie otnosheniia*, 73–74; MacMurray, *Treaties*, 1:81; Bounds, "Secret Treaty," 119–20.

93. "Cassini Convention," *NCH*, Oct. 30, 1896, 739–41; Cordier, *Histoire des relations*, 3:343–48. As Simanskii and Romanov both point out, the "Cassini Convention" that appeared in the English-language press gave a fairly accurate version of the treaty. Romanov is probably right in suggesting that it was based on a copy of an early draft leaked from the Russian legation (Simanskii, *Sobytiia*, 1:81; Romanov, *Russia in Manchuria*, 100–1). Li did not take its confidentiality too seriously and "accidentally" left it on his desk when he stepped out of his office during a meeting with Gérard in 1897 (*DDF*, 13:299–303; Gérard, *Ma mission*, 146). The first official Russian admission of the treaty's existence came in an editorial in the government's paper, *Pravitelstvennyi vestnik*, on March 30, 1902. Glinskii, *Prolog*, 184. On British reactions to the "Cassini Convention," see Neilson, *Britain*, 182–84.

94. The Russian gauge is 1.52 meters between the rails. See Westwood, *History of Russian Railways*, 30–31; Karl Baedeker, *Russia with Teheran, Port Arthur, and Peking* (Leipzig: Karl Baedeker, 1914), xx.

95. Romanov, *Russia in Manchuria*, 83; Malozemoff, *Russian Far Eastern Policy*, 79.

96. Chinese Eastern Railway, *Sbornik dokumentov, otnosiashchikhsia k Kitaiskoi Vostochnoi zheleznoi dorogi* (Harbin: K V Zh D, 1922), 11–16; Grimm, *Sbornik dogovorov*, 110–13; Skachkov, *Russko-kitaiskie otnosheniia*, 74–77; MacMurray, *Treaties*, 1:74–77.

97. Witte to Nicholas, memorandum, September 1896, RGIA, f. 1622, o. 1, d. 118, l. 1.

98. Paine, *Imperial Rivals*, 187; Hou, *Foreign Investment*, 65. See also Kent, *Railway Enterprise*.

99. MacMurray, *Treaties*, 1:86. The statutes are in ibid., 1:84–88.

100. If Peking chose to exercise this option, it would have had both to purchase the CER's shares and to assume its debt. Witte was confident that the concession would remain in Russian hands for the full 80-year period (Witte to Nicholas, memorandum, September 1896, l. 1).

101. Romanov, *Russia in Manchuria*, 88; Malozemoff, *Russian Far Eastern Policy*, 82.

102. Nilus, *Istoricheskii obzor*, 1:23; Glinskii, *Prolog*, 42; Solovev, *Vospominaniia*, 72–73.

103. Nilus, *Istoricheskii obzor*, 1:24.

104. Leroy-Beaulieu, *La rénovation*, 137–38.

105. Glinskii, *Prolog*, 61; Gurko, *Features and Figures*, 258–59; Laue, *Sergei Witte*, 151–52.

106. Gurko, *Features and Figures*, 259.

107. I. Ia. Korostovets to E. I. Alekseev, letter, Dec. 27, 1901, RGAVMF, f. 32, o. 1, d. 60, l. 23. Paine cites a very similar letter by Korostovets to Izvolskii in 1908: "In concluding the contract of 1896, given the weakness of China at that time, we had in mind nothing other than the annexation, in due course, if not all, then at any rate of the northern part of Manchuria" (*Imperial Rivals*, 178).

108. Simanskii, *Sobytiia*, 1:84.

109. Willem Jacobus Oudendijk, *Ways and By-Ways in Diplomacy* (London: P. Davies, 1939), 47.

110. Bounds, "Secret Treaty," 112.

111. Solovev, *Vospominaniia*, 35.

112. Radolin to Hohenlohe, memorandum, July 14, 1895, *GP*, 9:357.

9: Kaiser Wilhelm and Port Arthur

1. Two studies are Ronald Robinson, John Gallagher, and Alice Denny, *Africa and the Victorians: The Climax of Imperialism in the Dark Continent* (New York: St. Martin's

Press, 1961); and Henk L. Wesseling, *Verdeel en Heers: De Deling van Afrika, 1880–1914* (Amsterdam: Uitgeverij Bert Bakker, 1991).

2. Münster to Hohenlohe, memorandum, Nov. 24, 1898, *GP,* 13:244. Kaiser Wilhelm II concurred. In the margin he penciled: "Especially in Asia!" (246).

3. Thomas J. McCormick, *China Market: America's Quest for Informal Empire, 1893–1901* (Chicago: Quadrangle Books, 1967), 62.

4. Gérard, *Ma mission,* 54–67, 129–35; MacMurray, *Treaties,* 1:26–35; Pierre Renouvin, *La question d'Extrême Orient, 1840–1940* (Paris: Hachette, 1946), 167–68; Huenemann, *Dragon,* 49; Kent, *Foreign Railway Enterprise,* 159–60.

5. Wilgus, *MacDonald,* 77–95.

6. MacMurray, *Treaties,* 1:94–98, 104–6, 402–4; Huenemann, *Dragon,* 54; Renouvin, *Question,* 172; Langer, *Diplomacy,* 1:476–78.

7. R. Hart to J. D. Campbell, letter, Dec. 5, 1897, *I. G. in Peking,* 2:1146.

8. One Russian diplomat stationed in Peking at the time characterized these years as a Sino-Russian "honeymoon." See Solovev, *Vospominaniia,* 72; Langer, *Diplomacy,* 1:412.

9. Cassini to Lobanov, dispatch, Jan. 2, 1896, AVPRI, f. 143, o. 491, d. 114, pt. 1, ll. 1–2; Cassini to Lobanov, dispatch, Nov. 20, 1895, AVPRI, f. 133, o. 468, d. 66, ll. 237–41; also in Russia, *Russko-Iaponskaia voina,* pt. 1-a, 78–81; A. I. Pavlov to M. N. Muravev, dispatch, Oct. 7, 1897, AVPRI, f. 143, o. 491, d. 114, ch. 2, l. 133.

10. Cassini to Lobanov, telegram, July 15, 1896, AVPRI, f. 133, o. 491, d. 143, l. 32. In the margin Prince Lobanov exulted, "Excellent."

11. The latter was particularly frustrating, since the German Army and the British Navy were both furnishing advisors to help train the Qing military. See Cassini to Lobanov, dispatch, Feb. 17, 1896, AVPRI, f. 143, o. 491, d. 114, pt. 1, ll. 5–7; Lamsdorf, note, Jan. 20, 1898, GARF, f. 568, o. 1, d. 59, l. 6; A. I. Pavlov to M. N. Muravev, telegram, Nov. 20, 1897, AVPRI, f. 138, o. 467, d. 167, l. 3; Wilgus, *MacDonald,* 148–51; Simanskii, *Sobytiia,* 1:139–54. Cassini suggested that the Chinese had rejected Col. Wogack's ambitious plan to reorganize the Chinese army because of the officer's pro-Japanese sentiments during the recent war (Cassini to Lamsdorf, letter, Feb. 19, 1897, GARF, f. 568, o. 1, d. 527, l. 26).

12. Oskar P. Trautmann, *Die Sängerbrücke: Gedanken zur russichen Außenpolitik von 1870–1914* (Stuttgart: Union Deutsche Verlagsgesellschaft, 1940), 135.

13. Alfred von Tirpitz, *Erinnerungen* (Berlin: K. F. Koehler, 1927), 61, 63; Ganz, "German Navy," 115; Langer, *Diplomacy,* 2:449.

14. Wilhelm II to Hohenlohe, telegram, Nov. 17, 1894, *GP,* 9:245–46.

15. Hohenlohe to Wilhelm II, memorandum, Mar. 19, 1895, *GP,* 9:253–58; Irmer, "Die Erwerbung von Kiautschou," 9–12; Ralph A. Norem, *Kiaochow Leased Territory* (Berkeley: University of California Press, 1936), 11; O. Franke, *Die Großmächte in Ostasien von 1894 bis 1914: Ein Beitrag zur Vorgeschichte des Krieges* (Brunswick: George Westermann, 1923), 124–25.

16. Elisabeth von Heyking, *Tagebücher aus vier Weltteilen 1886–1904* (Leipzig: Koehler & Amelang, 1926), 224.

17. Tirpitz, *Erinnerungen,* 61–62. The distinguished Prussian geographer, Baron Ferdinand von Richthofen, had already alerted his compatriots to the value of the port after his extensive East Asian travels in the 1860s and 1870s. See Ferdinand, Freiherr von Richthofen, *China, Ergebnisse eigener Reisen und darauf gegründeter Studien,* vol. 2 (Berlin: Dietrich Reimer, 1877–1911). The geographer also published a briefer description of the region in Ferdinand, Freiherr von Richthofen, "Kiautschou, seine Weltstellung und voraussichtliche Bedeutung," *Preußische Jahrbücher* 91, no. 1 (January 1898): 167–71. The German debate about a suitable location for a naval station is described in

Irmer, "Die Erwerbung von Kiautschou," 15–41; Norem, *Kiaochow,* 13–27.

18. Lt. Bukharin, report, Dec. 24, 1895, AVPRI, f. 143, o. 491, d. 1487, ll. 24–25; Lamsdorf to Nicholas, memorandum, Nov. 11, 1897, GARF, f. 568, o. 1, d. 527, l. 12; Simanskii, *Sobytiia,* 1:87n.7; Glinskii, *Prolog,* 42–43.

19. Cassini to Lamsdorf, letter, Dec. 8, 1897, GARF, f. 568, o. 1, d. 527, l. 50; Cassini to Lobanov, telegram, Aug. 28, 1896, *KA,* 87:29.

20. A. Marschall, memorandum, June 19, 1896, *GP,* 14:31.

21. Irmer, "Die Erwerbung von Kiautschou," 28. Curiously, Tirpitz makes no mention of this comment when describing his conversation with Alekseev in his memoirs (*Erinnerungen,* 64).

22. Among the tsar's first words to his mother after the kaiser returned to Germany were "Thank God the German visit is over. . . ." Nicholas to Marie Fedorovna, letter, Aug. 1, 1897, GARF, f. 642, o. 1, d. 2324, l. 9; also in Bing, *Letters of Tsar Nicholas and Empress Marie,* 128.

23. Lamar Cecil, "William II and His Russian 'Colleagues,'" in Carole Fink et al., eds., *German Nationalism and the European Response* (Norman: University of Oklahoma Press, 1985), 124–31.

24. Nicholas to Marie Fedorovna, letter, July 23, 1897, GARF, f. 642, o. 1, d. 2324, l. 3; also in Bing, *Letters of Tsar Nicholas and Empress Marie,* 128. Nicholas was writing to a sympathetic audience. As a former princess of Denmark, the empress dowager despised the Prussians, who had seized the duchies of Schleswig and Holstein from the Danish king during a brief war in 1864. See Kuropatkin, diary, Mar. 14, 1898, RGVIA, f. 165, o. 1, d. 1871, l. 18; Cecil, "William II," 119–23.

25. B. Bülow to Ministry of Foreign Affairs, telegram, Aug. 11, 1897, *GP,* 14:58–59; Witte, *Memoirs,* 269; Romanov, *Russia in Manchuria,* 132; Irmer, "Die Erwerbung von Kiautschou," 44–45.

26. As recorded by Bülow in French, the text read: "His Majesty the Emperor of Germany having asked His Majesty the Emperor of Russia if Russia has any claims (*vues*) to Kiaochow Bay, His Majesty answered that, in fact, Russia desired to assure access to the bay until it had obtained a port more to the north, which it was already considering (Pyongyang). The German Emperor having inquired whether Emperor Nicholas objected if German ships, in case of need and after having obtained the consent of Russian naval authorities, were to anchor in Kiaochow Bay, the Russian Emperor responded negatively." See B. Bülow to Ministry of Foreign Affairs, telegram, Aug. 11, 1897, *GP,* 14:58; Hohenlohe to M. N. Muravev, letter, July 29, 1897, *KA,* 87:33–34.

27. German Foreign Ministry to Russian Ministry of Foreign Affairs, letter, Sep. 4, 1897, AVPRI, f. 138, o. 467, d. 166, l. 3; also in *KA,* 87:34; H. Radolin to B. Bülow, memorandum, Sep. 21, 1897, *GP,* 14:60–61.

28. The Wilhelmstrasse was no doubt well aware of this, since a number of German naval officers, including Adm. Tirpitz, had recently reconnoitered the bay. See A. I. Pavlov to M. N. Muravev, dispatch, Oct. 7, 1897, AVPRI, f. 143, o. 491, d. 114 ch. 2, ll. 133–34; Tirpitz, *Erinnerungen,* 63; Irmer, "Die Erwerbung von Kiautschou," 29, 41.

29. A. I. Pavlov to M. N. Muravev, dispatch, Mar. 6, 1897, AVPRI, f. 143, o. 491, d. 114, ch. 2, l. 28–35. Li Hongzhang said much the same to Heyking when the German minister informed him in September of his navy's plans to use Kiaochow for the winter with St. Petersburg's consent: "This is of no concern to the Russians. Kiaochow is after all Chinese territory" (Heyking to Ministry of Foreign Affairs, telegram, Oct. 1, 1897, *GP,* 14:61–62).

30. Lamsdorf to H. Tschirschky, letter, Oct. 2, 1897, *KA,* 87:34; Tschirschky to Hohenlohe, telegram, Oct. 14, 1897, *GP,* 14:62–64.

31. Solovev, *Vospominaniia*, 73.

32. Ganz, "German Navy," 125

33. "The Murder of the Two German Missionaries," *NCH*, Dec. 17, 1897, 1096–97; Joseph W. Esherick, *The Origins of the Boxer Uprising* (Berkeley: University of California Press, 1987), 123–27; Langer, *Diplomacy*, 2:451n.14. As Esherick and Langer both point out, it is unclear whether the murder was an expression of antiforeign hostility carried out by a xenophobic secret society or simply banditry.

34. Wilhelm II to Ministry of Foreign Affairs, telegram, Nov. 6, 1897, *GP*, 14:67.

35. Wilhelm II to B. Bülow, telegram, Nov. 7, 1897, *GP*, 14:70. The original texts of both this telegram and the response was in English, like all such correspondence between the two monarchs.

36. Nicholas to Wilhelm II, telegram, Oct. 26, 1897, *KA*, 87:37. The English original of the first sentence is from Wilhelm II to Hohenlohe, telegram, Nov. 7, 1897, *GP*, 14:69.

37. Wilhelm to Hohenlohe, telegram, Nov. 7, 1898, 69; W. Rotenhan to H. Tschirschky, telegram, Nov. 8, 1897, *GP*, 14:72.

38. Georg Franzius, *Kiautschou: Deutschlands Erwerbung in Ostasien* (Berlin: Schall & Grund, 1901), 129–42; John Schrecker, *Imperialism and Chinese Nationalism: Germany in Shantung* (Cambridge, Mass.: Harvard University Press, 1971), 34; Cordier, *Histoire des relations*, 3:352–53. For a summary of the bay's history under German rule, see Karl-heinz Graudenz, *Die deutschen Kolonien* (Munich: Südwest Verlag, 1982), 294–311.

39. Witte claims that during the meeting in Moscow with Li Hongzhang, Prince Lobanov nearly signed a version of the pact that would have obligated Russia to protect China against attack by *any* foreign power. Fortunately, the alert finance minister spotted the error in time to have a corrected version initialed by the dignitaries (*Memoirs*, 233–43).

40. E. E. Ukhtomskii, editorial, *SPBVed*, Nov. 30, 1897, 1,

41. E. E. Ukhtomskii, editorial, *SPBVed*, Nov. 20, 1897, 1.

42. Cassini to Lamsdorf, letter, Dec. 8, 1897, GARF, f. 568, o. 1, d. 527, l. 51.

43. Lt. Col. Muravev-Amurskii to Kuropatkin, dispatch, Dec. 25, 1897, AVPRI, f. 143, o. 491, d. 1488, l. 148; also in *KA*, 87:61–62.

44. Foreign observers noticed that the Russian press was quite hostile to the move. See "The Occupation of Kiao-Chau," *Times* (London), Dec. 4, 1897, 7; "Germany and China," *Times* (London), Dec. 14, 1897, 7. Bülow even ordered his ambassador in St. Petersburg, Hugo Prince von Radolin-Radolinski, to ask Muravev that he keep the papers in line (Bülow to Radolin, telegram, Dec. 18, 1897, *GP*, 14:126–27).

45. *GP*, 14:104n.

46. Russia's Korean adventure is described in two recent archivally based studies by Korean scholars. The dissertation of a promising young historian, Choi Dokkiu, is grounded in the records of the navy and the Finance Ministry in St. Petersburg: *Rossiia v Koree: 1893–1905 gg. (Politika Ministerstva finansov i Morskogo ministerstva)* (St. Petersburg: Zero, 1996). Pak Chon Ho's monograph focuses on diplomatic sources in Moscow: *Rossiia i Korea 1895–1898* (Moscow: Moskovskii Gosudarstvennyi universitet, 1993). See also Simanskii, *Sobytiia*, 1:200–61; Glinskii, *Prolog*, 65–70. For an English--language account, see Lensen, *Balance*, 2:514–716. A study focusing on Japan's role can be found in Peter Duus, *The Abacus and the Sword: The Japanese Penetration of Korea, 1895–1910* (Berkeley: University of California Press, 1995), esp. 103–68. For a British perspective, see *BDFA*, pt. I, ser. E, 6:224–401. See also George Alexander Lensen, ed., *Korea and Manchuria between Russia and Japan, 1895–1904: The Observations of Sir Ernest Satow* (Tallahassee, Fl.: Diplomatic Press, 1966), 43–100.

47. R. R. Rosen to M. N. Muravev, letter, Mar. 23, 1897, AVPRI, f. 138, o. 467, d.

153/159, ll. 71–72; M. N. Muravev to P. S. Vannovskii, letter, May 14, 1897, Simanskii, *Sobytiia*, 1:221.

48. Romanov, *Russia in Manchuria*, 149–50; Ignatev, *Vitte*, 64; Langer, *Diplomacy*, 1:408.

49. See, for example, F. V. Dubasov to Aleksei Aleksandrovich, "Ocherk politicheskago polozheniia na krainem Vostoke," GARF, f. 543, o. 1, d. 176, ll. 28–46

50. Rosen, *Forty Years*, 1:131. A posting to the Danish court was a good career move during the reign of Nicholas II. Aleksandr Izvolskii was also the ambassador in Copenhagen when the tsar tapped him to become his new foreign minister in 1906.

51. Hardinge, *Old Diplomacy*, 69. For other British views, see Neilson, *Britain*, 65.

52. A. Kiderlein-Wächter to F. Holstein, letter, Jan. 15, 1897, in Friedrich von Holstein, *The Holstein Papers: The Memoirs, Diaries, and Correspondence of Friedrich von Holstein*, ed. Norman Rich and M. H. Fisher, 4 vols. (New York: Cambridge University Press, 1955), 4:3. Many Russian colleagues fully agreed with these negative opinions. Witte, referring to the hero of Gogol's play *The Inspector General*, called him "the son of Ivan Aleksandrovich Khlestakov" (Suvorin, *Dnevnik*, 209). See also Witte, *Memoirs*, 262–63; Izvolskii, *Mémoires*, 160; Rosen, *Forty Years*, 1:131; Kalmykow, *Memoirs*, 98–99; Eugene Schelking, *Recollections of a Russian Diplomat: The Suicide of Monarchies (William II and Nicholas II)* (New York: Macmillan, 1918), 162–64.

53. M. N. Muravev to Nicholas, memorandum, Oct. 26, 1897, *KA*, 87:37–38; M. N. Muravev to P. P. Tyrtov, letter, Oct. 26, 1897, AVPRI, f. 138, o. 467, d. 166, l. 18; also in *KA*, 87:38; M. N. Muravev to Pahlen, telegram, Oct. 27, 1897, AVPRI, f. 133, o. 470, d. 54, l. 290; M. N. Muravev to Pahlen, telegram, Oct. 28, 1897, AVPRI, f. 133, o. 470, d. 54, l. 291. These last two telegrams are also in *KA*, 87:38–40 (translated from French), and excerpts are published in *GP*, 14:73–74. Malozemoff explains that "the right of first anchorage" was often invoked by European powers when claiming areas on unsettled or "uncivilized" coasts. He adds, however, that it was probably not applicable to established nations, such as China (*Russian Far Eastern Policy*, 281n.40).

54. Wilhelm II, marginal note on W. Rotenhan to Wilhelm II, telegram, Nov. 10, 1897, *GP*, 14:74.

55. N. D. Osten-Sacken to N. M. Muravev, telegram, Oct. 31, 1897, GARF, f. 568, o. 1, d. 127, l. 6; also in *KA*, 87:40.

56. Lamsdorf, notes to minister's report, Nov. 4, 1897, GARF, f. 568, o. 1, d. 58, l. 64.

57. N. M. Muravev to Nicholas, memorandum, Nov. 11, 1897, GARF, f. 568, o. 1, d. 127, ll. 11–18; also in *KA*, 52:103–8.

58. Ibid., l. 11.

59. Nicholas to N. M. Muravev, note, Nov. 11, 1897, GARF, f. 568, o. 1, d. 127, l. 11; also in *KA*, 52:102. Emphasis in original.

60. Russia, *Russko-Iaponskaia voina*, pt. 1-a, 216.

61. Chancellery of the Finance Ministry, "Istoricheskaia Spravka o vazhneishchikh dlia Rossii sobytiiakh na Dalnem Vostoke v trekhletie 1898–1900," RGIA, f. 1622, o. 1, d. 935, ll. 4–9; Glinskii, *Prolog*, 44–46; Russia, *Russko-Iaponskaia voina*, pt. 1-a, 215–17; Simanskii, *Sobytiia*, 1:99; Ignatev, *Vitte*, 66–68. Gurko's recollections of the proceedings seem somewhat faulty (*Features and Figures*, 255).

62. Witte, *Memoirs*, 274.

63. Simanskii, *Sobytiia*, 1:100–1; Solovev, *Vospominaniia*, 75.

64. It is unclear which of these arguments carried the day. Witte told the new war minister, Aleksei Kuropatkin, that Muravev "deceived" (*obmanul*) the tsar into believing the latter, i.e., that China invited Russia to take possession of Port Arthur (Kuroptakin, diary, Dec. 20, 1897, RGVIA, f. 165, o. 1, d. 1871, l. 6). Muravev alluded to this justification himself

two days later in a conversation with Kuropatkin (Kuropatkin, diary, Dec. 22, 1897, RGVIA, f. 165, o. 1, d. 1871, l. 7). However, most other sources, including Witte's own memoirs, suggest that Muravev invoked the English bogey to convince Nicholas to change his mind. Lamsdorf, notes to minister's report, Nov. 27, 1897, GARF, f. 568, o. 1, d. 58, l. 71; Witte, *Memoirs*, 275, Izvolskii, *Mémoires*, 161; Simanskii, *Sobytiia*, 1:100–3; Russia, *Russko-Iaponskaia voina*, pt. 1-a, 217. It is also likely that Muravev's concerns about German relations also played a role. Lamsdorf, notes to minister's report, Jan. 13, 1898, GARF, f. 568, o. 1, d. 59, l. 3; memorandum, addressed to Nicholas, Nov. 25, 1897, AVPRI, f. 138, o. 467, d. 166, l. 20.

65. F. Bertie to Admiralty, letter, Dec. 14, 1897, *BDFA*, pt. I, ser. E, 6:277; E. MacGregor to Foreign Office, Dec. 17, 1897, *BDFA*, pt. I, ser. E, 6:277–78; A. Buller to Admiralty, dispatch, Dec. 15, 1897, *BDFA*, pt. I, ser. E, 6:287; Young, *British Policy*, 49–50; Arthur J. Marder, *The Anatomy of British Sea Power: A History of British Naval Policy in the Pre-Dreadnought Era, 1880–1905* (New York: Alfred A. Knopf, 1940), 304. In December 1897, two British China Station cruisers, the *Immortalité* and the *Iphigenia*, would be ordered to Port Arthur, but their captains were interested in discovering what the Russians were up to there, not in claiming it for the Queen. By the time the cruisers arrived at the harbor, they spotted four Russian ships there. See A. Buller to Admiralty, dispatch, Jan. 3, 1898, *BDFA*, pt. I, ser. E, 6:304; Morse, *International Relations*, 3:116.

66. A. I. Pavlov to N. M. Muravev, dispatch, Nov. 2, 1897, AVPRI, f. 143, o. 491, d. 114, ch. 2, l. 146; also in *KA*, 87:42; A. I. Pavlov to N. M. Muravev, dispatch, Nov. 12, 1897, AVPRI, f. 134, o. 491, d. 114, ch. 2, ll. 151–58; also in *KA*, 87:51–55; Pokotilov to Witte, telegram, Nov. 16, 1897, AVPRI, f. 143, o. 491, d. 1487, l. 73; A. I. Pavlov to M. N. Muravev, telegram, Dec. 4, 1897, AVPRI, f. 143, o. 471, d. 114, l. 160; Simanskii, *Sobytiia*, 1:106–7.

67. H. Tschirschky to Ministry of Foreign Affairs, telegram, Dec. 1, 1897, *GP*, 14:106; B. Bülow to H. Radolin, telegram, Dec. 2, 1897, *GP*, 14:107; H. Radolin to B. Bülow, telegram (Russian decryption), Dec. 4, 1897, AVPRI, f. 133, o. 470, d. 53, l. 25.

68. N. M. Muravev to Osten-Sacken, telegram, Dec. 2, 1897, *GP*, 14:121.

69. P. P. Tyrtov to F. V. Dubasov, telegram, Dec. 1, 1897, GARF, f. 568, o. 1, d. 127, ll. 33–34.

70. Russia, *Russko-Iaponskaia voina*, pt. 1-a, 220–22.

71. Wilhelm II to Nicholas, telegram, Dec. 19, 1897, *GP*, 14:129–30.

72. F. V. Dubasov to P. P. Tyrtov, telegram, Dec. 6, 1897, GARF, f. 568, o.1, d. 127, l. 37.

73. A. I. Pavlov to M. N. Muravev, telegram, Nov. 23, 1897, AVPRI, f. 138, o. 467, l. 5; A. I. Pavlov to M. N. Muravev, dispatch, Dec. 4, 1897, AVPRI, f. 43, o. 491, d. 114, ch. 2, ll. 164–66; Lung Chang, *La Chine à l'aube du XXe Siècle: Les relations diplomatiques de la Chine avec les puissances depuis la guerre sino-japonaise jusqu'à la guerre russo-japonaise* (Paris: Nouvelles Editions Latines, 1962), 178.

74. A. I. Pavlov to M. N. Muravev, dispatch, Dec. 19, 1897, AVPRI, f. 143, o. 491, d. 114, ch. 2, ll. 176–77; A. I. Pavlov to M. N. Muravev, dispatch, Feb. 7, 1898, AVPRI, f. 143, o. 491, d. 115, ll. 18–19.

75. Simanskii, *Sobytiia*, 1:115.

76. Russian Ministry of Foreign Affairs to Zongli Yamen, note, Feb. 20, 1898, AVPRI, f. 143, o. 491, d. 115, ll. 31–34; M. N. Muravev to A. I. Pavlov, telegram, February 1898, GARF, f. 568, o. 1, d. 128, l. 13; AVPRI, f. 138, o. 467, d. 169. Much of the latter is also in "Perepiska o podkupke kitaiskikh sanovnikov Li-Khun-Chzhana i Chzhan-in-Khuana," *KA*, 2:287–93.

77. A. I. Pavlov to M. N. Muravev, dispatch, Mar. 22, 1898, AVPRI, f. 143, o. 491, d. 115, ll. 43–44.

78. Ibid., ll. 43–44; Solovev, *Vospominaniia*, 77.

79. Russia, Ministère des Affaires Etrangères, *Receuil de traités et documents diploma-*

tiques concernant l'Extrême Orient 1895–1905 (St. Petersburg: A. M. Mendeleevich, 1906), 331–37; Skachkov, *Russko-kitaiskie otnosheniia,* 78–80; MacMurray, *Treaties,* 119–21.

80. Westel W. Willoughby, *Foreign Rights and Interests in China* (Baltimore: Johns Hopkins University Press, 1920), 228–44.

81. F. M. Knobel to W. H. de Beaufort, memorandum, Jan. 7, 1898, *RGP,* 138:578; W. H. de Beaufort to F. M. Knobel, letter, Feb. 21, 1898, *RGP,* 138:609; Michael H. Hunt, *Frontier Defense and the Open Door: Manchuria in Chinese-American Relations, 1895–1911* (New Haven, Conn.: Yale University Press, 1973), 29–30.

82. See, for example, the map reproduced in Langer, *Diplomacy,* 2:684; Charles William De la Poer, Lord Beresford, *The Break-Up of China: With an Account of Its Present Commerce, Currency, Waterways, Politics, and Future Prospects,* 2 vols. (New York: Harper & Brothers, 1899).

83. The idea of a rapprochement was first mooted by Lord Salisbury, who instructed his ambassador in St. Petersburg, Sir Nicholas O'Conor, in January 1898 to approach the Russian government with the suggestion that "It is better . . . that we should come to an understanding. We should go far to further Russian commercial objects in the North, if we could regard her as willing to work for us." His proposal was for the two traditional adversaries to refrain from competing in each other's spheres, namely, the Yangzi River region for Britain and Zhili and Manchuria for Russia (O'Conor to N. M. Muravev, letter, Aug. 31, 1898 [N.S.], AVPRI, f. 143, o. 467, d. 163/165, l. 6). The reaction at the Choristers' Bridge was not overwhelmingly enthusiastic. See Lamsdorf, note, Jan. 20, 1898, l. 5; Lamsdorf, note, Jan. 19, 1899, GARF, f. 568, o. 1, d. 60, l. 4; Lamsdorf to Nicholas, memorandum, Jan. 29, 1898, AVPRI, f. 318, o. 467, d. 163/165, ll. 3–5; Lamsdorf to E. E. Staal, letter, Feb. 12, 1898, GARF, f. 568, o. 1, d. 128, ll. 4–5. A more modest agreement was finally signed in St. Petersburg by Count Muravev and the new British ambassador, Sir Charles Scott (Salisbury to Bax-Ironside, telegram, *BDOW,* 1:40–41). The Russian side is covered in *KA,* 25:111–34, and relevant British diplomatic correspondence is published in *BDOW,* 1:5–18, 38–41. See also A. W. Palmer, "Lord Salisbury's Approach to Russia, 1898," *Oxford Slavonic Papers* 6 (1955): 102–14; Neilson, *Britain,* 184–204; Simanskii, *Sobytiia,* 1:175–83; Langer, *Diplomacy,* 2:680–83. On the Chinese reaction, see M. N. Giers to N. M. Muravev, dispatch, May 21, 1899, f. 143, o. 471, d. 116, ll. 88–89; Glinskii, *Prolog,* 87.

84. Kang Yuwei, "The Reform of China and the Revolution of 1898," *Contemporary Review* 76 (August 1899): 184.

85. Suvorin, *Dnevnik,* 218.

86. "The Present Situation," *NCH,* Dec. 3, 1897, 1.

87. Oldenburg, *Last Tsar,* 1:127–29. Oldenburg does not provide a citation.

10: Righteous and Harmonious Fists

1. R. Hart to J. D. Campbell, letter, Jan. 23, 1898, *I. G. in Peking,* 2:1149; Robert Hart, "Peking Legations: A National Uprising and an International Episode," in *"These from the Land of Sinim": Essays on the Chinese Question* (London: Chapman Hall, 1901), 8.

2. Korsakov, *V starom Pekine,* 343.

3. Cordier, *Histoire des relations,* 3:408–9.

4. The "Hundred Days" and their immediate aftermath are described in A. I. Pavlov to N. M. Muravev, dispatches, Aug. 19, 1898–Sep. 10, 1898, AVPRI, f. 143, o. 471, d. 115, ll. 105–30; S. K. Kwong, *A Mosaic of the Hundred Days: Personalities, Politics, and Ideas of 1898* (Cambridge, Mass.: Harvard University Press, 1984); Lo Jung-Pang, ed., *K'ang Yu-wei: A Biography and a Symposium* (Tucson: University of Arizona Press,

1967), 83–114; Morse, *International Relations*, 3:128–55; Sergei Leonidovich Tikhvinskii, *Dvizhenie za reformy v Kitae v kontse xix veka* (Moscow: Nauka, 1980).

5. Wilgus, *MacDonald*, 233–40; Korsakov, *V starom Pekine*, 344; Tikhvinskii, *Dvizhenie*, 248–54.

6. Pavlov to Muravev, dispatch, Sep. 10, 1898, l. 118.

7. Ibid., l. 120. On Japan's involvement in the "Hundred Days," see Marius B. Jansen, *Japan and China: From War to Peace, 1894–1972* (Chicago: Rand McNally, 1975), 138–40; Richard C. Howard, "Japan's Role in the Reform Program of Kang Yu-wei," in Lo, *K'ang*, 280–312.

8. Putiata, *Kitai*, 265.

9. A. I. Pavlov to N. M. Muravev, dispatch, Aug. 28, 1898, AVPRI, f. 143, o. 471, d. 115, ll. 116–17; Finance Ministry, "Istoricheskaia spravka," 82–83n.; Glinskii, *Prolog*, 97.

10. Pavlov to Muravev, dispatch, Sep. 10, 1898, ll. 124–25.

11. M. N. Giers to N. M. Muravev, dispatch, Jan. 21, 1899, AVPRI, f. 143, o. 471, d. 116. ll. 1–3.

12. M. N. Giers to N. M. Muravev, dispatch, Aug. 2, 1899, AVPRI, f. 143, o. 471, d. 116, ll. 120–26; Ministry of Foreign Affairs, "Otchet MID 1899," AVPRI, f. 137, o. 475, d. 128, p. 117; Finance Ministry, "Istoricheskaia Spravka," 70–78; Glinskii, *Prolog*, 91–95.

13. M. N. Giers to N. M. Muravev, dispatch, Dec. 28, 1899, AVPRI, f. 143, o. 471, d. 116, ll. 232–34.

14. M. N. Giers to Lamsdorf, letter, Dec. 5, 1898, GARF, f. 568, o. 1, d. 433, l. 61; M. N. Giers to N. M. Muravev, dispatch, AVPRI, f. 143, o. 471, d. 116, ll. 64–67; Korsakov, *V starom Pekine*, 330–34; R. Hart to J. D. Campbell, letter, Jan. 14, 1900, *I. G. in Peking*, 2:1216.

15. Morse, *International Relations*, 3:161–69.

16. Paul A. Cohen, *History in Three Keys: The Boxers as Event, Experience, and Myth* (New York: Columbia University Press, 1997), 69–95, 117–18; Esherick, *Origins*, 173–81. Esherick's book is the most thorough social history of the Boxer rising's beginnings. The diplomatic and political background are covered in Victor Purcell, *The Boxer Uprising: A Background Study* (Cambridge: Cambridge University Press, 1963); and Chester C. Tan, *The Boxer Catastrophe* (New York: Octagon Books, 1967). Unlike most Western-based scholars, Tan devotes a fair bit of attention to Russia's role. An interesting cultural approach is taken by Cohen, *History in Three Keys*.

Among Russian works on the Boxers, the report written by Witte's agent in China, Dmitrii Pokotilov, remains an intelligent survey: Pokotilov to Witte, memorandum, Dec. 23, 1900, RGIA, f. 560, o. 28, d. 79, ll. 161–211. Although somewhat dated, another valuable study, by a Russian Orientalist who used primarily Chinese sources, is A. Rudakov, *Obshchestvo I-khe-tuan i ego znachenie v poslednikh sobytiakh na Dalnem Vostoke* (Vladivostok: T-va Sushchinskii, 1901). See also Nina Mikhailovna Kaliuzhnaia, "O kharaktere tainogo soiuza 'Ikhetuan,'" in V. P. Iliushechkin, ed., *Tainye obshchestva v starom Pekine* (Moscow: Nauka, 1970), 85–107.

17. Esherick, *Origins*, 170–73.

18. Esherick, *Origins*, 38–63; Susan Naquin, *Millenarian Rebellion in China: The Eight Trigrams Uprising of 1813* (New Haven, Conn.: Yale University Press, 1976); Spence, *Search for Modern China*, 112–13, 184–88. Although somewhat one-dimensional, a reasonable summary of popular risings during the late Qing and Republican periods is Jean Chesnaux, *Le mouvement paysan chinois: 1840–1949* (Paris: Editions du Seuil, 1976). See also Albert Feuerwerker, *Rebellion in Nineteenth-Century China* (Ann Arbor: University of Michigan Press, 1975).

19. Spence, *Search for Modern China*, 30–31; Purcell, *Boxer Uprising*, 162–64. Thus, although the *Yihequan* exercises involve fists, they bear little relation to the pugilism popular in the West. See Cohen, *History in Three Keys*, 16; Esherick, *Origins*, xiii.

20. Edward Harper Parker, *China and Religion* (London: John Murray, 1905), 2–16.

21. Purcell, *Boxer Uprising*, 139.

22. Rudakov, *Obshchestvo*, 29.

23. I. Ia. Korostovets to Ministry of Foreign Affairs, attachment to dispatch, June 12, 1900, *KA*, 14:13. Although most of the Boxers were peasants, their membership included elements of other groups, including unemployed bargemen, former soldiers and deserters, small tradesmen, and what one scholar calls the "lumpen intelligentsia," i.e., dissident intellectuals, failed civil-service examination candidates, monks, geomancers, etc. Soviet and post-1949 Chinese historiography notwithstanding, it would be misleading to see the Boxer rising purely as class conflict. Jonathan Spence's observation about unrest during the seventeenth century was still true two centuries later: "the idea of class warfare presumes a level of economic cohesion and self-consciousness concerning one's role in society that seems to have been lacking in China at the time" (*Search for Modern China*, 45). See also Feuerwerker, *Rebellion*, 2–3; Esherick, *Origins*, 235–40; Kaliuzhnaia, "O kharaktere," 94–96.

24. Morse, *International Relations*, 3:194.

25. Ralph Edward Glatfelter, "Russia in China: The Russian Reaction to the Boxer Rebellion" (Ph.D. diss., Indiana University, 1975), 66; Parker, *China*, 241–42, 244.

26. M. N. Giers to N. M. Muravev, dispatches, 1899, AVPRI, f. 143, o. 471, d. 116; Ministry of Foreign Affairs, Annual Report, 1899, AVPRI, f. 137, o. 475, d. 128, pp. 109–21.

27. M. N. Giers to N. M. Muravev, dispatch, Jan. 21, 1900, AVPRI, f. 143, o. 471, d. 117, ll. 21–23.

28. M. N. Giers to N. M. Muravev, dispatch, Feb. 29, 1900, AVPRI, f. 143, o. 471, d. 117, l. 65.

29. Simanskii, *Sobytiia*, 2:14–15.

30. Cohen, *History in Three Keys*, 36; Esherick, *Origins*, 285.

31. However, claims by Rudakov and other early-twentieth-century sinologists of the Qing dynasty's complicity in starting the rebellion have since been disproved. See Tan, *Boxer Catastrophe*, 36–43.

32. Ibid., 62; Esherick, *Origins*, 285–90.

33. On the situation in Peking during the Boxer rising, there are three published diaries by Russian government officials resident there at the time: Dmitrii Dmitrevich Pokotilov, *Dnevnik osady evropeitsev v Pekine* (Yalta: N. V. Vakhtin, 1900); and Pokotilov, *Dnevnik s 2–go po 31–oe avgusta 1900 goda* (St. Petersburg: V. F. Kirshbaum, 1900); Dmitrii Matveevich Pozdneev, *56 dnei pekinskago sidenia v sviazi s blizhaishimi k nemu sobytiiami pekinskoi zhizni* (St. Petersburg: V. F. Kirshbaum, 1901); Pavel Stepanovich Popov, "Dva mesiatsa osady v Pekine," *Vestnik Evropy* 36, no. 2 (February 1901): 517–36; no. 3 (March 1901): 5–37. See also Korsakov, *Pekinskiia sobytiia*. Two interesting Chinese perspectives are J. J. L. Duyvendak, ed., *The Diary of His Excellency Ching-shan* (Leiden: E. J. Brill, 1924); and "Journal d'un bourgeois de Pekin," in Baron d'Anthouard, *La Chine contre l'étranger: Les Boxeurs* (Paris: Librairie Plon, 1902), 294–343. First-hand Western accounts include R. Hart, "Peking Legations," 1–59; Lancelot Giles, *The Siege of the Peking Legations: A Diary*, ed. L. R. Marchant (Nedlands: University of Western Australia Press, 1970); and d'Anthouard, *La Chine*.

34. M. N. Giers to N. M. Muravev, dispatch, May 13, 1900, AVPRI, f. 143, o. 471, d. 117, l. 116.

35. M. N. Giers to N. M. Muravev, dispatch, May 7, 1900, AVPRI, f. 143, o. 491,

d. 117, ll. 106–9; Giers to Muravev, May 13, 1900, ll. 116–121; N. M. Giers to Guangxu Emperor, letter, May 23, 1900, AVPRI, f. 143, o. 491, d. 117, l. 143; Pokotilov, *Dnevnik,* 4; Simanskii, *Sobytiia,* 2:14–15.

36. Glatfelter, "Russia in China," 70.

37. D. M. Pozdneev to Bulgakov, letter, May 22, 1900, f. 590, o. 1, d. 112, l. 483. Although probably apocryphal, the conversation described by the journalist Dmitrii Ianchevetskii with a diplomat at Port Arthur in mid-May nicely conveys this attitude as well: Dmitrii Ianchevetskii, *U sten nedvizhnago Kitaia* (St. Petersburg: Tovarishchestvo Khudozhestvennoi pechati, 1903), 5. See also Ivan Iakovlevich Korostovets, *Rossiia na Dalnem Vostoke* (Peking: Vostochnoe Prosveshchenie, 1922), 9–11.

38. M. N. Giers to N. M. Muravev, telegram, May 27, 1900, GARF, f. 568, o. 1, d. 126, l. 14; also in *KA,* 14:14; Korostovets, *Rossiia,* 16; Simanskii, *Sobytiia,* 2:17.

39. Pokotilov to Witte, telegram, May 29, 1900, RGIA, f. 560, o. 38, d. 180, l. 88.

40. Glatfelter, "Russia in China," 73.

41. V. P. Mesherskii, "Dnevnik," *Grazhdanin,* June 13, 1900, 21.

42. "Rossiia i Kitai," *NV,* June 8, 1900, 2.

43. Vlas Mikhailovich Dorosevich, "Kitai," *Rossiia,* June 13, 1900, 2. Also published in Aleksandr Valentinovich Amfiteatrov and Vlas Mikhailovich Dorosevich, *Kitaiskii vopros* (Moscow: I. D. Sytin, 1901), 1–14. On Dorosevich's views more generally, see Louise McReynolds, "V. M. Dorosevich: The Newspaper Journalist and the Development of Public Opinion in Civil Soviety," in Edith W. Clowes et al., eds., *Between Tsar and People: Educated Society and the Quest for Public Identity in Late Imperial Russia* (Princeton, N.J.: Princeton University Press, 1991), 233–47.

44. See, for example, Vlas Mikhailovich Dorosevich, "Gzha Tsivilizatsii," in Amfiteatrov and Dorosovich, *Kitaiskii,* 15–16. Ukhtomskii made the same comparison (Schiemann, *Deutschland,* 1:373).

45. Amfiteatrov, "Kitaiskaia Groza," in Amfiteatrov and Dorosovich, *Kitaiskii,* 28–29.

46. N. B., "K sobytiam na Dalnem Vostoke," *SPBVed,* June 14, 1900, 2.

47. Nicholas, annotation on Giers to Muravev, June 15, 1900, l. 116; Nicholas to Marie Fedorovna, letter, Aug. 11, 1900, GARF, f. 642, o. 1, d. 2326, ll. 61–62l; Nicholas, annotation on Lamsdorf to Urusov, letter, Aug. 24, 1900, *KA,* 14:31.

48. Witte to Nicholas, memorandum, Aug. 11, 1900, RGIA, f. 560, o. 28, d. 218, ll. 66–73. Also summarized in A. A. Polovtsov, "Iz dnevnika A. A. Polovtsova," *KA,* 46:131–32; Witte, *Memoirs,* 278–79; Ignatev, *Vitte,* 130–32. N. M. Muravev to E. I. Alekeev, telegram, June 5, 1900, GARF, f. 568, o. 1, d. 129, l. 33. Muravev's thinking about the Boxers is laid out in N. M. Muravev to Nicholas, memorandum, June 4, 1900, *KA,* 14:14–15.

49. Kuropatkin, diary, June 8, 1900, RGVIA, f. 165, o. 1, d. 1889, l. 84.

50. Nicholas, annotation on M. N. Giers to Lamsdorf, dispatch, Sep. 29, 1900, AVPRI, f. 143, o. 471, d. 117, l. 127; Bogdanovich, *Tri poslednykh,* 255.

51. Bogdanovich, *Tri poslednykh,* 255; C. S. Scott to Salisbury, dispatch, June 28, 1900, *BDFA,* pt. I, ser. E, 24:28–29; Cordier, *Histoire des relations,* 3:507.

52. Bompard, *Mon ambassade,* 2–3; Izvolskii, *Mémoires,* 178; Hardinge, *Old Diplomacy,* 70; A. A. Polovtsev, "Dnevnik A. A. Polovtseva," *KA,* 3:137; Barbara Vogel, *Deutsche Rußlandpolitik: Das Scheitern der deutschen Weltpolitik unter Bülow 1900–1906* (Düsseldorf: Bertelsmann Universitätsverlag, 1973), 250n.22; Schelking, *Recollections,* 165–66.

53. Kalmykow, *Memoirs,* 139.

54. Lamsdorf, *Dnevnik 1894–1896,* 155.

55. Bompard, *Mon ambassade,* 4.

56. Izvolskii, *Mémoires,* 164; Kalmykow, *Memoirs,* 140. Witte went so far as to

claim credit for Lamsdorf's appointment to the post (*Memoirs*, 287).

57. Russia, *Russko-Iaponskaia voina*, pt. 1-a, 383–85; Korostovets, *Rossiia*, 12.

58. Korostovets, *Rossiia*, 20–21.

59. Kuropatkin to Nicholas, memorandum, Aug. 3, 1900, RGIA, f. 560, o. 28, d. 218, ll. 13–19.

60. Bogdanovich, *Tri poslednykh*, 254. The Order of St. George, which had four classes, was Imperial Russia's highest military decoration. See V. A. Durov, *The Orders of Russia* (Moscow: Voskresenie, 1993), 36–51.

61. C. Hardinge to Salisbury, dispatch, Oct. 26, 1900, *BDOW*, 2:17.

62. Kuropatkin, diary, Aug. 9, 1900, RGVIA, f. 165, o. 1, d. 1889, l. 94; Nicholas to Marie Fedorovna, letter, Dec. 22, 1900, GARF, f. 642, o. 1, d. 2326, ll. 101–2.

63. Nicholas to Marie Fedorovna, letter, Aug. 27, 1900, GARF, f. 642, o. 1, d. 2326, ll. 67–68. Nicholas made a very similar comment in the margin of a note from his foreign minister: "Russia's mission in the East thoroughly differs from the policies of the European governments" (Nicholas, annotation on M. N. Muravev to Nicholas, memorandum, June 4, 1900, *KA*, 14:15).

64. N. M. Muravev to Nicholas, memorandum, May 25, 1900, *KA*, 14:13–14; Romanov, *Russia in Manchuria*, 178.

65. Russia, *Russko-Iaponskaia voina*, pt. 1-a, 403–6. Russian participation in the campaign in Zhili province is also described in A. S. Grishinkii and V. P. Nikolskii, eds., *Istoriia russkoi armii i flota*, vols. 13–15 (Moscow: Obrazovanie, 1911), 13:50–63.

66. Russia, *Russko-Iaponskaia voina*, pt. 1-a, 411–43, 462–71.

67. "Otpravka iz Port-Artura v Taku ekspeditsionnago otriada," *Kronstadskii Vestnik*, June 23, 1900, 2.

68. Kuropatkin, diary, June 23, 1900, RGVIA, f. 165, o. 1, d. 1889, l. 87; Glinskii, *Prolog*, 107–8; Ford, "Russian Far Eastern Diplomacy," 262.

69. Ministry of Foreign Affairs, Annual Report, 1900, AVPRI, f. 137, o. 475, d. 130, l. 81; Lamsdorf to Nicholas, memorandum, June 30, 1900, *KA*, 14:18–19; Simanskii, *Sobytiia*, 2:78–79; Ignatev, *Vitte*, 131–33; Glatfelter, "Russia in China," 84–92.

70. Li Hongzhang to Witte, telegram, June 13, 1900, RGIA, f. 560, o. 28, d. 190, l. 1. Li also approached other governments, including the United States. See William J. Duiker, *Cultures in Collision: The Boxer Rebellion* (San Rafael, Calif.: Presidio Press, 1978), 145–48. Tan's suggestion that the Russian government rejected Li's proposal is misleading (*Boxer Catastrophe*, 122).

71. Witte to Li Hongzhang, telegram, July 20, 1900, RGIA, f. 560, o. 28, d. 190, l. 35; Witte to Nicholas, memorandum, July 13, 1900, RGIA, f. 560, o. 28, d. 190, l. 24; P. P. Tyrtov to Witte, letter, July 30, 1900, RGIA, f. 560, o. 28, d. 190, l. 57; Li Hongzhang to Witte, telegram, June 1900, RGIA, f. 560, o. 28, d. 290, l. 9.

72. Romanov, *Russia in Manchuria*, 179–89; Korostovets, *Rossiia*, 65; Ignatev, *Vitte*, 133; Morse, *International Relations*, 3:273; Tan, *Boxer Catastrophe*, 120–25; Langer, *Diplomacy*, 2:698.

73. Pokotilov to Witte, telegram, Jan. 4, 1900, *KA*, 14:27; Ianchevetskii, *U sten*, 423–35; Korostovets, *Rossiia*, 70; Morse, *International Relations*, 3:280.

74. Tan, *Boxer Catastrophe*, 129–56, 215–36; Esherick, *Origins*, 311; MacMurray, *Treaties*, 1:278–308; Cordier, *Histoire des relations*, 3:537–545. The talks are described in John S. Kelly, *A Forgotten Conference: The Negotiations at Peking, 1900–1901* (Geneva: Librairie Droz, 1963).

75. Simanskii, *Sobytiia*, 2:34–42; Malozemoff, *Russian Far Eastern Policy*, 133–35.

76. Lamsdorf to diplomatic representatives in Paris, Berlin, London, Vienna,

Rome, Washington, and Tokyo, telegram, Aug. 12, 1900, *KA*, 14:28–29.

77. Popov, "Dalnevostochnaia," 50.

78. R. Hart to J. D. Campbell, letter, Sep. 29, 1900, *I.G in Peking*, 2:1239.

79. Langer, *Diplomacy*, 2:695.

80. Wilhelm II marginal comment on Radolin to Ministry of Foreign Affairs, telegram, Aug. 30, 1900, *GP*, 16:109.

81. De Bezaure to Delcassé, dispatch, June 10, 1900, *DDF*, 16:269.

82. For a recent biography, see Vladimir Vasilevich Pustogarov, *". . . S palmovoi vetviu mira . . ." F. F. Martens: Iurist, diplomat, publitsist* (Moscow: Mezhdunarodnye otnosheniia, 1993).

83. F. F. Martens to Lamsdorf, memorandum, August 1900, *KA*, 20:177–85.

11: Manchurian Quicksand

1. Hosie's estimate of 17,000,000 seems somewhat high when compared to other accounts. See Alexander Hosie, *Manchuria: Its People, Resources, and Recent History* (London: Methuen, 1904), 155.

2. Owen Lattimore, *Manchuria: Cradle of Conflict* (New York: Macmillan, 1935), 13–24; Robert H. G. Lee, *The Manchurian Frontier in Ch'ing History* (Cambridge, Mass.: Harvard University Press, 1970), 3–20, 87–93; Hosie, *Manchuria*, 135–217. A thorough description of Manchuria's geography is given in Gustav Fochler-Hauke, *Die Mandschurei: Eine geographisch-politische Landeskunde* (Heidelberg: Kurt Vowinckel, 1941), 7–209. Written by one of its China hands, the work commissioned by the Russian Finance Ministry is also quite useful: Dmitrii Matveevich Pozdneev, *Opisanie Manchzhurii*, 2 vols. (St. Petersburg: Ministerstvo Finansov, 1897). A much briefer contemporary guide is A. Dombrovskii and V. Voroshilov, *Manchzhuriia* (St. Petersburg: N. V. Vasilev, 1897).

3. Hunt, *Frontier Defense*, 5.

4. Ibid., 15.

5. Lee, *Manchurian Frontier*, 22. For a fascinating study of Manchu ethnic consciousness in the last century of the Qing dynasty, see Pamela Kyle Crossley, *Orphan Warriors: Three Generations and the End of the Qing World* (Princeton, N.J.: Princeton University Press, 1990).

6. Lattimore, *Manchuria*, 108.

7. Lee, *Manchurian Frontier*, 6–7, 101–5; Peter Mikhailovich Golovachev, *Rossiia na Dalnem Vostoke* (St. Petersburg: E. D. Kuskovoi, 1904), 121–25.

8. Nilus, *Istoricheskii obzor*, 1:122; "Istoricheskaia spravka," 92.

9. Wolff, *Harbin Station*, 25–29, 35–41; Nilus, *Istoricheskii obzor*, 1:126–33.

10. Nilus, *Istoricheskii obzor*, 1:131–34, 171–73; Glinskii, *Prolog*, 61–62.

11. Nilus, *Istoricheskii obzor*, 1:156–70. The finance minister characteristically claimed credit for the port's new name (Witte, *Memoirs*, 278n.). There was much sparring between him and War Minister Kuropatkin over who would have jurisdiction over the port. In 1899 the entire leasehold was placed under the authority of a navy officer, although the Finance Ministry would retain much responsibility over Dalnii, with Port Arthur becoming a Russian military base. See minutes, council of Mar. 1, 1899, and Mar. 7, 1899, RGIA, f. 560, o. 38, d. 179, ll. 23–39; Minutes, council of Apr. 5, 1899, RGIA, f. 1622, o. 1, d. 167, l. 1.

12. Nilus, *Istoricheskii obzor*, 1:200, 503–11; Glinskii, *Prolog*, 111; Quested, *"Matey" Imperialists*, 99–100; McDonald, *United Government*, 12. The Guards' most famous veteran was Aleksandr Guchkov, the future leader of the moderately conservative Octobrist

Party in the Duma, Russia's prerevolutionary legislature (Nilus, *Istoricheskii obzor,* 1:507).

13. Malozemoff, *Russian Far Eastern Policy,* 188.

14. Beveridge, *Russian Advance,* 25–33. The Midwestern legislator saw nothing wrong with this advance. As he wrote elsewhere in his book: "We find [Manchuria] rapidly undergoing the same process with which we in the Philippines were, with so much difficulty engaged; with which Germany in Shan-tung, with so much outlay of wealth; with which England in South Africa was engaged with blood and bayonet . . . and the [Russian] soldier appears, as yet, to be the least important instrument of dominion. Thus far Russian elements of empire seem to be brick and mortar, shovel and wagon, quarry and wall, houses and homes, woman and children, order and system" (27).

15. Kuropatkin to Nicholas, memorandum, Aug. 3, 1900, RGIA, f. 560, o. 28, d. 218, l. 14.

16. Olga Bakich, "Origins of the Russian Community on the Chinese Eastern Railway," *Canadian Slavonic Papers* 27 (March 1985): 2; Jules Legras, "La Mandchourie russe," *Revue des Deux Mondes* 10 (July 1, 1902): 119; Lattimore, *Manchuria,* 108; Wolff, *Harbin Station,* 30. Some contemporary descriptions of the *Manchzhurtsy* (Russians in Manchuria) are given in Golovachev, *Rossiia,* 131–40.

17. A. Khvostov, "Russkii Kitai: Nasha pervaia koloniia na Dalnem Vostoke," *VE* 37, no. 10 (October 1902): 653–96; no. 11 (November 1902): 181–208; Paine, *Imperial Rivals,* 277; Bakich, "Origins," 2.

18. Chinese generally earned a daily wage of 40 kopeks in summer and double that amount in winter. By comparison, a Siberian laborer could expect to earn more than 2 rubles a day. See Beveridge, *Russian Advance,* 29; Quested, *"Matey" Imperialists,* 97–98; Wolff, *Harbin Station,* 31.

19. Nilus, *Istoricheskii ocherk,* 2:78.

20. Wolff, *Harbin Station,* 47.

21. Nilus, *Istoricheskii obzor,* 1:182–84.

22. Hosie, *Manhuria,* 80; Beveridge, *Russian Advance,* 16. Some critically minded Russians were less sanguine. Golovachev observed, "Despite Prince Ukhtomskii's assurances that Asians are considered by Russians to be 'their blood relatives,' eye-witnesses unanimously assert that the latter's sentiments are nowhere nearly so positive about Manchuria. . . ." (*Rossiia,* 132).

23. Quested, *"Matey" Imperialists,* 25–26, 34.

24. M. N. Giers to N. M. Muravev, dispatch, Nov. 13, 1899, AVPRI, f. 143, o. 491, d. 116, l. 180.

25. M. N. Giers to N. M. Muravev, dispatch, Nov. 5, 1899, AVPRI, f. 143, o. 491, d. 116, l. 170.

26. Simanskii, *Sobytiia,* 2:90; Morse, *International Relations,* 3:169; Glatfelter, "Russia in China," 59.

27. Dugald Christie, *Thirty Years in the Manchu Capital: In and around Moukden in Peace and War* (New York: McBride, Nast, 1914), 130.

28. Ibid., 132.

29. Nilus, *Istoricheskii obzor,* 1:190–93; Simanskii, *Sobytiia,* 2:90–91.

30. Romanov, *Russia in Manchuria,* 180.

31. However, Kuropatkin was not as eager to march into Manchuria as Witte suggests. The finance minister's recollection that his colleague was delighted with the rebellion because it would give Russia "grounds for taking Manchuria" seems apocryphal (Witte, *Memoirs,* 279).

32. Witte to Nicholas, memorandum, June 15, 1900, RGIA, f. 560, o. 38, d. 180,

ll. 104–5; Witte to Nicholas, memorandum, June 19, 1900, RGIA, f. 560, o. 28, d. 190, l. 8; Kuropatkin to Nicholas, memorandum, Aug. 3, 1900, RGIA, f. 560, o. 28, d. 218, ll. 13–19; Glinskii, *Prolog*, 111–14; Simanskii, *Sobytiia*, 2:100–1.

33. Nilus, *Istoricheskii obzor*, 1:190–215; Glinskii, *Prolog*, 113–14; Christie, *Thirty Years*, 135–42; Malozemoff, *Russian Far Eastern Policy*, 135–38; Hunt, *Frontier Defense*, 18.

34. According to Quested, there are no statistics for the number Russian civilian casualties in Manchuria during the Boxer rising, but she suggests that they were minimal (*"Matey" Imperialists*, 50).

35. V., "Blagoveshchenskaia 'utopiia,'" *VE* 45, no. 7 (July 1910): 231–41; Malozemoff, *Russian Far Eastern Policy*, 139–41; George Alexander Lensen, *The Russo-Chinese War* (Tallahassee, Fl.: Diplomatic Press, 1967), 89–103; Paine, *Imperial Rivals*, 213–14.

36. Grishinskii, *Istoriia russkoi armii*, 13:63–82; Simanskii, *Sobytiia*, 2:102–6; Nilus, *Istoricheskii ocherk*, 2:217–19; Quested, *"Matey" Imperialists*, 50. Russian accounts of the conflict include P. N. Krasnov, *Borba s Kitaem* (St. Petersburg: Russkoe imenie, 1901); Aleksandr Vasilevich Vereshchagin, ed., *Na voine: Razskazy ochevidtsev* (St. Petersburg: R. Golike, 1902); Vereshchagin, "Po Manchzhurii 1900–1901," *VE* 37, no. 1 (January 1902): 103–48; no. 2 (February 1902): 573–627; no. 3 (March 1902): 130–73; Konstantin Porfirevich Kushakov, *Iuzhno-manchzhurskie besporiadki v 1900 godu* (Ashkabad: Ashkabadskaia obshchina Zakaspiiskogo otdela Rossiiskogo obshchestva Krasnogo Kresta, 1902); Ianchevetskii, *U sten*, 507–618. The only English-language history of the campaign is Lensen, *Russo-Chinese War*.

37. Nicholas to Marie Fedorovna, letter, Dec. 22, 1900, GARF, f. 642, o. 1, d. 2326, ll. 101–2.

38. A good summary of the debate surrounding the evacuation of Ili is given in N. K. Giers to Aleksandr II, memorandum, July 15, 1879, RNB, f. 590, o. 1, d. 35, ll. 210–12.

39. For the text, see Morse, *International Relations*, 3:305; Simanskii, *Sobytiia*, 2:109–10; Glinskii, *Prolog*, 137.

40. Glinskii, *Prolog*, 120.

41. Witte to Nicholas, memorandum, Aug. 11, 1900, RGIA, f. 560, o. 28, d. 218, l. 72. About the memorandum, see Simanskii, *Sobytiia*, 2:107–9; Glinskii, *Prolog*, 119–20. Witte made a similar argument two months later (Witte to Nicholas, memorandum, Oct. 11, 1900, RGIA, f. 560, o. 38, d. 180, ll. 224–25). See also Witte to D. S. Sipiagin, letter, Aug. 10, 1900, *KA*, 18:39–40.

42. Witte to Nicholas, memorandum, Aug. 11, 1900, l. 69.

43. Ibid., l. 69.

44. Ibid., l. 66.

45. In the words of his minister to Tokyo, Baron Rosen was "a willing and devoted instrument" of the finance minister (Rosen, *Forty Years*, 1:200).

46. Lamsdorf to Kuropatkin, letter, Mar. 18, 1900, RGVIA, f. 165, o. 1, d. 759, ll. 1–2. See also Kuropatkin to V. V. Sakharov, letter, June 18, 1901, RGVIA, f. 165, o. 1, d. 702, l. 2.

47. Lensen, *Russo-Chinese War*, 278.

48. I. P. Balashev to Nicholas, memorandum, Mar. 12, 1902, GARF, f. 543, o. 1, d. 180, l. 4.

49. Ibid., l. 6.

50. Rosen, *Forty Years*, 1:120; Korostovets, *Rossiia*, 5–6; Oudendijk, *Ways and By-Ways*, 123; Anton Ivanovich Denikin, *The Career of a Tsarist Officer: Memoirs* (Minneapolis: University of Minnesota Press, 1975), 92; Avarin, *Imperializm*, 1:65.

51. Witte, *Memoirs*, 365.

52. Lamsdorf to L. P. Urusov, letter, Oct. 6, 1899, BA, MS coll. Urusov, box 1.

53. Korostovets, *Rossiia*, 11, 25,

54. Alekseev to Kuropatkin, letter, Mar. 6, 1901, RGAVMF, f. 32, o. 1, d. 123, ll. 1–7; Alekseev to Kuropatkin, telegram, July 27, 1901, RGVIA, f. 165, o. 1, d. 704, l. 1.

55. Alekseev to Kuropatkin, letter, Mar. 6, 1901, RGAVMF, f. 32, o. 1, d. 123, l. 6.

56. Kuropatkin, diary, Aug. 30, 1901, RGVIA, f. 165, o. 1, d. 1871, ll. 51–52; Kuropatkin, diary, Feb. 4, 1902, RGVIA, f. 165, o. 1, d. 1871, l. 68; Kuropatkin, diary, Oct. 20, 1902, RGVIA, f. 165, o. 1, d. 1871, l. 92; Lamsdorf, note, Mar. 19, 1902, AVPRI, f. 138, o. 467, d. 205/206, l. 1; Kuropatkin, diary, Dec. 31, 1902, KA, 2:17; Ministerial conference, minutes, Jan. 25, 1903, KA, 52:119.

57. Kuropatkin to Nicholas, memorandum, Mar. 14, 1900, l. 54.

58. Kuropatkin to Nicholas, memorandum, Aug. 3, 1900, RGIA, f. 560, p. 28, d. 218, ll. 13–19. Glinskii alludes to this memorandum in his Prolog, 118.

59. Kuropatkin to Nicholas, memorandum, Aug. 3, 1900, l. 16. He wrote much the same in his report to Nicholas earlier that year (Kuropatkin to Nicholas, Mar. 14, 1900, l. 55).

60. Kuropatkin to Nicholas, memorandum, Aug. 3, 1900, l. 15.

61. G. Montebello to T. Delcassé, dispatch, July 3, 1900, DDF 16:322.

62. Kuropatkin, draft for report, Feb. 8, 1900, RGVIA, f. 165, o. 1, d. 594, l. 22.

63. Simanskii, Sobytiia, 2:111–12; Glinskii, Prolog, 139.

64. For the text, see Romanov, Russia in Manchuria, 427–28.

65. I. Ia. Korostovets, the diplomat who conducted the negotiations on behalf of Alekseev at Port Arthur, describes the talks in his history of the Boxer rebellion (Rossiia, 125–30).

66. "General powers of control" was a mistranslation of article 7, which, according to Romanov's text, stated: "The chiang-chün [governor-general in Mukden] shall be provided with a Russian commissar for convenience of communication with the central authority in Kwantung province [i.e. Adm. Alekseev]. This commissar must be informed as to all more important matters and as to the chiang-chün's decrees" (Russia in Manchuria, 428). See "A Manchurian Agreement," Times (London), Jan. 3, 1901, 3; Glatfelter, "Russia in China," 193–94.

67. Lord Selborne to G. N. Curzon, letter, Apr. 19, 1901, in D. G. Boyce, ed., The Crisis of British Power: The Imperial and Naval Papers of the Second Earl of Selborne, 1895–1910 (London: Historians' Press, 1990), 114. Other Britons were more cynical. King Edward VII told Sir Ernest Satow, his minister to Japan: "Of course we had known all along that they would not evacuate, but why did they promise to do so?" (Lensen, Russo-Chinese War, 265).

68. Pak Chon Ho, Russko-Iaponskaia voina 1904–1905 gg. i Koreia (Moscow: Vostochnaia Literatura, 1997), 33–38; Popov, "Dalnevostochnaia," 48; Duus, Abacus, 134–68; W. G. Beasley, Japanese Imperialism, 1894–1945 (Oxford: Oxford University Press, 1987), 75; Grigorii Nikolaevich Trubetskoi, Russland als Grossmacht (Stuttgart: Deutsche Verlags-Anhalt, 1917), 50–51.

69. For example, as he set off for his new posting in Tokyo, Rosen wrote Foreign Minister Muravev: "I am growing convinced that every move on our part to treat Japan, in relation to its affairs in Korea, as a negligible quantity would be extremely dangerous and full of incalculable consequences" (R. R. Rosen to N. M. Muravev, letter, Mar. 23, 1897, AVPRI, f. 138, o. 467, d. 153/159, l. 172). See also Rosen, Forty Years, 1:142–47. In 1897, shortly after he was invited to become the new war minister, Gen. Kuropatkin already saw Japan as Russia's principal adversary in the Far East (Kuropatkin, diary, Dec. 20, 1897, RGVIA, f. 165, o. 1, d. 1871, l. 3).

70. Ian H. Nish, The Origins of the Russo-Japanese War (London: Longman, 1985), 45; Beasley, Japanese Imperialism, 79.

71. W., "England and Japan in the Far East," *Fortnightly Review* 65 (1895): 870.

72. Chihiro, "Japanese Policies," 354–55; Simanskii, *Sobytiia,* 1:209–11; Langer, *Diplomacy,* 1:406–7.

73. Rosen, *Forty Years,* 1:159; Simanskii, *Sobytiia,* 1:267; Langer, "Origins," 12–13.

74. A. P. Izvolskii to L. P. Urusov, letter, May 3, 1901, BA, MS coll. Urusov, Box 1.

75. Izvolskii to L. P. Urusov, letter, March 9, 1901, BA, MS coll. Urusov, Box 1.

76. Lamsdorf to Witte, Kuropatkin, and P. P. Tyrtov, letter, May 22, 1901, GARF, f. 568, o. 1, d. 175, ll. 2–3.

77. On Ito's career, see J. Morris, *Makers of Japan* (London: Methuen, 1906), 119–53.

78. Shumpei Okamoto, *The Japanese Oligarchy and the Russo-Japanese War* (New York: Columbia University Press, 1970), 24–31; Ian H. Nish, *Japanese Foreign Policy, 1869–1942* (London: Routledge & Kegan Paul, 1977), 59–62; Langer, *Diplomacy,* 2:747–48.

79. Okamoto, *Japanese Oligarchy,* 62. On Japanese public opinion and the press between 1900 and 1904, see ibid., 57–69; Nish, *Origins,* 95–97.

80. Lamsdorf, notes for report, Nov. 20, 1901, GARF, f. 568, o. 1, d. 62, ll. 43–45; Lamsdorf to Nicholas, memorandum, Nov. 22, 1901, *KA,* 63:44–45; Lamsdorf to Izvolskii, telegram, Nov. 22, 1901, *KA,* 63:47–48; Nish, *Anglo-Japanese Alliance,* 186, 196–200; Simanskii, *Sobytiia,* 2:159–72; Langer, *Diplomacy,* 2:764–70; Trubetskoi, *Russland als Grossmacht,* 68–69.

81. B. Bülow, memorandum, Nov. 4, 1901, *GP,* 18/1:39. The navy minister was equally opposed to a Japanese presence in Korea, since that would deprive him of the possibility of a naval station on the peninsula. See P. P. Tyrtov to Lamsdorf, letter, Nov. 30, 1901, GARF, f. 568, o. 1, d. 177, ll. 1–3.

82. For a history of the talks based on British and Japanese sources, see Nish, *Anglo-Japanese Alliance,* esp. 143–228. Hayashi's memoirs have been translated but according to Nish are not entirely reliable (394). See Pooley, *Secret Memoirs of Count Tadasu Hayashi.*

83. Malozemoff, *Russian Far Eastern Policy,* 173; Neilson, *Britain,* 223–25.

84. L. P. Urusov to Lamsdorf, letter, Jan. 31, 1902, AVPRI, f. 138, o. 467, d. 208/209, l. 1. In a letter to his ambassador in Paris, Lamsdorf told him not to be bothered by "the Anglo-Japanese arrangement, which makes so much noise in the world. It is always prudent to take things seriously, but I refuse to consider this so-called treaty as a tragedy" (Lamsdorf to L. P. Urusov, letter, Feb. 7, 1902, AVPRI, f. 138, o. 467, d. 208/209, l. 3).

85. Tan, *Boxer Catastrophe,* 170–72.

86. They are listed in ibid., 173. For a text of the final draft, which was approved by Witte, Lamsdorf, and Kuropatkin on January 28, see Romanov, *Russia in Manchuria,* 209–10.

87. Tan, *Boxer Catastrophe,* 174.

88. Pokotilov to Witte, telegram, Mar. 1, 1901, RGIA, f. 560, o. 38, d. 181, l. 64; Witte to Pokotilov, telegram, Mar. 13, 1901, RGIA, f. 560, o. 38, d. 181, l. 74; Romanov, *Russia in Manchuria,* 213–14.

89. Ministry of Foreign Affairs, Annual Report, 1900, AVPRI, f. 137, o. 475, d. 130, l. 85; Pokotilov to Witte, telegram, Feb. 21, 1901, RGIA, f. 560, o. 38, d. 181, l. 52; Kuropatkin, diary, Mar. 23, 1901, RGVIA, f. 165, o. 1, d. 1896, l. 32. Japanese and British efforts are described in Lensen, *Korea,* 1:127–96.

90. Lensen, *Korea,* 1:131.

91. Tan, *Boxer Catastrophe,* 190; also cited in Masataka Kosaka, "Ch'ing Policy over Manchuria (1900–1903)," *Papers on China* 16 (December 1962): 131.

92. Romanov, *Russia in Manchuria,* 232.

93. Kuropatkin, diary, Feb. 2, 1902, RGVIA, f. 165, o. 1, d. 1871, l. 67; Witte to Lamsdorf, letter, Feb. 20, 1902, GARF, f. 568, o. 1, d. 133, ll. 53–56; Lamsdorf to P. M.

Lessar, telegram, Feb. 20, 1902, GARF, f. 568, o. 1, d. 133, l. 57; Lamsdorf to Kuropatkin, letter, Feb. 22, 1902, GARF, f. 568, o. 1, d. 133, ll. 58–59.

94. For the text, see Russia, *Receuil*, 538–43; MacMurray, *Treaties*, 1:326–29; Glinskii, *Prolog*, 180–83.

95. P. M. Lessar to Lamsdorf, letter, Mar. 27, 1902, GARF, f. 568, o. 1, d. 133, ll. 60–61. The second paragraph of article 2 read: "Le Gouvernement Russe, en vue de cette obligation assumée par Sa Majesté l'Empereur de Chine, consent, de son côté, dans le cas où il n'y aura pas de troubles quelconques et si la manière d'agir des autres puissances n'y met pas obstacle, à retirer graduellement toutes ses troupes de la Mandchourie. . . ."

12: The Last Lap

1. A. S. Suvorin, "Malenkiia pisma," *NV*, Feb. 22, 1903, 3, cited but incorrectly dated as Feb. 20, 1903, in *BDFA*, pt. I, ser. A, 2:395. See also "Kitaiskaia zheleznaia doroga," *NV*, May 3, 1902, 2; N. Kravchenko, "S Dalniago Vostoka, pismo XVXIV," *NV*, Oct. 22, 1902, 2; Benedict Humphrey Sumner, *Tsardom and Imperialism* (Hamden, Conn.: Archon Books, 1968), 17. Already in 1901, when discussing the matter with Kuropatkin, Witte was "almost in tears" over the many complaints against the CER (Kuropatkin, diary, Aug. 30, 1901, RGVIA, f. 165, o. 1, d. 1871, l. 51).

2. Laue, *Sergei Witte*, 195–211. On Witte and Grand Duke Aleksandr Mikhailovich, see Aleksandr Mikhailovich to Witte, letter, Apr. 7, 1902, RGIA, f. 1622, o. 1, d. 31, l. 1; Kuropatkin, diary, Oct. 17, 1902, RGVIA, f. 165, o. 1, d. 1871, ll. 90–91; Kuropatkin, diary, Feb. 2, 1903, *KA*, 2:29; Witte, *Memoirs*, 309–10; Grand Duke Alexander [Mikhailovich], *Once a Grand Duke* (New York: Farrar & Rinehart, 1932), 208–9. On Plehve and Witte, see Kuropatkin, diary, Oct. 27, 1902, RGVIA, f. 165, o. 1, d. 1871, l. 98; Witte, *Memoirs*, 305.

3. Laue, *Sergei Witte*, 211–22.

4. McDonald, *United Government*, 39–40.

5. Simanskii, *Sobytiia*, 2:215–16.

6. A. M. Bezobrazov, business plan, Mar. 28, 1900, RGIA, f. 1622, o. 1, d. 680, ll. 1–3.

7. Aleksandr Mikhailovich to Nicholas, memorandum, Mar. 5, 1899, GARF, f. 601, o. 1, d. 720, l. 3.

8. Nicholas to Witte, note, Jan. 12, 1903, RGIA, f. 1622, o. 1, d. 680, l. 5.

9. Savinskii, *Recollections*, 44; Rosen, *Forty Years*, 1:211.

10. Dmitriev-Mamonov to Pokotilov, letter, Jan. 24, 1903, RGIA, f. 560, o. 28, d. 277, l. 20.

11. Dmitriev-Mamonov to Finance Ministry, letter, Feb. 2, 1903, RGIA, f. 560, o. 28, d. 275, l. 8. See also Pokotilov to Putilov, telegram, Feb. 6, 1903, RGIA, f. 1622, o. 1, d. 188, l. 1.

12. Protasev to Putilov, telegram, Jan. 28, 1903, RGIA, f. 1622, o. 1, d. 185, l. 1.

13. Girshman to Romanov, telegram, Feb. 7, 1903, RGIA, f. 560, o. 28, d. 275, l. 20; Pokotilov to Finance Ministry, telegram, Feb. 16, 1903, RGIA, f. 1622, o. 1, d. 192, l. 1; Witte to Nicholas, June 20, 1903, RGIA, f. 560, o. 38, d. 183, l. 161; Dmitriev-Mamonov to Putilov, telegram, Mar. 31, 1903, RGIA, f. 560, o. 1, d. 275, l. 210; Pokotilov to Witte, telegram, Mar. 20, 1903, RGIA, o. 28, d. 275, l. 179; Dmitriev-Mamonov to Pokotilov, letter, Mar. 6, 1903, RGIA, f. 560, o. 28, d. 277, l. 22.

14. Ultimately some 500 men, mostly "former Chinese soldiers," were hired for this purpose. Reports of their excesses on the Manchurian side of the border led to an official complaint from the Chinese legation in St. Petersburg. See Alekseev to

Lamsdorf, telegram, May 1, 1903, RGIA, f. 560, o. 28, d. 277, l. 18; Chinese legation to Russian Ministry of Foreign Affairs, note, Apr. 20, 1903, RGIA, f. 560, o. 28, d. 277, l. 2.

15. Witte to Nicholas, memorandum, July 25, 1903, RGIA, f. 560, o. 38, d. 183, l. 187.

16. Pokotilov to Witte, Feb. 14, 1903, RGIA, f. 1622, o. 1, d. 189, l. 1.

17. Pokotilov to Witte, Feb. 15, 1903, RGIA, f. 560, o. 28, d. 275, l. 39.

18. Iugovich to Witte, telegram, Mar. 14, 1903, RGIA, f. 1622, o. 1, d. 201, ll. 1–2.

19. Alekseev to Lamsdorf, letter, Mar. 12, 1903, RGVAMF, f. 32, d. 123, ll. 33–34.

20. Girshman to Romanov, letter, Mar. 11, 1903, RGIA, f. 560, o. 28, d. 275, l. 136.

21. A. M. Bezobrazov to Nicholas, memorandum, June 23, 1903, RGVIA, f. 165, o. 1, d. 876, l. 2.

22. Ministerial council, minutes, May 7, 1903, RGIA, f. 1622, o. 1, d. 685, ll. 2–3. The minutes of the 10-day Port Arthur conferences are in RGIA, f. 1622, o. 1, dd. 211–20.

23. Kuropatkin, diary, Aug. 19, 1903, *KA*, 2:58.

24. The Finance Ministry acted with the tsar's approval, as shown by his penciled notation on the document. See E. D. Pleske to A. M. Bezobrazov, letter, Oct. 27, 1903, RGIA, f. 560, o. 28, d. 277, l. 40.

25. Malozemoff, *Russian Far Eastern Policy*, 222.

26. Rosen, *Forty Years*, 1:210.

27. Kuropatkin, diary, Mar. 16, 1903, *KA*, 2:38.

28. Lensen, *Korea*, 210.

29. P. Lessar to Lamsdorf, dispatch, Sep. 20, 1902, AVPRI, f. 143, o. 491, d. 119, l. 206–8; Simanskii, *Sobytiia*, 3:18–22.

30. Minutes, Oct. 27, 1902, RGIA, f. 1622, o. 1, d. 718, ll. 2–3; Kuropatkin, diary, Nov. 3, 1902, RGVIA, f. 165, o. 1, d. 1871, l. 101.

31. Minutes, Jan. 25, 1903, RGIA, o. 1, d. 718, ll. 11–20; also in *KA*, 52:110–24.

32. This was decided at a conference two weeks earlier at the Choristers' Bridge chaired by Lamsdorf with senior ministry officials. See minutes, council, Jan. 11, 1903, RGIA, o. 1, d. 718, ll. 4–10.

33. G. A. Plançon to Prince Qin, note, Apr. 5, 1903, AVPRI, f. 143, o. 491, d. 120, ll. 12–13.

34. G. A. Plançon to Lamsdorf, May 3, 1903, telegram, AVPRI, f. 143, o. 491, d. 45, l. 6; G. A. Plançon to Lamsdorf, dispatch, May 3, 1903, AVPRI, f. 143, o. 491, d. 120, ll. 9–11; G. A. Plançon to Prince Qin, note, May 3, 1903, AVPRI, f. 143, o. 491, d. 120, ll. 23–24.

35. P. M. Lessar to Lamsdorf, telegram, May 30, 1903, AVPRI, f. 143, o. 491, d. 45, ll. 92–96.

36. P. M. Lessar to Lamsdorf, telegram, June 28, 1903, AVPRI, f. 143, o. 491, d. 46, l. 2; Lamsdorf to Nicholas, memorandum, July 2, 1903, AVPRI, f. 143, o. 491, d. 46, l. 17.

37. Although Nicholas coined the term, B. A. Romanov popularized it among historians to describe the growing ascendance of Bezobrazov.

38. Romanov, *Russia in Manchuria*, 284.

39. Ibid. Citation paraphrased from translation for clarity.

40. Malozemoff, *Russian Far Eastern Policy*, 218.

41. Minutes, May 7, 1903, RGIA, f. 1622, o. 1, d. 686.

42. Kuropatkin, who was away on an official visit of Japan, was represented by his deputy, Gen. V. V. Sakharov.

43. Lamsdorf to Nicholas, memorandum, May 28, 1903, AVPRI, f. 138, o. 467, d. 215/216, ll. 3–4; Nicholas to Lamsdorf, letter, May 29, 1903, AVPRI, f. 138, o. 467, d. 215/216, ll. 5–6.

44. Minutes, June 18, 1903, RGIA, f. 1622, o. 1, d. 211, l. 1.

45. Minutes, June 24, 1903, RGIA, f. 1622, o. 1, d. 216, ll. 1–4.

46. Minutes, June 21, 1903, RGIA, f. 1622, o. 1, d. 214, ll. 1–4; Pokotilov to Witte, telegram, June 21, 1903, RGIA, f. 560, o. 29, d. 79, l. 443.

47. Lamsdorf to Nicholas, letter, July 26, 1903, RGIA, f. 1622, o. 1, d. 718, l. 26.

48. Nicholas to Alekseev, telegram, Sep. 10, 1903, RGVAMF, f. 417, o. 1, d. 2865, l. 31.

49. Nicholas to Witte, letter, Aug. 16, 1903, RGIA, f. 1622, o. 1, d. 34, l. 1.

50. Witte, *Memoirs*, 312.

51. Kuropatkin, diary, Aug. 1, 1903, *KA*, 2:45–46; Kuropatkin, diary, Aug. 4, 1903, *KA*, 2:49.

52. I. Ia. Korostovets to Alekseev, letter, Sep. 18, 1903, RGAVMF, f. 32, o. 1, d. 132, l. 39.

53. Savinskii, *Recollections*, 52.

54. Simanskii, *Sobytiia*, 3:136.

55. Neilson, *Britain*, 231.

56. Rosen, *Forty Years*, 1:219.

57. Gurko, *Features and Figures*, 281.

58. Langer, "Origins," 26–28.

59. Cassini to Lamsdorf, telegram, June 12, 1903, AVPRI, f. 143, o. 491, d. 45, l. 138; Cassini to Lamsdorf, telegram, June 13, 1903, AVPRI, f. 143, o. 491, d. 45, l. 146.

60. Langer, "Origins," 26–28.

61. Lt. Col. Wingate, Deputy Assistant Quartermaster for Intelligence, China, "Note on Russian Position in China," July 29, 1903, *BDOW*, 2:211.

Conclusion

1. Avarin, *Imperializm*, 1:68.

2. Osterhammel, *China*, 395–96.

3. See, for example, "Obzor sobytii v Azii za 1894 god," *Grazhdanin*, Jan. 3, 1895, 2; N. T., "Neskolko slov po povodu K-Ia. voiny, *Grazhdanin*, Mar. 31, 1895, 1.

4. Aleksandr Rediger, *Istoriia moei zhizni: Vospominaniia voennogo ministra*, vol. 1 (Moscow: Kanon-Press-Ts., 1999), 316.

5. Kushakov, *Iuzhno-manchzhurskie besporiadki*. A very similar perspective is provided by *Novyi Krai*'s correspondent. See Ianchevetskii, *U sten*.

6. Kushakov, *Iuzhno-manchzhurskie bezporiadki*, 95, 171.

7. Ibid., 69.

8. Ibid., 133–35, 187–88.

9. Tzin, "Stoletie Rossii na Vostok," *Novyi Krai*, Jan. 1, 1901, 1.

10. Avarin, *Imperializm*, 1:68.

11. Simanskii, *Sobytiia*, 3:63.

12. Glinskii, *Prolog*, 259n.1; also cited in Langer, "Origins," 38n.121.

13. I. P. Balashev to Nicholas, memorandum, Mar. 12, 1902, GARF, f. 543, o. 1, d. 180, ll. 4, 6. "Master of the Hunt to the Court" Ivan Petrovich Balashov was the president of the Russian Timber Partnership established in March 1903 to exploit the Yalu River concession. See Russian Timber Partnership Charter, May 31, 1903, RGIA, f. 560, o. 28, d. 276, l. 85; Romanov, *Russia in Manchuria*, 271, 299.

14. Voenno-istoricheskaia kommissiia, *Russko-iaponskaia voina*, 1:430. For more details, see my "Russian Military Intelligence on the Manchurian Front, 1904–05," *Intelligence and National Security* 11, no. 1 (January 1996): 22–31.

15. Helene Iswolsky, *No Time*, 19.

16. René Füllop-Miller, *Rasputin, the Holy Devil* (New York: Viking, 1928), 127. The standard account of the Buriat's peculiar career is V. P. Semennikov, "Tibetskii

vrach i russkaia monarkhiia," in *Za kulisami tsarizma,* iii–xxxiv. Another good study is Igor Vladimirovich Lukoianov, "Dalnevostochnaia avantiura P. A. Badmaeva," (Unpublished paper, Sankt-Peterburskii filial Institut Rossiiskoi Istorii, 1992). See also G. V. Arkhangelskii, "Peter Badmaev: Znakhar, predprinimatel' i politik," *Voprosy Istorii,* no. 2 (February 1998): 74–84. The biography written by Badmaev's grandson is less than scrupulously objective: Boris Gusev, "Moi ded Zhamsaran Badmaev," in Gusev, ed., *Doktor Badmaev: Tibetskaia meditsina, tsarskii dvor, sovetskaia vlast* (Moscow: Russkaia kniga, 1995), 5–104.

17. Semennikov, *Za kulisami tsarizma,* 49–75.

18. Ibid., 72. Emphasis in original.

19. Ibid., 77–81.

20. Ibid., 81.

21. P. A. Badmaev to P. M. Romanov, dispatch, Mar. 21, 1896, GARF, f. 601, o. 1, d. 700, l. 3; Semennikov, *Za kulisami tsarizma,* 22.

22. Malozemoff, *Russian Far Eastern Policy,* 49.

23. Semennikov, *Za kulisami tsarizma,* xx.

24. P. A. Badmaev to Nicholas, memorandum, June 6, 1900, GARF, f. 601, o. 1, d. 700, l. 13.

25. Nicholas's published diary entries for 1895 and 1896 mention several meetings with Badmaev (*Dnevnik,* 71, 73, 77, 185). In later years, toward the end of the Romanov dynasty, Badmaev's ties to the court grew even more intimate, and he would be accused of being closely linked to Rasputin's circle; see Elisabeth Heresch, *Rasputin: Das Geheimnis seiner Macht* (Munich: Langen Müller, 1995), 200–4. Badmaev's name is frequently mentioned in the inquiry conducted by the Russian Provisional Government after the February 1917 revolution. See Russia, Chrezvyshainaia Sledstvennaia Komissiia Vremennago Rezhima, *Padenie Tsarskogo Rezhima,* ed. P. E. Shchegolov, vols. 1–7 (Moscow: Gosudarstvennoe Izd-vo, 1924–1927). For a fascinating late Soviet perspective on this aspect of Badmaev's controversial life, see *Agonia,* directed by Elem Klimov (Mosfilm, 1975).

26. Kuropatkin, diary, Apr. 7, 1898, RGVIA, f. 165, o. 1, d. 1871, l. 19; diary, Sep. 22, 1877, RGVIA, f. 165, o. 1, d. 1889, l. 36; notes to report, Feb. 8, 1900, RGVIA, f. 165, o. 1, d. 594, l. 22.

27. Kuropatkin, diary, Feb. 16, 1903, *KA,* 2:31.

28. Derk Bodde, *Tolstoy and China* (Princeton, N.J.: Princeton University Press, 1950), 46. Translation slightly altered for clarity.

29. Ibid., 45.

30. Ibid., 46.

31. Ministry of Foreign Affairs, Annual Report, 1900, AVPRI, f. 137, o. 475, d. 130, l. 76. See also the report by the Finance Ministry's agent, Pokotilov to Witte, memorandum, Dec. 23, 1900, ll. 161–211.

32. G. Sh. Polkovnik Lazarev, "Krizis v Kitae," *Sbornik materialov po Kiatiu* 1 (1900): 1.

33. Evgenii Vasilevich Bogdanovich, *Rossiia na Dalnem Vostoke* (St. Petersburg: Obshchestvo Krasnago Kresta, 1901).

34. The prince was a frequent dinner guest at Bogdanovich's home (Bogdanovich, *Tri poslednykh,* 226, 250, 253–54, 269, 278, 420–21).

35. A. Bokhanov, "Introduction," in Bogdanovich, *Tri poslednykh,* 6.

36. Kuropatkin, diary, Apr. 19, 1901, RGVIA, f. 165, o. 1, d. 1896, l. 38.

37. Bogdanovich, *Rossiia,* 8–9.

38. Ibid., 9–10.

39. Ibid., 21.

40. A. I., "O politke v kitaiskikh delakh," *SPBVed,* June 27, 1900, 2. Ukhtomskii's own views about the Boxers are in his *K sobytiiam v Kitae.*

41. Nor was the paper particularly profitable. It was long supported by subsidies from the tsar's purse. See Kuropatkin, diary, Apr. 11, 1902, RGVIA, f. 165, o. 1, d. 1871, l. 73; Vika, "Kniaz Meshcherskii 'Opyt nekrologii,'" *Znamia,* Apr. 16, 1903. On Meshcherskii, see Zaionchkovskii, *Russian Autocracy,* 37–41.

42. "Iz obshchestvennoi khroniki," *VE* 31, no. 2 (February 1896): 904–10.

43. Meshcherskii, "Dnevnik," *Grazhdanin,* June 13, 1900, 20.

44. Meshcherskii, "Dnevnik," *Grazhdanin,* June 4, 1900, 21.

45. Meshcherskii, "Dnevnik," *Grazhdanin,* June 13, 1900, 20.

46. Meshcherskii, "Dnevnik," *Grazhdanin,* June 15, 1900, 23.

47. Meshcherskii, "Dnevnik," *Grazhdanin,* Aug. 31, 1897, 13.

48. Meshcherskii, "Dnevnik," *Grazhdanin,* Mar. 19, 1898, 21–22.

49. Sumner, *Tsardom and Imperialism,* 15.

50. Popov, "Dalnevostochnaia," 42.

51. Sumner, *Tsardom and Imperialism,* 16.

52. Mikhail Pavlovich Fedorov, *Sopernichestvo torgovykh interesov na Vostoke* (St. Petersburg: N. Ia. Stoikovoi, 1903), 335.

53. Golovachev, *Rossiia,* 177.

54. Avarin, *Imperializm,* 1:77.

55. Fedorov, *Sopernichestvo,* 84.

56. Golovachev, *Rossiia,* 144.

57. Schiemann, *Deutschland,* 3:286.

58. Laue, *Sergei Witte,* 131.

59. Ibid., 132.

60. Oldenburg, *Last Tsar,* 1:65–66.

61. Propper, *Was Nicht,* 226; Laue, *Sergei Witte,* 133.

62. "Innotrannyi obzor," *VE* 29, no. 9 (September 1894): 379–81.

63. Sigma, "Ex Oriente Nox," *NV,* Mar. 12, 1895, 3.

64. Relations between Russians and Asians in the tsar's Pacific provinces were comparatively harmonious. Although outbursts of violence against Chinese migrants were not unknown, most notoriously at Blagoveshchensk in summer 1900, racial relations at the turn of the century seem to have been not nearly as troubled in Russia's Far East as on North America's West Coast. This point is made most emphatically in Quested, *"Matey" Imperialists.* See also John J. Stephan, *The Russian Far East: A History* (Stanford, Calif.: Stanford University Press, 1994), 71–80. In his popular book about Russia's Far East, D. I. Shreider went to great lengths to emphasize the positive contributions of the *manzy* to the local economy (*Nash Dalnyi Vostok* [St. Petersburg, A. F. Devrien, 1897], 48–67). Stephan speculates that the Russian slang for local Chinese was derived from the word "Manchurian" (*Russian Far East,* 73).

65. Shreider, *Nash Dalnyi Vostok,* 56.

66. A *desiatina* was a unit of land measure used in Imperial Russia, equivalent to 2.7 acres; see Lekha Vilgelmna Zhukova, *Ideologicheskie obosnovaniia Russko-Iaponskoi voiny* (Candidate's diss., Moskovskii Gosudarstvennyi Universitet, 1996), 85.

67. Ibid., 83.

68. Charles de Varigny, "Kitaitsy v Amerike," *SPBVed,* Aug. 25, 1895, 1. Although other Russian papers reprinted similar articles, *Sankt-Peterburskie Vedomosti* naturally stopped running such pieces after Prince Ukhtomskii became its editor the following year.

69. Nikolai Konstantinovich Mikhailovskii, *Posledniia sochineniia N. K. Mikhailovskago*, vol. 1 (St. Petersburg: N. N. Klobukov, 1905), 334.

70. The standard biography is Andrei Konstantinovich Lebedev, *Vasilii Vasilevich Vereshchagin: Zhizn i tvorchestvo 1842–1904* (Moscow: Iskusstvo, 1972). A good sense of the artist's ideas about the Central Asian and Turkish wars he painted is given in the autobiographical *Vasili Verestchagin: Painter, Soldier, Traveler* (New York: American Art Association, 1888). For a recent English-language study, see Vahan D. Barooshian, *V. V. Vereshchagin: Artist at War* (Gainesville: University Press of Florida, 1993). My understanding of the painter was also helped by two papers: Daniel Brower, "Images of the Russian Orient: Vasily Vereshchagin and Russian Turkestan," *Working Papers of the Center for German and East European Studies*, no. 3.5 (March 1993); and Pamela Jill Kachurin, "'Off with their Heads!' Decapitation and Display in the Works of V. V. Vereshchagin" (Unpublished paper, American Association for the Advancement of Slavic Studies, 1997).

71. Barooshian, *Vereshchagin,* 149–51.

72. Twentieth-century Soviet and American art historians generally argue that Vereshchagin's Central Asian paintings were meant to be antiwar statements. See Lebedev, *Vereshchagin,* 112–66; Barooshian, *Vereshchagin,* 26–46.

73. V. V. Vereshchagin, "Iz zapisnoi knizhki," *Novosti i Birzhevie Vedomosti,* July 25, 1900, 2.

74. V. V. Vereshchagin, "Iz zapisnoi knizhki," *Novosti i Birzhevie Vedomosti,* Aug. 22, 1900, 2.

75. Ibid.

76. V. V. Vereshchagin, "Iz zapisnoi knizhki," *Novosti i Birzhevie Vedomosti,* July 17, 1900, 2.

77. V. V. Vereshchagin, "Iz zapisnoi knizhki," *Novosti i Birzhevie Vedomosti,* Aug. 22, 1900, 2.

78. V. V. Vereshchagin, "Iz zapisnoi knizhki," *Novosti i Birzhevie Vedomosti,* July 25, 1900, 2.

79. Ibid.

80. Editorial, *Novyi Krai,* June 2, 1900, 3.

81. A. S. Suvorin, "Malenkiia pisma," *NV,* Mar. 4, 1895, 1.

82. "Morskie Razgovory," *NV,* July 18, 1902, 3; A. B., "Chingis-Khan," *NV,* Aug. 3, 1902, 3.

83. Notovitch, *Nicolas II,* 100.

84. Dmitrii Narkisovich Mamin-Sibiriak, *Polnoe sobranie sochinenii,* vol. 12 (Petrograd: A. F. Marks, 1917), 188.

85. I. S. Levitov, *Zheltaia rasa* (St. Petersburg: G. A. Bernstein, 1900); Levitov, *Zheltaia Rossiia* (St. Petersburg: G. A. Bernstein, 1901); Levitov, *Zheltyi Bosfor* (St. Petersburg: G. A. Bernstein, 1903).

86. Levitov, *Zheltyi Bosfor,* 11.

87. Ibid., 80–82.

88. Lamsdorf to ambassadors in Paris, London, Berlin, Vienna, etc., letter, May 31, 1901, GARF, f. 568, o. 1, d. 175, l. 10. The count used a similar line of reasoning in a conversation with Bülow, the German chancellor, at the Baltic port of Reval (Bernhard von Bülow to Metternich, letter, Aug. 8, 1902, *GP,* 18/1:66).

89. Michael Hunt, *Ideology and U.S. Foreign Policy* (New Haven, Conn.: Yale University Press, 1987), xi.

90. Walter McDougall, *Promised Land, Crusader State: The American Encounter with the World since 1776* (Boston: Houghton Mifflin, 1997).

Sources

Note about the Archives

Toward the Rising Sun is based on research in a number of Russian archives. The most useful collections in Moscow dealing with East Asian policy are those of the Archive of Foreign Policy of the Russian Empire (AVPRI), the State Archive of Russian History (GARF), and the Russian State Military Historical Archive (RGVIA). The most important repositories in St. Petersburg arc the Russian State Historical Archive (RGIA) and the holdings of the Russian Geographical Society, the city's branch of the Russian Academy of Sciences, and the Russian State Archive of the Navy (RGAVMF).

AVPRI is the principal archive for the study of tsarist diplomacy. This institution preserves the records of the prerevolutionary Ministry of Foreign Affairs and its predecessor, the College of Foreign Affairs. Ministerial documents are arranged both by function and by desk. In the case of China, fond 143, *Kitaiskii Stol* (China Desk) contains the relevant dispatches and much other pertinent material. Other collections are the ministry's annual reports in fond 137, and fond 138, *Sekretnyi Arkhiv* (Secret Archive), which includes important classified memoranda and council minutes.

RGVIA preserves the papers of Aleksei Kuropatkin, the war minister from 1898 until the Japanese war, in fond 165. Anyone interested in military history and court politics during the early years of Nicholas's reign will find much precious material in the extensive diaries kept by the war minister. Although those for 1902 through 1904 were published in the second issue of *Krasnyi Arkhiv*, Kuropatkin edited a typed version of the preceding years of his ministry when he sold them to the archive in the 1920s. Two other useful collections are fond 400, with the holdings of the Main Staff's Asian Section, and fond 447, which deals with China.

GARF, the former Central State Archive of the October Revolution, retains the papers both of the imperial family and of a number of important officials. Nicholas II's own diaries are frustratingly laconic, but the letters and documents he received (collected in fondy 601 and 54) are more helpful. Fond 568, which holds the papers of Foreign Minister Count V. N. Lamsdorf, is particularly valuable. Count Lamsdorf meticulously kept his correspondence and much other paperwork, thereby bequeathing an invaluable source to diplomatic historians.

In the former imperial capital, RGIA houses the files of many ministries involved in domestic affairs, including finance (especially in fond 560). Since that department took a leading role in tsarism's Far Eastern adventure when Sergei Witte was its chief, its records merit close attention. Two other important collections are fond 1622 (Sergei Witte's personal papers) and fondy 1070 and 1072 (Prince Esper Ukhtomskii).

The navy was also busy in the Pacific at the time. Its archive holds the papers of Admiral Evgenii Alekseev (fond 32) and the navy's Main Staff (fond 417). Researchers will also find a wealth of material in the extensive file of diaries, memoirs, and other documents collected by the navy for its official history of the war (fond 637). Two archives under the aegis of the Russian Academy of Sciences, those of its St. Peterburg branch and of the Russian Geographical Society, boast rich collections of relevant sources as well, including the papers of Nikolai Przhevalskii, which are in the latter.

Archives

MOSCOW, RUSSIA

Arkhiv vneshnei politikii Rossiiskoi Imperii (AVPRI)
    Fond 133—Kantseliariia MID
    Fond 137—Otchety MID Rossii
    Fond 138—Sekretnyi arkhiv Ministra
    Fond 143—Kitaiskii stol

Gosudarstvennyi arkhiv Rossiiskoi Federatsii (GARF)
    Fond 543—Kollektsiia rukopisei tsarskoselskogo dvortsa
    Fond 568—Lamzdorf, Vladimir Nikolaevich
    Fond 601—Nikolai II
    Fond 640—Aleksandra Fedorovna
    Fond 642—Mariia Fedorovna
    Fond 645—Aleksandr Mikhailovich
    Fond 662—Kseniia Aleksandrovna
    Fond 677—Aleksandr III
    Fond 681—Aleksei Aleksandrovich
    Fond 713—Badmaev, Petr Alexandrovich

Rossiiskii Gosudarstvennyi voenno-istoricheskii arkhiv (RGVIA)
    Fond 165—Kuropatkin, A. N.
    Fond 400—Glavnyi Shtab Aziatskaia chast
    Fond 401—Voenno-uchenyi komitet glavnago shtaba
    Fond 447—Kitai
    Fond 2000—Glavnoe upravlenie generalnogo shtaba

Otdel Rukopisei, Rossiiskaia gosudarstvennaia biblioteka (RGB)
    Fond 75—Golytsin, V. M.
    Fond 169—Miliutin, D. A.
    Fond 218—Edinnykh postupitelnyi
    Fond 363—Veniukov, M. N.

ST. PETERBURG, RUSSIA

S. P. B. filial Arkhiva Rossiiskoi Akademii Nauk (RAN)
    Fond 208—S. F. Oldenburg
    Fond 775—V. P. Vasilev

Nauchnyi arkhiv, Russkoe Geograficheskoe Obshchestvo (RGO)
    Fond 13—Uchenyi arkhiv Przhevalskii, N. M.

Rossiiski gosudarstvennyi istoricheskii arkhiv (RGIA)
Fond 560—Obshchaia kantseliaria ministra finansov
Fond 632—Russko-Kitaiskii bank
Fondy 1070, 1072—Ukhtomskii, E. E.
Fond 1273—Komitet Sibirskoi zheleznoi dorogi
Fond 1622—Vitte, S. Iu.

Rossiiski gosudarstvennyi arkhiv Voenno-Morskogo Flota (RGAVMF)
Fond 32—Alekseev, E. I.
Fond 417—Glavnyi Morskoi shtab
Fond 763—Dnevniki, zametki, zapiski, vyrezki iz gazet o Russko-Iaponskoi voiny.

Rukopisnyi Otdel, Institut russkoi literatury (IRLI)
Fond 314—Ukhtomskii, Esper Esperovich

Otdel Rukopisei, Rossiiskaia natsionalnaia biblioteka (RNB)
Fond 590 Pozdncevy, D. M., and A. M. Pozdneevy

NEW YORK CITY, USA

Bakhmeteff Archive, Columbia University (BA)
Lev Pavlovich Urusov Papers
Sergei Iulevich Witte Papers

Newspapers

Grazhdanin (St. Petersburg)
North-China Herald (Shanghai)
Novoe Vremia (St. Petersburg)
Novyi Krai (Port Arthur)
Rossiia (St. Petersburg)
Sankt-Peterburgskie Vedomosti (St. Petersburg)
Times (London)
Zhizn v vostochnoi okraine (Chita)

Published Document Collections

Bantysh-Kamenskii. *Diplomaticheskoe sobranie del mezhdu rossiiskim i kitaiskim gosudarst-vami s 1619 do 1792 god.* Kazan: Tipografiia Imperatorskago Universiteta, 1882.
Bourne, Kenneth, and D. Cameron Watt, eds. *British Documents on Foreign Affairs: Reports and Papers from the Foreign Office Confidential Print.* Part I, ser. A, vol. 2; ser. E, vols. 5–8. [Frederick, Md.]: University Press of America, 1983–1989.
Burtsev, Vladimir L. *Tsar i vneshniaia politika: Vinoviki russko-iaponskoi voiny po tainym dokumentam: Tainaia zapiska Gr. Lamsdorfa i malinovaia kniga.* Berlin: Eberhart Frowein, 1910.
Chinese Eastern Railway. *Sbornik dokumentov, otnosiashchikhsia k Kitaiskoi Vostochnoi zheleznoi dorogie.* Harbin: K.V.Zh.D., 1922.
France. Ministère des affaires étrangères. *Documents diplomatiques français (1871–1914), 1ère Série (1871–1900).* Vols. 11–16. Paris: Imprimerie nationale, 1947.

Gooch, G. P., and Harold Temperley, eds. *British Documents on the Origins of the War, 1898–1914.* Vols. 1–2. London: His Majesty's Stationery Office, 1927.

Grimm, Ervin Davidovich. *Sbornik dogovorov i drugikh dokumentov po istorii mezhdunarodnykh otnoshenii na dalnem vostoke (1842–1925).* Moscow: Institut Vostokovedeniia, 1927.

Krasnyi Arkhiv. Moscow: Tsentralnyi arkhiv RSFSR, 1922–1941.

    Vol. 2 (1922), "Dnevnik A. N. Kuropatkina," 5–112; "Perepiska o podkupke kitaiskikh sanovnikov Li-khun-Chzhana i Chzhan-in-Khuana," 287–93.

    Vol. 3 (1923), "Dnevnik A. A. Polovtseva," 75–172.

    Vol. 14 (1926), "Bokserskoe vosstanie," 1–49.

    Vol. 17 (1926), "Bezobrazovskii kruzhok letom 1904 g.," 70–80.

    Vol. 18 (1926), "Tsarskaia diplomatiia o zadachakh Rossii na Dalnem Vostoke," 3–29.

    Vol. 20 (1927), "Zapiska F. F. Martensa 'Evropa i Kitai,'" 175–85.

    Vol. 25 (1927), "Anglo-russkoe soglashenia o razdele Kitaia (1899)," 111–34.

    Vols. 41–42 (1930), "V shtabe adm. E. A. Alekseeva (is denvnika E. A. Plansona)," 148–204.

    Vol. 45 (1931), "Pisma V. V. Vereshchagina Nikolaiu Romanova v 1904 g.," 167–71.

    Vol. 46 (1931), "Iz dnevnika A. A. Polovtsova (1895–1900)," 110–32.

    Vols. 47–48 (1931), "Proekt zakhvata Bosfora v 1896 g.," 50–70.

    Vol. 52 (1932), "Pervye shagi russkogo imperializma na Dalnem Vostoke, 1888–1903," 34–124.

    Vol. 53 (1932), "Tserkov i russifikatsiia buriato-mongol pri tsarisma," 100–126.

    Vol. 58 (1933), "Vilgelm II o zaniatii tsarskoi Rossiei Port-Artura," 150–55.

    Vol. 63 (1934), "Nakanune Russko-Iaponskoi voiny," 3–54.

    Vol. 87 (1938), "Zakhvat Germaniei Kiao-Chao v 1897 g.," 19–63.

Lepsius, Johannes, et al., eds. *Die grosse Politik der Europäischen Kabinette 1871–1914: Sammlung der diplomatichen Akten der Auswärtigen Amptes.* Vols. 9, 12–14, 16, 18. Berlin: Deutsche Verlagsgesellschaft für Politik und Geschichte, 1922–1927.

MacMurray, John V. A. *Treaties and Agreements with and concerning China, 1894–1919.* Vol. 1. New York: Oxford University Press, 1921.

Mayers, William Frederic. *Treaties between the Empire of China and Foreign Powers.* Shanghai: North-China Herald, 1906.

Mezhdunarodnye otnosheniia v epokhu imperializma. Dokumenty iz arkhivov tsarskogo i vremennogo pravitelstv. Moscow: Gos. sotsialnoekon. izd-vo, 1931.

Russia. Ministère des Affaires Etrangères. *Receuil de traités et documents diplomatiques concernant l'Extrême Orient 1895–1905.* St. Petersburg: A. M. Mendeleevich, 1906.

Russia. Osobyi Komitet Dalnego Vostoka. *Dokumenty kasaiushchikhsia peregovorov s Iaponieiu v 1903–1904 godakh.* St. Petersburg: Sanktpeterburgskaia Sinodalnaia tipografiia, 1905.

Rijks Geschiedkundige Publicatiën. grote serie. Vols. 100, 138. The Hague: Martinus Nij-hoff, 1905–.

Sbornik sekretnykh dokumentov iz arkhiva byvshago ministerstvo inostrannykh del. Petrograd: NKID, 1917.

Semennikov, V. P., ed. *Za kulisami tsarizma: Arkhiv tibetskago vracha Badmaeva.* Leningrad: Gosudarstvennoe izdatelstvo, 1925.

Skachkov, P. E., and V. S. Misnikov, eds. *Russko-kitaiskie otnosheniia 1689–1916: Ofitsialnye dokumenty.* Moscow: Vostochnaia literatura, 1958.

Tikhvinskii, Sergei Leonidovich, ed. *Russko-kitaiskie otnosheniia v XVII veke: Materialy i dokumenty.* Vol. 2. Moscow: Nauka, 1972.

Tikhvinskii, Sergei Leonidovich, et al., eds. *Russko-kitaiskie otnosheniia v XVIII veke. Materialy i dokumenty.* Moscow: Nauka, 1978.

Troianovskii, K. M. *Siniaia kniga. Sbornik tainykh dokumentov izvlennykh iz arkhiva byvshago MID.* Moscow: Narkomindel, 1918.

Other Sources

A. G. *Nashi zadachi na Vostoke.* St. Petersburg: A. S. Suvorin, 1904.

A. I. "Beglyi ocherk morskikh operatsii russko-iaponskoi voiny." *Morskoi Sbornik* 369, no. 4 (April 1912): 103–82; 370, no. 6 (June 1912): 53–117.

Abrikossow, Dmitrii Ivanovich. *Revelations of a Russian Diplomat: The Memoirs of Dmitrii I. Abrikossow.* Edited by George Alexander Lensen. Seattle: University of Washington Press, 1964.

Adams, Brooks. *The Law of Civilisation and Decay: An Essay on History.* London: Swan Sonnenschein, 1895.

Adoratskii, Ieromonach Nikolai. "Pravoslavnaia missiia v Kitae za 200 let eia sushchestvovaniia." *Pravoslavnyi sobesednik,* February 1887, 252–65; March 1887, 317–51; April 1887, 460–507; September 1887, 30–58; October 1887, 188–213; November 1887, 287–343.

Aikman, David. "Russia Could Go the Asiatic Way." *Time,* July 6, 1992, 80.

Aldanov, Mark. "Count Witte." *Russian Review* 1, no. 1 (November 1941): 56–64.

Aldrich, Robert. *Greater France: A History of French Overseas Expansion.* New York: St. Martin's Press, 1996.

Alekseev, Aleksandr Ivanovich. *Amurskaia ekspeditsiia 1849–1855 gg.* Moscow: Mysl, 1974.

———. *Osvoenie russkogo Dalnego Vostoka, konets XIX v—1917 g.* Moscow: Nauka, 1989.

Alekseev, Mikhail. *Voennaia razvedka Rossii ot Riurika do Nikolaia II.* Vol. 1. Moscow: Russkaia Razvedka, 1998.

Alexander, Grand Duke [Aleksandr Mikhailovich]. *Once a Grand Duke.* New York: Farrar & Rinehart, 1932.

Ambler, Effie. *Russian Journalism and Politics, 1861–1881: The Career of Aleksei Suvorin.* Detroit: Wayne State University Press, 1972.

Amfiteatrov, Aleksandr Valentinovich, and Vlas Mikhailovich Dorosevich. *Kitaiskii vopros.* Moscow: I. D. Sytin, 1901.

Ananich, Boris Vasilevich, ed. *Krizis samoderzhaviia v Rossii 1895–1917.* Leningrad: Nauka, 1984.

———. *Rossiia i mezhdunarodnyi kapital, 1897–1914. Ocherki istorii finansovykh otnoshenyi.* Leningrad: Nauka, 1970.

———. "S. Iu. Vitte i izdatelskaia deiatelnost 'bezobrazovskaia kruzhka,'" *Knizhnoe delo v Rossii vo vtoroi polovine XIX–nachale XX veka: Sbornik nauchnykh trudov,* no. 4 (1989): 59–78.

Ananich, Boris Vasilevich, and Rafail Sholomovich Ganelin. "Opyt kritiky memuarov S. Iu. Vitte." In *Voprosy istorii i istochnikovedeniia istorii SSSR.* Leningrad, 1963.

———. *Sergei Iulevich Vitte i ego vremia.* St. Petersburg: Dmitrii Bulanin, 1999.

———. *S. Iu. Vitte: Memuarist.* St. Petersburg: Sankt-Peterburgskii filial Instituta rossiiskoi istorii RAN, 1994.

"A. N. Kuropatkin." *Razvedchik* 11, no. 378 (Jan. 13, 1898): 25–27.

Andreev, Aleksandr Ivanovich. *The Buddhist Shrine of Petrograd.* Ulan Ude: EcoArt Agency, 1992.

———. *Ot Baikala do sviashchennoi Lkhasy.* St. Petersburg: Agni, 1997.

Andrew, Christopher. *Théophile Delcassé and the Making of the Entente Cordiale.* London: Macmillan, 1968.

Anthouard, Albert François Ildefonse Baron d'. *La Chine contre l'étranger: Les Boxeurs.* Paris: Librairie Plon, 1902.

Aretin, K. O. von, and W. Conze, eds. *Deutschland und Russland im Zeitalter des Kapitalismus 1871–1914.* Wiesbaden: Harrasowitz, 1977.

Arkhangelskii, Georgii Vladimirovich. "Petr Badmaev—znakhar, predprinimatel i politik." *Voprosy Istorii,* no. 2 (February 1998): 74–84.

Artamanova, G. Sh. Polkovnik, ed. *Sbornik materialov po Kitaiu s miatezhnym dvizniem "Bolshikh kulakov" 1898–1900 gg.* Vol. 1. St. Petersburg: Voenno-Uchennyi Komitet Glavnago Shtaba, 1900.

Asakawa, K. *The Russo-Japanese Conflict: Its Causes and Issues.* Boston: Houghton, Mifflin, 1904.

Avarin, Vladimir Iakovlevich. *Imperializm v Manzhurii.* 2 vols. Moscow-Leningrad: Ogiz, 1934.

Avdeev, V. A. "'Sekrety' Russko-iaponskoi voiny." *Voenno-Istoricheskii Zhurnal,* no. 9 (1993): 87–88.

———. "Ternovyi venets Generala A. N. Kuropatkina." *Voenno-Istoricheskii Zhurnal,* no. 4 (1995): 68–75

Baddeley, John F., ed. *Russia, Mongolia, China: Being Some Record of the Relations between Them from the Beginning of the XVIIth Century to the Death of Tsar Aleksei Mikhailovich.* 2 vols. London: Macmillan, 1919.

Badmaev, Petr Aleksandrovich. *Osnovy vrachebnoi nauki Tibeta Khud-Shi.* Moscow: Nauka, 1991.

———. *Rossiia i Kitai.* St. Petersburg: A. S. Suvorin, 1905.

Baedeker, Karl. *Russia with Teheran, Port Arthur, and Peking.* Leipzig: Karl Baedeker, 1914.

Bakich, Olga. "Origins of the Russian Community on the Chinese Eastern Railway." *Canadian Slavonic Papers* 27 (March 1985): 1–14.

Bakunin, Mikhail. "Réponse d'un international à Massini." In *Michel Bakounine et l'Italie 1871–1872.* Leiden: E. J. Brill, 1961.

Baring, Maurice. *The Puppet Show of Memory.* London: W. Heinemann, 1922.

Barnhart, Michael A. *Japan and the World since 1868.* London: Edward Arnold, 1995.

Barooshian, Vahan D. *V. V. Vereshchagin: Artist at War.* Gainesville: University Press of Florida, 1993.

Bartol, Robert Anthony. "A. S. Suvorin and His Malenkiia Pisma: A Publisher's Commentary on Tsarist Russia, 1900–1906." Ph.D. diss., Michigan State University, 1972.

Bartold, Vasilii Vladimirovich. *Istoriia izucheniia Vostoka v Evrope i Rossii.* Leningrad: Tov. Alekseeva, 1925.

———. *Akademik Bartold—Sochineniia.* Moscow: Vostochnaia literatura, 1963.

Basily, Nicolas de. *Memoirs.* Stanford, Calif.: Stanford University Press, 1973.

Bassin, Mark. "Expansion and Colonialism on the Eastern Frontier: Views of Siberia and the Far East in Pre-Petrine Russia." *Journal of Historical Geography* 14, no. 1 (1988): 3–21.

———. *Imperial Visions: Nationalist Imagination and Geographical Expansion in the Russian Far East, 1840–1865.* Cambridge: Cambridge University Press, 1999.

———. "Inventing Siberia: Visions of the Russian East in the Early Nineteenth Century." *American Historical Review* 96 (1991): 763–94.

———. "Russia between Europe and Asia: The Ideological Construction of Geographical Space." *Slavic Review* 50, no. 1 (1991): 1–17.

Baumgart, Winfried. *Imperialism: The Idea and Reality of British and French Colonial Expansion, 1880–1914.* Oxford: Oxford University Press, 1982.

Becker, Seymour. "The Muslim East in Nineteenth-Century Russian Popular Historiography." *Central Asian Survey* 5, nos. 3–4 (1986): 25–47.

Beasley, W. G. *Japanese Imperialism, 1894–1945*. Oxford: Oxford University Press, 1987.

Belknap, Robert. "O Pushkinskoi Rechi Dostoevskogo." Unpublished conference paper, Smolensk Ped. Inst., 1993.

Belomor, A. E. *Pisma o flote*. St. Petersburg: M. M. Stasiulevich, 1896.

Belov, E. A. "Tibetskaia politika Rossii (1900–1914 gg.)." *Vostok*, no. 3 (1994): 99–109.

Bely, Andrei. *Petersburg*. Translated by Robert A. Maguire and John E. Malmstad. Bloomington: Indiana University Press, 1978.

Benckendorff, Count Costantine. *Half a Life: The Reminiscences of a Russian Gentleman*. London: Richards Press, 1955.

Benningsen, Alexandre. *Russes et chinois avant 1917*. Paris: Flammarion, 1974.

Bensidoun, Sylvain. *Alexandre III*. Paris: CEPES, 1990.

Berdiaev, Nikolai. *Dream and Reality: An Essay in Autobiography*. Translated by Katharine Lampert. London: Geoffrey Bles, 1950.

———. *Konstantin Leontiev*. Paris: YMCA Press, 1926.

———. *The Russian Idea*. Translated by R. M. French. London: Geofrey Bles, 1947.

Beresford, Charles William De la Poer, Lord. *The Break-Up of China: With an Account of Its Present Commerce, Currency, Waterways, Politics, and Future Prospects*. 2 vols. New York: Harper & Brothers, 1899.

Berg, Lev Semenovich. *Vsesoiuznoe geograficheskoe obshchestvo za sto let*. Moscow: Akademiia Nauk SSSR, 1946.

Bernstein, Herman. *With Master Minds: Interviews by Herman Bernstein*. New York: Universal Series Publishing, 1913.

Besançon, Alain. *Education et société dans le second tiers du XIX siècle*. Paris: Mouton, 1974.

———. *La falsification du bien. Soloviev et Orwell*. Paris: Julliard, 1985.

Beskrovnyi, Liubomir Grigorevich. *Russkaia armiia i flot v XIX v.* Moscow: Nauka, 1973.

Beskrovnyi, L. G., and A. L. Narochnitskii. "K istorii vneshnei politiki Rossii na Dalnem Vostoke v XIX v." *Voprosy Istorii*, no. 6 (1974): 14–36.

Betteley, Roy D. R. *Fabergé*. Bangkok: Chitralada Palace, 1986.

Beveridge, Albert J. *The Russian Advance*. New York: Harper, 1903.

Beyrau, Dietrich. *Militär und Gesellschaft im vorrevolutionären Rußland*. Cologne: Böhlau, 1984.

Bezobrazov, Aleksandr Mikhailovich. "Le conflit russo-japonais." *Le Correspondant* 291 (May 25, 1923): 577–615.

Bilof, Edwin George. "The Imperial Russian General Staff and China in the Far East, 1880–1888." Ph.D. diss., Syracuse University, 1974.

Bing, Edward J., ed. *The Letters of Tsar Nicholas and Empress Marie*. London: Ivor Nicholson & Watson, 1937.

Bishop, Isabelle Bird. *Korea and Her Neighbors*. New York: Fleming H. Revel, 1898.

Bland, J. O. P. *Li Hung-chang*. New York: Henry Holt and Company, 1917.

Bliokh, Ivan Stanislavovich [Jan Bloch]. *Budushchaia voina v tekhnicheskom, ekonomicheskom i politicheskom otnosheniiakh*. 6 vols. St. Petersburg: Tip. I. A. Efrona, 1899.

Blok, Aleksandr. *Polnoe sobranie stikhotvorenii v dvukh tomakh*. Vol. 1. Leningrad: Sovetskii Pisatel, 1946.

Bodde, Derk. *Tolstoy and China*. Princeton, N.J.: Princeton University Press, 1950.

Boeß, Otto. *Die Lehre der Eurasier: Ein Betrag zur russischen Ideengeschichte des 20. Jahrhunderts*. Wiesbaden: Harrasowitz, 1961.

Bogdanov, M. N. *Ocherki istorii buriat-mongolskogo naroda*. Verkhneudinsk: Buriat-mongolskoe izd-vo, 1926.

Bogdanovich, Aleksandra Viktorevna. *Tri poslednikh samoderzhtsa.* Moscow: Novosti, 1990.

Bogdanovich, Evgenii Vasilevich. *Rossiia na Dalnem Vostoke.* St. Petersburg: Obshchestvo Krasnago Kresta, 1901.

Bompard, Maurice. *Mon ambassade en Russie (1903–1908).* Paris: Plon, 1937.

Botkin, Petr Sergeevich. *Kartinki diplomaticheskoi zhizni.* Paris: E. Sialskii, 1930.

Boulay, N. W. H. du. *An Epitome of the Chino-Japanese War, 1894–95.* London: Her Majesty's Stationery Office, 1896.

Boulger, Demetrius C. "The 'Yellow Peril' Bogey." *Living Age* 240, no. 3109 (Feb. 6, 1904): 321–29.

Bounds, Marcella. "The Sino-Russian Secret Treaty of 1896." *Papers on China* 23 (July 1970): 109–25.

Bowlt, John E. *The Silver Age: Russian Art of the Early Twentieth Century and the "World of Art" Group.* Newtonville, Mass.: Oriental Research Partners, 1979.

The Boxer Rising: A History of the Boxer Trouble in China. Reprinted from the "Shanghai Mercury". New York: Paragon, 1967.

Boyce, D. G., ed., *The Crisis of British Power: The Imperial and Naval Papers of the Second Earl of Selborne, 1895–1910.* London: Historians' Press, 1990.

Brahm, Heinz. "Sowjetische Intellektuelle über die 'chinesische Gefahr.'" *Berichte des Bundesintitutes für ostwissenschaftliche und internationale Studien,* no. 60 (1977).

Brandt, Max von. *Drei Jahre ostasiatischer Politik 1894–1897.* Stuttgart: Strecker & Moser, 1898.

Braun, Peter C. M. S. *Die Verteitigung Indiens 1800–1907.* Cologne: Böhlau, 1968.

Bridge, Sir Cyprian. "The Russo-Japanese Naval Campaign of 1904." In *The Naval Annual 1905,* edited by T. A. Brassey, 97–172. Portsmouth: J. Griffin, 1905.

Brooks, Jeffrey. *When Russia Learned to Read: Literacy and Popular Literature, 1861–1917.* Princeton, N.J.: Princeton University Press, 1985.

Brower, Daniel R. "Images of the Russian Orient: Vasily Vereschagin and Russian Turkestan." *Working Papers of the Center for German and European Studies,* no. 3.5 (March 1993).

———. "Imperial Russia and the Orient: The Renown of Nikolai Przhevalsky." *Russian Review* 53, no. 3 (July 1994): 367–82.

———. "Siberia in Paris: Russia at the 1900 Paris World's Fair." Unpublished conference paper, American Association for the Advancement of Slavic Studies, 1988.

Brower, Daniel, and Edward J. Lazzerini, eds. *Russia's Orient: Imperial Borderlands and Peoples, 1700–1917.* Bloomington: Indiana University Press, 1997.

Brunschwig, Henri. *Mythes et réalités de l'impérialisme colonial français 1871–1971.* Paris: Librairie Armand Colin, 1960.

Brunnhofer, Hermann. *Russlands Hand über Asien: Historisch-Geographische Essays zur Entwicklungsgeschichte des russischen Reichsdenkens.* St. Petersburg: n.p., 1897.

Buchanan, Meriel. *Ambassador's Daughter.* London: Cassel, 1958.

Buksgevden, Baron Aleksei. *Russkii Kitai: Ocherki diplomaticheskoi snoshenii Rossii s Kitaem.* Port Arthur: Novyi Krai, 1902.

Bülow, Bernhard, Prince von. *Memoirs.* 4 vols. London: Putnam, 1931.

Bushkovitch, Paul. "What is Russia? Russian National Consciousness and the State, 1500–1917." Unpublished conference paper, Columbia University, 1994.

Byrnes, Robert. *Pobedonostsev: His Life and Thought.* Bloomington: University of Indiana Press, 1968.

Cahen, Gaston. *Histoire des relations de la Russie avec la Chine sous Pierre le Grand (1689–1730).* Paris: E. Alcan, 1912.

Cameron, Meribeth E., et al., eds. *China, Japan, and the Powers*. New York: Ronald Press, 1952.

Carlson, Maria. *"No Religion Higher than Truth": A History of the Theosophical Movement in Russia, 1875–1922*. Princeton, N.J.: Princeton University Press, 1993.

Carlton, Eric. *War and Ideology*. Savage, Md.: Barnes and Noble Books, 1990.

Carter, James H. "Sino-Russian Relations up to the Treaty of Nerchinsk." Unpublished graduate paper, Yale University, 1991.

Cassels, Alan. *Ideology and International Relations in the Modern World*. London: Routledge, 1996.

Cassini, Arthur Pavlovich. "Russia in the Far East." *North American Review* 178, no. 570 (May 1904): 681–89.

Cassini, Marguerite. *Never a Dull Moment: The Memoirs of Countess Marguerite Cassini*. New York: Harper & Brothers, 1956.

Cecil, Lamar. "William II and His Russian 'Colleagues.'" In *German Nationalism and the European Response*, edited by Carole Fink et al., 95–134. Norman: University of Oklahoma Press, 1985.

———. *Wilhelm II: Prince and Emperor, 1859–1900*. Chapel Hill: University of North Carolina Press, 1989.

Chang Tao-shing. *Russia, China, and the Chinese Eastern Railway*. Stanford, Calif.: Hoover Institution Press, 1973.

Charykov, Nikolai Valerievich. *Glimpses of High Politics: Through War and Peace, 1855–1929*. New York: Macmillan, 1931.

Chekhov, Anton Pavlovich. *The Cherry Orchard; Uncle Vanya; The Cherry Orchard;* and *The Wood Demon*. In *The Oxford Chekhov*, translated by Ronald Hingley, 57–112. Oxford: Oxford University Press, 1965

———. *The Duel and Other Stories*. Translated by Constance Garnett. New York: Macmillan, 1920.

Cheng Lin. *The Chinese Railways: A Historical Survey*. Shanghai: China United Press, 1935.

Chéradame, André. *Le monde et la guerre russo-japonaise*. Paris: Plon, 1906.

Chesnaux, Jean. *Le mouvement paysan chinois: 1840–1949*. Paris: Editions du Seuil, 1976.

Chicherin, Georgii Vasilevich. "Rossiia i aziatskie narody." In *Stati i rechi po voprosam mezhdunarodnoi politiki*. Moscow: Sots.-ekon. Literatury, 1961.

Chihiro, Hosoya. "Japan's Policies toward Russia." In *Japan's Foreign Policy, 1868–1941: A Research Guide*, edited by James Morley. New York: Columbia University Press, 1974.

Chirol, Valentine. *The Far Eastern Question*. London: Macmillan, 1896.

———. *Fifty Years in a Changing World*. New York: Harcourt, Brace, 1928.

Choi Dokkiu. "Morskoe ministerstvo i politika Rossii na Dalnem Vostoke (1895–1903)." *Ezhegodnik Sankt-Peterburgskogo nauchnogo obshchestva istorikov i arkhivistov* 1 (1996): 145–71.

———. *Rossiia v Koree: 1893–1905 gg. (Politika Ministerstva finansov i Morskogo ministerstva)*. St. Petersburg: Zero, 1996.

Christ, David S. "Russia's Far Eastern Policy in the Making." *Journal of Modern History* 14, no. 3, (September 1942): 317–41.

Christie, Dugald. *Thirty Years in the Manchu Capital: In and around Moukden in Peace and War*. New York: McBride, Nast, 1914.

Christoff, Peter. *An Introduction to Nineteenth-Century Russian Slavophilism*. Vol. 1, A. S. Xomjakov; vol. 2, I. V. Kireevskij. The Hague: Mouton, 1961–1972.

———. *K. S. Aksakov: A Study in Ideas*. Princeton, N.J.: Princeton University Press, 1982.

Chu, Samuel C., and Kwang-Ching Liu. *Li Hung-chang and China's Modernization*. Armonk, N.Y.: M. E. Sharpe, 1984.

Churchill, Rogers Platt. *The Anglo-Russian Convention of 1907*. Cedar Rapids, Iowa: Torch Press, 1939.

Cioran, Samuel D. *Vladimir Solovev and the Knighthood of the Divine Sophia*. Waterloo, Ont.: Wilfred Laurier University Press, 1977.

Clarke, Sir George Sydenham. *Russia's Sea Power Past and Present*. London: John Murray, 1898.

Clubb, O. Edmund. *China and Russia: The "Great Game"*. New York: Columbia University Press, 1971.

Cohen, Paul A. *History in Three Keys: The Boxers as Event, Experience, and Myth*. New York: Columbia University Press, 1997.

———. "Wang T'ao's Perspective on a Changing World." In *Approaches to Modern Chinese History*, edited by Albert Feuerwerker et al., 133–62. Berkeley: University of California Press, 1967.

Conger, Sarah Pike. *Letters from China with Particular Reference to the Empress Dowager and the Women of China*. Chicago: A. C. McClurg, 1909.

Connaughton, Richard. *The War of the Rising Sun and the Tumbling Bear*. London: Routledge, 1991.

Connelly, Matthey, and Paul Kennedy. "Must it Be the Rest against the West?" *Atlantic Monthly* 274, no. 6 (December 1994): 69.

Conrad, Joseph. "Geography and Some Explorers." In *Last Essays*. Garden City: Doubleday, Page, 1926.

Coons, Arthur Gardiner. *The Foreign Public Debt of China*. Philadelphia: University of Pennsylvania Press, 1930.

Corbett, Julian S. *Maritime Operations in the Russo-Japanese War, 1904–1905*. Annapolis, Md.: Naval Institute Press, 1994.

Cordier, Henri. *Histoire des relations de la Chine avec les puissances occidentales, 1860–1902*. Vol. 3. Paris: Félix Alcan, 1902.

Courant, Maurice. *La Sibérie: Colonie russe jusqu'à la construction du Transsibérien*. Paris: Félix Alcan, 1920.

Crisp, Olga. "The Russo-Chinese Bank: An Episode in Franco-Russian Relations." *Slavonic and East European Review* 52, no. 127 (April 1974): 197–233.

Crossley, Pamela Kyle. *Orphan Warriors: Three Generations and the End of the Qing World*. Princeton, N.J.: Princeton University Press, 1990.

Curzon, George N. *Problems of the Far East: Japan—China—Korea*. London: Longmans, Green, 1894.

———. *Russia in Central Asia in 1889 and the Central Asian Question*. London: Longmans, Green, 1889.

Danilevskii, Nikolai Iakovlevich. *Rossiia i Evropa*. St. Petersburg: Tip. Bratev Panteleevykh, 1869.

Davidson-Houston, James Vivian. *Russia and China: From the Huns to Mao Tse-tung*. London: Robert Hale, 1960.

Davis, Clarence B., and Kenneth E. Wilburn, Jr., eds. *Railway Imperialism*. New York: Greenwood Press, 1991.

Decornoy, Jacques. *Péril jaune, Peur blanche*. Paris: Bernard Grasset, 1970.

Demidova, Natalia Fedorovna, and Vladimir Stepanovich Miasnikov. *Pervye russkie diplomaty v Kitae ("Rospis" I. Petlina i stateinyi spisok F. I. Baikova)*. Moscow: Nauka, 1966.

Denikin, Anton Ivanovich. *The Career of a Tsarist Officer: Memoirs*. Minneapolis: University of Minnesota Press, 1975.

Diachenko, Boris, ed. *Zheltaia opasnost*. Vladivostok: Voron, 1996.

Dilks, David. *Curzon in India*. London: Hart-Davis, 1970.

Dillon, Emil Joseph. *The Eclipse of Russia*. New York: George H. Doran, 1918.

———. "Two Russian Statesmen." *Quarterly Review* 236, no. 469 (October 1921): 404.

Dittmer, Helen Roth-Bergman. "The Russian Foreign Ministry under Nicholas II." Ph.D. diss., University of Chicago, 1977.

Dmitriev-Mamonov, A. I., ed. *Ot Volgi do Velikogo okeana: Putevoditel po Velikoi Sibirskoi zheleznoi doroge s opisaniem Shilko-Amurskago vodago puti i Manchzhurii*. St. Petersburg: T-vo khudozh. pechati, 1900.

Dmitriev-Mamonov, A. I., and A. F. Zdiarskii, eds. *Guide to the Great Siberian Railway*. St. Petersburg: Artistic Printing Society, 1900.

Dmytryshyn, Basil, et al., eds. *To Siberia and Russian America: Three Centuries of Russian Eastward Expansion*. 3 vols. Portland: Oregon Historical Society, 1985–1989.

Dombrovskii, A., and V. Voroshilov. *Manchzhuriia*. St. Petersburg: N. V. Vasilev, 1897.

Dostoevsky, Fedor Mikhailovich. *Crime and Punishment*. Translated by Constance Garnett. New York: Macmillan, 1928.

———. *Diary of a Writer*. Translated by Boris Brasol. 2 vols. New York: Scribner, 1949.

Drage, Geoffrey. *Russian Affairs*. London: John Murray, 1904.

Dubrovin, Nikolai Fedorovich. *Nikolai Mikhailovich Przhevalskii, Biograficheskii ocherk*. St. Petersburg: Voennaia Tipografiia, 1890.

Duiker, William J. *Cultures in Collision: The Boxer Rebellion*. San Rafael, Calif.: Presidio Press, 1978.

Duus, Peter. *The Abacus and the Sword: The Japanese Penetration of Korea, 1895–1910*. Berkeley: University of California Press, 1995.

Duyvendak, J. J. L., ed. *The Diary of His Excellency Ching-shan*. Leiden: E. J. Brill, 1924.

Eagleton, Terry. *Ideology: An Introduction*. London: Verson, 1991.

Edkins, Joseph. *The Revenue and Taxation of the Chinese Empire*. Shanghai: Presbyterian Mission Press, 1903.

Edwards, E. W. *British Diplomacy and Finance in China, 1895–1914*. Oxford: Oxford University Press, 1987.

Edwards, Michael. *Playing the Great Game: A Victorian Cold War*. London: Hamish Hamilton, 1975.

Elridge, C. C. *England's Mission: The Imperial Idea in the Age of Gladstone and Disraeli*. Chapel Hill: University of North Carolina Press, 1974.

Emerson, Caryl. *Boris Godunov: Transpositions of a Russian Theme*. Bloomington: Indiana University Press, 1986.

Emets, Valentin Alekseevich. "Mekhanizm priniatiia vneshnepoliticheskikh reshenii v Rossii do i v period pervoi mirovoi voiny." In *Pervaia mirovaia voina: Diskussionye problemy istorii*, edited by Iu. A. Pisarev and V. L. Malkov, 57–71. Moscow: Nauka, 1994.

Enselme, Hyppolite. *A Travers la Mandchourie: Le chemin de fer de l'est chinois*. Paris: J. Rueff, 1904.

Epanchin, Nikolai Aleseevich. *Na sluzhbe trekh imperatorov*. Moscow: Nashe Nasledie, 1996.

Erdmann, Ada von. "Nikolaj Karlovic Giers, russischer Außenminister 1882–1895: Eine politische Biographie." *Zeitschrift für Osteuropäische Geschichte* 9 (1935): 481–540.

Ermakova, T. V. "Issledovaniia buddizma v Rossii (konets XIX–nachalo XX v.)." *Vostok*, no. 5 (1995): 139–48.

Esherick, Joseph W. *The Origins of the Boxer Uprising.* Berkeley: University of California Press, 1987.

Esin, B. I. "Russkaia legalnaia pressa kontsa XIX–nachala XX veka." In *Iz istorii russkoi zhurnalistiki kontsa XIX–nachala XX v.* Moscow: Moskovskii Universitet, 1973.

Esthus, Raymond A. "Nicholas II and the Russo-Japanese War." *Russian Review* 40, no. 4 (October 1981): 396–411.

Estournelles de Constant, Paul d'. "Le péril prochain: l'Europe et ses rivaux." *Revue des Deux Mondes* 134, no. 3 (Apr. 1, 1896): 651–86.

Evtuhov, Catherine. *The Cross and the Sickle: Sergei Bulgakov and the Fate of Russian Religious Philosophy.* Ithaca, N.Y.: Cornell University Press, 1997.

Evtuhov, Catherine, et al., eds. *Kazan, Moscow, St. Petersburg: Multiple Faces of the Russian Empire.* Moscow: O.G.I., 1997.

Fabritskii, S. S. *Iz proshlago: Vospominaniia fligel-adiutanta gosudaria Imperatora Nikolaia II.* Berlin: Zinaburg, 1926.

Fairbank, John K., ed. *The Cambridge History of China.* Vol. 11, pt. 2. Cambridge: Cambridge University Press, 1980.

———. *The Chinese World Order: Traditional China's Foreign Relations.* Cambridge, Mass.: Harvard University Press, 1968.

Faligot, Roger. *Histoire mondiale du renseignement.* Vol. 1. Paris: R. Laffont, 1994.

Fay, Sidney. "The Kaiser's Secret Negotiations with the Tsar." *American Historical Review* 24, no. 1 (October 1918): 48–72.

Fedorov, Mikhail Pavlovich. *Sopernichestvo torgovykh interesov na Vostoke.* St. Petersburg: N. Ia. Stoikovoi, 1903.

Fedorov, Nikolai Fedorovich. *Filosofiia obshchevo dela.* 2 vols. Vernyi: Tip. Semirechensk-ago obl., 1906.

———. *Sobranie sochineniia v chetyrekh tomakh.* 2 vols. Moscow: Progress, 1995.

Ferenczi, Caspar. *Außenpolitik und Öffentlishkeit in Rußland 1906–1912.* Hussum: Matthiesen Verlag, 1982.

Ferro, Marc. *Nicholas II: The Last of the Tsars.* London: Penguin, 1991.

Feuerwerker, Albert. *Rebellion in Nineteenth-Century China.* Ann Arbor: University of Michigan Press, 1975.

Fieldhouse, David K. *The Colonial Empires: A Comparative Survey from the Eighteenth Century.* Houndmills: Macmillan, 1982.

———. "Imperialism: An Historiographical Revision," *Economic History Review,* 2d ser., 14, no. 2 (1961): 187–209.

Filchner, Wilhelm. *Sturm über Asien.* Berlin: Neufeld & Heinius, 1924.

Fischer, Raymond H. *The Russian Fur Trade, 1550–1700.* Berkeley: University of California Press, 1943.

Fleming, Peter. *Bayonets to Lhasa: The First Full Account of the British Invasion of Tibet in 1904.* New York: Harper, 1961.

———. *The Siege at Peking.* New York: Harper & Brothers, 1959.

Ford, Harold Perry. "Russian Far Eastern Diplomacy: Count Witte and the Penetration of China, 1895–1904." Ph.D. diss., University of Chicago, 1950.

Foster, John W. *Diplomatic Memoirs.* 2 vols. Boston: Houghton Mifflin, 1909.

Foust, Clifford M. *Muscovite and Mandarin: Russia's Trade with China and Its Setting, 1727–1805.* Chapel Hill: University of North Carolina Press, 1969.

Fox, Martynna A. "The Eastern Question in Russian Politics: Interplay of Diplomacy, Opinion, and Interest, 1905–1917." Ph.D. diss., Yale University, 1993.

Franke, Otto. *Die Großmächte in Ostasien von 1894 bis 1914*. Brunswick: Verlag Georg Westermann, 1923.

Franklin, Anthony Lawrence. "The Chinese Response to British and Russian Encroachment in Northwestern China." Ph.D. diss., St. John's University, 1978.

Franzius, Georg. *Kiautschou: Deutschlands Erwerbung in Ostasien*. Berlin: Schall & Grund, 1901.

Friedjung, Heinrich. *Das Zeitalter des Imperialismus*. Vol. 1. Berlin: Neufeld & Henius, 1922.

Fuller, William C. *Civil-Military Conflict in Late Imperial Russia*. Princeton, N.J.: Princeton University Press, 1985.

———. *Strategy and Power in Russia, 1600–1914*. New York: Free Press, 1992.

Füllop-Miller, René. *Rasputin, the Holy Devil*. New York: Viking, 1928.

Galdanova, Galina Rinchinovna, et al. *Lamaizm v Buriatii XVIII-nachala XX veka*. Novosibirsk: Nauka, 1983.

Ganz, A. Harding. "The German Navy in the Far East and the Pacific: The Seizure of Kiaochow and After." In *Germany in the Pacific and Far East, 1870–1914*, edited by J. A. Moses and P. D. Kennedy, 115–36. St. Lucia: University of Queensland Press, 1977.

Garin, Nikolai Georgievskii. *Iz dnevnikov krugosvetnugo puteshestvlia (po Koree, Manchzhurii i Liadunskom poluostrovu)*. Moscow: Gos. izd-vo. Geograficheskoi literatury, 1950.

Gattrel, Peter. *The Tsarist Economy, 1850–1917*. London: B. T. Batsford, 1986.

Gaus, Christian, ed. *The German Emperor as Shown in His Public Utterances*. New York: Charles Scribner's Sons, 1915.

Gavrilenkov, Vasilii Mikhailovich. *Russkii puteshestvennik N. M. Przhevalskii*. Smolensk: Moskovskii rabochii, 1989.

Gavrilenkova, Evgeniia. "Chekhov i Przhevalskii." *Rabochii put*, Aug. 23, 1980, 3.

———. "Spletnia: Przhevalskii i Stalin. Pochemu sviazyvaiut eti imena?" *Rabochekretstiabnskii korrespondent*, no. 2 (1990): 26–29.

Geishtor, Iosif Emilevich. *Torgovlia Rossii na Dalnem Vostoke*. St. Petersburg: P. O. Iablonskii, 1903.

Geiss, Imanuel. *German Foreign Policy, 1871–1914*. Boston: Routledge & Kegan Paul, 1976.

George, Martin. *Mystische und religiöse Erfahrung im Denken Vladimir Solovevs*. Göttingen: Vandenhoeck & Ruprecht, 1988.

Georgievskii, Sergei Mikhailovich. *Vazhnost izucheniia Kitaia*. St. Petersburg, I. N. Skorokhodova, 1890.

Geraci, Robert Paul. "Window on the East: Ethnography, Orthodoxy and Russian Nationality in Kazan, 1870–1914." Ph.D. diss., University of California at Berkeley, 1995.

Gérard, Auguste. *Ma mission en Chine, 1894–1897*. Paris: Plon, 1918.

———. *Memoires d'Auguste Gérard*. Paris: Librairie Plon, 1928.

Gerrare, Wirt. *Greater Russia: The Continental Empire of the Old World*. New York: Macmillan, 1903.

Gerschenkron, Alexander. "Russia: Patterns and Problems of Economic Development, 1861–1958." In *Economic Backwardness in Historical Perspective*. Cambridge, Mass.: Harvard University Press, 1962.

Geyer, Dietrich. "Modern Imperialism? The Tsarist and Soviet Examples." In *Imperialism and After: Its Continuities and Discontinuities*, edited by W. J. Mommsen, 49–62. London: Alen & Unwin, 1986.

———. *Russian Imperialism: The Interaction of Domestic and Foreign Policy, 1860–1914*. New Haven, Conn.: Yale University Press, 1987.

———, ed. *Wirtschaft und Gesellschaft im vorrevolutionären Rußland*. Cologne: Kiepenheuer & Witsch, 1975.

Giles, Lancelot. *The Siege of the Peking Legations: A Diary,* edited by L. R. Marchant. Nedlands: University of Western Australia Press, 1970.

Gillard, David. *The Struggle for Asia, 1828–1914: A Study in British and Russian Imperialism.* London: Methuen, 1977.

Gillès, Daniel. *Chekhov: Observer without Illusion.* New York: Funk & Wagnalls, 1968.

Girardet, Raoul. *L'idée colonial en France de 1871 à 1962.* Paris: La Table Ronde, 1972.

Girault, René. *Emprunts russes et investissements français en Russie 1887–1914.* Paris: Librairie Armand Colin, 1973.

———. "Les relations economiques et financieres entre la France et la Russie de 1887 à 1914." Ph.D. diss., Université de Paris 1, 1971.

Glatfelter, Ralph Edward. "Russia in China: The Russian Reaction to the Boxer Rebellion." Ph.D. diss., Indiana University, 1975.

Glinskii, Boris Borisovich, ed. *Prolog Russko-Iaponskoi voiny: Materialy iz arkhiva Grafa S. Iu. Vitte.* Petrograd: Brokgauz-Efron, 1916.

Godlewska, Anne, and Neil Smith, eds. *Geography and Empire.* Oxford: Blackwell, 1994.

Gollwitzer, Heinz. *Europe in the Age of Imperialism, 1880–1914.* New York: W. W. Norton, 1969.

———. *Die Gelbe Gefahr.* Göttingen: Vandenhoeck & Ruprecht, 1962.

———. *Geschichte des weltpolitischen Denkens.* Vol. 1. Göttingen: Vandenhoeck & Ruprecht, 1972.

Golovachev, Petr Mikhailovich. *Rossiia na Dalnem Vostoke.* St. Petersburg: E. D. Kuskovoi, 1904.

Golovnin, Vasilii Mikhailovich. *Japan and the Japanese: Comprising the Narrative of a Captivity in Japan.* 2 vols. London: Colburn, 1853.

Golowin, K. *Russlands Finanzpolitik und die Aufgaben der Zukunft.* Translated by M. Kolossowski. Leipzig: Otto Wigand, 1900.

Gordin, Ia. "Chto uvleklo Rossiiu na Kavkaz?" *Zvezda,* no. 10 (1997): 94–111.

Gourvitch, Evgenia. *Wladimir Solowjow, der Mensch.* Hersbruck: H. J. Windelberg, 1986.

Grand-Charteret, Jean. *Nicolas ange de la Paix, empereur du knout.* Paris: Louis Michaud, 1906.

Graudenz, Karlheinz. *Die deutschen Kolonien.* Munich: Südwest Verlag, 1982.

Gray, Camilla. *The Russian Experiment in Art, 1863–1922.* London: Thames and Hudson, 1986.

Gray, Jack. *Rebellions and Revolutions: China from the 1800s to the 1980s.* Oxford: Oxford University Press, 1990.

Great Britain. Historical Section of the Committee of Imperial Defence. *Official History (Naval and Military) of the Russo-Japanese War.* 3 vols. London: His Majesty's Stationery Office, 1910–1920.

Great Britain. Naval Intelligence Division. *A Handbook of Siberia and Arctic Russia.* London: His Majesty's Stationery Office, n.d.

Grebenshchikov, Igor. "N. M. Przevalskij und N. N. Miklukho-Maklaj (Klassik und Romantik in der russischen geographischer Forschung)." *Forschungen und Fortschritte* 28, no. 3 (March 1954): 72–78.

Green, Martin. *Dreams of Adventure, Deeds of Empire.* London: Routledge & Kegan Paul, 1980.

Greenfield, Liah. *Nationalism: Five Roads to Modernity.* Cambridge, Mass.: Harvard University Press, 1992.

Gregory, Paul. *Before Command: An Economic History of Russia from the Emancipation to the First Five-Year Plan.* Princeton, N.J.: Princeton University Press, 1994.

Grenard, F. "L'Angleterre et la Russie au Tibet." *Bulletin du comité de l'Asie française* 7, no. 79 (October 1907): 375–83.

Grigoriev, Vasilli Vasilevich. *Rossiia i Aziia.* St. Petersburg: Tip. brat. Panteleevich, 1878.

Grimm, Claus. "Graf Witte und die deutsche Politik." Inaugural diss., Albert-Ludwig-Universität zu Freiburg, 1930.

Grünig, Irene. *Die russische öffentliche Meinung und ihre Stellung zu den Großmächten 1878–1894.* Berlin: Ost-Europa Verlag, 1929.

Grunwald, Constantin de. *Le Tsar Nicolas II.* Paris: Berger-Levrault, 1965.

———. *Trois siècles de diplomatie russe.* Paris: Carlmann-Lévy, 1945.

Grünwedel, Albert. *Mythologie du Bouddhisme en Tibet er Mongolie basée sur la collection lamaïque du Prince Ukhtomsky.* Leipzig: F. A. Brockhaus, 1900.

Grishinkii, A. S., and V. P. Nikolskii, eds. *Istoriia russkoi armii i flota.* Vols. 13–15. Moscow: Obrazovanie, 1911.

Guillen, Pierre. *L'Expansion 1881–1898.* Paris: Imprimerie nationale, 1984.

Gurko, Vladimir Iosifovich. *Features and Figures of the Past: Government and Opinion in the Reign of Nicholas II.* Stanford, Calif.: Stanford University Press, 1939.

Guroff, Gregory. "The State and Industrialization in Russian Economic Thought, 1909–1914." Ph.D. diss., Princeton University, 1970.

Gusev, Boris. "Moi ded Zhamsaran Badmaev," in *Doktor Badmaev: Tibetskaia meditsina, tsarskii dvor, sovetskaia vlast.* Moscow: Russkaia kniga, 1995.

———. "Zhamsaran i ego doch." In *Vykhod iz okruzheniia.* Leningrad: Sovetskii pisatel, 1989.

Guzin, A. S. "Tailandskii vopros na rubezhe XIX i XX vv. i pozitsiia Rossii." In *Vzaimot-nosheniia narodov Rossii, Sibirii i stran Vostoka: Istoriia i sovremennost.* Irkutsk: Irkutskii gos. ped. institut, 1995.

Hagerman, Herbert J. *Letters of a Young Diplomat.* Santa Fe: Rydal Press, 1937.

Halde, P. J. B. Du. *Description géographique, historique, chronologique, politique et physique de l'Empire de la Chine et de la Tartarie Chinoise.* Vol. 4. Paris: P. G. Lemercier, 1735.

Hallgarten, Georg W. F. *Imperialismus vor 1914.* 2 vols. Munich: Beck, 1963.

Halperin, Charles J. *Russia and the Golden Horde: The Mongol Impact on Medieval Russian History.* Bloomington: Indiana University Press, 1985.

———. "Russia and the Steppe: George Vernadsky and Eurasianism." *Forschungen zur Ost–europäische Geschichte* 36 (1985): 55–194.

Hambly, Gavin, ed. *Zentralasien.* Frankfurt a/M: Fischer, 1966.

Hamilton, Angus. *Korea.* Charles Scribner's Sons, 1904.

Hardinge, Charles. *Old Diplomacy: The Reminiscences of Lord Hardinge of Penhurst.* London: John Murray, 1947.

Hart, B. H. Liddel. "John Bloch: A Neglected Prophet." *Military Review* 37, no. 3 (June 1957): 31.

Hart, Robert. *The I. G. in Peking: Letters of Robert Hart Chinese Maritime Customs, 1868–1907.* 2 vols. Cambridge, Mass.: Harvard University Press, 1975.

———. "The Peking Legations." *Cosmopolitan* 30, no. 2 (December 1900): 136.

———. *"These from the Land of Sinim": Essays on the Chinese Question.* London: Chapman Hall, 1901.

Hauner, Milan. *What is Asia to Us? Russia's Asian Heartland Yesterday and Today.* Boston: Unwyn Hyman, 1990.

Hauser, Oswald. *Deutschland und der English-Russische Gegensatz, 1900–1914.* Berlin: Musterschmidt Verlag, 1958.

Häusler, Eugen. *Der Kaufmann in der russischen Literatur.* Königsberg: Gräfe und Unzer, 1935.

Hearn, Lafcadio. "China and the Western World: A Retrospect and a Prospect." *Atlantic Monthly* 77, no. 462 (April 1896): 450–64.

Hedin, Sven. *General Prschewalski in Innerasien.* Leipzig: F. A. Brockhaus, 1928.

Heldt, Barbara. "'Japanese' in Russian Literature: Transforming Identities." In *A Hidden Fire: Russian and Japanese Cultural Encounters,* edited by J. Thomas Rimer, 170–83. Stanford, Calif.: Stanford University Press, 1995.

Heresch, Elisabeth. *Rasputin: Das Geheimnis seiner Macht.* Munich: Langen Müller, 1995.

Heretz, Leonid. "Russian Apocalypse, 1891–1917: Popular Perceptions of Events from the Year of Famine and Cholera to the Fall of the Tsar." Ph.D. diss., Harvard University, 1993.

Heyking, Elisabeth von. *Tagebücher aus vier Weltteilen 1886–1904.* Leipzig: Koehler & Amelang, 1926.

Hoare, J. E. "Komundo-Port Hamilton." *Asian Affairs* 17, pt. 3 (October 1986): 298–308.

Hoetzsch, Otto. *Die weltpolitische Kraftverteilung seit den Pariser Friedensschlußen.* Leipzig: Treubner, 1933.

——. *Rußland in Asien: Geschichte einer Expansion.* Stuttgart: Deutsche Verlags-Anstallt, 1966.

Hohenlohe-Schillingsfürst, Fürst Chlodwig zu. *Denkwürdigkeiten der Reichskanzlerzeit.* Stuttgart: Deutsche Verlags-Anstalt, 1931.

Holstein, Friedrich von. *The Holstein Papers: The Memoirs, Diaries, and Correspondence of Friedrich von Holstein.* Edited by Norman Rich and M. H. Fisher. 4 vols. New York: Cambridge University Press, 1955.

Hopkirk, Peter. *The Great Game: On Secret Service in High Asia.* London: John Murray, 1990.

——. *Setting the East Ablaze: Lenin's Dream of an Empire in Asia.* New York: W. W. Norton, 1984.

——. *Trespassers on the Roof of the World: The Race for Lhasa.* London: John Murray, 1982.

Hosie, Alexander. *Manchuria: Its People, Resources, and Recent History.* London: Methuen, 1904.

Hosking, Geoffrey. *Russia: People and Empire, 1552–1917.* Cambridge, Mass.: Harvard University Press, 1997.

Hou, C. M. *Foreign Investment and Economic Development in China, 1840–1937.* Cambridge, Mass.: Harvard University Press, 1965.

Howe, Susanne. *Novels of Empire.* New York: Columbia University Press, 1949.

Hsie, T. A. "Demons in Paradise: The Chinese Images of Russia." *Annals of the American Academy of Political and Social Science* 349 (September 1963): 27–37.

Hsü, Immanuel C. Y. "The Development of the Chinese Foreign Office in the Ch'ing Period," in *The Times Survey of Foreign Ministries of the World,* edited by Zara Steiner, 119–33. London: Times Books, 1982.

——. "The Great Policy Debate in China, 1874: Maritime Defense vs. Frontier Defense." *Harvard Journal of Asiatic Studies* 25 (1965): 212–28.

——. *The Ili Crisis.* Oxford: Oxford University Press, 1965.

——. *The Rise of Modern China.* Oxford: Oxford University Press, 1983.

——. "Russia's Special Position in China during the Early Ch'ing Period," *Slavic Review* 23, no. 4 (1964): 688–700.

Hsü Shushi. *China and Her Political Entity.* New York: Oxford University Press, 1926.

Huenemann, Ralph William. *The Dragon and the Iron Horse: The Economics of Railroads in China, 1876–1937.* Cambridge, Mass.: Harvard University Press, 1984.

Hummel, Arthur W., ed. *Eminent Chinese of the Ch'ing Period.* Vol. 1. Washington, D.C.: U.S. Government Printing Office, 1943.

Hunczak, Taras, ed. *Russian Imperialism.* New Brunswick, N.J.: Rutgers University Press, 1974.

Hunt, Michael H. *Frontier Defense and the Open Door: Manchuria in Chinese-American Relations, 1895–1911.* New Haven, Conn.: Yale University Press, 1973.

——. *Ideology and U.S. Foreign Policy.* New Haven, Conn.: Yale University Press, 1987.

Hyde, Francis E. *Far Eastern Trade, 1860–1914.* London: Adam & Charles Black, 1973.

Iadrintsev, Nikolai Mikhailovich. *Sibir kak koloniia.* St. Petersburg: I. M. Sibiriakov, 1892.

Ianchevetskii, Dmitrii. *Groza s Vostoka: Zadachi Rossii, Zadachi Iaponii na Dalnem Vostoke.* Revel: Revelskie Izvestiia, 1907.

——. *U sten nedvizhnago Kitaia.* St. Petersburg: Tovarishchestvo Khudozhestvennoi pechati, 1903.

Ignatev, Anatolii Venediktovich. *Russko-angliiskie otnosheniia nakanune pervoi mirovoi voiny.* Moscow: Mezhdunarodnye otnosheniia, 1962.

——. *S. Iu. Vitte: Diplomat.* Moscow: Mezhdunarodnye otnosheniia, 1989.

Ignatev, Anatolii Venediktovich, et al., eds. *Rossiiskaia diplomatiia v protretakh.* Moscow: Mezhdunarodnye otnosheniia, 1992.

Ignatev, Nikolai Pavlovich. *Ochetnaia zapiska.* St. Petersburg: V. V. Komarov, 1895.

Irmer, Arthur Julius. "Die Erwerbung von Kiautschou, 1894–1898." Inaugural diss., Rheinischen Friedrich-Wilhelm Universität zu Bonn, 1930.

Iriye, Akira. *Pacific Estrangement: Japanese and American Expansion, 1897–1911.* Cambrige, Mass.: Harvard University Press, 1972.

——. "Public Opinion and Foreign Policy: The Case of Late Ch'ing China." In *Approaches to Modern Chinese History,* edited by Albert Feuerwerker et al., 216–38. Berkeley: University of California Press, 1967.

Isachenko, Anatolii Grigorevich, ed. *Russkoe Geograficheskoe Obshchestvo: 150 let.* Moscow: Progress, 1995.

Ismail-Zade, D. I. "Illarion Ivanovich Vorontsov-Dashkov." In *Istoricheskie siluety,* edited by S. V. Tiutiukin, 20–62. Moscow: Nauka, 1991.

Iswolsky, Helene. *No Time to Grieve: An Autobiographical Journey.* Philadelphia: Winchell, 1985.

Iutkevich, Sergei. *Sobranie Sochinenii.* Vol. 2. Moscow: Iskusstvo, 1991.

Iuzefovich, Leonid. *Samoderzhets pustyni: Fenomen sudby barona R. F. Ungern-Shterna.* Moscow: Ellis Luck, 1993.

Ivanov, Georgii. *Kniga o poslednem tsarstvovanii.* Orange, Conn.: Antiquary, 1990.

Izvolskii, A. P. *Mémoires de Alexandre Iswolsky: Ancien ambassadeur de Russie a Paris.* Paris: Payot, 1923.

Jansen, Marius B. *Japan and China: From War to Peace, 1894–1972.* Chicago: Rand McNally, 1975.

Jelavich, Barbara. *A Century of Russian Foreign Policy.* Philadelphia: Lippincott, 1964.

——. "Giers and the Politics of Russian Moderation." In *New Perspectives in Modern Russian History,* edited by Robert B. McKean, 24–42. Houndmills: Macmillan, 1992.

Jelavich, Charles, and Barbara Jelavich, eds. *Russia in the East, 1876–1880.* Leiden: E. J. Brill, 1959.

Jeshurun, Chandran. *The Contests for Siam, 1889–1902.* Kuala Lumpur: Penerbit University Kebangsaan Malaysia, 1977.

Joll, James. "1914: The Unspoken Assumptions." In *The Origins of the First World War: Great Power Rivalry and German War Aims,* edited by Hans-Joachim Wolfgang Koch, 309–16. New York: Taplinger, 1972.

Johnson, K. Paul. *Initiates of Theosophical Masters.* New York: State University of New York Press, 1995.

Judge, Edward H. *Plehve: Repression and Reform in Imperial Russia, 1902–1904.* Syracuse, N.Y.: Syracuse University Press, 1983.

Kabuzan, Vladimir Maksimovich. *Dalnevostochnyi krai v XVII-nachale XX vv.* Moscow: Nauka, 1985.

Kachurin, Pamela Jill. "'Off with their Heads!' Decapitation and Display in the Works of V. V. Vereshchagin." Unpublished paper, American Association for the Advancement of Slavic Studies, 1997.

Kalesnik, Stanislav Vikentevich. *Geograficheskoe Obshchestvo za 125 let.* Leningrad: Nauka, 1970.

Kaliuzhnaia, Nina Mikhailovna. "O kharaktere tainogo soiuza 'Ikhetuan.'" In *Tainye obshchestva v starom Pekine,* edited by V. P. Iliushechkin, 85–107. Moscow: Nauka, 1970.

Kalmykow, Andrew D. *Memoirs of a Russian Diplomat: Outposts of the Empire, 1893–1917.* New Haven, Conn.: Yale University Press, 1971.

Kang Yuwei. "The Reform of China and the Revolution of 1898." *Contemporary Review* 76 (August 1899): 180–98.

Kappeler, Andreas. *Russland als Vielvölkerreich: Entstehung, Geschichte, Zerfall.* Munich: C. H. Beck, 1993.

Karataev, Nikolai Mikhailovich. *Nikolai Mikhailovich Przhevalskii: Pervyi issledovatel prirody Tsentralnoi Azii.* Moscow: Akademiia Nauk SSSR, 1948.

Kariov, E. A., ed. *Russkaia literatura i Vostok.* Tashkent: Fan, 1988.

Karlinsky, Simon. "Gay Life before the Soviets." *Advocate,* Apr. 1, 1982, 31–34.

Kashani-Sabet, Firoozeh. "Charting the Globe: The Emergence of Geographical Societies in Europe." Unpublished conference paper, Yale University, 1996.

Katkov, George, and Michael Futrell. "Russian Foreign Policy 1880–1914." In *Russia Enters the Twentieth Century,* edited by Erwin Oberländer et al., 9–33. New York: Schocken, 1971.

Kazemzadeh, Firuz. *Russia and Britain in Persia, 1864–1914.* New Haven, Conn.: Yale University Press, 1968.

Kelly, John S. *A Forgotten Conference: The Negotiations at Peking, 1900–1901.* Geneva: Librairie Droz, 1963.

Kennan, George F. *The Decline of Bismarck's European Order: Franco-Russian Relations, 1875–1890.* Princeton, N.J.: Princeton University Press, 1979.

——. *The Fateful Alliance.* New York: Pantheon Books, 1984.

Kennedy, Paul M. *The Rise and Fall of British Naval Mastery.* London: Ashfield Press, 1986.

——. *The Rise and Fall of the Great Powers: Economic Change and Military Conflict from 1500 to 2000.* New York: Vintage Books, 1989.

——. *The Rise of the Anglo-German Antagonism, 1860–1914.* London: George Allen & Unwin, 1980.

——. "The Theory and Practice of Imperialism." *Historical Journal* 20, no. 3 (September 1977): 761–69.

Kent, Percy H. *Railway Enterprise in China.* London: Edward Arnold, 1908.

Khalfin, N. A. *Prisoedinenie Rossii v Srednei Azii.* Moscow: Nauka, 1975.

Khan, Mohammad Anwar. *England, Russia, and Central Asia.* Peshawar: University Book Agency, 1963.

Khisamutdinov, Amir. *The Russian Far East: Historical Essays.* Honolulu: Center for Russia in Asia, 1993.

Khodarkovsky, Michael. *Where Two Worlds Met: The Russian State and the Kalmyk Nomads, 1600–1771.* Ithaca, N.Y.: Cornell University Press, 1992.

Khudozhestvennyi albom "Mandzhuriia" (Russko-Iaponskaia voina). St. Petersburg: A. V. Martynov, 1906.

Kim, C. I. Eugene, and Han-kyo Kim. *Korea and the Politics of Imperialism, 1876–1910.*

Berkeley: University of California Press, 1967.

Kim, G. F., and P. M. Shastitko, eds. *Istoriia otechestvennogo vostokovedeniia do serediny XIX veka*. Moscow: Nauka, 1990.

Kiniapina, Nina Stepanovna. *Vneshniaia politika Rossii vtoroi polovine XIX veka*. Moscow: Vysshaia shkola, 1974.

Kirby, E. Stuart. *Russian Studies of China: Progress and Problems of Soviet Sinology*. London: Macmillan, 1975.

Kiuner, Nikolai Vasilevich. *Ocherki noveishei politicheskoi istorii Kitaia*. Khabarovsk: Knizhnoe delo, 1927.

———. *Snosheniia Rossii s Dalnim Vostokom na protiazhenii tsarstvovaniia doma Romanovykh*. Vladivostok: Vostochnyi Institut, 1914.

Klein, Alfred. "Der Einfluss des Grafen Witte auf die deutsch-russischen Beziehungen." Inaugural diss., Westfälischen Wilhelms-Universität zu Münster, 1931.

Kliashtornyi, S. G., and A. I. Kolesnikov. *Vostochnyi Turkestan glazami russkikh puteshestvennikov*. Alma Ata: Nauka, 1988.

Klug, Ekkehart. "Das 'asiatische' Russland: Über die Entstehung eines europäischen Vorurteils." *Historische Zeitschrift* 245 (1987): 265–89.

Kluge, Rolf-Dieter. *Westeuropa und Rußland im Weltbilt Aleksandr Bloks*. Munich: Verlag Otto Sagner, 1967

Knight, Nathaniel. "Constructing the Science of Nationality: Ethnography in Mid-Nineteenth-Century Russia." Ph.D. diss., Columbia University, 1995.

Koltsova, N. K. *Kolonizatsionno-pereselencheskaia politika tsarizma v Iuzhno-Ussuriiskom krae v kontse XIX–nachale XX vv*. Tomsk: Geograficheskoe obshchestvo, 1952.

Koot, John Theodore. "The Asiatic Department of the Russian Foreign Ministry and the Formation of Policy toward the Non-Western World, 1881–1894." Ph.D. diss., Harvard University, 1980.

Korelin, A. P., and S. A. Stepanov. *S. Iu. Vitte: Finansist, politik, diplomat*. Moscow: Terra, 1998.

Korostovets, Ivan Iakovlevich. *Rossiia na Dalnem Vostoke*. Peking: Vostochnoe Prosveshchenie, 1922.

———. *Kitaitsy i ikh tsivilizatsiia*. St. Petersburg: M. M. Lederle, 1896.

———. *Pre-War Diplomacy: The Russo-Japanese Problem*. London: British Periodicals, 1920.

———. "Russkaia dukhovnaia missiia v Pekine." *Russkii Arkhiv* 31, no. 9 (1893): 57–86.

———. *Von Cinggis Khan zur Sowjetrepublik: Eine kurze Geschichte der Mongolei unter besonderer Berücksichtigung der neuesten Zeit*. Berlin: Walter de Gruyter, 1926.

Korostowetz, Wladimir. *Graf Witte: Der Steuerman in der Not*. Translated by Heinz Stratz. Berlin: Bruckenverlag, 1929.

Korsakov, Vladimir Vikentevich. *Pekinskiia sobytiia: Lichnyia vospominaniia uchastnika ob osade v Pekine*. St. Petersburg: A. S. Suvorin, 1901.

———. *Piat let v Pekine*. St. Petersburg, Trud, 1902.

———. *V prosnuvshemsia Kitae*. Moscow: S. P. Iakovlev, 1911.

———. *V starom Pekine*. St. Petersburg: Trud, 1904.

Kozlov, Innokenti Varfolomeevich. *Velikii puteshestvennik*. Moscow: Mysl, 1985.

Kozlov, Petr Kuzmich. "Nikolai Mikhailovich Przhevalskii." *Russkaia Starina*, 149 (January 1912): 144–59.

———. *Nikolai Mikhailovich Przhevalskii: Pervyi izsledovatel prirody Tsentralnoi Azii*. St. Petersburg: N. Ia. Stokovaia, 1913.

Kozlova, Marina Georgievna. *Rossiia i strany Iugo-Vostochnoi Azii*. Moscow: Nauka, 1986.

Krasnov, P. N. *Borba s Kitaem*. St. Petersburg: Russkoe imenie, 1901.

Krause, Alexis. *Russia in Asia*. London: Grant Richards, 1899.

Kravchenko, Nikolai Ivanovich. *V Kitae! Putevye zametki nabroski khudozhnika.* St. Petersburg: Tovarishchestvo P. Golitke i A. Viborg, 1904.

Krenistyn, N. V. *Polet russkogo orla v Indiiu.* Moscow: Obshestvo rasprostraneniia poleznykh knig, 1903.

Krivchenko, Vasilii Silovich. *Puteshestvie Ego Imperatorskago Vysochestva Naslednika Tsesarevicha na Vostok ot Gatchiny do Bombeia.* St. Petersburg: Tip. Min. Vnutrennykh Del, 1891.

Krupinski, K. *Rußland und Japan: Ihre Beziehungen bis zum Frieden von Portsmouth.* Königsberg: Ost-Europa Verlag, 1940.

Krylov, Ivan Andreevich. *Krylov's Fables.* Translated by Bernard Pares. Westport, Conn.: Hyperion, 1977.

Kuleshov, Nikolai Stepanovich. "Agvan Dorjiev: The Dalai Lama's Ambassador." *Asian Affairs* 79 (February 1992): 20–31.

———. *Rossiia i Tibet v nachale XX veka.* Moscow: Nauka, 1992.

Kuo Heng-yü. *China und die "Barbaren": Eine geistesgeschichtliche Standortbestimmung.* Pfullingen: Verlang Günther Neske, 1967.

Kuo Sung-Ping. "Chinese Reaction to Foreign Encroachment with Special Reference to the First Sino-Japanese War and Its Immediate Aftermath." Ph.D. diss., Columbia University, 1954.

Kuropatkin, Aleksei Nikolaevich. *Deistviia otriadov generala Skobeleva v Russko-Turetskoiu voiny 1877–78 godov: Lovcha i Plevna.* St. Petersburg: Voennaia Tipografiia Glavnogo Shtaba, 1885.

———. "Iaponskie dnevniki A. N. Kuropatkina." *Rossiiskii Arkhiv,* no. 6 (1994): 393–444.

———. "Iz vospominanii generala A. N. Kuropatkina 1867–1882 gg." *Istoricheskii Arkhiv,* no. 4 (1994): 185–95.

———. *Kashgariia: Istoriko-geograficheskii ocherk strany, eia voennyia sily, promyshlennost i torgovlia.* St. Petersburg: Imperatorskoe Russkoe Geograficheskoe Obshchestvo, 1879.

———. *Lovcha, Plevna i Sheinovo: Iz istorii Russko-Turetskoi voiny.* St. Petersburg: V. A. Poletika, 1881.

———. "Ocherk dvizheniia russkikh voisk v Sredniuiu Aziiu." In *Voennyia besedy ispolnennya v shtabe voisk gvardii i peterburgskago voennago okruga v 1885–1887 gg.* Vol. 1. St. Petersburg: Voisk Gvardiia, 1887.

———. "Ocherk voennykh deistvii v Srednei Azii s 1839 do 1836." In G. A. Leer, ed., *Obzor voin Rossii ot Petra Velikogo do nashikh dnei.* Vol. 2, pt. 3. St. Petersburg: Izd-vo. Glav. upr. voenn-ucheb. zavedenii, 1889.

———. *Otchet o sluzhebnoi poezdke Voennago Ministra v Turkestanskii voennyi okrug v 1901 godu.* St. Petersburg: Voennaia tipografiia, 1902.

———. *Otchet voennago ministra po poezdke na Dalnem Vostoke v 1903 godu.* 3 vols. St. Petersburg: Voennaia tipografiia, 1903.

———. "Razvedivatelnaia missiia v Turtsiu." *Voenno-Istoricheskii Zhurnal,* no. 4 (1994): 68–77.

———. *Russko-kitaiskii vopros.* St. Petersburg: A. S. Suvorin.

———. *The Russian Army and the Japanese War.* Translated by A. B. Lindsay. 2 vols. New York: E. P. Dutton, 1909.

———. *Russko-Iaponskaia voina: Iz dnevnikov A. N. Kuropatkina i N. P. Linevicha.* Edited by M. N. Pokrovskii. Leningrad: Gosudarstvennoe Izdatelstvo., 1925.

———. *Vsepoddanneishii otchet Generala-Leitenanta Kuropatkina o poezdke v Teregane v 1895 godu.* St. Petersburg, ca. 1896.

———. *Zadachi Russkoi armii.* Vol. 3. St. Petersburg: V. A. Berezovskii, 1910.

———. *Zavoevanie turkmenii.* St. Petersburg: V. Berezovskii, 1899.

Kushakov, Konstantin Porfirevich. *Iuzhno-manchzhurskie besporiadki v 1900 godu*. Ashkabad: Ashkabadskaia obshchina Zakaspiiskogo otdela Rossiiskogo obshchestva Krasnogo Kresta, 1902.

Kutakov, Leonid Nikolaevich. *Rossiia i Iaponiia*. Moscow: Nauka, 1988.

Kutuzov, Graf Peter. *Zhelatelniia osnovy russko-kitaiskago soglasheniia*. St. Petersburg: V. P. Meshcherskii, 1900.

Kwong, S. K. *A Mosaic of the Hundred Days: Personalities, Politics, and Ideas of 1898*. Cambridge, Mass.: Harvard University Press, 1984.

Lamb, Alistair. *Asian Frontiers: Studies in a Continuing Problem*. New York: Praeger, 1968.

———. *British India and Tibet, 1766–1910*. London: Routledge & Kegan Paul, 1986.

———. "Some Notes on Russian Intrigue in Tibet." *Journal of the Royal Central Asian Society* 46, no. 1 (January 1959): 46–65.

Lambert, R. S., ed. *Grand Tour: A Journey in the Tracks of the Age of Aristocracy*. New York: E. P. Dutton, 1937.

Lamsdorf, Vladimir Nikolaevich. *Dnevnik 1886–1890*. Moscow: Gosudarstvennoe Izdatelstvo, 1926.

———. *Dnevnik 1891–1892*. Moscow: Academia, 1934.

———. *Dnevnik 1894–1896*. Moscow: Mezhdunarodnye otnosheniia, 1991.

Landgraf, Dieter. *Amur, Ussuri, Sachalin: 1847–1917*. Neuried: Hieronymus, 1989.

Landon, Perceval. *The Opening of Tibet: An Account of Lhasa and the Country and People of Central Tibet and of the Progress of the Mission Sent There by the English Government in the Year 1903–4*. New York: Doubleday, Page, 1906.

Landor, A. Henry Savage. *China and the Allies*. 2 vols. New York: Charles Scribner's Sons, 1901.

Laney, Frank M. "The Military Implementation of the Franco-Russian Alliance, 1890–1914." Ph.D. diss., University of Virginia, 1954.

Langer, William L. *The Diplomacy of Imperialism*. 2 vols. New York: Alfred A. Knopf, 1956.

———. *European Alliances and Alignments, 1871–1890*. New York: Alfred A. Knopf, 1931.

———. "The Origins of the Russo-Japanese War." In *Explorations in Crisis: Papers on International History*, edited by Charles E. and Elizabeth Schorske, 3–45. Cambridge, Mass.: Harvard University Press, 1969.

Lantzeff, George V., and Richard A. Pierce. *Eastward to Empire: Exploration and Conquest on the Russian Open Frontier to 1750*. Montreal: McGill-Queen's University Press, 1973.

Larenko, P. *Stradnye dni Port-Artura: Khronika voennykh sobytii i zhizni v osazhennoi kreposti s 26-go ianvaria 1904 g. do 9-e ianvariia 1905 g.* Vol. 1. St. Petersburg: Shreder, 1906.

L'Armée russe et ses chefs en 1888. Paris: Librairie Moderne, 1888.

Lattimore, Owen. *Inner Asian Frontiers of China*. Boston: Beacon Press, 1962.

———. *Manchuria: Cradle of Conflict*. New York: Macmillan, 1935.

———. *Pivot of Asia: Sinkiang and the Inner Asian Frontiers of China and Russia*. Boston: Little, Brown, 1950.

Laue, Theodore H. von. *Sergei Witte and the Industrialization of Russia*. New York: Columbia University Press, 1963.

———, ed. "Sergei Witte on the Industrialization of Russia" *Journal of Modern History* 26, no. 1 (March 1954): 60–74.

Lavrin, Janko. "Vladimir Solovev and Slavophilism." *Russian Review* 20, no. 1 (January 1961): 11–18.

Layton, Susan. *Russian Literature and Empire: Conquest of the Caucasus from Pushkin to Tolstoy*. Cambridge: Cambridge University Press, 1994.

Lebedev, V. T. *V Indiiu: Voenno-statisticheskii i strategicheskii ocherk*. St. Petersburg: Ti-pografiia A. A. Pokhorovshchikova, 1898.

Lederer, Ivo J., ed. *Russian Foreign Policy*. New Haven, Conn.: Yale University Press, 1962.

LeDonne, John P. *The Russian Empire and the World, 1700–1917: The Geopolitics of Expansion and Containment*. New York: Oxford University Press, 1997.

Lee, Chong-sik. *The Politics of Korean Nationalism*. Berkeley: University of California Press, 1963.

Lee, Ki-baik. *A New History of Korea*. Cambridge, Mass.: Harvard University Press, 1984.

Lee, Robert H. G. *The Manchurian Frontier in Ch'ing History*. Cambridge, Mass.: Harvard University Press, 1970.

Legras, Jules. "La Mandchourie russe." *Revue des Deux Mondes* 10 (July 1, 1902): 115–58.

———. "S. Y. Witte (Souvernirs personnels)." *La Vie des Peuples* 9 (January–April 1923): 812–25.

Lemann, Jean-Pierre. *The Image of Japan from Feudal Isolation to World Power, 1850–1905*. London: George Allen & Unwin, 1978.

Lensen, George Alexander. "The Attempt on the Life of Nicholas II in Japan." *Russian Review* 20, no. 3 (July 1961): 232–53.

———. *Balance of Intrigue: International Rivalry in Korea and Manchuria, 1884–1899*. 2 vols. Tallahasee: University Press of Florida, 1982.

———. *The Russian Push towards Japan: Russo-Japanese Relations, 1697–1875*. Princeton, N.J.: Princeton University Press, 1959.

———. *The Russo-Chinese War*. Tallahassee, Fl.: Diplomatic Press, 1967.

———, ed. *The d'Anethan Dispatches from Japan, 1894–1910: The Observations of Baron Albert d'Anethan, Belgian Minister Plenipotentiary and Dean of the Diplomatic Corps*. Tokyo: Sophia University Press, 1967.

———, ed. *Korea and Manchuria between Russia and Japan, 1895–1904: The Observations of Sir Ernest Satow*. Tallahassee, Fl.: Diplomatic Press, 1966.

———, ed. *Russia's Eastward Expansion*. Engelwood Hills, N.J.: Prentice-Hall, 1964.

Leonov, G. A. "K istorii lamaiskogo sobraniia Gosudarstvennogo Ermitazha." In *Buddizm i literaturno-khudozhestvennoe tvorchestvo narodov Tsentralnoi Azii*, edited by R. E. Pubaev, 101–15. Novosibirsk: Nauka, 1985.

Leontev, Konstantin Nikolaevich. "Vostok, Rossiia i slavianstvo." In *Sobranie sochinenyi*. Vol. 6. Moscow: V. Sablin, 1912.

Leontev, Viktor Petrovich. *Inostrannaia Ekspansiia v Tibete v 1888–1919 g*. Moscow: Akademiia Nauk SSSR, 1956.

Leontovich, Fedor Ivanovich. *Drevnii mogolo-kalmytskii ili oraitskii ustav*. Odessa: G. Ulrich, 1879.

Leroy-Beaulieu, Pierre. *La rénovation de l'Asie: Sibérie—Chine—Japon*. Paris: Armand Colin, 1900.

Levitov, I. *Zheltaia rasa*. St. Petersburg: G. A. Bernstein, 1900.

———. *Zheltaia Rossiia*. St. Petersburg: G. A. Bernstein, 1901.

———. *Zheltyi Bosfor*. St. Petersburg: G. A. Bernstein, 1903.

Levitskii, Nikolai Arsenevich. *Russko-iaponskaia voina 1904–1905 gg*. Moscow: Narkomat oborony soiuza SSR, 1936.

Lieven, Dominic. *Nicholas II: Emperor of All the Russias*. London: John Murray, 1993.

———. *Russia and the Origins of the First World War*. New York: St. Martin's Press, 1983.

———. *Russia's Rulers under the Old Regime*. New Haven, Conn.: Yale University Press, 1989.

Lin, Chen. *The Chinese Railways: A Historical Survey*. Shanghai: China United Press, 1935.

Lincoln, W. Bruce. *Petr Petrovich Semenov-Tian-Shansky: The Life of a Russian Geographer*. Newtonville, Mass.: Oriental Research Partners, 1980.

Liszkowski, Uwe. *Zwischen Liberalismus und Imperialismus*. Stuttgart: Ernst Klett Verlag, 1974.

Lo Hi-min, ed. *The Correspondence of G. E. Morrison*. Vol. 1. Cambridge: Cambrige University Press, 1876.

Lo Jung-Pang, ed. *K'ang Yu-wei: A Biography and a Symposium*. Tucson: University of Arizona Press, 1967.

Lobanov-Rostovsky, Andrei. *Russia and Asia*. Ann Arbor, Mich.: George Wahr, 1951.

Losev, Aleksei Fedorovich. *Vladimir Solovev i ego vremia*. Moscow: Progress, 1990.

Lukashevich, Stephen. *N. F. Fedorov (1828–1903): A Study in Russian Eupsychian and Utopian Thought*. Newark: University of Delaware Press, 1977.

Lukoianov, Igor Vladimirovich. "Dalnevostochnaia avantiura P. A. Badmaeva." Unpublished paper, Sankt-Peterburskii filial Institut Rossiiskoi Istorii, 1992.

———. "S. Iu. Vitte i plany sooruzheniia Sibirskoi zheleznoi dorogi: k predistorii russko-iaponskoi voiny." *Novyi Chasovoi*, no. 4 (1996): 45–52.

Lung Chang. *La Chine à l'aube du XXe Siècle: Les relations diplomatiques de la Chine avec les puissances depuis la guerre sino-japonaise jusqu'à la guerre russo-Japonaise*. Paris: Nouvelles Editions Latines, 1962.

Lvov, F. A. *Likhodiei biurokraticheskago samovlastiia kak neposredstvennye vinovniki pervoi russko-iaponskoi voiny*. St. Petersburg: Energiia, 1906.

Lynch, George. *The War of the Civilisations: Being the Record of a "Foreign Devil's" Experiences with the Allies in China*. London: Longmans, Green, 1901.

McClellan, Robert. *The Heathen Chinee: A Study of American Attitudes toward China, 1890–1905*. Columbus: Ohio State University Press, 1971.

McCormick, Thomas J. *China Market: America's Quest for Informal Empire, 1893–1901*. Chicago: Quadrangle Books, 1967.

McCully, Newton A. *The McCully Report: The Russo-Japanese War, 1904–1905*. Edited by Richard A. von Doenhoff. Annapolis, Md.: Naval Institute Press, 1977.

McCune, George M. "Russian Policy in Manchuria, 1895–1898." *Far Eastern Survey* 26 (Sep. 26, 1945): 272–74.

McDonald, David Maclaren. *United Government and Foreign Policy in Russia, 1900–1914*. Cambridge, Mass.: Harvard University Press, 1992.

MacDonald, Robert H. *The Language of Empire: Myths and Metaphors of Popular Imperialism, 1880–1980*. Manchester: Manchester University Press, 1994.

McDougall, Walter. *Promised Land, Crusader State: The American Encounter with the World since 1776*. Boston: Houghton Mifflin, 1997.

MacGregor, Sir Charles. *The Defence of India: A Strategical Study*. Simla: Government Central Branch Press, 1884.

MacGregor, John. *Tibet: A Chronicle of Exploration*. London: Routledge & Kegan Paul, 1970.

MacKenzie, David. "Turkestan's Significance to Russia, 1850–1917." *Russian Review* 33, no. 2 (April 1974): 167–88.

MacKenzie, John, ed. *Imperialism and Popular Culture*. Manchester: Manchester University Press, 1986.

———. *Orientalism: History, Theory and the Arts*. Manchester: Manchester University Press, 1995.

Mackerras, Colin. *Western Images of China*. Hong Kong: Oxford University Press, 1989.

MacKinder, Halford. "The Geographical Pivot of History." *Geographical Journal* 23, no. 4 (April 1904): 421–44.

McLean, D. "The Foreign Office and the First Chinese Indemnity Loan, 1895." *Historical Journal* 16, no. 2 (June 1973): 303–21.

McReynolds, Louise. *The News under Russia's Old Regime*. Princeton, N.J.: Princeton University Press, 1991.

———. "V. M. Dorosevich: The Newspaper Journalist and the Development of Public Opinion in Civil Society." In *Between Tsar and People. Educated Society and the Quest for Public Identity in Late Imperial Russia*, edited by Edith W. Clowes et al., 233–47. Princeton, N.J.: Princeton University Press, 1991.

Madison, Frank. "The Russians in Manchuria." *Harper's Weekly*, Apr. 16, 1904, 582–84.

Magarshack, David. *Chekhov the Dramatist* (London: John Lehmann, 1952

Maguire, Robert. "Macrocosm or Microcosm? The Symbolists on Russia." *Review of National Literatures* 3, no. 1 (spring 1972): 125–52.

Maksimov, Aleksandr Iakovlevich. *Na Dalekom Vostoke. Polnoe sobranie sochinenii*. Vol. 4. St Petersburg: K. L. Pentkovskii, 1899.

———. *Nashi zadachi na Tikhom Okeane*. 4th ed. St. Petersburg: K. L. Pentkovskii, 1901.

Malozemoff, Andrew. *Russian Far Eastern Policy, 1881–1904: With Special Emphasis on the Causes of the Russo-Japanese War*. Berkeley: University of California Press, 1958.

Maltsev, S. S. *Zheltaia opasnost (Kitaisko-evropeiskii konflikt 1900g.)*. Warsaw: Tsentralnaia tipografiia, 1900.

Mamin-Sibiriak, Dmitri Narkisovich. "Poslednie ogonki." In *Polnoe sobranie sochinenii*. Vol. 12. Petrograd: A. F. Marks, 1917.

Mancall, Mark. *China at the Center: 300 Years of Foreign Policy*. New York: Free Press, 1984.

———. *Russia and China: Their Diplomatic Relations to 1728*. Cambridge, Mass.: Harvard University Press, 1971.

Marc, Pierre. *Quelques années de la politique internationale: Antécédants de la guerre russo-japonaise*. Leipzig: K. F. Koehler, 1914.

Marder, Arthur J. *The Anatomy of British Sea Power: A History of British Naval Policy in the Pre-Dreadnought Era, 1880–1905*. New York: Alfred A. Knopf, 1940.

Marinov, V. A. *Rossiia i Iaponiia pered pervoi mirovoi voinoi (1905–1914 gody). Ocherki istorii otnoshenii*. Moscow: Nauka, 1974.

Markov, Sergei. *Liudy velikoi tseli: N. M. Przhevalskii, N. N. Miklukho-Maklai*. Moscow: Sovetskii Pisatel, 1944.

Marks, Steven G. *Road to Power: The Trans-Siberian Railroad and the Colonization of Asian Russia, 1850–1917*. Ithaca, N.Y.: Cornell University Press, 1991.

Marriott, Sir J. A. R. *Anglo-Russian Relations, 1689–1943*. London: Methuen, 1944.

Martens, Fedor Fedorovich. *Le conflit entre la Russie et la Chine*. Brussels: C. Muquardt, 1880.

———. *Russland und England in Zentralasien*. St. Petersburg, 1880.

Martin, Janet. *Treasure of the Land of Darkness: The Fur Trade and Its Significance for Medieval Russia*. Cambridge: Cambridge University Press, 1986.

Marvin, Charles. *The Russian Advance towards India: Conversations with Skoboleff, Ignatieff, and Other Distinguished Russian Generals and Statesmen, on the Central Asian Question*. London: Sampson Low, 1882.

Masaryk, T. G. *The Spirit of Russia: Studies in History, Literature, and Philosophy*. 3 vols. London: Allen & Unwin, 1968.

Maslin, M. A., ed. *Russkaia ideia*. Moscow: Respublika, 1992.

Massie, Robert K. *Dreadnought: Britain, Germany, and the Coming of the Great War*. New York: Random House, 1991.

———. *Nicholas and Alexandra*. New York: Athenium, 1968.

Maylunas, Andrei, and Sergei Mironenko, eds. *A Lifelong Passion: Nicholas and Alexandra, Their Own Story*. London: Weidenfeld & Nicholson, 1996.

Meade, Marion. *Madame Blavatsky: The Woman behind the Myth*. New York: G. P. Putnam's Sons, 1980.

Mehlinger, Howard D., and John M. Thompson. *Count Witte and the Tsarist Government in the 1905 Revolution*. Bloomington: Indiana University Press, 1972.

Meng, S. M. *The Tsungli Yamen: Its Organization and Functions*. Cambridge, Mass.: Harvard University Press, 1962.

Menhert, Klaus. *Peking and Moscow*. New York: G. P. Putnam's Sons, 1963.

Menning, Bruce. *Bayonets before Bullets: The Russian Imperial Army, 1861–1914*. Bloomington: Indiana University Press, 1992.

Meshcherskii, Kniaz Vladimir Petrovich. *Moi vospominaniia*. 3 vols. St. Petersburg: V. P. Meshcherskii, 1897–1912.

Meyendorff, Alexandre, ed. *Correspondance diplomatique de M. de Staal (1884–1900)*. 2 vols. Paris: M. Rivière, 1929.

Meyer, Karl E., and Shareen Blair Brysac. *Tournament of Shadows: The Race for Empire and the Great Game in Central Asia*. New York: Counterpoint, 1999.

Miasnikov, Vladimir Stepanovich. *The Ch'ing Empire and the Russian State in the Seventeenth Century*. Moscow: Progress Publishers, 1985.

———. *Dogovornymi statiami utverdili*. Khabarovsk: Priamurskoe Geograficheskoe Obshchestvo, 1997.

Mikhailovskii, Nikolai Konstantinovich. *Posledniia sochineniia N. K. Mikhailovskago*. Vol. 1. St. Petersburg: N. N. Klobukov, 1905.

Miliutin, Dmitrii Aleksandrovich. "Kriticheskoe izsledovanie znacheniia voennoi geografii i voennoi statistiki." *Voennyi Zhurnal*, no. 1 (1846).

———. *Dnevnik*. Vol. 1. Moscow: Bilioteka im. Lenina, 1947.

Miller, Henry. "Russian Development of Manchuria." *National Geographic Magazine* 15, no. 3 (March 1904): 113–27.

Mirsky, D. S. "The Eurasian Movement." *Slavonic and East European Review* 6 (1927): 311–20.

Mochulsky, Konstantin. *Andrei Bely: His Life and Works*. Translated by Nora Szalavitz. Ann Arbor, Mich.: Ardis, 1977.

———. *Vladimir Solovev: Zhizn i uchenie*. Paris: YMCA, 1951.

Mommsen, Wolfgang. *Grossmachtstellung und Weltpolitik 1870–1914: Die Außenpolitik des Deutschen Reiches*. Frankfurt a/M: Ullstein, 1993.

———. *Theories of Imperialism*. Translated by P. S. Falla. Chicago: University of Chicago Press, 1982.

Morgan, Gerald. *Anglo-Russian Rivalry in Central Asia, 1810–1895*. London: Cass, 1981.

Morley, James, ed. *Japan's Foreign Policy, 1868–1941: A Research Guide*. New York: Columbia University Press, 1974.

Morrill, Dan L. "Nicholas and the Call for the First Hague Conference." *Journal of Modern History* 46, no. 2 (June 1974): 296–313.

Morris, J. *Makers of Japan*. London: Methuen, 1906.

Morse, Hosea Ballou. *The International Relations of the Chinese Empire*. Vol. 3. London: Longmans, Green, 1918.

Mosolov, Aleksandr Aleksandrovich. *Pri dvore poslednego imperatora*. St. Petersburg: Nauka, 1992.

Mosse, Werner E. *The European Great Powers and the German Question, 1848–1871*. Cambridge: Cambridge University Press, 1958.

———. "Imperial Favourite: V. P. Meshchersky and the Grazhdanin." *Slavonic and East European Review* 59, no. 4 (October 1981): 529–47.

———. *Perestroika under the Tsars*. London: I. B. Tauris, 1992.

Murfett, Malcolm H. "An Old Fashioned Form of Protectionism: The Role Played by British Naval Power in China from 1860 to 1941." *American Neptune* 50, no. 3 (summer 1990): 178–91.

Murphy, Agnes. *The Ideology of French Imperialism, 1871–1881*. New York: Howard Fertig, 1968.

Murzaev, Eduard Markovich. *N. M. Przhevalskii*. Moscow: Geografiz, 1953.

———. "Slovo o Przhevalskom." *Moskva*, no. 4 (1989): 153–60.

———. *V dalekoi Azii*. Moscow: Akademiia Nauk SSSR, 1956.

Mutsu Munemitsu. *Kenkenroku: A Diplomatic Record of the Sino-Japanese War, 1894–1895*. Princeton, N.J.: Princeton University Press, 1982.

Nabokoff, Constantine D. *Ordeal of a Diplomat*. London: Duckworth, 1921.

Nabokov, Vladimir, translator. *The Song of Igor's Campaign*. New York: McGraw-Hill, 1960.

Nadin, P. "Kitaisko-vostochnaia zheleznaia doroga." *Vestnik Evropy* 39, n. 6, (June 1904): 593–620.

Nahm, Andrew C. *Korea: Tradition and Transformation: A History of the Korean People*. Elizabeth, N.J.: Hollym International, 1988.

Naquin, Susan. *Millenarian Rebellion in China: The Eight Trigrams Uprising of 1813*. New Haven, Conn.: Yale University Press, 1976.

Narochnitskii, A. L. "Agressiia evropeiskikh derzhav i SShA na Dalnem Vostoke v 1882–1895 gg." Dissertation Abstract: Institut Istorii, 1955.

Neilson, Keith. *Britain and the Last Tsar: British Policy and Russia, 1894–1917*. Oxford: Oxford University Press, 1995.

Nelson, M. Frederic. *Korea and the Old Orders in Eastern Asia*. Baton Rouge: Louisiana State University Press, 1945.

Nemirovich-Danchenko, V. I. *Na voinu*. Moscow, 1904.

Neumann, Iver B. *Russia and the Idea of Europe: A Study in Identity and International Relations*. London: Routledge, 1996.

Nevelskoi, G. I. *Podvigi russkikh morskikh ofitserov na krainem Vostoke Rossii 1849–1855*. St. Petersburg: A. S. Suvorin, 1897.

Nicholas II. *Dnevnik Imperatora Nikolaia II*. Berlin: Slovo, 1923.

———. *Dnevniki Imperatora Nikolaia II*. Moscow: Orbita, 1991.

Nidermuller, Vice Admiral A. G. von. *Ot Sevastopolia do Tsushimy: Vospominaniia*. Riga: M. Didkovskii, 1930.

Nikhamin, V. P. "Russko-iaponskie otnosheniia i Koreia 1894–1895 gg." Candidate's diss., Vysshaia diplomaticheskaia shkola, 1948.

Nikitin, D. V. "Kak nachalas voina s Iaponiei." In *Port-Artur: Vospominaniia uchastnikov*. New York: Chekhov, 1955.

Nilus, E. Kh., ed. *Istoricheskii obzor Kitaiskoi vostochnoi zheleznoi dorogi, 1896–1923 gg.* Vol. 1. Harbin: Tipografiia K.V.Zh.D., 1923.

Nish, Ian H. *The Anglo-Japanese Alliance: The Diplomacy of Two Island Empires, 1894–1907*. London: Athlone Press, 1966.

———. *Japanese Foreign Policy, 1869–1942*. London: Routledge & Kegan Paul, 1977.

———. *The Origins of the Russo-Japanese War*. London: Longman, 1985.

———. "The Royal Navy and the Taking of Weihawei, 1898–1905." *Mariner's Mirror* 54 (1968): 39–54.

Nivat, Georges. "Du 'Panmogolisme' au mouvement Eurasien." In *Vers la fin du mythe russe: Essais sur la culture russe de Gogol à nos jours*. Lausanne: L'Age d'Homme, 1988.

Nolde, Boris. *L'alliance franco-russe: Les origines du système diplomatique d'avant-guerre*. Paris: Librairie Droz, 1936.

————. *La formation de l'empire russe.* 2 vols. Paris: Institut d'Etudes Slaves, 1952.

Norem, Ralph A. *Kiaochow Leased Territory.* Berkeley: University of California Press, 1936.

Norman, Henry. *The Peoples and Politics of the Far East.* New York: C. Scribner's, 1895.

Notovich, Nicolas. *L'Empereur Nicolas II et la politique russe.* Paris: Paul Ollendorf, 1895.

Okamoto, Shumpei. *The Japanese Oligarchy and the Russo-Japanese War.* New York: Columbia University Press, 1970.

Oldenburg, Sergei Sergeevich. *Last Tsar: Nicholas II, His Reign, and His Russia.* 4 vols. Gulf Breeze, Fl.: Academic International Press, 1975.

Oliphant, Nigel. *A Diary of the Siege of the Legations in Peking during the Summer of 1900.* London: Longmans, Green, 1901.

Osterhammel, Jürgen. *China und die Weltgesellschaft.* Munich: C. H. Beck, 1989.

————. *Colonialism: A Theoretical Overview.* Princeton, N.J.: Markus Wiener, 1997.

Oudendijk, Willem Jacobus. "Russia and China." *Journal of the Royal Central Asian Society* 22, no. 3 (July 1935): 369–402.

————. *Ways and By-Ways in Diplomacy.* London: P. Davies, 1939.

Pagden, Anthony. *Lords of All the World: Ideologies of Empire in Spain, Britain, and France, c. 1500–c. 1800.* New Haven, Conn.: Yale University Press, 1995.

Paine, S. C. M. *Imperial Rivals: China, Russia, and Their Disputed Frontier.* Armonk, N.Y.: M. E. Sharpe, 1996.

Pak, B. B. "375 dnei v rossiiskoi missi." *Vostok,* no. 5 (1997): 27–37.

Pak Chon Ho. *Rossiia i Korea 1895–1898.* Moscow: Moskovskii Gosudarstvennyi universitet, 1993.

————. *Russko-iaponskaia voina 1904–1905 gg. i Koreia.* Moscow: Vostochnaia Literatura, 1997.

Paléologue, Maurice. *Guillaume II et Nicolas II.* Paris: Plon, 1934.

Palmer, A. W. "Lord Salisbury's Approach to Russia, 1898." *Oxford Slavonic Papers* 6 (1955): 102–14.

Pamiati Nikolaia Mikhailovicha Przhevalskogo. St. Petersburg: A. S. Suvorin, 1890.

Pares, Bernard A. *The Fall of the Russian Monarchy: A Study of the Evidence.* London: Jonathan Cape, 1939.

————. *A History of Russia.* New York: Alfred A. Knopf, 1926.

Parker, Edward Harper. *China and Religion.* London: John Murray, 1905.

Parry, Albert. "Russian (Greek Orthodox) Missionaries in China, 1689–1917: Their Cultural, Political, and Economic Role." *Pacific Historical Review* 9, no. 4 (December 1940): 401–24.

————. "Russian (Greek Orthodox) Missionaries in China, 1689–1917: Their Cultural, Political and Economic Rôle." Ph.D. diss., University of Chicago, 1938.

Pasvolsky, Leo, and Harold G. Moulton. *Russian Debts and Russian Reconstruction: A Study of the Relation of Russia's Foreign Debts to Her Economic Recovery.* New York: McGraw-Hill, 1924.

Pearson, Charles H. *National Life and Character: A Forecast.* London: Macmillan, 1893.

Pelensky, Jaroslaw. *Russia and Kazan: Conquest and Imperial Ideology (1438–1560s).* The Hague: Mouton, 1974.

Pethybridge, R. W. "British Imperialists in the Russian Empire." *Russian Review* 30, no. 4 (October 1971): 346–55.

Pierce, Richard A. *Russia in Central Asia, 1867–1917: A Study in Colonial Rule.* Berkeley: University of California Press, 1960.

Pierrot, Jean. *The Decadent Imagination, 1880–1900.* Translated by Derek Coltman. Chicago: University of Chicago Press, 1981.

Pinon, René. *La lutte pour le Pacifique: Orgines et résultats de la guerre russo-japonaise.* Paris: Perrein et Cie., 1906.

Pobedonostsev, Konstantin Petrovich. *L'autocratie russe. Mémoires politiques, correspondence officielle et documents inédits relatifs à l'histoire du règne de l'empereur Alexandre III.* Paris, 1927.

———. *Reflections of a Russian Statesman.* Ann Arbor: University of Michigan Press, 1973.

———. *Velikaia lozh nashego vremeni.* Moscow: Russkaia kniga, 1993.

Pogodaev, Nikolai Petrovich. "Russkaia burzhuazno-monarkhicheskaia i angliiskaia burzhuaznaia pressa kak istochnik po Anglo-russkim otnosheniiam v 1906–1909 gg." Candidate's diss., Universitet Kuibesheva, 1984.

Pokotilov, Dmitrii Dmitrevich. *Dnevnik osady evropeistev v Pekine s 22-go maia do 1-e avgusta.* Yalta: N. V. Vakhtina, 1900.

———. *Dnevnik s 2-go do 31-oe avgusta 1900 godu.* St. Petersburg: V. F. Kirshbaum, 1900.

Pokrovskii, Mikhail Nikolaevich. *Diplomatiia i voiny tsarskoi Rossii v XIX stoletii.* Moscow: Krasnaia Nov, 1923.

———, ed. *Perepiska Vilgelma II s Nikolaem II.* Moscow: Gosudarstvennoe izdatelstvo, 1923.

Poliakov, I. S. "Loshad Przhevalskogo, zoologicheskii ocherk." *Izvestiia* 17, no. 1 (January 1881): 1–20.

Polvinen, Tuomo. *Imperial Borderland: Bobrikov and the Attempted Russification of Finland, 1898–1904.* London: Hurst, 1995.

Pooley, A. M., ed. *The Secret Memoirs of Count Tadasu Hayashi.* New York: G. P. Putnam's Sons, 1915.

Popov, A. "Dalnevostochnaia politika tsarizma v 1894–1901 gg." *Istorik Marksist* 11, no. 11 (November 1935): 38–58.

———. "Iz istorii zavoevaniia Srednei Azii." *Istoricheskie zapiski* 9 (1940): 198–242.

———. "Rossiia i Tibet." *Novyi Vostok* 18 (1927): 101–19; 19 (1928): 20–21, 33–54.

Popov, Pavel Stepanovich. "Dva mesiatsa osady v Pekine." *Vestnik Evropy* 36, no. 2 (February 1901): 517–36; no. 3 (March 1901): 5–37.

Portal, Roger. *La Russie industrielle de 1881 à 1927.* Paris: Centre de Documentation Universitaire, n.d.

Portugalskii, R. M., et al. *Pervaia mirovaia v zhizneopisaniiakh russkikh voenachalnikov.* Moscow: Elakos, 1994.

Powell, Ralph L. *The Rise of Chinese Military Power, 1895–1912.* Princeton, N.J.: Princeton University Press, 1955.

Pozdneev, Aleksei Matveevich. *Ob otnosheniiakh evropeitsev k Kitaiu.* St. Petersburg: A. M. Volf, 1887.

———. *Ocherki byta buddiiskikh monastirei i buddiiskago dukhovenstva v Mongolii.* St. Petersburg: Imperatorskaia Akademiia Nauk, 1887.

———. "Tretie puteshestvie v Tsentralnoi Azii." *Zhurnal Ministerstva Narodnago Prosveshcheniia* 232 (March 1884): 316–51.

Pozdneev, Dmitrii Matveevich. *Opisanie Manchzhurii.* 2 vols. St. Petersburg: Ministerstvo Finansov, 1897.

———. *56 dnei pekinskago sidenia v sviazi s blizhaishimi k nemu sobytiiami pekinskoi zhizni.* St. Petersburg: V. F. Kirshbaum, 1901.

Price, Don C. *Russia and the Roots of the Chinese Revolution, 1896–1911.* Cambridge, Mass.: Harvard University Press, 1974.

Pritchett, V. S. *Chekhov: A Spirit Set Free.* New York: Random House, 1988.

Propper, Stanislav Maksimilianovich. *Was Nicht in die Zeitung Kam: Erinnerungen des*

Chefredakteurs der "Birschewyja wedomosti". Frankfurt a/M: Frankfurter Societäts Druckerei, 1929.

Przhevalskii, Nikolai Mikhailovich. "Avtobiografiia N. M. Przhevalskago." *Russkaia Starina* 19, no. 11 (November 1888): 528–43.

———. "Dnevnik polednego puteshestviia N. M. Przhevalskogo v 1888 g." *Izvestiia* 72, nos. 4–5 (1940): 630–40.

———. "Dnevnik vtorogo puteshestviia N. M. Przhevalskogo v Tsentralnuiu Aziiu." *Izvestiia* 72, nos. 4–5 (1940): 501–606.

———. *From Kulja, across the Tian-Shan to Lob-Nor.* Translated by E. Delmar Morgan. London: S. Low, Marston, Searle & Rivington, 1876.

———. "Inorodicheskie naselenie v iuzhnoi chasti Primorskoi Oblasti." *Izvestiia* 5, no. 5 (October 1869): 185–201.

———. *Iz Zaisana cherez Khami v Tibet.* St. Petersburg: V. S. Balashev, 1883.

———. *Mongolia, the Tangut Country, and the Solitudes of Northern Tibet.* Translated by E. Delmar Morgan. 2 vols. London: S. Low, Marston, Searle, & Rivington, 1876.

———. *Ot Kiakhty na istoki Zheltoi Reki.* St. Petersburg: V. S. Balashev, 1888.

———. *Puteshestvie v Ussuriiskom Krae, 1867–1869 gg.* St. Petersburg: N. Nekliudov, 1870.

———. "Sovremennoe polozhenie Tsentralnoi Azii." *Russkii Vestnik* 186 (December 1886): 473–524.

———. "Vospominaniia okhotnika." *Izvestiia* 72, nos. 4–5 (1940): 488–500.

Purcell, Victor. *The Boxer Uprising: A Background Study.* Cambridge: Cambridge University Press, 1963.

Pustogarov, Vladimir Vasilevich. *". . . S palmovoi vetviu mira . . ." F. F. Martens: Iurist, diplomat, publitsist.* Moscow: Mezhdunarodnye otnosheniia, 1993.

Putevoditel po Kitaiskoi vostochnoi zheleznoi dorogi. St. Petersburg: Golike i Viborg, 1903.

Putiata, Polkovnik G. Sh. Dmitrii Vassilevich. *Kitai: Ocherki geograficheskago sostoianiia administrativnago i voennago ustroistva Kitaia.* St. Petersburg: Voennaia tipografiia, 1895.

———. *Vooruzhennyia sily Kiataia.* St. Petersburg: Voennaia tipografiia, 1889.

Pyman, Avril. *A History of Russian Symbolism.* Cambridge: Cambridge University Press, 1984.

———. "The Scythians." *Stand* 8:3 (1966 1967): 23–33.

Quested, Rosemary. "A Fresh Look at the Sino-Russian Conflict of 1900 in Manchuria." *Journal of the Institute of Chinese Studies* 8 (1978): 159–91.

———. *The Expansion of Russia in East Asia, 1857–1860.* Kuala Lumpur: University of Malaysia Press, 1968.

———. "Local Sino-Russian Political Relations in Manchuria." *Journal of Oriental Studies* 10 (July 1972).

———. *"Matey" Imperialists? The Tsarist Russians in Manchuria, 1895–1917.* Hong Kong: University of Hong Kong, 1982.

———. *The Russo-Chinese Bank: A Multinational Financial Base of Tsarism in China.* Birmingham: University of Birmingham, 1977.

———. *Sino-Russian Relations: A Short History.* Sydney: George Allen & Unwin, 1984.

Radde, Gustav I. *23,000 mil na iahte "Tamara": Puteshestvye ikh Imperatorskikh Vysochestv Velikikh Kniazei Aleksandra i Sergeiia Mikhailovichei v 1890–1891 gg.* 2 vols. St. Petersburg: Eduard Goppe, 1892.

Radzinskii, Edvard. *Stalin: The First In-Depth Biography Based on Explosive New Documents from Russia's Secret Archives.* New York: Doubleday, 1996.

Radziwill, Princesse Catherine. *Nicolas II le dernier tsar.* Paris: Payot, 1933.

Raeff, Marc. *Michael Speransky: Statesman of Imperial Russia.* The Hague: Martinus Nij–hoff, 1969.

Raptchinsky, Boris. *Blank en Geel in het Verre Oosten*. Zutphen: W. J. Thieme, 1933.

Raskin, Jonah. *The Mythology of Imperialism: Rudyard Kipling, Joseph Conrad, E. M. Forster, D. H. Lawrence, and Joyce Cary*. New York: Random House, 1971.

Rayfield, Donald. *Chekhov: The Evolution of His Art*. London: Paul Elek, 1975.

———. *The Dream of Lhasa: The Life of Nikolay Przhevalsky (1839–88), Explorer of Central Asia*. [Athens]: Ohio University Press, 1976.

Rediger, Aleksandr. *Istoriia moei zhizni: Vospominaniia voennogo ministra*. Vol. 1. Moscow: Kanon-Press-Ts., 1999.

Renouvin, Pierre. *La question d'Extrème Orient, 1840–1940*. Paris: Hachette, 1946.

Repin, Leonid. *Otkryvateli*. Moscow: Molodaia gvardiia, 1989.

Rees, J. D. "The Czar's Friend." *Fortnightly Review*, no. 412 (Apr. 1, 1901): 612–22.

Riasanovsky, Nicholas V. "The Emergence of Eurasianism." *California Slavic Studies* 4 (1967): 39–72.

———. "'Oriental Despotism' and Russia." *Slavic Review* 22, no. 4 (1964): 644–49.

———. "Russia and Asia: Two Nineteenth-Century Russian Views." *California Slavic Studies* 1 (1960): 170–81.

Rich, David Alan. *The Tsar's Colonels: Professionalism, Strategy, and Subversion in Late Imperial Russia*. Cambridge, Mass.: Harvard University Press, 1998.

Richardson, James L. *Crisis Diplomacy: The Great Powers since the Mid-Nineteenth Century*. Cambridge: Cambridge University Press, 1994.

Richthofen, Ferdinand, Freiherr von. *China, Ergebnisse eigener Reisen und darauf gegründeter Studien*. Vol. 2. Berlin: Dietrich Reimer, 1877–1911.

———. "Kiautschou, seine Weltstellung und voraussichtliche Bedeutung" *Preußishce Jahrbücher* 91, no. 1 (January 1898): 167–71.

Ritchie, Galen B. "The Asiatic Department during the Reign of Alexander II 1855–1881." Ph.D. diss., Columbia University, 1970.

Rhie, Marilyn M., and Robert A. M. Thurman. *Wisdom and Compassion: The Sacred Art of Tibet*. New York: Abrams, 1991.

Robinson, Ronald, John Gallagher, and Alice Denny. *Africa and the Victorians: The Official Mind of Imperialism*. London: Macmillan, 1981.

Roborovskii, Vsevolod Ivanovich. "Nikolai Mikhailovich Przhevalskii v. 1878–1888 gg." *Russkaia Starina* 23, no. 1 (Januuary 1892): 217–38; 23, no. 3 (March 1892): 653–74.

Rockhill, William Woodville. *China's Intercourse with Korea from the XVth Century to 1895*. London: Luzac, 1905.

Rohrbach, Paul. "Fürst Ukhtomski über russisch-deutsche Politik." *Preußische Jahrbücher* 92 (1898): 337–46.

Rollins, Patrick J. "Imperial Russia's Africa Colony." *Russian Review* 27, no. 4 (October 1968): 432–51.

Romanov, Boris Aleksandrovich. *Russia in Manchuria, 1892–1906*. Translated by Susan Wilbur Jones. Ann Arbor, Mich.: Edwards, 1952.

———. "Vitte kak diplomat (1895–1903 gg.)." *Vestnik leningradskogo universiteta*, nos. 4–5 (1946): 150–72.

Romanova, Galina Nikolaevna. *Ekonomicheskie otnosheniia Rossii i Kitaia na Dalnem Vostoke XIX–nachalo XX vv*. Moscow: Nauka, 1987.

Roosevelt, Theodore. "National Life and Character." *Sewanee Review* 2, no. 3 (May 1894): 353–76.

Rosen, Baron Roman Romanovich. *Forty Years of Diplomacy*. Vol. 1. London: Allen & Unwyn, 1922.

Rosenbaum, A. "Manchurian Bridgehead: Anglo-Russian Rivalry and the Imperial Russian

Railways of North China, 1897–1902." *Modern Asian Studies* 10 (1976): 41–64.

Rosengarten, Adolph G. "John Bloch: A Neglected Prophet." *Military Review* 37, no. 1 (April 1957): 27–39.

Rosenthal, Bernice Glatzer. *Dmitrii Sergeevich Merezhkovsky and the Silver Age: The Development of a Revolutionary Mentality.* The Hague: Martinus Nijhoff, 1975.

——, ed. *The Occult in Russian and Soviet Culture.* Ithaca, N.Y.: Cornell University Press, 1997.

Rostovskii, S. "Tsarskaia Rossiia i Sin-Tzian v XIX–XX vekakh." *Istorik Marksist,* no. 3 (1936): 26–53.

Rostunov, Ivan Ivanovich, ed. *Istoriia Russko-iaponskoi voiny 1904–1905 gg.* Moscow: Nauka, 1977.

Rouire, A. M. F. *La rivalité anglo-russe au XIXe siècle en Asie.* Paris: Colin, 1908.

Rudakov, A. *Obshchestvo I-khe-tuan i ego znachenie v polednikh sobytiakh na Dalnem Vostoke.* Vladivostok: T-va Sushchinskii, 1901.

Rupen, Robert A. *Mongols of the Twentieth Century.* 2 vols. Bloomington: Indiana University, 1964.

Rusin, Aleksandr Ivanovich. "Iz predistorii russko-iaponskoi voiny: Doneseniia morskogo agenta v Iaponii A. I. Rusina (1902–1904 gg.)." *Russkoe proshloe* 6 (1996): 55–86.

Russia. Chrezvychainaia Sliedstvennaia Komissiia Vremennogo Pravitelstva. *Padenie Tsarskogo Rezhima,* edited by P. E. Shchegolov. 7 vols. Moscow: Gosudarstvennoe Izd-vo, 1924–1927.

Russia. Generalnyi shtab. *Sbornik geograficheskikh, topograficheskikh i statisticheskikh materialov po Azii.* 87 vols. St. Petersburg: Voen. tip., 1883–1914.

Russia. Istoricheskaia Komissiia pri Morskom Generalnom Shtabe. *Russko-Iaponskaia voina 1904–1905 gg. Deistviia flota.* Edited by A. F. Heiden et al., pt. 1-a. Petrograd: Morskoi generalnyi shtab, 1918.

Russia. Ministerstvo Finansov. *Ministerstvo Finansov 1802–1902.* 2 vols. St. Petersburg: Ekspeditsiia zagotovleniia gosudarstvennykh bumag, 1902.

Russia. Ministerstvo Inostrannykh Del. *Ocherk istorii Ministerstva Inostrannykh Del 1802–1902.* St. Petersburg, 1902.

Russia. Nikolaevskaia voennaia akademiia. *Comptes rendus publiés par le Rousski Invalid des conférences sur la guerre russo-japonaise.* Vol. 1. Paris: Henri Charles-Lavauzelle, 1907.

Russia. Pereselencheskoe Upravlenie. *Aziatskaia Rossiia.* 3 vols. St. Petersburg: A. F. Marks, 1914.

Russia. Shtaba Turkestanskogo voennogo okruga. *Svedeniia kasaiushchiasia stran, sopredelnykh s turkestanskim voennym okrugom.* Vols. 3–28. Tashkent, 1898–1901.

Russia. Tsentralnyi statisticheskii komitet M. V. D. *Ot Vladivostoka do Uralska: Putevoditel k puteshchestviiu Ego Imperatorskago Vysochestva gosudaria naslednika tsesarevicha.* St. Petersburg: Tip. T-va A. Transhel, 1891.

Russia. Voenno-istoricheskaia kommissiia po opisaniiu Russko-Iaponskoi voiny. *Russko-iaponskaia voina 1904–1905 gg.* Vols. 1–2. St. Petersburg: A. S. Suvorin, 1910.

Rybachenok, Irina Sergeevna. "Dalnevostochnaia politika Rossii 90-kh godov XIX v. na stranitsakh russkikh gazet konservativnogo napravleniia." In *Vneshnaia politika Rossii i obshchestvennoe mnenie,* edited by A. L. Narochnitskii, 125–46. Moscow: Institut Istorii SSSR, 1988.

——. "Rossiia i gaagskaia konferentsiia po razoruzheniiu 1899 g." *Novaia i Noveishaia Istoriia,* no. 4 (1996): 169–92.

——. *Soiuz s Frantsiei vo vneshnei politiki Rossii v kontse XIX v.* Moscow: Institut istorii SSSR, 1993.

Rywkin, Michael, ed. *Russian Colonial Expansion to 1917*. London: Mansell Publishing, 1988.
Ryzhenkov, Mikhail Rafailovich. "Rol voennogo vedomstva Rossii v razvitii otechestvennogo vostokovedeniia v XIX–nachale XX vv." Candidate's diss., Institut vostokovedeniia, 1990.
Sabler, S. V., and I. V. Sosnovskii. *Sibirskaia zheleznaia doroga*. St. Petersburg, 1903.
Sacke, Georg. *W. S. Solowjews Geschichtsphilosophie: Ein Beitrag zur Charakteristik der russischen Weltanschauung*. Berlin: Ost-Europa Verlag, 1929.
Sahni, Kalpana. *Crucifying the Orient: Russian Orientalism and the Colonization of Caucasus and Central Asia*. Bangkok: White Orchid Press, 1997.
Said, Edward A. *Culture and Imperialism*. New York: Alfred A. Knopf, 1993.
———. *Orientalism*. New York: Vintage, 1979.
Samokhin, Andrei. *Kitaiskii Krug Rossii*. Frankfurt a/M: Possev, 1981.
Samoilov, N. A. "Aziia (konets xix–nachalo xx veka) glazami russkikh voennykh issledovatelei." *Strany i narody Vostoka* 28 (1994): 292–34.
Sandberg, Graham. *The Exploration of Tibet: Its History and Particulars from 1623 to 1904*. Calcutta: Thacker, Spink, 1904.
Sanders, Ewoud. "Przewalskipaard." *NRC Handelsblad*, Sep. 2, 1996, 18.
Sarkisyanz, Emanuel. *Geschichte der orientalischen Völker Rußlands bis 1917*. Munich: R. Oldenbourg, 1961.
———. "Russian Attitudes toward Asia." *Russian Review* 13, no. 4 (October 1954): 245–54.
———. *Russland und der Messianismus des Orients*. Tübingen: J. C. B. Mohr, 1955.
Sands, William Franklin. *Undiplomatic Memories*. New York: McGraw-Hill, 1930.
Saul, Norman E. *Concord and Conflict: The United States and Russia, 1867–1914*. Lawrence: University Press of Kansas, 1996.
Savinskii, Aleksandr Aleksandrovich. *Recollections of a Russian Diplomat*. London: Hutchinson, 1927.
Savitsky, P. N. "Geopoliticheskie zametki po russkoi istorii." In *Nachertanie russkoi istorii*, edited by G. V. Vernadsky, 234–60. Prague: Evraziiskoe knigoizdatelstvo, 1927.
Saxton, Alexander. *The Indispensible Enemy: Labor and the Anti-Chinese Movement in America*. Berkeley: University of California Press, 1971.
Sazonov, Serge. *Fateful Years, 1909–1917: The Reminiscences of Serge Sazonov*. London: F. A. Stokes, 1928.
Sbornik pervyi o Vladimire Soloveve. Moscow: Tipografiia Imperatorskogo Moskovskogo Universiteta, 1911.
Schäfer, Ernst, ed. *Tibet und Zentralasien*. Stuttgart: Henry Goverts, 1965.
Scheider, William H. *An Empire for the Masses: The French Popular Image of Africa, 1870–1900*. Westport, Conn.: Greenwood Press, 1982.
Schelking, Evgenii Nikolaevich. *Recollections of a Russian Diplomat: The Suicide of Monarchies (William II and Nicholas II)*. New York: Macmillan, 1918.
Schelting Alexander von. *Russland und Europa im Russischen Geschichtsdenken*. Bern: A. Franke, 1948.
Shchegolev, I. *Vospominaniia Port-Artura 1903–1904 g*. Odessa: Tipografiia Iuzhno-Russkago Obshchestva Pechatnago Dela, 1905.
Schiemann, Theodor. *Deutschland und die große Politik*. 14 vols. Berlin: Georg Reimer, 1902–1915.
Schimmelpenninck van der Oye, David H. "Russian Military Intelligence on the Manchurian Front." *Intelligence and National Security* 11, no. 1 (January 1996): 22–31.
———. "The Russo-Japanese War" In *The Military History of Tsarist Russia*, edited by Frederick Kagan and Robin Higham. New York: St. Martin's Press, forthcoming in 2001.

———. "Svet s Vostoka." *Rodina* 6, no. 11 (November 1995): 30–33.

———. "Tsarist Military Intelligence and the Younghusband Expedition of 1904." In *Intelligence and International Politics from the Civil War to the Cold War*, edited by Jennifer Siegel. Westport, Conn.: Greenwood, forthcoming in 2002.

Schmidt, V. *Die deutsche Eisenbahnpolitik in Shantung, 1898–1914: Ein Betrag zur Geschichte des deutschen Imperialismus in China*. Wiesbaden: Harrasowitz, 1976.

Schorkowitz, Dittmar. *Die soziale und politische Organisation bei den Kalmücken (Oiraten) und Prozesse der Akkulturation von 17. Jahrhundert bis zur Mitte des 19. Jahrhunderts*. Frankfurt a/M: P. Lang, 1992.

Schrecker, John. *Imperialism and Chinese Nationalism: Germany in Shantung*. Cambridge, Mass.: Harvard University Press, 1971.

Schumpeter, Joseph Alois. "The Sociology of Imperialisms." In *Imperialism and Social Classes*, translated by Heinz Norden, 3–130. New York: Augustus M. Kelley, 1951.

Schuyler, Eugene. *Turkistan: Notes of a Journey in Russian Turkistan, Kokand, Bukhara and Kuldja*. 2 vols. New York: Scribner, Armstrong, 1876.

Schwartz, Harry. *Tsars, Mandarins, and Commissars: A History of Chinese-Russian Relations*. Philadelphia: J. B. Lippincott, 1964.

Semenov-Tian-Shanskii, Petr Petrovich. *Istoriia poluvekovoi deiatelnosti Imperatorskogo Russkogo Geograficheskogo Obshchestva, 1845–1895*. 3 vols. St. Petersburg: V. Bezobrazov, 1896.

Semenov, Svetlana Georgievna. *Nikolai Fedorov: Tvorchestvo i zhizni*. Moscow: Sovetskii pisatel, 1990.

Sergeev, Evgenii Iurevich. *Politika Velikobritanii i Germanii na Dalnem Vostoke*. Moscow: Institut Vseobshchei Istorii, 1998.

Setnitskii, N. A. *Russkie mystliteli o Kitae (V. S. Solovev i N. F. Fedorov)*. Harbin: n.p., 1926.

Seton-Watson, Hugh. *The Russian Empire, 1801–1917*. Oxford: Oxford University Press, 1967.

Shaumian, Tatiana L. *Tibet v mezhdunarodnykh otnosheniiakh v nachale XX veka*. Moscow: Nauka, 1977.

Shelkovnikov, B. "Voennoe moguchestvo Kitaia." In *Voennyi Almanach na 1901 god*, edited by B. L. Tageeva, supplement, 1–32. St. Petersburg: V. S. Balashev, 1901.

Shin, Peter Yong-Shik. "The Otsu Incident: Japan's Hidden History of the Attempted Assassination of Future Emperor Nicholas II of Russia in the Town of Otsu, Japan, May 11, 1891, and Its Implication for Historical Analysis." Ph.D. diss., University of Pennsylvania, 1989.

Shoemaker, Michael Myers. *The Great Siberian Railway: From St. Petersburg to Pekin*. New York: G. P. Putnam's Sons, 1903.

Shreider, D. I. *Nash Dalnyi Vostok*. St. Petersburg, A. F. Devrien, 1897.

Shteinberg, Evgenii Lvovich. *Borba russkogo naroda za vykod v Tikhii okean*. Moscow: Voennoe izdatelstvo, 1940.

Shteinfeld, Nikolai. *Russkoe delo v Manchzhurii s XVIII veka do nashikh dnei*. Harbin: Luan-dun-bao, 1910.

Siegelbaum, Lewis. "Another 'Yellow Peril': Chinese Migrants in the Russian Far East and the Russian Reaction before 1917." *Modern Asian Studies* 12, no. 2 (April 1978): 307–30.

Simanskii, Panteleimon Nikolaevich. *Sobytiia na Dalnem Vostoke*. 3 vols. St. Petersburg: Voennaia tipografiia, 1910.

Simmons, Ernest J. *Chekhov: A Biography*. New York: Atlantic Monthly Press, 1962.

Sinor, Denis, ed. *The Cambridge History of Early Inner Asia*. Cambridge: Cambridge University Press, 1990.

———. "Le mongol vue par l'Occident." In *Studies in Medieval Inner Asia*. Vol. 9. Ashgate: Variorum, 1997.

Skalkovskii, Konstantin Apollonovich. *Les ministres des finances de la Russie 1802–1890*. Translated by P. de Nevsky. Paris: Guillaumin et Cie., 1891.

———. *Vneshniaia politika Rossii i polozhenie inostrannykh derzhav*. St. Petersburg: A. S. Suvorin, 1897.

Skrynnikov, Ruslan Grigorevich. *Sibirskaia ekspeditsiia Ermaka*. Novosibirsk: Nauka, 1982.

Sladkovskii, Mikhail Iosifovich. *Istoriia torgovo-ekonomicheskikh otnshenii narodov Rossii s Kitaem (do 1917 g.)*. Moscow: Nauka, 1974.

———. "Otnosheniia mezhdu Rossiei i Kitaem v seredine XIX v." *Novaia i noveishaia istoriia,* no. 3 (1975): 55–64.

Slezkine, Yuri. *Arctic Mirrors: Russia and the Small Peoples of the North*. Ithaca, N.Y.: Cornell University Press, 1994.

Smith, Charles Emory. "The Young Tsar and His Advisers." *North American Review,* no. 458 (January 1895): 21–28.

Snelling, John. *Buddhism in Russia: The Story of Agvan Dorzhiev, Lhasa's Emissary to the Tsar*. Shaftesbury: Element, 1993.

Snesarev, Andrei Evgenevich. *Indiia kak glavnyi faktor v Sredne-Aziatskom voprose*. St. Petersburg: A. E. Suvorin, 1906.

Snyder, Jack. *Myths of Empire: Domestic Politics and International Ambitions*. Ithaca, N.Y.: Cornell Univesity Press, 1991.

Sokol, K. G. *Monumenty Imperii*. Moscow: Geos, 1999.

Sokolsky, George E. *The Story of the Chinese Eastern Railway*. Shanghai: North-China Daily News, 1929.

Solovev, Iurii Iakovlevich. *Vospominaniia diplomata 1893–1922*. Moscow: Sotsialnoekonomicheskaia literatura, 1959.

Solovev, S. M. *Zhizn i tvorcheskaia evoliutsiia Vladimira Soloveva*. Brussels: Zhizn s Bogom, 1977.

Solovev, Vladimir Sergeevich. *Chteniia o Bogochelovechestve; Stati; Stikhotovreniia i poema: Iz trekh razgovorov*. St. Petersburg: Khudozhestvennaia literatura, 1994.

———. *Sobranie sochineniia Vladimira Sergeevicha Soloveva*. Vols. 6–9. St. Petersburg: Prosveshchenie, n.d.

———. *Sochineniia v dvukh tomakh,* 2 vols. Moscow: Pravda, 1989.

———. *A Solovev Anthology*. Edited by S. L. Frank. New York: Charles Scribner's Sons, 1950.

———. *War and Christianity: From the Russian Point of View*. New York: G. P. Putnam's Sons, 1915.

Sorokin, Aleksandr Ivanovich. *Russko-Iaponskaia voina 1904–1905 gg*. Moscow: Ministerstvo Oborony Soiuza SSR, 1956.

Spector, Stanley. *Li Hung-chang and the Huai Army*. Seattle: University of Washington Press, 1964.

Spence, Jonathan D. *The Chan's Great Continent: China in Western Minds*. New York: Norton, 1998.

———. *The Search for Modern China*. New York: Norton, 1990.

Steinberg, John Warner. "The Education and Training of the Russian General Staff: A History of the Imperial Nicholas Military Academy, 1832–1914." Ph.D. diss., Ohio State University, 1990.

Steinberg, Jonathan. "Germany and the Russo-Japanese War." *American Historical Review* 75 (1970): 1965–86.

Steinberg, Mark D., and Vladimir M. Krustalëv, eds. *The Fall of the Romanovs: Political*

Dreams and Personal Struggles in a Time of Revolution. New Haven, Conn.: Yale University Press, 1995.

Steiner, Zara, ed. *The Times Survey of Foreign Ministries of the World.* London: Times Books, 1982.

Steinmann, Friedrich von. "Russlands Politik im fernen Osten und der Staatssekretär Bezobrazov." Inaugural diss., Friedrich-Wilhelms Universität zu Berlin, 1931.

Stepanov, A. "K voprosu o panmongolisme." *Pravoslavnyi Sobesednik* 50, no. 3 (March 1905): 427–40; no. 4 (April 1905): 667–86.

Stephan, John J. *The Russian Far East: A History.* Stanford, Calif.: Stanford University Press, 1994.

Sternkopf, Joachim. *Sergei und Vladimir Solov'ev: Eine Analyse ihrer Geschichtstheoretischen und geschichtsphilosophischen Anschauungen.* Munich: Otto Sagner, 1973.

Strémooukhoff, D. *Vladimir Soloviev et son oeuvre messianique.* Lausanne: L'Age d'Homme, 1975.

Struve, Petr. "Graf S. Iu. Vitte: Opyt Kharakteristiki." *Russkaia Mysl* 36, no. 3 (March 1915): 9–13.

Sumner, Benedict Humphrey. *Tsardom and Imperialism.* Hamden, Conn.: Archon Books, 1968.

Sutton, Jonathan. *The Religious Philosophy of Vladimir Solovyov: Towards a Reassessment.* New York: St. Martin's Press, 1988.

Suvorin, Aleksei Sergeevich. *Dnevnik.* Moscow: L. D. Frenkel, 1923.

Svechin, A. A. *Russo-Iaponskaia voina.* Oranienbaum: Izdatel'stvo Ofitserskoi Strelkovoi Shkoli, 1910.

Swart, Koenraad W. *The Sense of Decadence in Nineteenth-Century France.* The Hague: Martinus Nijhoff, 1964.

Tan, Chester C. *The Boxer Catastrophe.* New York: Octagon Books, 1967.

Tang, Peter S. H. *Russian and Soviet Policy in Manchuria and Outer Mongolia, 1911–1931.* Durham, N.C.: Duke University Press, 1959.

Taranovski, Theodor. "The Politics of Counter-Reform: Autocracy and Bureaucracy in the Reign of Alexander III, 1881–1894." Ph.D. diss., Harvard University, 1976.

Tarle, Evgenii Viktorovich. *Graf S. Iu. Vitte: Opyt kharakteristiki vneshnei politiki.* Leningrad: Knizhnye novinki, 1927.

Taube, Baron Michel de. *La politique russe d'avant-guerre.* Paris: Librairie Ernest Leroux, 1928.

Trease, Geoffrey. *The Grand Tour.* New York: Holt, Rinehart and Winston, 1967.

Teng Ssu-yü and John K. Fairbank, eds. *China's Response to the West: A Documentary Survey, 1839–1923.* Cambridge, Mass.: Harvard University Press, 1954.

Terentev, Mikhail Afrikanovich. *Istoriia zavoevaniia Srednei Azii.* 3 vols. St. Petersburg: V. V. Komarov, 1906.

Tettau, Freiherr von. *Kuropatkin und seine Unterführer.* Berlin: Ernst Siegfried Mittler, 1913.

Thaden, Edward C. *Conservative Nationalism in Nineteenth-Century Russia.* Seattle: University of Washington Press, 1964.

Thompson, Richard Austin. *The Yellow Peril, 1890–1924.* New York: Arno Press, 1978.

Thornton, A. P. *Doctrines of Imperialism.* New York: John Wiley & Sons, 1965.

Tikhvinskii, Sergei Leonidovich, ed. *Chapters from the History of Russo-Chinese Relations 17th-19th Centuries.* Moscow: Progress Publishers, 1985.

———. *Dvizhenie za reformy v Kitae v kontse xix veka.* Moscow: Nauka, 1980.

Tikhvinskii, Sergei Leonidovich, et al., eds. *Istoriia Rossiiskoi Dukhovnoi Missii v Kitae: Sbornik Statei.* Moscow: Sviato-Vladimisrskoe Bratstvo, 1997.

Tirpitz, Alfred von. *Erinnerungen.* Berlin: K. F. Koehler, 1927.

Tiutchev, Fedor Ivanovich. *Sochineniia.* St. Petersburg: Trenke & Friusno, 1886.

Tokheim, Andrea. "Przhevalskii: Journey to Lob-Nor." Unpublished undergraduate paper, Yale University, 1993.

Tompkins, Stuart Ramsay. "Witte as Minister of Finance 1892–1903." *Slavonic Review* 11, no. 33 (April 1933): 590–606.

Towle, George M. *England and Russia in Asia.* Boston: Osgood, 1885.

Trautmann, Oskar P. *Die Sängerbrücke: Gedanken zur russichen Außenpolitik von 1870–1914.* Stuttgart: Union Deutsche Verlagsgesellschaft, 1940.

Treadgold, Donald. *The Great Siberian Migration: Government and Peasant in Resettlement from Emancipation to the First World War.* Princeton, N.J.: Princeton University Press, 1957.

Trench, F. *The Russo-Indian Question.* London, MacMillan, 1869.

Treue, Wilhelm. "Russland und die Eisenbahnen im Fernen Osten." *Historische Zeitschrift* 157 (1938): 504–40.

Trubetskoi, Evgenii. *Mirosozertsanie Vl. S. Soloveva.* 2 vols. Moscow: A. I. Mamontov, 1913.

Trubetskoi, Grigorii Nikolaevich. *Russland als Grossmacht.* Stuttgart: Deutsche Verlags-Anhalt, 1917.

Trubetskoi, Nikolai Sergeevich. *The Legacy of Genghis Khan and Other Essays on Russia's Identity.* Ann Arbor: Michigan Slavic Publications, 1991.

Tschizewskij, Dmitrij. *Russian Intellectual History.* Ann Arbor, Mich.: Ardis, 1978.

Tsion, Ilia F. *M. Witte et les finances russes.* Lausanne: B. Benda, 1895.

———. *Où la dictature de M. Witte conduit la Russie.* Paris: Librarie Haar et Steinert, 1897.

Tsybikov, Gonbochzhab Tsebekovich. *Izbrannie trudi.* 2 vols. Novosibirsk: Nauka, 1981.

Tsyvinskii, Admiral G. F. *50 let v Imperatorskom flote.* Riga: Orient, n.d.

Tupper, Harmon. *To the Great Ocean: Siberia and the Trans-Siberian Railway.* Boston: Little, Brown, 1965.

Twitchett, Denis, and John K. Fairbank, eds. *The Cambridge History of China.* Vols. 10–11. Cambridge: Cambridge University Press, 1980.

U. . ., Kniaz, [S. D. Urusov]. *Imperator Nikolai II: Zhizn i deianiia Ventsenosnago Tsaria.* Nice: Ia. E. Kleidman, 1910.

Ukhtomskii, Kniaz Esper Esperovich. "The English in Tibet." *North American Review* 179 (1904): 24–29.

———. *Iz kitaiskikh pisem.* St. Petersburg: Vostok, 1901.

———. *Iz oblasti Lamaizma.* St. Petersburg: Vostok, 1904.

———. *Iz proshlogo.* St. Petersburg: Vostok, 1902.

———. *Iz putevykh nabroskov i vospominanii.* St. Petersburg: Vostok, 1904.

———. *K sobytiiam v Kitae. Ob otnosheniiakh Zapada i Rossii k Vostoku.* St. Petersburg: Vostok, 1900.

———. *Kto zhaleet? Poema.* St. Petersburg: Obshchestvennaia polza, 1885.

———. *Ot Kalmytskoi stepi do Bukhary [Putevye ocherki].* St. Petersburg: Kniaz V. P. Meshcherskii, 1891.

———. *Ot sostoianii missionerskago voprosa v Zabaikale, v sviazi s prichinami, obuslovlivaiushchimi malouspeshnost khristianskoi propovedi sredi buriat.* St. Petersburg: Sinodalnaia tipografiia, 1892.

———. *Pered groznym budushchim. K russko-iaponskomu stolknoveniu.* St. Petersburg: Vostok, 1904.

———. *Travels in the East of His Imperial Majesty Czar Nicholas II of Russia, when Cesarewitch, 1890–1891.* 2 vols. Westminster: Constable, 1900.

———. *V tumanakh sedoi stariny. K variazhskou voprosu. Anglo-Russkaia sviaz v davnie veka.* St. Petersburg: Sankt-Peterburgskiia Vedomosti, 1907.

Ular, Alexandre. *Un empire Russo-Chinois.* Paris: Félix Juven, [1900?].

Ulianov, Danbo. *Predskazaniia Buddy o Dome Romanovykh.* St. Petersburg: Tsentralnaia tipo-litografiia, 1913.

Unkrig, W. A. "Aus den letzten Jahrzehnten des Lamaismus in Rußland." *Zeitschrift für Buddhismus und verwandte Gebiete* 7, no. 2 (1926): 135–51.

V-b. "Nikolai Mikhailovich Przhevalskii i ego zaslugi v dele geograficheskikh otkrytii." *Russkaia Mysl* 11, no. 5 (May 1890): 122–47.

Vaganova, N., ed. *Przhevalskii, Zametki o filme.* Moscow: Goskinoizdat, 1952.

Vagts, Alfred. "Der chinesisch-japanische Krieg 1894/95." *Europäische Gespräche* 9, no. 5 (May 1931): 234–52; no. 6 (June 1931): 285–301.

Vaillant, Robert Britton. "Japan and the Trans-Siberian Railroad, 1885–1905." Ph.D. diss., University of Hawaii, 1974.

Valuev, Petr Aleksandrovich. *Dnevnik P. A. Valueva, 1865–1876.* 2 vols. Moscow: AN SSSR, 1961.

Vambéry, Arminius. *The Coming Struggle for India.* London: Cassell, 1885.

Varigny, C. de. "l'Invasion chinoise et le socialisme aux Etats-Unis." *Revue des Deux Mondes* 29, no. 3 (Oct. 1, 1878): 589–613.

Vasilev, Vasilii Pavlovich. *Otkrytie Kitaia.* St. Petersburg: Izd. zhurnala Viestnik vsemirnoi istorii, 1900.

Veniukov, Mikhail Ivanovich. *Ocherk politicheskoi etnografii stran lezhashchikh mezhdu Rossieiu i Indeiu.* St. Petersburg: V. Bezobrazov, 1878.

———. *Ocherki sovremennogo Kitaia.* St. Petersburg: V. Bezobrazov, 1874.

———. *Rossiia i Vostok.* St. Petersburg: V. Bezobrazov, 1877.

———. *Starye i novye dogovory Rossii s Kitaem.* St. Petersburg: V. Bezobrazov, 1863.

Veresaev, Vikentii Vikentevich. *In the War: Memoirs of V. Veresaev.* New York: Mitchell Kennerley, 1917.

Vereshchagin, Aleksandr Vasilevich, ed. *Na voine: Razskazy ochevidtsev.* St. Petersburg: R. Golike, 1902.

Vernadsky, George. *The Mongols and Russia.* New Haven, Conn.: Yale University Press, 1953.

Verner, Andrew M. *The Crisis of Russian Autocracy: Nicholas II and the 1905 Revolution.* Princeton, N.J.: Princeton University Press, 1990.

Vesin, L. "N. M. Przhevalskii i ego puteshestviia." *Vestnik Evropy* 138, no. 7 (July 1887): 145–67; no. 8 (August 1887): 512–29.

Vigasin, A. A., et al., eds. *Istoriia otechestvennogo vostokovedeniia s serediny XIX veka do 1917 goda.* Moscow: Vostochnaia Literatura, 1997.

Vladimir [Zenone Volpicelli]. *The China-Japan War.* New York: Charles Scribner's Sons, 1896.

———. *Russia on the Pacific and the Siberian Railway.* London: Sampson Low, Marston, 1899.

Vodovozov, V. V. *Graf S. Iu. Vitte i Imperator Nikolai II.* Peterburg: Mysl, 1992.

Vogel, Barbara. *Deutsche Rußlandpolitik: Das Scheitern der deutschen Weltpolitik unter Bülow 1900–1906.* Düsseldorf: Bertelsmann Universtitätsverlag, 1973.

Vonliarliarskii, Vladimir Mikhailovich. *Moi vospominaniia 1852–1939 gg.* Berlin: Russkoe natsionalnoe izdatelstvo, n.d.

———. "Why Russia Went to War with Japan: The Story of the Yalu Concession." *Fortnightly Review* 87 (1910): 816–31, 1030–43.

Voorheis, Peter. "The Perception of Asiatic Nomads in Medieval Russia: Folklore, History, and Historiography." Ph.D. diss., Indiana University, 1972.

Voskressenski, Alexei D. *The Sino-Russian St. Petersburg Treaty of 1881: Diplomatic History.* Commack, N.Y.: Nova Science Publishers, 1986.

Vucinich, Alexander. *Darwin in Russian Thought*. Berkeley: University of California Press, 1988.

Vucinich, Wayne S., ed. *Russia and Asia: Essays on the Influence of Russia on the Asian Peoples*. Stanford, Calif.: Stanford University Press, 1972.

Walicki, Andrzej. *A History of Russian Thought from the Enlightenment to Marxism*. Stanford, Calif.: Stanford University Press, 1973.

———. *The Slavophile Controversy: History of a Conservative Utopia in Nineteenth-Century Russian Thought*. Translated by Hilda Andrews-Rusiecka. Oxford: Oxford University Press, 1975.

Wallace, Donald Mackenzie. *Russia: On the Eve of War and Revolution*. Princeton, N.J.: Princeton University Press, 1984.

Waller, Derek. *The Pundits: British Exploration of Tibet and Central Asia*. Lexington: University Press of Kentucky, 1990.

Walder, David. *The Short Victorious War: The Russo-Japanese Conflict, 1904–1905*. London: Hutchison, 1973.

Walsh, Warren B. "The Imperial Russian General Staff and India: A Footote to Diplomatic History." *Russian Review* 16, no. 2 (April 1957): 53–58.

Wang, Chin Chun. "The Chinese Eastern Railway." *Annals of the American Academy of Political and Social Science* 122 (November 1925): 57–79.

Warth, Robert D. "Before Rasputin: Piety and the Occult at the Court of Nicholas II." *Historian* 47, no. 3 (May 1985): 323–37.

———. *Nicholas II: The Life and Reign of Russia's Last Monarch*. Westport, Conn.: Praeger, 1997.

Weale, Bertram Lenox Putnam. *Indiscreet Letters from Peking* New York: Dodd, Mead, 1907.

———. *Manchu and Muscovite*. London: Macmillan, 1907.

Webb, James. *The Harmonious Circle: The Lives and Work of G. I. Gurdjieff, P. D. Ouspensky, and Their Followers*. New York: Shambhala, 1987.

Weeks, Morris. *The Last Wild Horse*. Boston: Houghton Mifflin, 1977.

Weeks, Theodore R. *Nation and State in Late Imperial Russia: Nationalism and Russification on the Western Frontier, 1863–1914*. DeKalb: Northern Illinois University Press, 1996.

Wehler, Hans Ulrich, ed. *Imperialismus*. Cologne: Kiepenheuer & Witsch, 1970.

Wei Ken-shen. *Russo-Chinese Diplomacy, 1689–1924*. Shanghai: Commercial Press, 1928.

Wells, David, and Sandra Wilson, eds. *The Russo-Japanese War in Cultural Perspective*. New York: St. Martin's Press, 1999.

Wen Ching Yin. *Le système fiscal de la Chine*. Paris: Imprimerie du Montparnasse et de Persan Beaumont, 1929.

Wesseling, Henk L. *Verdeel en Heers: De Deling van Afrika, 1880–1914*. Amsterdam: Uitgeverij Bert Bakker, 1991.

Westwood, J. N. *A History of Russian Railways*. London: George Allen and Unwin, 1964.

———. *Japan against Russia, 1904–1905: A New Look at the Russo-Japanese War*. Albany: State University of New York Press, 1986.

White, John. *The Diplomacy of the Russo-Japanese War*. Princeton, N.J.: Princeton University Press, 1964.

Widmer, Eric. *The Russian Ecclesiastical Mission during the Eighteenth Century*. Cambridge, Mass.: Harvard University Press, 1961.

Wilgus, Mary H. *Sir Claude MacDonald, the Open Door, and British Informal Empire in China, 1895–1900*. New York: Garland, 1987.

Wilhelm II. *Letters from the Kaiser to the Czar*. New York: Frederick A. Stokes, 1920.

Wilhelm II and Nicholas II. *Correspondence entre Guillaume II et Nicolas II 1894–1914*. Paris: Plon, 1924.

Williams, Samuel Wells. *A History of China: Being the Historical Chapters from "The Middle Kingdom."* 2 vols. New York: Charles Scribner's Sons, 1901.

Willoughby, Westel W. *Foreign Rights and Interests in China.* Baltimore: Johns Hopkins University Press, 1920.

Winks, R. W., and James R. Rush, eds. *Asia in Western Ficton.* Manchester: Manchester University Press, 1990.

Wishnick, Elizabeth. "Russia in Asia and Asians in Russia." *SAIS Review* 20, no. 1 (winter–spring 2000): 87–101.

Witte, Sergei Iulevich. "Dokladnaia zapiska Vitte Nikolaiu II." *Istorik Marksist*, nos. 2–3 (February–March 1935): 130–39.

———. *Erzwungene Aufklärungen aus Anlaß des Berichtes des Generaladjutanten Kuropatkin über den Krieg mit Japan.* Vienna, 1911.

———. *Konspekt lektsii o narodnom i gosudarstvennom khoziaistve, chitannykh Ego Imperatorskomu Vysochestvu Velikomu Kniaziu Mikhailu Aleksandrovichu v 1900–1902 gg.* St. Petersburg: Brockhaus i Efron, 1912.

———. *Po povodu natsionalizma: Natsionalnaia ekonomiia i Fridrikh List.* St. Petersburg: Brockhaus i Efron, 1912.

———. *The Memoirs of Count Witte.* Translated and edited by Sydney Harcave. Armonk, N.Y.: M. E. Sharpe, 1990.

———. "Russia's Work in Manchuria." *Harper's Weekly*, Apr. 9, 1904, 544–45.

———. *Samoderzhavie i zemstvo.* Stuttgart: J. H. W. Diest, 1903.

———. "Sergei Witte on the Industrialisation of Imperial Russia." *Journal of Modern History* 26, no. 1 (March 1954): 60–74.

———. *Vynuzhdeniia raziasneniia po povodu otcheta Gen-Ad. Kuropatkina o voine s Iaponiei.* St. Petersburg: I. D. Sytin, 1911.

Wittschewsky, Valentin. *Russlands Handels-, Zoll-, und Industriepolitik von Peter dem Grossen bis auf die Gegenwart.* Berlin: Ernst Siegfried Miller, 1905.

Wittfogel, Karl A. "Russia and the East: A Comparison and Contrast." *Slavic Review* 22, no. 4 (1963): 627–43.

Wittram, Reinhard. "Das russische Imperium und sein Gestaltwandel." *Historische Zeitschrift* 187 (1959): 568–93.

Wolff, David. *To the Harbin Station: The Liberal Alternative in Russian Manchuria, 1898–1914.* Stanford, Calif.: Stanford University Press, 1999.

Wood, Carlton Leroy. "Die Beziehungen Deutschlands zu China (Eine historische Betrachtung in politischer und ökonomischer Hinsicht vom 19. Jahrhundert bis zum Jahre 1934)." Inaugural diss., Ruprecht-Karls-Universität zu Heidelberg, 1934.

Woodman, Dorothy. *Himalayan Frontiers: A Political Review of British, Chinese, Indian, and Russian Rivalries.* New York: Praeger, 1969.

Woodward, David. *The Russians at Sea: A History of the Russian Navy.* New York: Praeger, 1965.

Wren, Melvyn C. *The Western Impact upon Tsarist Russia.* Chicago: Holt, Rinehart and Winston, 1971.

Wright, Mary Clabaugh. "The Adaptibility of Ch'ing Diplomacy: The Case of Korea." *Journal of Asian Studies* 17, no. 3 (May 1958): 363–81.

———. *The Last Stand of Chinese Conservatism: The T'ung-Chih Restoration, 1862–1874.* Stanford, Calif.: Stanford University Press, 1957.

Wu, Aitchen K. *China and the Soviet Union: a Study of Sino-Russian Relations.* London: Methuen, 1950.

Yokoyama, Toshio. *Japan in the Victorian Mind: A Study of Stereotyped Images of a Nation,*

1850–80. London: Macmillan, 1987.

Yorck von Wartenburg, Maxmillian Graf. *Das Vordringen der Russischen Macht in Asien*. Berlin: Ernst Siegfried Mittler und Sohn, 1900.

Young, C. Walter. *The International Relations of Manchuria: A Digest and Analysis of Treaties, Agreements, and Negotiations concerning the Three Eastern Provinces of China*. New York: Greenwood Press, 1969.

Young, George M., Jr. *Nikolai F. Fedorov: An Introduction*. Belmont, Mass.: Nordland, 1979.

Young, Leonard Kenneth. *British Policy in China 1895–1902*. Oxford: Clarendon, 1970.

Young, M. B. *The Rhetoric of Empire: American China Policy, 1895–1901*. Cambridge, Mass.: Harvard University Press, 1968.

Zabel, Rudolf. *Deutschland in China*. Leipzig: George Wigand, 1902.

Zabriskie, E. H. *American-Russian Rivalry in the Far East: A Study in Diplomacy and Power Politics, 1895–1914*. Philadelphia: University of Pennsylvania Press, 1946.

Zaionchkovskii, Petr Andreevich. *The Russian Autocracy in Crisis, 1878–1882*. Gulf Breeze, Fl.: Academic International Press, 1979.

———. *Samoderzhavie i russkaia armiia na rubezhe XIX–XX stolety*. Moscow: Mysl, 1973.

Zelenin, A. V. *Puteshestvia N. M. Przhevalskago*. 2 vols. St. Petersburg: Soikina, 1899.

Zernov, Nicolas. *Three Russian Prophets: Khomiakov, Dostoevsky, Soloviev*. London: S. C. M. Press, 1944.

Zhukova, Lekha Vigelmna. "Ideologicheskoe obosnovanie russko-iaponskoi voiny." Candidate's diss., Moskovskii Gosudarstvennyi Universitet, 1996.

Zühlke, Herbert. *Die Rolle des Fernen Ostes in den Politischen Beziehungen der Mächte, 1895–1905*. Berlin, 1927.

Zvonarev, K. K. *Agenturnaia razvedka*. Vol. 1. Moscow: IV upravlenie shtaba Rab.-Kr. Armii, 1929.

Index

NORWAY

SWEDEN

FINLAND

★
St. Petersburg

BARENTS
SEA

ARCT

NOVAIA ZEMLIA

KARA SEA

● Arkhangelsk

VOLGA

URALS

OB

ENISEI

● Kazan

Ekaterinburg

RUSS

● Orenburg

Tiumen

● Tobolsk

Omsk

● Tomsk

ANGA

IRTYSH

TRANS-SIBERIAN RAILWAY

ARAL-
SEA

LAKE
BALKHASH

ALTAI MOUNTAINS

● Tashkent

Verny

● Kulja

TIEN SHAN

XINJIANG

AFGHANISTAN

Kashgar

TAKLAMAKAN
DESERT

KARAKORAM

INDIA

KUNLUN MOUNTAINS

Asian Rus

KM/Verst

0

Miles